Alphabetical Index to the First Lines of *All* Stanzas of Poetry by John and Charles Wesley

Alphabetical Index to the First Lines of *All* Stanzas of Poetry by John and Charles Wesley

COMPILED AND EDITED BY
S T Kimbrough, Jr.

FOREWORD BY
Randy Maddox

☙PICKWICK *Publications* · Eugene, Oregon

ALPHABETICAL INDEX TO THE FIRST LINES OF ALL STANZAS OF POETRY
BY JOHN AND CHARLES WESLEY

Copyright © 2017 S T Kimbrough, Jr. All rights reserved. Except for brief quotations in critical publications or reviews, no part of this book may be reproduced in any manner without prior written permission from the publisher. Write: Permissions, Wipf and Stock Publishers, 199 W. 8th Ave., Suite 3, Eugene, OR 97401.

Pickwick Publications
An Imprint of Wipf and Stock Publishers
199 W. 8th Ave., Suite 3
Eugene, OR 97401

www.wipfandstock.com

PAPERBACK ISBN: 978-1-5326-1720-1
HARDCOVER ISBN: 978-1-4982-4173-1
EBOOK ISBN: 978-1-4982-4172-4

Cataloguing-in-Publication data:

Names: Kimbrough, S T, Jr. | Maddox, Randy, foreword

Title: Alphabetical Index to the First Lines of All Stanzas of Poetry by John and Charles Wesley / S T Kimbrough, Jr. ; foreword by Randy Maddox.

Description: Eugene, OR: Pickwick Publications, 2017.

Identifiers: ISBN 978-1-5326-1720-1 (paperback) | ISBN 978-1-4982-4173-1 (hardcover) | ISBN 978-1-4982-4172-4 (ebook)

Subjects: LCSH: Wesley, Charles, 1707–1788—Indexes. | Wesley, John, 1703–1791—Indexes.

Classification: BX8495.W4 K563 2017 (print) | BX8495.W4 K563 (ebook)

Manufactured in the U.S.A. 06/18/18

Contents

List of All Wesley Works Indexed in Volume 13 of *The Poetical Works of John and Charles Wesley (PW)* by George Osborn | vii

Foreword by Randy Maddox | xi

Acknowledgments | xiii

Abbreviations | xiv

Introduction to the Alphabetical Index | xv

Part 1

Alphabetical Index of the First Lines of All Stanzas of Poems in *PW*, edited and expanded by S T Kimbrough, Jr. | 1

First Lines not included in *PW* and *UP* | 322

- First lines of all stanzas of Wesley poems in the *Arminian Magazine (AM)*.
- First lines of all stanzas of the Wesley poem: Hymn for Mary Langston, Hymn I and II.
- First lines of all stanzas of the C. Wesley poem: I. Hymn [for the King].
- First lines of all stanzas of the C. Wesley poem: II. Hymn for the Queen.
- First line of the stanza of the C. Wesley poem: On the Rev'd John Wesley.
- First lines of all stanzas of the C. Wesley poem: [III.] Hymns for King George, 1769.
- First line of an untitled C. Wesley stanza "Would Peter's zeal have sold."

Part 2

Alphabetical Index of the First Lines of All Stanzas of Poems in *The Unpublished Poetry of Charles Wesley (UP)*, vols. 1–3 | 325

List of All Wesley Works Indexed in Volume 13 of *The Poetical Works of John and Charles Wesley*, edited by George Osborn

Contents of the Osborn Volumes[1]

Volume 1

Hymns and Sacred Poems, 1739	1–194
Hymns and Sacred Poems, 1740	195–370

Volume 2

A Collection of Psalms and Hymns, 1741	1–42
Hymns and Sacred Poems, 1742	43–366

Volume 3

Hymns on God's Everlasting Love, first series, 1741	1–38
Hymns on God's Everlasting Love, second series, 1741–42?	39–106
An Elegy on the Death of Robert Jones, Esq., 1742	107–128
Poems extracted from the third volume of *A Collection of Moral and Sacred Poems*, 1744	129–180
Hymns on the Lord's Supper, 1745	181–342
Gloria Patri, etc., or Hymns to the Trinity, 1746	343–356

Volume 4

Hymns for Times of Trouble and Persecution, second edition enlarged, 1745	1–26
Hymns in Time of Persecution	27–50
Hymns to be Sung in a Tumult	51–56
Hymns for Times of Trouble, for the Year 1745	57–82
Hymns for Times of Trouble, 1745?	83–90
Hymn for the Public Thanksgiving-Day, Oct. 9, 1746	91–104
Hymns for the Nativity of our Lord, 1745	105–26
Hymns for Our Lord's Resurrection, 1746, third edition	127–50
Hymns for Ascension-Day, 1746	151–62
Hymns of Petition and Thanksgiving for the Promise of the Father, 1746	163–204
Hymns for Those that Seek, and Those that Have Redemption in the Blood of Jesus Christ, 1747	205–82
Hymns and Sacred Poems, 1749, Volume 1, Part 1	283–480

1. The list of mostly original titles included in the contents of PW is printed here so that one may check a text against the published version, and at times the manuscript version of the text, as found on the website of the Duke Divinity School Center for Studies in the Wesleyan Tradition. See the printed and manuscript sources at: http://www.divinity.duke.edu/initiatives-centers/cswt/wesley-texts/manuscript-verse.

WORKS INDEXED IN *THE POETICAL WORKS OF JOHN AND CHARLES WESLEY*

Volume 5

Hymns and Sacred Poems, 1749, Volume 1, Part 2	1–138
Hymns and Sacred Poems, 1749, Volume 2, Part 1	139–288
Hymns and Sacred Poems, 1749, Volume 2, Part 2	289–484

Volume 6

Hymns for a Protestant	1–6
Hymns for New Year's Day, 1750	7–16
Hymns Occasioned by the Earthquake, March 9, 1750	17–28
Hymns Occasioned by the Earthquake, Part 2	29–52
An Epistle to the Reverend Mr. John Wesley, 1755	53–64
An Epistle to the Rev. Mr. George Whitefield, 1771	65–70
Catholic Love, 1755	71
Hymns for the Year 1756, Particularly for the Fast-Day, February 6	73–96
Hymns for the Preachers Among the Methodists (so-called), 1760	97–108
Hymns of Intercession for All Mankind, 1758	109–46
Hymns for the Expected Invasion, 1759, and for The Thanksgiving Day, November 20, 1759	147–86
Funeral Hymns, first series, 1746?	187–212
Funeral Hymns, second series, 1759	213–88
Funeral Hymns, third series	289–366
Hymns for Children, 1763	367–465

Volume 7

Hymns for the Use of Families, and on Various Occasions, 1767	1–200
Hymns on the Trinity, 1767	201–348
Preparation for Death, in Several Hymns, 1772	349–422
An Elegy on the Late Rev. George Whitefield, M.A., 1771	423–442

Volume 8

Versions and Paraphrases of Select Psalms	1–262
Hymns Written in the Time of the Tumults, June 1780	263–80
Hymns for the Nation, in 1782, 1781	281–308
Hymns for the National Fast, Feb. 8, 1782	309–36
Prayers for Condemned Malefactors, 1785	337–53
Hymns for Love	354–87
Hymns and Poems (Chiefly relating to events in the personal history of the Rev. C. Wesley)	388–432
Epitaphs	433–39
Miscellaneous Hymns and Poems	440–48
The Protestant Association (Written in the midst of tumults, June 1781)	449–87

Volume 9

Short Hymns on Select Passages of the Holy Scriptures, 1762 Genesis—Isaiah	1–471

Volume 10

Short Hymns on Select Passages of the Holy Scriptures, 1762 Jeremiah—Gospel of Mark	1–502

Volume 11

Short Hymns on Select Passages of the Holy Scriptures, 1762 Gospel of Mark—Gospel of John	1–512

WORKS INDEXED IN *THE POETICAL WORKS OF JOHN AND CHARLES WESLEY*

Volume 12

Short Hymns on Select Passages of the Holy Scriptures, 1762   3–456
Gospel of John—Acts

Volume 13

Short Hymns on Select Passages of the Holy Scriptures, 1762   3–242
Romans—Revelation

Foreword

The reader holds in his/her hands a labor of love that pulls together a lifetime of service in Wesley Studies.

Over the last thirty years there have been several major developments in the field of Wesley Studies. Among these, none is more significant than the recovery of Charles Wesley's distinctive voice and perspective, alongside that of his brother John. And no one has contributed more to this recovery than S T Kimbrough, Jr. His passion for broader awareness of and benefit from the theological resources bequeathed by Charles Wesley to the whole church bore its initial fruit in the publication (with Oliver A. Beckerlegge) of three volumes of Wesley's verse that had neither been put in print by Wesley during his life nor included in the long-standard thirteen-volume collection, *The Poetical Works of John and Charles Wesley*, edited by George Osborn (1868–72). In the midst of the appearance of these three volumes of *The Unpublished Poetry of Charles Wesley* (1988–92), Kimbrough was also a prime mover in forming The Charles Wesley Society, which took as its mission both the reproduction of Charles Wesley texts and the fostering of secondary scholarship upon these texts. Kimbrough served as editor of the facsimile reprints issued by the CWS, as well as the *Proceedings* of the society. And he authored over twenty scholarly essays himself, along with several books on Wesley's "lyrical theology."

Dwelling in this way on both sides of intersection between producing primary texts of a historic figure and writing interpretive essays about that figure, Kimbrough could not help but recognize the importance of resources that assist interpreters in accessing the full range of the texts of the figure whom they are studying. In the case of the massive body of Charles Wesley's verse, there has been a long-standing need for a comprehensive and reliable index.

This need is created by several factors. To begin with, most people encounter Charles Wesley's hymns initially in recent hymnals, where there is little sense of their original setting or notation of any editorial changes. We need a guide to this original setting, or a standard edition, if we want to engage the hymn with scholarly integrity. Again, if our interest in a particular theme in Wesley is awakened by some hymn, we could use help in locating other settings in which he might treat that theme. Then there are some specific problems (which Kimbrough describes in greater detail in his introductory remarks) created by Osborn's collection—particularly in its later volumes, where Osborn intermixes sources and often gives abridged versions. Kimbrough and Beckerlegge rightly include

complete versions of this same material in their volumes. But this creates the need for a resource that helps readers of Osborn to know when a more complete version of a hymn might be found elsewhere.

To highlight just one more situation where readers will particularly appreciate the current resource, anyone studying spiritual biographies knows that the formative power of hymnody is often reflected by persons invoking a phrase or stanza from a favorite hymn. But this favored stanza is often not the first stanza of a hymn (on which most indices are based). So how does one find the complete hymn for a citation? Perhaps Kimbrough has received as many inquiries for help on this problem as I have had to field. This may be what convinced him to accept the task—though it increased the amount of labor exponentially—of providing an index of the first line of *every* stanza in Wesley's corpus of hymns and religious verse, not just of the first lines of the first stanza.

Whatever Kimbrough's motivation for taking up this herculean task, the present volume stands as a fitting capstone of a lifetime devoted to helping foster among "the people called Methodists" and the church as a whole a deeper exposure to and appreciation for the rich contribution of Charles Wesley.

Randy L. Maddox

William Kellon Quick Professor of
Wesleyan and Methodist Studies
Duke Divinity School

Acknowledgments

The deepest possible gratitude is expressed to my late wife, Sarah Ann Robinson Kimbrough (1930–2016), for her patient forbearance and enduring encouragement in this tedious and time-consuming project. In the wake of her death, her patience and encouragement continued to motivate me to work long hours every day until the index was completed. I shall remain in her debt for such sustained support.

I express sincere gratitude to the Reverend Charles A. Green for his assistance in technical matters and proof reading. In addition, I am grateful to Mr. Barry Johnston, for his careful reading of the index material and for many helpful suggestions.

Abbreviations

AM	*Arminian Magazine*
EGW 1771	*An Elegy on the late Reverend George Whitefield, M.A.* 1771
HGEL 1741, 1742	*Hymns on God's Everlasting Love,* 1741, 1742
HI 1758, 1759	*Hymns of Intercession for All Mankind,* 1758, 1759
HLS 1745	*Hymns for the Lord's Supper* 1745
HNL 1745	*Hymns for the Nativity of our Lord* 1745
HSP 1739	*Hymns and Sacred Poems* 1739
HSP 1740	*Hymns and Sacred Poems* 1740
HSP 1742	*Hymns and Sacred Poems* 1742
HSP 1749	*Hymns and Sacred Poems* 1749, vols. 1 & 2
HUF 1767	*Hymns for the Use of Families,* 1767
HUTD 1759	*Hymns to be Used on the Thanksgiving Day, Nov. 29,* 1759
MARC	Methodist Archives and Research Centre, The Rylands University Library, Manchester, England
MSACTS	MS Acts 1764
MSF	MS Fish 1742
MSHL	MS Hymns for Love
MSJN	MS John 1763
MSLK	MS Luke 1765
MSMT	MS Matthew 1766
MSMK	MS Mark 1766
MSMH	MS Miscellaneous Hymns 1747
MSPS	MS Psalms 1740
MSSH	MS Scriptural Hymns 1783
PS 1741	"Promise of Sanctification" 1741
RH 1747	*Hymns for Those that Seek, and Those that Have Redemption in the Blood of Jesus Christ* 1747
SH 1762	*Short Hymns on Select Passages of the Holy Scriptures* 1762

Introduction to the Alphabetical Index

This is the first attempt to create an index of the first line of every stanza of all the poems and hymns in the publications of John and Charles Wesley, as well as those of other authors[1] included in their publications. Two primary sources have been used as the basis for the creation of the index: (1) George Osborn, *The Poetical Works of John and Charles Wesley*, thirteen volumes published between 1868 and 1872; (2) S T Kimbrough, Jr., and Oliver A. Beckerlegge, *The Unpublished Poetry of Charles Wesley*, three volumes published in 1988, 1990, 1992.

The index on pages 291 to 529 of volume 13 of *PW* was Osborn's attempt to produce a first line index of all stanzas of the poems included in the thirteen-volume work. Unfortunately there were hundreds of omissions and to date no attempt has been made to correct this flaw. There are also occasional misspellings, though they are not prevalent. Because of lack of space in *PW* first lines were often abbreviated, thus providing often only portions of first lines. In this index all first lines of poem stanzas are printed in full, omissions are included, and misspellings are corrected.

Technical Matters of Importance

1. No attempt has been made to fuse the indices of *PW* and *UP*. They are printed separately.

2. The index in volume three of *UP* published in 1992 includes *only* the *first lines* of the first stanzas of all hymns and poems in the three volumes. The expanded index here includes the first lines of *all* stanzas of the hymns and poems in the three volumes with the exception of the texts in the section, "Hymns and Poems of Doubtful Authorship" in volume three, which is omitted.

3. The *PW* index of Osborn's thirteen volumes is *not* reproduced as originally published. It is fully corrected, including hundreds of omitted first lines of stanzas. They have been inserted in this volume and appear in italics.

---

1. On the website of the Center for Studies in the Wesleyan Tradition, see "Other Author Hymns First Line Index": http://www.divinity.duke.edu/initiatives-centers/cswt/wesley-texts/manuscript-verse.

In addition, first lines by Osborn from other published sources have also been inserted in italics with the citation of the original source with volume (if applicable) and page number.

Generally, punctuation is regularized, and archaic spellings remain essentially unchanged since word searches in online original sources require same. There is a discrepancy in capitalization of nouns in this index since the English language was going through major changes in the eighteenth century, especially the movement away from some Anglo-Saxon grammatical practice, e.g. capitalization of nouns. Furthermore, in some instances earlier archaic spellings were often changed in later publications, e.g. burthen and burden, murtherer and murderer. Hence, both spellings are found in the index. While the spectrum of Wesley publications across almost fifty years reflects these changes, no attempt has been made here to regularize them. Early publications may include capitalization of nouns, later ones may not. At times this discrepancy may have had more to do with printer preference than with that of the Wesleys.

4. A few words appear in captial letters or italics for apparent emphasis.

5. When identical first lines are repeated in the same or different poems in the *PW* and *UP* indices, usually the second line, or the first part of it, is included immediately following the first line separated by a solidus for sake of clarity, for example:

> O Thou to whom all hearts are known / My latest
>
> O Thou to whom all hearts are known / Who dost

Since the first lines are identical, the second line, or portion thereof, clearly differentiates between the two stanzas. If there is not enough space to include the second line or portion thereof after the solidus, it appears in the footnotes. If the second lines are also identical, the third line is printed in the footnotes. If complete stanzas are identical, this is cited in the footnotes.

There are some first lines that appear with such frequency that the second line or portion thereof is usually included to distinguish between the repetitions, even when they appear in different volumes of *PW* and *UP*. Some examples are:

> Come, Father, Son, and Holy Ghost
>
> Father, Son, and Holy Ghost
>
> To Father, Son, and Holy Ghost
>
> Holy, holy, holy Lord
>
> Come, let us anew
>
> Salvation to God

INTRODUCTION TO THE ALPHABETICAL INDEX

6. Opening quotation marks are used in the index only when a quotation is completed within the first line or as the first line of a hymn or poem.

7. When Osborn published *PW*, he often included portions of previously unpublished texts, e.g. four stanzas of a five-stanza poem, without providing any information about manuscript sources or omitted lines or stanzas. This is particularly characteristic of volumes 9–14, which purport to be the reproduction of *Short Hymns on Select Passages of the Holy Scriptures*, the two-volume work published in 1762. Charles Wesley's original publication included 2,349 hymns and poems, whereas *PW* included 1,328 for the Old Testament and 3,491 for the New Testament, or a total of 4,820. Where Osborn included incomplete hymns and poems, they were published in their complete form in *UP*. This means there is some repetition of lines in both *PW* (namely, Osborn's inclusion of lines or stanzas from previously unpublished lyrics) and *UP*. When repetition of lines caused by this occurrence appears in both indices, the repeated first lines of stanzas of poem portions published in *PW* are noted in the footnotes of the *UP* index with the specific reference to their location in *PW*. For example a footnote might read: "The stanza beginning with this line [meaning the line to which the footnote number is affixed] appears in *PW* 4:316." There is a cross reference in the *PW* index for citations of occurrences of corresponding texts in *UP*, e.g., *UP* 1:281.

    Osborn further confused matters for the reader and researcher by combining portions of different poems into a single stanza or poem without citing the source(s) of the portions. So far as possible as pertains to first lines, this has been documented for *PW* and *UP*.

8. One of the major difficulties with Osborn's index is that in approximatly ten per cent of the first lines listed he has changed the wording. Hence, those lines do not reflect what the Wesleys originally wrote. Of course, what they preferred for a first line sometimes differed from edition to edition. However, in this index every effort has been made to correct changes Osborn made and to restore first lines as they were first printed or appeared in the manuscripts. Therefore, the lines in this index may be considered authentic Wesley first lines. Of course, at times printed sources and manuscript sources differ. In any case, Osborn's changes to first lines have been dismissed, and so far as possible, the earliest versions of the lines have been used. Where Osborn changed the first word in a line, this has been footnoted, since it changes the position in the index. All other internal changes are made without notation.

    In addition, some changes have been made for the purpose of fluid reading. The eighteenth-century printing practice of abbreviating the "ed" of the past tense form of a verb with an apostrophe and "d", e.g. assum'd, has been eliminated and an "e" replaces the apostrophe, hence, assumed. When the definite article, or another word ending in a vowel, precedes a noun beginning with a vowel, throughout the Wesley publications this is printed in two

xvii

different ways, e.g. the' intercession or th' intercession, to' approve or t' approve. Throughout the index this practice has been regularized to the latter.

The capitalization of pronouns, Thee, Thou, Thine, Thy, He, His, Him, Me, My, Mine in reference to divinity has been eliminated and they are written with lower case. The abbreviation of auxiliary helping verbs such as coud, woud, shoud, etc. has been eliminated and they are written in full.

See "Charles Wesley's Manuscript Verse, An online collection of verse, including precursors to many items in published collections" at http://www.divinity.duke.edu/initiatives-centers/cswt/wesley-texts/manuscript-verse.

9. In 1778 John Wesley began publishing monthly the *Arminian Magazine,* cited as *AM,* in response to the Calvinst publications, the *Christian Magazine* and *Gospel Magazine. AM* was to present and defend the theological position of God's universal offer of salvation to all. The final pages of each issue were devoted to poetry. While in some of the early publications John Wesley included some previously published hymns and poems of his brother Charles, in later issues he included many previously unpublished lyrics of Charles. Most of the unpublished Wesley poems that appeared in *AM* were included by Osborn in *PW.* A few poems, however, were not included by him. The first lines of the stanzas of these poems appear at the end of the Osborn index followed by the date of the *AM* issue and page number.

These are followed by the first lines in italics of all stanzas of additional poems that appeared neither in *PW* nor in *UP.* The first lines are followed by the abbreviations of their original sources with volume and page designations.

If anyone is aware of first lines of hymns and poems of John or Charles Wesley that have not been included here, please notify the editor, S T Kimbrough, Jr., via the publisher with appropriate documentation and inclusion will be considered for an updated edition.

PART 1

Alphabetical Index of First Lines of All Stanzas of Poems in *The Poetical Works of John and Charles Wesley* by George Osborn, edited and expanded by S T Kimbrough, Jr.

Volume I

A better gift he us provides	221
A better heritage he sought	212
A devil to myself I am	274
A faithful Witness of my grace	206
A man that looks on glass[1]	31
A miracle of grace and sin	95
A monster to myself I am	252
A patient, a victorious mind[2]	162
A place he should possess at last	212
A power to choose, a will t' obey	311
A rest of lasting joy and peace	370
A rest where all our soul's desire	370
A sigh thou breath'st into my heart[3]	65
A stately dome he raises now[4]	19
A thousand specious arts essayed	84
A wretch from sin and death set free?	252
Abate the purging fire	267
Abba, Father! hear my cry	322
Abba, Father! hear thy child	193
Abraham, when severly tried	214
Absent from thee, my exiled soul	50
Absent in our flesh from home	363
Abundant sweetness, while I sing[5]	175
Accept, dear youth, a sympathizing[6]	19
Accused, his mouth he opened not	80
Adam's likeness, Lord, efface	184
Adverse to earth's rebellious throng	180
After thy likeness let me rise	307
Ah! dear, redeeming Lord	337
Ah, foolish man, where are thine eyes?[7]	60
Ah, give me, Lord, myself to feel	77
Ah, give me now, all-gracious Lord[8]	349
Ah! give us, Lord, to know	317
Ah! let it not my Lord displease	243
Ah, Lord! enlarge our scanty thought[9]	266
Ah, Lord!—If thou art in that sigh	258
Ah, Lord! Wouldst thou within me live	253
Ah, Love! thy influence withdrawn[10]	141
Ah, my dear, angry Lord[11]	49

1. George Herbert.
2. From the German of Johann A. Freylinghausen, translated by John Wesley.
3. George Herbert.
4. George Herbert.
5. From the Spanish of David Israel Lopez Laguna.
6. John Gambold.
7. George Herbert.
8. From the German of Nikolaus von Zinzendorf, translated by John Wesley.
9. From the German of Nikolaus von Zinzendorf, translated by John Wesley.
10. From the German of Paul Gerhardt, translated by John Wesley.
11. George Herbert.

INDEX OF FIRST LINES OF POETRY BY JOHN AND CHARLES WESLEY

Ah! my dear Lord, whose changeless love	131
Ah, my dear Master! can it be	292
Ah no! ne'er will I backward turn[12]	72
Ah! rescue me from earth and sin	293
Ah, show me, Lord, my depth of sin[13]	223
Ah! what avails my strife	267
Ah! who is as thy servants blind	314
Ah! why did I so late thee know[14]	176
Aid me, ye hovering spirits near	50
All glory to th' eternal Three[15]	130
All glory to the sacred Three[16]	117
All heaven thou fill'st with pure desire[17]	109
All may of thee partake[18]	31
All things are busy round but I[19]	30
All things in earth and air and sea[20]	163
All thy hosts to battle bring	297
All ye that in my word believe	208
Almighty universal Lord	295
Already springing hope I feel[21]	86
Although I fail, I weep[22]	70
And art thou grieved, O sacred Dove[23]	43
And can I see my comfort gone	246
And can I yet delay	268
And can it be, that I should gain	105
And live I yet by power Divine	74
And now in age I bud again[24]	45
And now their idle fury view	295
And shall I, Lord, confine thy love	312
And shall I slight my Father's love	92
And shall I still the cup decline	26
And shall not we the call obey	213
And well I know thy tender love[25]	86
And well thou know'st I did not seek	293
And whatsoe'er thou will'st[26]	126
And while I felt thy blood within[27]	349
And will he now forsake his own	181
And wilt thou not this havoc see	369
And wilt thou yet be found	266
Angel of God, whate'er betide	294
Angels and archangels join	297
Angels, attend, ('tis God commands,)	303
Angels stood trembling at the sight[28]	119
Arise; if thou dost not withstand[29]	87
Arise, my soul, arise	146
Arise, stir up thy power[30]	158
Arm me with thy whole armour, Lord[31]	90
Arm of the Lord, awake, awake!	346
Around me clouds of darkness roll	131
Art thou all Justice? shows thy Word[32]	63
Art thou idle? Canst thou play?[33]	221
Art thou idle? Sits there now[34]	221
Art thou not touched with human woe	275
As flowers their opening leaves display[35]	168
As in a strange, though promised land	212

12. From the German of Gerhard Tersteegen, translated by John Wesley.
13. From the German of Maria Böhmer.
14. From the German of Johann Angelus Scheffler, translated by John Wesley.
15. From the German of Nikolaus von Zinzendorf, translated by John Wesley.
16. George Hickes.
17. From the German of Nikolaus von Zinzendorf, translated by John Wesley.
18. George Herbert.
19. George Herbert.
20. From the German of Nikolaus von Zinzendorf, translated by John Wesley.
21. From the German of Christian Friedrich Richter, translated by John Wesley.
22. George Herbert.
23. George Herbert.
24. George Herbert.
25. From the German of Christian Friedrich Richter, translated by John Wesley.
26. From the German of Paul Gerhardt, translated by John Wesley.
27. From the German of Nikolaus von Zinzendorf, translated by John Wesley.
28. Altered from John Norris.
29. George Herbert.
30. From the German of Johann Angelus Scheffler, translated by John Wesley.
31. From the German of Wolfgang Dessler, translated by John Wesley.
32. George Herbert.
33. Altered from George Herbert.
34. Altered from George Herbert.
35. From the German of Gerhard Tersteegen, translated by John Wesley.

PART 1: THE POETICAL WORKS OF JOHN AND CHARLES WESLEY

As incense to thy throne above[36]	169	A goodly, formal saint	116
As no return the shower can know	208	A land of corn, and wine, and oil	303
Ask not, who ended here his Span[37]	9	A land where milk and honey flow	255
Assist me thou, at whose command	13	A lifeless form we still retain	358
Assured the Saviour should appear	214	A little strength thou see'st we have	356
Astonished at thy frowning brow[38]	142	A monster to myself I am	91
At first thou gav'st me sweetnesses[39]	36	A new, a living life I live	247
At him my mounting spirit aims	304	A poor, blind child, I wander here	258
At last (alas, how late!) I've seen[40]	342	A powerless form, a lifeless sound	353
At last I own it cannot be	84	A royal priesthood to ordain	326
Author of Being, Source of Light[41]	1	A sinner in thine hands I am	122
Author of Faith, appear!	337	A stranger intermeddleth not	165
Author of Faith, Eternal Word	209	A time to thee I will not set	103
Awake from guilty nature's sleep	301	A vile, backsliding sinner, I	233
Awake, sad drooping heart, awake![42]	87	A vile, unworthy worm, my eyes	82
Awake, sad heart, whom sorrows drown[43]	87	Absolute, unchangeable	267
Awake, the woman's conquering seed	84	Accomplished is our sister's strife	184
Away, vain world! my heart resign[44]	341	Accomplished is thy legal war	49
Away, ye shades, while light I rise[45]	39	According to thy faithful word	310
Awed by a mortal's frown, shall I[46]	178	Act for thine own and *Sion's* sake	164
Awhile amazed I was to see[47]	119	Adam descended from above	249
		Adam, flesh, and self, and pride	68
		Adored by angels, mocked by men	70
## Volume II		After all that I have done	265
		After thy love, if I continue hard	10
A body natural it lies	185	*Again the kind revolving year*	22
A child, a fool, a thing of nought	259	Against his God the creature calls	70
A double portion, from above	344	Ah! leave us not to mourn below	227
A few thou still hast left who stand	354	*Ah! my dear, loving Lord*	114
A golden girdle binds his breast	340	Ah! my Lord, if thou art near	262

36. From the German of Nikolaus von Zinzendorf, translated by John Wesley.
37. John Gambold.
38. From the German of Johann Angelus Scheffler, translated by John Wesley.
39. George Herbert.
40. Altered from John Norris.
41. Samuel Wesley, Sr.
42. George Herbert.
43. George Herbert.
44. Altered from John Norris.
45. George Herbert.
46. From the German of Johann Joseph Winckler, translated by John Wesley.
47. Altered from John Norris.

Ah! tell me that I shall not sin	129
Ah! wherefore did I ever take	101
Ah! wherefore did I ever doubt	259
Ah! woe is me! my joy is fled	121
Ah, woe is me! to evil sold	100
Alarmed at their successful toil[48]	62
Alas! I know not how to pray	205
All earthly comforts I disdain	258
All hail the Saviour's hallowed cross	94
All may from him receive	230
All nations of the earth are blest	310

48. From the German of August Gottlieb Spangenberg, translated by John Wesley.

All power is to our Jesus given	334	Away my flattering hopes and fears	130
All praise to him who dwells in bliss	27	*Away, my unbelieving fear*	198
All souls are thine: and thou for all	72	*Away, vain thoughts that stir within*	246
All the struggle then is o'er	306		
Allured by unresisted grace	203		
Alpha and Omega, save me	96		

Volume III

Already, Lord, I feel thy power	233
Although the vine its fruit deny	199
Amazing height of Jesu's love	195
Amazing height of love Divine	338
Amen to all that God hath said	358
An alien from the life Divine	109
An heart in every thought renewed	78
An heart resigned, submissive, meek	77
An heaven begun on earth we feel	362
An humble, lowly, contrite heart	78
An inward baptism, Lord, of fire	196
And must I yield to black despair	65
And must that which is so good	211
And shall my sins thy will oppose	142
Angels, behold the bleeding Lamb	195
Angels catch th' approving sound	190
Anger and lust thou wilt expel	141
Anger I no more shall feel	278
Answer, dear Lord, thy Spirit's groan	300
Answer that gracious end in me	132
Answer their challenge, Lord	327
Answer thy death's design in me	146
Arise, my soul, arise	323
Arise, O jealous God	328
Arm of God, thy strength put on	89
Arrest our nature's headlong course	331
As a grain of mustard-seed	292
As flowers from mother-earth we rise	28
As gods we did in glory shine	235
As many waters sounds his word	341
As shadows glide o'er hills and dales	28
As the apple of an eye	124
Assailed with doubt, and fear, and grief	232
Assembled here with one accord	228
At thy last gasp the graves displayed	71
Author of faith, to thee I lift	14
Avert from us the heavy doom	351
Awake, Jerusalem, awake	168

A Branch shall in that gospel Day	144
A dying saint can true believers mourn	126
A feast of holy joy, and love	154
A feast prepared for all mankind	153
A feast where milk and honey flow	154
A fountain gushes from his side	233
A man I am of lips unclean	134
A people glorious all within	HSP 1749, 1:34
A ransom for my soul was paid	27
A real, fiery, sulphurous hell	25
A remnant shall be left behind	137
A tenth shall still return, and grow	137
A virtuous maid, for twenty years	176
A world he suffered to redeem	4
A wretched slave of sin, to thee	159
Aaron for us the blood hath shed	248
Above the clouds I will aspire	148
Above the stars of God once more	148
Accept, all-gracious as thou art	331
Acceptance through his only name	309
Adam descended from above	23
Adieu, dear dying saint, adieu	174
Again thy love reveal	45
Against the storm he turned his steady face	120
Against the truth ye stop your ears	136
Against them will I set my face	149
Ah! do not let me trust	46
Ah, do not, Lord, thine own forsake	251
Ah, do not of my goodness doubt	21
Ah! foolish souls, and blind!	82
Ah! gentle, gracious Dove	34
Ah, give me, Lord, my sins to mourn	220
Ah, give us, Saviour, to partake	295
Ah! let it not my Lord displease	160
Ah poor misguided soul!	51
Ah, tell us no more	282

PART 1: *THE POETICAL WORKS OF JOHN AND CHARLES WESLEY*

Ah! What availed him then the gentle mind	110
Ah! when shall I awake	61
Ah! whither should I go	89
Ah woe is me! aghast I said	134
Alas for me! constrained to dwell	160
All glory and praise / To the Ancient	334
All glory and praise / To the God	348
All glory and praise To Jesus our Lord!	337
All glory to God	353
All hail, Redeemer of mankind!	308
All Hail, thou mighty to atone	311
All Hail, thou suffering Son of God	295
All-loving, all-redeeming Lord	281
All might be saved, but all are not	70
All my hopes on thee depend	250
All our salvation is of God	65
All praise to God above	335
All praise to the Lord, All praise is his due	320
All the hindrance is in me	10
All the new earth is now at rest	146
All the power of sin remove	240
All worship and praise	354
Amazing mystery of love!	241
Amazing love to mortals showed	318
An hidden life in Christ I live	166
And can I see thee die unmoved	173
And can we call to mind	297
And can we forbear, In tasting our food	371
And can we forget, In tasting our meat	372
And canst thou, Lord, incline our heart	70
And did they fright the child	50
And is he gone to his eternal rest	109
And shall he not have	334
And shall I let him go	276
And shall not we his death partake	234
And since it cannot please alone	331
And will he not his purchase take	300
Angel, and Son of God, come down	257
Angel of gospel grace	251
Angel of gospel peace he came	34
Angel-powers the throne surround	293
Angels here his servants are	165
Angels in fixed amazement	338
Another and another goes	157
Arise, O God, arise	37
Arise, O God, maintain thy cause!	5
Arm of the Lord, whose vengeance laid	331
Armed with this fiery dart	47
Around our lower orb they burn	261
As Dives would his brethren warn	26
As trees that cast their leaves retain	137
As was from the beginning	349
Assured we shall acceptance find	322
At last I yield, I yield	91
At thy cross behold me lying	278
Author of life Divine	244
Author of our salvation, thee	236
Avenge us of our foe	84
Away with all our trouble	371
Away, ye clouds of unbelief	174
Away, ye dreams of future rest	43

Volume IV

A begging Bartimeus I	379
A child of faithful Abraham I	382
A chosen, saved, peculiar race[49]	316
A daily death I die through fear	356
A darker soul did never yet	324
A day of gloominess and dread	71
A drop of love's eternal sea	474
A faith that doth the mountain move	460
A God that hides himself he is	323
A guilty soul, by sin oppressed	378
A law shall soon from me proceed	301
A leper at thy feet I fall	379
A man of strife to all on earth	354
A mourner for sin	366
A mystery of grief and sin	431
A peace on earth he brings	115
A poor unloving wretch to thee	340
A proverb of reproach below	33
A royal race of priests Divine	309
A secret, slow, internal fire	376

49. See *UP* 2:455.

IDEX OF FIRST LINES OF POETRY BY JOHN AND CHARLES WESLEY

A sinner now undone and lost	468	Alas! thy gracious day is past	346
A spirit dark, and damned I am	332	*All-conquering Lord,*	
A stranger to hope	363	*Whom sinners adore*	53
A stranger to thy people's joys	263	All fulness of peace, All fulness of joy	241
A suffering fight we wage	36	*All glory to God, And peace upon earth*	112
A touch, a word, a look from thee	373	*All glory to God in the sky*	125
A wandering discontented Cain	384	All glory to God, Who ruleth on high	107
A weaker worm did never yet	468	*All-good, Almighty God*	432
Abandoned to the fury's will	423	*All hail the true Elijah*	149
Absorbed in ceaseless woe	427	All in vain for death I languish	352
Accepting my pain	363	All Israel have trangressed thy law	5
According to his word	272	All kind of ill they falsely say	27
Accurst without thy love I am	335	All may in thee our gracious Lord	5
After all that I have done	444	All ocean's waves may swell and roar	78
After thee with joy we come	35	All our desert, we own, is hell	6
Again at God's right hand	147	All power to our great Lord	155
Again my mournful sighs	326	*All praise to our redeeming Lord*	252
Again thou Spirit of Burning come	189	All thanks be to God	210
Ah! do not let me longer live	352	All the day long he meekly stands	29
Ah! give me, Lord, the tender heart	443	All the kingdom from above	194
Ah! give them, Lord, a longer space	29	All things I want, but One is nigh	378
Ah! gracious Lord, forgive	402	All thy resurrection's power	148
Ah, how could I grieve	414	All to God's free grace is owing	107
Ah! Lord, if I again may dare	393	All we like sheep have gone astray,	
Ah! Lord, if it be thou indeed	456	/ Have	69
Ah! Lord, if thou indeed art ours	135	All we like sheep have gone astray,	
Ah never let thy servant rest	236	/ To	290
Ah! no; my spirit's desperate wound	392	*All-wise, all-good, almighty Lord*	120
Ah! no; thy laughter ceases there	346	*All ye that pass by*	371
Ah! tell me, Lord, for whom I pine	475	*All ye that seek the Lord who died*[50]	129
Ah! what availed the shortlived power	385	Amen our hearts reply	184
Ah! what avails it now, that I	384	An earthquake hath the cavern shook[51]	129
Ah! what shall I do?	416	An heavenly birth	114
Ah! what shall I say?	412	An herald from the heavenly King	106
Ah! where am I now!	409	An outcast from thy blissful face	329
Ah! wherefore is this evil come	10	An unregenerate child of man	247
Ah! woe (eternal woe) is me	368	Ancient of Days, why didst thou come	343
Ah! woe is me, condemned to bear	351	*And are our joys so quickly fled*	454
Ah! woe is me, constrained to dwell	28	And art thou not the Saviour still	374
Ah! wretch that I am!	410	*And can I in sorrow lay down*	239
Alas for us, to evil sold	70	*And have I measured half my days*	322
Alas for us, whose eyes are held	136		
Alas, it must be so!	436		
Alas! they cannot buy thy peace	345		

50. *UP* 3:111.
51. *UP* 3:112.

And here will I lie	123
And if I go away	184
And is he removed	156
And is the lovely shadow fled	245
And must thou perish in thy blood	347
And shall I complain	367
And shall I dare mine eyes lift up	368
And shall we now turn back	44
And shall we not hope	120
And shall we not sing	211
And shall we not sing Our Master	52
And when thou dost his spirit receive	26
And when thy dear love	274
And while we are here	114
Angel Divine, who still art near	223
Angels, behold that Infant's face	119
Angels our servants are	231
Angels, rejoice in Jesus' grace	160
Angels speak, let men give ear	107
Arm me with thy great power	15
Arm of the Lord, awake, awake, / The terrors	186
Arm of the Lord, awake, awake! / thine own	302
Arm of the Lord, awake for me	222
Armed with thy strength alone	48
Arrest our fierce pursuers' speed	224
Art thou not our Forerunner gone	159
As a woman in her throes	193
As chaff before the whirlwind drive	30
As fire on crackling stubble feeds	72
As herbs revived by vernal dew	291
As horsemen harnessed for the fight	71
As in the ancient days appear	302
As she soon forgets to mourn	193
As snow behold his garment white[52]	130
As women, when their time draws nigh	291
Assert thy claim, receive thy right	447
Assist me then to come once more	401
At distance heaped on either hand	303
At Immanuel's birth	113
Atonement he made For every one	298

Author of every work Divine	198
Author of faith, to thee I cry	324
Author of never-failing peace	201
Awake and sing, ye souls that dwell	291
Awake as in the ancient days	223
Awake, Jerusalem, awake	305
Awakened by thy threatenings, Lord	287
Away my fond and needless fears	334
Away with our fears! / The Godhead appears	113
Away with our fears, / Our troubles and tears	203

Volume V

A clod of living earth	15
A country of joy	338
A desolate soul, thou know'st I am	337
A drop of that unbounded sea	419
A faithful steward of my Lord	96
A faithful witness of thy grace	138
A feeble, helpless child of man	70
A man of sin and strife	118
A minister of heavenly love	420
A pardon written with his blood	64
A pardoning God of mercy, I	93
A perfect soundness faith shall give	310
A perfect soundness it imparts	312
A royal coronet	85
A servant to thy servants thou	18
A spark of that ethereal fire	419
A thousand times o'erwhelmed with woe	176
A thousand ways and means we try	154
A witness of thy truth I stand	146
A worm hath smote my verdant bower	190
A wretch for years consigned	366
Abandoned to the tempter's power	157
Above the reach of care	357
According to our faith in thee	331
According to thy will	237
Actual and inbred sin	48
Afflicted and grieved, Forlorn	350

---

52. UP 3:112.

IDEX OF FIRST LINES OF POETRY BY JOHN AND CHARLES WESLEY

Afflicted, and hated of men	255	Already, Lord, I feel	347
Afflicted by thy gracious hand	392	Ambition in his breast	84
After my lowly Lord to go	483	Amen, amen, my God and Lord	111
Again we lift our voice	214	Amidst that bright ethereal train	219
Ah! do not let thy sheep depart	243	Amidst the storms of life I stand	356
Ah! do not suffer us to stray	167	Among the slaughtered souls might I	199
Ah! foolish man, where are thine eyes	327	An outcast from thy blissful face	292
Ah! foolish world, forbear	367	*And are we yet alive*	466
Ah! give me all thy grace to know	91	And can I, dearest Lord, not love	414
Ah! let it not my Lord displease	198	And can I the dear soul forget	434
Ah! Lord, if thou hast bid me lead	90	*And did my Lord on earth endure*	149
Ah! Lord, regard my endless woe	247	And hast thou died, O Lamb of God	325
Ah! Lord, the grievous havoc see	248	And if it be thy sovereign will	410
Ah, what a wretch am I!	261	*And is the happy spirit fled*	87
Ah, whither, or to whom	171	*And let our bodies part*	462
Ah! who that piteous sight can bear	3	*And must I give him up?*	445
Ah! wouldst thou, Lord once more awake	246	And shall a worm refuse to stoop	18
		And shall I, Lord, the cup decline	69
Alas, for them, that will not know	250	And shall I not live	29
Alas, he knows it all	170	And shall I not relief afford	19
Alas! if their report be true	328	And shall we mourn to see	215
All are not lost, or wandered back	466	*And shall we not sing*	283
All glory and praise To Jesus	321	*And shall we then abide in sin*	328
All hail, thou lengthener of my days	77	And therefore our God The outcasts hast	391
All honour, and praise	403	And this I shall prove	24
All my business and concern	302	Angel of covenanted grace	65
All my treasure is above	21	Angels all, the men behold	354
All of mine be cast aside	383	Angels your march oppose	272
All on earth is vanity	445	Anna-like within the temple	275
All our works in thee be wrought	426	Answer on him thine own request	416
All power he hath to quell	45	Appear, as when of old confessed	122
All power is thine in earth and heaven	159	Appear in me, bright Morning Star	7
All praise to God on high	83	Appointed by thee, we meet in Thy name	427
All praise to the Lamb!	25		
All praise to the Lord	378	Apprize them of the ruin near	242
All thanks to the Lamb, Who gives us to meet	468	*Are there not in the labourer's day*	17
		Arise, ye men of war	44
All things are possible to him	300	Arise, your strength renew	46
All things are possible to God	301	*Arm of the Lord, awake, arise*	295
All together bound with him	256	As a wide extended river	426
All worship and love	221	As sent, to bless me, from above	422
All worship and praise Are Jesus's due	350	As shipwrecked mariners desire	199
Allow, dear Lord, the widow's plea	337	As sorrowful I, Yet always rejoice	350
Almighty God of truth and love	375	As sure as now thy cross I bear	70

PART 1: THE POETICAL WORKS OF JOHN AND CHARLES WESLEY

Ask, (thyself hast said), and have	240
Assured thy fulness to receive	292
At charity's almighty call	18
At Jesus's call We freely sell all	440
At Jesus's call We gave up our all	387
At Jesus's feet Transported we sit	57
At once their pardon they received	86
At this thrice welcome time of grace	226
Attended by the sacred dread	49
At this solemn noon of night	187
Author of faith, thy love we praise	77
Author of faith, we seek thy face	233
Author of friendship's sacred tie	408
Author of the peace unknown	426
Away my needless fears	448
Away with my fears!	400
Awhile in flesh disjoined	460
Awhile she lay detained beneath	89

Volume VI

A bush unburned amidst the flame	160
A Christian good, without pretence	248
A daily death through life he died	345
A doer of the word he heard[53]	309
A faithful memory bestow	421
A father to the sick and poor	351
A formal self-deceiving race	38
A gazing-stock to fiends and men	106
A leopard watches o'er	124
A man of passions like to ours	354
A murderer convict I come	5
A nursing mother to the poor	270
A peace on earth he brings	115
A servant in his earliest years[54]	308
A sinner that has cloaked his shame	4
A steward just, and wise, and good	351
A stranger in the world below	217
A stranger to thy grace	1
A taste of that mysterious cup	285
A voice out of the temple cries	26

53. UP 3:336.
54. UP 3:355.

A witness of his boundless love	228
A zealous instrument of good	281
Abandoned to extreme despair	428
Above all sin, and doubt, and fear	312
Absent, alas! from God	208
Accept our desire, And give us thy love	440
Accepting our deliverance, Lord	32
Adorn thee with thy richest dress	89
Affliction, poverty, disease	270
Affliction's kind, unfailing friend	353
Ah, dire effect of female pride	436
Ah, give me other eyes	393
Ah! give me to bow my faint head	189
Ah, let us not receive	420
Ah lovely appearance of death	193
Ah! lovely Christlike soul, adieu	263
Ah! might I, Lord, the virtue prove	402
Ah! most compassionate High-Priest	118
Ah! my dear departed friend	365
Ah! never let me speak a word	381
Ah! never suffer them to leave	108
Ah, no:—I still may turn and live	429
Ah, no! we would not have him back	257
Ah, sister in Jesus, adieu	188
Ah! Wherefore did we ever seem to part	70
Ah! whither should ye fly	124
Ah! who are as thy servants blind	116
Ah! wouldst thou in their hearts begin	127
Alas! How distant now, how desolate	58
Alas! I knew not then	2
All glory to God	34
All honour and praise Are Jesus's due	195
All nations, tongues, and people bless	113
All our time and vigour give	424
All power to save, O Lord, is thine	383
All praise to the Lord, All praise is his due	287
All praise to the Lord, Whose trumpet we hear	13
All thine attributes we own	381
Allured by his prevenient grace	358
Almighty God, to thee I cry	380
Almighty Lord of hosts	89
Aloft the spirit flies	205

Amidst impending plagues and woes	42	As born her relatives to please	296
Among the morning-stars	206	As heretics and Lollards still	131
An house we call our own	44	As lightning launched from east to west	138
And am I born to die	426	As listed on Abaddon's side	112
And am I only born to die	432	As pilgrims to the world unknown	315
And are thy plagues and mercies, Lord	31	Ascending to that world of light	234
And can we now our loss regret	357	At the noon of life prepared	290
And can we wish him doomed again	257	Attentive to thy people's prayers	120
And hath he bowed his head	244	*Author and End of my desires*	385
And if the sword a few destroys	160	*Awake, ye guilty souls, awake*	32
And if we must win The crown, like our God	441	Away my tears, and selfish sighs	267
And is he then set free	348	*Away with our sorrow and fear*	197

Volume VII

And is the struggle past	201		
And let this feeble body fail	218		
And must I be to judgment brought	401	*A Child on us bestowed*	233
And O! Almighty Son of God	38	A fond imagination vain	325
And shall I for his bliss repine	258	A Fountain of bliss he freely o'erflows	213
And shall we not press	210	A house with hands not made	137
And when our spirits we resign	403	A lion in my house, shall I	162
And while th' angelic army sings	448	A mother may perhaps neglect	193
And yet this thing impossible is done	60	*A personal distinction see*	210
Angels rejoice! a child born	258	A power to believe We humbly request	28
Anguish if her Lord employs	337	A prisoner of the Lord	139
Answer on them that end of all	407	*A real Unity*	311
Answer, thou bleeding Love Divine	129	A sanctuary the faithful find	205
Answer, thou who hear'st the prayer	291	*A sinner ready to expire*	368
Answer thy own bride and Spirit	143	A sinner saved! (be then my cry)	377
Appalled, o'erwhelmed with conscious fear	21	A sinner saved myself from sin	164
Appalled we saw th' invader's sword	171	*A thousand oracles Divine*	312
Appear in the skies, Thou Saviour of men	48	*A transgressor from the womb*	369
		A witness of his frantic ways	169
Appear with clouds on *Sion's* hill	96	*A wonderful plurality*	216
Are they not of wisdom void	423	Absolute, as one he were	267
Arise into thy resting-place	82	Accomplish then thy gracious end	101
Arm of the Lord, awake, awake	122	Accomplish thy redeeming plan	20
Armed with thine all-sufficient grace	101	Acknowledging the Author	26
Arrested by the pains of hell	133	Added to thy lambs and sheep	38
Arrived above, the stranger stands	257	*Admonished of deliverance nigh*	417
Art thou the God of the Jews alone	138	Adorned in pearl and rich array	74
As a ripe shock of corn brought home	243	Again thou didst, in council met	266
As a wild ass's colt is man	413	Ah, do not let him stay	78
As born her earthly lord to please	327	Ah, Lord, in them the work begin	329

Ah, make me, ere I hence remove	410	Awed, and delighted with a God unknown	426
Ah, suffer not my faith to fail	395		
Ah, take me, Saviour, at my word	141		
Ah, what avails superior light	77		

Volume VIII

Ah, what shall we do, Our pardon to gain	37	A child of sorrow from the womb	426
Ah, when shall we increase	320	*A Christian here her glorious journey ends*	436
Alien from the life of God	391	A day's a thousand years to thee	349
All hail, mysterious Trinity	304	A father of the fatherless	149
All my heart to thee I give	151	A few at this tremendous hour	312
All my hope and consolation	383	A few more days imprisoned here	371
All that is past, my God, forgive	404	*A follower of the bleeding Lamb*	436
All the ill which I have done	403	A general consternation spreads	267
All things in all the Father doth	298	A man for this great end designed	484
All things unto Christ, as man	234	*A man of misery and sin*	381
All who partake of Christ, partake	238	*A meek and lowly follower of the Lamb*	437
Allowed to kiss my Saviour's feet	191	A monster to the world I am	159
Almighty Redeemer of all	27	A nation whom no oaths can bind	300
Along the hill or dewy mead	179	A ray he darted from his throne	32
An heir of endless bliss	137	A ruffian drenched in guiltless blood	353
An issue foul Hath filled my soul	187	A seed shall first their Lord confess	45
And is my Whitefield entered into rest	425	A sinner hanging o'er the grave	354
And let this gross corporeal clay	103	A sinner self-condemned I am	258
And summoned to the mountain-top	410	A smoke out of his nostrils poured	31
And when he has prepared our place	46	A stranger to the blissful grace	354
And when I sink among the dead	402	A strife we are to all around[55]	162
Another day preserved by grace	35	A thousand at thy side shall lie	175
Another in distress and pain	120	A watchman in our Church he was	407
Answer now my mournful prayer	357	A wounded spirit, by sin distressed	117
Answer on her thy wisdom's end	71	Abroad the sword our kin devours	414
Answer, thou suffering Son of man	121	Accomplished see thy own desires	355
Answer to God for me	379	Accomplishing thine own desire	379
Appear my Sanctuary from sin	135	After the fight, ye breathe anew	470
Armed with thy love and patient mind	55	Aghast, ye stood, nor dared oppose	469
As dead already here	139	Again I take the words to me[56]	432
Ask if a mother's heart is kind	193	Again thy Spirit of grace	418
Ask, if the sun doth once mistake	193	Against his peaceable ally	124
Assenting to the letter	343	*Agreed! let it be as the patriots hope*	480
At morning, noon, and evening	26		
At this solemn turn of fate	55		
Author, and End of my desires	386		
Author of godly sorrow, meet	140		
Author of my desires	414		
Away with my fears	369		

55. *UP* 2:447.
56. In MARC, MA 1977/583/32, #19, the first line reads, "I take the words prescribed to me."

IDEX OF FIRST LINES OF POETRY BY JOHN AND CHARLES WESLEY

Ah! do not at a distance stand	160	Among the sons of men I dwell	127
Ah give me first the rapturous powers	386	An army of associators	450
Ah! leave me not, my God and Lord	88	Ancient of days! thy name	177
Ah! Lord, regard the pains I feel	121	And if he comes with shows of love	94
Ah! suffer not my foe to boast	24	*And if I may not testify*	343
Ah! suffer not their hearts to say	77	*And if you wish in peace to live*	475
Ah, who the ways of Providence can know	44	*And is it not a dream?*	242
Alas, what shall we do	314	*And let these wretched bodies die*	345
All-conquering King	394	*And lo! before thy face t' appear*	346
All counsels to sum up in one	475	*And may we not to Satan yield*	419
All glory to God	395	*And must I sink among the dead*	347
All glory to God! Plucked out of the flame	280	*And now from street to street they roam*	454
All glory to our gracious Lord	204	*And O! beneath thy mercy's wings*	266
All my bones, my strength shall bless thee	78	And thou, my soul, thy Saviour praise	75
All my days like smoke expire	186	And which we cordially agree[58]	405
All my heart hath sought thy face	210	*And while thy mercy's utmost power*	345
All my promises renew	442	Answering in us thy Spirit's cries	485
All my sins I called to mind	217	Answering to thy Spirit's call	367
All our foes by thy right hand	40	Appear as crucified for me	360
All thanks and all praise To thee will I give	255	Are not his servants kings? and rule	105
All that go by pluck off her grapes[57]	163	Arise, O God, arise!	20
All that on this Rock are stayed	108	Arise, O Lord, into thy rest	248
All the day long I wait on thee	49	Arise, O Lord of hosts, arise	301
All the men whose hearts are right	141	Arise, O Lord, thine arm make bare	14
All the power of pride and passion	78	*Arise, thou jealous God, arise*	404
All their wickedness consume	132	Arm of the Lord, awake	268
All these I from my youth have broke	347	*Arm of the Lord, awake, awake*	273
All things are possible to God	415	Arm the man of thy right hand	269
All those that see me bruised and torn	42	*Arms, and the good old cause I sing*	450
All thy church of creatures new	142	Around his church the angels stand	151
All thy mighty works are wrought	113	Around thy plenteous table spread	244
All who of their downfall hear	141	As an eagle swift and strong	190
All-wise omnipotent creators	476	As arrows in the giant's hand	243
All ye that fear the Lord, draw near	146	As grass on the house-top decays	246
Almighty God, to whom alone	178	As hungry wolves they come from far	318
Although in distress, I labour and strive	255	As in religion's cause they join	267
America her felons pours	276	As lovers in the appointed hour	455
America, we trust shall show	308	As round Jerusalem	240
Among the gods there's none like thee	170	As servants whom their lords chastise	238
		As sheep appointed to be slain / By cruel	266

57. *UP* 2:448.

58. Osborn rewrote: O may we in thy love agree.

PART 1: *THE POETICAL WORKS OF JOHN AND CHARLES WESLEY*

As sheep appointed to be slain / The victims	285
As strong, and glorying in my might	428
As sure as God brought back our head	28
As sworn their Maker to dethrone	4
As the hart, with fleeing faint	95
As waters let them pass away	129
Ask, and the Gentile world receive	5
At morn we see the fiery void	461
At this most alarming crisis	291
Awake, O Lord, for us arise	102

Volume IX

A charge to keep I have	60
A Christian, should I fly, or yield	224
A church which may remain	471
A fallen, sinful child of man	11
A favourite child of Providence	344
A few good days I long to live	313
A few more days preserve me here	30
A guilty, weak, and helpless worm	311
A living principle of grace	255
A mother principled with grace	349
A multitude of sinners	296
A nation God delights to bless	268
A novice, to myself unknown	98
A pleasant heritage is mine	131
A poor afflicted sojourner	142
A prostrate soul desiring	408
A rebel to this present hour	100
A Saviour I have	407
A sojourner and stranger	294
A thousand secret checks within	21
A trembling, persecuted slayer	128
A voice is in his blood	164
A voice of shrieking fear	464
Aaron a transient blessing gave	61
Aaron lifts up his praying hands	61
Above what we can ask or hope	190
Accepting what the poor bestowed	193
According to my faith in thee	331
Acquiring his first spot of ground	25

Adam descended from above	415
Afraid to think the vision true	453
After I have attended	283
After we have endured a while	158
Again to Satan's yoke I bow	136
Ah! foolish souls, th' accursed race	87
Ah, how can I my heart prepare	213
Ah, leave us not in danger's day	221
Ah! Lord, with thee we ask, How long	76
"Ah, no," the faithless spies reply	73
Ah! rid me of this fear and doubt	30
Ah! save me from a worse extreme	63
Ah, show me that happiest place	362
Ah! why should ye be stricken more?	369
Ah, woe is me, by lust enticed!	140
Ah, woe is me, immersed in sin	377
Alas for sinners that obtain	71
Alas, when seeming to repent	41
All in ourselves the straitness lies	190
All Israel shall see	288
All my life of grace is thine	239
All power, O God, in earth and heaven	159
All thanks to heaven let Britain pay	230
All that command is love!	104
All that in his footsteps tread	78
All that on thy name believe	451
All which thou hast heard above	450
All ye that Sion love	466
Almighty God of love	469
Almighty to persuade thou art	16
Am not I the wildered sheep?	331
An abject slave I long have been	210
An Advocate in heaven we have	155
An alien to my mother's sons	305
An hidden God indeed thou art!	420
An offering to their God	470
And dare we our perfection boast?	14
And have not I ungrateful been	110
And let my body languish	244
And let my carcase fall	78
And shall we in ourselves confide	233
Angel Divine, who goest before	45
Answers my almighty Lord	434
Appear, Great God, appear to me	271

Are there, Saviour, can there be	273	A pastor who o'erlooks the rest	499
Arise, and shine with borrowed rays	451	A perfect confidence inspire	311
Arm me with jealous care	60	A Pharisee his neighbours blames	459
Arm of the Lord, O Christ, thou art	403	A Pharisee the law defends	461
Armed with Jesu's two-edged sword	90	A preacher of repentance true	445
Armed with the presence of my Lord	120	A prisoner for religion's sake	244
Armed with thy patient Spirit	283	A proud philosopher forsakes	328
Armed with your Lord's authority	267	A rich man saved! it cannot be	327
Art thou not at leisure now	284	A sinner still, though saved I am	261
As a wide-extended river	276	A sinner, though he truly know	320
As an eagle cleaves the air	51	A sinner's heart by lust possessed	481
As children we continue long	378	A sinner's penitential prayer	291
As due to my most righteous deed	227	A soul that hungers for the word	280
As eagles fluttering o'er their nest	399	A time, I know there is t' obey	175
As giants may they run their race	134	A time there is to live alone	306
As many as on earth are found	439	A true forerunner of his Lord	445
As my day my strength hath been	113	A type of modern parents see!	335
Ascending to be clothed upon	188	A wicked priest to hell consigned	381
"Ask what ye will," 'tis Jesu's word	185	A withered hand the miser is	462
Assisted by preventing grace	274	Above my Lord I would not be	468
Assure me, thou my debt hast paid	162	Absolute faith, O Lord, I owe	359
At evening to myself I say	146	Absolute Lord, and Judge supreme	252
At the close of life's short day	319	According to my faith bestowed	210
Attentive to their feeblest cry	412	According to thy faithful word	132
Awake, the woman's heavenly Seed	7	Actions he more than words requires	204
Away with your oblations vain	371	Adopted by the Father's grace	442
		Advancement in thy kingdom here	336
		After all that I have done	5
		After his own almighty power	385

Volume X

		Again the hidden God appears	74
A crime resolved upon	496	Ah, canst thou find it in thy heart	6
A death devoted race	53	Ah, foolish man, who hears thy word	206
A father if I more esteem	242	Ah, give me, Lord, in thee to find	44
A follower of thy suffering[59] Son	404	Ah give me, Lord, to use aright	302
A fountain of infectious blood	485	Ah! leave us not to venture	182
A grain of grace may we not see	274	Ah, Lord, preserve my soul from sin	242
A guide and master-builder wise	460	Ah! Lord, we must with shame confess	323
A length of years in sin and pain	486	Ah! Lord, with late regret I own	3
A life of piety severe	333	Ah, Lord, with trembling I confess	165
A loose morality proceeds	299	Ah, no: we disavow	363
A maid cannot forget her dress	5	Ah! Saviour, keep my trembling heart	315
A moment's joy they dearly buy	212	Ah, simple souls, who fondly dream	14
A pastor should consider long	460	Ah, whither shall I run	447
		Ah! why am I left to complain	26

59. Osborn changed "suffering" to "patient."

Ah wouldst thou, Lord, My soul inspire	39	Asunder sawn with anxious thought	128
Ah! wretched souls, who urged by shame	240	At first our wisely silent Lord	488
		Attached to earth, and dead within	456
Alas, shall I stand idle still	332	Attended by thy Spirit's power	471
All are Gergesenes in heart	219	Author of faith, on me confer	310
All glory to God	221	Author of faith, the grace impart	110
All hail, thou suffering Son of Man	215	Author of faith, the pregnant grace	298
All kinds and all degrees of sin	263	Avenger of his slighted laws	87
All! shall all forgiven be!	469	Awake, thou guilty world, awake	86
All, the awful Judge to see	383	Away my faithless fear	198
All the good things which now I claim	84	Away this soft, luxurious pride!	215
All these sacred words I read	277	Awed by the righteous doom of them	391
All thy commands I shall fulfil	325	Awed by thy continual presence	405
All thy cures are mysteries	160		
Allured and strengthened from above	145		
Allured into the desert	73		

Volume XI

Almighty Lord of earth and skies	117
Among the dead in vain	437
An end of all these earthly things	72
An entrance through thy speaking blood	200
An humble instrument of God	452
An hundred pence! How small the debt	320
An ignorant crowd Of sinners we join	228
An instrument of Jesus' grace	297
And can we doubt a future day	498
And dost thou not thyself suspect	69
And shall thy followers, Lord, complain	412
Angel and mediator	129
Angel of covenanted grace, / The	79
Angel of covenanted grace, / Come	129
Applause from man he cannot bear	324
Are words the proof of sin forgiven?	263
Arise in the power of thy love	479
Arise, thou Sun of righteousness	134
As I have believed, O Lord	212
As lord he o'er his fellows reigns	379
As many as in Adam died	400
As many as in Adam fell	337
As taught by thee, O God, I pray	80
Ask we, now the storm is laid	480
Assist me, Lord, against that day	186
Assist me, Lord, to lay aside	193

A child of hell with Satan joins	431
A church of living members	58
A grateful soul cannot defer	252
A guide of souls will not retain	163
A happy instrument of grace	145
A hidden kingdom in the skies	178
A humble heart he makes his shrine	60
A late-returning child	237
A leprous soul that feels	144
A life thou hast which ne'er begun	424
A mere helpless sinner I	258
A messenger required to speak	433
A minister should burn and shine	373
A monument of mercy's power	303
A murderer from the first	85
A pastor fraught with Jesu's grace	160
A pastor good in God's esteem	454
A pastor should his flock prepare	505
A pastor with courageous zeal	53
A preacher should with freedom use[60]	191
A priest corrupt whom avarice blinds	281
A prosperous minister	143
A ready way repentance makes	124
A rich man saved! it cannot be / Ye that	34
A rich man saved! it cannot be / Till	262
A saint quite off his guard	206

60. *UP* 2:117.

INDEX OF FIRST LINES OF POETRY BY JOHN AND CHARLES WESLEY

A Saviour born, in love supreme	117	All must confess thy power	296
A sheep before the shearers brought	295	All my powers shall then be brought	358
A sign admired by thy redeemed	121	All my worldly wisdom lose	259
A sin there is which far exceeds	128	All that voice of God shall hear	479
A sinner blind and poor	37	All who went his birth before	41
A sinner in thy sight	236	Allured by his Redeemer's love	263
A sinner long possessed by sin	218	All-wise, all-good, almighty Lord	318
A sinner now I come to thee	498	Amidst the worldly noise	492
A sinner once to sight restored	442	An advocate the sinner needs	80
A soul by sacred infancy	31	An answer plain and full we give	447
A stranger to the judge she was	255	An apostolic prelate hopes	36
A stranger to the truth of grace	456	An herald from the King of kings	116
A Teacher come from God, and more	340	An herald of the grace Divine	401
A teacher sent from God designs	403	An humble saint will never praise	110
A token he for good receives	161	An image of the Gentiles see	39
A true disciple of the Lord	286	An impotent desire I feel	365
A vessel of mere mercy I	155	An Israelite indeed	330
A vision true is proved by fear	102	An upper room will soon be found	73
A voice, and nothing more	349	And have they not agreed it now	445
A widow poor, forlorn, oppressed	255	And let the railing world exclaim	448
A wonder of grace To angels and men!	359	And me—may every soul subjoin	468
A youth possessed by sin	187	And shall I his lot refuse	286
Able to break th' infernal band	71	And shall mere man of men demand	372
Accompanied it needs must be	252	And shall not we who Christ embrace	101
Accomplish then thy love's design	379	And still we trust in thee	307
Adam descended from above	341	And what though every man condemn	418
Adjudged to die he is by all	81	And while he ready makes our place	65
After I have endured awhile	250	Angel, and Porch, and Pool thou art	364
After we have affliction seen	134	Angels, saints, and men are glad	233
Ah do not from thy people go	65	Angels the banquet share	239
Ah, leave us not, above our power	202	Annexed to means improbable	335
Ah, Lord, direct my aim aright	206	Answer then thy blessed design	459
Ah, Lord, enlarge my selfish heart	348	Answer thine own design	215
Ah, Lord, my ignorance I own	487	Answer thy mercy's whole design	115
Ah, tell it, Lord, to me	56	Answering to their pastor's zeal	414
Ah, wretched man when God requires	51	Appear, to us appear	96
Alas for him! whose teaching pride	72	Are there not still who would receive	496
Alas for us, who need beware[61]	273	Art thou not able to convert	44
Alas, ye scorn the Lord to fear	243	As a wild ass's colt is man	39
All his treasure here he views	228	As heretics and foes	354
All in their wretched selves alone[62]	347	As members of that heavenly Man	423
		As patriots wise and good	482
		As walking in a shadow vain	17
61. UP 2:186.		Ask the ancient prophecies	294
62. UP 2:223.			

At each unrighteous judgment seat	83	A zealot of the straitest sect	236
As his feet that harlot see	167	A zealous servant of the Lord	336
At length the time is quite fulfilled	400	Accepted in the Well-beloved[65]	100
At the great feast of God	239	According to your law indeed	409
Author of faith and Finisher	388	Added to the chosen seed	328
Author of faith, appear	94	Adopt me by thy grace	229
Author of faith implant in	387	Adorable captivity	70
Avenge us, Saviour, of our	273	Adored by the acclaiming crowd	271
Awake out of your pleasing dream	375	After he hath sent his Son	47
Away then all your boastings vain	157	Again th' angelic hosts adore	48
		Against distress foreshown	384

Volume XII

		Ah, never Lord in anger grant	279
A bigot obstinately wrong	425	Ah, what can outward wonders do	67
A captive, poor, despised, and bound	450	Ah, whither will ye fly	233
A casual unexpected guest	227	Ah! wretched souls, who once in grace	22
A Christian innocently may	325	Alarmed by mercy's sudden stroke	267
A convert purged of all his stains	398	Alarmed in vain the truth he hears	414
A criminal they could not doom	74	Alas, what shall, or can I do	323
A faithful soul will never stay	118	All, all the blessings prove	122
A few compendious words	439	All, except the children? No	323
A fisher of men Will others invite	114	All glory and power	445
A judge so late, he quits his place	407	All harmoniously combine	120
A king to God above	421	All is grace and mystery!	87
A magistrate corrupt and lewd	413	All our hopes and souls we venture	4
A man may his Creator fear	243	All power he to the Man hath given	151
A man of God, like holy Paul	394	All that to the truth belong	76
A picture of my life I view	437	All the comfortable aid	355
A plain indisputable case![63]	222	All the sins of all mankind	88
A preacher full of faith and zeal	397	All this mountain load remove	11
A present help in trouble	438	All thy other works are wrought	305
A rich inheritance they buy	80	Almighty Redeemer of men	211
A sinner poor and lame	160	Always as pardoned sinners here	373
A soul by man forsaken	45	Always ready thee we know	358
A soul who hath the Saviour known	101	Amazed the scoffers stand	282
A stronger reason to take heed	400	Amazed the strange effects we see	277
A sufferer for his Saviour's cause	433	Ambassador of the Most-High	55
A universal pest	409	Amen! we thus our seal set to	133
A warm concern for Jesu's name	354	Among the branches found no more	22
A while[64] in Jesus' servant blessed	383	An apostolic minister[66]	353
A word, a look from thee	233	An envious, proud, and selfish man	355
		An old disciple of thy Lord	386

63. UP 2:319.
64. Osborn error: Awhile.
65. UP 2:278.
66. UP 2:387.

And can a messenger be proud	291	A few may scruple to confess	102
And let the Spirit bind	374	A fountain of life and grace	240
And let the world his servants chase	290	A life of poverty and toil	262
And shall not, Lord, the heathens rise	419	A Man of griefs thou didst appear	99
And shall not we the same require[67]	94	A sinless saint he was not yet	55
And shall thy followers complain	74	A sinner saved through Jesu's grace	37
Anointed, sent from him	17	A taste of thy tormenting fears	130
Anxious thy followers' lives alone	67	A thousand times I faint	159
Apostle of thy Father thee	107	A token of thy favour	45
"Apply to Jesus' minister"	247	A wretched man of sin	177
Are there not found instructors still	354	Abraham did for the promise stay	134
Arm me Lord with double grace	377	Absolved from all which we have done	114
Armed with authority the man	78	Accepted first through faith alone	170
Armed with the power of Jesu's grace	88	Accounted just through faith Divine	171
Art thou the Lamb of God	228	Afflicted by a gracious God	158
As champions for the church they stand	404	Afflicted I cry To God for relief	176
As evil when they cast us out	29	After he had been tempted, tried	134
As for religion's cause	362	After his few days of mourning	117
As his only Son and heir	60	Against your Luciferian pride	186
As in the watery glass	200	Ah do not at a distance stand	254
As light and heat the solar rays	251	Ah, do not thou our souls forsake	211
As soon as suffering saints require	320	Ah, give me constantly to feel	58
As truth his record we receive	131	Ah, give me wisdom to discern	37
Assaulted, but not hurt, he found	351	Ah, grant me, Lord, in death to find	104
Assured I am by Jesus' rise	344	Ah, Saviour. Now in me reveal	105
At thy command we rise	17	Aiming at the noblest end	21
Atoning blood and water		All glory and praise To Jesus our Lord	248
clean	SH 1762, 2:264	All our best performances	42
Author of immortality	171	All that desperate sinners want	137
Author of our salvation, thee	7	All their banded powers we dare	247
Author of our sure salvation	321	All things that I may clearly see	230
Authority in things Divine	307	All we, like sheep, have gone astray	283
Away with him from earth, they cry	391	All who read, or hear, are blessed	219
Away with our fears!	46	Almost o'erpowered, compelled	185
		And let th' apostle still forbear	54

Volume XIII

		And shall the chief of every sect	35
		And when our faith in vision ends	71
A body natural, by food	39	Angels, where'er we go, attend	118
A city we seek from above	162	Answer the blessed end	201
A conscious unbeliever	44	Are we justified by grace	24
A crown of righteousness	111	Are we not plainly here forbid	207
A dog, and worse, alas, am I	191	Arm me with thy gracious mind	68
		Arm us with thy patient mind	20
67. *UP* 2:277.		Armed with the dear Redeemer's mind	235

As beautiful, as useful there	228	Blest be the Name that sets thee free	181
As favours from my kindest Lord	84	Blind from my birth to guilt and thee	263
As motion raised by vital heat	170	Blind we were, but now we see	291
As on my dying bed	257	Bold may I wax, exceeding bold	180
As soon a hellish fiend accurst	281	*Bold shall I stand in thy great day*[73]	347
As soon as in him we believe	240	Bold we ask through Christ the Son	357
As to a loathsome carcase joined	10	Bound down with twice ten Thousand ties	271
As when the active soul is fled	172	Boundless wisdom, power Divine[74]	281
Astonished at thy patient love	194	Bow thine ear, in mercy bow	115
Author of our faith, we look	41	Brood thou o'er our nature's night	189
		Brother in Christ, and well-beloved, / Attend	227

Volume I

		Brother in Christ, and well-beloved, / To	340
Back recalled, I know not how	321	Build us in one body up	356
Be all into subjection brought	228	Burdened beneath this fleshly load	243
Be all my added life employed	75	Buried in sin, thy voice I hear	133
Be heaven even now our soul's abode[68]	163	Buried, o'erwhelmed, and lost in sin	94
Be I, O thou my better part[69]	344	Burst we then the bands of death	158
Be it unto angels known	364	But, alas! I soon rebelled	320
"Be still—and know that I am God!"	235	But altered now, and fall'n he is[75]	61
Be thou my joy; be thou my dread	241	But art thou not already mine	326
Be thou, O Rock of Ages, nigh	128	But art thou not our Father now?	368
Before thy face, O Lord Most High[70]	104	But as I raved, and grew more wild[76]	39
Before us make thy goodness pass	238	But if thou tarriest, why must I?[77]	64
Behold, for me the Victim bleeds	327	But I of means have made my boast	234
Behold the Saviour of mankind[71]	117	But, lo! a place he hath prepared	306
Being of beings, God of Love	34	But, lo! thy anger kindled is	368
Being of beings, may our praise[72]	168	But, O! forgivenss is with thee	256
Believe who will that human pain	314	But, O! his tyranny is o'er!	335
Believing in the woman's Seed	211	But, O! how soon thy wrath is o'er	327
Beneath th' afflictive stroke I fall	247	But, O, in vain the tempter tries	309
Blessed, peaceful state! Where, lulled to sleep	245	But, O! the mightier work of grace	323
Blest be the God that calls thee home	183	But, O the power of grace Divine	288
Blest be the God whose tender care	191	But, O! what offering shall I give[78]	160
Blest be the God whose bounty's store	191		

68. From the German of Nikolaus von Zinzendorf, translated by John Wesley.
69. Altered from George Sandys.
70. From the German of Johann A. Freylinghausen, translated by John Wesley.
71. Samuel Wesley, Sr.
72. From the German of Gerhard Tersteegen, translated by John Wesley.
73. From the German of Nikolaus von Zinzendorf, translated by John Wesley.
74. From the German of Anna Dober, translated by John Wesley.
75. George Herbert.
76. George Herbert.
77. George Herbert.
78. From the German of Joachim Lange, translated by John Wesley.

But, O! with our transgressions stained	79	Be it according to thy word, / Ready to meet	69
But shall thy creature ask thee why?	237	Be it according to thy word, / This moment[88]	270
But since thy will my bounds of life assigned[79]	44	Be it according to thy word! / Redeem me	305
But soon he'll break Death's envious chain[80]	118	Be thou, O Love, whate'er I want	74
But stay—What read I written there[81]	42	Before thee I my heart persuade	311
But thou didst reckon, when at first[82]	41	Before they see the realms of light	354
But thou, they say, art passing by	263	Before thou dost in vengeance come	346
But though my life henceforth be thine	277	Before thy people's face they cast	349
But we now extol his name	289	Behold, for thee I ever wait	197
But when abroad at once I view[83]	38	Behold, he comes! and every eye	339
But when all in me is sin[84]	108	Behold him, all ye that pass by	74
But when thou dost the sense repress[85]	46	Behold, his flock from every side	18
But while I grow, as heaven were mine[86]	45	Behold, the Lord your God shall come	51
But will he not our souls sustain	302	Behold the Servant of my grace	171
But, working still, within my soul[87]	103	Behold, thou standest at the door	361
By faith expiring Jacob knew	216	Behold, to thee our souls aspire	228
By faith he left th' oppressive land	218	Behold, ye souls that mourn for God	164
By faith he slew the typic Lamb	218	Beholding as with open face	360
By faith the handmaid of the Lord	213	Believing on my Lord, I find	203
By faith the holy men of old	210	Beneath my load he faints, and dies	71
By faith we know thee strong to save	209	Beneath thy shadow let us sit	362
By faith, when now to manhood grown	217	Better that I had never felt	100
By faith, while Israel's host surrounds	219	Better that I had never known	100
		Better that we had never known	359
		Bid me bear the hallowed cross	155

Volume II

		Bind, Father, hand and foot thy son[89]	15
Baffled, I still my foes defied	202	Bind in me the strong man, bind	67
Baffled, o'ercome, I yield at last	81	Blasted, the vigour of the young	56
Baptized into my Saviour's name	246	Blessing and honour, praise and love	337
Barren although my soul remain	199	Blessing, honour, thanks, and praise	188
Be his dread name on earth confest	24	Blessings on all he pours	230
		Blessings, the payment of the poor	25
		Blest are they, entirely blest	318
		Blest be the dear, uniting love	221
		Blest, O Israel, art thou	307
		Blind as I am, with both my hands	108

79. George Herbert.
80. Samuel Wesley, Sr.
81. George Herbert.
82. George Herbert.
83. George Herbert.
84. George Herbert.
85. George Herbert.
86. George Herbert.
87. George Herbert.

88. The first and last stanzas of this hymn have identical lines 1 and 2, but lines 3 and 4 differ.
89. From the German of Gottfried Arnold, translated by John Wesley.

Bliss to carnal minds unknown	218
Bold shall we stand in thy great might	348
Born from above, I soon shall praise	182
Born into the world above	190
Break forth into joy, Your Comforter sing	170
Break off the yoke of inbred sin	145
Break, stubborn heart; and sigh no more	139
Break the dire confederacy	31
Breathe the breath of simple life	67
Burdened am I, and opprest	146
But that thou art my wisdom, Lord[90]	12
Burning with unhallowed fires	105
But ended is the shameful hour	253
But have ye not his being known	54
But how shall I to thee attain	84
But let us hasten to the day	222
But let us plead for sin no more	350
But let us to the end endure	356
But make us faithful unto death	348
But O, above all thy kindness we praise	177
But O, how soon from glory driven	202
But, O! the jealous God the blame	116
But Oh! they soon forsook their God	58
But shall human weakness dare	283
But shall I throw on God the blame	101
But the righteousness of faith	241
But they who wait upon the Lord	148
But thou canst preserve from sin	155
But thou canst wash the leper clean	148
But we, alas! deserve thy blame	349
But while I thus dispute and grieve[91]	13
But while thou, my Lord, art nigh	268
But will he not at last appear	165
But wilt thou let thy foe devour	127
Butter and honey did I eat	120
By faith I every moment stand	233
By impious feet no longer trod	168
By me, O my Saviour, stand	125

90. Altered from George Herbert.
91. Altered from George Herbert.

Volume III

Back to the presence of the Lord	25
Be everlasting praise	347
Be it according to thy will	20
Be it so! they all reply	293
Because he hides his face	276
Because he saith, Do this	277
Because I would not come to him	19
Before his name I knew	31
Before I at his bar appear	27
Before thou hadst the debt laid down	68
Begin the great millennial day	342
Behold the all-atoning Lamb	96
Behold the Lamb of God, who takes	4
Behold the Lamb of God, who bears	20
Beneath thy bruising hand I fall	325
Bids all men everywhere repent	67
Blessing, and praise to thee	99
Blessing to God, for ever blest	369
Blest be the Lord, for ever blest	263
Blest be the love, for ever blest	280
Break to me now the hallowed bread	257
Bring in the kingdom of his peace	140
Bring near the glad day	283
Burdened with guilt and misery	153
But both in Jesus join	268
But can I fear thy justice nigh	65
But canst thou not thy work revive	341
But dost thou give thy special grace	69
But ended is the grief unknown	179
But first of the celestial train	261
But hath thy love excepted none?	69
But if my gracious day is past	18
But if thy written Word be true	70
But is it possible that I	43
But is thy grace less free	30
But none, like this mysterious rite	245
But O, forbid it, Lord!	57
But O! if mercy is with thee	18
But O! What words the mighty joy can paint	125
But oh! my strivings all are vain	158
But soon the morning vapor passed	110

But soon the subtle fiend	46
But soon the tender life will die	242
But thy love hath taught us better	364
But you may rest secure	50
By faith and hope already there	285
By faith even now we see	316
By faith we nail them to the tree[92]	317
By grace we draw our every breath	95
By my own hands, not his, I fall	27
By nature only free to ill	94
By that great sacrifice	328
By the cross we abide	324
By the picture of thy passion	277
By thine agonizing pain	228
By thine all-atoning blood	265
By thy meritorious dying	226

Volume IV

Base wretch that I am!	414
Be faithful unto death, he	40
Be it a vale of tears	399
Be it according to thy will	341
Be it according to thy word, / Now let me	325
Be it according to thy word, / Accomplish	373
Be saved from hell, from sin, and fear	29
Be this my one great business here	317
Be with him in that darkest hour	66
Because from sin we turn away	38
Because thou lovedst, and diedst for me	344
Before his dreadful camp the Lord	73
Before I all thy people shame	385
Before me place in dread array	316
Before their face an Eden blooms	71
Before with fruitless horror we	104
Behold, and in his footsteps tread	300
Behold me prostrate at thy feet	454
Believing against hope	14
Believing still in Jesu's name	175

Beneath my love's almighty shade	56
Beneath thine anger's present weight	11
Bent to devour the total prey	97
Bent to redeem a sinful race	225
Beset on every side	267
Betake thee to the secret place	292
Better she is than richest mines	234
Beyond the world and Satan's power	369
Bishop of souls, regard our cry	65
Blessing, and praise, and thanks, and love	256
Blest for ever be the name	463
Blow ye the trump, in Sion blow	70
Blow ye the trumpet's loudest blast	74
Bold they return to sure success	97
Born his creatures to restore	107
Born thy people to deliver	116
Borne by the prayer of faith I lie	380
Break forth into praise! Our Surety and head	145
Break not off my weakest hold	421
Breathe, O breathe thy loving Spirit	219
Brethren, the end is near	17
Bring the sweet spices of your sighs[93]	129
Britons, rejoice, the Lord is King!	93
Bruised by the oppressor's hand	34
Burdened with a world of grief	221
But all in vain for me they grieve	339
But can it be, that I should prove	479
But God, we know, is given indeed	175
But I felt it too soon	410
But I hear a voice say	213
But I my servants' word fulfil	299
But I the Lord thy Saviour am	304
But I, the righteous Lord, on all	306
But if from him I turn mine eye	456
But if thou nothing hast to plead	347
But is it possible	398
But it is thy gracious pleasure	465
But lo! in our distress we see	455
But, Lord, I trust in thee	14
But neither threats nor smiles can move	288
But now I seek to touch my Lord	453

92. Osborn changed to: We nail the old Adam to the tree.

93. *UP* 3:111.

But O, forgivenesses are thine	4	Barren and withered trees	55
But O! thou seest my desperate case	381	Be it weariness and pain	178
But rather let him freely take	294	Be jealous for thy glorious name	167
But shall my bold presumption dare	369	Be near to defend	27
But surely at the last	274	Be this, dear Lord, my chief desire	394
But they who, sunk in self-despair	291	Be this my constant care	202
But thou, my Lord, art nigher still	471	Be this my hospitable care	345
But thou, my Lord, art rich in grace	470	Be this my whole employ below	99
But we have only evil wrought	3	Be thou his mouth and wisdom, Lord	107
But we know by faith and feel	176	Because our God they have not known	259
But we thy warning take	20	Before my faith's enlightened eyes	92
But where is all his furious boast	304	Before the morning watch her cry	88
But whether thou hast ever healed	361	Before thy glorious eyes we spread	419
But who of all your hosts can tell	160	Before thy sheep, great Shepherd, go	229
But will I not confirm my word	310	Beguiled, alas, by Satan's art	244
But wilt thou not at last appear	264	Beguiled, alas, of their reward	245
But woes, redoubled woes	19	*Behold the servant of the Lord!*	10
But ye that fear the Lord	18	*Being of beings, God of love*	291
By earth and hell pursued in vain	303	Believe on his name,	
By faith already there	162	Till inwardly clean	322
By faith they conquered kingdoms	85	Believe, that Jesus died for thee	123
By faith we catch thy mantle	150	Believing against hope	172
By faith we see the glory	80	Believing on our common Lord	318
By him into existence brought	119	Beneath their anger's utmost weight	260
By that highest point of passion	139	Betrothed to the Son of God, I abide	350
By the coming of thy Spirit	140	Better for me to die, than live	191
By the earnest of thy Spirit	167	Between the saints, and Holy One	287
By the Holy Ghost we wait	181	Beyond the bounds of time, and space	168
By the pomp of thine ascending	139	Bid me of men beware	269
By the sense of sin forgiven	194	Big with earnest expectation	297
By this the Saviour of mankind	106	Blessing, and thanks, and love,	
By thy bonds my soul release	360	and might	280
By thy fasting and temptation	138	*Blest be the Lord! by earth and heaven*	298
By thy first blood-shedding heal us	138	Body, and soul at once restore	238
By thy own right-hand of power	142	Both shall reach the happy shore	452
By thy sorer sufferings save us	139	Both with calm impatience press on	456
By thy Spirit, Lord, reprove	357	Bounds I will not set to thee	291
By whom shall I thy sorrows cheer?	306	Bow every soul at Jesu's name	35
		Brandish in faith till then	42
		Break hearts of stone	58
		Breathe on us, Lord, in this our day	470

Volume V

Baffle the crooked serpent's skill	233	Breathes as in us both one soul	453
Balm into wounded spirits it pours	111	Breathless leave this heavy clod	206
		Bring us every moment nearer	456

Burning before the Sovereign Sire	287
But above all afraid	270
But above all, lay hold	41
But above all thy power display	166
But can I now the loss lament	194
But chiefly would I make my moan	97
But (for I know my wretched heart	414
But God is to his promise just	296
But I trust thou wilt stay	27
But Jesus shall show his fulness of power	334
But let the terrors of thy law	126
But let us all abide	273
But let us now the promise prove	319
But lo! when Jonathan was dead	420
But lo! with humble faith I bow	5
But may we not strive	320
But, my Lord, I cry to thee	444
But now, my gracious God, thy love	376
But now we would thy word obey	252
But O! suffice the season past / We now	131
But O! suffice the season past / That we	154
But O thou faithful God of love	102
But oh! thou wouldst not have me live	372
But, oh! your evil day is past	362
But our great God, who reigns on high	251
But shall I then depart	171
But shall not sin remain	47
But still the world refuse	370
But still we remain	266
But that the faithless world may know	238
But this we can tell	31
But thou art ready still to run	79
But thou canst my soul transform	303
But thou hast given a loud alarm	269
But thou know'st, a sharper pain	100
But thou know'st this heart of mine	100
But thy tender pity saw	386
But we who now our Lord confess	382
But who on earth with thee is blest	404
But who the dreadful word receive	154
But will his desperate madness go	396
But wilt thou not at last appear	252
But wilt thou not thy cause maintain	257
But worse than all my foes, I find	268
But worse than all thou seest within	102
By all thou hast done	290
By anger, malice, hatred, pride	130
By bosom friends betrayed, forsook	198
By deep distress a suppliant made	79
By faith we are come	457
By faith we now the veil look through	278
By faith we now transcend the skies	382
By fools accounted mad	258
By her example fired I rise	87
By human wolves encompassed round	165
By Jesu's dying merit	443
By love, mere pitying love, inclined	292
By mercy alone	57
By no private wants compelled	277
By sin no longer bound	366
By that which every joint supplies	320
By the blood of the Lamb	28
By thy reconciling love	52
By works let us show	320

Volume VI

Be still, ye isles, and wait your doom!	174
Because he bought me with his blood	450
Because thy lingering love defers	170
Before its mouth it opens wide	33
Before the Lord's fierce anger come	33
Before the yawning cavern close	237
Before thou all thy wrath reveal	76
Before thy chosen servant go	123
Begotten again, And principled right	441
Being benign, whose name is Love	78
Beneath our earthly load	207
Beneath thy chastening hand we stoop	262
Beneath thy kind protection keep	133
Beneath thy wings secure	154
Bent to preserve our favoured race	182
Beyond our vale of woe	230
Bid him from this moment be	353
Bid me in thine image rise	384
Blasphemers of thy awful name	128

Blessed be the love that led thee on	229	But if we live in vice and sin	418
Blessed with his lowly, loving mind	264	But is th' almighty God restrained	121
Blessed are the servants, Lord	24	*But is the hasty spirit fled?*	266
Blessing, and love, and thanks, and praise	260	But is thine anger turned aside	185
		But Jesus' throne Immovable stands	92
Blessing, and thanks, and power, and praise[94]	308	But, lo, he lives again	349
		But lo! The snare is broke, the captive's freed	70
Blest in our returning Saviour	142	But lo! the soul-ensnaring fiend	282
Blind with intoxicating pride	170	But man his liberty of will	394
Blooming innocence, adieu	365	*But more than all let those be clean*	116
Blow ye the trumpet blow	12	But must I from his glorious face	429
Blow ye the trumpet's loudest blast	84	But need we now our grief conceal	264
Boldly he braved the stormy deep	182	But, numbered with the British sheep	321
Born for this intent we are	386	But, O Almighty God of love	410
Born that others might rejoice	336	But O! my dying God	2
Born to distress and woe	348	But O! prevent the misery	50
Bowed beneath the deepest sense	77	But, O they rashly took	373
Bowels of compassion, sound	221	But O! thou dreadful righteous Lord	22
Bridegroom of souls, reply	239	But O, thou righteous God, how long	237
Bring back those wondrous days of old	130	But, O to thee for help we cry	386
Bring the heavenly city down	364	*But O, we hope for better things*	418
Bring the kingdom of thy Spirit	45	But O, with what reluctant strife	414
Britons, arise with one accord	181	But oh! my gracious God to me	6
Burdened with a load of clay	364	But oh! suffice the season past	3
But ah! what means this frantic noise	164	But oh! the Saviour of mankind	19
But blinder still, the rich and great	22	But our almighty Lord	398
But chiefly blessed the womb that bare	235	But our defence is sure	125
But chiefly to thy mild command	119	But praised be the Lord, Our Refuge and Hope	183
But chiefly who in Christ believed	351		
But Christ, the Object of her love	243	But rather than live	406
But did she then herself conceal	271	But see, whom God hath made his heir	261
But do not, Lord, from us remove	102	But shall we e'er ourselves forget	103
But do ye thus the Lord requite	165	But shining in her properest sphere	296
But does she still exist in more than sound	55	But should the bold usurping spirit dare	56
		But suffice the season past	423
But, for thou hast not yet forbid	172	But their greatest happiness	379
But, gaining now whom she requires	300	But those who in their heart have Jesus known	56
But hast thou finally forsook	136		
But hath not heaven, who first bestowed	253	But thou hast saved the chosen seed	179
But have we by their ruin rose	171	But vain our vows, we know	416
But if so thy will ordain	23	*But we, by divers ways*	397
But if, to scourge our nation's sin	176	But we by faith's illumined eye	260
		But what are all the blessings, Lord	388

[94]. UP 2:335.

INDEX OF FIRST LINES OF POETRY BY JOHN AND CHARLES WESLEY

But when she heard the gospel-sound	267	Before my eyes of faith confessed	194
But whether they thine hand will see	31	*Before my Judge severe*	379
But while we render thee thine own	167	Before my soul and body part	406
But who can paint the strong desire	241	Begotten again, And born from above	317
But who or guile or falsehood use	424	Behold me with thy closing eye	352
But who sufficient is to lead	409	Beneath their burden groaning	345
But who to teach Almighty grace shall dare	60	Beneath thy wings, their sure defence	420
		Bending beneath the burden	113
But will the gracious Lord	152	Benumbed by sin I long have been	187
But wilt thou let the fountains fail	132	Best for her so soon to die	84
But wilt thou let the leopards tear	49	Better than life thy favour is	125
But wilt thou not thine own secure	41	Better than my boding fears	61
By all the powers of love pursued	250	Betwixt the mountain and the multitude	437
By all the rage of fiends and men	240	Beyond our utmost thought	338
By faith we already behold	198	Bid her live in peace Divine	143
By faith we find the place above	27	Bid then my new-born soul	380
By folly taught, by nature led	437	Bidden in time of trouble	118
By God approved, by man unknown	439	Bleeding love—I long to feel it	384
By heavenly indignation struck	76	Blessed be the sacred Three in One	278
By his own flesh forsook	348	*Blessing, and praise, and thanks, and love*	66
By ministerial spirits conveyed	199	Born again, and led by him	252
By our old companion left	363	Born again that thee we may	34
By ten years' siege the fort they take	410	Born in the dregs of sin and time	71
By that unerring Spirit led	228	Born of the Spirit now divinely led	428
By the signals of thy coming	92	*Bowels of Divine compassion*	334
By the Spirit of grace	454	Brethren in our Creator's eyes	160
By thee if rightful monarchs reign	121	*Bridegroom of his church, and head*	211
By timely grief the woe prevent	83	Brought from the gates of death, I give	95
By wisdom meek, and patient pain	135	Brought through the dread hour And torturing fires	143
By wisdom pure and peaceable	326		
By works of righteousness she showed	248	But ah, thou know'st a heavier care	51
		But chiefly let my dying cries	405

Volume VII

		But Christ the God maintains his throne	222
		But give us through thy Spirit's power	211
Banished now out of thy sight	369	But God the Spirit's things are known	255
Baptized into one only name	277	But grounded on thy written word	218
Baptized into thy name	306	But he my flesh and blood assumed	384
Be it so, thou glorious God	268	But if, disdaining to receive	257
Be thyself our whole desire	38	But if now thy prescience sees	70
Because his time to tempt and try	354	But if our cry hath reached thy heart	121
Before her weary eyes display	66	But if the gospel we obey	173
Before his strong arrest I feel	399	But if thou foreknow'st it best	82
Before I render up my breath	378	*But if thou otherwise ordain*	53
		But is there no salvation	113

But Jesus to his church is known	206
But let not us the demon please	72
But let us to our God return	257
But lo! An ampler field appears in view	430
But lo, I from thy justice, Lord	394
But most I long to prove	145
But now the Lord, who sends by whom he will	426
But O, before the fixed decree	118
But shall my partial fond presumption dare	434
But shall my will prescribe to thee?	130
But shall sinful man complain	83
But since without thy Spirit's might	99
But thou draw'st me after thee	304
But thou hast fulfilled thy word	242
But till our souls are born again	314
But we have by his unction known	250
But we thy mind have understood	263
But we would receive the power	96
But when that Spirit pours	29
But who the kingdom shall behold	184
But wilt thou not at last appear	181
But wilt thou not the balm apply	108
But wilt thou suffer me to bear	51
By a blessed anticipation	343
By all thou did'st on earth endure	352
By duteous and respectful awe	170
By faith Divine perceiving	220
By faith I now inherit	335
By faith the upper choir we meet	313
By God sanctified Our Father we love	297
By his residence below	252
By justice doomed to die	362
By mercy set free	80
By mercy's sweet attraction	32
By our bosom-foe beset	16
By providential love bestowed	157
By Satan's subtilty beguiled	73
By the dreadful exhibition	384
By the Father, and the Son	290
By the Redeemer certified	371
By the Spirit of thy love	38
By the travail of thy soul	142
By the travail of thy Spirit, / By thine	57
By the travail of thy Spirit, / me sustain	59
By the virtue of thy blood	38
By this thy churches know	238
By thy most severe temptation	57
By whispering love into my heart	412

Volume VIII

Baffled for once, the mob retreat	456
Be cautioned by good advice	474
Be merciful, O God, to me!	127
Be thou exalted, Lord, above	127
Be thou my strong defence and tower	159
Because the rebels mocked his word	195
Because thou hangedst on a tree	345
Because thou hast said, Do this for my sake	440
Before my soul and body part	377
Before the righteous wrath of men	346
Before we gasp our latest breath	342
Begirt with hosts of enemies	205
Behold how good a thing	250
Behold them rush from jail to jail	455
Behold them with that pitying eye	298
Being of beings, Source of love	349
Beneath a daughter of affliction lies	436
Beneath thine anger, Lord, we droop	173
Bent on evil, every one	140
Bereaved by his revoking word	423
Besides, ourselves the city guard	471
Better a day thy courts within	166
Better it is in God to trust	204
Blaspheming multitudes we hear	265
Blasphemous thought, away	380
Bless us, that we may call thee blessed	207
Blessed are the pure in heart	208
Blessed be the God of pardoning love	152
Blessed be the Lord! for he hath heard	56
Blessed be the Saviour-God	64
Blessed is the man, and none but he	3
Blessed is the man, supremely blessed, / Whose	65

Blessed is the man, supremely blessed, / Who	72	But I, a slighted worm, in vain	42
Blessed is the man that dares confide	91	But I (all love, and thanks, and praise	120
Blessed is the man that fears the Lord	244	But I will thy power confess	132
Blessed is the man, to whom his Lord	65	*But if again, by sin brought low*	196
Blessed is the man whose kind relief	93	But if thou in anger frown	328
Blessed supremely blessed is he	142	But if thy sovereign, awful will	351
Blessed the people are that own	69	But, jealous of myself, I hope	384
Blessed with constant power to mourn	363	But Jesus is my God, the Lord	181
Blessed are the creatures new	208	But Jesus shall for ever reign	18
Blessing and thanks to God most high	397	But let all who seek thy favour	158
Body and soul at once revive	413	But let my faithful friends rejoice	77
Body and soul thy judgments feel	11	But let not them that seek thy face	155
Bolder I with my fellows grew	390	But let the men that seek thy name	93
Borne down the irremeable	172	But let the saints, with grateful joy	148
Bought with his blood	366	But let them still abide	241
Bound every heart which Christ inspires	397	*But lo! at the appointed time*	463
Bow down, O Lord, thy gracious ear	169	But my God is still the same	187
Britain then thy hand shall own	269	But my straitened spirit mourned	88
Britain thou again wouldst choose	332	But my whole desire thou art	30
Britain, thou hast to traitors sold	332	But never can ye place	137
Britons at home with Britons fight	414	But now, enervated by age	429
Broke off from thee, by passion grieved	377	But now the dupes of meek condition	451
Brought by his sweet attracting grace	106	But now your courage is returned	474
Built by his almighty hands	112	But O! I still with sinners dwell	122
But, alas! thy threatenings sound	97	But, O! my suit to thee is known	156
But all my wants to thee are known	87	But O, thou humbled soul, look up	26
But as for me, with humble fear	10	But O! What death doth he require	457
But chiefly them, who dared employ	270	But oh! what penal woes shall seize	123
But chiefly those they hate and fear	458	But peace, and power, and love	241
But didst thou, Lord, thy kingdom send	322	But raise me up, my gracious God	95
But do ye king and soldiers think	469	But rich in grace, thou hast not yet	276
But drunk with insolence of power	315	But shall I to my foes give place?	12
But give I God a sacrifice	433	But sinners shall consume away	73
But God hath quelled their angry pride	239	But soon, if worthy of the grace	433
But God in our defence shall stand	396	But soon their evil day shall come	319
But God on the throne	395	But still, in patient hope	136
But God rewards his own	85	But, still regardless of the wrong	87
But God shall cast into the pit	124	But the great God in whom we trust	345
But God shall vindicate my wrong	119	But the Lord who dwells above	22
But he indeed hath heard my prayer	146	But the men who fear thy name	329
But he that dealt the treacherous wound	123	But the righteous, Lord, at last	140
But he that, to salvation wise	199	But they in my adversity	75
But hear my agonizing prayer	423	But those that serve the prince of hell	27
		But thou, alas! hast put to shame	100

But thou art a shield for me	6		Backward alas, too long, and slack	128
But thou art he, O God, through whom	43		Balm of my wounded spirit, Lord	418
But thou canst yet his soul revive	408		Be blessed for my sake,	
But thou hast told us in thy word	375		With permanent good	445
But thou nearer art, O Lord!	230		Be bold in Jesus to confide	441
But thou, O God, confound their power	129		Be it according to thy will	93
But thou, O Lord, art full of grace	79		Be it my only wisdom here	260
But thou, O Lord, shalt vengeance take	126		Be they strong, or void of might	211
But thou requirest all our hearts	115		Bear me to the sacred scene	281
But thou, without the help of man	485		Bear with me then, most patient Lord	415
But trouble will not always last	426		Bears transformed with oxen graze	385
But trusting in the word	63		Beckoning with mine uplifted hand	433
But turn their hearts again	273		Before another's mote you spy	267
But vain, without a nod of thine	269		Before he put the covering on	57
But vain your hope of a reprieve	464		Before I render up my breath	112
But we who truly fear thy name	321		Before its strong arrest I feel	30
But when the poor his help implore	73		Before that everlasting day	456
But when to folly they returned	196		Before the last great day	468
But while an exile here I live	423		Before the saints to glory go	184
But while the showers of vengeance come	319		Behold your due in Uzzah dead	165
But while through pride I held my tongue	66		Being of Beings, make	35
But while thy way is in the deep	425		Believing I my seal set to	424
But who can all his errors tell	38		Believing now in Jesu's name	279
But who regards the wrath Divine	173		Beloved for Jesu's sake	469
But who shall his strongholds o'erthrow	133		Beneath a mountain-load of grief	460
But who shall quit this low abode	47		Bereft of my peace	286
But why is no discovery made	467		Besieged by all the powers of night	124
But woe is me! constrained	234		Better be wise among the few	52
But ye that hope in him	65		Bewildered, lost, I must stand still	215
By a world of foes surrounded	14		Beyond the bounds of space and time	447
By an almighty arm we own	274		Beyond the reach of sin and hell	404
By factious demagogues gainsaid	290		Blessed be the day that I was born	231
By faith we now the cloud look through	486		Blessed by our everlasting Lord	204
By famine, pestilence, and sword	414		Bondmen indeed! too long we lived	222
By him the hungry soul is fed	195		Bound in sin and misery	407
By his bloody cross and passion	292		Branch of Jesse's stem, arise	383
By his mighty fiat made	68		Brayed in trouble's mortar I	354
By thee I have a troop broke through	33		Breathe in praise of your Creator	343
By thy most benign command	383		Bright with lustre not her own	367
By vengeance terribly o'ertook	349		But all may now to God draw nigh	64
By whom—but we inquire in vain	286		But all who Jesus' spirit breathe	159
By whom, O God, shall Britain rise, / So	286		But as a beggar I	263
By whom, O God, shall Britain rise? / Not	286			

Volume IX

But betwixt hope and sad despair	350
But canst thou not the whole remit	53
But faith in thy redeeming blood	314
But first, through virtue of thy word	125
But, for the glory of thy name	135
But for thy endless mercy's sake	312
But for thy truth and mercy's sake	448
But how much pleasanter to see	358
But how shall I the promise plead	447
But I am all to sin inclined	299
But if by thy sufficient grace	277
But if thou pronounce the word	385
But Jesus hath our sentence borne	9
But Jesus, our triumphant Lord	86
But kings may spare their labour vain	177
But lest we from our City stray	88
But lo, the Lord for ever lives	197
But lo! unless our hands sustain	165
But no such rigid law we fear	228
But now the better hope brought in	69
But now (the warm Enthusiast cries	216
But now whate'er was done by man	195
But O! I now with shame confess	264
But O my kind, Almighty Lord	278
But O! our feeble strains of praise	225
But O! the house of living stones	227
But, O thou patient God, forgive	50
But O! thy changeless word is passed	464
But on the day of sacred rest	49
But shall he still devour	373
But shall I then through fear forbear	266
But thou dost for ever live	376
But we a mighty Daysman know	239
But when, most gracious God and true	375
But while the Judge a moment stays	375
But will he not again	427
But wilt thou suffer me to die	422
By all who neither love nor fear	195
By Boaz, yet divinely, taught	145
By faith and hope I now draw nigh	198
By faith I on his strength lay hold	120
By faith we know, the world was made	1
By Gentiles nourished and caressed	457
By his gracious wise commands	219
By humble faith and active love	212
By mercy sealed in lasting sleep	106
By Moses doomed to die	355
By numbers urged, o'erpowered we are	211
By secret influence from above	236
By thee from Egypt led	89
By thine unerring Spirit led	43
By this assuredly we know	38
By thy own Spirit's might	98
By thy passion on the tree	388
By young corrupters lured	355

Volume X

Barren, light, and void, and vain	147
Be it according to thy word	7
Be mindful of thy promise Lord	195
Before the final, general doom	374
Before the threatened curse takes place	21
Before us still, great Shepherd, go	402
Before ye lose your stumbling feet	22
Behold him walking on the wave	284
Behold the adverse sect arise	209
Behold the miracle renewed!	68
Beneath my sins he bowed his head	431
Beneath this mountain-load of grief	253
Bid me step into the pool	445
Blacker far in my own eyes	484
Blind to our own through selfish love	192
Blind to thee, O Lord, and lame	341
Blindly we asked for pain and loss	335
Bound in chains of hidden night	219
Break this Babylonish yoke	47
Breathe into this foul heart of mine	13
Brought into the fire I am	125
Brought into the fire, Thy wonderful power	125
Brought to the point, a sinner still	489
Brought to thy followers in vain	309
But ah, we lost the grace bestowed	446
But canst thou take it all away	82
But Christ shall work at his return	373
But Christ, who the abuse foresees	221

But did he not our nature take 150
But doth it, Lord, thy wonder raise 212
But he who gave the slighted word 414
But his presence we implore 220
But hope I have in thee 208
But how much greater, O my God 293
But I more than all would know 394
But I without delay 216
But if Christ the bread impart 500
Bt if for me his bowels plead 78
But if I cheerfully forego 243
But if the everlasting pain 400
But if thou let 90
But if thou thyself impart 10
But if thou wilt not save us here 68
But if thy grace my soul defend 413
But Jesus by a sinner seen 483
But lo, a deeper mystery 374
But lo, at last with joy I hear 486
But long as I my sins repeat 42
But loosed by thy captivity 416
But, Lord, I trust, thy gracious skill 85
But me thy word forbids 358
But my most inveterate ill 161
But O! in vain the world I shun 19
But, O Lord of Hosts, in thee 47
But O, my Lord and God thou art 470
But O, they shall once more 366
But O, thy grace which comes to all 456
But O, what numbers turn 370
But oh, how desperately proud 27
But shall I doubt thy will 207
But shall the men that call him Lord 340
But the Most-High shall cast you down 360
But then in his extreme distress 489
But those who bear the Christian's name 420
But thou dost send forth the light 286
But thou, my Saviour, must confer 464
But thy love doth not despise 480
But we a kingdom here receive 155
But we our great High-Priest admire 429
But we who now thy grace implore 384
But what thou didst for sinners shed 12
But when a penitent we see 221
But when he undertakes to heal 213
But when his faith begins to fail 488
But when I all my sins confess 417
But where, alas, may such be found 493
But where thou didst for ages dwell 8
But while we Pharisees condemn 298
But will not our Almighty Lord 169
By a miracle of grace 113
By faith accounted just 102
By faith I Babel's fall foresee 102
By faith I set me on the tower 102
By faith I to the fountain fly 123
By faith we our Example trace 325
By faith we see our Lord descend 114
By miracle the crowd he fed 256
By my own backslidings I 4
By not appearing on thy side 262
By oaths they learn their God to scorn 170
By office greater far than John 249
By one almighty word begin 490
By Satan, or his instrument 152
By the legal goat foreshowed 447
By the malicious fiend possessed 465
By this stone to powder ground 66
By thy death the living way 432
By thy most mysterious pain 36
By thy Spirit's outstretched hand 34
By turning now to thee our Lord 363

Volume XI

Baptized into his name we own 129
Be it according to thy word 385
Be it Lord in me fulfilled 136
Be this my whole employment here 68
Be this, dear[95] Lord, our constant care 61
Because they will not understand 12
Because thou sav'st us from our fall 369
Because unworthy of thy grace 162
Because we could not keep thy laws 403
Before he saw him in the tree 263
Before mine eyes of faith appear 435

95. Osborn changed "dear" to "O."

Before the rising morn	281	But if his stubborn pride disdain[97]	249
Before thy holiness	143	But if I can believe in thee	26
Behold a favourite of the skies	243	But if in me revealed thou art	387
Behold him high above all height	321	But if thou appoint me still	291
Beholding as with open face	497	But if thou the Father show[98]	360
Believing all thy fulness mine	47	But if we cast thy word aside	64
Below he lifts his haggard eyes	244	But if you needs must work before	251
Beneath a mask of piety	271	But is it possible, that I	24
Betrayed by pride insensible	82	But Jesus came the world to save	414
Beyond the rage of fiends and men	96	But Jesus on the tree	89
Blasphemous Jews may still deride	302	But lo, the sentence to prevent[99]	267
Blessed be the Lord, for ever blessed	112	But man averse in heart and mind	50
Blessed with the faith that works by love[96]	371	But mercy doth the dread remove	110
Blind at thy call I rise SH 1762, 2:208		But now through faith we may	301
Blind to ourselves by nature we	15	But O I never, never need	368
Blind to the Christian mystery	184	But O most gracious God and true	445
Boasters of a religious show	412	But O, thy blood the sorrow buys	300
Bold I may of thee inquire	33	But our redeeming Lord	142
Bold we then to thee apply	203	But partial, ignorant, and blind	404
Born blind I was, and bred in sin	447	But present in thy Spirit still	439
Born of the flesh, to flesh alone	341	But rather what of Christ they say	18
Borne upon the wings of love	380	But should we not the truth declare	53
Bowed down to the ground, But prisoners of hope	219	But souls unconscious of their wants	112
		But stranger far, and more profound	500
Bread of God, for thee I lift	382	But strangers to his saving grace	470
Broken the Man of griefs appears	435	But stricter still the union is	505
Built by the most holy God	42	But surely thou hast cast on me	218
Burdened with our griefs and cares	86	But taught of God we wait the end	226
Buried where Jesus lies	92	But that I may pray like thee	150
But a believing child of grace	462	But the men of learning proud	164
But ah! we know not what we say	185	But the wise, and learned, and proud	453
But armed with thy undaunted zeal	222	But them the flock will never hear	458
But better taught by grace	231	But thicker darkness overspread	304
But born in sin and misery	352	But thy true disciples pray	421
But breathing in the sacred leaves	392	But we now by faith adore thee	408
But conscious of our constant wants	73	But we the base throng Our voices may raise	219
But deaf to nature's voice	397		
But faith, and hope of joys above	42	But we who God in Jesus know	280
But his silence intercedes	84	But when thou dost our souls convert	149
But I for Jesu's Spirit pray	305	But whoe'er thy word receive	97
But I my good Physician know	367		

96. *UP* 2:235. This is a variant of the MS verse: "If blest by faith that works by love."

97. *UP* 2:161.
98. *UP* 2:330.
99. *UP* 2:177.

By faith I touched th' incarnate God SH 1762, 2:203	
By faith we shall see him promised of old	118
By fellow-worms caressed, beloved	375
By his tyrannising sin	6
By preaching thy word	139
By riches lawfully acquired	209
By taking all my sins away	205
By that inspoken word of thine[100]	362
By the guilt and tyranny	427
By the needy widow taught	59
By thee instructed we suppress	395
By thee preserved in our distress	172
By this celestial sign	326
By thy example, Lord, repress	401
By thy own mercy brought	38

Volume XII

Baptized into his nature	280
Be according to thy word	14
Be it all my business Lord	77
Be it our greatest joy below	260
Be it to all the nations known	172
Be it to every nation known	342
Be satisfied! We thirst for thee[101]	94
Bear as ye list, ye whirlwinds bear!	438
Because the truth they cannot bear	30
Before a man of God we lose	231
Before his Father's face	215
Before the world's foundation	43
Behold him bleeding on the tree!	90
Behold th' Apostles of the Lamb	189
Behold the Man, the prisoner there!	416
Believe in God; believe in him	373
Believers of old Who Jesus confessed[102]	155
Believing into Jesus' Name	172
Beloved by all thou call'st thine own	125
Beneath the purposes of men	419
Beyond his persecutors' sight[103]	365
Bishop supreme, thy people bless	381
Bitter implacable and proud	73
Blameworthy they suppose	399
Bleeding from their bosom rent	221
Blessed with my felicity	432
Blind infidels, ye must contend	455
Bold he sets his steadfast face	400
Bold in our Almighty Lord	288
Bonds for ornaments we take	187
Born from above, their heavenly birth	245
Born of the flesh, I mocked the men	395
Born to fulfil the promises	206
Both strength and righteousness	160
Both the clashing sects unite	337
Bought with the blood	378
Bound he is, yet truly free	451
Bound to the altar see	84
Branches we could not be	20
Brought before kings, he stands	421
Built, through the sacred oracles	411
But ah suffice the season passed	209
But arm us for that fiery hour	392
But by Jesus' word alone	131
But by the Holy Ghost baptized	252
But can Paul be justified?	389
But chiefly, Lord, the gifts of grace	272
But did he not refuse the cause	349
But few alas, depend	436
But first your present need	447
But followers of the Nazarene	452
But freely justified	20
But God the poor attends	270
But how can we their guilt retain?	108
But I can to thee appeal	124
But if this counsel is Divine	194
But Jesus Christ is he	226
But Jesus' death hath set us free	302
But let the season past suffice	78
But lo, in Christ alone	6
But millions now with lips profane	262
But nothing can obstruct thy way	110

100. *UP* 2:232.
101. *UP* 2:277: "We long for thee."
102. *UP* 2:290.
103. *UP* 2:398.

But O the Way came down	7
But our High Priest above	237
But our triumphant head	369
But rest not in the work begun	373
But slighted and repulsed by men	209
But suffice the season passed	130
But the Antitype much more	213
But the King of kings decrees	271
But thou our sins and curse hast took[104]	98
But vain the striving zeal	403
But when our Lord intends to cheer	434
But when the dreary hour is o'er	115
But when the honour of thy name	146
But when the lettered man	393
But who are ye, or whence your power	361
But who thy heavenly doctrine hear	31
But without their Lord Their efforts are vain	114
But words will not suffice alone	123
But you who thus refuse to see	454
By countless acts of wickedness	190
By divination to prevail	223
By faith we walk in thee	6
By faith your sins effaced ye know	373
By his nakedness he owns	86
By his own Almighty Spirit	191
By his Spirit made known	122
By his wonderful name	212
By nature we incline	237
By one Spirit inspired and led	57
By prayer disposed to hear the word	315
By tenderness of love to man	262
By that prophetic impulse stirred	401
By the miracle of grace	59
By thy example Lord	5
By thy Spirit's inspiration	299
By thy Word and Spirit led	117
By virtue from the Root	21
By wild impetuous passion led[105]	78
By wisdom pure, and humble love	254
By works of outward righteousness	298

Volume XIII

Basis of our steadfast hope	136
Be double honour paid	180
Be not high-minded then, but fear	55
Before he sacrificed his child	170
Before the throne my Saviour stands	140
Before us o'er the desert go	268
Believe, and saved this moment be	22
Believing the pure fountain flowed	113
Beneath his dereliction	46
Blessed are the pure in heart	250
Blessing to God the heavens cry	234
Boldly we approach the throne	143
Born a sad heir of endless pain	9
Born (again from heaven) to please	182
Bought by a thousand pangs divine	283
Bridegroom of thy Church appear	241
Brightness of th' Eternal Glory	116
Brimfull of all evil, and void of all good	245
But ah! they damp our eager thirst	189
But art thou willing now to own	169
But canst thou account me just	204
But chiefly through my pride of heart	35
But Christ, the co-eternal Son	131
But could the chief apostle grieve	79
But did the great apostle fear	32
But did the saints of God, the dead	88
But didst thou not on earth appear	206
But him we now exalted see	120
But how shall I my wish obtain	165
But if even we, the least of all	195
But if the fire thy work consume[106]	28
But if thou bid'st us mortify	88
But lo, we every grace put on	76
But, Lord, my heart is known to thee	43
But may the righteous man	148
But may we not at once spring up	175
But must I always feel within	15
But must my heart, to sin inclined	205

104. Osborn changed "hast took" to "didst take."

105. *UP* 2:270.

106. *UP* 2:463.

But now enlightened from above	4
But now my misery I confess	229
But now, the gospel-plan	135
But O, take heed, ye souls unskilled	27
But O thou patient mournful Man	90
But on thy guardian care	149
But our unworthiness	265
But say, thou all-atoning Lamb	145
But should we not believe the men	208
But taught of God, we come to do	148
But taught of God, we surely know	67
But that every moment I	153
But the blind world their pardoning Lord	123
But the pure gospel-grace	31
But till the love of Christ we gain	209
But thou expiring on the tree[107]	36
But thou on whom our souls depend	152
But thronging round, with busiest love	119
But trusting in the martyred Lamb	235
"But we now, the prize t' attain	80
But when he hath my patience proved	158
But when the Lord hath closed thine eyes	224
But while for thee we mourn	141
But wilt thou give me up	8
But with a believing eye	153
But ye that tremble at his frown	187
By endless conflicts tried	185
By faith persuaded more and more	151
By nature, Lord, I evil love	17
By sea and by land	163
By the blood of the Lamb	235
By the Spirit of our head	220
By the Spirit of thy grace	233
By this, divinely warned, we knew	108
By wilful sin the man who wrongs	216
By wrestling on in instant prayer	190

Volume I

Can out of weakness make us strong	345
Can these assuage the wrath of God	276
Canst thou forget thy days of flesh	275

107. *UP* 2:465

Canst thou love more when from a body freed[108]	16
Canst thou withhold thy Healing grace[109]	64
Captain of my salvation, hear!	179
Careless through outward cares I go	172
Carnal, and sold to sin, no more[110]	348
Cast out thy foes, and let them still	264
Cease, foolish heart, thy fond complaints	244
Cease, my child, thy worth to weigh[111]	168
Champion of God, thy Lord proclaim	229
Cheered by thy Saviour's sorrows rise[112]	87
Cheerless and all forlorn I droop	131
Cherubs with seraphs join[113]	156
Christ, by highest heaven adored	183
Christ, from whom all blessings flow	361
Christ in us; in him we see	170
Christ, my life, my inward heaven	224
Christ, of all our hopes the seal	170
Christ, our head, gone up on high	359
Christ our Lord and God we own	115
"Christ the Lord is risen to-day"	185
Christ, the true, the heavenly vine	358
Christ, to all believers known	358
Christ; who, now gone up on high	188
Christ, whose glory fills the skies	224
Circled round with angel powers	187
Close by thy side still may I keep[114]	129
Closer knit to thee our head	361
Cold, weary, languid, heartless, dead	131
Come, all ye Magdalens in lust	92
Come, and all our sorrows chase	292
Come, and let us sweetly join	350
Come, and possess me whole	268

108. Monsigneur De Renty.
109. George Herbert.
110. From the German of Nikolaus von Zinzendorf, translated by John Wesley.
111. George Herbert.
112. George Herbert.
113. From the German of Johann Angelus Scheffler, translated by John Wesley.
114. From the German of Christian Friedrich Richter, translated by John Wesley.

IDEX OF FIRST LINES OF POETRY BY JOHN AND CHARLES WESLEY

Come, dearest Lord! my soul's desire[115]	65	Come, Saviour, come, of old decreed	120
Come, Desire of Nations, come	184	*Come, Saviour Jesu, from above*[128]	110
Come, Divine and peaceful Guest	189	Come then, bright flame, my breast inspire	15
Come, Father, Son, and Holy Ghost, / And seal me	372	Come then, if, mighty to redeem	15
Come hither, all who serve the Lord	332	Come then, my God, mark out thy heir	164
Come hither all, whom careless joy[116]	112	Come then, my Hope, my Life, my Lord	76
Come hither all, whom searching pain[117]	112	Come, then, O my Saviour, come	257
Come hither all, whom tempting wine[118]	112	Come, then, our heavenly Adam, come	33
Come hither all, whose groveling taste[119]	111	Come then, thou all-embracing Love	315
Come hither all, whose idol-love[120]	112	Come, thou high and lofty Lord	351
Come hither, all ye slaves of sin	332	Come thou, my dear Redeemer, come	285
Come, Holy Ghost, all-quickening fire[121]	164	"Come to Judgment, come away!" / (*Hark*,[129]	11
Come, Holy Ghost, all-quickening fire	165	*Come to Judgment, come away!* / *This the*[130]	11
Come, Holy Ghost, all-quickening fire[122]	240	*Come to Judgment, come away!* / *Lingering*[131]	11
Come, Holy Ghost, all-quickening fire[123]	242	*Come to Judgment, come away!* / *Wide*[132]	11
Come, Holy Ghost, (for moved by thee	239	Come to Judgment, come away! / help[133]	12
Come, Holy Ghost, my heart inspire	308	Come to my help, come quickly, Lord	303
Come, Holy Ghost, our hearts inspire	238	Come to the Living Waters, come!	205
Come, Holy Ghost, the Saviour's love	34	Come, ye kindred souls above	364
Come, holy, holy, holy Lord	346	*Commit thou all thy griefs*[134]	125
Come, let us lengthen out the feast	302	Conqueror of hell, and earth, and sin	284
Come, my Beloved, O come away[124]	344	Conscience and Reason's power deride[135]	39
Come, O my guilty brethren, come	92	Convinced my work was but begun	334
Come, O my Joy, my Love, my heart[125]	106	Corrupt my will, nor half subdued	73
Come, O my Light, my Feast, My Strength![126]	106		
Come, O my Saviour, come away	372		
Come, O my Way, my Truth, my Life[127]	106		

115. George Herbert.
116. George Herbert.
117. George Herbert.
118. George Herbert.
119. George Herbert.
120. George Herbert.
121. Line 2 for pages 164 and 165: "Come, and in me delight to rest."
122. Line 2: "Come, and my hallowed heart inspire."
123. Line 2: "my consecrated heart inspire."
124. Altered from George Sandys.
125. George Herbert.
126. George Herbert.
127. George Herbert.

128. From the French, Antoinette Bourignon.
129. George Herbert.
130. George Herbert.
131. George Herbert.
132. George Herbert.
133. George Herbert.
134. From the German of Paul Gerhardt, translated by John Wesley.
135. George Herbert.

Could each one see his neighbour's heart[136]	19
Couldst thou know, as thou art known	331
Couldst thou the Redeemer see	331
Crown the agonizing strife	189
Cursed for the sake of wretched man	32

Volume II

Call me in my last agony[137]	15
Call on us, by thy Spirit call	346
Calmly to thee my soul looks up	319
Can earth afford that secret place	84
Can life and death together dwell	162
Can the Ethiop change his skin	298
Can the self-same fountain yield	112
Can unholy actions suit	111
Cause me, O God, myself to know	68
Cause me to walk in Christ my way	320
Children, have you aught to eat	221
Children of wrath and slaves of sin	172
Chose from the world if now I stand	319
Christ hath the foundation laid	291
Christ, my hidden Life, appear	262
Christ, my Master and my Lord	219
Christ, our Brother and our Friend	218
Christ, our head, and common Lord	224
Christ shall make thee free indeed	307
Christ, the head, the Corner-Stone	291
Christ the tempted, hear my crying	96
Christ, thou in our eyes art glorious	32
Clear as the trumpet's voice he speaks	340
Closer and closer let us cleave	222
Clothe me with thy holiness	94
Come, dearest Lord, no longer stay	42
Come, glorious Lord, the rebels spurn	335
Come, gracious Lord, we wait thy day	340
Come in, come in, thou heavenly Guest	361
Come joy or grief, come life or death	103
Come, let us join our God to bless	16

Come, let us who in Christ believe	191
Come, Lord, and help me to rejoice	302
Come, Lord, and make me pure within	182
Come, Lord, our souls are on the wing	227
Come, Lord, the drooping sinner cheer	145
Come, Lord! thy Spirit bids thee come	234
Come, Lord, we groan to see thy day!	196
Come, O come, all-gracious Lord	257
Come, O my comfort and delight	74
Come, O my God, thyself reveal	366
Come, O thou greater than our heart	332
Come, O thou Traveller unknown	173
Come, O thou universal Good!	73
Come, see how Christians wail their dead	185
Come then, and claim me for thine own	143
Come then, and loose my stammering tongue	234
Come, to the house of mourning, come	183
Come, ye absent souls who love	224
Comfort, ye ministers of grace, / Comfort my	165
Comfort, ye ministers of grace, / Comfort the	49
Confident now of faith's increase	243
Confound, o'erpower me with thy grace	323
Conqueror of sin, and hell, and death	362
Contented now upon my thigh	176
Convert, and send forth more	342
Could I of thy strength take hold	104
Creaton's line his wisdom laid	52
Creation to his law submits	54

Volume III

Call me out of condemnation	270
Call on your reprobating god	75
Can it, Father, can it be?	305
Can thy justice aught reply	306
Can we enjoy thy richest love	281
Can ye doubt if God is love	88
Cheer us with immortal wine	241
Christ our Passover for us	275

---

136. George Herbert.
137. From the German of Johann Angelus Scheffler, translated by John Wesley.

Christ, the true and living Light	99	Call on him now, ye watchmen call[138]	314
Christ we praise, our God above	104	Call, on the name of Jesus call	348
Clear us by thy condemnation	270	Calm on tumult's wheel they sit	16
Clearly do I see the way	9	Can there a malady be found	361
Clothed in his righteousness, receive	331	Canst thou deny thy love to me	343
Come, all who long his face to see	254	Canst thou reject our dying prayer	461
Come, all who truly bear	224	Captain of our salvation, hear	30
Come down from above, Whose mercies abound	74	*Captain, we look to thee*	55
		Careful, without care I am	215
Come, dear Redeemer of mankind	243	Cast for our sins into the deep	145
Come, Holy Ghost, set to thy seal	220	Cast we off our needless fear	117
Come, Holy Ghost, thine influence shed	266	Caught in the toils of death thou art	347
Come in thy Spirit down	253	Changed by his mighty love	49
Come, let us join our friends above	93	Chief of apostate spirits, I groan	360
Come, let us join with one accord	283	Children of faithful Abraham these	300
Come, let us who in Christ believe	64	Children of the resurrection	148
Come near, ye people of my Lord	76	*Christ, our living head, draw near*	148
Come quickly in, thou heavenly Guest	66	*Come all who love the slaughtered Lamb*	39
Come quickly, Lord, for whom we mourn	290	Come, almighty to deliver	219
Come quickly, Lord, the Spirit cries	341	Come, and display the power below	184
Come then, our dying Lord	223	Come, and partake the gospel feast	276
Come, thou everlasting Spirit	226	Come, and wipe away my tears	180
Come, thou Spirit of contrition	330	*Come, Holy celestial Dove*	195
Come, thou Witness of his dying	226	Come in, come in, thou Prince of Peace	457
Come, through the dark valley come	172	Come in, with thy disciples sit	137
Come to the feast, for Christ invites	258	Come, little flock, (my people now	292
Come, to the supper come	221	*Come, Lord, come quickly from above*	349
Come to thy house again	269	*Come, Lord, from above*	213
Come we that record	323	*Come, O my chosen people, come*	65
Comfort every longing heart	359	*Come, our redeeming Lord*	266
Communion closer far I feel	254	Come quickly from above	178
Compassed with an host of foes	13	Come quickly, dearest Lord, that I	121
Confiding in thy only love	326	Come quickly then, my Lord, and take	447
Conformed to an expiring God	178	Come see the rising triumph	149
Conformed to his death	324	Come, sinners, to the gospel feast	274
Conscience, the worm that never dies	25	Come, the contrite heart's Desire	102
Constrained by ecstacies too strong to bear	112	Come then, and show thine art	327
		Come then at my call	365
		Come, then, dear Lord, thyself reveal	173
		Come then from above	365
## Volume IV		Come then, O Lord, my sins forgive	377
		Come then, thou Prophet of the Lord	136
Call on him, and he yet shall live	348		

138. UP 2:453.

Come then, thou soul-dividing sword	185
Come then to heaven, your native home	33
Come then to those who want thine aid	187
Come then to thy servants again	126
Come then, ye souls by sin opprest	276
Come thou greater than my heart	419
Come, thou long expected Jesus	116
Come ye that seek the Lord	143
Come, ye weary sinners, come	220
Compelled though I am	364
Confer not thou with flesh and blood	276
Confound whoe'er his ruin seek	22
Confounded for their envious hate	289
Confusion, misery, and shame	4
Conquerors of our intestine foes	103
Conscious of my unbelief	332
Consider, gracious Lord	426
Convince the souls, who feel their sin	187
Convinced of sin and unbelief	199
Could neither seal nor stone secure[139]	130
Cover his enemies with shame	25
Cover, O earth, my blood	395
Covered with guilty shame	394
Cut off our dependence vain	228

Volume V

Call aloud on Jesu's name	281
Call them into thy wondrous light	483
Called to distress, and patient grief	155
Calm he eyes them from above	293
Calm, O calm my troubled breast	303
Can a true believer doubt	351
Can I my own dear child forget	396
Can it anger the Lamb	29
Can the good God his grace deny	329
Canst thou despise our fear and pain	168
Canst thou forget	61
Canst thou reject thy Spirit's cry	240
Captain, God of our salvation	274
Captain of our salvation, hear	311
Carried about from God's own ways	319

Carry on thy victory	134
Caught up in the air I soon shall ascend	420
Cause us thy record to receive	470
Ceaseless I mourn my children lost	247
Centre of our hopes thou art	426
Children we lived, alas! too long	319
Choked by the thorns of worldly care	247
Christ, of all our conversation	456
Claim for thine each faithful sservant	54
Come all the members far and near	472
Come all, whoe'er have set	386
Come catch the blood	58
Come, Divine Immanuel come	133
Come down, all-glorious Lord, come down	93
Come in this accepted hour	309
Come in thy pleading Spirit down	176
Come, Jesus, and cleanse	290
Come, Jesus, and loose	
The stamnerer's tongue	469
Come let us anew / Our pleasures pursue	282
Come, let us anew / Our journey pursue	387
Come let us arise, / And aim at the prize	320
Come, let us arise, / And press to the skies	424
Come, let us ascend	457
Come let us rejoice In confident hope	333
Come let us try if Jesu's love	397
Come, let us who to Christ are joined	316
Come, Lord, be manifested here	7
Come, Lord, the glorious Spirit cries	228
Come, Lord, with thy disciples sit	471
Come my partner in the patience	447
Come, O my soul, the call obey	141
Come, O thou all-victorious Lord	124
Come O thou Lamb,[140] for sinners slain	312
Come, O thou Prophet, Priest, and King	325
Come on, my partners in distress	168
Come the heavenly peace Divine	432
Come then, dear Lamb, for sinners slain	312
Come then, my friendly foes	214
Come then, my health,	
my Hope, my Home	73

---

139. *UP* 3:112.

140. Osborn changed to: Come, O thou, Lamb.

Come then, my Jesu, from above	145
Come then, the saving grace impart	131
Come, then, ye sinners, to your Lord	64
Come, threatening world, Thy prisoner take	145
Come, thou omniscient Son of Man	315
Come, ye followers of the Lord	177
Come, ye real widows, come	353
Come ye, then, my servants dear	354
Companions to the Man of Woe	243
Conclude us first in unbelief	124
Confiding in that name alone	392
Conscious to myself, I pray	100

Volume VI

Call in the ruthless sons of Rome	81
Called back by an ungrateful race	171
Called in the morning of their day	414
Calmly didst thou run thy race	232
Can I describe a worth like thine	331
Can she her sucking child forget	250
Can we forget from whence our union came	68
Can we 'scape the desolation	168
Can you her artless warmth forget	242
Canst thou forgive the impious crowd	81
Captain, God of our salvation	161
Captain of our salvation, take	408
Celestial charity expands	320
Childish, now, alas! we are	403
Children have a right to sing	457
Choke not the seed of heavenly love	83
Christ, the Friend of sinners, bought her	278
Close behind the tribulation	144
Close follower of the Lamb	231
Clothed with humility and grace	438
Come, Desire of nations, come	48
Come Father, Son, and Holy Ghost, / thou Three in One	137
Come, Father, Son, and Holy Ghost, / To whom	407
Come, glorious God, our souls unbind	113
Come, Holy Ghost, the grace impart	375
Come, let us anew / Our journey pursue	14
Come, let us embrace	399
Come let us join our friends above	215
Come, let us join the hosts above	445
Come, let us join with one accord	430
Come, let us our good God proclaim	447
Come, let us rival those above	395
Come, let us with our Lord arise	395
Come, Lord, and display Thy sign in the sky	195
Come, my companions dear	463
Come, O my Saviour, come	202
Come on, my Whitefield! (since the strife is past	67
Come Saviour arrayed With glory and power	92
Come, see in this pale shadowy form	313
Come then, the Life, the Truth, the Way	419
Come then, thou great Deliverer come	136
Come then to my rescue, (I pray	191
Come then to thy languishing bride	197
Come then, ye hostile bands	152
Come thou, our longing hearts' Desire	342
Come, thou Conqueror of the nations	160
Come, to thy drooping servants come	262
Come with them, O thou Man in white	79
Comissioned by the dying God	236
Commences now the Christian race	325
Condemned like haggard Cain to rove	237
Confiding in our fleshly arm	156
Confound the misbelieving pride	38
Conscious of dissolution near	296
Conscious of his pardon sealed	352
Constant, unwarped from first to last	272
Contemplating his blessed estate	347
Convince the wretches who deny	37
Could actions, words, or looks express	320
Could I like rapid Young aspire	331
Could the greedy grave devour	366
Covered and blind is every seer	175
Covered with conscious shame	396

PART 1: *THE POETICAL WORKS OF JOHN AND CHARLES WESLEY*

Covered with honourable shame[141]	302

Volume VII

Call to mind that unknown anguish	57
Called by a common name	312
Called by the Holy Ghost alone	246
Can I forget the solemn day	94
Can I seek the grace in vain	357
Can I the memorable day forget	426
Can we of ourselves resign	96
Cast as a broken vessel by	99
Cast on the fidelity	61
Caught as in the toils of hell	142
Challenge now thine humble dwelling	307
Child of my age so late bestowed	126
Child of prayer, by grace Divine	92
Children of God who Christ receive	230
Come away to the skies	198
Come, Father and Son	8
Come, Father, in the Son, / And in the Spirit[142]	29
Come, Father, in the Son, / And in the Spirit[143]	320
Come, Father, Son, and Holy Ghost[144]	310
Come Father, Son, and Holy Ghost[145]	326
Come, heavenly Lord	37
Come, Holy Ghost, thou God most high	245
Come Holy Ghost, thou Lord most high	278
Come Holy Ghost, thyself reveal	250
Come, Jesus, and build thy temples below	28
Come, let us anew / Our calling pursue	158
Come, Lord, from the skies	176
Come quickly, Lord, the veil remove	135
Come, Son of Abraham and of God	12
Come then, and to my soul reveal	194
Come then, Divine Interpreter	249
Come then from above	9
Come then, great God, thyself reveal	385
Come then, his life, his strength, His peace	148
Come then my Consolation	104
Come then my hope of glory	111
Come then, my present Saviour	360
Come then, thou Triune God unknown	315
Come then, thou universal Good	178
Come then, thy servant to release	421
Come then to thy creature, and tell	318
Come, thou all-inspiring Spirit	47
Come, thou eternal Spirit of God	261
Come, thou everlasting Lord	196
Come Wisdom, Power, and Grace Divine	43
Command us to rise Of pardon possessed	319
Concerning this we now agree	328
Confiding in thy word	393
Conscious of his pardoning power	7
Constrained by pure delight we own	49
Contrary to thee by nature	389
Count we now our mournful gains	83
Covered by the darkest shade	261
Creeds and books can nothing do	303

Volume VIII

Called out of Babylon	417
Can the disciples of our Lord	326
Can ye so suddenly forget	468
Canst thou deny thyself	374
Cast in the mould of sin I am	115
Cast me not off in feeble age	160
Cast thy concern away	81
Cast up, cast up an iron road	398
Caught by the men who steal for God	407
Cause me in thy paths to go	213
Celebrate th' eternal God	262
Charged by the sovereign King of kings	176
Christ shall bless thy going out	236
Clap your hands, ye people all	110
Cleansed by the sacred blood	52
Clothed with humility and love	106

---

141. *UP* 3:333.
142. Line 3: "Purify our inward parts."
143. Line 3: "Glorious, Triune majesty."
144. Line 2: "Whom One all-perfect God we own."
145. Line 2: "Restorer of thine image lost."

Clothed with humility and grace[146]	422	Crushed by thine almighty hand	332
Come, and maintain thy righteous cause	103	Crushed by thy heavy hand, I groan	86
Come, behold th' almighty Lord	108	Cut short thy work in righteousness	298
Come Father, Son, and Holy Ghost[147]	441		
Come, Finisher of sin and woe	426		

Volume IX

Come, Lord, to a soul That waits in thy ways	440	Can all be prophets then? are all	71
Come, Lord, with love my soul inspire	382	Can all her fleets and armies save	196
"Come," my cheerful brethren said	237	Can aught we do in faith, or give	358
Come, O thou common Lord	326	Can confident assertions prove	353
Come, Saviour, from above	388	Can I forget the wondrous ways	96
Come then in all thy glory	370	Can reason save from passion's power	278
Come then, in blessings from above	431	Captain of Israel's host, and Guide	43
Come then, Jehovah crucified	371	Captain of my salvation, show	162
Come, then, O my Friend Divine	369	Cast off for thy unfaithfulness	441
Come then, the all-victorious Name	399	Casual howe'er our steps may seem	145
Come then, thou slaughtered Lamb Divine	360	Caught in the toils of hell and sin	214
		Cause of my own undoing	338
Come then, to vindicate thine own	381	Cautious in all his works and deeds	395
Come, thou choicest gift of heaven	334	Centre of unity	32
Come thyself into my heart	373	Chastened I all my days have been	268
Comfort and make thy sufferers glad	174	Chastised and afflicted below	261
Command iniquity to cease	15	Chastised by my God	391
Commit unto the Lord	81	Chief Captain of Jehovah's host	121
Compassed round with hostile nations	291	Children I have nursed up and bred	369
Compel triumphant Gallia's pride	301	Christ and the promised land in view	184
Compelled at last the loyal bands	464	Christ appears! my sin and sadness	318
Concord, on a distant shore	335	Christ, our Passover, is slain	42
Conformed to an expiring God	157	Christ, the Church's head with thee	450
Confound the tyrant's power	21	Christ, the Lord our God, thou art	83
Confound their devilish art	273	Clothed with the skins of victims slain	10
Confounded are all they	182	Come all the lost race, Redeemed from your fall	444
Confusion o'er my soul is spread	101		
Conqueror of sin, and death, and hell	5	Come, Divine effectual power	461
Contemned and hated for thy cause	239	Come, eternal King, surrounded	390
Conviction's sharpest arrows dart	340	Come, Father, Son, and Holy Ghost, / One God	65
Counsel they take, but not by thee	484		
Creation, varied by his hand	200	Come heavenly Dove	300
Crown of my rejoicing, Lord	430	Come, if the Sun of Righteousness	374
Crushed beneath thine anger, I	186	Come in thou Supplicant Divine	101
		Come, Jesus, come, my heart inspire	265
		Come just as ye are, For Jesus invites	445
		Come, Lord, thy glorious face display	290

146. *UP* 3:286.
147. Line 2: "Revealed in the baptismal flood."

Come O thou uncreated Word	323	Can the Ethiop change his skin	22
Come on ye faithful souls, come on	75	Can these dry bones perceive	59
Come, taste, and confess		Can they discharge the debt in hell	168
The goodness Divine	445	Can we believe this precious word	317
Come then, my unbelief to end	447	Can we follow Christ in vain?	259
Come then, that thy great name		Can we from the world conceal	165
may be	425	Canst thou at sin astonished be	24
Come then, the true celestial Vine	255	Canst thou then without compassion	294
Come them, thy Father's will to do	428	Canst thou with specious words deceive	204
Come, thou heavenly Solomon	167	Captain, God of my salvation	404
Come, thou universal Blessing	16	Caught by th' Almighty Hand	58
Come to me, if such thy case	298	Celebrate Immanuel's name	141
Come, victorious Captain, come	126	Chastened thus, O Lord, I know	4
Come with thy salvation, Lord	323	Cheered by his word and Spirit's light	284
Comforter of all that mourn	266	Christ and his truth when all desert	434
Coming in a way of grace	446	Christ and whoe'er his doctrine preach	471
Commanded, Lord, and drawn by thee	422	Christ the head and corner-stone	347
Condemned to die, of death afraid	123	Christ, the true anointed Seer	139
Conducted by his gracious power	220	Christ, whose glory fills the skies	56
Confiding in the promised power	262	Christ's is the religion pure	462
Confined in a dungeon of clay	298	Clothed in our flesh and blood	148
Confirm their word, and prove it thine	398	Collected, perfected in one	108
Consume our lusts as rotten wood	179	Come, Jesus, now thy foe t' exclude	20
Continue then thy son to please	173	Come, let us to the Lord return	76
Corrupt alas, in every part	369	Come, let us use the grace divine	46
Crush the head he strives to hide	8	Come, Lord, to all, far off and near	119
Cut me not off, almighty Lord	240	Come, my God, Jehovah, come	126
Cut off my dependence vain	376	Come, O thou Breath divine	61
		Come, the Lord our Righteousness	103
		Come then, dear Lord, into my heart	13
## Volume X		Come then the purging flame	130
		Come then, with all thy	
Called by nature's glimmering light	352	wounds confessed	172
Called to sustain the hallowed cross	164	Companion to the world he lives	380
Calm retreat and fervent prayer	501	Compassion for a dying race	229
Can a law from God proceed	166	Confirm in our degenerate days	25
Can a minister complain	235	Conflicts I cannot require	185
Can a servant of the Lord	296	Confounded by thy glory near	206
Can a true follower of thine	168	Conscious from whom your	
Can all the art of devilish man	435	blessings flow	271
Can God remove the stone within	57	Conscious of our infirmity	150
Can one of the soft gentle kind	497	Conscious of what my sins demand	51
Can the bands of death detain	81	Could I but ask, and ask aright	198
Can the dark Ethiop change his skin	22	Covered with flesh and skin	60

Crown thy impatient people's hope	88
Cut off from those he once oppressed	380

Volume XI

Caesar his own dignity	115
Call (and give me ears to hear)	149
Called by thy gospel messenger[148]	261
Called to the marriage of the Lamb	335
Calling thy mercies past to mind	289
Can injured innocence complain	80
Canst thou deliberate which to choose	242
Captain, God of our salvation	311
Casting a dying look[149]	90
Cautious, the door of sense I close	67
Changed the strong bent of nature's will	336
Charged with the universal load	325
Checked by the worldly throng	261
Children of God by faith we owe	430
Christ and his friends the poor relieve	509
Christ by the youth's escape makes known	80
Christ doth not hear, or answer those	297
Christ himself the precept gives	374
Christ no further effort makes	13
Christ of himself, and Christ alone	17
Christ the character express	465
Christ the God of our salvation	195
Christ to suffer it behooved	314
Christians, alas, like Pilate are	85
Come all, and see our Saviour here!	329
Come all to Christ, who all receive	179
Come in thy gracious kingdom[150]	267
Come, let us with speed To Bethlehem go	118
Come, Lord, and tame the tiger's force	156
Come O thou Day-spring from on high	440
Come Saviour, by thy promise bound	140
Come then, my God, the promise seal	45
Come, then, O Lord, thy light impart	115
Come thine exiles to remove[151]	278

148. UP 2:232.
149. UP 2:69.
150. UP 2:180.
151. UP 2:189.

Comfort though thou dost not give us	11
Coming in thy great Father's name	375
Commendable excess	69
Confessing whom our hearts adore	399
Conqueror in one temptation, see	132
Conscience, thou voice of God in man	416
Conscience when we refuse to hear	49
Conscious of this plague within	148
Content to blast their wicked aim	416
Continual need of thee I have	368
Continuing in the outward word	426
Contrary sects we see	354
Conviction is from God	450
Convinced of sin I cannot be	431
Could we see that dreadful sight	77
Could Zachary, the just	103
Countless miracles unseen	378
Covered with outward sufferings here	36

Volume XII

Caesar their only king they know	83
Called from above, I rise[152]	397
Calm he hears their furious cry	398
Calmer of the troubled heart	3
Can I gain by losing thee?	37
Can priests with Sadduccees agree	137
Can the grave a Christian scare	102
Can the great God his creatures need?	341
Can we in unbelievers find	353
Can we mourn as broken hearted	3
Candid and honourable men	406
Canst thou, O Saul, believe	218
Cast th' usurper from his throne	39
Challenge we the world to show	73
Champion of God, in Jesus' might	199
Chariots it doth and ships ascend	138
Chased from home we cannot be	259
Chiefly, when the Lord of all	221
Chosen by God's immediate will	273
Christ our head and heavenly Lord	61
Christ presenting to their view	338

152. UP 2:410.

Christ returning to the skies	103	Can it never be fulfilled?	20
Christ the times and seasons knows	36	Can suffering purge my inbred sin	131
Christ to his servants condescends	121	Can ye the Spirit's course confine	238
Christian piety sincere	352	Captain, we thy command obey	76
Christians as men profane	390	Chastised by an indulgent God	155
Christians he exults to meet	450	Children of God, through Jesu's love	13
Christians make the same reply	356	Children, ye have as truly known	199
Christ's little flock who vex and tear	329	Christ for ever lives to pray	136
Christ's ministers apart are set	274	Christ is the one Foundation laid	26
Closer knit to God and thee	57	Christ is the Tree of life Divine	223
Clothed with majesty Divine	331	Christ shall on them a name bestow	224
Cognizance of your slighted cause	351	Christ, the saving Power Divine	179
Come holy, hallowing Flame	256	Christians indeed are creatures new	69
Come out from those who know not God	152	Close followed by their works they go	236
Come then, and claim thy property	305	Come, Divine Interpreter	219
Come then, celestial Guest	14	Come, Holy Ghost, supply the want	61
Come thou holy One of God	61	Come, King of saints, so long concealed	241
Comfort of all believing hearts	4	Come, let us obey	162
Compunction of heart, If Jesus bestow	151	Come let us rise with Christ our head	85
Concerned for justice, not for him	391	Come then, and by thy death release	146
Confirmed by daily miracle	276	Come then, and dwell in me	45
Confounded in the dust I would	72	Come then, my hope, my rest	205
Conscience and remorse for sin	86	Come then, O my Saviour come	202
Conscious of Jesus near	121	Come then our heavenly Friend	142
Conscious of my happiness	432	Come then, thou very God	201
Conscious of the indwelling God	15	Come, thou beatific Spirit	48
Consenting to my Lord and God	112	Come, thou everlasting Son	241
Constrained by Jesus' love	369	Comforter of all that mourn	270
Constrained I do at last believe	111	Coming through our great High-priest	136
Contemplating the great reward	149	Confiding in thy name	64
Contemplating thy shining face	300	Conformed to my expiring Head[153]	257
Contempt he justly might express	349	Conformed to our head In outward distress	14
Contrary to custom's law	349	Conscience of ill! How sharp the pain!	145
Convinced I of the truth may be	224	Conscious of all that I have done, / Of evils	144
		Conscious of all that I have done, / Since first	146
		Constraineth us, to what?	48
		Could sufferings heighten or complete	120

Volume XIII

Called after thee I am	107
Called to fill up the measure	18
Calmly with submission mourn	269
Can I be angry, and not sin?	72
Can it mercenary be	154

[153]. Osborn notes this is a poem by J. Leifchild.

IDEX OF FIRST LINES OF POETRY BY JOHN AND CHARLES WESLEY

Volume I

Daily growth the members find	237
Dark and cheerless is the morn	224
Darksome I still remain and void	95
Dead as I am, and cold my breast	13
Dead in the midst of life I was	332
Dear, lovely, gracious souls, to me	246
Death is still digging like a mole[154]	40
Death, the latest foe, destroy	292
Death's sentence in myself I feel	255
Deliverance to my soul proclaim	270
Delusive world, thy hour is past	24
Depth of mercy! Can there be	271
Descend, and let thy lightning burn	269
Did I then my soul deceive?	325
Didst thou for this forsake Thy throne?[155]	67
Dies, and revives the dying flame	95
Divinely warned of judgments near	212
Doom, if thou canst, to endless pains	236
Doom them an endless death to die	313
Doth thy Lord prolong his stay	331
Doubtless through one eternal now	313
Doubtless thy heavenly Father could[156]	42
Dust and ashes, though we be[157]	281

Volume II

Darkness and clouds surround Thy throne	194
Darkness they make with light agree	351
Dead with my gracious Lord and God	247
Dear as the apple of his eye	58
Dear Object of our faith and love	193
Deferred my hope, and sick my heart	196
Depart, ye ransomed souls, depart	171
Departed is the Lord from me	107

154. George Herbert.
155. George Herbert.
156. George Herbert.
157. From the German of Anna Dober, translated by John Wesley.

Descend, pass by me, and proclaim	301
Did I not believe and feel	111
Did I not my soul deceive	113
Didst thou not die, that I might live	133
Didst thou not in the flesh appear	133
Didst thou only bid me leap	104
Die all of self to live no more	69
Die the gay flower of human pride	51
Do as thou findest in thy heart	84
Doubtless thou art of purer eyes	82
Doubtless thou art our Father still	60
Draw near, O Son of God, draw near	341
Draw near, ye strangers to our God	184
Drive him to th' infernal region	31
Drooping soul, shake off thy fears	293
Drop down in showers of love	230
Dust and ashes is my name	211

Volume III

Dead, already dead, within	85
Dear dying Lord, thy Spirit breathe	29
Dear, loving, all-atoning Lamb	23
Dear Saviour of all, Attend while we sing	8
Defend thy mercy's cause	82
Destruction if thy body shed	255
Determined all thy will t' obey	327
Did Jesus ordain / his supper in vain	282
Did not his word the fiends expel	21
Did they toward the altar turn	311
Did thine ancient Israel go	311
Dies the glorious Cause of all	230
Dives, and I, and Judas there	25
Divinely taught to make the sober feast	117
Divinely warned to meet the mortal hour	125
Draw near, ye blood-besprinkled race	265
Drawn, and redeemed, and sealed	347
Drooping soul, rejoice, rejoice	162
Dying friend of sinners, hear us	226
Dying, whom thy hands have made	305

Volume IV

Dare I lift again mine eyes	405
Darkness he makes his secret place	323
Dead in sin too long I was	331
Dead to praise, and wealth, and beauty	384
Deeper plunged in guilt and shame	428
Deeper than hell, it plucked me thence	446
Defeat, confound, oppress	23
Descending from above	192
Desperate soul, what must I do	387
Destruction from the Lord is come	71
Destruction may come	88
Determined nothing else to know	472
Did I not oft beseech thee, Lord	400
Didst thou ever see a soul	390
Didst thou not in thy person join	121
Didst thou not plead above	184
Dies a never-dying death	462
Dignified with worth Divine	229
Disturbed the nations are	267
Do not begin to make excuse	275
Do not let me live to sin	391
Do not look upon me	413
Do not suffer me to live	444
Do with me as thou wilt	435
Dost thou not all my sufferings know	338
Dost thou not see our labouring heart	261
Dost thou refuse to hear	433
Dost thou, to break my pride	433
Doth thy justice still withstand	358
Dragged from their graves, they then shall call	292
Draughts of iniquity I drink	392
Drawn by his grace we come from far	124
Drawn by the evangelic sound	374
Dreadful sin-chastising God	68
Driven out from my God	411
Drunk with the bold aspiring hope	96
Drunken, but not with wine	394
Dying in sin, condemned and lost	269

Volume V

Dead as I am to God	171
Dead, dead are all my hopes below	190
Dear dying Lamb, for whom alone	251
Dear Lamb, if thou for me couldst die	72
Death is all swallowed down	38
Deceitful workers, in thy name	249
Deceiving and deceived, they glide	249
Despisers of the gospel word	130
Devoted to my God below	338
Did he evade the pain, and shame	142
Didst thou not make us one	423
Disconsolate tenant of clay	181
Distinct by characters Divine	92
Divinely confident I am	74
Do for him, dearest Lord	435
Does it injure thy blood	29
Dogs, and wolves in vain appear	293
Dost thou not, Lord, our trouble see	175
Doth he in deed or word gainsay	143
Drink of life's exhaustless river	457
Drink to a thirsty Christ I give	19
Drunkards, and slaves of lewd excess	252

Volume VI

Dangers and snares abound	398
Dare we again for respite cry	171
Dark and bottomless the pit	378
Darkness and clouds surround thy throne	175
Dead! dead! The child I loved so well!	252
Dead to the things above	373
Deeper we sink, and deeper still	436
Departed hence in perfect peace	227
Depressed by the cross, He mounted the higher	287
Descending on his azure throne	141
Destroy the souls—which cannot end!	140
Destruction is the dreadful cry!	87
Devotion in tears Expresses its love	307
Did he not labour day and night	284

Did he not triumph in the cross	284	Did we, Lord, in every step	331
Did not her alms and prayers arise	324	Dispersed th' assassinating band	274
Did they, O God, ascribe to thee	170	Dispersing th' infernal gloom	486
Did such a soul the witness want	312	*Divided 'gainst itself so long*	292
Didst shed thy blood to pay	2	Divinely struck with sudden dread	150
Didst thou not walk with Christ in white	229	Do I presume to preach thy word	404
Dissolved are nature's closest ties	428	Do thou the true discernment give	290
Do not, Lord, for ever chide	221	*Dost thou request a feeble worm*	376
Drawn by a secret power, he flew	282	Draw me out of the snare	61
Drawn down by public crimes	153	Dreadful in number and in power	125
		Dreadful in power, as rich in grace	198
		Dumb I for a while became	90
		Dwell within thy ramparts peace	238
		Dying once to die no more	412

Volume VII

Day after day I mourn	165
Dearer than life, thy love bestow	402
Dearest of thy gifts below	96
Death I no more desire	114
Delight, and softest sympathy	191
Departing from their sinful way	170
Departing in thee	373
Didst thou not in our flesh appear	194
Different from the Father then	212
Disconsolate, distressed	29
Do not suffer him to live	70
Do thou, if so thy love ordain	404
Drawn by a dying sinner's prayer	378
Dying every mournful day	418

Volume IX

Dark as the shades of endless night	421
Darkness and clouds around me roll	174
David's Son by heaven adored	201
David's true, celestial Son	173
Dawned that gospel-day Divine	387
Dead souls I will anew create	413
Dearer than life, thou know'st I love	332
Death in the pot! 'tis always there	192
Death's sentence in myself receive	9
Deep sunk in nature's base desire	194
Deepen the wound thy hands have made	111
Delivered now into mine hand	96
Despicable, frail, and dying	19
Destroyed of God, the slanderer	319
Determined after thee I bear	144
Did God reject the pious prayer	82
Did I not lingering stand	20
Discerning thee, my Saviour, stand	276
Disconsolate, forsook	379
Discouraged at our wayward ways	415
Dispersed the powers of darkness see	412
Distracted by thought And care without end	445
Do we not all from thee receive	203
Doctrines, experience to try	380
Dost thou not, Lord, with pity see	110

Volume VIII

Daring as Charles's spurious brood	482
Darkness and clouds surround	181
Darkness he made his secret place	32
Daughter of heaven, though born on earth	105
Death as the wages of our sin	345
Deep to deep with horror calls	97
Deepen and fix the enmity	356
Defeat the men, with Satan joined	92
Deny us arms? We cannot see	471
Detached from every creature now	417
Devils believe, and tremble too	348
Did we in our evil day	331

Doth Christ expect what cannot be	377	Deliver us from evil, Lord	202
Doth God regard the outward show	183	Descending from thy Father's throne	385
Doth the great God, and Judge severe	237	Deserving in thy proper right	462
Draw me, and I with vigour new	361	Determined then thy lot expect	413
Drawn by thy grace the sons of night	452	Devils must at Christ's command	7
Drawn by thy messenger's report	209	Did his own apostles need	275
Duller than beasts the human herd	369	Did Jesus for the world atone?	325
		Did our love the pardon buy?	167
		Did they not see to life restored	89
		Didst thou not leave thy Father's throne	503

Volume X

Dare ye spurn the just command	426	Dispenser of the joyful word	180
Darkness in ourselves, we shine	165	Do it thyself in me[158]	196
Darkness the whole earth o'erspreads	429	Do what thou wilt; it should be so	502
Death and the grave can never cool	435	Doth Jesus still the traitor spare	509
Deliver us from evil	183	Doubting your heavenly Father's care	14
Deliverance is on Sion's hill	92	Doubts may in true disciples rise	391
Desperate is the sinner's case	383	Drawn by efficacious grace	393
Destroy me not by thy delay	17	Drawn by the secret power of grace	236
Detached from every good below	216	Drawn I was, and taught by thee	331
Determined I am Through Jesus's grace	96	Drinking cannot quench or cool	355
Devoted to eternal fire	318	Driven by stronger grace[159]	205
Didst thou in me thyself reveal	485		
Directed by the Father's will	314		

Volume XII

Dismissed I calmly go my way	72	Darkened by th' excess of light	396
Dispensers of the joyful word	467	Darkness was light, and rugged plain	267
Do I not still for mercy pray	197	David the man of war	214
Dost thou not, Lord, with pity see	229	David's immortal Son	215
Doth Christ the passive people lead	449	Day after day distressed	159
Doth justice then to man enjoin	171	Dead in sins and trespasses	424
Draw me, Saviour, from above	36	Death and the grave their baleful power	92
Drawn by my Redeemer's love	361	Death, everlasting death, I own	97
Drawn by thine extended fame	161	Death, hell, and sin are now subdued[160]	100
Dreadful, pride-chastising word	124	Debtor both to Greek and Jew	448
Dreadful soul-o'erwhelming word	25	Deceit and force are still employed	206
Drunkards, and murderers, and thieves	344	Deeply, justly sensible	221
		Defenders of his witnesses	403
		Depending on their faithful Lord	SH 1762, 2:257
		Deserted at thy greatest need	98

Volume XI

Daily do you yourselves deny	243
Daily we see the arm revealed	146
Dangers we will not rashly brave	133
Dear objects of their Shepherd's care	31
Deceived by Truth we cannot be	411

158. *UP* 2:119.
159. *UP* 2:130.
160. *UP* 2:279.

Deserters willing to come back	310	Egypt unfolds her golden blaze	217
Didst thou ever yet intend	225	Embolden by thine outstretched arm	295
Didst thou forget, thou Man of Grief	97	End of my every action thou!	173
Discord they bring, and civil strife	330	Enlarge my heart to make thee room	324
Discoursing from the written word[161]	337	*Enslaved to sense, to pleasure prone*	32
Dispensers of the gospel grace	309	Enter thyself, and cast out sin	261
Dispute and fierce contention springs	388	Enthroned above yon sky[165]	156
Disturbers of the public peace	317	Equal with God Most-High	147
Divided tongues of fire	142	Ere long, when Sovereign wisdom wills[166]	9
Do ye not still, ye ruling men	171	Ere yet the time was come	100
		Error, and sin, and death are o'er	50
		Essay your choicest strains	152

Volume XIII

		Eternal beam of Light Divine	128
Daily I now myself deny	190	*Eternal depth of Love Divine*[167]	173
Dared the chief apostle say	58	Eternal streams of pity flow[168]	66
Darkly through a glass we see	48	Eternity thy fountain was[169]	144
Deliver from the wrath to come	184	Even heathens feel thy power[170]	157
Did holy Paul himself require	55	Ever now your speaking cries	365
Didst thou at once spring up	185	Ever upward let us move	188
Didst thou not leave thy throne	201	Excluded from my Saviour's prayer	24
Does it extenuate thine offence	166	*Exempted from the general doom*	211
Dost thou desire to know and see	224	Extended on a cursed tree[171]	232
Doth the Lord for oxen care	102	Expand thy wings, prolific Dove	239
Down to the gates of hell	186	Eye hath not seen, ear hath not heard	367
Draw we then through Jesus near	144		
Dreamers of your salvation sure	172		
Dying to my Father look	154		

Volume II

Each hand and heart that lend us aid	19
Each thought and deed his piercing eyes	27
Each to each ye then shall say	252
Earnest of benefits behind	254
Easily I fall away	276

Volume I

Each moment draw from earth away[162]	72
Eager for thee I ask and pant	164
Eager he rushes now to war[163]	19
Earth, rejoice; the Lord is King	296
Earth then a scale to heaven shall be	33
Earth they beheld with generous scorn	220
Effulgence of the Light Divine[164]	161

161. *UP* 2:378.
162. From the German of Gerhard Tersteegen, translated by John Wesley.
163. George Herbert.
164. From the German of Johann A. Freylinghausen, translated by John Wesley.
165. From the German of Johann Angelus Scheffler, translated by John Wesley.
166. John Gambold.
167. From the German of Nikolaus von Zinzendorf, translated by John Wesley.
168. George Herbert.
169. From the German of Ernst Lange, translated by John Wesley.
170. From the German of Johann Angelus Scheffler, translated by John Wesley.
171. From the German of Paul Gerhardt, translated by John Wesley.

Enter his heart, possess him whole	216	Ephraim, my pleasant child, shall say	56
Established by Almighty hands	357	Ere I utter my complaint	458
Eternal God, come down	328	*Eternal Paraclete, descend*	184
Eternal life to all mankind	310	*Eternal power of Jesu's name*	268
Eternal, spotless Lamb of God	337	*Eternal Spirit, come*	167
Eternal, undivided Lord	12	Eternal triune Lord	255
Ever fainting with desire	274	Even now the momentary grace	440
Every day the Lord of Hosts	239	Even now the waves of passion rise	455
Every moment am I falling	96	Even now thou bidd'st my fears depart	333
Every one that seeks shall find	294	Even now we taste the pleasures there	263
		Ever hoping against hope	458
		Evil alas! thou know'st, and few	353
		Evil and sad my days have been	323

Volume III

Eager I urge my soul request	160	Excused, alas! why should you be	275
Earth and heaven together meet	164	Excused from coming to a feast!	275
Effectual let the tokens prove	266	Exposed to man's oppressive power	27
Endless scenes of wonder rise	230	Exposed to shame, and want, and pain	40
Enkindle now the heavenly zeal	237	Extend to these thy pardoning grace	252
Enlarge my heart to all mankind	29		
Enlightened once I was	56		
Envious I hear the passing bell	159		

Volume V

Envious I view that faded check	174	Ears to hear the gospel sound	134
Equip me for the war	78	Earth and hell their counsel take	186
Erect thy tabernacle here	342	Emptied of all thy greatness here	18
Eternal God of truth and grace	176	Encompassed with so great a cloud	362
Eternal Spirit, gone up on high	298	End, Lord, the fierce temptation	442
Expect we then the quickening word	259	Enlarge, inflame, and fill my heart	106
Expiring in the sinner's place	233	Entered into his work I am	114
Extend thy arms, and take me in	163	Ere long we shall fly	32
Extend to me the cleansing tide	23	Eternal death's sad sentence	207
		Eternal Spirit, descend from high	389
		Even now, all-loving Lord	117
		Even now he hath heard	379

Volume IV

Each moment applied	366	Even now his arms receive	83
Eager I urge my sole request	385	Even now his heart inspire	435
Earth to her centre quakes	268	Even now the earnest he reveals	226
Eighteen, or eight and thirty years	377	Ever careful to abound	359
Empty of him, who all things fills	324	Evil to my charge they laid	384
Encompassed by the dogs of hell	396	Exposed in this bleak wilderness	395
Entangled in the fowler's snare	423	Exposed we seem to Satan's will	257
Enter into the Rock	12	Extend thine arms, and take her in	240
Enter into thy secret place	65	Extol his kingly power	36
Entering into my closet, I	259		

INDEX OF FIRST LINES OF POETRY BY JOHN AND CHARLES WESLEY

Volume VI

Eager she drinks their praises in	437
Eager to drink his deepest cup	265
Early from our vale of tears	334
Earth unhinged, as from her basis	93
Endue with wisdom from above	127
Enduring, with that patient Lamb	330
Enrolled with that harmonious throng	246
Enter into the Rock, and hide	32
Entering into their closet, Lord	118
Ere the soul and body part	352
Ere the threatened ruin come	323
Error and ignorance remove	407
Escape to a country above	192
Eternal Judge of all	52
Eternity stands forth in sight!	200
Even as life the heavenly flame	328
Even now the heavenly convoy waits	277
Even now thou dost the stroke suspend	78
Even now thy piercing eye	90
Even now we taste the heavenly powers	200
Even now with them we meet	153
Even of ourselves shall men arise	107
Even then thou didst our Guardian stand	76
Every eye shall now behold him	143
Every fresh alarming token	93
Every part its curse sustains	378
Evil from me far off remove	451
Exempt from nature's agonies	330
Exercise the potter's power	380
Exposed to want and woe	238
Extol the Lamb of God	12
Exulting with her head to rise	325

Volume VII

Each person, absolutely Lord	309
Each person of the mystic three	283
Each person properly Divine	277
Early in the temple met	47
Ease of every heart-oppression	367
Easy to be entreated, mild	164
Equal to the Most High he lives	226
Ere with my lips I pray	364
Essence of eternal love	369
Eternal life begun below	195
Even from the sacred laver take	63
Even now I faint o'erwhelmed with dread	54
Even now I taste the raptures there	177
Even now the cordial hope my sorrow cheers	440
Ever able to cleanse	9
Every chosen instrument	237
Every present soul receiving	33
Evil communication	91
Exposed I long have been	139
Extol the great Jehovah's name	197
Except the Lord conduct the plan	42

Volume VIII

Earnest of my full possession	98
Earnestly remember them	339
Earth, tremble on, with all thy sons	200
Earth's haughty kings their Lord oppose	4
E'en now with eagle's eye	324
Encompassed by the dogs of hell	44
Ere at thy word the mountains rose	172
Ere yet on Christ their souls were stayed	194
Escaping for their wickedness	307
Eternal death must be their doom	341
Eternally blessed And joyful in thee	41
Even now he lifteth up my head	54
Even now his word doth swiftly run	304
Even now our Lord doth pour	251
Even now thou canst disarm their rage	285
Even then my path to thee was known	257
Every appetite subdue	368
Every evil word and way	213
Every evil thought and vain	225
Every soul from thee departs	22
Every stubborn spirit bow	335
Every word enjoined by thee	233
Evil do thou eschew	84

Evil eager they pursue	140
Evil he shall soon reward	121
Examine me, O Lord	52
Except the house Jehovah raise	243
Exposed to thy vindictive ire	321
Extinct we see the fatal blaze	465
Extirpating th' ungodly race	307

Volume IX

Eager alas, for sensual good	9
Eager my utmost Saviour	409
Earth and hell thy law opposes	72
Earth shall then with love o'erflow	387
Earth's greatest kings and queens shall be	433
Ease to an afflicted soul	342
Effect of righteousness Divine	402
Eldad, they said, and medad there	70
Empty us then, most gracious Lord	191
Enclosed with walls of living fire	458
Engraven with an iron pen	431
Enlarge thy dwelling-place, extend	440
Enter, ye guilty slaves of sin	376
Entered on the vast wilderness	43
Eternal God, my refuge now	115
Eternal Lord of earth and skies	422
Eternal Rock, project thy shade	400
Eternal Spirit, spread	68
Eternal Sun of Righteousness	65
Even I, the meanest servant I	399
Even in the most degenerate days	182
Even now whoe'er in thee believes	423
Evil I from the womb have been	424
Expand thy wings, celestial Dove	2
Expecting me on earth to reign	434
Expecting now to be restored	426

Volume X

Earth explains the plaintive cry	432
Earth rejoice, the Lord hath raised	30
Earthly things who counts his gain	484
Employment for our active zeal	321
Empower me by thy Spirit within	382
Empty the lamp, till thou impart	382
Enabled by thy word, I rise	12
Enter Lord this troubled heart	286
Entering into my God's design	408
Equal and just are all thy ways!	395
Ere my weary eyes I close	254
Essence incomprehensible	42
Essence of holinesses	184
Eternal Judge of quick and dead	304
Even here he bids us triumph	74
Even now a sketch I see	436
Even now my tempted spirit faints	94
Even those unhappy souls he bought	SH 1762, 2:180
Every charitable deed	393
Every deed and word and thought	238
Every gospel-minister	295
Every gospel-scribe should be	277
Every one who thee believes	197
Evil I then must be	203
Evil, or good, thou lovest us all	173
Exalted on thy glorious throne	455
Excused from every needless care	216
Expecting, Lord, thine awful day	135

Volume XI

Each should the word receive	214
Earthly kingdoms soon decline	105
Earth's remotest countries now	221
Eclipsed the Sun of Righteousness	304
End of our enlarged desires	383
Endeavouring to restrain	173
Engrave her doom upon my heart	254
Enlarged beyond the narrow space	511
Enlightened by his God alone	441
Enough for him who only means[172]	290
Entered upon his final scene	510
Enthroned again above the skies	487

---

172. *UP* 2:194.

Envious and proud in every age	447	Every sinner's King and mine	86
Envy, when time began	85	Every soul for them should plead	294
Erase the character of sin	32	Everything the Son receives	9
Ere the righteous Judge appear	19	Excused from earthly cares	196
Essential Truth, thy words are his	425	Exempt a Christian would not be	423
Eternal Judge of quick and dead	371	Expecting at Jesus's grave	103
Eternal thanks to thee	420	Expecting that appointed day	344
Even we, the vulgar know	449	Expiring in the sinner's stead[175]	94
Every knee shall bow before	290		

Volume XII

Each party calls the coat their own	87
Each precious opportunity	314
Eager to repair the wrong[173]	238
Eager to see the men suppressed	329
Earth and heaven and hell agree	148
Elders, and priests, and rulers rage	177
Elders commend their catholic zeal	404
Elders if the church ordain	293
Emblem of our sins, he groans	83
Emboldened through the name	283
Emboldened by grace, The mount we ascend	386
Employ in every place	449
Enrobed and crowned in mockery	79
Enrobed with majesty and power	164
Enslaved to the world I have been	211
Entreated with humanity	435
Envious and wicked priests appear	169
Error, ye Pharisees sincere[174]	425
Escaped from the tempestuous sea	446
Estranged alas from God	202
Even I through thy desert	280
Even now my affliction he sees	104
Even now we know 'tis he, 'tis he!	115
Even saints by grace renewed	291
Even the zeal which God bestows	69
Even you, the holy fathers, you	406
Every confessor and servant	217
Every shepherd under thee	126

Volume XIII

Each Person we alike adore	24
Empowered through Moses' hallowing hands	129
Emptied of selfishness and pride	255
Engraven on my heart and mind	138
Entangled in the worldly snare	256
Enter with all thy fulness in	231
Entered the holy place above	140
Enthroned at God's right-hand he sits	86
Essence of happiness, appear	94
Even now we sweetly call to mind	249
Every gift on me bestowed	21
Every Israelite indeed	59
Every moment we live	93
Exposed continually I am	255
Eye hath not seen, ear hath not heard	224

Volume I

Fain would I go to thee my God	133
Fain would I know, as known by thee	77
Fain would I know my utmost ill	88
Fain would I leave this earth below	50
Fain would I rise, and get me hence	250
Fain would I spread through earth abroad	335
Faint is my head, and sick my heart[176]	63
Faint we were, and parched with drought	291
Faith lends its realizing light	210
Faith to be healed, thou know'st I have	271

---

173. *UP* 2:328.
174. *UP* 2:427.
175. *UP* 2:276.
176. George Herbert.

Faithful, and often owned of God	227	First-born of many brethren thou![183]	266
Famed for their faith, all these believed	221	Fix my new heart on things above	305
Far as our parent's fall	151	Fix, O, fix my wavering mind[184]	281
Far as the heavens that earth surpass	207	Fixed on this ground will I remain[185]	280
Far, far above thy thought[177]	127	Fleeting he deemed them all, and vain	217
Far from fear, from danger far	292	Fondly my foolish heart essays	132
Far from me my God is gone	324	Foolish, and impotent, and blind	324
Far in some lonely, desert place	251	Foolish Vanity, farewell[186]	18
Farewell Honour's empty pride![178]	17	For as in Adam all have died	312
Father, behold thy son	96	For as the snow from heaven comes down	208
Father, forgive thy froward child	327	For charged with all their guilt he stood	82
Father, hail, by all adored	354	For ever here my rest shall be	283
Father, I long my soul to raise	78	For every man he tasted death	311
Father, I want a thankful heart	77	For I, the holy God and true	207
Father! if justly still we claim[179]	166	For love is swift of foot[187]	70
Father, if now thy breath revives	345	For me I now believe he died!	277
Father, if thou my Father art	307	For more we ask; we open then	34
Father of all, in whom alone	237	For, O! thy face is turned aside	368
Father of lights, from whom proceeds	76	For ten long, legal years I lay	333
Father of mercies, God of love	251	For thee my spirit often pants	88
Father of mercies, hear my call!	73	For thee my thirsty soul does pant[188]	175
Father, our eyes we lift to thee	190	For thee we leave our native shore	230
Father, Son, and Spirit, hear	356	For thee, within myself, for thee	243
Father, thy everlasting grace[180]	279	For them his heaven he hath prepared	214
Father, whose hand on all bestows	308	For this let men revile my name[189]	178
Fear not hence that ill should flow	184	For this, no longer sons of night	288
Feebly then thy hands lift up	331	For this the heavenly Dove	317
Few as they are, and void of art[181]	47	For this the saints lift up their voice	288
Fight the good fight, and stand secure	229	For this we lift our longing eyes	32
Fill me with all the life of love	225	For thou hast granted my request[190]	102
Fill not my life's short hour with pain[182]	63		
Fill with inviolable peace	249		
Finished your course, and fought your fight	345		
Fired with the thought, I see thee now	182		

177. From the German of Paul Gerhardt, translated by John Wesley.
178. From the French, Antoinette Bourignon.
179. Henry More.
180. From the German of Johann Andreas Rothe, translated by John Wesley.
181. George Herbert.
182. George Herbert.
183. From the German of Nikolaus von Zinzendorf, translated by John Wesley.
184. From the German of Anna Dober, translated by John Wesley.
185. From the German of Johann Andreas Rothe, translated by John Wesley.
186. From the French, Antoinette Bourignon.
187. George Herbert.
188. From the Spanish of David Israel Lopez Laguna.
189. From the German of Johann Joseph Winckler, translated by John Wesley.
190. George Herbert.

For thus the mighty God hath said	207	Fully redeemed, I fain would rise	285
For what to thee, O Lord, we give	216	Fully thy heavenly mission prove	227
For whom didst thou the cross endure	274	Fully thy quickening Spirit impart[198]	340
For you the purple current flowed	93	Fury is not in thee, my God	261
For your imputed guilt he bled	80		
For zeal I sigh, for zeal I pant[191]	12		
Forbid it, gracious Lord, that I	234		

Volume II

Forth at thy call, O Lord, I go	302	Faded my virtuous show	116
Forth in thy strength, O Lord, I go	239	Fain would I learn of thee, my God	145
Forward I now in duties go	325	Fain would I the truth proclaim	297
Fountain of all the good we see	191	Fainting soul, be bold, be strong	293
Fountain of Being, Source of Good	31	Faith freed me from the iron yoke	248
Fountain of blessings, Source of good	191	Faith in thy power thou seest I have	310
Fountain of Good, all blessing flows[192]	142	Faith is lost in unbelief	277
Frail, dark, impure, I still remain	84	Faith, mighty faith, the promise sees	311
Free as the Muse, my wishes move[193]	38	Faith to be healed thou know'st I have	282
Friend of sinners, King of saints	192	Faith, when it comes, breaks every chain	304
From all eternity with love[194]	141	Faithful and True, we now receive	290
From earth unpainfully released	211	Faithful to thy Spirit's leading	96
From every evil motion freed	371	Faithless heart! be this thy grief	88
From grief and sin I then should cease	253	Faithless heart! to Jesus bow	88
From guilt and pain ye shall be freed	208	Far be it from my wretched heart	101
From heaven reveal thy vengeful ire	367	Far, far above all earthly things	121
From hence the Christian race I ran	334	Far spent is the Egyptian night	242
From my own works at last I cease	82	Father, behold we claim	230
From one old man the race did rise	213	Father, hear; to thee I cry	212
From parents' eye, and paths of men[195]	51	*Father, I stretch my hands to thee*	13
From sin, the guilt, the power, the pain	265	*Father, in the mighty name*	213
From thy blest wounds our life we draw[196]	169	*Father of all, whose powerful voice*	335
		Father of Jesus Christ,—my Lord	309
Fruit of a virgin's womb	147	*Father of Lights, to thee, from whom*	25
Fruit of the Saviour's prayer	100	*Father of mercies, hear our prayers*	16
Fruitless, till thou thyself impart	235	*Father of mercy, hear our prayer*	21
Full of myself, I oft forsook[197]	52	*Father of my dying Lord*	279
		Father of our dying Lord	228
		Father of uncreated light	194
		Father, Son, and Holy Ghost	180
		Father, supply my every need	321
		Father, thy long-lost son receive	12
		Father, 'tis thine each day to yield	336
		Feebly if I now begin	125

191. From the German of Sigmund Gmelin.
192. From the German of Johann Angelus Scheffler, translated by John Wesley.
193. George Herbert.
194. From the German of Paul Gerhardt, translated by John Wesley.
195. John Gambold?
196. From the German of Nikolaus von Zinzendorf, translated by John Wesley.
197. John Gambold?
198. From the German of Ludwig Andreas Gotter, translated by John Wesley.

First and Last, in me perform	207	From every earthly low desire	324
First the dead in Christ shall rise	187	From every sickness, by thy word	363
Five bleeding wounds he bears	323	From God to all his church below	338
Flesh and blood cry out amain	284	From the bear and lion's paws	237
Flesh, earth, and hell deny	327	From the hand of hell retrieve her	30
Followed by their works they go	189	From the idle babbler, man	261
Foolish heart, unjust and vain	87	From th' oppressive power of sin	120
For all he hath on us bestowed	57	From the world of sin, and noise	263
For ever be his name adored	248	From thee no more shall I depart	287
For ever in thy Christ built up	17	From thence flow plenteous streams and clear	26
For ever is thy mercy gone	65		
For every fight Is dreadful and loud	198	From whom have all my blessings flowed	203
For Jesus my Lord Is now my defence	177	Fruit of thy gracious lips, on me	78
For Jesus the Lord hath comforted man	170	Fruit that I may bear, ordain	277
For my selfishness and pride	119	Fulfil, fulfil my large desires	366
For not as fugitives that try	171	Full of concupiscence and pride	131
For their dear suffering Saviour's sake	345	Full of pain and sin am I	99
For this he hung upon the tree	326	Full of truth and grace thou art	200
For this in steadfast hope I wait	282	Full oft in fruitless, fond desire	81
For this my jealousy is stirred	169		
For this only thing I pray	120		
For those who kindly founded this	17		

Volume III

For thou art their boast, Their glory and power	177	Factors for hell, ye strive in vain	150
		Faded and thunderstruck thy brow	147
For thus the Lord your God hath said	169	Fain we would be all like thee	332
For us he in the wilderness	16	Faith ascends the mountain's height	288
Forgive me, O long-suffering God	161	Faith in thy pardoning love we have	222
Forgive me then my follies past	161	Far above their noblest songs	12
Forgive the sins through which we groan	138	Farther than this I cannot go	60
		Fasting he doth, and hearing bless	245
Forlorn, forsaken, and alone	121	*Father, accept our sacrifice*	258
Fountain of life and all my joy	181	*Father, behold I come to do*	324
Fountain of Life, to all below	225	Father, behold thy dying Son!	310
Fountain of power, when he is near	172	Father, behold thy favourite Son, / And hear	17
Freed am I now, for ever freed	253		
Freely am I justified	265	*Father, behold thy favourite Son, / They*	305
Friend of sinners, in thy heart	134	Father, for us, even us, he bleeds	311
From a thing like me unclean	283	*Father, Friend of human race*	366
From actual and from inbred sin	338	*Father, God, who seest in me*	304
From all filthiness of flesh	106	Father, hear the blood of Jesus	225
From all iniquity, from all	305	*Father, I offer thee thine own*	264
From all remaining filth within	321	*Father, if I have sinned, with thee*	32
From all ungodliness and sin	324	*Father, if thou willing be*	327
From anger set our spirits free	332		

Father, in thee we taste the bread	368
Father, into thy hands alone	326
Father, let the sinner go	306
Father, live, by all things feared	345
Father, Lord of earth and heaven	350
Father of all above, below	352
Father of earth and heaven / All glory be	104
Father of earth and heaven / The hungry	357
Father of everlasting love	251
Father of Jesus Christ our Lord	100
Father of Jesus Christ the Just	16
Father of mankind, Be ever adored	347
Father of mankind, whose love	99
Father of mercies, hear	328
Father of our common Saviour	101
Father of our dear Lord	98
Father, on us the Spirit bestow	330
Father, our sacrifice receive	332
Father, see the Victim slain	304
Father, Son, and Holy Ghost, / All glory be	100
Father, Son, and Holy Ghost, / thee, with all	104
Father, Son, and Holy Ghost, / One in Three[199]	333
Father, Son, and Holy Ghost, / One in Three	334
Father, Son, and Holy Ghost, / thy Godhead	354
Father, Son, and Spirit bless us	102
Father, the grace we claim	268
Father, through thy Son receive	368
Father, thy feeble children meet	332
Father, thy own in Christ receive	221
Father, to him we turn our face	310
Father, we render thee thine own	369
Father, whose everlasting love / thy only	3
Father, whose everlasting love / Draws every	96
Fill our flesh with killing anguish	330
Fill the heart of each believer	271

199. The stanzas on pages 333 and 334 are identical.

First-born of many sons	316
Flesh and blood shall not receive	291
Following where my Lord hath led	327
For all that joy which now we taste	296
For all the sins of all mankind	16
For every man he tasted death	93
For I (the Lord of Hosts hath said	149
For in this holy mount shall rest	155
For lo! to us a Royal heir	138
For me, and all mankind	72
For me, for me the Saviour	33
For me, for us, and all mankind	65
For mercy I languish and faint	363
For them, and not for all mankind	66
For this alone I breathe	73
For this alone we pine	370
For those who at the judgment day	4
For thou in his distress hast been	152
For thou the staff of sin hast broke	138
For us all thy great salvation	101
For whom didst thou die	8
Forgive, the Saviour cries	228
Fountain of Deity	345
Fountain of unexhausted love	18
Free as air thy mercy streams	9
Freed from the inward cross	52
From all thy grief, and pain, and fear	145
From house to house they broke the bread	339
From the first feeble thought of good	95
From this thrice hallowed shade	304

Volume IV

Fain would I all thy goodness feel	259
Fainting in all the streets they lie	306
Faith in thy blood, thou seest, I have	471
Faith in thy changeless name I have	374
Faithful and good thou art	41
Fallen as I am once more	387
Fallen from thy pardoning grace	386
Famine, and sword, have laid thee waste	305
Far better goods we have above	38

Far from the paths of men, to thee	259	For thine own sake I pray	242
Far off he is, yet always near	323	For this, alas! I mourn	207
Fast by the streams of paradise	295	For this my heart sighs	213
Father, admit our lawful claim	170	For this my streaming eyes o'erflow	386
Father, and can it be	447	For this only thing I wait	251
Father, behold with gracious eyes	270	For this we reckon all things loss	32
Father, glorify thy Son	175	For thy dear sake we suffer wrong	37
Father, God, to us impart	142	For thy own mercy sake	435
Father, God, we glorify	141	For thy own truth, and mercy sake	469
Father, I in thy strength arise	429	For thy transient outward presence	183
Father, I seek thy face	437	For us wast thou not lifted up	461
"Father, if now thou hear'st it cry	349	For what you have done	371
Father, in me reveal thy Son	237	For years I have my vileness seen	384
Father in whom we live	254	For you, and for me	372
Father of endless majesty	225	Force our hardened souls to fear	60
Father of everlasting grace	165	Forerunner of mankind	154
Father of Jesus Christ, my Lord	259	Forth with our armies went	99
Father of Jesus Christ, the Just	227	*Fountain of power, from whom descends*	23
Father of mercies hear	329	*From the jaws of black despair*	390
Father, on thee whoever call	166	From anger and contemptuous pride	40
Father, our hearts we lift	114	From heaven he shall once more	169
Father, regard thy pleading Son	261	From him I farther still have strayed	391
Father, we ask in Jesu's name	261	From now my weary soul release	371
Fear not, my own peculiar race	297	From Pharaoh, and th' Egyptian's power	326
Fear not the taunts of short-lived man	302	From the world of care release us	139
Filled with faith's eternal Spirit	148	From thy feeble helpless creature	466
Find in Christ the way of peace	212	Furthered in faith, or hope, or love	280
Finish then thy new creation	219	Fury is not in me; to all	294
First-fruits of yonder land above	203		
Fly, to the mountains, fly	19		
Fools as we are, and slow of heart	136		
Foolish is all their strife, and vain	297	Volume V	
Foolish world, thy shouts forbear	450	Fain would I be clean	290
For as the plants in garden grow	312	Fain would we love the God we fear	131
For I the righteous Lord, and true	310	Fairer than the sons of men	21
For lo! the Lord from heaven comes down	65	Faith asks impossibilities	307
For lo! the Lord's great day is near	61	Faith cries out, It is the Lord	80
For sinners like me	273	Faith in the blood of Christ I have	308
For Sion's sake I will not cease	312	Faith in thy sovereign name I have	66
For thee, not without hope I mourn	266	Falsely accused I hold my peace	146
For thee our hearts we lift	168	*Falsely to thee the great pretend*	404
For thine only love I pant	251	Far from the soul removed	430
For thine own compassion's sake	406	Far from the world a place provide	416
		Far from the world thy calm retreat	405

IDEX OF FIRST LINES OF POETRY BY JOHN AND CHARLES WESLEY

First line	Page
Farewell thou once a sinner	216
Father, at thy footstool see	408
Father, God, thy love we praise	280
Father, in these reveal thy Son	388
Father of all, whose Sovereign will	393
Father of lights, to thee I lift	411
Father of mercies, hear! / Who didst of old	267
Father of mercies, hear / And send the	434
Father of mercies, hear my cry	292
Father, Son, and Holy Ghost, / Be to us what	408
Father, Son, and Holy Ghost / In solemn	389
Father, Son, and Holy Ghost / Mysterious	454
Father, take thy plague away	186
Father, thy will be done, not mine	82
Father, to thee I lift mine eyes	49
Father, to thee my soul I lift	374
Father, thou know'st he bought my peace	292
Feeble, and languishing in pain	237
Fellowship to the world unknown	477
Fellow-prisoners beneath	223
Find the ease for which I pant	339
Fisher of men ordained by thee	125
Fix on thee our whole affection	456
Fluttering soul, what dost thou here	444
Fly, my friends, with treacherous speed	179
Foe to nature as thou art	68
Following on with earnest haste	339
Foolish, we come to learn of thee	323
Foolish world, who canst not find	405
Fools, and madmen let us be	333
Fools that we are, and slow of heart	154
For a moment of pain	223
For her the plaintive turtle	239
For his mate the turtle moans	119
For me he meekly bows his head	3
For me thou hast died	304
For that heavenly prize	201
For thee delightfully employ	51
For their dead, the heathen mourning	344
For this a suffering life I live	112
For this alone / I make my moan	60
For this alone I live below	137
For this do I call	304
For this do I pray	305
For this do I wail	290
For this do we keep	266
For this do we mourn	222
For this do we wait	32
For this hope displayed before us	448
For this I humbly wait on thee	392
For this I in thy Spirit groan	337
For this I part with him below	432
For this immortal hope	430
For this my soul exults in hope	77
For this she counted all things loss	88
For this the pleading Spirit groans	481
For this we strive, for this we pray	167
For this with all thy saints we praise	110
For us, by men and fiends distressed	242
For what thou hast already done	130
Forbid it, O most gracious God	396
Foremost of created things	408
Forgetting still the things behind	335
Forgive them, Lord, but O! restrain	250
Forgive us for thy mercy sake	95
Forth in thy name, O Jesus send	107
Forth in thy name, O Lord, I go	50
Fountain of good, from thee alone	413
Frail alas! my nature is	9
Free from anger, and from pride	53
Free from sin, and servile fear	293
Free from sin I soon shall live	68
Free from sin we here shall live	332
Friend of my soul, its griefs he shares	421
Friend of all who seek thy favour	455
Friendship Divine! thy praise I sing	403
Friendship self, celestial guest	445
From actual blame	289
From all I suffer here	208
From all iniquity redeem	230
From all iniquity to save	326
From all of woman born	356
From all our foes, our sins redeem	299
From every sinful wrinkle free	483

From him our mingled blessings flow	477
From him the quickening Spirit flows	319
From idol loves, and vain desires	234
From strength to strength go on	44
From the faithless sons of men	185
From the things that are seen	200
From the world I remove	201
From thee that I no more may part	374
From this inbred sin deliver	297
Fronting the throne a crystal sea	287
Fulfil at last my heart's desire	396
Full gladly then for thee I grieve	69
Full of the wicked one, and born	151

Volume VI

Fain I would be as thou art	442
Fain I would, I would believe	415
Fain I would to thee be brought	441
Faithful she then in little was	240
Far away the aliens chase	78
Far from his generous bosom chase	123
Far oft from them the woe remove	50
Farewell, my best, my happiest friend!	341
Farewell (since heaven ordains it so)	254
Farewell, thou best of friends, farewell	318
Father, accept them in thy Son	408
Father, accept thine own	396
Father, and God of Abraham, hear	33
Father, for Jesu's sake alone	386
Father, hear the remnant's prayer	169
Father, I wake thy love to praise	450
Father, in thee our hearts confide	262
Father, Lord of earth and heaven	251
Father of compassions, hear us	168
Father of everlasting grace	383
Father of everlasting love	112
Father of faithful Abraham, hear	136
Father of harmony, farewell!	344
Father of lights, and God of love	260
Father of mercies, show	389
Father, the kind instruction give	403
Father, thy mercies past we own	16
Father, thy righteous will be done!	292
Father, to thee our souls we raise	421
Father, to thee thine own we give	388
Father, to us thy Spirit give	413
Father, to us vouchsafe the grace	280
Father, we make thy deed our own	259
Father, we on that Name depend	363
Father, with joy we praise	416
Fear to offend or God or man	326
Filled up with love and life Divine	243
Fire, vapour, and storm Accomplish His word	91
Fly, happy spirit, fly	237
Foe to the Popish boast	1
Followed by the hosts of heaven	161
Foolish, ignorant, and blind	393
For converse formed by art Divine	327
For friendship formed, her constant heart	320
For great in majesty Divine	178
For her a suffering life he lived	346
For her, whom her apostate sons despise	62
For I have heard a voice of woes	89
For I the just, the jealous God	84
For Immanuel's sake	454
For lo! a voice with awful sound	86
For my life, and clothes, and food	390
For O! my people have not known	87
For them she toiled with Martha's hands	295
For these, howe'er in flesh disjoined	72
For this habitually prepared	350
For this I ever pray	393
For this in faith we call	208
For this on earth she could not rest	300
For this premonished from above	173
For this thou hear'st thy Spirit groan	114
For this, ye sinners, howl and cry	84
For thou hast bid the creatures be	141
For thus the Lord vouchsafes to speak	83
For thus their angry Lord hath spoke	88
For us is prepared	211
For us thy guardian hand	89
For whether I am born to blush above	68
For works that I had wrought	2
Forced by the public crimes	HI 1759, 6

Forgive me, O thou jealous God	3	Father, for Jesus' sake	166
Forgive us, Lord, for such we were	38	*Father full of soft compassion*	341
Forth from the midst of Babel brought	71	*Father, God of pitying love*	81
Forth from the midst of Babel call	113	Father, if such thy sovereign will	71
Forth in thy strength, O Lord, we go	100	Father in Jesus reconciled	215
Found in the paths of righteousness	317	Father, in the name I pray	60
Fountain of power and dignity	126	Father, kindly draw, and give us	337
Free from that partial, blind respect	273	Father, manifest thy Son	304
Free from the busy worldling's cares	271	*Father of all, by whom we are*	72
Free from the law of sin and death	280	*Father of all, to thee I come!*	393
Freely his all for her he gave	310	*Father of all, whose bowels move*	408
Friendly, faithful soul, adieu	232	Father of compassions, show	363
From heaven angelic voices sound	141	*Father of earth and heaven*	165
From hence the fight of faith begun	240	*Father of everlasting grace*	155
From her and every creature torn	297	*Father of light, thy needful aid*	76
From love's soft witchcraft free	205	*Father of omnipresent grace*	18
From those who did her Father's will	360	Father of our patient Lord	86
From us, as we from him, secure	253	Father, Son, and Holy Ghost / For good	61
From violent and perfidious foes	120	Father, Son, and Holy Ghost / heal thy	308
From whence these dire portents around	24	*Father, Son, and Holy Spirit, / Saved by thee*	336
Fruit of Jesus' lips and prayer	232	*Father, Son, and Holy Spirit, / One*	337
		Father, Son, and Spirit come / Enter now	68, 69

Volume VII

Fain we would obedient prove	85	Father, Son, And Spirit, come / And with	33
Fain would I, Lord, obtain the grace	195	Father, Son, and Spirit, descend	324
Fairer than the sons of men	151	*Father, Son, and Spirit, hear*	303
Faith echoes to his prayer above	156	*Father, thy froward children*	118
Faith in thy powerful love I have	100	*Father, thy glory we confess*	289
Faith, though rational, is founded	333	*Father, thy gracious warning*	114
Far above the world of pain	82	Father, till thou revealest	31
Far from myself to thee	102	*Father, to thy protection*	335
Far from passion, and from pride	418	*Father, who know'st the things we need*	157
Far from thy family removed	155	Finish the first transgression, thou	407
Far from thy mad fantastic ways	179	First in the primitive offence	65
Father, and Friend of humankind	62	Fixed on the Athanasian mound	315
Father, and Son, and Spirit join	286	Foes to God and unforgiven	148
Father, and Son, and Spirit joined	230	Foolish, and blind to what is best	120
Father and Son for ever join	265	For all who thine appearing love	184
Father and Son in nature join	216	For friendship formed by nature and by grace	436
Father, by saints on earth adored	22	For Jesus' sake my son retrieve	147
Father, by the tender name	85	For mercy and grace We only can cry	37
Father, draw him from his birth	68		

For One all-perfect God we plead	263
For redemption I call	322
For the sake of thy Son	8
For thee, not without hope, we mourn	183
For this alone I wish to live	106
For this alone on earth we wait	224
For this, as tottering over	104
For this I pant, Athirst and faint	190
For this we ask in faith sincere	76
For thy glory we are	199
For thy nature's sake forgive me	341
For when the rich a proffered Christ reject	434
Forerunner of the Lord their God	209
Fountain and root of all beside	177
Fountain of Divine compassion	306
Fountain of endless mercies	25
Fountain of life Divine	291
Fountain of unexhausted love	146
Free for whate'er thy love ordains	182
Free from low, distracting care	151
From sudden unexpected death	409
From the evils which surround us	14
From the pit of condemnation	14
From thee I must be driven	189
From thee our being we receive	266
Fulfilled in us we daily own	250
Full credence we give	302
Full of trembing expectation	57
Full of themselves, with learned pride	328
Fully certified thou art	307
Fulness of energy Divine	297
Fulness of joy his presence gives	103
Furnished with intellectual light	315

Volume VIII

Fail mine eyes with looking up	226
Fain I would on thee rely	96
Faints my soul with strong desire	368
Fairer than all the earth-born race	102
Faith which sweetly works by love	430
Faithful and true, thy word we plead	340
Faithful soul, pray always, pray	235
False witnesses against me rise	55
False witnesses rose up to blast	75
Far from me, O Lord, remove	211
Far from the Truth[200] and living Way	129
Farewell, my dearest child, farewell	433
Fast by the Baybylonish tide	252
Fast by the streams of Paradise	3
Father, for thy own mercy's	424
Father, if still we have	314
Father of everylasting love / In Jesu's name	317
Father of everlasting love / The only refuge	284
Father, regard his powerful prayer	342
Father, Son, and Holy Ghost, / Present with	443
Father, to thee we bring	303
Fearless of the scorner's power	216
Fifty thousand Britons brave	328
Fight with those that strive t' annoy me	78
Filled with abiding peace Divine	245
Fired with the hope so rich a treasure	456
First for themselves the patriots care	481
Fisher of men, ordained by Christ alone	434
Fishers of men, by Satan sent	318
Flushed with success, without their head	452
Fly every touch of blame	182
Folded as a garment, they	189
Following after righteousness	215
Foolish world, thy vain reply	330
For his people in distress[201]	108
For his people in distress[202]	109
For in my haste I said	64
For Israel's sake the sinner spare	155
For Jesus the Lord, though lofty and high	255
For lo! the Lord a seed hath chose	249

200. Osborn changed "Truth" to "true."
201. Lines 2 and 3 read: "The God of Jacob stands; / Keeps us, till our troubles cease."
202. Lines 2 and 3 read: "The God of Jacob stands; / Bears us, til our troubles cease."

First Line	Page
For, lo! the reign of hell	240
For my friends' and brethren's sake	238
For not by their own arm or sword	99
For not in my own sword or bow	100
For, O! I always falling am!	87
For, O, my sins I now confess	115
For, O! thy love to me is great	171
For refuge, Lord, to thee I fly!	259
For these thy ransomed ones we claim	441
For this a dying life I live	366
For this at thy feet / Expecting I sit	421
For this I have forsook	52
For this raised up by thee	388
For this shall every child of God	66
For this ten thousand faithful souls	323
For this we still remain	389
For thou hast immortality	172
For thou hast revealed thy nature unknown	255
For thou hast saved my soul from death	126
For thou in power and love art great	170
For thou my soul hast known	62
For thou, O Lord, my cause hast gained	18
For thy lovingkindness, Lord	113
For us he in thy presence stands	343
For who, except the Lord, is God?	33
Forbid the flood our land t' o'erflow	268
Foremost of the celestial train	169
Forfeited by Britain's sin	334
Foul their mouth, and filled with lies	131
Fraught with the policy of Rome	301
Freely where'er I would, I went	428
Friend of all the sinful race	339
From Aaron's beard it rolls	251
From every secret foe	303
From his high and holy place	188
From my misdeeds avert thy face	116
From the malice of men	394
From the precepts of thy law	222
From the throne of God there springs	107
From the time that thee I know	247
From trouble's abyss	350
Frowning on us, he seems awhile	307
Full of providential love	143
Furiously the heathen raged	108

Volume IX

First Line	Page
Fain would I in my earliest days	358
Fain would I, Lord, from earth remove	91
Fain would I, Lord, my household lead	19
Fain would I put my trust in thee	446
Fain would I to that fountain fly	279
Faint my head, and sick my heart	81
Fair as the unclouded moon	366
Faith and love the breast-plate make	60
Faith lays hold on thy great might	99
Faithful and True, we trust in thee	35
Faithful, O God, thy threatening word	212
Faithful, O Lord, thy mercies are	55
Far from the crowd	301
Farther, and farther[203] still	306
Farther and farther still I run	6
Fast found with the fetters of woe	269
Father, help, by covenant ours	211
Father, how kind thou art	352
Father, I dare believe	334
Father, I do at last relent	64
Father, I joyfully believe	26
Father, I know my day is nigh	106
Father, if thou my Father art	15
Father, in Abraham's steps I tread	17
Father, in Christ my Father, thou	229
Father, in Christ we seek thy face	221
Father, inspire my altered heart	7
Father, instruct my docile heart	94
Father, let thy faithfulness	63
Father of all, the Just, the True	419
Father of boundless grace	468
Father of Christ, the sinner's Friend	141
Father of everlasting grace / Be mindful	207
Father of everlasting grace / thou hast in us	381
Father, see this living clod	3
Father, show to me thy glory	54

203. Osborn changed to: Further and further.

Father, Son, and Holy Ghost, / In council join	2
Father, that I may keep thy law	359
Father, the ancient greeting hear	223
Father, the thing impossible	417
Father, thine eyes are open now	175
Father, thou call'st me by my name	23
Father, thou didst chastise our Lord	439
Father, thou dost conduct the blind	417
Father, thou dost forgive	318
Father, thou dost not gladly grieve	356
Father, thou dost our Prophet hear	156
Father, thou hast bestowed	427
Father, thou hast raised him up	103
Father, thou still dost lead	66
Father, though late, I turn to thee	137
Father, thy merciful design	93
Father, thy promise we embrace	77
Father, thy will be done	68
Father, to my heart appear	252
Father, to that first-born of thine	26
Father, trusting in thy Son	61
Father, we humbly wait to hear	463
Fathers their heavenly Father knew	48
Favour, and grace to Israel shown	221
Fear not, for I thy God am here	410
Fear of God before mine eyes	251
Find we in the hallowed place	52
First, the great almighty Lord	271
Flesh, earth, and Satan joined	118
Fly, sinners, fly to David's Son	161
For a departing friend I grieve	170
For as I once to Noah swore	442
For evil may I good return	163
For half an age of mournful years	316
For I my Sion's peace	466
For I, the Lord, thy God abide	411
For I who to my promise stand	459
For lo, my wrath is pacified	454
For lo! the Lord will come	467
For pleasure, and praise, And riches ye pant	445
For this I at thy footstool wait	448
For this only thing I wait	251
For this thou art gone up on high	396
For thy people's rest I sigh	91
Foretold by the converted seer	84
Forgetting still the things behind	304
Forgive my partial selfishness	23
Forward! but whither shall we go	45
Fountain of light thy Saviour is	458
From hence, most gracious Lord, from hence	92
From her dark, inconstant state	367
From infancy to hoary hairs	424
From nature's different mixtures free	58
From our own inventions vain	357
From sin preserved in thee	114
From thence thy heralds run	468
Fruit of the true immortal Vine	360
Full, but not satisfied	206
Full of thy holy love I rise	101
Full of unutterable grace / *Thus the true*	171
Full of unutterable grace / *Jesus mine eye*	335
Full oft thou hast my helper been	326

Volume X

Fain would I, Lord, admittance find	325
Fain would I my affection show	434
Fain would I wash my soul from sin	11
Fain would we cease from sinning	183
Faith is the source of prayer	343
Faith sends me, Jesus, in thy name	237
Faith to be healed thou know'st I have	39
Faithful, and true, for this we wait	88
False confidence the tempter gives	153
False friendship in its last excess	302
Far from a world of noisy care	144
Far from his sour hypocrisy	459
Father, by right Divine	179
Father, create my heart again	186
Father, for Jesus' merit	181
Father, for Jesu's sake alone	40
Father, for power I groan	176
Father, how wide thy glories shine	239
Father, I all thy fulness want	196

First Line	Page
Father, I ask in Jesu's name	201
Father, I now my sin confess	52
Father, I now th' atonement plead	417
Father, I will, I do repent	14
Father, if thou must reprove	21
Father, in our hearts reveal	64
Father, in thy beloved Son	149
Father, instruct my childlike heart	188
Father, make good thy word of grace	130
Father, now to Israel raise	63
Father of earth and sky	178
Father of everlasting grace	103
Father of Jesus Christ, our Lord	138
Father of the fatherless	45
Father, the good in secret done	175
Father, the prayer thou dost require	177
Father, thy heavenly voice I own[204]	148
Father, thy heavenly voice I own[205]	150
Father, thy kind design explain	98
Father, to me the faith impart	300
Father who art in heaven	179
Feeblest of all thy people, I	121
Feet on my helpless soul bestow	294
Few on their ministry attend	454
First his own peculiar race	349
First our Lord vouchsafes to praise	247
Fishers of men 'tis thine to make	158
Fit mansion for the spirit impure	262
Followers of the silent Lamb	426
Foolish world, who brand the men	468
Fools themselves the just esteem	383
For a moment's labour here	394
For every sinful action	183
For the hiding of thy face	51
For th' Omniscient's information	177
For these I would in secret grieve	19
For thy truth and mercy's sake	37
Forbear, my foe, thy triumph vain	98
Forbid it, Lord, that I should be	326
Forbid it, Lord, that I should strive	169
Forgiveness is the children's bread	292
Forth-issuing from Jehovah's throne	88
Forth the zealous servants went	350
Foulest of the sinful race	148
Friend, how darest thou enter in	351
From him his ministers should learn	449
From servile fear and flattery free	449
From spitting, shame, and scorn	412
From the fools reputed wise	252
From trials unexempted	182
Fulfil thine own intense desire	254
Fulfilling thy own prayer	184
Full of earnest expectation	379
Full of himself, and swollen with pride	461
Fulness of the Deity	141
Fulness of power in earth is thine	441
Fulness of power in heaven is thine	440
Furnished thus, O Lord, by thee	277

Volume XI

First Line	Page
Fain would I my Redeemer see	488
Faith enables us to bear	249
Faith for his proofs is wanting still	247
Faith is not on all bestowed	393
Faith to be healed even now	224
Faith to be healed I have	38
Faithful and good, thy Saviour hear	22
False we must ourselves confess	5
Far above all competitors	231
Far from the house of God most-high	223
Father, behold thy Son	299
Father, I still confess	237
Father, if thou willing be	291
Father in thy hands we are	405
Father of all, in me	381
Father of me, and all mankind	200
Father thou hast our hearts inclined	386
Father, through thy Son to me	204
Father thy boundless love we find	155
Father, thy word, thy oath we plead	113
Father, we in the joy rejoice	194
Father, we trust thy Spirit of grace	125

204. Line 2: "thy gracious majesty."
205. Line 2: "Propitious through thy favourite Son."

Fear for a moment may withhold	281
Fear, joy, astonishment oppose	313
Fearful, fluttering heart be still	277
Fed, and strengthened by the word	175
Few will risk the consequence	445
Filled with the power procured for me	153
Fisher of men ordained	144
Fix in us that quiet spirit	277
Followed, and by the church deplored	162
Following Christ when danger's near	290
For long unfruitfulness	43
For me the answer came	492
For pardon I believed	174
For precious souls he cares	260
For the sick of sin we plead[206]	99
For thee I in thy temple stay	368
For this, as taught by thee, I pray	45
For this I pray, and long, and trust	40
For this into their hands he goes	469
For this thou dost thy life lay down	460
For this we magnify thy name	195
For those eternal things designed	242
For what thou didst bestow	180
For wisdom, Lord, on thee I wait	404
Foreign and false the riches here	242
Forgive my foes? It cannot be	155
Forgiveness is the foremost grace	48
Formed in the region of the air	388
Forth by our good desires we go	472
Foul lepers, by ourselves abhorred[207]	251
Founded on the rock of peace	159
Fountain of life to all that live	318
Fountain of purity Divine	502
Fountain of truth for ever full	424
Free from pain recline my head	470
Freely he left his throne above	350
From every golden string	239
From Jesus, manifest below	117
From Jesu's sacrifice	72
From sin and misery	265
From spiritual to sensual good	14
From the calm repose of prayer	186
From the close hypocrisy	207
From the impious and profane	137
From the man, outrageous spite	444
From the tribunal of thy cross	493
Full of designs for living here	210
Full of the greatness of his Lord	324
Full of the Holy Ghost he comes	131
Fulness of his sanctity	465

Volume XII

Faith beholds th' invisible	441
Faith cannot pray in vain	369
Faith cannot unfruitful prove	324
Faith comes by hearing of the word	112
Faith effects the wondrous union	105
Faith through the apostolic word	56
Faith we surely know and feel	16
Faith, which when it comes, sets free	296
Faithful and merciful High-Priest	56
Faithfully I would declare	372
Far better 'tis that righteous men[208]	418
Far off we need not rove	342
Fast bound in chains of hellish night	322
Father, forgive the sinful race	95
Father, I ask in Jesus' name	40
Father I would thy will obey	281
Father, in the powerful name	28
Father of Christ our Saviour	42
Father of our gracious Lord	60
Father regard thy Spirit's groans	346
Father, the narrow path	201
Father, the promised bliss I claim	147
Father, thine offspring own	343
Father, thy name be sanctified!	23
Father who always hear'st our Friend	13
Favour against the good	416
Festivals observed to God	352
Few alas! the need confess	357
Fill my heart with watchful love	377
Filled with his purity and power	410

206. *UP* 2:71.
207. *UP* 2:162.
208. *UP* 2:422.

Filled with the same almighty grace	190	Faith, hope, and love thou dost bestow	36
Filled with the Spirit of holiness	143	Faith in thy blood if thou bestow	145
First for the twelve he intercedes	47	Faith is the grace	161
First to the Jews was Shiloh sent	167	Faith lends an ear	161
Five thousand added in a day	169	Faith the foundation sure remains	36
Followers of the Crucified	36	Faith without works is not the true	172
Foolish men, your hope is vain	435	Faith's appropriating power	62
For evil in a garden done	65	Faithful I account thee, Lord	95
For that farther revelation	15	False-witnesses may rise	83
For this let fiery zealots seize	429	Far from all the smell of fire	247
For thy own sake pronounce the word	97	Farther th' apostle dared not say	35
For whom dost thou endure the cross	98	Father, behold, I calmly wait	97
"Forgive them," gasps his parting breath	95	Father, from every bosom chase	174
"Forgive them," still the Saviour cries	95	Father, I still his passion plead	128
Forgotten of God and forsook	104	Father, if I may call thee so	130
Forth against all the world he goes	237	Father, if mine in Christ thou art	98
Fountain of life and light Divine	132	Father, into my heart convey	93
Fountain of life, I gasp for thee	14	Father, into thy arms of love	52
Free from nature's fond excess	221	Father, manifest thy Son	182
Free from self-exalting pride	312	Father, obedient to thy will	12
Freedom the cause of God requires	431	Father of all, we trust in thee	211
Freely he lays the ransom down	66	Father of all, we worship thee	24
Freely pardoned they were	304	Father of Jesus Christ our Lord, / Our sins	195
Fresh fatigue for Jesus' sake[209]	369		
Frightened by a servant's word	145	Father of Jesus Christ our Lord, / With Jesus	212
From all the power of passion free	385		
From Christ the unction flows	383	Father, on me the grace bestow	167
From his submissiveness we know	254	Father, send into our hearts	42
From men who harden their own hearts	358	Father, thy kind advice I take	52
From Noah's down to Moses' days	308	Father, thy love in Christ reveal	61
From spirits glorified	242	Father, thy most benign intent	10
From the curious vain desire	130	Father, to thee and to the Lamb	234
From their bleeding bosom rent	221	Father, that we are truly thine	157
Fruit of faith and charity	23	Father, we give thee all the praise	71
Full of a false misguided zeal	306	Feeble in body, and in mind	256
Full power to thee thy Father gave	48	Filled with the blessedness of hope	113
Fulness of power the world to save	62	Flesh out of his flesh we are	76
		Flowed from him an open fountain	117
		Foolish, alas! the hope, and vain	251

Volume XIII

		For all it was shed	235
Fain would I, Lord, the word receive	227	For me obtained he is	72
Fain would I the compassion prove	98	For names the Christian world contend	68
		For this, thou faithful Lord, I come	269
		For thy glory in the sky	154

209. *UP* 2:401.

For universal peace I pine	19	Glory to thee, whose powerful word	231
For who by faith your Lord receive	87	Glory to thy great Name alone	240
From endless death to save	205	Go then the secret cause explore[217]	42
From hence he shall our comforts raise	249	Go where the darkest tempest lowers	227
From his heavenly throne descending	117	God from above, with ready grace	171
From the mystic volume hearing	218	God in their every work was praised	172
Full of the pure immortal hope	232	*God of Love, incline thine ear!*	323
Full well the labour of our hands	18	God of my life and all my powers[218]	51
Furnished out of thy treasury	110	God of my life, what just return	75
		God of my life, whose gracious power[219]	322
		God, the everlasting God	188

Volume I

		God through himself we then shall know	239
Gently will he lead the weak	351	God, without faith, we cannot please	211
Gideon and Barak claim the song	219	God, your God, shall surely come	291
Give me back my innocence	321	God's mighty Spirit fills the dome[220]	166
Give me thine all-sufficient grace	294	Good God! that any child of thine	309
Give me thy might, thou God of power	180	Grace our every thought controls	170
Give me thy strength, O God of power[210]	179	Grace we implore; when billows roll[221]	163
Give me thy wings, celestial Dove	262	Grace will I sing, through Jesu's name	314
Give them conceptions worthy thee	314	*Gracious soul, to whom are given*	330
Give them to hear the word as thine	240	Grant this, O holy God, and true![222]	167
Give to my eyes refreshing tears[211]	177	Grant this, O Lord; for thou hast died	226
Give to the winds thy fears[212]	127	Grant, though parted from our sight	188
Give we to the Lord above	288	*Granted is the Saviour's prayer*	188
Giver of concord, Prince of peace	298	Great are the things which Thou hast done	120
Giv'st thou me honour? All shall see[213]	28	Groaning I languish at his stay	326
Giv'st thou me knowledge? It shall still[214]	28	Grov'ling on earth we still must lie	32
Gladly the toys of earth we leave[215]	168	Guilty I stand before thy face	277
Glorious in soul, he mounts and flies[216]	58		
Glory, and praise, and love to thee	240		
Glory be to God on high	115		
Glory to God, and praise, and love	299		
Glory to God, whose sovereign grace	287		

Volume II

Gather those outcasts who remain	19
Gently he lifts the fallen up	56

210. From the German of Johann Joseph Winckler, translated by John Wesley.
211. From the German of Johann Angelus Scheffler, translated by John Wesley.
212. From the German of Paul Gerhardt, translated by John Wesley.
213. George Herbert.
214. George Herbert.
215. From the German of Gerhard Tersteegen, translated by John Wesley.
216. George Herbert.

217. George Herbert.
218. John Gambold?
219. Line 2 reads: "Through various deaths my soul hath led."
220. Henry More.
221. From the German of Nikolaus von Zinzendorf, translated by John Wesley.
222. Henry More.

Gifts, alas! cannot suffice	274	Grant me comfort, or deny	214
Gigantic lusts come forth to fight	313	Grant me now the bliss to feel	276
Give me a new a perfect heart	320	Grant, O grant my last request	135
Give me, Lord, a holy fear	125	Grant that every moment I	277
Give me, Lord, the victory	152	Grant this, and then from all below	139
Give me the grace, the love I claim	300	Great helper of the friendless thou	331
Give me thy life; for thou my death	146	Great Searcher of the heart and reins	351
Give me thyself, from every boast	150		
Give me to feel thy agonies	71		
Give the pure gospel word	343		

Volume III

Give the pure word of general grace	343	Gainst those that faithless prove	50
Give them an ear to hear the word	342	Gathered to the well-known sign	50
Giver and Guardian of my sleep	140	Get thee behind me, fiend!	277
Giver of peace and unity	333	Give each to thee as seemeth best	269
Gladly therefore will I boast	294	*Give us, O Lord, the children's bread*	299
Glitter his feet like polished brass	341	*Give us this day, all-bounteous Lord*	278
Glory be to God above	220	Give us to hear the dreadful sound	221
Glory to God, whose gracious care	77	Give we to our Lord the glory	101
Glory to God, whose gracious power	217	*Glorious Saviour of my soul*	10
Glory to his name belongs	252	*Glory, love, and praise, and honour*	364
Glory to the name of Jesus	32	*Glory to God, and peace on earth*	141
Go, into every nation, go!	49	*Glory to God on high!*	348
God, arise, thou jealous God	106	*Glory to God the Father give*	350
God is thine; disdain to fear	306	Glory to God who reigns above	300
God of all power, and truth, and grace	319	*Glory to him who freely spent*	245
God of all power, and truth, and love	285	Glory to the Eternal Spirit!	346
God of compassion, Lord of love	41	Go, foolish worms, his word deny	262
God of Daniel, hear my prayer	266	Go forth, and speak my word to all	135
God of eternal Majesty	60	Go, sinner, in her footsteps tread	177
God of Israel's faithful three	267	Go tell the reprobates their doom	136
God of my salvation, hear	200	*Go, wretched soul, to meet thy doom*	24
God of our health, in thy great name	138	God, ever merciful and just	67
God of our life, at thy command	138	God forbid that I should dare	15
God of Truth, and Power and Love	66	God in this dark vale of tears	11
God of unexhausted grace	179	*God incomprehensible*	258
God of unspotted purity	358	God is both the Gift and Giver	102
God only doth the victory give	186	God is the thing I sought	31
God only wise, and great, and strong	55	God is unchangeable	47
God, the gracious God and true	307	*God of all-pardoning grace*	58
God was once my glorious dress	156	*God of all-redeeming grace*	321
God, who him to life restored	187	*God of infinite compassion*	101
God's almighty word shall stand	307	*God of unexampled grace*	229
Gold that can bear the fiery test	360	God of unfathomable grace	43
Good tidings show to Judah's race	51		

God sees in you no sin	48
God the Father through the Spirit	102
God, the Good, the Just, I clear	16
God was in Christ, and all mankind	68
Grace only doth from sin restrain	95
Gracious and True, set to thy seal	29
Gracious thou art to all	62
Grant my importunate request	19
Great are thy miracles of grace	152
Great Friend of mankind, We trust in thy blood	98
Great is thy faithfulness and love	264
Great witness of God, To thee we appeal	9
Grief hath shook the house of clay	162
Gross misconceit be far away!	266

Volume IV

Gather and sanctify the crowd	74
Gaze on that helpless Object	112
Get thee behind us, fiend	45
Give him, and us, and all to see	98
Give him, before he bows his head	48
Give him th' indubitable sign	48
Give him thy little flock to feed	24
Give him thy pardoning love to feel	350
Give him, when now the day draws near	47
Give me back my guilty load	387
Give me the faith to hold me up[223]	450
Give me to bow, with thee, my head	249
Give to mine eyes refreshing tears	442
Give us thy strength, O God of love	28
Gladness and joy far off remove	441
Gladness and joy shall there be found	300
Glorious head, triumphant Saviour	140
Glory be to God on high, / And peace on	108
Glory be to God on high, / God in whom	221
Glory be to God the Giver	108
Glory to God! they all shall cry	285
Glory to the righteous God	478
Go see the King of Glory	111
Go tell the followers of your Lord[224]	130
Go tell the vile deserters!—No	134
Go then, my angry Master said	76
Go then, my Lord again enjoined	276
Go through the gates, ('tis God commands,)[225]	315
God in the flesh below	154
God is gone up on high	154
God is in this, in every place	324
God of all consolation, take	380
God of all power, and truth, and grace[226]	54
God of all power, and truth, and grace[227]	290
God of everlasting grace	221
God of God, and Light of light	181
God of infinite compassion	7
God of love, that hear'st the prayer	228
God of love, who hear'st the prayer	101
God of my life, to thee I raise	353
God of my salvation, hear	464
God of the patriarchal race	224
God, only God hath all my heart	56
God only is unchangeable	302
God only knows the love of God	341
God ruleth on high, Almighty to save	51
God sitting on his holy seat	95
Good Physician, show thine art	359
Gracious God, what shall I do?	427
Grafted in him they all shall share	294
Grant me for thy mercy sake	180
Grant me (not as childish men	180
Grant me (not as mortals give	180
Grant us in this awful crisis	101
Grant us still to pray and grieve	69
Grieved with the penal want of grace	384
Guard him from all who dare oppose	21
Guilty because they know not him	187
Gushing from thy wounded side	359

---

223. *UP* 3:203.
224. *UP* 3:113.
225. *UP* 2:464.
226. Line 2: "All our iniquity remove."
227. Line 2: "thou hast increased the holy seed."

Volume V

Gather the outcasts in, and save	121
Gather them in on every side	482
Gentle Jesu, Lovely Lamb	21
Gentle thou, and meek in heart	303
Get thee behind me, fiend! no more	307
Give glory to Elijah's God	109
Give glory to Jesus our head	357
Give him thy meek and quiet mind	75
Give me a sober mind	270
Give me, Lord, thy Holy Spirit	297
Give me on thee to call	262
Give me that second rest	118
Give me the faith which can remove	105
Give me the thing thou long'st to give	294
Give me to bear thy easy yoke	51
Give me to catch them by thy grace	127
Give me to triumph in thy shame	197
Give me what God to thee did give	294
Give us ourselves and thee to know	124
Give, when thou wilt, the blessing	472
Giver of life, and strength renewed	377
Gladly before rulers brought	383
Gladly I drink thy mercy's cup	70
Gladly I hasten to decay	113
Gladly I own the promise true	111
Glory and thanks, and praise	128
Glory and thanks to God we give	381
Glory, honour, thanks, and praise	380
Glory, Lord, to thee we give	106
Glory to Christ be given	116
Glory to God above	268
Glory to the God unknown	187
Glory to that victorious grace	81
Glory to the awful God!	180
Go, in peace my children go	132
Go meet him in the sky	285
Go up, with Christ, your head	271
Go with me thou in all my ways	91
God do so to me, and more	133
God forbids his longer stay	80
God hath ordained that I should see	308
God of all good gifts the Donor	425
God of all grace, and majesty	372
God of all grace, thy saving name	473
God of all power, and grace	235
God of all-redeeming grace	406
God of almighty love	56
God of my life, for thee I pine	71
God of my life, how good, how wise	193
God of my life, thy love I praise	78
God of my life, to thee	15
God of my life, to thy decree	193
God over all his state maintains	287
God they extol above the sky	288
God was in Christ, and dwelt with men	298
Gracious Lord, how long shall I	443
Gracious Redeemer shake	262
Grant me first the rest from sin	161
Great Author of my being	202
Great Searcher of hearts	439
Greatest of all O let him be	416

Volume VI

'Gainst these by thee sent forth to fight	101
'Gainst vice we partially declaim	37
Gentle Jesus, meek and mild	441
Gently she their will inclined[228]	336
Give glory to God Who sits on the throne	184
Give him then, and always give	387
Give me thy bliss to share	206
Give the never failing peace	174
Give us an humble, active mind	421
Glorious God, accept a heart	381
Glory, and thanks, and love	285
Glory, and thanks, and praise	223
Glory be to God alone	465
Glory to God, and praise	446
Glory to God belongs	434
Glory to God, if we receive	426
Glory to God on high	338
Glory to the Redeemer give[229]	300

228. *UP* 3:339.
229. *UP* 3:332.

Go, blessed saint, to Jesus go	295	Give us quietly to tarry	48
Go, blessed spirit, from earth set free	228	Giver of all good gifts, on me	173
Go, claim thy full, immense	341	*Giver of every good*	101
Go, envious fiend, and force	275	*Giver of every useful gift*	140
Go then to thy glorious estate	192	*Giver of godly woe*	362
God is good and great alone	395	*Giver of the nightly songs*	11
God is goodness, wisdom, power	386	*Giver of unfeigned repentance*	14
God of all-alluring grace	376	*Giver, Lord, of life and death*	363
God of all power, and truth, and love	323	Giver of penitential pain	397
God of awful majesty	23	Glad to pray, and labour on	47
God of glorious majesty	20	Glorious God, like them we bless thee	301
God of unbounded power	151	Glorious, Triune God of love	269
God of unfathomable grace	281	*Glory to our God most high*	87
God only can our sight restore	392	*Glory to the paternal God*	200
God, our soul's eternal Lover	278	God by nature we confess	288
God over all supreme	230	*God did the testament enjoin*	240
God over all, thy work we praise	181	*God distinct in persons three*	303
God over-ruling all we own	183	God doth to our King attend	10
God we absolutely trust	252	God from hence, the God supreme	273
God, within our hearts reside	404	God hath answered all our prayers	83
God's image she in man revered	328	God hath Israel visited	271
Good of himself he only is	426	God in persons three, appear	308
Good Physician, show thine art	352	God inaccessible, unknown	331
Good thou art, and good thou dost	461	*God made known the mystery*	236
Grace, in answer to his prayer	391	*God of a truth in us resides*	293
Gracious God, my sins forgive	391	*God of all consolation*	253
Great Builder of thy church below	127	*God of all grace and patience, hear*	406
Great God of all-victorious grace	163	*God of eternal truth and love*	71
Great God of love, prepare my heart	247	God of her complete salvation	64
Great God, if now thy day is near	41	*God of love, his doom prevent*	153
Great God, who, ready to forgive	19	*God of love, with pity see*	95
Great God, whose wrath in ancient times	79	God of my life and health restored	93
Great Guardian of Britannia's land	105	*God of my life preserved by grace*	109
Great Guardian of thy church below	172	*God of my thoughtless infancy*	133
Great King of saints, to thee alone	255	God of the patriarchal race	197
Greaten my contracted mind	445	*God of unfathomable grace*	116
Guide of our weak, unstable youth	418	*God only wise, almighty, good*	75
Guide to her natural allies	360	*God our Teacher we embrace*	291
		God over all for ever blessed	177
		God over all we bless thy name	225
		God, th' eternal persons three	268
		God the Father his whole will	293
		God, the offended God most high	217
		God they went, the persons three	271

Volume VII

Give me the hidden bliss to feel	105
Give me to believe aright	324

God, t' enhance her joy above	84	God most merciful, most high	107
God unsearchable, unknown	311	God of all grace and patience, hear	313
God, very God indeed	300	*God of faithful Abraham, hear*	401
God was in Christ, th' eternal Sire	215	*God of infinite compassion*	97
God were manifested there	269	*God of love, thy gracious token*	278
God, who did the Spirit bestow	251	*God of my righteousness*	7
God whom we in Christ adore	286	God of our salvation, thee	143
God, whose eye doth all things see	70	*God of tremendous power*	313
Good incommunicated, pure	263	God of truth and power and grace	441
Governed by thine only will	46	God of unfathomable love	114
Governed by the engrafted word	150	God omnipotent, arise	268
Grant me this, I ask no more	353	God on me his blessings showers	190
Great Author of my being	132	*God on us his grace bestow*	147
Great Fountain-head of Deity	232	God shall judge the faithless race	22
Great omnipresent One in Three	289	God, th' almighty God, hath made	183
Great things I do not, Lord require	419	*God, the omnipresent God*	106
Great Triune God, whose ruling power	347	God who doth appoint the end	331
Guilt my troubled spirit harrows	112	*God, who wouldst a world forgive*	305
Guilty, guilty we confess	242	God without faith I cannot please	348
		Good it is for me t' have known	219
		Gospel-grace to each extend	335
Volume VIII		Grace every morning new	251
		Grace if thou forbear to give	385
'Gainst me my mortal foes conspire	94	Gracious, merciful, and kind	190
'Gainst our anointed Lord	313	Granting my incessant suit	364
Gird on thy thigh the Spirit's sword	103	*Great God incomprehensible*	375
Girded with almighty power	143	Great God, we know not what to do	287
Give him the sting of death to feel	352	Great is our redeeming Lord	111
Give me love, and let me die	383	Grieved at human vanity	89
Give sentence, Lord, with me	51	*Guardian of my hoary hairs*	430
Given, his joys and griefs to share	302	Guilty we must receive our hire	349
Glorious is the Lord Most high	110		
Glory to our redeeming Lord	304	**Volume IX**	
God, be mercifully near	409		
God be mindful of thy prayers	39	'Gainst me thou writest bitter things	245
God beholds and loves his own	22	'Gainst the man of sin in me	159
God ever near to the distressed	351	Give him in thee to view	320
God hath built his church below	237	Give me not up to Satan's power	330
God in Christ, to whom I pray	364	Give me that enlarged desire	312
God in his holiness hath sworn	133	Give then thyself, Jehovah, give	292
God in that spacious firmament	36	Glorious in majesty	114
God is not in their thoughts, or way	312	Glorious indeed (though fools despise)	166
God is the Lord that shows us light	208	Glory and thanks to him belongs	340
God keeps off the hostile bands	111		

Go forth, ye ransomed people, flee	425	God is not slack; if long he stay	387
Go on, thrice happy soul, go on	404	God is the plenitude of good	325
God hath all our actions wrought	205	God never alienates his right	319
God inaccessible thou art	317	God of eternal truth and grace	100
God of all-sufficient grace	18	God of heaven, appear below	67
God of all power, and truth, and love	236	God of truth, we wait on thee	34
God of the upright ones	113	God on man the grace bestows	295
Gone out against my body, Lord	143	God over all and Judge supreme	441
Good; for 'tis there our Lord we find	35	God over all, for ever blessed	458
Grace vouchsafed for Jesu's sake	346	God over all, thy power I own	30
Grace which sure salvation brings	126	God, whose mercies never end	54
Gracious Lord, who stand'st between	93	God's servants true they will not hear	346
Gracious thou, when most severe	202	Good for us, thy joy to share	305
Great Angel of the Lord most high	134	Good, I feel it is, for me	50
Great Author of all my desires, / The thing	307	Good is the saying of my Lord	58
		Good Lord, for thy own goodness sake	28
Great Author of all my desires, / thy beauty	391	Good news of sin forgiven	369
		Gospel-faith on me bestow	255
Great God of Hosts, against my foe	200	Gospel indeed! th' eternal God	444
Great God, to me the sight afford	54	Grace, and the will through Christ alone	226
Great God, unknown, invisible	271	Grant me that bold simplicity	278
Great God, we to thy servant go	272	Great Builder of thy church, appear	109
Great God, who dost the proud abase	151	Great Founder of thy church, in thee	116
Great heir of David's throne	382	Great in Divine fecundity	354
Great in the field of battle, great	167	Great in evil is the day	33
Great is the truth, and must prevail	154	Great Triune God, thy servants own	442
Greater than ancient Israel, we	92	Greater than Solomon is he	265
Grieved at his heart is God for me	15	Greatest of all his works below	188
Guilty whene'er my sin I own	316	Greatest of the prophetic race	248
		Guide of my youth hast thou not been	6

Volume X

Volume XI

Gather the nations in that day	108		
Gentle and meek he comes to those	338	Gather we still the fragments up	378
Give glory to your God and Lord	21	Gifts will not evidence our grace	508
Give me, Lord, if thou art he	245	Give me, O Lord, my soul t' abase	225
Glad to be hid, unknown, obscure	452	Give me on thee, the living Bread	390
Glory and thanks to thee we give	91	Give us, Lord, the grace to give	212
God as he will his grace bestows	502	Give us this day our daily bread	201
God in Christ, appear; and seal	55	Gladly I believe the word	478
God in mercy sent again	349	God and his hellish enemy	428
God in mercy to our race	461	God by his almighty word	108
God is love and holiness	385	God cannot take delight to grieve	437

God commands the grass to grow	377	Go, sacred ship, from stormy seas	449
God did in Christ himself reveal	114	God (as yet they did not see)	447
God is rich, and God alone	240	God bids, To all my name confess	176
God let his vineyard out to man[230]	49	God doth thus to kings declare	271
God lets his closest followers know	93	God heard the acceptable prayer	52
God made his mind to prophets known	351	God himself prepares our way	259
God made man on earth appeared	383	God his suffering servants sees	265
God o'er the heathen reigns	52	God in Christ is love to me	59
God of Israel, see	106	God in his Son incarnate	280
God omnipotently near	377	God is my hope and portion here	411
God only can his Son reveal	455	God is not partial in his love	249
God over all for ever blessed	368	God is the King by kings adored	278
God over all unless thou art	340	God, my father's gracious God	396
God supreme, who diedst for me	327	God of grace, vouchsafe to me	298
God was in Christ on earth revealed	112	God passes kings and conquerors by	269
God's accepted worshipper	357	God permits his works to be	170
Good out of all these ills he brings	276	God sent him to bless	168
Goods and time, and gifts, and grace	214	God, th' eternal God and true	252
Goods for many years laid up!	210	God to apostolic men[231]	309
Gospel to every soul of man	97	God, to make his mercy known	184
Grace unconditional and free	202	God who his creatures' love requires	182
Great before God is great indeed!	103	God who on Sinai's top came down	142
Great Judge, and Lawgiver supreme	29	God will not needlessly be seen	240
Great Searcher of the mazy heart	156	God's work to ruin or prevent	194
Great the steward's labour is	215	Good in myself whereon to ground	62
Great things in the Satanic hour	64	Grace doth not the rich prefer	328
Great words an evil tree may bear	157	Great things ordained for thee to do[232]	238
Greater and more than man is he	103	Greater love is not in man	26
Greater things Nathanael viewed	332	Greater miracles than these[233]	360
Gripped by th' arresting hand of death	244	Greater than the Son, as man	16
Guilty of death thou art indeed	81	Gross darkness, such as may be felt	98
		Guarded by thy loving care	185

Volume XII

Gentiles and Jews at once believed	288
Gifts extraordinary bestowed	357
Gifts to the saints at Rome	455
Give, Jesus, give th' uniting grace	96
Give me now myself to know	38
Give them to feel the irksome pain	426
Give us Lord like them t' inherit	326
Giver of repentance, thee	257

Volume XIII

Gentle then to all, and kind	66
Give all thy saints to find in thee	242
Give me now to find thee near	153
Give me this hour thy help to find	253
Give then the bliss for which I pray	51

230. UP 2:62.
231. UP 2:369.
232. UP 2:326.
233. UP 2:391.

Give us in our dejected state	268	Hardly at last I all gave o'er	333
Give us our ministers to love	35	Hark how all the welkin rings	183
Give us to walk as in thy sight	262	Hark how he groans! while nature shakes[237]	117
Glad the general servant be	66		
Gladly I take thy love's advice	229	Hark how the woods with music ring[238]	57
Glory ascribe and endless praise	77	Hark! the wastes have found a voice	290
Go on? but how? from step to step?	132	Harlots, and publicans, and thieves	301
Go on to take his name in vain	55	Hasten, hasten the glad hour	224
God [hath] on us his Spirit bestowed[234]	24	Have I not heard, have I not known	275
God in mortal flesh revealed	101	Have mercy, Lord! Lo, I confess	62
God of boundless pity spare	270	He bore the curse of all	151
God of Elijah hear	265	He breaks the power of cancelled sin	300
God of universal nature	271	He called: I answered to his call	333
God on us his Spirit bestowed	24	He came—O, my Redeemer dear[239]	64
God over all, for ever blessed	63	He ever lives for me to pray	278
God, who didst so dearly buy	31	He, for the presence of his flesh[240]	165
God's everlasting Son	141	He glorified Jehovah's name	213
Grace, the fountain of all good	219	He knew in whom he had believed	215
Gracious Lord, implant in me	42	He left his Father's throne above	105
Great and marvellous in grace	237	He left his throne above	148
Great is the storm that works within	253	He makes thy gifts occasion more[241]	41
Guilt the serpent's sting I feel	152	He owns a God—but eyes him not[242]	60
		He raised himself upon the bed	216
		He rested in Jehovah's power	215

Volume I

		He shines on earth adored	147
Ha! what do I here written see?[235]	42	He speaks; and listening to his voice	300
Had he not in mercy spared	289	He to us hath come unsought	288
Hail! by all thy works adored	115	He triumphed in his glorious shame	218
Hail, Everlasting Lord	147	He (while the world that disbelieved	212
Hail, Galilean King!	148	He who requires his creature's time[243]	47
Hail, holy martyrs, glorious names	345	He would that all his truths should own	312
Hail the day that sees him rise	187	Headlong we cleave the yawning deep	231
Hail the heavenly Prince of Peace!	183	Health's slowly-lingering, vain return[244]	37
Hail the life-giving Lord	149	Hear, and inspire my stammering tongue	310
Hail, the Lord of earth and heaven!	186	Hear; for thou, O Christ, alone	116
Hail, venerable train[236]	157		
Hail your dread Lord and ours	152		
Happy souls, whose course is run	365		
Harder were they than the rock	289		

234. *UP* 2:460.
235. George Herbert.
236. From the German of Johann Angelus Scheffler, translated by John Wesley.
237. Samuel Wesley, Sr.
238. George Herbert.
239. George Herbert.
240. Henry More.
241. George Herbert.
242. George Herbert.
243. George Herbert.
244. George Herbert.

Hear him, ye deaf; his praise, ye dumb	301	High on thy Father's throne	155
Hear, holy, holy, holy Lord	310	*High praise to thee, all-gracious God*[254]	339
Hear, Holy Spirit, hear[245]	99	High-throned on heaven's eternal hill[255]	142
Hear, Holy Spirit, hear	101	Him though highest heaven receives	187
Hear in mercy my complaint	257	Him we love, as yet unseen	355
Hear, Jesu! hear my broken heart![246]	67	Him we only taste below	171
Hear, Jesu, hear my helpless cry	83	His evil let the sinner leave	207
Hear then, and thankfulness impart[247]	41	His Israel himself shall clear	256
Hearken to me with earnest care	206	His joys are double—and his pains[256]	58
Heaven his sole treasure now he loves[248]	18	His looks like cedars planted on[257]	344
Heaven's glory is thy awful throne[249]	144	His numerous seed he now shall see	81
Heavenly Adam, Life Divine	194	His own on earth he sought	148
Heavenly Father, Lord of all	192	His portion thou, he burns no more	26
Heavenly Father, Sovereign Lord	290	His Providence supplies our needs	302
Heavenward our every wish aspires	34	His seed elect, his heir foretold	215
Hell's armies tremble at thy nod[250]	143	His steady way he still pursued	218
Helpless to thee for aid I cry	293	His son the father offered up	215
Hence may all our actions flow	354	His would I wholly be	151
Hence our hearts melt, our eyes o'erflow[251]	266	Hither my actions righteous deemed	226
		Hither my spotted soul be brought	226
Henceforth may no profane delight[252]	111	Ho! every one that thirsteth, come!	313
Henceforth thy only will I choose	249	*Ho! every one that thirsts, draw nigh*	205
Here from afar the finished height[253]	34	Hold not thy peace at Sion's woe	369
Here, in thine own appointed ways	235	Holy and true, the key	319
Here the sinner that believes	355	Holy Ghost, no more delay	194
Here then, my God, vouchsafe to stay	304	Holy, Holy, Holy Lord / Live by heaven	115
Herod and Pilate both combined	295	*Holy Lamb, who thee receive*[258]	280
Hid; till Christ, our Life, appear	186	Horror to think that God is hate!	313
Hide me! If thou refuse to hide	293	Hosts of heaven, begin the song	364
High above every name	138	How blest are they who still abide[259]	265
		How can it be, thou heavenly King[260]	266

245. The six lines of stanzas 1 and 11 of the same poem, which begin with this line are identical.
246. George Herbert.
247. George Herbert.
248. George Herbert.
249. From the German of Ernst Lange, translated by John Wesley.
250. From the German of Johann Angelus Scheffler, translated by John Wesley.
251. From the German of Nikolaus von Zinzendorf, translated by John Wesley.
252. From the French, Antoinette Bourignon.
253. John Gambold?
254. From the German of Ludwig Andreas Gotter, translated by John Wesley.
255. From the German of Johann Angelus Scheffler, translated by John Wesley.
256. George Herbert.
257. Altered from John Norris.
258. From the German of Anna Dober, translated by John Wesley.
259. From the German of Nikolaus von Zinzendorf, translated by John Wesley.
260. From the German of Nikolaus von Zinzendorf, translated by John Wesley.

How canst thou brook his foolishness?[261]	59
How cold this clime! And yet my sense[262]	343
How could I, Lord, hold out so long	248
How do thy mercies close me round!	306
How good thou art! how large Thy grace![263]	123
How hapless is th' applauded virgin's lot[264]	22
How long, great God, how long must I[265]	342
How shall I ask, and ask aright?	253
How shall I lift my guilty eyes	248
How shall I teach the world to love	75
How shall we thy great arm revere[266]	125
How swiftly wafted in a sigh[267]	124
How strong, how stately does he go![268]	118
How thou wilt now thy servant use[269]	37
Howe'er I rove, where'er I turn[270]	140
Humble, and teachable, and mild	241
Humble each vain aspiring boast	227
Humbly, behold, we sit	318
Humbly I now the rod revere	247
Husband of thy church below	359

Volume II

Happiest souls, (if such are here)	192
Happiness is not in me	105
Happy he whom Christ shall find	193
Happy soul who sees the day	251
Happy they whose joys abound	317
Hardly convinced, I own at last	131
Hark, a voice divides the sky!	189
Hark! in the wilderness a cry	50
Hast thou been with me, Lord, so long?	166
Hast thou not died to purge our sin	290
Hast thou not heard, hast thou not known	56
Hast thou not invited all	98
Hast thou not made me willing, Lord? / Do I not now	205
Hast thou not made me willing, Lord? / Would I not die	271
Hast thou not reversed my doom?	279
Hast thou not said, who canst not lie	321
Hath not my Saviour died to make	205
Have mercy, Lord, thy wrath remove	65
Having done all, by faith I stand	314
He all shall break through; his truth and his grace	198
He bids me ask, and I shall have	102
He brought them through the wondrous way	59
He burst the barriers of the tomb	247
He clothed us in these robes of light	235
He delivers by his love	267
He died, that we to sin might die	326
He ever lives above For me	323
He found us in the desert	20
He, high enthroned above all height	52
He in the hollow of his hand	52
He is our Comforter and Light	20
He knows thee now as he is known	364
He left true bliss and joy above[271]	11
He lives, when thou hast fully	363
He magnified his saving power	58
He meted out the earth, and poised	52
He neither hopes nor fears	85
He pities now my sad estate	102
He prospers all his servants' toils[272]	63
He rescued when to evil sold	58
He sends them from the skies	230
He tells me he will quickly come	243
He visits now the house of clay	365

261. George Herbert.
262. Altered from John Norris.
263. Samuel Wesley, Sr.
264. John Gambold.
265. Altered from John Norris.
266. George Herbert.
267. George Herbert.
268. Altered from John Norris.
269. George Herbert.
270. From the German of Paul Gerhardt, translated by John Wesley.
271. Altered from John Norris.
272. From the German of August Gottlieb Spangenberg, translated by John Wesley.

He waits that he may gracious be	102	His grace, which I abused so long	180
He walks in glorious liberty	363	His image view in us displayed	235
He was from all eternity	338	His mercy then he called to mind	58
He will perform the work begun	242	His mighty arm, his high right-hand	172
He willeth not the sinner's death	344	His sacred limbs they stretch, they tear	71
He wills that I should holy be	243	His sacred unction from above	272
Health I shall have, if that be best	281	His sheep he shall protect, and feed	52
Hear, all that will, the Spirit hear	346	His sickness feel, endure his pain	216
Hear, Jesu; hear, the First and Last	347	His spotless purity of soul	340
Hear me still myself bemoan	114	His to thine own afflictions join	216
Hearken to the solemn voice	191	Hold of thy righteousness I take	295
Heaven I shall have within my breast	327	Holy, and true, and righteous Lord	322
Hell in vain against us rages	33	*Holy and True, who hast the key*	355
Hell was ready to devour	32	Holy Ghost, set to thy seal	179
Help us to build each other up	136	Holy Ghost, the Comforter	229
Help us to help each other, Lord	136	Hoping against hope, I wait	135
Help us to praise our glorious King	314	How beauteous nature now!	27
Here I rejoice to bless thy name	217	*How beautiful his feet appear*	169
Here let my soul's sure anchor be	273	How blest, if always thus we might	24
Here many a faithful soul is found[273]	64	How canst thou stay? Think on the pace	41
Here will I set up my rest	315	How could I, Lord, thy goodness grieve?	180
Hide her till the storm be over	30	How dark and dreary is my heart!	90
Hide me, dearest Saviour, hide	98	How good to Israel's chosen race!	57
High enthroned at God's right hand	257	*How happy is the man*	85
High on his everlasting throne[274]	61	How happy the man Whose heart is set free	176
Him and his god, and sin and death	345	*How happy they, O King of kings!*	18
Him eye to eye shall they behold	170	How have I thy Spirit grieved	264
Him in all my works I seek	317	How know I, if thou shouldst me raise[277]	13
Him shall they see with wrath return	339	How long, great God, have we appeared	359
Him to know is life and peace	316	How shall I find the living way	128
His arm he hath bared, his mercy and grace	170	How shall I thank thee for the grace, / On me	73
His[275] body was destroyed, when nailed	247	How shall I thank thee for the grace, / The trust	233
His call we now obey	330		
His eye the world at once looks through[276]	62		
His form is as the Son of Man	340		

273. From the German of August Gottlieb Spangenberg, translated by John Wesley.
274. From the German of August Gottlieb Spangenberg, translated by John Wesley.
275. Osborn changed "his" to "Its."
276. From the German of August Gottlieb Spangenberg, translated by John Wesley.

Volume III

Had not thy grace salvation brought	94
Hail, Father, Friend, of human race	348
Hail, Holy Ghost! alike adored	352
Hail, holy, holy, holy Lord / Thrice	349

277. Altered from George Herbert.

Hail Mary's Son! thy mercies never end	112	He spake: and all the temple shook	134
Hail, thou all-alluring Spirit	101	He still respects thy sacrifice	301
Happy soul, depart in peace	171	He suffers both from man and God	217
Happy soul, from prison freed	172	He tasted death for every one	289
Happy the man to whom 'tis given	265	He that believes in thee	58
Happy the saints of former days	339	He that in thee believes	58
Happy the souls that followed thee	322	He that on the throne doth reign	295
Happy the souls to Jesus joined	286	He took into his hands the cup	215
Happy the soul whom God delights	165	He wept, because thou wouldst not see	22
Hark, he calls his exile home	171	He whom we remember here	288
Hast thou not sent us forth	59	He will, our hearts reply he will	300
Hath he pleasure in your pain	88	He will the steadfast mind impart	139
He bids me eat the bread	277	He willeth not that all should come	66
He bids us drink and eat	273	He willeth (so they judge their God	66
He bids us taste his Grace	336	He worketh once to will in all	94
He cannot me pass by	54	Hear an incarnate devil preach	26
He did not them bereave	36	Hear his blood's prevailing cry	304
He died for all, he none passed by	64	Hear, Jesu, hear my dying call	28
He dies, as now for us he dies	321	Hear me, Lord, my sins confessing	278
He dispels our sin and sadness	367	Hear, sinners, hear an human fiend	26
He ever lives, and prays	303	Hear the old hellish murderer roar	71
He gives them damning grace	81	*Hearts of stone, relent, relent*	232
He hallowed the cup Which now we receive	286	Help us thy mercy to extol	3
		Here all thy blessings we receive	246
He justly claims us for his own	335	Here let me ever lie	63
He lives for us to intercede	321	Hereafter none can take away	326
He made it possible for all / To turn again	65	Hidden their life with God above	144
		Him even now by faith we see	315
He made it possible for all / his gift of	96	Him the true ark and mercy-seat	310
He marked the city of our God laid low	121	His blood, for all a ransom given	94
		His blood procured our life and peace	242
He now hath wiped away their tears	180	His body is the seat	244
He now stands knocking at the door	65	His body torn and rent	303
He now thy nature hath expelled	147	His everlasting arms are spread	175
He only meant to warn	49	His grace doth once to all appear	136
He pours his Spirit into my soul[278]	170	His grace to me salvation brings	165
He prays for those that shed his blood	22	His grace would every soul restore	64
He promised all mankind to draw	96	His love is manna to my taste	166
He reads, while we beneath	303	His mercies flow to all mankind	139
He shall by his renewing grace	155	His mercy cast a pitying look	241
He shall the pride of man abase	156	His name the sinner hears	72
He sleeps; and from his open side	299	His offering did thy guilt remove	135
		His sacramental pledge we take	290
		His servants shall be	323

278. Free paraphrase of the German of Christian Friedrich Richter by Charles Wesley.

His threatenings all are vain	49	Humble the proud oppressive king	245
His threatenings are a jest	50	Humbly own it is the Lord!	326
His will is good and just	277		
His word subdued at once the carnal will	113		
His wrath he might on all have shown	68		

Volume IV

Holy, and just, and gracious God	66	Hadst thou not purged our stain	183
Holy Ghost, all-quickening Fire	99	*Hail, Jesus, hail, our great High-Priest*	157
Holy, meek, and gentle Lamb	10	Hallow, and make thy servants meet	226
Honour and endless love	347	Happy beyond description he	234
Hopeless, my damned estate I mourn	26	Happy in thy glorious love	222
Horror of horrors! hell of hell!	26	*Happy Magdalene, to whom*	132
Horror of horrors! spawn of hell!	67	Happy soul as silver tried	319
Hosannah in the highest	337	Happy soul from self and sin[280]	321
Hosannah to the Son! / Hosannah cry aloud	106	Happy soul, who now renewed	320
Hosanna to the Son / Of David on his throne HGEL 1741, 31		Happy soul whose active love	321
		Happy souls that Christ obey	16
Hovering around the new-born heir	175	*Happy the man who finds the grace*	234
How art thou humbled to the ground	147	Happy the man who Wisdom gains	235
How can heavenly spirits rise	256	Happy who trust in him	19
How could my folly dare	53	Harden to adamant his brow	66
How did thy pity grieve HGEL 1741, 31		Harder than the flinty rock	406
		Hardly yet do I know	410
How dreadful is the mystery	255	Hast died that I might live	242
How glorious is the life above	290	Hast thou not surely seen my grief?	326
How happier far was I	53	Hast thou not wrought the sure belief	461
How happy are thy servants, Lord	338	Hast thou received the Holy Ghost?	346
How hath the Lord destroyed his power	146	Haste, O haste to my relief	390
How hath the proud oppressor ceased!	146	Haste then, ye souls that first believe[281]	130
How he did these creatures raise	258	Haste, to his tomb repair	131
How long, O God, how long	36	Hasten him, Lord, into our heart	173
How long, O Lord, shall we	269	Hasten the day, when we	177
How long, thou faithful God, shall I	257	Have I not fought against my God	391
How long, thou jealous God! how long	5	"Have me excused," why will ye say?	275
How long, ye wavering souls, how long	75	Have we not filled up the measure	7
How oft for thy hard-heartedness	22	Have we not then believed in vain	135
How richly is the table stored	248	He all his foes shall quell	141
How royal the cheer	365	He answered for all	371
How shall I commend the grace	12	He beckoned to the savage band	93
How vast the happiness I feel[279]	170	He bids me come! his voice I know	456
How, when it shall be	335		
Howl, ye base advocates for sin	151		

280. John Wesley's marginal note: "Happy soul from every sin."

279. Free paraphrase of the German of Christian Friedrich Richter by Charles Wesley.

281. *UP* 3:113.

He brings down them who dwell on high	287	Hear us to thee for succour cry	223
He comes from above	113	Hear, ye brethren of the Lord	133
He comes from on high	122	Hearken to me, my chosen race	300
He comes, he comes from far	153	*Hearken to me, who seek the Lamb*	300
He comes his own to claim	132	Hearken to me, ye souls who know	302
He cries, and weeps, and groans, and bleeds	261	Heavy laden with sin	364
		Help, gracious Lord, my deep distress	375
He deigns in flesh t' appear	110	*Help, Jesus, help against my foe*	257
He died to purge our guilty stain	187	*Help, Lord, to whom for help I fly*	476
He dies to atone / For sins not his own	372	Help me now, but let me still	465
He doth in all his saints reside	174	Help me, O thou Man of woe	420
He fills whom first he hath prepared²⁸²	315	*Help, O help, my great Creator*	465
He finds, who Wisdom apprehends	235	Help on thee, thou mighty One	464
He gives me now a token	87	Helper of every helpless soul	31
He hath opened a door	210	Helper of the helpless thou	463
He, he shall bid the temple rise	299	Helpless howe'er my spirit lies	377
He in the land of uprightness	288	Hence let all my troubles rise	420
He laid his glory by	109	Henceforth I ever live above	134
He lays the lofty city low	287	Her early short-lived excellence	245
He left me alone	415	Her hands are filled with length of days	235
He now mine inmost soul hath turned	311	Here for ever would I lie	133
He on our Israel's side	99	Here, Jesu, am I	416
He only can the words apply	179	Here let me still remain	438
He saw the serpent's egg break forth	95	Here then beneath my curse I stoop	338
He shall perform my word of grace	299	Here then I lay me down	434
He sits at God's right hand	141	Here will I ever, ever cry	375
He sunk; while Israel's chosen race	303	High on his holy seat	155
He takes his suffering people's part	39	Highly favoured soul! to her	132
He tells us he will quickly come	32	Him eye to eye we there shall see	281
He that believes on me	171	Him for thy glory's sake	22
He visits now the troubled breast	173	Him the angels all adored	108
He (while the glorious angels stand	33	Him the purchase of thy passion	167
He will, I dare believe, he will	330	Him the world cannot receive	176
He will, Jehovah surely will	75	Him ye beheld, our conquering God	160
He will not refuse the song	118	Himself prepares his people's hearts²⁸³	315
He will not taste thy pardoning grace	288	His anger most of all I fear	424
Head of the martyr's noble host	225	His bleeding love 'tis thine to seal	188
Head of thy church triumphant	79	His bloody hand th' oppressor shakes	43
Head of thy suffering church below	47	His body doth the cure dispense	452
Hear all the Saviour's cry	171	His branching arms he wide shall spread	55
Hear in this accepted hour	466	His chamber let the bridegroom leave	74
Hear my earnest supplication	465	His death is my plea	372

---

282. *UP* 2:454.

283. *UP* 2:454.

IDEX OF FIRST LINES OF POETRY BY JOHN AND CHARLES WESLEY

His eye observed the dark design	95
His foes and ours are one	155
His hands confirm, his breast inspire	66
His happiness in part is mine	278
His hidden power controlled the foe	96
His inspiration now blaspheme	346
His judgments are abroad	17
His kingdom cannot fail	141
His kingdom from above	115
His love is mighty to compel	277
His mercy hath brought salvation to all	298
His mercy's wings are spread	19
His mild and gentle sway	77
His near approach ye know	18
His only trust is in thy blood	349
His pardoning love my heart constrains	441
His power is in our weakness shown	39
His sacred life defend	23
His saving power no limits knows	286
His truth and love are on my side	334
His warning voice I would not mind	445
His welcome cross we daily bear	39
Hold of thine arm we take	35
Honour, and majesty, and might	24
Honour, and praise, O Christ, receive	37
Honour the means ordained by thee	137
How are the mighty fallen! dead!	98
How can it be, our reason cries	135
How did I thy help implore	428
How happy are they	408
How happy are we Who trust in the Lord	88
How happy is the pilgrim's lot	278
How long, thou hidden God unknown	329
How mighty thou art	273
How oft shall I beseech thee, Lord	467
How shall a lost sinner in pain	418
How shall a sinner come to God?	451
How shall a sinner find	249
How then dare I presume	402
How weak was my heart	412
Humbled in the lowest deep	479

Volume V

Hail, great Physician of mankind	65
Hail holy, holy, holy Lord, / mysterious	345
Hallelujah they cry	458
Happy both, no matter then	351
Happy, could I through life declare	99
Happy, for ever happy I	198
Happy, if I their grief may cheer	19
Happy, if with my latest breath	113
Happy, might I obtain the grace	378
Happy might I the grace receive	346
Happy soul, above the rest!	407
Happy soul, enjoy thy gain	358
Happy soul, that safe from harms	293
Happy soul, thy days are ended	216
Happy soul! what wills he now?	341
Happy state of widowhood	338
Happy the souls that first believed	479
Happy we who trust in Jesus	344
Hardened in just despair	214
Hark, how the watchmen cry	271
Hark, how thy turtle-dove complains	232
Hast thou the work of grace begun	232
Hasten, Lord, the perfect day	333
Hasten that kingdom of thy grace	229
Hasten to grant my sole request	295
Haters of God, your madness mourn	123
Haters of those that would be good	131
Hath he not spoke the word	371
He by the holy men of old	299
He came from above	31
He can have a new heart	26
He can, he can, yourselves confess	4
He cannot love it now	84
He cannot now aspire	84
He chides his rash disciple's zeal	142
He comes, he comes to call	285
He comes of hellish malice full	34
He died from all sin Our souls to redeem	321
He died that we might be made whole	317
He died, that we to him might live	316
He from sin who saved me now	380
He hath our salvation wrought	332

He hath ransomed our race	31	Hereby thou favourest me, I know	108
He hath said, From all sin	320	Hereby we sweetly know	429
He hath the Bride, and he alone	112	Herein the faithful word is shown	114
He hears, and he will soon redeem	114	Higher let the torrent rise	164
He hears, he hears it now!	172	Him, and his powers below	37
He knows whate'er I want	449	Him, and his works at once destroy	232
He lives to die no more	85	Him Prophet, and King, And Priest we proclaim	390
He makes them apt to teach and guide	318	Him to the all-gracious Lender	441
He may be without sin	26	His blood by faith applied	370
He never will ensnare	370	His blood shall sanctify throughout	308
He prays, and cries!	58	His blood, we know, hath bought our peace	335
He shed his blood to wash us clean	317	His burden who bear	424
He soon shall appear	32	His everlasting arms receive	355
He that a sprinkled conscience hath	398	His faith is lost in sight	83
He to himself hath reconciled	298	His glorious reign	63
He who hath their cure begun	120	His goodness we praise	57
He wills, that I should holy be	308	His grace hath brought salvation	114
Head of thy church triumphant	454	His grace to our souls did	264
Head of thy church, whose Spirit fills	228	His grace which hath salvation nigh	473
Head of thy patient church beneath	165	His love, surpassing far	363
Health, pardon, and peace	25	His love we proclaim, And publish abroad	321
Hear me, Lord, my suit redouble	212	His nature to our souls make known	317
Hear me, Lord, myself bemoaning	211	His only righteousness I show	112
Hear, O Lord, the ceaseless prayer	255	His purity share	321
Hear, O thou Strength of Israel	256	His servant and disciple see	146
Hear our faith's effectual prayer	240	His suit is my own	436
Hear then the pleading Spirit's prayer	231	His truth, and love, and power	371
Hear then thy own petition	209	His welcome cross with joy she bore	87
Heavenly all-alluring Dove	408	His word for ever shall endure	299
Help a poor and needy soul	173	Holpen by him to suffer more	152
Help, gracious Lord, the time is come	155	*Holy sanctifying Dove*	428
Help, Lord! the busy foe	51	Honour, and endless thanks, and love	114
Help us to make our calling sure	229	Honour, and might, and majesty	288
Henceforth I will not comfort take	158	Honour, and might, and thanks, and praise	1
Her fervent zeal what tongue can tell?	89	Hovering o'er both his wings He spread	412
Her meat his counsel to fulfil	89	How blest whom Jesus calls his own	381
Her to the throne of grace we bear	239	*How can a sinner know*	363
Here is firm footing, here	449	How costly was the medicine, Lord	66
Here let me pour out all my tears	97	*How empty then the former boast*	375
Here only can I show my love	69		
Here then I doubt no more	450		
Here then my calling I discern	141		
Here then my foot of faith stands sure	309		
Here then to thee thine own I leave	11		

How happy are they	56	Have done thy Spirit worse despite	166
How happy, gracious Lord! are we	278	Have we not dragged the judgment down	156
How happy the pair, Whom Jesus unites	427	He bids us now partake	286
How long, thou suffering Son of God	153	He calls his own to see him rise	174
How many to th' angelic foe	248	He came, and warned her to depart	274
How oft didst thou my soul withhold	194	*He comes! he comes! the Judge severe*	141
How rich in the friends	402	He holds her still in life detained	340
How shall a slave released	365	He hymns the glorious Lamb alone	246
How shall I bless thy thwarting love	195	He in the house of God shall dwell	424
How shall I in thy presence dare	98	He justly claims the first-born son	254
How shall it but by this be known	91	He knows the texture of my heart	347
How truly blessed	60	He loves to be remembered thus	446
How weak my heart and blind	262	He makes us his peculiar care	448
		He owned the soul so dearly loved	249
		He reigns in the holiest place	193

Volume VI

		He sees the trial past	286
Hail! Father, Son and Holy Ghost	371	He speaks, and, yielding up the ghost	313
Had not thy mercy interposed	19	He speaks the powerful word	52
Handel, and all the tuneful train	344	He that hath practised no deceit	424
Happy at last might I	349	He the good fight of faith hath won	199
Happy beyond description he	459	He this flowery carpet spread	387
Happy child, who gained a place	414	He who set his love upon her	278
Happy, could we the secret find	265	He who so much for us hath done	418
Happy harmonist, to thee	365	He will, (our hearts cry out,) he will	200
Happy he doth and glorious live	395	*He's come, he's come, in peace and power*	303
Happy man whom God doth aid!	387	*He's come to set the prisoner free*	339
Happy, pure, impassive soul	333	*He's gone! The spotless soul is gone*	279
Happy Samuel, to God	414	*Head over all in earth and skies*	121
Happy the follower of his Lord	353	Hear all nature's groans proclaiming	144
Happy the man, who Jesus knows	375	Hear—and drop thy controversy	169
Happy the souls he leaves behind	355	Hear his all-commanding Spirit	169
Happy the well-instructed youth	424	Hear, then, thy children's call	416
Happy, and wise, and great, and good	262	Hear us, who now for mercy call	33
Happy who in Jesus live	211	Heathens, and Jews, and Turks may I	6
Happy whoe'er his wants supplied	235	Heaven expanded in her heart	338
Hark, hark! 'tis a voice from the tomb	332	Heaven is mine inheritance	445
Hark how all nature groans	46	Heavier woes he keeps in store	39
Has he, from his Lord above	423	Help us, thou heavenly Man of Woe	293
Haste, ye ministerial spirits	279	Her bliss no pause nor period knows	299
Hasten the long-expected day	50	Her convoy to those endless joys	322
Hastening the universal doom	357	Her desolate state too well we know	104
Hastening through this mortal vale	365	Her from the birth the Lord did draw	294
Haters of God, yet still they cry	101	Her genuine faith by works was known	359
		Her life from outward evil free	267

Her lovely excellence is fled	292	His soul in pure affection flowed	346
Her "morals, O thou bleeding Lamb"	269	His spirit, mounting on the wing	246
Her mourning days are finished soon	356	His Spirit's gentlest art	204
Her piety with life begun	357	His tears relieve our mournful pain	297
Her pious course with life began	324	His tokens we espy	46
Her precious hours employing there	358	His wisdom timed the lingering stroke	254
Her Saviour in his members seen	270	Hither by special mercy led	419
Her slumbering guides and watchmen rouse	114	Hither, ye worms, come up	36
		Hold me fast in thine embrace	442
Her solid piety unfeigned	268	*Holy Child, of heavenly birth*	401
Her soul was cleansed below	203	Holy, holy, holy Lord / Live by heaven and	387
Her soul we shall embrace once more	298	Honour, and majesty, and power	141
Her unopposing heart received	325	Honour and praise to Jesus pay	430
Her watchful foe shall keep her in	86	Honour, glory, and salvation	162
Here let thy Providence preside	412	Honour, glory, power is thine	397
Here let us spend our utmost zeal	103	Horror shall every heart assail	85
Here rests in hope, beneath this humble clod	292	*Hosanna to him Who ruleth on high!*	451
		Hosanna to the Son	400
Here then, O God, vouchsafe to dwell	105	Hosanna to God	209
Here then we calmly rest	154	*Hosannah to Jesus on high!*	190
High on Immanuel's land	44	How blessed is our brother, bereft	194
High on thy great white throne	44	How can I doubt my blissful end	329
Him beholding face to face	379	How can it sleep, when hostile heaven	156
Him for everything I praise	233	How careful then ought I to live	402
Him that sitteth on the throne	386	How could I, Lord, myself deceive	5
His astonishing birth	454	How did her generous bounty deal	241
His coming he foreshows	46	How did she entertain the spies	327
His course impetuous who can tell?	283	How did she put his bowels on	360
His crown of life shall soon be ours	317	How far below thy dazzling sphere	276
His faith was swallowed up in sight	317	How full of heaven his latest word	281
His few sad days of guiltless pain	258	*How hapless are the lettered youth*	410
His friends and partners in distress	311	*How happy are the little flock*	95
His goodness towards us all designed	254	*How happy every child of grace*	216
His grace if God on us confer	422	*How happy, Lord, thy children are*	419
His hand is lifted up	51	How happy the angels that fall	190
His heart, as tender as sincere	350	*How happy the dead, Who Jesus adored!*	307
His justice or grace Ye shortly shall prove	91	How happy then are we	44
His kingdom below	399	*How highly favoured then are we*	438
His life the proof substantial gave	350	*How ignorant the human mind*	392
His love endured the fiery test	311	How long shall Antichrist blaspheme	139
His majesty will not despise	445	How long shall I the standard see	87
His mercy every sinner claims	446	*How long, thou weapon of the Lord*	156
His son (and mine) is fled	223	How many whom thy judgments call	350
His soul doth on the Rock remain	312	*How, O thou sovereign Lord of Hosts*	129

How often hath thy goodness tried	78
How often when his arm was bared	9
How sad our state by nature is	413
How shall I leave my tomb?	427
How shall we sing and triumph there	227
How soon may God rebuke	43
How then ought I on earth to live	432
How vain, great God, and worse than	37
How vainly then the zealots blind	5
How weak the thoughts and vain	43
How wretched are the boys at school	417
However employed, Their joy was the same	439
Howe'er the wisdom of our God	42
Howsoever employed	435
Humble, like her Lord, and meek	335

Volume VII

Hail, co-essential Three	319
Hail, Father, Son, and Spirit, great	266
Hail, holy, holy, holy Lord, / Whom One	280
Hallelujah we sing	199
Happy day of his returning	41
Happy, if with my Best-beloved	184
Happy soul whom Jesus loves	15
Happy they, who never rest	309
Harassed by long domestic war	75
Hardened in sordid sin	167
Hast thou not many a soul relieved	399
Haste, thou God of our salvation	42
Have not we redemption found	10
He came a lost world to redeem	40
He challenges thy youthful days	272
He could not by a greater swear	239
He hath beheld the person joined	234
He hath to us made known	338
He in the kind physician came	95
He is our God alone	258
He is our Life, the Lord our God	290
He magnified the social state	197
He makes known the mystery	292
He now begins, from every weight set free	429
He sanctifies, without respect	327
He speaks—and dies! Transported to resign	EGW 1771, 26
He that hath seen th' Incarnate Son	233
He who cancelled our offences	7
He whom the world cannot receive	248
Head of the Church, appear, appear	49
Hear her help-imploring groan	82
Hear me, Lord, myself bemoan	357
Hear, O thou Friend of human kind	64
Hear us then, thou Man of grief	97
Help me to put thy bowels on	157
Help, my loving Lord and Saviour!	58
Help, the woman's heavenly Seed	90
Help us to look upon him	35
Helper of our infirmity	265
Helpless and lame In soul I am	187
Helpless babe, who from the womb	69
Hence, lying world, with all thy care	179
Here, as in the lions' den	17
Here betrothed to thee in love	151
Here I give myself to prayer	55
Here is knowledge rare, and hidden	149
Here would I maintain my station	342
Hide me by thy presence, Lord	413
Him as a Spirit of binding fear	107
Him let my blameless life reprove	170
Him let us tend, severely kind	73
Him we to thy grace commend	129
His blood from every sin	379
His blood has brought the general peace	371
His death is present now with thee	395
His death the sinner raises	105
His death to thee I show	379
His favour sealed in perfect peace	371
His free inexhaustible love	41
His kingdom was the gift of God	274
His oracles the answer give	386
His power the interceding Son	223
His precious blood both wounds and heals	191

His Son on us bestowed	305	Had we of God forgetful been	101
His sovereign grace vouchsafed a worm to choose	425	Hadst thou not left thyself a seed	276
		Hail the venerable name	237
His true Divinity, denied	235	Hangs my new-born soul on thee	247
Holy Child of heavenly birth	150	*Happy, for ever happy they*	319
Holy Ghost, apply thy word	247	Happy in him thy soul shall be	244
Holy Ghost, regard our prayers	246	Happy that she long may live	303
Holy, holy, holy Lord / mysterious One	323	*Happy the man that sees in thee*	254
Holy, holy, holy Lord / God the Father	308	Happy the man, to whom 'tis given / To	166
Holy, holy, holy Lord, / Favoured with a	345	Happy the man who always sees	244
Holy, holy, holy Lord, / One Almighty God	286	Hardened by long impunity	179
		Haste to my help, thy blood apply	259
Holy is our God alone	288	Haste to our help, thou God of love![284]	162
Holy Lamb, who thee confess	46	Hasten, Lord, my soul deliver	158
Horror of horrors! must I die	398	Hasten the promised hour	326
How beauteous on the mountain tops appear	434	Have[285] I ability t' obey	376
		Have I not known the Master's will	347
How blest the messenger whom Jesus owns	431	*Have mercy, Lord, for man hath none!*	125
How could God for sinners die?	241	Have mercy, Lord! the world restrain	238
How empty our external boast	331	Have mercy then once more	62
How fast the chains of nature bind	73	Have patience till, by thee renewed	116
How foolish was my hope and vain	353	Have we not lately heard and seen	288
How good and pleasant 'tis to see	17	Havoc, th' infernal leader cries!	267
How happy are they	36	He bids the little flock increase	198
How happy are we	175	He bowed the heavens, he left His throne	348
How happy we whom grace unites	46	He calls the man of his right hand	463
How have we heard his generous zeal exclaim	439	He forgives thy every sin	190
		He from his eternal throne	69
How pleasant and sweet	175	He hath preserved me by his might	124
How shall a young unstable man	150	He in sickness makes me whole	46
How shall I, Lord, the meetness gain	383	He is our defence and shield	70
How shall I walk my God to please	162	He knows their happy days	83
How shall we the gift improve	87	He launched the weapons of his war	32
How short, alas, our taste	22	He only hath the nations taught	179
Human tears may freely flow	85	He only is thy God and Lord	105
Humbly prostrate at thy feet	97	He plucked the prey out of their teeth	240
		He saved me in temptation's hour	31
		He sent his warrant from above	33
Volume VIII		He shall bless his ransomed ones	110
Had not the Lord for Israel stood	239		
Had not the Lord in danger's hour	180		
Had not the Lord, we now may cry	236		

284. *UP* 2:446.
285. Osborn changed "Have" to "Had."

He shall obtain the starry crown	48	Him will I praise, the Lord of all	203
He smiles, and makes the desert smile	198	Him with glorious majesty	17
He smote the gates that kept them in	196	Him with lute and harp record	184
He still th' united prayer shall hear	124	His all-sufficient help I found	205
He that in Christ his soul doth hide	175	His blessing makes the mother bear	243
He the people shall subdue	110	His faithful troops from every side	464
He then is blessed, and only he	261	His firmest friends, unbought, unknown	485
He to Israel's chosen race	183	His head thou hast crowned	
"he trusted in the Lord," they cry	43	With gold from above	40
Head of thy church, attend	417	His hearty request, thou, Lord,	
Hear him, our Advocate with thee	342	hast bestowed	40
Hear him, ye nations, and rejoice	153	His mercy shall to all appear	153
Hear me, Lord, in tender love	230	His peace he to his saints shall give	168
Hear me, O Lord my God! and weigh	24	His people all are just and clean	151
Hear me, O my gracious Lord!	230	*His praise their happy lives employ*	196
Hear, O Lord, my bitter cry	185	His righteousness I will proclaim	15
Hear, O Lord, my mournful prayer	90	His Spirit into my soul inspire[288]	427
Hear then his all-availing prayer	350	His vanquished foe full oft he reared	483
Hear thy afflicted people's prayer[286]	162	His verdant leaf shall never fade	4
Hear us, in this our evil day	300	His voice upon the waters is	57
Heathens he compels t' obey	111	His wise, permissive will	325
Help me in thy steps to tread	228	His word did out of nothing call	47
Help me! thou God of love and might	92	His words are all deceit and lies	79
Help me with eyes of faith to see	375	Hopeless, I must for ever die	348
Help, O help, thou Serpent-Bruiser!	77	Horror seized thy Sion's foes	112
Help, O Lord! the faithful fail	22	*How can I hate what nature loves*	358
Hence, by a glimmering ray of hope	298	How came mynherr our doom to know	466
Her boughs she stretched from sea[287]	163	How can we now preserve the nation	472
Her, my dearest earthly friend	409	How do I thy precepts love!	232
Her thou hast on all bestowed	302	*How do I thy precepts love! / my desires*	223
Here let me pause, and fix mine eye	392	How does the whole creation groan	246
Here my soul had almost failed	221	How gladly would I haste away	122
Here on thy promise, Lord	53	*How happy, Lord, are we*	323
Here, only here, thy love must save	12	How has thy love contrived to keep	392
Here then I quietly resign	417	How is the fervent love grown cold	408
High above all, at thy right hand	105	*How long, how often shall I pray*	431
High above all their Saviour sits	58	How long, O God, how long	333
Him as a guardian angel send	291	How long shall I inquire within	23
Him have I set before my face	28	How long shall Satan's rage prevail?	24
Him in whom they move and live	262	How long shall thy fierce anger burn?	174
Him let all the nations fear	68	*How long to thee, O God, shall I*	317
		How long wilt thou forget me, Lord	23

286. UP 2:446.
287. UP 2:447.
288. UP 1:315.

How long, ye sons of men	7	Have we not then a power from thee	106
How long, ye violent men	136	He a new song hath taught me	296
How lovely are thy tents, O Lord	165	He bids me seek him in the word	259
How precious all thy sayings are!	38	He by the pangs of death oppressed	142
How shall a weak, sinful youth	209	He can no longer sigh, nor droop	350
How shall I plead with thee? / Assist me	362	He did: the King invisible	175
		He found me in a desert place	107
How shall I plead with thee, / Saviour of	363	He hath in us his name revealed	426
		He hath my feet established	295
How shall we in his merits trust?	344	He heals the broken heart	343
How vast the mercy's store	64	He in the heathen's sight	467
How wisely timed the help that came	393	He laid his purple robes aside	166
Howe'er impatient to depart	386	He leaped the fatal ditch, where all	186
Howe'er the righteous thou conceal	284	He mourns his frustrated intent	15
Humbled in all thy paths I stayed	155	He saw the one great Sacriice	172
Humbly we hope for better things	419	He that by faith in Jesus lives	404
		He turned their water into blood	39
		He waits, that we from sin may turn	396
		He went, and touched Elisha's bones	197
		Hear, heaven and earth, your God's appeal	368

Volume IX

Had God foreknown it could not be	14	Heavenly Principle within	8
Had not the Lord reserved a seed	370	Heavy-laden and weary I faint	258
Hangs my new-born soul on thee	304	Help, eternal Spirit Divine	449
Happy as the first sinless man	115	Hence ye profane! far off remove	359
Happy beneath the Vine I sit	363	Her place intended to maintain	4
Happy day of union sweet	388	Hide me from the wrath of God	277
Happy, for ever happy I	80	Hide me in my Saviour's grave	250
Happy I am my wants to feel	397	High on the hill behold him stand	50
Happy is the man forgiven	17	High on thy heavenly throne	463
Happy is the righteous man	446	Him strong to redeem Ye islanders praise	417
Happy, Lord, thy people are	60	Him we in the furnace see	389
Happy soul, enjoy thy lot	84	His anger will the Lord retain	141
Happy the men who Jesus know	393	His government shall grow	382
Happy who in Christ delight	12	His hands he washed not in her blood	137
Hard it is, but not for thee	185	His life alas, I have not lived!	82
Hark! the sacred minstrel plays	189	His long-withheld assent to steal	395
Hast thou not undertook my cause	147	His name from east to west	427
Hasten, O God, the joyful day	397	His Name, his Nature, soars	382
Hated because we fear thy name	464	His soul's Delight, his Best-Beloved	414
Hated by fiends and men, who feel	26	His spiritual, believing seed	17
Haters of God, who still blaspheme	170	His strength in his obedience lay	139
Have I not always feared	354	Holy and Just, I fly to thee	128
Have I not often wished the same	74	Holy as thee, O Lord, is none	150
Have we not securely played	386		

Holy Child, our children take	153
How are the mighty fallen!	2
How backward man himself to blame!	7
How can we then complain or boast	48
How fond the self-deceiver's hope	158
How happy the people that dwell	406
How happy the sorrowful man	233
How in the slippery paths of youth	327
How justly, Lord, dost thou complain	435
How loath is God to strike, who stays	14
How loud the blood of Abel cries	13
How madly rash for puny man	72
How mean the gifts which earthly kings	229
How oft have I, like Pharaoh, proved	39
How often have I blindly done	70
How often, Lord, hath trouble brought	29
How pleasant a thing	343
How ready is the man to go	36
How safe the man in Jesus found	194
How safe, when God hath sealed	118
How shall a desperate slave of sin	262
How shall a sinful worm presume	317
How shall I keep the promise, how	262
How shall we offer to the skies	383
How shall we stand the hosts of Rome	383
How should I know unless from thee	421
How should we place to Satan give	195
How soon the fruits of sin appear!	6
How welcome to our fallen race	265
How went he to his grave in peace	198
How wisely, Saviour, doth thy love	43
Howe'er in humble words we all	243
Howe'er thou may'st to-morrow deal	198
Humbled like him, the Lord I fear	183

Volume X

Had they no true faith received	440
Hail all-redeeming Lord	122
Hail, Galilean King	412
Hail, holy, heaven-descended Child	143
Happy might I stationed be	427
Happy soul who Jesus knows	419
Happy the man who eyes receives	270
Happy the man who knows	187
Happy the place, but happier still	142
Happy the sin-sick soul to whom	451
Happy the soul who casts behind	158
Happy they and truly wise	381
Happy they, who humbly dread	133
Happy, when by faith I can	314
Happy who knows the Master's will	386
Happy whom God vouchsafes to praise	388
Hard struggling to comply in vain	171
Harkening to their Shepherd's voice	64
Hast thou forgot, thou Man of woe	430
Hast thou not heard my sad complaint	38
Hasten, Lord, the day of rest	33
Hasten, Lord, the promised day	127
Hasten the long-expected day	401
Hasten then the general peace	43
Have I not asked, and asked again	197
Have I not found that pearl Divine	276
Have I not sought a length of years	198
He comes! The heavenly bridegroom, comes	SH 1762, 2:186
He doth not learnedly declaim	449
He knew not where to lay his head	215
He never knew his Lord aright	389
He now had taught the favoured race	396
He preached th' incarnate God come down	249
He promises in life's short day	330
He rises glad to tend his Lord	451
He that hath least to do for God	387
He tramples on his Lord's command	234
He understands the word aright	472
He wears our feeble flesh, within	150
He, when the time of fruit drew near	345
He with Divine tranquillity	397
Head of thy church, for thee we look	108
Heal me, O gracious Lord, for well	29
Health into my spirit speak	161
Hear this, who at a trifle strain	362
Hear this, ye men of moral zeal	343
Hear ye dry bones, and feel	59
Hear ye, to whom your God imparts	271

Heathens, whatever called, they are	190	How am I healed, if still again	84
Heaven is for all alike prepared[289]	332	How base the inconsistent fear	389
Heaven's magnificence declares	170	How can a child of God	496
Hell's ministers by Satan taught	352	*How can I doubt thy will*	SH 1762, 2:151
Help me, Lord, on whom alone	292	How can I lose, if God is true	199
Here in depth of sweet distress	74	How can I my own heart renew?	53
Here on the earth he bids us come	393	How can it be most gracious Lord	197
Him dead and buried we confess	95	How can thine own apostles fall?	402
Him in every age the same	31	How difficult the task we find	317
Him whom wind and sea obeys	481	How dire the ball, the feast	497
Himself, and us, he cannot save	429	How disproportionate the toil	388
Himself he will not save, that we	429	How doth a single word of thine	343
Himself how shall a sinner know?	326	How dreadful is the sinner's fate	384
His blind exterminating zeal	274	How envy blinds the Pharisees!	259
His blood and body are the price	401	How few that saying understand	257
His body if a Christian slight	467	How great in excellence, above	354
His Father's Delight he comes for our sake	339	How great its efficacious power	355
His followers we their burden bear	228	How great our gain that serve a King	176
His glory he on Tabor shows	304	How great the goodness of our Lord	213
His heart it is that bleeds	317	How great the pardoning grace Divine	333
His life of soft luxurious ease	380	How great thy beauty who can tell	120
His mercies in Jesus renewed	49	How kindly, Lord, dost thou lament	364
His ministers he takes	466	How long shall I languish and moan	102
His name is Jesus Christ the just	261	How long wilt thou with us abide	309
His own renown, his own great name	450	How may we resemble God	172
His passions changed and sanctified	266	How mean he still on earth appears	246
His pity for the body's pain	280	How near ye to the confines run	261
His utmost rage and efforts vain	450	How often, Lord, have I believed	27
Holiness in sinners' hands	406	How often who can tell!	365
Holiness of Holinesses	72	How safe beneath thy wings we rest	371
Holy and unholy now	276	How shall he 'escape the hell within?	483
Holy, thou know'st, I fain would be	326	"How shall I give thee up?"	78
Hope of thy church and Saviour, hear!	24	How shall we then the spirits prove?	204
Horrible wish! thy murtherers dare	423	How small the gift it matters not	244
Hosanna to him, Whom angels adore	339	How then shall sinners meet the Lord	264
Hosannah to the Son[290]	118	How unlike the Person now	412
Hosannah to the Son[291]	139	How vain the care of Jesus' foes	435
		How welcome to man The kingdom He brings!	339
		Howe'er in serving him employed	452
		Humbly at thy cross adore	427
		Humbly do I inquire of thee	58

289. *UP* 2:32.

290. Lines 2 and 3 read: "Of David on his throne! / Lo, he comes, our Lord and King."

291. Lines 2 and 3 read: "Of David on his throne! / David's Son and King thou art."

Volume XI

Habitual sin shuts up the tomb	477
Had Christ descended from the cross	89
Hadst thou not cast a gracious look	147
Hadst thou, O Lord, been always here	472
Hail, all-redeeming Lord	79
Hail, Filial Deity	130
Hanging by humble faith on thee	106
Happiness for Adam's race	227
Happy he whose utmost patience	86
Happy his faithful worshippers	299
Happy, if then he hear	261
Happy, if watching to the end	67
Happy is the family	474
Happy poor who know your bliss	151
Happy the man who uses right	276
Happy the self-mistrusting man	451
Happy the soul who lives again	163
Happy the steward of his grace	179
Happy those who labour on	347
Happy through life if I	262
Happy thy faithful followers, Lord	13
Happy we, the friends of Jesus	195
Happy who finds his whole employ	179
Happy who in his house abide	21
Happy who the angels' word	118
Happy whom Jesus takes aside	8
Happy you by men abhorred	151
Happy you content to pine	151
Happy you to sorrow born	151
Hard to conceive without thy love	391
Hardened in his impenitence[292]	249
Hark how the hellish bloodhounds cry	416
Harmless in act, and word, and thought	296
Hast thou indeed done well?	381
Hasten that happiest gospel-day	201
He asks that he may give	354
He blasts the undeserving tree	42
He but to be remembered wants	303
He came from heaven to kindle fire	SH 1762, 2:235
He comes, he comes, on earth to reign	486
He comes, he comes to fetch his bride!	65
He comes (pretender vain) to pray	258
He curbs the struggling grief within	476
He dies—a death of pain and shame[293]	301
He disarms the hostile mind	411
He doth not in their error leave	324
He doth to us his mind declare	185
He eats with men of every sort	147
He for no invitation stays	264
He gathers fruit who sinners wins	361
He had the happiness he chose	245
He hath for all been offered up	483
He hath been lifted up for me	345
He holds us thus in humble fear	7
He in our mortal flesh revealed	322
He leaves them all in humble fear	395
He left on this auspicious night	510
He lifts the hands stretched out so late	316
He longed the rite t' ordain	283
He marks the church he left behind	66
He muses frequently retired	146
He must unjust or cruel seem	415
He offered them sufficient light	495
He only at God's glory aims	454
He rises in the power of love	417
He shows and does the work Divine	370
He shuns his murderers no more	469
He spake, and Jesus' word alone[294]	362
He spake that they might hear	372
He speaks by benefits bestowed	185
He spends his strength the world to please	235
He still vouchsafes to bless	94
He still with fixed attention sees	274
He teaches us to cast aside	416
He that doth his Pattern eye	139
He that hath ears to hear	219
He thus delights t' approve	94
He thus his word fulfils	95
He thus the way makes known	83

---

292. UP 2:161.

293. UP 2:202.

294. UP 2:233.

He to the conscious soul of man	15	His miracles had plainly told	270
He waits in hope to see and know	263	His oracles who disbelieve	247
He waits; to manifest his grace[295]	468	His own advantages of grace	324
He who rules the lower air	380	His own, and not another's sheep	455
He will not with his purchase part	348	His own great glory he intends	468
He winks at ignorance sincere	98	His passover precedes	283
He yields the infinite increase	490	His person, not his sin, I love	153
Hear, Jesus, hear their helpless cry	30	His promises kind	306
Hear this, thou prosperous wretched man	211	His public ministry to close	496
Hear what the wise and learned say!	446	His sacrifice pleads, His prevalent blood	102
Heathens mock our blessed hope	176	His servants in their low estate	110
Heathens shall in judgment rise	206	His Spirit drew me to the pool	441
Heavenly King, we still attend	41	His Spirit send to seal us his	386
Help me, Lord, to recollect	197	His Spirit's small and quiet voice	185
Help me to make the poor our friends[296]	241	His thanks abominably vain	258
Help, O help mine unbelief	327	His understanding's eyes	449
Her loss she never can forget	163	His voice the sheep rejoice to hear	455
Her vehemence did the judge provoke	256	His wishes, were they all fulfilled	235
Here I cannot seek in vain	374	His word, the sign of Jesus' will	363
Here then in vehement hope I rest	25	Holy, hallowing Spirit, come	127
Him and his friend they sought to slay	248	Holy sanctifying Lamb	282
Him in whom all fulness dwells	322	Horrible night for murder made	509
Him, only him we long to hear	185	House to house and field to field	228
Him we foolishly mistrust	208	How blessed the people are	56
His arm th' almighty Father bared	111	How blind the misconceiving crowd	389
His church is the floor, his saints are the wheat	128	How blind the priests who could not see	49
		How can we escape the fire	126
His course, but not his office ends	99	How dark the night which sin hath spread	15
His disciples sincere	306	How deep and unperceived in man	512
His foes the precious truth abuse	295	How does he take the lowest place	225
His foes with joy malicious hear	295	How fatal and unlike to these	333
His God he on the cross can see	303	How fervent is our Shepherd's love	95
His good is that to which he gives	34	How foolish is my heart	308
His goodness in externals lies	258	How good to visit Jesus' friends	481
His hand on us if Jesus lay	8	How happy is the Christian's lot	60
His heralds in his name we cry	114	How happy, Lord, are we	52
His last tremendous groan	89	How happy that distinguished pair	101
His life a daily death they see	343	How hard for you to think it hard	33
His love can find a thousand ways	131	How hath he loved us? how?	345
His minister the world should bear	433	How hopeless is a sinner's case[297]	508
		How ignorant and blind	260

295. *UP* 2:247.
296. *UP* 2:157.
297. *UP* 2:260.

How little of himself he knows	74	Happy the parting minister	370
How long hast thou vouchsafed to feed	379	Happy the souls allowed to hear	367
How oft beneath a show of zeal	27	Happy we as those above	368
How oft would I have gathered you	223	Happy were the church, could all	198
How pleasing is the harmony	489	Happy who for his conduct past	423
How pure the blessed spirits there	55	Happy who thus their Lord confess!	392
How rich in God's esteem	259	Hast thou forgot,[300] thou man of grief	97
How righteous is the sinner's doom	245	Have not I for forty years	277
How sad our state by nature is	436	Having fulfilled the charge enjoined	173
How sad the state of fallen man	8	He asks an undivided heart	230
How sad the triumph of an hour	71	He dares no more himself prefer	123
How shall I, a sinner, dare	127	He did not his assistants call	347
How shall we do the things enjoined	284	He did not scorn to make reply	254
How stubborn the presumptuous man	76	He doth not seek the light	234
How vain our strife to heal	173	He feels th' anticipated fear	413
How will he their reproaches bear	246	He first their wilfulness reproves	438
Howe'er our hasty nature fret[298]	170	He follows Christ unbidden	129
Howe'er the softening art of man	157	He for thy sake approves us	24
Humbly now, O Lord, I own	148	He gives the grace unknown	13
Humility prepares his way	264	He hath at last his heart's desire	263
Hungering after heavenly food	378	He is ready to prove	168
Hurricanes the ship defies	380	He knew th' apostles too, endued	361
		He knows his Saviour's mind	404
		He knows our depth of poverty	116
		He lost his ancient colleague's aid	311

Volume XII

		He made the direful place his own	141
Hadst thou left me, Lord, alone	214	He made their wickedness his own	350
Hadst thou not come to Adam's race	31	He must the wrath Divine appease	82
Happy alone we cannot rest	247	He now instructs us to receive	313
Happy church when all are joined	306	He now is sent to every heart	167
Happy loss of liberty	445	He pleads his privilege at last	325
Happy man with princes bred	273	He preaches Christ, and faith in him	413
Happy Paul to bonds consigned!	407	He sees him with the Saviour's eyes	321
Happy prisoner of the Lord	323	He sleeps! and lo his wounded side	89
Happy saint, so quickly driven	216	He speaks in tender pitying grace	116
Happy soul whom Jesus chooses	15	He thirsted for this soul of mine[301]	94
Happy the highly favoured man	70	He trembles, but he cannot stay	414
Happy the man by Jesus sent	297	He who breathed into our earth	424
Happy the man redeemed at last	394	He who furious inquisition	393
Happy the man through special grace	388	He who knew a father's mind	380
Happy the men who first partook	261		
Happy the multitude[299]	180		

298. *UP* 2:104.
299. *UP* 2:295.

300. Osborn changed "Hast thou forgot" to "Didst thou forget."
301. *UP* 2:276.

He whom winds and seas obey	436	His present power controls	13
He will not first bestow on me	299	His sight he first receives[304]	238
He would not have thy soul to wait	149	His Spirit attests	150
He would not urge the plea before	325	His Spirit in our hearts hath sealed	132
Head and members, Christ entire	60	His Spirit too declares	193
Hear a desperate sinner pray	173	His vouchers we are	250
Hear, earth and heaven, with wonder hear	97	His work is done, his sufferings passed	115
Hear the meek Lamb for sinners plead	95	His wrath he with his love reveals[305]	147
Hear this, thou persecutor hear	235	Holy Ghost, beneath whose power	274
Heathens hear what Jews	348	Holy Ghost, by him bestowed	40
Heathens in every age contend	87	Holy Ghost, convince my heart	38
Heathens it apprehends and Jews	138	Horrible apostasy!	213
Heathens stand amazed, affrighted	154	How august the hallowed place	382
Help me, Lord, to feed and keep	126	How beautiful the feet appear	318
Her house is opened with her heart	316	How can it be? A soldier good	244
Her spirit she gave up!	183	How can the governor withstand	408
Here a true specimen we see	184	How different Christ from Moses here	209
Here at the Temple's gate	158	How do you, alas, profane	183
Here lies of life th' immortal Prince	92	How does he break the law of God	412
Herod intends a saint to kill	264	How gross our nature's blindness is	209
Herod mounts the gorgeous throne	271	How happy the men[306]	155
Highly favoured them we call	314	How many days he doth not tell	136
Him do I seek by faith t' adore	67	How quickly changed my God, by thee	442
Him self-sufficient and alone	341	How should a prisoner poor and bound	435
Himself permitted to defend	423	How should Israel's sons commend	207
Himself with lifted hands and eyes	47	How soon a miser's fears are past	415
Hirelings without remorse or pain	169	How soon alas the selfish sin	182
His blood the cement was[302]	180	How wretched is the man	81
His consolation sweet	44	Howe'er the angry world oppose	189
His counsellors we cannot be	313	Howe'er your idols we despise	364
His counsels then we bear in mind	231	Human events we should attend	194
His death the prophecies fulfilled[303]	328	Humble and wise, they offer not	189
His innocence we daily find	77		
His love and righteousness	220		
His love by action spoken	129		

Volume XIII

Happy for ever happy I	169
Happy might I the grace receive	150
Happy the man, who poor and low	222
Happy we live, when God doth fill	18
Happy we, who humbly prove	143

His loving labour he repeats 446
His manner was, when it could be 327
His mind revealed I tell 376
His name through faith alone 162
His offering pure we call to mind 158

302. *UP* 2:295.
303. *UP* 2:378.
304. *UP* 2:327.
305. *UP* 2:288.
306. *UP* 2:289.

Hast thou not prepared the place	242	Holy Ghost, we know thou art	31
Hasten the joyful day	49	Holy Ghost, with grace inspire	65
Have I this hope thy face to see?	200	Holy, innocent, and pure	137
Have we suffered much for thee	164	Honour the king, who God adore	180
He can; but hath he said, he will?	40	Horrible lust of fame and power	174
He comes triumphant from above[307]	28	How backward is our flesh and blood	131
He dares not ask almighty power	175	How can the brethren testify	214
He died, that sin in us might die	10	How long thou awful God, how long	281
He doth by his presence arm	247	How shall I make my calling sure?	190
He entered once the holiest	139	How shall I that love attain	181
He flies at the sound Of Jesus's name	246	How strong the stream of error ran	61
He loved, and gave himself for me	62	How then shall I presume	148
He offered up himself entire	142	Howe'er the Nicolaitanes claim	213
He prays for his own: his	235	Howe'er untunable the voice	75
He saith, Ye shall be perfect here	5	Humble myself! it cannot be	187
He that made my conscience clean	144	Hymned by the bright angelic choirs	75
He walks to and fro, And seeks to devour	246		
He wills, that I should holy be	90		
Head of thy Church conflicting here	283		

Volume I

Hear us in our time of need	267
Hearing our feeble flesh complain	126
Help me, Saviour, to hold fast	122
Help then my desperate unbelief	145
Henceforth let none attempt in vain	70
Here let me ever lie	16
Here may I covet no reward	262
Here may it ever, ever burn	263
Here will I ever, ever lie	192
Him Prophet, Priest, and King we own	26
Himself a spotless sacrifice	139
Himself doth in his word declare	196
Himself he cannot perfect call	222
His arm stretched out we oft have seen	282
His death completes the sacrifice	120
His grace shall quickly lift us up	249
His love into the furnace cast	121
His mournful days of flesh are o'er	142
His promise stands, I will forgive	5
His Son whom all heaven's host obeyed	119
His witness within By faith we receive	248
Holy Ghost, remove the grief	62
Holy Ghost, the power inspire	21

I am no link of thy great chain[308]	30
I am the man who long have known	275
I ask thy grace to make me clean	226
I ask thy help; by thee sent forth	179
I bid you all my goodness prove	206
I cannot open, Lord, mine eyes[309]	29
I cannot rest, till in thy blood	265
I do the thing thy laws enjoin	235
I ever gasp in Christ to live	251
I fasted, read, and worked, and prayed	333
I feel, I feel thee now the same	275
I feel the power of Jesu's name	285
I felt my Lord's atoning blood	300
I forced thee first to disappear	327
I found, and owned his promise true	300
I groan from pride to be set free	371
I groan to break my prison-walls	253
I had forgot my heavenly birth[310]	113
I half believe (the deadly cold[311]	47
I have long withstood his grace	272

307. *UP* 2:463.
308. George Herbert.
309. George Herbert.
310. George Herbert.
311. George Herbert.

I have no might t' oppose the foe	324	I viewed thy furniture so fine[319]	36
I have no skill the snare to shun	323	I wait my vigour to renew	235
I have spilt his precious blood	272	I want the Spirit of power within	307
I hold thee with a trembling hand	328	I want thy love, I fear thy frown	253
I, I alone have done the deed![312]	232	I will complain, yet praise[320]	49
I know in thee all fulness dwells	204	I work, and own the labour vain	235
I know, my struggling nought avails	336	I would be thine, thou know'st I would	372
I know thou wilt accept me now	135	Idle mirth, where art thou now?[321]	222
I'll weary thee with my complaint	76	Idly we talk of harvests here[322]	65
I loathe myself, when God I see	328	If all may not thy mercy claim	310
I long to pour out all my soul	250	If done t' obey thy laws[323]	31
I long to see this Excellence[313]	343	If fury can in thee have place	310
I long to see thy face	267	If God refuse our heart to turn[324]	19
I look to former times, and strain	325	If I could hear thy quickening call	309
I look to see his lovely face	256	If I rightly read thy heart	273
I, my Beloved, am only thine[314]	344	If in this darksome wild I stray[325]	137
I my Master have denied	272	If now my nature's weight I feel	251
I need not urge my eager plea	336	If now thy influence I feel	164
I only live to find thee there	336	If pride, desire, wrath stirred anew[326]	349
I pant to feel thy sway	155	If rough and thorny be my way[327]	138
I rest beneath th' Almighty's shade	306	If still the sun should hide his face[328]	40
I rested in the outward law	234	If still thou goest about, to do	262
Isaac by faith declared his race	216	*If sufferings could thy love obtain*	HSP 1740, 56
I see the fiery trial near	323		
I see the perfect law requires	233	If the first glance, but opened now[329]	103
I see thy garments rolled in blood[315]	109	If thou art rigorously severe	256
I seek no motive out of thee	236	If thou impart thyself to me	264
I sent a sigh to seek thee out[316]	68	If thou still canst idle be[330]	222
I thank thee, Uncreated Sun[317]	177	If thy love to us hath given	360
I thirst, thou wounded Lamb of God[318]	265		
I too with thee shall walk in white	265		
I trust in him who stands between	235		

312. From the German of Paul Gerhardt, translated by John Wesley.
313. Altered from John Norris.
314. Altered from George Sandys.
315. From the German of Nikolaus von Zinzendorf, translated by John Wesley.
316. George Herbert.
317. From the German of Johann Angelus Scheffler, translated by John Wesley.
318. From the German of Nikolaus von Zinzendorf, translated by John Wesley.
319. George Herbert.
320. George Herbert.
321. Altered from George Herbert.
322. George Herbert.
323. George Herbert.
324. George Herbert.
325. From the German of Nikolaus von Zinzendorf, translated by John Wesley.
326. From the German of Nikolaus von Zinzendorf, translated by John Wesley.
327. From the German of Nikolaus von Zinzendorf, translated by John Wesley.
328. George Herbert.
329. George Herbert.
330. Altered from George Herbert.

First line	Page
If we now begin to be	356
Image of God Most High	316
Impotent, dumb, and deaf, and blind	264
In a dry land, behold, I place[331]	175
In all I do I feel thy aid[332]	176
In all I do, myself I feel	132
In all my ways thy hand I own	322
In blessing thee with grateful songs[333]	175
In darkness willingly I strayed[334]	176
Indignant kings stood up t' oppose	295
Infinite God, thy greatness spanned	230
In him complete we shine	152
In holiness within thy gates[335]	175
In life's short day let me yet more[336]	85
In my redeeming work employed	208
In part we only know thee here	341
In search of empty joys below	206
In suffering be thy love my peace[337]	141
In the devouring lion's teeth[338]	232
In thee I sure redemption have	285
In thee we languish to be found	238
In thee we move. All things of thee[339]	168
In thine appointed ways we wait	368
Into thy gracious hands I fall[340]	90
Inured to poverty and pain	306
In vain its pomps ambition spreads	217
In vain the mad Fanatic's dreams	14
In works of righteousness employed	367
Instructive Sound! I'm now convinced by thee[341]	10
Is anything too hard for thee	279
Is there a thing beneath the sun[342]	72
Is there a thing than life more dear	215
Is this the soul so late weighed down	182
Isaac by faith declared his race	216
It cannot be! Is this the heart[343]	48
Its inmost folds are known to thee	252

331. From the Spanish of David Israel Lopez Laguna.
332. From the Spanish of David Israel Lopez Laguna.
333. From the Spanish of David Israel Lopez Laguna.
334. From the German of Johann Angelus Scheffler, translated by John Wesley.
335. From the Spanish of David Israel Lopez Laguna.
336. From the German of Christian Friedrich Richter, translated by John Wesley.
337. From the German of Paul Gerhardt, translated by John Wesley.
338. From the German of Paul Gerhardt, translated by John Wesley.
339. From the German of Gerhard Tersteegen, translated by John Wesley.
340. From the German of Wolfgang Dessler, translated by John Wesley.

Volume II

First line	Page
I all thy holy will shall prove	287
I am all unclean, unclean	92
I am the man who long have known	165
I ask according to thy will	130
I ask in confidence the grace	286
I ask not sensible delight	127
I ask that I may do thy will	309
I cannot love thee little, Lord	302
I cannot praise thee as I would	231
I cannot pray, I cannot praise	81
I cannot rest, till pure within	206
I count not now the tedious years	311
I dare not speak, I cannot show	165
I doubt not, Lord, but there remains	161
I, even I, believe in him	312
I every hour In jeopardy stand	198
I fear nor earth, nor sin, nor hell	142
I feel and know him now in part	365
I feel that I have power with God	300
I feel that thou wouldst have me live	129
I feel what then shall raise me up	183
I fell, and sunk in self-despair	202
I felt my heart, and found a chillness cool	10
I find him lifting up my head	242
I from outward things withdraw	262

341. John Gambold.
342. From the German of Gerhard Tersteegen, translated by John Wesley.
343. George Herbert.

I hate my sins, no longer mine	143	I strive in all I do to please	149
I have always equal need	279	I thank thee for that gracious taste	231
I have lost the life Divine	156	I thank thee for the future grace	141
I have not a priest unmoved	134	I thank thee, whose atoning blood	234
I have not believed in vain	299	I the golden sceptre see	147
I have the keys of death and hell	341	I thought not of my God	117
I have the things for which I pray	309	*I too will magnify the Lord*	57
I have the things I ask of thee	141	I took the morning's wings, and fled	81
I know him by those prints of love	167	I trust that to the life Divine	285
I know it is not now renewed	160	I wait till he shall touch me clean	304
I know that my Redeemer lives, / And ever	243	I want a godly fear	209
		I want a sober mind	208
I know that my Redeemer lives; / he lives	182	I want a true regard	209
		I want an heart to pray	209
I know the terms: I cannot see	69	I want with all my heart	209
I know thee, Saviour, who thou art	175	*I will hearken what my Lord*	264
I leave it all to him alone	82	I will remove the sword of flame	347
I leave it all to thee alone	163	I would be truly still	86
I, like Gideon's fleece, am found	318	I would, (but thou canst tell,)	86
I live to God, who from the dead	247	I would: but thou must give the power	145
I long to know, and to make known	72	I wrestle not now, But trample on sin	179
I need not tell thee who I am	175	If aught can there enhance their bliss	22
I only wait for this glad hour	161	If but one good thought could buy	112
I rest upon thy word	208	If but one tempted soul may find	164
I right early shall awake	293	If every one that asks may find	164
I saw the port of Jesu's breast	100	If he can find it in his heart	82
I see an open door of hope	313	If I have begun once more	123
I see it now from Pisgah's top	255	If I have tasted of thy grace	272
I shall, a weak and helpless worm	282	If in this feeble flesh I may	281
I shall all in thee inherit	96	If now I have acceptance found	254
I shall be perfected in love	286	If now the bowels of thy love	205
I shall be redeemed from all	280	If now thou knockest at my heart	205
I shall from every sin be free	364	If now thou talkest by the way	167
I shall fully be restored	279	If, O Lord, I have found favour	96
I shall my ancient strength renew	282	If such a worm as I can spread	281
I shall not always make my moan	302	If thither he will us convey	18
I shall nothing know beside	278	If thou didst see me in my blood	204
I shall suffer and fulfil	278	If thy grace for all is free	152
I shall triumph evermore	278	If with the wretched sons of men	197
I sin in every breath I draw	234	I'll trust my Great Physician's skill[344]	11
I soon shall hear thy quickenng voice	238	In a land of corn and wine	306
I stand and admire thine outstretched arm	178	In calm, submissive grief	85
I start from the contempt of men	131		

344. Altered from John Norris.

In every messenger reveal	344	I cannot see his face, and live	134
In God we put our trust	245	I cannot trust my treacherous heart	60
In heaven thou reign'st, enthroned in light	335	I cheerfully comply	277
		I could believe that God is hate	60
In her no spot of sin remained	184	I could not be restored	54
In hope, against all human hope	310	I could the devil's law receive	60
In hope, believing against hope, / Jesus	199	I, even I, have purged thy sin	171
In hope believing against hope, / thy	285	I feel that thou hast lost thy sting	163
In love and pity to my soul	217	I feel thee willing, Lord	63
In patient hope for this I wait	163	I feel within me, unsubdued	60
In spirit joined, and one with thee	364	I gasp to end my wretched days	163
In the strength of God I rise	238	I groan to be redeemed from sin	160
In the strength of Jesu's name	237	I hasten where the deepest hell	25
In the time of my distress	207	I have thy salvation wrought	171
In the wilderness I stray	93	I heard him ask, Whom shall I send	135
In thee, who hast redeemed of old	295	I in their hearts will still remain	148
In this reanimated clay	182	I know my soul is foul as hell	28
In vain doth Satan rage his hour	334	I live and suffer all my care	158
In vain they bid me blindly fly	162	I loathe myself in my own sight	18
In vain thou strugglest to get free	174	I might have seen in that my day	42
In vain to Christ the slothful pray	17	I now believe in thee	92
In vain was Tophet moved	269	I now the broken cisterns leave[345]	169
Into that happy number, Lord	225	I own my punishment is just	28
Into their hands by sin betrayed	107	I saw my death with stony eye	24
Is crucified for me and you	75	*I saw the Lord in light arrayed*	133
Is it not enough that I	215	*I see my doom, but cannot feel*	HGEL 1742, 4
Is it thy will to save	329	I that speak in righteousness	227
Is not faith the same for ever?	31	I, the Father's favourite Son	227
Is there any divination	33	I this record leave behind	15
Is there no balm in thee to heal	126	I wait to catch thy parting breath	174
It mocks my strength, prevents my flight	102	I want the dear Redeemer's grace	254
		I will compel them to submit	148
It shall be so: I do not doubt	308	I will that those thou giv'st to me	292
It teaches us, and not in vain	325	I would not still deceive	90
		If after all my waste of love	43

Volume III

		If all long-suffering thou hast shown	19
		If all men have strayed, Of every one	8
I am into bondage brought	14	If all men were dead, And fell in the fall	8
I am not worthy, Lord	246	If any fail of promised rest	65
I can no longer trust	55	If any man thirst, And happy would be	7
I can no more rely	55		
I cannot, dare not now deny	165		
I cannot from destruction turn	24		

345. Free paraphrase of the German of Christian Friedrich Richter by Charles Wesley.

If by thy light I now perceive	59	It speaks me justified	59
If chiefly here thou mayst be found	281		
If God the seed did sow	48		

Volume IV

If his death we receive	324		
If once the spirit unclean	49	I am from all eternity	296
If reason can arrest his doom	67	I am never at one stay[346]	449
If so poor a worm as I	333	I am not worthy, Lord, that thou	379
If yet again my Lord returns	43	I am the man, the Jonas I	10
Impatient for my change I wait	160	I ask thy promised succours	86
In Adam we died, In thee we may live	8	I believe thy pardoning grace	416
In an accepted time of love	233	I bid th' unfathomed deep be dry	299
In fastings oft the hardy soldier was	115	I bow to the rod	367
In holy fellowship they lived	339	I cannot persevere in good	449
In Jesus we live, in Jesus we rest	286	I come, thy servant, Lord, replies	279
In memory of your dying God	267	I do not, dare not, Lord, mistrust	353
In rapture lost, on thee I gaze	33	I dread the human face Divine	337
In rapture lost, the heavenly choir	179	*I, even I, am he that cheer*	304
In rapturous bliss	282	I feel, I now divinely feel	475
In sure and steadfast hope again to find	126	I felt it; and still	415
In that sad memorable night	215	I felt it applied	273
In the rite thou hast enjoined	240	I find brought in a better hope	452
In thee do we live, thy daily supplies	371	I followed an heart	415
In them the strong delusion reigns	70	I followed with the thoughtless throng	453
In thine own appointments bless us	271	I, (for my Son hath died to seal	55
In this authentic sign	221	I glory in redemption found	454
In this barren wilderness	276	I hate the souls that preach a lie	310
In this expressive bread I see	216	I have no babes to hold me here	278
In this howling wilderness	235	I have no sharer of my heart	278
In vain he labours to persuade	280	I hope at last to find	448
In vain I take the broken bread	257	I hope thou able art to cleanse	361
In vain the subtle tempter tries	280	I hung the earth on empty space	298
In vain thy written Word	80	I keep it, I th' almighty Lord	294
Increase (if that can be)	80	I know my Saviour lives	197
Into our minds recall	270	I know not how thy love will deal	414
Into the fellowship	328	I know the tempest roars for me	11
Is it the dying Master's will	279	I know the work is only thine	325
Is not the cup of blessing, blest	266	I know thy justice wills	437
Is not the hallowed broken bread	267	I know t' alleviate my pain	360
Is this the man of hellish birth	148	I languish and pine	213
It bears us now on eagle's wings	285	I left my first zeal	415
It seals the universal peace	139	I lift my weary eyes	394
It seemed to my Redeemer good	253	I long thy coming to confess	121
It shall be so: my word shall stand	150		
It speaks me justified from all	17		

346. *UP* 3:202.

I must, I shall be born again	331	If now thy will his soul relents	350
I need not fear the burning pool	397	If on such a land as this	68
I never shall rise	411	If such be my doom	363
I now admire the worthies	85	If the ruin be decreed	60
I own, I have sinned in thy sight	425	If thou all compassion art	418
I rest in thine almighty power	480	If thou canst pardon me once more	441
I rode on the sky	409	If thou couldst stoop for me to die	344
I see stretched out to save me	87	If well I know the tuneful art	243
I shall, I surely shall	14	If, when I had put thee to grief	196
I sink if thou longer delay	419	If yet thou canst compassion have	269
I sought him in the secret cell	323	If yet thou canst my sins forgive	371
I speak th' irrevocable word	299	Immanuel's love Let sinners confess	113
I stop the wise, and drive them back	299	*Immortal King of kings*	81
I the bitter cup have tasted	383	*Immortal Potentate*	22
I, the bright Sun of Righteousness	297	Impart the salutary pain	186
I the diviner's skill confound	299	In all my griefs below	438
I the good fight have fought and won	67	In anguish, agony, and grief	291
I the weak sons of men o'errule	298	In answer to our fervent prayer	24
I throw mine eyes around	395	In base mistrust of finding God	330
I thwarted his will	415	In blessings will I then come down	55
I use, but trust in means no more	452	In calm and quiet peace	18
I want an heart to love my God	205	In different states the ransomed race	296
I water it with heavenly dew	294	In flesh we part awhile	272
I will my sovereign art display	55	In him we have immortal food	38
I will not let my sorrow go	205	In hope believing against hope	472
I will not let thee go	250	In judgment dost thou here reprieve	400
I will pursue, I will o'ertake	223	In love forbid my longer stay	216
I will, that they should holy be	310	In me the stubborn evil reigns	451
I will to the whole ransomed race	76	In me thine utmost mercy show	477
I would not live, and therefore go	338	In my weak sinful flesh appear	121
I would not, Lord, my soul deceive	337	In our forty days reprieve	9
I would not to thy foe submit	247	In patient distress	363
If, drawn by thine alluring grace	227	In restoring love again	406
If evil we, by nature know	170	In sickness make thou all his bed	350
If first thou chastise Our insolent boast	89	In thee, O Lord, I put my trust	479
If hope be in my end	399	In thee we have hope, In thee we have peace	90
If I have only known thy fear	236		
If in the vale of tears thy will	351	In this accepted hour	172
If me, even me thou yet canst spare	446	*In trouble I seek thee, O God*	424
If my blood could atone	367	In tumult and noise, We sing of Thy grace	52
If near the pit I rashly stay	477		
If now I lament after God	196	In tumult and war his tokens we hear	89
If now the stricken rock relents	440	In vain the dear departing saint	246
If now the Witness were in	236	In vain the subtil foe	45

In vain the world as madness brands	174	I come, O God, to do thy will	19
Incarnate Deity	255	I come to testify the grace	136
Infinite God, to thee we raise	224	I come, with eager joy I come	210
Infinite, unexhausted love!	440	I dare in thee confide	347
Iniquities increase	218	I dare no longer doubt	172
Inspire him with thy tender care	48	I dare not deprecate the cross	82
Inspire the living faith	197	I dare not hope to see	213
Instinct with living powers	153	I dare not, Lord, the gift refuse	413
Is he not to his Father gone	188	I feel applied	62
Is not thy power divinely shown	468	I feel it settled in my heart	144
Is there a soul on this side hell	351	I have felt it applied, The life-giving tide	28
Is there a thing too hard for thee?	361	I fill my Lord's afflictions up	20
Is there no balm in Gilead found?	413	I have faith in thy blood	27
Is there no balm of love	361	I have my Saviour always near	19
Is there on earth a loss too great	361	I hear, I feel the balmy word	355
Israel shall as the lily grow	55	I hear the providential word	82
Issues from thee a purer flood	453	*I, I am the man that have known*	264
Issuing forth from him and thee	181	I lift mine eye to thee	22
It challenged its stray	273	I lift my broken heart	189
It cost thy blood my heart to win	336	I lift my heart to thee	417
It may be, God, the God ye love	62	I lift up my voice, To pardon restored	35
It must be so; in me alone	337	I look for help in thee alone	79
It was not possible	147	I mourn for those that did run well	245
Its being with its power destroy	307	I never shall rest	289
Its virtue I tried	367	I now believe, and therefore speak	103
		I now on the scale Of friendship arise	419
		I now with all my brethren join	378

Volume V

		I quickly shall o'ertake	348
I aim at the prize	26	I seek, and pursue	26
I all have left for Jesu's sake	82	I shall feel it again	29
I already am blest	26	I shall throughly be clean	27
I am not as from thee I came	292	I sing of thy grace	401
I am sure it shall be	27	I sink with thee, with thee to rise	157
I ask nor joy, nor life, nor ease	295	I spend myself, that you may know	112
I ask not ease	60	I stand in thy might	25
I asked, but never hoped from thee	5	I struggle still, and fain	170
I believe thou hast died	29	*I thank thee, Lord, of earth and heaven*	103
I cannot fear, I cannot doubt	470	I the glory shall see	305
I cannot see thy face, and live!	94	I thirst to drink my Master's cup	153
I come at thy call	25	I to God shall be joined	30
I come for the grace	27	I trust thy image to regain	293
I come, if thou my strength restore	65	I wait thy will to do	16
I come, not like the sordid herd	391	I want a principle within	373
		I want an even strong desire	105

I will, I will obey thy word	80	*In Jesus's name On sinners I call*	34
I will not let thee go, unless	177	In life and death I bless his name	90
I will not point thee out the way	153	In loud hallelujahs they sing	358
I will not take the proffered sword	145	In patience I wait	30
I without sin on earth shall live	300	In patient distress	200
I would for thee my life resign	198	In patient hope I now give heed	7
I would from every sin	263	In quiet, calm distress	171
I would the precious time redeem	106	In sacred melancholy	202
If anxious here for their success	394	In safety lead thy little flock	234
If for their bodies I provide	394	In sickness will I make his bed	20
If for this th' uniting Spirit	425	In sight of God proceed	45
If I foolishly depart	12	In steadfast faith on thee I call	72
If I may be so greatly blessed	434	*In sure and steadfast hope to rise*	86
If mercy is indeed with thee	372	In sure and steadfast hope,	
If my God I cast behind	13	/ In view of	474
If sometimes he believes	436	In sure and steadfast hope	
If thee th' ungrateful world could hate	144	/ To be redeemed	330
If then I have acceptance found	91	In that Jerusalem above	
If thou canst, the whole remit	204	/ All is harmony	210
If thou didst the grace impart	428	In that Jerusalem above, / No pain	200
If thou ever didst discover	211	In the heavenly Lamb	24
If thou hast power and will to save	311	In the kingdom of thy patience	345
If to the right, or left I stray	374	In the skies we shall meet	305
If to us thy sacred Spirit	276	In the stream I drink the Fountain	452
If we have through him found favor	174	In the wedding-garb of love	349
If what I wish is good	450	In thee I confide	25
If what my soul requires	450	In thee together let us die	410
Impoverish, Lord, and then relieve	124	In them let all mankind behold	482
Impregnable it stands	44	In thy pilgrimage with men	276
In a rapture of joy	403	In vain, till thou the power bestow	244
In all his glorious image bright	300	In vain was he in flesh revealed	326
In answer to thy Spirit's prayer	417	In want my plentiful supply	50
In comfort, power, and peace	366	In weariness and pain	14
In every place, in every age	260	Infinitely dear and precious	456
In faith we wrestle for that soul	76	Inflamed with seraphical love	358
In fellowship; alone,	43	Into a world of ruffians sent	268
In haste to fill their measure up	257	Inwardly like other men	195
In heaven my heart and treasure is	65	Is it not his will to join	406
In hellish toils o'ertaken	442	Is she so near the burning lake	239
In him is bestowed	284	Is there in this low creation	440
In him we have peace	469	Is this the man of woe	464
In hope of that ecstatic pause	169	Is this the time, say, Jesu, say	471
In hope of that salvation	208	It bids the weary come	369
In Jesus we believe	474	It dazzles our eyes	30

It keeps our mind in perfect peace	312
It keeps, till I am born again	6
It must be so; thou say'st it must	151
It proffers happiness	369
It shall not always vex us here	297
It speaks to God, my God, for me	67
It washes the foul	28
Its proud aspiring brow	47

Volume VI

I, and my house, will serve the Lord	10
I aspire to things above	444
I cannot obey thy commands	462
I dare no longer trust	2
I despise all earthly things	445
I first, of ill o'ercome, shall yield	102
I, I shall conquer too	201
I, if here I love my Lover	459
I know her now possessed	201
I know not what to do or say	381
I laid me down in peace, and rise	450
I loved her for thy sake alone	276
I saw, and lo! the fruitful place	88
I saw, and lo! the mountains shook	87
I saw the earth by sin destroyed	87
I see a world of spirits bright	220
I see the generous friend sincere!	226
I shall live the simple life	442
I shall then show forth thy praise	443
I triumph in her bliss!	201
I trust thy utmost Saviour's love	341
I want (alas! thou know'st my heart)	276
I want—to love my foes like her	276
I will accept his offers now	429
I will, I will on Jesus trust	305
I will improve what I receive	429
I will not utterly consume	88
I would (but thou must give the power)	385
Idle boys and men are found	423
If earth its mouth must open wide	22
If God on us hath much bestowed	417
If his life a snare would prove	252
If his life would matter raise	252
If now, on such a land as this	158
If now the alien hosts break in	158
If now the dreadful charge is given	79
If now thou art nigh	399
If now thou dost thy work revive	115
If now thou standest at the door	402
If now we remove	406
If some defile the hallowed place	106
If this felicity were mine	460
If thou all his ways hast seen	222
If thou hast torn our child away	256
If thou hast wrought us, Lord, to this	256
If thou must in wrath reprove	77
If thou preserve our souls in peace	105
If thy dreadful controversy	92
If trouble for a moment seize	31
If unto us our friends are good	447
If we have filled up our measure	168
If well we anything have done	422
Impatient to be truly great	284
In a new world of light and bliss	260
In condescending love	316
In him if we believe	389
In his great name alone	434
In hope of that immortal crown	219
In hope to share thine happiness	318
In innocent songs, his coming we shout	405
In Jesus joined to God again	394
In love and every grace she grew	273
In lowly confidence Divine	315
In measure then reprove	125
In meek and quiet peace	231
In my earliest hour	453
In our most precarious state	76
In our useful employ	435
In prayer and praise we lift our voice	277
In self-mistrusting fear	225
In specious pride and envy bred	411
In the mansions of the blessed	363
In the means thou hast enjoined	376
In the morning of her day	334
In this acceptable hour	222
In us thy pardoning love reveal	263

In vain are children taught to pray	456	I trust him alone	80
In vain her strength and language fail	250	I view the Lamb in his own light	195
In vain the fierce invader swore	178	I wait the quickening word	388
In vain the Gnostic tempter tried	280	I want a pardon sealed	388
In wisdom as in years she grew	358	I want the faith my God to please	382
In wisdom infinite thou art	371	I want thy laws engraved within	382
In words like these the dying saint	330	I want to pour a sea of tears	191
Infected by their stain	373	I would in Abraham's footsteps go	160
Inspired with godliness sincere	269	If fore-ordained to see the light	62
Instructed from above	225	If my threatening sins were gone	363
Into the depths they sunk as lead	178	*If of the truth a proof ye seek*	294
Is this the guilty nation, Lord	157	If on thy promised grace alone	78
It is the Lord, whose will is done	356	If once to swell the virgin's womb	50
It stands securely high	207	If pure essential love thou art	44
		If stubborn, insolent, and proud	173
		If subject to Another's will	264

Volume VII

		If the morning's wings gain	260
I and my house will serve the Lord	163	If those who know not God	167
I ask for them the life of faith	156	If thou dost our sorrows share	122
I ask not ecstacies	361	If thou gav'st th' enlarged desire	48
I by myself the heavens expand	281	If thou hast a token given	342
I cannot haughtily contemn	171	If thou hast in mercy caught me	382
I cannot, Lord, of him despair	156	If thou wilt thine own revoke	96
I come, at Jesus' call I come	360	If to heaven I take my flight	260
I come but tremble to draw near	382	Implant by thy grace A church in this house	28
I fear, lest in my trying hour	54	In a dreary vale of woe	323
I feel the fatal moment nigh	397	In a state of nature sleeping	33
I know and feel it cannot be	384	In an agony of doubt	416
I know it, Lord: with humble fear	400	In an earthly habitation	39
I long thy smiling face to see	378	In answer to ten thousand prayers	193
I must, I do restore	117	In answer to the chosen race	347
I must the fair example set	163	*In anxious agony of doubt*	370
I must this instant now begin	31	In assurance of hope	200
I now for their awakening stay	157	In both the Holy Spirit know	314
I now from all my sins would turn	396	In childhood's giddy hour	391
I now perceive thy love's design	321	In complicate Distress I wait	186
I own thy kind design on me	101	In each person we revere	288
I received it not of man	237	In every hour of near access	154
I see his beauty in the flower	179	In God my Saviour I confide	55
I see those outstretched arms of love	177	In hope of that thrice happy[347] day	421
I seek not my repose below	140		
I sing the new triumphant song	376		
I then shall lift mine eyes	380		

347. Osborn changed "thrice happy" to "most joyful."

In Jesus' name behold we meet!	42	I feel thy yearning bowels move	27
In Jesus's name Jehovah is found	208	I found thy hand, again beset	393
In majesty one, In glory the same	336	I from every evil way	223
In manifested love explain	194	I glory in thy power to save	19
In me create that seeing eye	378	I have the wicked seen	85
In mercy infinite	380	I have thy commandments took	225
In mercy mitigate her pain	65	I heard my gracious Father say	5
In my bitterest affliction	59	I in the pardoning God confide	120
In my pilgrimage below	151	I mourn my heart to ill inclined	382
In mystic unity	224	I must by faith behold thee here	365
In number as my days decrease	109	I must, unless thy yearning heart	377
In our desolate estate	21	I myself will save th' oppressed	23
In peace incomprehensible	12	I never yet have seen	83
In presence of thy heavenly host	71	I now beneath their fury groan	126
In soft compassion mind us	31	I once unfeignedly believed	405
In soul and body blessed	389	I only live to win	357
In that day, Jehovah saith	241	I publish the divine decree	5
In the arms of faith and prayer	125	I said, when chastened by thy rod	94
In this thrice acceptable hour	12	I shall not die in sin, but live	206
In thy tabernacle keep	414	I shall then mine all to thee	121
In yon unbounded plain I see	180	*I shall yet record his praise;*	
Incapable of rest	145	*/ I shall thank*	96
Indulged with an obscure retreat	140	I shall yet record his praise,	
Indulged with this, I ask no more	401	/ See again the	97
Infallibly assured	330	I sing the goodness of the Lord	24
Inferiors as a sacred trust	161	*I sought the Lord in grief, in pain*	257
Inspirer of the sacred Book	259	I take the words prescribed to me[348]	432
Instruct me, Saviour, when to yield	154	I, too, the poorest sinner I	93
Into nothing sink before thee	368	I trust in an almighty Lord	54
Invited and urged to draw nigh	27	I wait for God, my soul doth wait	246
Invited by him	175	*I wait to prove thine utmost grace*	160
Is here a soul that knows thee not	30	I will increase their gracious store	249
Is it then, most gracious Lord	416	"I will instruct thy child-like heart"	67
Israel the Father calls his son	283	I will not let thee go	357
Israel's Lord and God supreme	259	I will to my words take heed	88
It must be so: the day is near	348	I would, but want the power to give	375
Its virtue sanctifying	114	I, (yet O, not I, but he	400
		If all who will receive it, may	376
		If bards on those who greatly dare	478
## Volume VIII		If fully purposed to destroy	322
		If he seem awhile to chide	59
I, alas! was hastening on	188		
I cannot all thy love declare	91	348. Osborn rewrote as: "Again I take the words to me."	
I cannot pray aright	361		

If in my word thy children stay	249	*In trouble's abyss, To God the Most High*	350
If mercy hath excepted none	341	*In true and patient hope*	135
If mob is totally suppressed	473	In vain alas, thy patience spares	297
If now in me thy Spirit stirs	356	*In vain doth the assassin dark*	272
If now in us thy Spirit cry	289	In vain our haughty lords required	253
If still I in thy grace abide	405	In vain your labour ye repeat	243
If thou forgive my debt immense	427	*In vengeance, Lord, rebuke me not*	86
If thou hast work prepared for him	411	Innocent love! it doth no ill	378
If thou our instant suit approve	351	Instructed by thy heavenly grace	173
If thou shouldst as my Judge appear	258	Instrument of saving them	431
If thou the genuine gospel bless	431	Into thy fold this moment take	441
If thou wilt work a work of grace	399	Is this, great God, my single aim	404
If through thy strength I have run well	384	It must, alas! continue whole	360
If willing to save all thou art	378		
In age and feebleness extreme	432		
In all the feebleness of sin	86		

Volume IX

In answer to these choking questions	466		
In condescending love	61	I am healed, I am healed	287
In death's uncomfortable shade	246	I ask my soul, What dost thou here	181
In each hellish insurrection	278	I bow me to my God's decree	10
In faith we ask a fresh reprieve	413	I call the world's Redeemer mine	254
In fetters confined Our body complains	350	I cannot, Lord, in judgment stand	210
In God I trust, the good, the true	126	I cannot lose what is not mine	231
In him when brethren join	252	I continue the song	288
In his providential reign	69	I dare not my own soul deceive	289
In honour of the incarnate God[349]	377	I envied oft the swine their meat	22
In late despair of human aid	257	I find it now: most gracious God	11
In lieu of seers and partriarchs old	106	I found him—crucified for me	365
In love he doth his sons chastise	305	I frowned for a small moment's space	441
In mercy take these sins away	260	I had my former children lost	432
In paths of righteousness	83	I have oft victorious been	133
In praises with his people join	133	I hold him with a trembling hand	365
In the dreadful day of fight	256	I know it: by thy hands and feet	431
In the earthy furnace tried	23	I know myself the same	5
In the name of the Lord	405	I know not what my God hath willed	241
In the records of thy love	210	I know the power was thine	22
In thee, O Lord, I put my trust	159	I lay the city's base alone	442
In thee, O Lord, I trust	61	I live to render thee the praise	425
In thine utmost indignation	12	I long to behold him arrayed	404
In this last tremendous blow	329	I may abide it—I	334
In trouble on the Lord I cried	204	I nothing else require	406
		I now my Consolation see	330
		I now reflect with grief and shame	100
		I now thy grace implore	263

349. Osborn changed "the incarnate" to "a suppliant."

I now thy love's design perceive	97	Immortal King, with pity see	228
I only wait till thou impart	405	Impatient of a Father's rod	231
"I saw, and coveted, and took!"	123	Impatient of opposers, see	350
I see him sweat great drops of blood	9	In calm repose	302
I see th' exceeding broad command	330	In childhood's earliest hour	354
I shall, (when he who saith I shall	102	In Christ to our celestial home	417
I then regenerate from above	299	In desertion and grief	286
I thirst for a life-giving God	298	In early prayer who seek his love	347
I too have left my worldly home	146	In every sacred exercise	202
I too have sinned against the Lord	169	In every state, in every turn	344
I too the broad command have seen	330	In grace and faith increasing	409
I triumphed in the grace begun	285	In heavenly majesty and grace	29
I trust in Jesu's death alone	419	In his capital descending	390
I trust in thee: for what?	339	In loudest songs thy joy declare	439
I trust, the works which thou hast done	292	In Moses's song The Lamb we proclaim	46
I turn to the true House of God	176	In my prosperity I said	285
I vow, resolve, and promise, Lord	311	In presence of thy heavenly Lord	458
I wait a few sorrowful years	252	In pride and delicacy bred	159
I want that pure acquaintance	256	In small events we daily prove	145
I went out full of youthful hope	145	In tears who sowed, in joy we reap	381
I will call on his name	325	In that millennial church below	459
I will thine officers create	457	In this identic body I	255
I will with other children bless	432	In unbelief confined	338
I wish not that the Lord was gone	448	In unbelief imprisoned fast	313
I would attend thy leisure	283	In vain for him, my heart's desire	258
Idols may triumph for an hour	154	In vain to screen you from his eye	375
If a fond credulous fool thou art	355	In vain we offer sacrifice	219
If but one Christian soul appear	166	In vain, ye fearful, faithless spies	73
If cursed with his wish, he obtains	293	In vain your longest prayers ye say	371
If God to one of all our race	376	In want and murmuring distress	161
If I perish forgot	287	In weariness, confirmed repose	392
If in David's steps we tread	202	Inexpressibly great	285
If justice stern reject my prayer	279	Infinite in compassion	337
If mercies without end could move	157	Inspired with life and vigour new	304
If mine were right, it could not be	196	Instructed by his error, Lord	264
If nature mixed with grace he find	395	Intestine wars and fightings cease	127
If now thou dost thy people feed	397	Into my dungeon's gloom	338
If now thou dwellest in my heart	144	Is anything too hard for God?	73
If punished after my desert	40	Is God's peculiar people mine?	25
If rational good he desire	293	Is it a moral sense in man	21
If such thou wilt indeed receive	161	Is it a thing so small	111
If thou command it, Lord, we may	102	Is it not thy blessing, Lord	192
If thou my pardoning God appear	379	Is there then a power in man	461
If thou vouchsafe thy face to show	460	Is this the man to God so dear	168

"Israel before their foes are fled!"	154
Israel, exult to prove	117
It holds us, when by grace set free	119
It must, O Lord, proceed from thee	279

Volume X

I ask not aught whereof to boast	196
I ask not, Lord, when time shall end	366
I bow to God in Jesu's name	134
I cannot faithful be	408
I cannot speak a word, or do	264
I cannot wash my heart	11
I do believe thou canst, thou wilt	227
I feel the meaning of this pain	52
I feel the voice that cries "Repent"	145
I follow on to know	77
I have mine idols multiplied	7
I have need of a physician	223
I hear, the rod I hear	98
I here beneath thy feet confess	292
I know the Judge is always near	375
I leave a careless world below	162
I look for enmity and war	241
I now my patient pattern see[350]	405
I see thee now to sinners joined	428
I seek the kingdom first	190
I shall, when thou bestow'st the power	156
I take him for my Lord	421
I take thee at thy word	38
I think him David's Son	357
I think him perfect Love	357
I think him still the same	357
I think him the Most-High	357
I too have oft preferred	420
I trust thy promise, Lord, to break	100
I wait for thy appearing	129
I wait the word Divine	209
I want that unreflecting love	395
I want the weeping prophet's heart	18
I will mine indignation pour	105

350. Osborn changed "patient pattern" to "meek example."

I will, through grace I will	11
I worship whom the world despise	425
"I would, and ye would not"	365
I would our desolate Sion mourn	18
If Christ on me his grace bestows	241
If few that find the narrow way	202
If for a world a soul be lost	303
If God the slothful wretch reject	391
If grace doth more than sin abound	33
If I have with God found favour	405
If in him it richly dwells	277
If Jesus answers not a word	291
If my obduracy impede	195
If my own party I approve	368
If now I know the Crucified	300
If only with our lips we pray	287
If still my heart be unrenewed	172
If such the punishment of those	436
If, taught of him, I understand	173
If those who after me are come	334
If thou dost thy gospel bless	32
If thou hast willed me to return	7
If thou my stubbornness convert	39
If thou the power of asking give	194
If thou the power of faith impart	171
If thou thy healing power exert	28
If thy time be fully come	82
If to thy hand of power I stoop	360
If wilful sin hath blinded me	193
If with my all I cannot part	187
Immensely great the debt of man	318
Impatient of control he flies	482
Impossible it is with man	327
In a world of evil tossed	480
In bliss assured and pardon sealed	235
In every age, the Saviour's grace	307
In every fiery hour	179
In flattery nursed, the lawless great	495
In honour of the Infant-God	144
In hope of perfect liberty	119
In justice to a sinful race	366
In patience we our souls possess	92
In Peter's faith and fall I see	302
In pitying tenderness of love	337

In proof, thou wilt not cease to love	43	I long to feel thy sway	296
In riotous excess	496	I must in Abraham's footsteps stay	429
In sin's and Satan's onsets	75	I now thy call obey	38
In tenderest pity to thine own	132	I own, alas, my desperate case!	29
In the dark abodes of death	218	I read, but cannot comprehend	487
In the discriminating day	133	I reckon on thy Spirit's power	232
In the feebleness of nature	184	I rise obedient to thy word	146
In the houses of the great	451	*I seek to touch my powerful Lord*	SH 1762, 2:214
In thy Father's presence own us	276	I set me on the watchman's tower	67
In thy sinless people show	57	I stand in thy sight my evils to own	264
In vain doth earthly bliss afford	95	I the greatest debtor am	166
In vain for Christ the tempter spread	151	I the miracles have seen	376
In vain for redemption I look	26	I too have done the same	292
In vain in their own lying words	230	I use the power by thee bestowed	321
In vain the promise of our Lord	153	I wait till thou my Lord repeat	480
In vain the Truth himself hath sworn	327	I want the faith which reasons not	409
In vain with angry hearts we dare	168	I want the true divinity	43
In vain with guilty, slavish fear	416	I who so oft have seen	142
In wondrous condescension	129	I will give you drink, and feed[352]	228
Indulge me in this one request	198	I will, I do arise	236
Innocence will not descend	411	I would be less and less	349
Insatiate still for more	362	I would believe that thou art he	423
Inspire me, Saviour, with that power	156	I would my sight receive	38
Inspired at God's command	61	I yield, I joyfully agree	30
Instructed thus, from man we cease	310	If all who holy things profane	337
Instruments of our salvation	93	If bathed in thine atoning blood	502
Intentions, hearts to God are known	192	If charged the holy Jesus be	295
Is there a sinner here	328	If God doth for a time defer	77
Is there a soul thou dost not call	36	If God justifies, Let all men condemn	265
Israel's, Judah's tribes command	63	If guilty why to be set free?	298
It cannot heal your pride to praise	15	If Jesus' saying we receive	156
It cannot heal your sloth, to say	14	If left alone with thee I am	417
It never was heard, It never was seen	229	If man forbid, and thou enjoin	367
		If ministers thy grace ordain	480

Volume XI

		If now thy previous grace I feel	423
I ask no more, how can it be?	340	If still thou dost with sinners eat	71
I ask the gift of righteousness	44	If the chief of saints confess	127
I cannot doubt the power Divine[351]	372	If the Son of God forbear	434
I do believe thy blood was spilt	25	If thou the fishers guide	142
I have but done my duty, Lord	251	If thou the grace of faith bestow	457
I know, most gracious Saviour	438	If thou vouchsafe to show	96

351. UP 2:237.

352. UP 2:150.

First Line	Page
If we in thy grace have tasted	11
Ignorance in which ye dwell	453
Imperfectly we have	284
In all the paths of righteousness	456
In every child of misery	196
In figures, types, and promises	434
In hell he pours a fruitless prayer	245
In momentary majesty	183
In our feeble nature clad	78
In ourselves the hindrance lies	375
In outward things alone[353]	150
In pain and darkness groaning	199
In pity to my cries	38
In pure obedience to thy will	293
In that perpetual summer, we	279
In the church whoe'er aspire	285
In the first infant church we view	169
In thee my Saviour I confide	47
In thee, O Lord, is all my trust	272
In them th' immortal seed remains	490
In this barren wilderness	11
In thy mysterious peace	260
In trouble I dare not complain	491
In unambiguous words and few	324
In us who Christ our God adore	486
In vain the self-deceiver stays	247
In vain they would decline	301
In works, in deeds thou dost declare	424
Incomprehensible to man	501
Inseparably one with thee	497
Insolent lie against the Lord!	132
Inspired with faith we come and see	328
Inspired with goodness from above	455
Instructed by his fall, I stand	75
Instructed by thy tenderest love	424
Insults in the improper hour	88
Into the hands of sinful men	78
Into the heathen judge's power	83
Invaders of the ministry	457
Is it not the Shepherd's voice	212
Is there a saint who doth not need	68
Is there benevolence in hell?	246
Is this the man who answered, "Lord	82
Israel spiritual renewed	332
Israelites indeed they stand	282
It is mine own infirmity!	347

353. *UP* 2:95.

Volume XII

First Line	Page
I ask not how or when	375
I do believe the record true	89
I every moment hope	159
I followed my immortal Guide	267
I for no favour sue	418
I have no right to ask thy love	41
I have nothing to do	128
I have other gods adored	214
I in this emblem see	158
I long with thee to bow my head	99
I the miracle admire	210
I turn from the creature away	104
I wait the powerful look	258
I will abide in thee, my Lord	19
I would not, Lord, thy Spirit bind	137
If all were left upon record	132
If but one faithless soul be here	110
If Christ his servant bless	253
If Christ to try our faith ordain	434
If first to Christ by night	91
If God the Holy Ghost impart	301
If God to man a promise make	202
If grafted into thee, the Vine	18
If hardened ye remain	283
If men the Sovereign Priest arraign	71
If now ye hear in vain	376
If one concise epistle read	308
If parting from a shepherd good	380
If then ye have the Spirit known	252
If thou call even us t' inherit	217
If thou ordain the minister	108
If to this selfsame thing, O Lord	136
If two agree in their request	269
Immortal Son of Man, appear	164
Imperfectly they knew	5
Impossible for man to read	132

Impotent attempt and vain	360	Is there such dire malignity	32
Impotent their rage and vain	399	Israel he from Egypt led	165
In a dark world I wander on	437	It cannot be a house of woe	324
In Abraham our God we find	203	It is the voice of my Beloved	104
In Abraham's sepulcher they rest	205	It visits as unsought	234
In all places and times	135	It was not possible	149
In[354] all their griefs, and sorrows shares	90		
In answer to our cry	366		
In Christ the holy One	19		

Volume XIII

In every time and place	201	I cannot doubt thy love for me	208
In his Spirit alone	46	I cannot rise, before I sink	165
In hunger, weariness, and pain	319	I come by thy meek Spirit led	92
In many a soul, and mine	157	I come to buy that richest dress	230
In order foremost of the Three	50	I do consider thee	155
In many a soul, and mine	157	I do with all my soul believe	193
In our degenerate years revive	153	I feel a strong immortal hope	91
In our redeeming Lord	364	I feel throughout my evil day	255
In ours, in every age are seen	408	I from this instant now repent	4
In outward things, with faith endued	435	I hear thy feeble children cry	11
In pagan times it might be so	30	I know in whom I have believed	105
In peace Divine unspeakable	49	I long to love my bleeding Lord	44
In presence of the Pagan crowd	442	I now come out from all their ways	52
In sad judicial blindness left	454	I seem desirous to repent	78
In Satan's cause they all combine	286	"I the good fight have fought"	110
In sin I long have dwelt	202	I thus the pious Jew offend	34
In solemn doubts of import great	141	I too, forewarned by Jesu's love	191
In suffering saints when Jesus cries	319	I too have done the same	151
In the council of the sky	433	I trust in thee alone	83
In the lonely desert place	210	I urge the race begun	159
In thee we then are creatures new	15	I want that better than the best	36
In this degenerate age	220	I want that wisdom from above	173
In this Divine epitome	147	I want the faith in Jesu's blood	203
In thy heavenly Father one	57	I want the witness, Lord	150
In thy state of exaltation	191	I would be of thy Spirit born	203
In vain of temperance he heard	415	I would be pure, complete, entire	165
In works of charity who hide	182	I would, more sensibly distressed	78
In worse than childish play	339	I would the precious time redeem	75
Inquisitive to know	339	I yield to be by thee prepared	238
Insatiate, filled with mad despite	222	If after God thou hear'st me pray	60
Inspired and actuated by love	184	If anger, vanity, desire	15
Inspiring me with faith Divine	63	If bold, the highest place I claim	34
Intreated as a criminal	450	If called his office to extol	37
		If children may the Scripture know	108

354. Oborn changed "In" to "he."

If death my friend and me divide	91
If faith in our dear dying Lord	109
If God enlighten through his word	124
If I ever felt thy drawing	271
If Jesus doth reign, And saves us from sin	30
If mercy let me go	149
If now we freely pardoned are	34
If others the commandments slight	75
If still I in the truth abide	214
If still, when justified by grace	195
If tempted in death, and forsook	105
If thou direct my paths aright	256
If thou gavest the piercing fear	271
If thou in us reside	43
If thou my bonds hast broke	64
If thou my constant Saviour art	94
If thou require my soul this night	193
If two or three in thy great name	282
If we, believing our own hearts	194
Impious, mischievous, unclean	137
In all our intercourse below	263
In all the works of faith	159
In each distressing hour	57
In each event	81
In hope of the salvation	107
In iron bondage bound	8
In Jesu's name and Spirit I	130
In pity give	161
In pity to thy children, blast	212
In proof that she indeed believed	220
In sorrow, as in grace, we grow	157
In spirit one	82
In thy members here beneath	220
In us the full obedience true	11
In vain for a reprieve he cries	67
In vain thou say'st in words alone	168
Indeed thou hast thy servant heard	50
Inscribing with the city's name	228
Inspirer of the ancient seers	109
Instructed after him we go	134
Is it, great God, to honour thee	54
Is it of nature or of grace	60
Is it thy will concerning me?	93
Is that cursed root in me	103
Is there a frailty of the saints	53
It cannot be thy will	202
It hath for me sufficient been	56
It is the Lord, who doth not grieve	230
It nought avails me to exclaim	251
Its energy exert	22
Its weakness inconceivable	58

Volume I

Jerusalem in ruins lies	369
Jesu, accept our sacrifice	216
Jesu, attend! thyself reveal!	341
Jesu, be endless praise to thee[355]	349
Jesu, behold, the wise from far[356]	116
Jesu, hear, and bow the skies	366
Jesu, if still the same thou art	258
Jesu, if still thou art to-day	262
Jesu, Lover of my soul	259
Jesu! my heart's desire obtain	88
Jesu, my God and King	152
Jesu, my great High-Priest above	87
Jesu! my Life, thyself apply	284
Jesu, mighty to redeem	292
Jesu! Redeemer, Saviour, Lord	270
Jesu, see my panting breast![357]	281
Jesu, the heavens bow	338
Jesu, the pure, the spotless Lamb[358]	116
Jesu, the Sinner's Friend, to thee	83
Jesu, the Strength of all that faint	255
Jesu! the weary wanderer's rest	128
Jesu, thine aid afford	266
Jesu! thou art my King	99
Jesu, thou art my Righteousness	283
Jesu, thou art our King	154
Jesu, thy all-victorious love	328

355. From the German of Nikolaus von Zinzendorf, translated by John Wesley.
356. George Hickes.
357. From the German of Anna Dober, translated by John Wesley.
358. George Hickes.

Jesu, thy blood and righteousness[359]	346	Jesus to my deliverance flew	75
Jesu, thy boundless love to me[360]	138	Join, earth and heaven, to bless	151
Jesu, thy light again I view[361]	159	Joseph by faith the flight foretold	216
Jesu! to thee I bow; / Th' Almighty's	148	Joy of my eyes the creature was	245
Jesu! to thee I bow, / Saved to the utmost	152	*Joy of my soul, when thou art gone*[369]	46
Jesu, to thee my heart I bow[362]	109	Joyful, all ye nations, rise	183
Jesu, to thee my soul aspires	134	Just through him, behold thy way	330
Jesu, vouchsafe my heart and will[363]	85	Justice and truth maintain	153

Volume II

Jesu, we the promise claim	351
Jesu, when this light we see[364]	281
Jesu, who by thine own love slain[365]	116
Jesu, who on the fatal wood[366]	116
Jesu, who to thy heaven again[367]	117
Jesu, whose glory's streaming rays[368]	89
Jesus! Answer from above	273
Jesus, come, my sickness cure	223
Jesus greater we proclaim	297
Jesus, if half-discerning now	24
Jesus, in whom the Godhead's rays	260
Jesus, in whom the weary find	249
Jesus, of all my hopes the ground	282
Jesus protects; my fears, be gone!	306
Jesus speaks, and pleads his blood	272
Jesus, the all-atoning Lamb	226
Jesus, the all-restoring Word	225
Jesus, the Lamb of God, hath bled	277
Jesus, the name that charms our fears	300

Jah, Jehovah is my Lord	251
Jehovah is unchangeable	56
Jesu, all his depths discover	31
Jesu, all power is given to thee	136
Jesu, all to thee is given	30
Jesu, claim thy ransomed creature	31
Jesu, come, and bind him, bind him	30
Jesu, for this we calmly wait	333
Jesu, for thy love I languish	96
Jesu, Friend of sinners, hear	119
Jesu, fulfil the Gospel word	248
Jesu, gentle, loving Lamb	97
Jesu, God of our salvation	29
Jesu, Great Redeemer, hear	75
Jesu, hear a sinner's prayer	95
Jesu, hear thy Spirit's call	257
Jesu, help, thou serpent-bruiser	29
Jesu, I come my doom to meet	66
Jesu, I fain would walk in thee	272
Jesu, I hang upon thy word	243
Jesu, I in thee believe	241
Jesu, if thou hast died	118
Jesu, is it past thy finding?	31
Jesu, let my nature feel	277
Jesu, let this soul find favour	30
Jesu, lo! I come to thee	298
Jesu, Lord, for this we wait	220
Jesu, manifest thy glory	29
Jesu, mighty to deliver	30
Jesu, mighty to renew	89
Jesu, my hiding-place, to thee	81

359. From the German of Nikolaus von Zinzendorf, translated by John Wesley.
360. From the German of Paul Gerhardt, translated by John Wesley.
361. From the German of Joachim Lange, translated by John Wesley.
362. From the German of Nikolaus von Zinzendorf, translated by John Wesley.
363. From the German of Christian Friedrich Richter, translated by John Wesley.
364. From the German of Anna Dober, translated by John Wesley.
365. George Hickes.
366. George Hickes.
367. George Hickes.
368. From the German of Wolfgang Dessler, translated by John Wesley.

369. George Herbert.

Jesu, my King, to thee I bow	312	Jesus, my strength, my Life, my Rest	203
Jesu, my life, appear within	271	Jesus shall his great arm reveal	334
Jesu, my Lord, mighty to save	142	Jesus, the great tremendous God	325
Jesu, my Saviour, Brother, Friend, / On whom	271	Jesus their toil delighted sees[371]	63
Jesu, my Saviour, Brother, Friend, / As I	273	Join we then with one accord	189
Jesu, my soul takes hold on thee	313	Joined in one Spirit to our head	221
Jesu, my strength, my hope	208	Joyful in hope, my spirit soars	244
Jesu, my trust is in thy Word	308		
Jesu, Redeemer of mankind	303		

Volume III

Jesu, see thine helpless creature	29	Jehovah shall lay to his hand	144
Jesu, shall he still devour?	30	Jesu, a soul receive	329
Jesu, shall I never be	276	*Jesu, at whose supreme command*	237
Jesu, Sin-atoning Lamb	146	Jesu, attend my cry	265
Jesu, take my sins away	153	*Jesu, dear, redeeming Lord*	240
Jesu, than the strong man stronger	30	Jesu, descend again With all	371
Jesu, the Life, the Truth, the Way	327	*Jesu, did they crucify*	332
Jesu, the Saviour of mankind	217	Jesu, hear! In bitterness	12
Jesu, the Truth, the Way	327	Jesu, let thy sufferings ease me	278
Jesu, thou for me hast died	319	*Jesu, my Hope, my help, my Power*	59
Jesu, thou hast bid us pray	255	*Jesu, my Lord and God, bestow*	263
Jesu, thou know'st my simpleness	128	*Jesu, my strength and hope*	329
Jesu, thy soul renew my own[370]	15	*Jesu, on thee we feed*	297
Jesu, thy wandering sheep behold!	343	*Jesu, our pardon we receive*	242
Jesu, to thee I now can fly	202	*Jesu, regard the plaintive cry*	271
Jesu, to whose supreme command	332	*Jesu, the blood apply*	268
Jesu, united by thy grace	158	*Jesu, the hindrance show*	89
Jesu, unto thee my sin	201	*Jesu, sinner's Friend, receive us*	274
Jesu, what hast thou bestowed	260	*Jesu, Son of God, draw near*	264
Jesu, wherefore dost thou	30	*Jesu, suffering Deity*	223
Jesu, wherewith shall I draw near	108	Jesu, thine own at last receive	335
Jesu, wound the dragon, wound him	29	*Jesu, thine own with pity see*	295
Jesu's love than sin is stronger	96	*Jesu, thy weakest servants bless*	249
Jesu's name the conquest won us	32	*Jesu, thy word is past! the grace*	69
Jesus, and him crucified	223	Jesu, to thee for help I fly	60
Jesus can to the utmost save	248	*Jesu, to thee for help we call*	239
Jesus, faithful to his word	187	*Jesu, to thee in faith we look*	328
Jesus, full of truth and grace	93	*Jesu, we follow thee*	313
Jesus hath died that I might live	140	*Jesu, we know that thou hast died*	317
Jesus I serve, to him alone	248	*Jesu, we thus obey*	273
Jesus is our common Lord	218	*Jesu, we thy promise plead*	359

370. From the German of Johann Angelus Scheffler, translated by John Wesley.

371. From the German of August Gottlieb Spangenberg, translated by John Wesley.

Jesu, we will not let thee go	281	Jesu, save me through thy name	463
Jesus again their life shall be	154	Jesu, seek thy wandering sheep	357
Jesus alone can I require[372]	170	Jesu, Shepherd of the sheep	449
Jesus appears to sacrifice	249	Jesu, show us thy salvation	138
Jesus drinks the bitter cup	230	Jesu, sin-atoning Lamb	8
Jesus, forgive the wrong	83	Jesu, the promised strength supply	330
Jesus, harmonious name!	72	Jesu, this eagerness of praise	376
Jesus hath said, we all shall hope	3	Jesu, thy chosen servant guard	25
Jesus hath spoke the word	277	Jesu, thy weak disciples see	36
Jesus, life-inspiring Saviour	364	Jesu, thy word for ever lives	378
Jesus, Lord, his soul receive	172	Jesu, we hang upon the word	172
Jesus, Master of the feast	276	Jesus, accept the praise	271
Jesus, my Jesus, hear	44	Jesus all the day long	409
Jesus, our outward wants relieve	360	Jesus, answer all thy name	359
Jesus terminates our hope	288	Jesus—but O! at last	398
Jesus, the Woman's Seed	102	Jesus, by faith I place me	85
Jesus, to whom all power is given	155	Jesus, full of truth and love	220
Jesus, to whom alone we live	357	*Jesus, God of my salvation*	466
Jesus, transporting sound!	72	*Jesus, God of peace and love*	194
Joined to the Lord her Righteousness	176	Jesus hath spoke the faithful word	170
Just it is, and good, and right	321	*Jesus, I behold thee now*[373]	449
		Jesus is glorified	168

Volume IV

		Jesus, let thy pitying eye	405
		Jesus, Lord, in pity hear us	167
Jacob, receive the word Divine	295	Jesus, Master, dying Lord	388
Jehovah is come down to raise	125	Jesus, mighty mediator	8
Jehovah, Jesus, Lord	154	Jesus my garments hath put on	311
Jesu, as taught by thee, I pray	248	*Jesus, my Lord, attend*	207
Jesu, convert and stir us up	101	*Jesus, my strength and righteousness*	232
Jesu, dear departed Lord	193	Jesus, on thy only name	390
Jesu, go not far from me	464	*Jesus, our exalted head*	181
Jesu help! thou sinner's Friend	462	*Jesus, our help in time of need*	30
Jesu, I believe thee near	416	Jesus, Redeemer of mankind	28
Jesu, I call thee by the name	360	Jesus, see thy fallen creature	353
Jesu, I cry for help to thee	216	Jesus shall impute his merit	209
Jesu, in honour of thy name	362	Jesus shall make us free indeed	293
Jesu, in thy gracious power	34	Jesus shall pitch his tent in me	469
Jesu, in us thyself reveal	457	Jesus shall soon descend	267
Jesu, on me bestow	427	*Jesus, take all the glory!*	258
Jesu, roll away the stone	59	Jesus, the forfeiture restore	393
		Jesus, the glory take!	41

372. Free paraphrase of the German of Christian Friedrich Richter by Charles Wesley.

373. *UP* 3:202, with different wording of the first line: "Jesu, I believe thee now."

Jesus, the heaven of heaven he is	245	Jesu, Lord, when shall it be?	183
Jesus, the holy child	115	Jesu, Lover of mankind	407
Jesus the merciful and just	188	Jesu, my all in all thou art	50
Jesus, the rising Lord of all	134	*Jesu, my good and faithful Lord*	306
Jesus the Saviour reigns	140	*Jesu, my Hope in life and death*	73
Jesus, thou all-redeeming Lord	380	*Jesu, my Hope, my Joy, my Rest*	294
Jesus, thou lovely bleeding Lamb	265	*Jesu, my Truth, my Way*	22
Jesus, thy far-extended fame	374	*Jesu, our Life, in us appear*	336
Jesus, thy righteous cause maintain	30	Jesu, regard the joint complaint	176
Jesus, thy word we dare believe!	173	Jesu, seek thy wandering sheep	294
Jesus, thy word we own	268	*Jesu, soft harmonious Name*	475
Jesus, to thee we fly		Jesu, take all the praise	459
/ From the devouring	13	*Jesu, the growing work is thine*	250
Jesus, to thee we fly, / On thee for help	161	*Jesu, thou all-redeeming Lord*	121
Jesus to you his fulness brings	275	*Jesu, thou only hast the key*	125
Jesus, visit us again	194	*Jesu, thou sovereign Lord of all*	174
Jesus, we long to know thy name	158	*Jesu, thou strength of all that turn*	311
Jesus, we on the words depend	179	*Jesu, thy legacy I take*	152
Jesus, we trust in thee alone	79	*Jesu, thy record I receive*	143
Join all who know the Name	99	*Jesu, to thee alone*	128
Join, all ye joyful nations	110	*Jesu, to thee our hearts we lift*	465
Judgment for those who slight		Jesu, we in thy name believe	324
Thy grace	289	*Jesu, we look to thee*	467
Judgment to execute is thine	100	*Jesu, whither shall I go*	11
Justly we all thine anger bear	5	Jesu, with us thou always art	389
		Jesu's praise is all our song	476

Volume V

		Jesu's tremendous name	273
Jealous for thy own great name	101	*Jesus, bestow the power*	269
Jesu, accept the grateful song	110	*Jesus comes with all his grace*	332
Jesu, approach, and touch his hand	75	Jesus, crown thine own desire	441
Jesu, at thy command	235	Jesus doth his spirit bear	293
Jesu, by highest heavens adored	18	Jesus for me the winepress trod	376
Jesu, call to mind thy word	241	Jesus for us our God raised up	298
Jesu, cast a pitying eye	305	Jesus, Friend of human kind	408
Jesu, come, my Hope of glory	297	*Jesus from whom all blessings flow*	481
Jesu, full of grace for me	172	Jesus from pride, from wrath, from lust	325
Jesu, great healer of mankind	79	*Jesus from sin shall save his own*	4
Jesu, great Shepherd of the sheep	33	*Jesus, fulfil his heart's desire*	416
Jesu, help thy fallen creature!	210	*Jesus, God of our salvation*	275
Jesu, in this hour be near	382	*Jesus, guard thy gathered sheep*	276
Jesu, I bless thy gracious power	2	Jesus hath died for you!	42
Jesu, Lord, we look to thee	52	Jesus hath undertook my cause	292
		Jesus, head, and Lord of all	282
		Jesus, hear our midnight cry	277

Jesus, if from thee I find	438
Jesus, in thine all-saving name	322
Jesus, in thy saving name	380
Jesus, Lord, whose only merit	440
Jesus, my constant Jesus stand	296
Jesus, my hope of glory	218
Jesus, my Master, and my Lord	268
Jesus, my strength, my peace	356
Jesus of Nazareth, look down	253
Jesus, our exalted Jesus	448
Jesus, pronounce the softening word	98
Jesus the Conqueror reigns	36
Jesus the Name, high over all	111
Jesus, the Name to sinners	111
Jesus the prisoner's fetters breaks	111
Jesus the soul of music is	398
Jesus, the Truth, and Power Divine	107
Jesus, thee alone I know	185
Jesus, thou soul of all our joys	399
Jesus, thy sovereign name I bless	69
Jesus to thee we bow	467
Jesus, to thee we look	330
Jesus, to thy preserving care	433
Jesus, to whom I fly	342
Jesus, was ever grief	14
Jesus, was ever love like thine	66
Jesus, why dost thou delay	161
Jesus, with kindest pity see	418
Jesus with us assembled is	472
Join all in earth, and all in heaven	35
Join all ye ransomed sons of grace	280
Join every soul that looks to thee	481
Joined to me my Maker is	343
Joy of mine eyes, and more beloved	194
Joyful again we hear	129

Volume VI

Jesu, save us from our sins	40
Jesu, thy waiting servants see	104
Jesus, all-redeeming Lord	398
Jesus, be now my friend with God	459
Jesus beneath the fig-tree saw	358

Jesus cheered the sinner here	364
Jesus, come! our utmost Jesus	208
Jesus hath saved our souls from death	164
Jesus, help! to thee we pray	424
Jesus, her ruinous walls rebuild	114
Jesus his own disciples chid	452
Jesus, Jehovah, Lord	150
Jesus let his whole church adore	140
Jesus, Lord, to whom we cry	21
Jesus, Lord, we cry to thee	404
Jesus, now assume thy power	279
Jesus, our great High-priest	12
Jesus our sure support thou art	255
Jesus, our true Elisha, Lord	132
Jesus, Son of David, hear	449
Jesus, take all the praise	245
Jesus, the Lord and God most high	458
Jesus the Lord our Shepherd is	446
Jesus, this be all my boast	444
Jesus, thy ministers inspire	314
Jesus, thy speaking blood	15
Jesus, vouchsafe a pitying ray	433
Jesus, we cast ourselves on thee	422
Jesus will not despise	400
Join all, whom God in Jesus spares	159
Joined to the hidden church unknown	72
Jointly praying, and apart	377
Just[374] ready to depart in peace	304

Volume VII

Jehovah by himself hath sworn	239
Jehovah come! thyself reveal	326
Jehovah entire In each we confess	317
Jehovah, ere the world begun	309
Jehovah, God and Lord	258
Jehovah, God the Father, bless	276
Jehovah, God the Son, reveal	276
Jehovah, God the Spirit, shine	276
Jehovah in three persons, come	310
Jehovah in thy person show	195
Jehovah is but One	275

374. Osborn changed "Just" to "Yet."

Jehovah is he Substantially love	319	Jesus, the fame Of thy great name	186
Jehovah receive The loftiest praise	208	Jesus, the just, the good	361
Jehovah the almighty Lord	274	Jesus, the Lord most high	166
Jehovah the Lord In him we confide	208	Jesus the Lord, thy nature pure	238
Jehovah, the true God most high	208	Jesus, the mightier works of grace	228
Jehovah's Spirit of purest love	256	*Jesus, the true Jehovah, hear!*	221
Jesu, thou hast to hoary hairs	358	Jesus, the true Jehovah, Lord	209
Jesus as God we magnify	223	Jesus the Truth, the Life, the Way	325
Jesus beheld my last distress	95	*Jesus, the truth we own*	216
Jesus blends them with his own	86	*Jesus, the virtue of thy name*	23
Jesus, by our prayers invited	39	*Jesus, the woman's conquering seed*	141
Jesus, call to mind thy word	221	Jesus, thou all-atoning Lamb	192
Jesus Christ, the good, the just	214	*Jesus, thou art the mighty God*	219
Jesus, come! (the mortal sentence	383	Jesus, thou precious Corner-stone	18
Jesus, display thy presence here	19	*Jesus, thou Son of Mary*	59
Jesus, evermore the same	97	Jesus, thou Son of the Most High	234
Jesus, (for whose only sake	87	*Jesus, thy blessed self impart*	401
Jesus, fulfil our one desire	45	*Jesus, thy precious passion*	330
Jesus, full of pity, see	20	*Jesus, to thee distressed I cry*	351
Jesus hath bought us with his blood	235	Jesus, to us impart	13
Jesus, help! no longer tarry	63	*Jesus, to whose omniscient mind*	377
Jesus, I at thy throne appear	156	*Jesus, we ask thy promised aid*	65
Jesus, I will not let thee go	172	*Jesus, we look to thee*	29
Jesus, Jehovah, God	239	Jesus, who bought us with his blood	236
Jesus, Jehovah, hear	220	Jesus, with loving fear	168
Jesus, Jehovah's Power	335	Joy of our eyes, our heart's desire	119
Jesus, Lord, we cry to thee	128	Joyous hope our sorrows cheering	42
Jesus, my faithful Guide	137	*Justly thou mightst in helpless age*	394
Jesus, my hope, my rest	139		
Jesus, my hope of heavenly rest	410	## Volume VIII	
Jesus, my Life in death, appear!	395		
Jesus, my Lord, my God	212	Jehovah from his throne surveyed	25
Jesus, my Master in the sky	159	Jehovah lifts the fallen up	261
Jesus' name in Satan's hour	71	*Jehovah's law all-perfect is*	37
Jesus, omnipotent to save	147	*Jehovah reigns on high*	177
Jesus, on me thy mercy show	226	*Jehovah's voice the cedar rends*	58
Jesus our Refuge in distress	124	Jerusalem, dear hallowed name	253
Jesus our Righteousness	220	*Jesu, dear redeeming Lamb*	427
Jesus, our tendered souls prepare	44	*Jesu, if I have found favour*	77
Jesus' praises we proclaim	10	*Jesu, mighty to deliver*	158
Jesus, preserve, till thou our souls receive	441	*Jesu, take the sinner's part*	29
Jesus shall there our hearts secure	46	*Jesus, from whom dominion springs*	290
Jesus, Son of Mary, hear	142	*Jesus, full of truth and grace*	70
Jesus, Son of the Most High	235		

Jesus, God o'er all supreme	401
Jesus his Redeemer dies	16
Jesus, (if I may once more	373
Jesus, into thy hands we fall	345
Jesus is gone up on high	110
Jesus is lifted up on high	207
Jesus is my defence	136
Jesus let all mankind adore	154
Jesus loves and guards his own	46
Jesus, mighty to deliver	203
Jesus, my Lord, my God	356
Jesus, my Lord, on thy great name	14
Jesus, my soul aspires	370
Jesus, our great High Priest	251
Jesus, our injured king incline	277
Jesus, our sanctuary thou art	265
Jesus, our true and faithful Lord	418
Jesus, regard a mother's sighs!	410
Jesus, supreme in majesty	295
Jesus the good Shepherd is	46
Jesus, the promise made by thee[375]	421
Jesus, thou all-redeeming Lord	345
Jesus, thy flaming eyes	332
Jesus, thy feeble servant see	412
Jesus, thy hated servant own	415
Jesus, thy name alone	271
Jesus, was ever love like thine!	352
Jesus, with complacence see	302
Join, all the friends of Jesus, join	396
Joined to all that fear the Lord	218
Joyful at thy word, as one	232
Joyful I fly this moment hence	374
Joyful in this blessed hope	135
Just and right are all thy ways	220
Justice, thy summons we obey	344
Justly by man condemned to die	341

Volume IX

Jacob then was free from blame	83
Jehovah for his servants cares	20
Jehovah from Jehovah pours	21

375. *UP* 3:286.

Jehovah's everlasting days	242
Jehovah-El, I thee adore	54
Jesu, thou seest my troubled breast	267
Jesu, thy work begin	299
Jesu's majesty we sing	389
Jesus, as taught by thee I plead	122
Jesus, bid our hearts be still	174
Jesus come, thy kingdom here	201
Jesus, command us to draw near	125
Jesus, confirm my heart's desire	59
Jesus, dear almighty Lord	428
Jesus, dear departing Lord	187
Jesus, for this we still attend	415
Jesus from our sins shall save us	275
Jesus, from thy holy place	403
Jesus, full of truth and grace, / Among	127
Jesus, full of truth and grace, / Show	312
Jesus, giver of contrition	200
Jesus, hail! thy grace appearing	451
Jesus hath fulfilled his word	430
Jesus, I believe thee near	445
Jesus, I cast my soul on thee	30
Jesus, I here abide	67
Jesus, I in thy promise trust	96
Jesus, I magnify thy grace	316
Jesus, if thou dost intend	273
Jesus, if thou thy power bestow	372
Jesus is a mouth to me	36
Jesus is vanished from thy sight	437
Jesus, let all thy lovers shine	133
Jesus, let the gospel-word	384
Jesus, Lord, to thee I look	38
Jesus, mighty to convert	81
Jesus, my balm for every ill	366
Jesus, my faith increase	390
Jesus my love, my life, my peace	364
Jesus, my Saviour and my Prince	293
Jesus, my soul to fill	200
Jesus, now on sin we tread	125
Jesus, now thine arm display	435
Jesus obtained us the reprieve	80
Jesus, omnipotent to save	314
Jesus, on me the grace bestow	322
Jesus, on me the power bestow	393

Jesus, on thee our souls are stayed	215	Jesus, we have long expected	402
Jesus shall still his people save	430	Jesus, we on thy word rely	402
Jesus, Son of God, thou art	107	Jesus, we wait to see	471
Jesus, taught by thee we know	99	Jesus, with pitying eye	282
Jesus that ladder is	27	Jesus, with thine o'ershadowing hand	220
Jesus, the Antitype thou art	161	Joshua from above, thy will	126
Jesus, the good thy saints desire	289	Just such a wretch am I	216
Jesus the Lord hath set us free	426	Justly, O Lord, thou dost require	212
Jesus, the man's defender be	340	Justly thou hast my soul forsook	327
Jesus, the merciful and true	80		
Jesus, the power belongs to thee, / And thee	333		

Volume X

Jesus, the power belongs to thee, / Set my	342	Jehovah from Jehovah sent	157
		Jehovah to his temple came	128
Jesus, the sinner's hiding place	290	Jehovah's eyes, With thee they are	116
Jesus, the wonders of thy name	436	Jesus, all-redeeming Lamb	81
Jesus, the word of mercy give	209	Jesus, almighty to convert	415
Jesus thine Anointed One	209	Jesus, Angel of the Lord	113
Jesus, thine efficacious word	132	Jesus answered not a word	419
Jesus, thou art a tree	5	Jesus, as in the ancient days	91
Jesus, thou art my Lord, my God	340	*Jesus, at thy command I go* SH 1762, 2:202	
Jesus, thou art the Power	294	Jesus, beneath the sense I groan	292
Jesus, thou dost not sue in vain	101	Jesus, bid the chains be broke	56
Jesus, thou hast spoke the word	387	Jesus' blackened follower may	468
Jesus, thou hast the faith bestowed	337	Jesus, by faith approaching thee	224
Jesus, thou hear'st thine Israel groan	34	Jesus, by thine almighty hands	115
Jesus, thou that Noah art!	13	Jesus, come, the world's Desire	110
Jesus, throughout my threescore years	32	Jesus competitors disdains	242
Jesus, thy coming we confess	85	Jesus, directed by thy word	196
Jesus, thy loving Spirit alone	340	Jesus, display thy sovereign skill	294
Jesus, thy name is my strong tower	351	Jesus, evermore the same	222
Jesus, thy name my Bezer stands	129	Jesus, extend thine hand of grace	306
Jesus, thy perfect love reveal	130	Jesus, fix thy kingdom here!	66
Jesus, thy power I dare confess	238	Jesus from, not in, our sins	141
Jesus, thy precious love I need	360	Jesus, I come to thee	207
Jesus, thy salvation bring	189	Jesus I faithfully receive	443
Jesus, thy sovereign will	124	Jesus I own my heart	187
Jesus, thyself impart	116	*Jesus, I to thy temple go* SH 1762, 2:151	
Jesus, to me the grace impart	437	Jesus, I wait the Spirit's power	490
Jesus, to my heart explain	376	Jesus, if mine thou art	49
Jesus, to thee	301	Jesus, if our faith be true	353
Jesus, to thy wounds I fly	373	Jesus, if thou thy servant guard	174
Jesus, we claim thee for our own	147	Jesus, if we aright confess	281
Jesus, we dare believe on thee	51		

Jesus in earth and heaven the same	322	Jesus, thy Spirit drags him thence	482
Jesus in every age the same	231	Jesus, thy Spirit's power exert	201
Jesus let all his saints revere	412	Jesus, thy wisdom give	367
Jesus, Lord, assume thy right	97	Jesus, to thee I cry	260
Jesus, Lord, our hearts inspire	31	Jesus truly doth forgive	259
Jesus, my desperate helplessness	403	Jesus, turn the chaff to wheat	147
Jesus, my vehement spirit pants	107	Jesus, united by thy fear	132
Jesus, on me the want bestow	162	Jesus, was ever love like thine!	431
Jesus on the celestial hill	112	Jesus, what grace dost thou bestow	121
Jesus on us in this our day	245	Jesus when by faith we see	440
Jesus prepare thy meanest guest	352	Jesus, who disdain'st a part	78
Jesus, rebuke my fiery zeal	191	Jesus, who is a God like thee!	99
Jesus shall I always be	501	Jesus, who now art passing by	337
Jesus, the church is our strong-hold	97	Jesus with eyes of faith I see	424
Jesus, the church redeemed by thee	283	Jointly, Lord, we come to thee	37
Jesus, the crowning grace impart	163	Joy unmixed I would not know	438
Jesus the formal teachers leaves	288	Joyful news I would proclaim	394
Jesus, the grace re-give	258	Judah and Israel's house incline	9
Jesus, the infinite I AM	252	Judah now, the land of praise	31
Jesus the King of earth and heaven	385	Justice Divine with sharpest sword	120
Jesus the Lord again we sing	74	Justice severe demands the whole	318
Jesus, the mortal Son of Man	455	Justly may'st thou give me up	25
Jesus, the needy sinner's Friend	282		
Jesus, the soul's and body's ills	214		
Jesus, the true, immortal Vine	401		

Volume XI

Jesus, the truth of simple love	343	Jehovah by himself hath sworn	113
Jesus, the word, by which alone	151	Jehovah doth himself conceal	110
Jesus, the Word, the Life, the Way	360	Jehovah in our form appears	501
Jesus, thee in faith we claim	86	Jehovah to Jehovah	57
Jesus, thee thy works proclaim	160	Jehovah, with Jehovah one	459
Jesus, thine eye with pity sees	455	Jehovah's co-eternal Son	100
Jesus, thou art th' Anointed One	245	Jehovah's Fellow, and his Son	121
Jesus, thou know'st our envious foes	410	Jehovah's name is Love	345
Jesus thou seest my trembling heart	348	Jesu's charity adore!	307
Jesus, thou seest thy creature's pain	223	Jesu's real witnesses	466
Jesus, thou Son of David, stay	226	Jesus a captive made	293
Jesus, thy contrite Spirit shed	494	Jesus a sinful soul converts	361
Jesus, thy gracious nature tell	79	Jesus alone the room supplies	186
Jesus, thy messengers prepare	471	Jesus answered them, to show	464
Jesus, thy minister ordain	157	Jesus attend my cry	187
Jesus, thy name we bless	118	Jesus, before he sheds his blood	20
Jesus, thy patient power I feel	425	Jesus, believing in thy name	32
Jesus, thy people's hearts inflame	93	Jesus, believing on thy name	352
Jesus thy saving power employ	441		

Jesus bleeding on the tree	230	Jesus, my long-sequestered God[378]	130
Jesus by his mere word, alone	421	Jesus, my Lord, I cry to thee	26
Jesus by his stupendous grace	247	Jesus, my soul's infirmity	468
Jesus by whom redeemed I live	253	Jesus, my trust is in thy name	308
Jesus commends the faith in me	253	Jesus no exception leaves	18
Jesus declines the umpire's place[376]	209	Jesus now gone up on high[379]	233
Jesus, descended from the sky	392	Jesus omnipotent to heal	25
Jesus, Divine Interpreter	309	Jesus our souls receive	301
Jesus doth not enjoin	180	Jesus prove thy word on me	137
Jesus, eternally the same	273	Jesus, Purity Divine	43
Jesus' faithful minister	123	Jesus, quickening Spirit, come	480
Jesus, for this I wait	37	Jesus risen from the dead	93
Jesus! formidable name	98	Jesus, send forth thy truth and light	404
Jesus fulfil the title	87	Jesus sojourning below	150
Jesus full of holiness	150	Jesus, Son of God and man, / thy Person	294
Jesus full of truth and grace	426	Jesus, Son of God and man, / To the	344
Jesus hath left his house below	66	Jesus, Son of the Most-High	105
Jesus here his wisdom shows	376	Jesus' soul and body are	338
Jesus hides himself from those	443	Jesus spake the word to all	181
Jesus his benefits bestows	508	Jesus, succeed our ministry	315
Jesus, how great thy servants are	491	Jesus that Bread of life we own	387
Jesus, I believe in thee	419	Jesus, the gift Divine I know	355
Jesus, I belong to thee	28	Jesus the Good Shepherd, good	233
Jesus I thy wisdom need	399	Jesus the gospel-grace impart	511
Jesus, I wait till thou display	109	Jesus, the holiness impart	56
Jesus, if thou thy Spirit give[377]	222	Jesus, th' irrevocable word	44
Jesus, incline thine ear	188	Jesus the Patron of mankind	9
Jesus, inspire the watchful power	68	Jesus, the power and kingdom's thine	132
Jesus keeps the soul in view	359	Jesus the power impart[380]	213
Jesus, kind, inviting Lord	30	Jesus, the purchase of thy blood	101
Jesus lays the ransom down	87	Jesus, the Sabbath's Lord we praise	443
Jesus, lengthen out my day	269	Jesus, the stumbling-block and sign	122
Jesus, Light of life Divine	494	Jesus, thee I surely know	394
Jesus, Lord, for thee I stay	358	Jesus, thou art the House of Grace	364
Jesus, Lord, I fain would stoop	504	Jesus, thou dost the sinner see	224
Jesus, Lord, to thee I give	407	Jesus, thou hast the hindrance shown	477
Jesus, Lord, to thee I run	33	Jesus, thou know'st what is in man	339
Jesus more than conqueror	134	Jesus, thou only canst abase	285
Jesus multiplies to give	12	Jesus, thou say'st I shall receive	47
Jesus must first for Peter die	512	Jesus, thou that Spirit art	128
Jesus my Advocate hath been	287		

376. *UP* 2:136.
377. *UP* 2:148.
378. *UP* 2:88.
379. *UP* 2:153.
380. *UP* 2:140.

Jesus, thy disciples here	444	Jesus, believing in thy name	113
Jesus, thy killing quickening power	121	Jesus, by the judge allowed	85
Jesus, thy ministers receive	401	Jesus coming to thine own	208
Jesus, thy preaching servants raise	103	Jesus, dost thou not ordain	28
Jesus thy record we receive	350	Jesus, eternally the same	367
Jesus, thy travelling church below	169	Jesus exalted is	225
Jesus to heaven is gone[381]	270	Jesus filled with sanctity	17
Jesus' upright confessor	444	Jesus for him employs	395
Jesus vouchsafes to recompense	162	Jesus, from hell and earth, and sin	270
Jesus, we now with pure delight[382]	360	Jesus from thee I surely know	89
Jesus we own the angels' Bread	388	Jesus, full of truth and love	407
Jesus, we testify thy power	481	Jesus hath made me free indeed	267
Jesus, we thy mercy bless	353	Jesus I humbly seek	228
Jesus weeps for sinners blind[383]	475	Jesus I long that grief to feel	125
Jesus weeps, our tears to see	475	Jesus I thy merits plead	11
Jesus! where is he to be found	442	Jesus, I would with joy embrace	69
Jesus, while yet a Man of woe	490	Jesus, if thou my Master art	307
Jesus who dost alone contain	424	Jesus, if thou the faith impart	151
Jesus who in his church below	107	Jesus in all times and places	303
Joy in our enjoyments here	355	Jesus, in the sacred book	229
Joyful to see the light appear	373	Jesus, in whom I now believe	62
Judas might cast out devils	194	Jesus instructs his servants here	232
Just as he lists, the Spirit blows	342	Jesus is first perceived and known	118
Justly doth our humble Lord	433	Jesus is my light within	173
		Jesus, Jehovah's equal Son	51
		Jesus, King of Righteousness	76

Volume XII

		Jesus' messenger at last	431
Jacob gathered up his feet	88	Jesus, of Jesse's line	279
Jehovah doth the heavens bow	142	Jesus, on this thy solemn day	106
Jehovah sends by whom he will, / his grace	175	Jesus our Desire and Hope	309
		Jesus our head to heaven is gone	63
Jehovah sends by whom he will, / And let	249	Jesus sometimes by slow degrees	116
		Jesus, speak the word to me	105
Jehovah's Son, declared with power	113	Jesus, that new command of thine	26
Jesu's every harbinger	280	*Jesus, the cause belongs to thee*	*SH* 1762, 2:267
Jesu's followers all confess	109		
Jesu's love I cannot feel[384]	239	Jesus the faithful pastors keep	378
Jesus and him alone	455	Jesus the Father's darling Son	203
Jesus at last arise	202	Jesus the Lord I would confess	230
		Jesus the oft repeated call	67
		Jesus, the only faultless Man	77
381. *UP* 2:182.		Jesus the poor with pity sees	116
382. *UP* 2:30.		Jesus the previous knowledge gives	381
383. *UP* 2:248.		Jesus the royal prophet's Lord	149
384. *UP* 2:328: "Jesus' love I cannot feel."			

Jesus, the spirit of Jealousy	260
Jesus the true fidelity	25
Jesus the woman's conquering Seed	361
Jesus, thee my God and Saviour	111
Jesus thee the head we own	57
Jesus their true and constant Guide	297
Jesus, thine own defend	440
Jesus, thou know'st the nations still	223
Jesus, thou tak'st thy servant's part[385]	348
Jesus through faith alone	160
Jesus through thy atoning blood	163
Jesus thy church inspire[386]	181
Jesus, thy dear redeeming grace	70
Jesus thy Father's child I am	63
Jesus, thy prayer is answered now	49
Jesus thy preaching servants bless	261
Jesus, thy servants bless	456
Jesus thy spirit shows	374
Jesus, thy weakest followers hear	12
Jesus, thy word till time shall end	107
Jesus, to me appear	427
Jesus, to our supplication	217
Jesus to thy Father gone	10
Jesus to us apostles raise	181
Jesus, was ever love like thine	55
Jesus wept! and never chid	380
Jesus, what hast thou done?	75
Jesus while the world despise thee	82
Jesus who divinely know	360
Jesus, with heavenly bread	121
Jesus, with thy Father come	58
Jesus' word doth first convey	106
Jews may clamour for his blood	422
Jews the prophecy fulfil	391
Join we, Lord, as taught by thee	71
Joined no longer to the Tree	21
Joy in the Lord, or grief confessed	145
Joyful to share his happy toil	261
Just in your own eyes, Who Jesus reject	454
Justice none could he obtain	227
Justified through faith alone	297

385. UP 2:384.
386. UP 2:298.

Volume XIII

Jehovah manifest below	99
Jehovah's charioteers surround	119
Jehovah's co-eternal Son	3
Jehovah's Son, appear	204
Jesu thy goodness I proclaim	268
Jesus, assist us to believe	89
Jesus be mercifully nigh	267
Jesus, come, my soul's Physician	241
Jesus doth with us remain	247
Jesus, for this to thee I cry	255
Jesus holds us by the hand	247
Jesus, I fain would find	230
Jesus, I from thee receive	65
Jesus I look to thee	154
Jesus, if such thy saving name	12
Jesus, in sore temptation's hour	253
Jesus, in thy great name I go	223
Jesus, in whose name I trust	269
Jesus, is there not in thee	270
Jesus, let our faithful mind	264
Jesus, let thy kingdom come	221
Jesus, life of the believer	91
Jesus, my only Hope thou art	145
Jesus, my refuge in despair	192
Jesus, our true and faithful Lord	193
Jesus, out of our hearts remove	215
Jesus, plant thy Spirit in me	66
Jesus, rebuke our teaching pride	35
Jesus, Redeemer of mankind	209
Jesus, reveal thy love to me	94
Jesus, suffering Son of God	70
Jesus, that perfect good unknown	80
Jesus, th' appropriating grace	124
Jesus, the first and last	221
Jesus, the Just appears	177
Jesus, the passive grace bestow	165
Jesus, the promised grace we claim	210
Jesus the righteous Judge shall come	96
Jesus, the Son of God, in thee	225
Jesus, the Spirit of faith bestow	109
Jesus, the wise discerning mind	29
Jesus, the word bestow	22

Jesus, thou art that Morning-Star!	226	Kept by the strength of Jesus	87
Jesus, thou dear redeeming Lord	242	Kindle the flame of love within	260
Jesus, thou my labours bless	178	Know'st thou not where to find	131
Jesus, thy bleeding love	141		
Jesus, thy blood hath purged my sin	181		
Jesus, thy feeblest servant fill	125		

Volume V

Jesus, thy grace suffices	57
Jesus, thy promised Spirit impart	230
Jesus, thy promised Spirit supply	21
Jesus, thy sanctifying will	123
Jesus, thy word I plead	64
Jesus, to me the joy impart	214
Jesus, to me thy mind impart	183
Jesus, to me vouchsafe the grace	16

Keep him, till th' appointed hour	256
Keep me then, my Lord, my Love	180
Keep me then, my Saviour, keep	9
Keep us till then in perfect peace	34
Kept in awe by my own heart	443
Kind remembrancer, to thee	68

Volume VI

Jesus to thee I would look up	253
Jesus, we steadfastly believe	212
Jesus, with thee thy cross I share	127
Join all who feel th' atoning blood	248
Join with me the heavenly choirs	246
Joined to our head in Christ we are	50
Joy shall then my heart o'erflow	66
Justly we call the Father ours	214

Keep me from the great offence	442
Keep me thus to God resigned	401
Knowledge, and power, and glory meet	262
Known by her God, and well approved	295

Volume VII

Kindler of seraphic fire	342
Kindler of seraphic fires	369
Kindly then thine own receive	408

Volume I

Kindled his relentings are	272
King of glory, Soul of bliss	186
King of Saints, to whom are given	362

Volume VIII

Keep (for I nothing else desire)	423
Keep me from the hands of men	256
Keep me, who in thee confide	29
Kept by all-sufficient grace	442
Kept by him, I cannot fear	6
Kept by him, we scorn to fear	107
Kindly do the showers distil	144
Kindreds, and tongues, and nations	36
Know, for himself the Lord	8
Know, that the Lord is God	185
Known on earth to none but thee	211

Volume II

Keep us through faith to that thy day	250
Known unto him are all our needs	16

Volume III

Kept by the mercy of our God	95
Knows the ox his master's stable	365

Volume IV

Keep, till this Jewish state is past	248

Volume IX

Kedar shall all its flocks present	453
Keeping my heavenly Guide in view	345
Kept by constant miracle	156
Kept by that hand, I cannot fear	70
Kept by the almighty Lord	127
Kept in the way by Power Divine	417
Kept off by Lot, the fiery rain	21
King of kings, I cry to thee	199

Volume X

King of kings Jehovah made	348
Kings of earth, from Christ alone	425
Know the wise and faithful servant	379

Volume XI

Keep us to that solemn hour	177
Kindly for his own he cares	233
King of saints, thy right assume	105
King of the inward Jews thou art	302
Kings of earth, on Jesus wait	41

Volume XII

Kindly thou dost chastise, reprove	18
King of the Jews and Gentiles	75
King proclaimed in different tongues	85
Know all who doubt or fear to know	188
Know all who help bestow	447

Volume XIII

Keep the souls whom now we leave	264
Kept by thine almighty hand	41
Kept from sin, the world, and hell	179
Know this, ye infidels in heart	172
Knowing that reconciled thou art	189
Knowledge howe'er sublime	31

Volume I

Lame at the pool I still am found	263
Lament, unhappy heart, lament[387]	42
Lead us in the way of peace	291
Learn thou the whole of mortal state[388]	35
Leave not thy work undone	338
Leave to his sovereign sway[389]	127
Leave us not below to mourn	292
Let air, and earth, and skies obey	231
Let earth no more my heart divide	241
Let earth's remotest bound	153
Let God's high praises still resound[390]	122
Let it for thee new life afford	190
Let it hence to all be known	360
Let me—I know not how to pray	251
Let me not languish, then, and spend[391]	30
Let me thy righteous doom applaud HSP 1740, 57	
Let the fruits of grace abound	351
Let this my every hour employ	305
Let us for this faith contend	353
Let us in life, in death[392]	128
Let us join ('tis God commands,)	352
Let us thee, though lost, regain	184
Let us then as brethren love	352
Let us triumphantly ride on	315
Let war's devouring surges rise[393]	121
Life his healing blood imparts	363
Life of the world, our souls to feed	190
Lift to him thy weeping eye	330
Light of the world below	316
Like mighty wind, or torrent fierce[394]	167
Like withered leaves we fade away	368

387. George Herbert.
388. John Gambold?
389. From the German of Paul Gerhardt translated by John Wesley.
390. Samuel Wesley, Sr.
391. George Herbert.
392. From the German of Paul Gerhardt translated by John Wesley.
393. Henry Pitt.
394. Henry More.

Live we now in Christ our head	357	Lord, how in silence I despise[401]	37
Lives again our glorious King	186	Lord, how long, how long shall I	254
Lo! abundantly they bloom	290	Lord, I adjudge myself to grief[402]	43
Lo! for us the wilds are glad	290	*Lord, I believe a rest remains*	370
Lo, God is here! him day and night[395]	168	Lord, I believe the precious blood[403]	347
Lo, God is here! Let us adore[396]	167	Lord, I believe the price is paid[404]	347
Lo! I cumber still the ground	272	Lord, I believe the promise sure	259
Lo! I cut off the dear right hand	248	Lord, I believe the promise true	293
Lo, I tread on deaths and snares	224	Lord, I believe, were sinners more[405]	347
Lo! to faith's enlightened sight	297	Lord, I confess my sin is great[406]	62
Lo! to the hills I lift mine eye	270	Lord, I despair myself to heal	82
Lo! we commend thee to his grace	228	Lord, I have now invited all[407]	112
Load me with scorn, reproach, and shame	25	Lord, I will not let thee go	193
Loathsome, and foul, and self-abhorred	263	Lord, if indeed, without a bound	314
Lone, unfrequented wilds they trod	221	*Lord, if to me thy grace hath given*	94
Long did all hell its powers engage	181	Lord, let the angels praise thy name[408]	59
Long did my coward flesh delay	293	Lord of my soul, bow down thine ear[409]	66
Long have I seemed to serve thee, Lord	233	Lord of the wide-extended main	229
Long have I vainly hoped and strove	84	Lord over all, sent to fulfil[410]	162
Long have I waited in the way	263	Lord, we believe; and taste thee good	302
Long my imprisoned spirit lay	105	Lost and undone, for aid I cry[411]	85
Long my reluctant folly held	247	Love can bow down the stubborn neck	329
Long o'er my formless soul	99	Love only can the conquest win	328
Look, and be saved from sin!	337	Love, thine image Love, restore	224
Look on my sorrows, mark them well[397]	66	Love's mysterious work is done!	170
Look unto him, ye nations; own	301	Love's redeeming work is done	185
Loosed from my God, and far removed	249		
Lord and God of heavenly powers	114		
Lord, arm me with thy Spirit's might[398]	161		
Lord, at thy feet I fall	268		
Lord God of armies, ceaseless praise[399]	105		
Lord, how happy is a heart[400]	18		

395. From the German of Gerhard Tersteegen, translated by John Wesley.
396. From the German of Gerhard Tersteegen, translated by John Wesley.
397. George Herbert.
398. From the German of Joachim Lange, translated by John Wesley.
399. From the German of Johann A. Freylinghausen, translated by John Wesley.
400. From the French, Antoinette Bourignon.
401. George Herbert.
402. George Herbert.
403. From the German of Nikolaus von Zinzendorf, translated by John Wesley.
404. From the German of Nikolaus von Zinzendorf, translated by John Wesley.
405. From the German of Nikolaus von Zinzendorf, translated by John Wesley.
406. George Herbert.
407. George Herbert.
408. George Herbert.
409. George Herbert.
410. From the German of Johann A. Freylinghausen, translated by John Wesley.
411. From the German of Christian Friedrich Richter, translated by John Wesley.

Volume II

Lame as I am, I take the prey	176
Lamb of God for sinners slain	98
Lay to thy mighty hand	328
Lay to thine hand, O God of grace	132
Lead me, till my few evil years	77
Lead us till all our toil is past	250
Leave me, my friends, the mourner leave	258
Lebanon brings her stores in vain	53
Led through the howling wilderness	204
Less grievous will the judgment-day	359
Let all my father's children be	259
Let earth and all her fulness still	314
Let future times thy name confess	217
Let it still my heart constrain	123
Let me gain my calling's hope	275
Let me never, never more	112
Let me no more, in deep complaint	322
Let others hug their chains	245
Let others rush with trembling haste	331
Let the pangs that fill my breast	214
Let the stronger sons of God	317
Let the world bewail their dead	189
Let the world lament and grieve	222
Let the world lament their dead	186
Let the world their virtue boast	317
Let thy merit as a cloud	207
Let us go forth, 'tis God commands	17
Let us hold fast the pledge of good	352
Let us never, never rest	219
Let us now to thee aspire	224
Let us then sweet counsel take	220
Let us thy word of patience keep	356
Let us walk with Christ in white	219
Lift up, and fix our steadfast eye	332
Lift up thy feet of burnished brass	351
Lift up your eyes to things on high	55
Lift up your heads, ye lofty gates	23
Light as the balance-dust, and small	53
Lighter than vanity, and less	53
Lion of the tribe of Judah	32
Listen to my ceaseless cries	210
Live without sin! If God is true	296
Lo! an exceeding great reward	51
Lo! I take thee at thy word	265
Lo! in my prayer I ever mourn	65
Lo! on dangers, deaths, and snares	268
Lo! the Levite me espies	157
Lo! the priest comes down in vain	156
Lo! the prisoner is released	188
Lo! the tall sons of Anak rise	313
Long did thy loving Spirit strive	109
Long hath thy good Spirit strove	154
Long have I laboured in the fire	202
Long have I viewed, long have I thought[412]	10
Lord, and am I yet alive	212
Lord, and is thine anger gone	123
Lord, at thy feet we fall as dead	341
Lord, I am blind; be thou my sight	259
Lord, I am sick; my sickness cure	259
Lord, I believe and rest secure	244
Lord, I believe thy every word	280
Lord, I believe thy work of grace	363
Lord, I cannot cease from sinning	96
Lord, I confess my sins to thee	159
Lord, I glorify thy grace	298
Lord, I look to be made clean	280
Lord, if I on thee believe	275
Lord, my head burns, my heart is sick	41
Lord, my time is in thy hand	264
Lord, my time is in thine hand	294
Lord of the harvest, hear	342
Lord, regard my earnest cry	150
Lord, we believe, and wait the hour	290
Lord, we believe to us and ours	227
Lord, we confess our sins to thee	288
Lord, we renounce whoe'er oppose	350
Lost are they now, and scattered wide	343
Love alone can match in fight	240
Love, mighty Love, my heart o'erpower	197
Love, perfect Love, expels all doubt	355
Love the dear atoning Lamb	223

412. Altered from John Norris.

Low as this mortal frame must lie[413]	9	Like as in Egypt's evil day	140
Lowly, loving, meek, and pure	278	Little, and base, and mean	79
		Live, our Eternal Priest	303
		Live our great God on high	351

Volume III

		Lo, he comes triumphant down	288
Labours for thee my struggling soul	173	Lo! he feeds on living Bread	165
Lamb of God, for whom we languish	270	Lo! his clothing is the Sun	164
Lamb of God, whose bleeding love	228	Lo, his glorious banner spread	288
Leave a world of sin and pain	172	Lo! I at thy summons come	163
Leave me then, without relief	363	Lo, in the gap my Surety stands	17
Let all who truly bear	218	Lo! in thy hand I lay	92
Let both Jews and Gentiles join	325	Lo! my necessary meat	362
Let but thy ark the walls surround	260	Lo, on thy bloody sacrifice	252
Let earth and heaven agree	71	Long have I groaned thy grace to gain	272
Let heaven and earth agree	347	Long in the mortal toils she lay	178
Let heaven and earth proclaim	315	Long we for thy love have waited	275
Let him to whom we now belong	335	Look as when thy closing eye	296
Let it not plunge their soul	84	Lord, as with my latest breath	13
Let me on the image dwell	162	*Lord, if now thou passest by us*	351
Let my flesh be troubled still	327	*Lord, not unto me, (The whole I disclaim)*	6
Let no savour of the grave	264	Lord of all, thy creatures see	358
Let the beasts their breath resign	86	Lord of life, thy followers see	240
Let the dust return to dust	172	Lord, thou know'st my simpleness	296
Let the ordinance be sealing	271	Lord, thou seest our willing heart	332
Let the sons of Belial rage	HSP 1749, 1:39	Lord, we bless thee for thy grace	231
Let the wisest mortal show	256	Lord, we forget thou once didst take	68
Let thy blood, by faith applied	229	Lord, we forget thy dying groans	68
Let us in silence wait	64	Lost, and undone, and damned am I	42
Let us the Good Spirit bless	104	Louder than gathered waters	337
Let us through thy curse inherit	270	Love was once my pleasant meat	361
Let us with solemn awe	269	Loving to every man, / Of tenderest pity	81
Life of the world, come down	360	Loving to every man thou art	33
Lift your eyes of faith, and look	227		
Lift your eyes of faith, and see	293		

Volume IV

Light in thy only light I see[414]	170		
Light of life, to thee I haste[415]	168	*Lamb of God, we follow thee*	34
Like as a father feels	81	*Lamb of God, who bear'st away*	59
		Laugh the world, secure and glad	193
		Lay but thine hand upon my soul	381
		Lay thy hand upon my soul	358
		Lay thy weighty cross on me[416]	449
		Lay to thy hand, Almighty Love	269

413. David Lewis.
414. Free paraphrase of the German of Christian Friedrich Richter by Charles Wesley.
415. Free paraphrase of the German of Wolfgang Christoph Dessler by Charles Wesley.

416. *UP* 3:202: "Lay thy mighty cross on me."

Leader of faithful souls, and Guide	262	Look, as when thy languid eye	408
Let angels and archangels sing	118	Look, as when thy pity saw	407
Let earth and heaven combine	109	Look, as when thy weeping eye	407
Let me alone,—that all my wrath	260	Look, as when thine eye pursued	407
Let me from this moment give	459	Look not on me, a beast, a fiend	333
Let me, while my faith is trying	467	Look through the tutelary cloud	223
Let my punishment be o'er	391	Look with that soul piercing look	388
Let others walk with thee	356	Lord, I believe the sure	172
Let sinners possessed	366	Lord, I believe thee true and good	470
Let th' effect of Jacob's pain	60	Lord, I cannot let thee go	418
Let thy dying love constrain	59	*Lord, I know not how to pray*	458
Let us, for conscience sake, revere	22	Lord, I my unbelief confess	457
Let us then our Prince proclaim	118	Lord, if thou hast bestowed	448
Let us then with angels gaze	117	Lord, if thou wilt, I *do* believe	373
Leviathan, that subtle fiend	293	*Lord of Hosts, we look to thee*	64
Lift up for all mankind to see[417]	315	Lord, thou hast bid thy people pray	25
Lift up your eyes, the heavens survey	301	*Lord, to thee what shall I say?*	428
Lift up your heads, ye gates	154	*Lord, we have all forsook*	48
Light are the pains we now endure	43	Lord, we receive the grace, and thee	125
Light of those whose dreary dwelling	116	Lord, we with joy embrace	171
Like Hagar's son I lift mine hand	354	Lord, when thine hand is lifted up	289
Like him would I be	123	*Love Divine, all love's excelling*	219
Listen to my plaintive moans	259	*Love Divine for thee I languish*	439
Lo! at his word th' embattled powers	71	Love, only love, thy heart inclined	343
Lo! he lays his glory by	117	Low in the deepest dungeon laid	354
Lo! I come with joy to do	214	Lured by the grateful scent of blood	95
Lo! I thy soul have freely loved	306		
Lo! in the arms of faith and prayer	21		
Lo! on a narrow neck of land	316		

Volume V

Lo! the audacious hopes of Rome	97		
Lo! the false prophets rise	218	*Lamb, lovely Lamb, for sinners slain*	72
Lo! to my Father I ascend!	134	Laid in the lowest deep of sin	292
Long as thou lengthen'st out our days	94	Lay the foundation then no more	317
Long did our lusts and passions reign	289	Lead me into every deed	341
Long have I bowed to sin's command	326	Lead us, thou, our constant Guide	428
Long have I drank the bitter cup	354	Learning should I strive to gain	12
Long have I lived in grief and pain	451	Leave no unguarded place	41
Long have I murmured to be clean	445	Less cannot suffice	27
Long have you heard and known	217	Less than the least of saints, I join	228
Long may he guard thy people's rest	25	Lest again we start aside	386
Look, as when condemned for them	407	Let all in Satan's counsel join	198
Look, as when thy grace beheld	407	*Let all in thy great praise agree*	334
		Let all mankind in Christ rejoice	317
		Let all men rejoice, By Jesus restored!	390

417. UP 2:454.

Let all the God of Daniel praise	108	Long as I live beneath	16
Let all who for the promise wait	479	Long as in the vale I live	180
Let all with thankful hearts confess	107	Long as on earth I stay	347
Let heathens murmur and complain	338	Long as our fiery trials last	177
Let him through thine almighty name	416	Long as the guilt of sin shall last	245
Let it in our souls be seen	407	Long as the war subsists within	166
Let Jews their slightest wrong repay	155	Long may he to thy glory live	76
Let me know my Shepherd's voice	294	Long the lost souls of men I sought	126
Let me of thy life partake	10	Long the wily soothing foe	359
Let me then on thee rely	184	Long, too long we went astray	385
Let me trample on the foe	383	Look from the tree	59
Let none forsake the fold, and fly	254	Look through us with thine eyes of flame	315
Let none unwarily give place	254	Loose me from the chains of sense	10
Let others from themselves remove	310	Lord, I believe for me, even me	470
Let others human succour seek	156	Lord, I will not deprecate	186
Let others madly hug their chains	311	Lord, if I now thy drawings feel	483
Let others plead for sin's remains	334	Lord, if thou didst indeed inspire	228
Let others to the creature fly	66	Lord, my time is in thy hand	196
Let the gathering storm descend	186	Lord, we believe, and rest secure	329
Let the living stones cry out	332	Lord, we believe; and wait the hour	331
Let the promised inward grace	389	Lord, we believe, and with calm zeal	313
Let the punishment suffice	204	Lord, we believe the promise true	76
Let truth the girdle be	41	Lord, we the call obey	129
Let us both together rise	426	*Lord, we thy will obey*	428
Let us each for other care	53	Lost in a labyrinth of sin	175
Let us patiently endure	178	Love moved him to die	31
Let us the word hold fast	474	Love only can the conquest win	148
Let us then rejoice in hope	333	Love us, though far in flesh disjoined	478
Let us then with joy remove	53	*Lovely Lamb, I come to thee*	302
Let us thus with even pace	433	Lover of souls, thou know'st to prize	122
Let us together wait	473	Lovers of pleasure more than God, / For you	122
Lift up your eyes, ye sons of light	113	Lovers of pleasure, more than God, / We	130
Lift up your hearts to things above	478	Lulled in imaginary peace	246
Light of life, seraphic Fire	309		
Light of the world, thy beams I bless	17		
Listed into the cause of sin	397		
Live, till all thy life I know	294		

Volume VI

Live till the Lord in glory come	479
Lo! he in the clouds descends	353
Lo! here we are, thy truth to prove	311

Lo! I receive it at thy hand	69	Laid to the root with conscious awe	9
Lo! in the arms of faith and prayer	238	*Lamb of God, I fain would be*	443
Lo! the rains descend, o'erflow	164	*Lamb of God, I look to thee*	442
Lo! thy sister is gone back	132	Learning's redundant part and vain	407

IDEX OF FIRST LINES OF POETRY BY JOHN AND CHARLES WESLEY

Less dreadful will the punishment	79	Lo! from their roots the mountains	26
Less pestilent the men who dare	139	Lo! he comes with clouds descending	143
Let all that breathe Jehovah praise	458	*Lo! in a thankful loving heart*	4
Let all the faithless nation cry	38	Lo! our all at stake we see	77
Let children proclaim Their Saviour and King	405	Lo! 'tis he! our heart's Desire	145
Let every instrument disclaim	183	Lo! we to our promise stand	251
Let God, the mighty God	149	Long he on Tabor's top abode[420]	309
Let God, who comforts the distressed	111	*Long in the toils of death she lay*	339
Let heathenish boys	434	*Long in those peaceful pleasant ways*	268
Let infidels and heathen mourn[418]	301	Long was he tossed below	245
Let me, above all, fulfil	443	Look down, thou happy spirit, look down	255
Let me in thy footsteps tread	444	Lord, I abhor, renounce, abjure	6
Let me to my betters bend	401	Lord, I accept the sign	201
Let mercy attend	454	Lord, I at last recant, reject	5
Let none within the pale be found	116	Lord, I the welcome word receive	219
Let others draw with fierce despite	6	Lord, if thou hast our hearts inclined	411
Let the blind sons of Rome bow down	3	Lord of earth and skies, again	415
Let the potsherds of the earth	444	Lord of Hosts, thine arm reveal	174
Let the punishment suffice	222	*Lord of hosts, we bow before thee*	45
Let them alone, thy wisdom cries	103	*Lord of the gospel harvest, send*	119
Let thy love possess me whole	445	*Lord over all, if thou hast made*	138
Let thy will on me be done	385	*Lord, that I may sing to thee*	455
Let us in God confide	43	Lord, we behold thy mighty hand	173
Let us now to Jesus turn	424	Lord, we present it now	420
Let us the shining path pursue[419]	301	Lord, we will not cease to pray	222
Let us then to God aspire	387	Lord, while after thee we mourn	364
Let us things excellent discern	421	Love, that makes us creatures new	404
Let us, with all his saints, agree	447	*Lover of little children, thee*[421]	448
Life and death depend on thee	251	Lover of little children, thee	449
Life is to her rescue come	337	Loving he is to all his sons	447
Lift we then our hearts to God	386	Loving Jesus, gentle Lamb!	443
Lift your heads, ye friends of Jesus	144		
Light of the world, thy beams impart	119		
Like her, who now supremely blessed	266	## Volume VII	
Like him, her thirty years and three	265	Lead to the streams of paradise	178
Like Moses caught to his embrace	362	Least of all thy mercies we	16
Like Moses on the mountain laid	251	*"Leave the stump and roots behind"*	273
Like thunder confined In caverns He roars	91	*Left from my birth to thee my God*	404
Little and vile in his own eyes	375		

418. *UP* 3:332.
419. *UP* 3:333.
420. *UP* 3:336
421. The four-line stanzas that begin with this line on pages 448 and 449 are identical.

Less than thy least of mercies, I	115	Love inflicts the plague severe	85
Let her long a witness live	98	Love moved thee to die	9
Let him now unclose his eyes	154	Love of my expiring Saviour	59
Let Ishmael live Devoted to God	79	Love our real holiness	346
Let me alone this only year	396	*Lovely-fair, but breathless clay*	82
Let me now thy help secure	58	*Lover, Friend of human kind*	97
Let no affections foolish	91	Lover of mankind, his life he gave	439
Let on us thy Spirit rest	196	Lover of souls, to rescue mine	25
Let the balm be now applied	98	Loving thee with all my heart	366
Let the redeemed by grace	144		
Let the redeemed give thanks and praise	107		

Volume VIII

Let the sense of joys above	404	Laid on the altar of thy Son	118
Let the sense of sin forgiven	384	Lead me in all thy righteous ways	10
Let them pant, and never rest	84	Leave me, then, to Jesus leave me	13
Let thy dying love constrain us	14	Less fierce the saints of forty-one	451
Let thy own bowels move thee	186	Less had I felt the deadly blow	123
Let Us, saith the Lord, descend	267	*Let earth be glad, the Lord is king*	307
Life and death are in thine hand	86	Let earth's inmost centre quake	107
Light in thy light O may I see	400	*Let every prophet cry aloud*	311
Listening to his plaintive moan	122	*Let God, the glorious God, arise*	148
Lo, like one of Us the man	267	Let heaven and earth his goodness sing	157
Lo, on the margin of the grave	411	Let her then triumphant stand	303
Lo the great God will come	244	*Let life itself with language fail*	253
Long I every means have tried	415	Let me here my title see	428
Long in prayer and supplication	381	Let me in thine image live	234
Long in the land my days have been	417	Let mercy bring salvation near	174
Long in the toils of hell she lay	67	Let the people praise thee, Lord	147
Long in prayer and supplication	381	Let their lips show forth thy glory	158
Long may he live to serve thy will	124	Let them hear thy dying cries	339
Loosed and detached I cease from man	181	Lift thyself up, awake for me	15
Lord, for this alone I stay	92	Live for deeper grief to cry	362
Lord, I magnify thy power	60	Lo! again in tender love	109
Lord, I the messengers receive	39	Lo! he comes with clouds! he comes	184
Lord, if thou didst the wish infuse	164	Lo! his triumphal chariot waits	49
Lord, if thou didst thyself inspire	42	Lo! on thy Son our souls we cast	343
Lord, if thou hast on me bestowed	168	Lo! the Lord's all-seeing eye	70
Lord of Hosts, upon thy throne	303	Lo! the wicked bend their bow	21
Lord of Hosts, we bow before thee	300	Lo! this was he, the man (they cry)	119
Lord over all, and God most high	163	Lo! they still my steps surround	30
Lord over all, I at thy feet	227	Lo, they whet their tongues like swords	140
Lord, thou hitherto hast brought us	40	Long as my God shall lend me breath	260
Love Divine, for whom I languish	367	*Long have I groaned my sin to feel*	156
Love Divine, th' afflicted see	121		
Love excludes the selfish passion	390		

Long I wandered from my God	218		
Long life he desired, To spend in thy praise	41	Leaving myself behind	232
Long may he here thy image live	485	Led by his Light, I dared pursue	260
Long may he live to serve thy cause	415	Left to myself, I now confess	217
Look on them with thy flaming eyes[422]	164	Less than the least of saints, on me	152
Loose all your bars of massy light	48	Less than thy least of mercies I / myself	29
Loosed from the chains of unbelief	393	Less than thy least of mercies I / A grain	351
Lord, attend my earnest prayer	134	Let all in joyful songs record	215
Lord, for this I wait on thee	131	Let all mankind adore	465
Lord, for thy mercy's sake draw near	156	Let angels wonder at the sight!	24
Lord, how long shall thy displeasure	13	Let earth and hell their powers engage	163
Lord, I am and will be thine	228	Let heathen scorn and vilify	167
Lord, I have with strong desire	228	Let heaven my sad confession hear!	128
Lord, I on thy help depend	130	Let Jacob's favoured race	27
Lord, I unto thee have cleaved	213	Let judgment in the desert stay	402
Lord, I will exalt thy grace	58	Let me alone, (amazing word!)	53
Lord, I with thankfulness adore	403	Let me cast myself aside	392
Lord, if thou the grace impart	247	Let me well conclude my race	274
Lord, if thy sovereign majesty	431	Let others of their virtue boast	309
Lord, in thy wrath no more chastise	11	Let others when your fruits they see	353
Lord, my life is in my hand	224	Let Sodom's governors give ear	370
Lord of Hosts, and God Most High	328	Let the angel of the Lord	42
Lord of Hosts, and King of kings	268	Let the house of Saul give place	164
Lord of Hosts, thine arm reveal	130	Let the Spirit of our head	383
Lord, regard my earnest cry	233	Let there be light (again command)	2
Lord, thou hast thy word fulfilled	218	Let this feeble body droop	310
Lord, thou know'st my simpleness	29	Let thy Spirit of grace o'erflow	403
Lord, thou know'st my uprightness	226	Let us, with mild discerning eye	347
Lord, thy humble suppliant hear	139	Lift up thy countenance serene	65
Lord thy word's unerring light	224	Light of life eternal, rise	452
Love Divine shall still embrace	47	Like him, I smote, engaged with sin	197
Love only doth our souls secure	378	Like him, in piety's decay	180
Love the channels of his grace	237	Lo! I in simplicity	335
Love would all my evils heal	368	Lo! in longing hope I stand	90
Love would all my wishes fill	368	Lo, the church with gradual light	366
Love would my salvation be	368	Lo! the house of holiness	173
Lover thou art of purity	104	Lo! the pious monarch stands	174
Loving to the whole ransomed race	305	Long as on earth by faith I live	341
Lurking in their dens all day	131	Long as our faith's capacity	190
		Long as our hands are lifted up	50
		Long enthralled to low desires	327
		Long in a tempted state forlorn	97
		Lord, am not I at ease?	401

422. UP 2:448.

Lord, I adore thy righteous will	171	Let Judah's joyous house	101
Lord, I believe thy mercy's power	94	Let me, according to thy word	57
Lord, I confess thy judgments just	311	Let me thus her zeal record	398
Lord, I have sinned, but now relent	136	Let nature of itself despair	327
Lord, I thy charge obey	68	Let none presume, let none despair	334
Lord, I thy truth proclaim	115	Let not the follower of the Lord	154
Lord, if I have with thee found grace	152	Let not the wise his wisdom boast	20
Lord, if indeed from thee I know	23	Let others, curious to inquire	366
Lord, if some secret sin of mine	123	Let the God of truth and love	86
Lord, if thou from me hast broke	64	Let the horrific king appear	67
Lord, if thou let the sinner go	276	Let the infernal lion roar	71
Lord, in kind compassion hear	223	Let the rain descend, the flood	206
Lord, in the strength of grace	203	Let the Spirit of our head	142
Lord in thy light, I see	389	Let the world in eager chase	50
Lord, may not I thy promise claim	15	Let the world my Lord despise	278
Lord of hosts, and God of love	211	Let the world profusely vain	314
Lord of Hosts, thy power assume	386	Let thy church in danger prove	112
Lord of hosts, to thee we bow	187	Let us by our lives declare	55
Lord, of thee we fain would learn	384	Let us, Lord, with humblest care	297
Lord, that I may learn of thee	392	Let us with lawful violence strive	477
Lord, that I may truly fear	130	Life a temptation is	447
Lord, thy saying I embrace	102	Lion of Judah's tribe, draw near	87
Lord, to thee I lift mine eyes	281	Live without sin! it cannot be!	114
Lord, we before the world profess	220	Living and dead together joined	226
Lost, perplexed with doubts and fears	89	Lo! it comes, Jehovah's day	133
Lust is a fire that fiercely burns	262	Lo, the fiends expect their prey	219
Lusting to shed his brother's blood	12	Lo, the heavenly Bridegroom comes!	382
		Lo, the opened graves declare	433
		Lo! the sin-avenging Lord	123
		Lo! the Son of Man appears	418

Volume X

		Lo the wedding is prepared	350
Labouring as one that labours not	188	Loathsome, foul, and self-abhorred	452
Lead me not into temptation	184	Long an outcast from my Lord	50
Led blindfold by the blindfold guide	202	Long as the things of earth ye love	146
Left in dark uncertainty	385	Long forms of prayer ye say	362
Left in the persecutor's power	284	Long we have our burden borne	57
Left to themselves the strong give place	434	Lord, as taught by thee, we pray	67
Legion the true infernal name	483	Lord from such we turn away	377
Lend me thy wings, celestial Dove	19	Lord, give me that pacific mind	163
Let all adore th' immortal King	140	Lord, give us wisdom to suspect	267
Let earth and hell their powers employ	68	Lord, help me that I never may	120
Let every answering bone	60	Lord, I believe thy power the same	287
Let heathens mock what God enjoined	186	Lord, I believe thy sprinkled blood	213
Let him alone, the blindfold guide	289	Lord, I can, I do believe	453

Lord, I fain would learn of thee	255	Let all the God of mercy praise	146
Lord, I look for thy salvation	98	Let all their great Redeemer praise	112
Lord, I revoke my hasty prayer	96	Let every child of Adam own	437
Lord, if I have indeed believed	457	Let him, Lord, my heart inspire	326
Lord, if thou giv'st the hearing ear	475	Let me with like eagerness	139
Lord, if thou the tempest chide	480	Let mine injurious brother own[423]	248
Lord, if thou wilt, thou canst from sin	208	Let my elder brethren chide	259
Lord, impart thy grief to me	463	Let Pharisees affect	3
Lord in thy humanity	410	Let the furious sons of Rome	190
Lord of Hosts, almighty Lord	111	Let the rich their wish obtain	59
Lord of Hosts, from thee we take	111	Let us to the mount retreat	414
Lord of the hallowed day	258	Life to a soul if Jesus give	483
Lord, on thy promise I rely	290	Light of my soul, I follow thee	320
Lord over all, thy Spirit pour	65	Light of the world, appear to all	439
Lord, the builders still reject	347	Light of the world they him confess	469
Lord, thou forbiddest me in vain	168	Lightened by thy interior ray	319
Lord, thou know'st, I would be seen	175	Like him with confidence of love	91
Lord, we answer to thy call	10	Listening at the Master's feet	139
Lord, we long to see thy glory	275	Living to dispense thy grace	214
Lord, we thy Spirit's call obey	160	Long as eternal ages last	388
Lord, we with awful thanks confess	48	Long as my day of life remains	438
Lord, what is man's distinguished race	266	Long as thy mangled form appears	300
Lord, while at thy command	60	Long did I seek in vain	220
Lord, with joyful lips and heart	131	Long undisturbed the tempter keeps[424]	204
Lost by the first, the second Man	156	Longing to be all thine own	259
Love, all-sufficient love alone	354	Looking for the grace of God	175
Love as generous as sincere	397	Loosed from the bands of sin we bring	40
Love in me intensely burn	147	Lord, I at times in thee believe	24
Love, only love in justice great	354	Lord, I believe, and enter in	458
Loved for a time, they might have been	78	Lord, I believe, and stand secure	347
Loving my friends I freely pay	171	Lord, I believe, thou wilt forgive	24
Lured by the grateful scent of blood	374	Lord, I by faith my seal set to	10
		Lord I come by faith to thee	159
		Lord, I have counted first the cost	231
		Lord, I would be brought to thee	259

Volume XI

		Lord, I would my sight	
		receive	SH 1762, 2:208
Labour is by God enjoined	211	Lord, if my sin-sick soul	174
Lamb without spot, who didst give	191	Lord, if thou hast sent forth me	348
Learn from hence, who now with power	137	Lord, if thou my soul convert	126
Learning and power contend	449	Lord, if thou the grace supply	18
Led to a court (our heavenly Lord	297		
Left to his own feebleness	79		
Less will in his hands suffice	377		
Lest this my dreadful end should be	508		

423. *UP* 2:161.
424. *UP* 2:129.

Lord, if thy grace I have	171	Long undesired with foes he stayed[425]	352
Lord of all, with pure intent	119	Loosed from his bands, awhile restored	400
Lord of himself, he takes his flight	234	Lord appear, the wrongs redress	208
Lord of souls he truly was	286	Lord, I ask it in thy name	11
Lord, on thee thy people wait	11	Lord, I would thy servant be	129
Lord our life of faith and prayer	177	Lord, if at thy command	260
Lord, that I may the doctrine know	402	Lord, if thou dost my faith approve	299
Lord, they asked a good unknown	383	Lord, in these thy Spirit's days	161
Lord, thou dost thy followers seek	312	Lord of hosts, our God and Lord	178
Lord, thou hast spoke me whole	SH 1762, 2:218	Lord of the gospel-harvest, give	312
		Lord the cause belongs to thee	179
Lord, thou seest me in the snare	63	Lord, the figure we look through	207
Lord thy promise we believe	256	Lord, the sacred terror send	185
Lord thy saying I receive	478	Lord, thy testamental will	59
Lord thy wisdom we adore	136	Lord we with thanks adore	93
Lord we our seal set to	260	Lord, whoe'er resist thy will	148
Love is the source of every good	158	Lord with open heart and ear	166
Love only did my Lord constrain	461	Lover of souls he cannot rest	362
		Lovers of earthly things defer	344
		Luke and Aristarchus too	434

Volume XII

Labouring till all our work is done	332
Learning itself cannot withstand	346
Learning secular, profane	207
Learning unsanctified	393
Led by the word's attractive power	282
Led into captivity	450
Legal impurity they dread	73
Less by action than by patience	127
Let fiends and men their wisdom join	263
Let heathens force by force repel	69
Let infidels fear	440
Let teachers false their sentence close	308
Let the great and wise confess	174
Let the self-condemned and poor	420
Let the true servant of the Lord	253
Let the whole house of Israel know	150
Let us without delay	231
Life, through the virtue of thy love	113
Lo, he stands with arms extended	217
Lo, the thing impossible	226
Lo with furious malice wild	179

Volume XIII

Lamb of God, thy right we own	232
Lamb of God, we would submit	29
Least of thy faithful people I	254
Left to myself, in paths of vice	116
Less than the least in his own eyes	57
Let all be done in love!	43
Let all mankind abase	257
Let all the sons of light	237
Let all who speak in Jesu's name	183
Let God omnipotent arise	282
Let me then thy cup receive	154
Let others, then, in man confide	61
Let the fond joy of grace decay	38
Let the Spirit before his throne	219
Let the winds blow, and billows roll	135
Let thy Spirit to me explain	250
Liberty in Christ we have	70
Liberty from my own sin	71
Lift up your hearts to things above	249

---

425. UP 2:386.

Listening to thy people's cries	270	Me for thine own thou lov'st to take	206
Lo! in the world I have distress	269	Me to thy suffering Self conform	294
Lo th' incarnate God appears!	246	Me will ye mete with reason's line	207
Long as I watch, I keep	237	Meanwhile I whispering heard a Friend[429]	107
Long as the flesh and spirit	57	Meek and lowly be my mind	192
Long as thy love residing	198	Meekly then persist to mourn	332
Long have I waited, Lord	250	Meet and right it is to sing	286
Lord, I believe, thy mercy's power	217	Mercy for all thy hands have made	311
Lord, I want thy power and peace	20	Mercy I sing, transporting sound	311
Lord, is it for thy sake that I	47	Mercy the fatal bar removed	311
Lord of earth, and air, and sea	264	'Midst danger's blackest frown[430]	157
Lord, throughout our evil day	40	Mild he lays his glory by	184
Lord, thy real work revive	81	Mild he shines on all beneath	185
Lord, to thee I feebly look	153	Ministerial spirits, know	365
Lord, to thy cross I flee	226	Mixed with the choirs that hover round	182
Lord, unto me the knowledge grant	203	*Monarch of all, with lowly fear*[431]	104
Lord, we long to see that day!	96	More dear than life itself, thy love[432]	175
Lord, we with joy thy word obey	100	More hard than marble is my heart[433]	139
Lord, when I am of thee possessed	100	More of thy life, and more I have	284
Lord, while I in thy name believe	121	Moses by faith from death was saved	217
Lord, whom winds and seas obey	263	Move, and actuate, and guide	362
Love, causeless love, our God inclined	114	Murderers, and all ye hellish crew	301
Love Divine, thyself impart	202	My dying Saviour, and my God	283
Love incompatible with sin	255	My enemies and friends were joined	334
Love, only love thy law fulfils	99	My eyes no longer drowned in tears[434]	124
		My Father, O my Father, hear	346
		My feeble flesh refused to bear	74
		My feeble knees I bend again	131

Volume I

Made unto me, O Lord, my God	282	My flesh chastised with torturing paid[435]	37
Make me to the end endure	224	*My God! I know, I feel thee mine*	328
Make us all in thee complete	352	*My God, (if I may call thee mine*	133
Man cannot serve thee: all his care[426]	60	My God, my God, on thee I call	326
Man doth not live by bread alone	192		
Man for the simple life Divine[427]	35		
Many are we now, and one	362		
Many a spring since here I grew[428]	45		
Master, thy greatness wants not me	243		
Master, to us reveal	318		
Master, (will we ever say,)	187		
May see the tokens of thy hand	296		

429. George Herbert.
430. From the German of Johann Angelus Scheffler, translated by John Wesley.
431. From the German of Johann A. Freylinghausen, translated by John Wesley.
432. From the Spanish of David Israel Lopez Laguna.
433. From the German of Paul Gerhardt, translated by John Wesley.
434. Samuel Wesley, Sr.
435. George Herbert.

426. George Herbert.
427. John Gambold?
428. George Herbert.

My God, thy name man cannot praise[436]	60		My soul draws nigh, and cleaves to thee[448]	176
My God, what is a human heart?[437] / Silver	29		*My soul extols the mighty Lord*	120
My God, what is a human heart?[438] / thou	29		My soul, in all its powers renewed[449]	103
			My soul it easily besets	252
My gracious Master, and my God	300		My soul, while still to him it flies	256
My hand performs, my heart aspires	277		My spirit mourns, by thee forgot	255
My health, my light, my life, my crown[439]	140		My steadfast soul, from falling free	329
My heart did heave, and there came forth[440]	43		*My stock lies dead, and no increase*[450]	40
My heart from all pollution clean[441]	130		My sufferings all to thee are known	274
My heart, my will I here resign	248		My suit is made, my prayer is o'er[451]	124
My heart thou wilt anew create	276		My weary eyes look out in vain	242
My humbled soul, when thou art near	327		My will be swallowed up in thee	242
My inward holiness thou art	284		My worthless heart to gain	268
My Joy, my Life, my Crown of bliss[442]	47			
My life, my blood I here present[443]	179			
My Life, my Portion thou	269			

Volume II

My Lord, (I still will call thee mine	274
My Love, my Saviour, hear my cry[444]	67
My nature re-exchange for thine	74
My one desire is this	269
My peace, my life, my comfort now	164
My peace returns, my fears retire	275
My peevish passions chide	267
My Saviour, how shall I proclaim[445]	232
My Saviour, thou thy love to me[446]	139
My soul before thee prostrate lies[447]	85

Make clean as wool my filthy heart[452]	14
Make good their apostolic boast	342
Make us into one spirit drink	139
Man, foolish man, his virtue shows	51
Man his own deity reveres	54
Mark the hard travail of my soul	144
Master, on thee my soul is stayed	142
May all the pleasing pains you share	26
May he to every bounteous friend	23
May he your pious alms regard	26
May heart, and voice, and life combine	25
May I, may all who humbly wait	244
May we this life improve	27
May we with calm and sweet repose	28
Me as a bowl if now he turn	83
Me, behold, thy mercy spares	251
Me from perdition what can save	159
Me thou wouldst not disregard	114
Me to save if thou hast died	97

436. George Herbert.
437. George Herbert.
438. George Herbert.
439. From the German of Paul Gerhardt, translated by John Wesley.
440. George Herbert.
441. From the German of Nikolaus von Zinzendorf, translated by John Wesley.
442. George Herbert.
443. From the German of Johann Joseph Winckler, translated by John Wesley.
444. George Herbert.
445. From the German of Paul Gerhardt, translated by John Wesley.
446. From the German of Paul Gerhardt, translated by John Wesley.
447. From the German of Christian Friedrich Richter, translated by John Wesley.

448. From the Spanish of David Israel Lopez Laguna.
449. George Herbert.
450. George Herbert.
451. George Herbert.
452. From the German of Gottfried Arnold, translated by John Wesley.

Meek, patient Lamb of God, to thee[453]	14
Mercy for all be all their song	344
Mercy he doth for thousands keep	301
Mercy then there is for me	154
Mine; and yours, whoe'er believe	251
Mine is wisdom, power is mine	299
Mine own and not another's eyes	183
Monster of sin! How can it be	102
More and more let love abound	220
Mountains and rocks, on you I call	91
My earth thou water'st from on high	366
My Father, my God, I long for thy love	178
My Father, O my Father, hear	203
My feeble soul gives o'er the strife	100
My fig-leaves now are cast aside	90
My first estate I could not keep	121
My flesh, which cries, It cannot be	296
My fluttering spirit fatigues my breast	365
My God, I cannot let thee go	160
My God is my guide, thy mercies abound	178
My God is reconciled	324
My heart, thou knows't, can never rest	78
My heart, which now to God aspires	131
My Jesus, why dost thou delay	128
My life I know thou canst repair	281
My Lord and God I then could see	231
My Lord in my behalf appears	313
My Lord, thou wilt not long delay	273
My mind by thy all-quickening power	12
My mouth is stopped, and guilty now	110
My nature I obeyed	115
My old affections mortify	270
My own glory still I seek	211
My people have been long opprest	169
My prayer hath power with God; the grace	175
My sin and nakedness	115
My soul breaks out in strong desire	150
My stony heart thy voice shall rent	72
My strength is gone, my nature dies	174
My time and life are in thy hand	281
My time, O God, is in thine hand	163
My whole regard still may I place	273

Volume III

Me, the sinner most distrest	305
Mean are our noblest offerings	320
Melt, happy soul, in Jesu's blood[454]	168
Memorial of thy sacrifice	308
Messias, Prince of Peace	63
Ministerial spirits, come[455]	168
Mixed with the sacred smoke we rise	320
Moab shall first be trodden down	155
More than conquerors at last	294
Most justly then my day is past	42
Mourn the good-natured soft voluptuous crowd	116
My dear Redeemer, and my God	29
My earnest of eternal bliss	279
My feeble soul would fain aspire	331
My friend, how shall I let thee go?	173
My God and my Lord, thy call I obey	7
My greedy soul knows no remorse	34
My hands hang down, my feeble knees	42
My life I here present	37
My life to thee I fain would give	160
My love shall all your foes control	140
My mountains shall lift up their head	150
My people shall in dwellings sure	143
My soul could yield to every vice	60
My soul is on thy promise cast	32
My soul it harrows up	82
My spirit wound (but oh! be near	325
My strength will I ascribe to thee	61
My wound I slightly healed	52

---

453. From the German of Gottfried Arnold, translated by John Wesley.

454. Free paraphrase of the German of Christian Friedrich Richter by Charles Wesley.

455. Free paraphrase of the German of Wolfgang Christoph Dessler by Charles Wesley.

Volume IV

Made flesh for our sake	114
Made perfect first in love	110
Madness and misery	230
Make not as thou wouldst farther go	137
Make this the acceptable hour	378
Mark the men, who deeply sigh	68
Master, we call thy word to mind	27
Me for their dear redeeming Lord	33
Me if thou canst still restore	405
Me, Lord, thou never wilt forsake	474
Me, the vilest of the race	390
Me to thy suffering self conform	471
Meanest of all thy servants, I	271
Meet am I for the great	246
Men, devils engage, The billows arise	51
Men of dignity and power	229
Men of worldly, low design	228
Merciful God, to thee we cry	9
Mere mercies they are	362
Messiah! Joy of every heart	225
Might I find thy pardoning love	421
Might I in thy sight appear	358
Mine arms shall judge the world below	301
Mine indignation's dreadful cup	306
More desperate in my damned estate	392
Most helpless is my soul	327
Most holy, pure, and perfect thou	287
Mourn awhile for God thy rest	319
My anchor this, which cannot move	266
My every weakness she betrays	423
My Father's children feel my care	339
My feeble heart cannot conceive	361
My folly returned To Egypt and burned	415
My God hath saved me from all sin	311
My God, incline thine ear, and hear	6
My God, my God, what shall I say	362
My good and faithful servant thee	34
My gracious God, how shall I shun	475
My heart, which now to thee I raise	373
My Jesus, my hope, When will he appear	257
My just desert is more	397
My lusts have re-ursurped the sway	385
My mercy will I cause to rest	301
My message as from God receive	277
My only trust is in thy blood	471
My pardon I claim	372
My poor despairing soul she racks	424
My present help in trouble	84
My refuge is this	416
My righteousness shall soon appear	301
My righteousness shall stand alone	301
My Saviour prays for me	433
My sin's incurable disease	373
My solemn engagements are vain	477
My Son from all, who come to him	294
My Son I have for sinners given	304
My sore disease, my desperate sin	375
My soul doth magnify the Lord	311
My soul in sin so rooted stands	361
My soul shrinks back—but O! to whom	424
My soul with thy whole armour arm	476
My strong propensity to ill	381
My trespass is grown up to heaven	446
My vehement soul cries out for death!	396
Myself alas! I cannot raise	381

Volume V

Made like the first happy pair	408
Made perfect through woe	440
Made unto salvation wise	163
Make him as the troubled sea	241
Make us of one heart and mind	52
Master, come, no more delay	240
Master, I have not learned thee so	150
Master, I own thy lawful claim	157
Master, if thee the world blasphemed	144
Master, is it not for thee?	196
Master, thy promised help I claim	101
Master, we call thy word to mind	259
Me he called, a woman grieved	352
Me if thou hadst never sent	196
Me if thy grace vouchsafe to use	11
Me in my blood thy love passed by	1
Me my consort hath outrun	339

Me to retrieve from Satan's hands	302	My gifts and comforts all, I know	421
Meanest of all thy sons, on me	413	"My God hath called me hence," she cried	90
Meanest of the number I	339		
Meek, patient Son of God and man	242	*My God, I am thine*	24
Meek, simple followers of the Lamb	480	My God, my all, O Christ, thou art	66
Meet and right it is to sing	279	My God supply thy servant's need	103
Meet for the fellowship above	86	My goodness thou art	29
Men, devils agree To tell us in vain	333	My heart, alas, is dead	170
Men of like passions once ye were	362	My heart's desire, and prayer to thee	246
Mercy and peace your portion be	479	*My Jesus my All, thy name I confess*	419
Mercy I keep for all mankind	93	*My Jesus, my Lamb, / All weakness I am*	27
Might I now escape away	206	My Jesus, my Lamb, / I trust in thy name	303
Mine eyes' and heart's desire is gone	355		
Mine eyes prevent the morning ray	7	My Jesus, my Lord, thy grace I commend	427
Mine utter helplessness I own	145		
Misers, his life for you he paid	123	My Jesus to know	24
Mollify our harsher will	476	My Joshua, bid the sun stand still	295
More favoured than the saints of old	94	My joy in thee, my pure delight	159
More than resigned in mortal pain	89	My life is hid with Christ above	6
Moses thy backward parts might view	94	My longing soul prepare	430
Most meek, and tender-hearted Lamb	74	*My Lord, by sinners crucified*	97
Moved by the Spirit's softest wind	113	My Lord from above	29
Must I from him so much receive	434	My loving labour I repeat	19
My all of comfort here	418	My mourning days shall quickly end	355
My Alpha is here	304	My needy Jesus I descry	20
My basest want of love I feel	98	My pain is relieved, my sorrow is past	35
My body that dies	305	My pardon is sure, If I always endure	290
My bosom fill with soft distress	96	My pattern here I plainly see	147
My bosom-friend receive	429	My peace it is made	25
My brethren beloved, Your calling ye see	390	My poor heart vouchsafe to dwell in	297
My comfort and stay	251	My remnant of days	403
My comfort is fled	200	My residue of days	430
My comforts are blasted	207	*My Saviour and King*	28
My company is gone	348	My son I will to thee restore	397
My cup it runs o'er	26	My sorrows I forget	15
My ever-living Lord	347	My soul, and all its powers	16
My every idol I resign	191	My soul on thee, O Lord, relies	6
My every weak, though good, design	11	My soul, with just ambition fired	153
My faith is not vain	30	My spirit by thy pangs is torn	157
My first concern their souls to rear	394	My spirit, Lord, alarm	270
My first of comforts here below	412	My stony heart thy wrath defies	2
My former desperate wound to heal	433	My talents, gifts, and graces, Lord	106
My former friend (for ever dear	420	My total fall I never knew	310
My friend! by pitying grace bestowed	433	Myself, alas, I cannot heal	393

Myself I cannot save, myself I cannot keep	263

Volume VI

Made ready here by patient love	266
Maker, Saviour of mankind	384
Many a soul is lodged before us	209
Master at thy command we rise	103
Master, on us, even us bestow	265
Me, they say, thy hands have made	449
Meanest and least of all her sons, may I	61
Meek and lowly may I be	443
Meek like him, and just, and pure	291
Meekly we our vow repeat	251
Meet and right it is that I	464
Memorial of her faith unfeigned	248
Men in their own eyes Were children again	440
Merciful God, almighty King	75
Merciful God, how shall we raise	10
Merciful God thy love we sing	182
Mercy alone deferred our doom	159
Mercy, and love, and endless grace	372
Mercy is thy heavenly nature	169
Mercy o'er thy works presides	461
Mercy, that heaven-descending guest	270
Mercy prolonged his dying hours	403
Met in those permanent abodes	298
Methinks e'en now I hear him say	453
Millions more thou ready art	462
Mindful of thy chosen race	48
Mine earthly happiness is fled	253
Mixed with the virgin train	206
More esteemed as nearer viewed	336
Most gentle of all the soft kind	332
Most gracious God, what shall we say	169
Most patient God, regard our prayer	128
Mould them according to thy will	412
Mountains, alas! on mountains rise	409
Moved by our long continued cry	119
Murderer of souls, thou know'st he lives	236
Muster thy host, great God of war	130

My body I disdained t' incline	3
My bowels yearn with deep distress	86
My brethren, friends, and kinsmen these	72
My faith is all in thee	3
My father, my guide, (Our Israel may say	307
My first and last unalienable Friend	55
My furious wrath they still shall know	85
My God, in Jesus reconciled	450
My God to me his grace hath given	303
My Hutchinson himself survives	226
My Master calls: at his command	322
My peace thou hast already made	402
My prayers are sealed, my child has fled	258
My rebels shall with panic dread	88
My works of righteousness	2

Volume VII

Made apt by thy sufficient grace	75
Made apt to teach, he points them out the way	430
Made by pure consummate love	414
Made capable of heavenly rest	379
Make her, Lord, thy constant care	144
Make thy goodness pass before me	334
Man's intemperate offence	89
Manna spiritual and hidden	336
Many Gods we disclaim	301
Marked for an angel of the church below	427
Master, be thou my might, my mouth	182
Master supreme, I look to thee	160
May I not suffer his distress	146
Me baptized into thy passion	59
Me, me for his dear sake alone	107
Meet and right it is to praise	16
Meet for the fellowship above	404
Melted by thy creature's tears	97
Merciful God, on me	6
Merciful God, what hast thou done	177
Mercy I ask to seal my peace	193
Mercy we ask in Jesus' name	148
Might I on my Lord reclined	407
Might we, Lord, thy love attain	84

Mightier than the mighty, seize	11	My sin reluctant I confess	126
Mighty to redeem from pain	144	My soul an offering to my God	413
Mindful of thy servant, Lord	416	My soul in life detain	380
Mindful of thy suffering days	122	My Spirit then set free	389
Mine, alas, can never pay	127	My stiff-necked stubbornness of will	354
More grace is on the humble man bestowed	433	My virtues false and vain	102
		My zeal be warm, and wise, and meek	171
More highly favoured we than those	346	*Mysterious God in persons three*	328
Most sensibly declining	110		
Move their hearts, and more stir up	246		

Volume VIII

Moved by the Holy Ghost to minister	428	Make a loud and cheerful noise	183
Must I th' infernal language hear	169	Make me, through thy wondrous name	385
My bowels of compassion	117	Make the little ones thy care	409
My burden unable to bear	40	Make their tongues themselves betray	141
My deathless soul, my mouldering dust	394	Makers of wrecks, a desperate race	481
My every choice, desire, design	180	Malice ventures not to blame	302
My every creature-good remove	53	Man is a creature of a day	172
My fairest prospects I forego	174	Man's justice can no more demand	349
My feeble heart's extreme desire	375	Many a time, may Israel say	245
My finished work, my conflicts past	377	Me and mine I fain would give	401
My flesh again to dust shall turn	400	Me, for thy truth and mercy's sake	383
My God and Lord, thy counsel show	40	Me from my Lord	367
My God in Christ the sinners' Friend	417	Me from my youth thou, Lord, hast taught	160
My God, thou art in Jesus mine	176	Me he hath counted for his name	396
My God, thou wilt not leave me	104	Me Lord, thou didst begin to turn	155
My God, who from my earliest age	419	Me, me, thy meanest messenger	416
My head with Jesus bending	115	Me the proud have greatly scorned	216
My heart all other means defies	24	Me the proud with lies pursued	218
My heart he turns to earthly things	354	Me to redeem from sin and hell	378
My heart, which then to thee I give	385	Me to that great salvation keep	386
My immortality thou art	103	Me when thou hast taught thy way	233
My ingratitude to heal	357	Meantime in spite of all your covers	467
My last, my most momentous days	401	Meantime the resolute crusaders	451
My life, a copy fair from thine	172	*Men of true piety, they know not why*	444
My life I know secured above	62	*Mercies, Lord, belong to thee*	362
My life of faith and prayer	165	Merciful God, to them extend	346
My love they amply will repay	39	*Merciful God, what hast thou done*	390
My notions true are notions vain	315	Mercy and truth in concert sweet	168
My only Hope, in sad despair	370	Mercy they can ne'er receive	339
My only resource in despair	41	Mighty and numberless my foes	88
My only want, desire, and hope	401	Mighty to save, his love we sing	35
My paradise is lost and gone	134		
My rest on earth to toil for thee	182		
My Saviour from the wrath to come	50		

Mine ear shall hearken to his cry	177
Mine eye with sorrow fails	62
Mine eyes no longer drowned in tears	201
Mine eyes to God I ever lift	50
Mischief thy heart doth now devise	119
Mixed with the sheep on thy right-hand	341
Monarchs with their armies met	112
More righteous than ourselves are they	318
More than all my teachers I	223
Mortals shall revere thy voice	143
Most righteous God of boundless power	275
Most wretched of the sinful race	349
Mourning I go beneath thy frown	86
Musing on the former days	96
My blood poured out like water is	43
My clothes they equally divide	44
My foes are strong and numberless	154
My foes I challenged forth to fight	34
My friends can yield me no relief	87
My God alone I fain would love	426
My God, my God! I cry to thee!	42
My heart and flesh cry out for God	165
My heart is fixed, O God, my heart	128
My heart is full of Christ, and longs	102
My heart is pained within my my breast	122
My heart, to every vice inclined	79
My hope I ground on this alone	377
My lips shall glory in the song	161
My sins have swept me far from God	86
My soul, distressed on every side	54
My soul, inspired with sacred love	260
My soul out of the dungeon bring	258
My soul pursues and hangs on thee	139
My soul with infinite desire	386
My spirit faints by grief oppressed	259
My spirit humbly I commend	343
My spirit utterly had failed	55
My trust is in thy gracious power	24
My vows I will to his great name	202
My wretchedness to thee convert	116

Volume IX

Make me, Saviour, as thou art	281
Make this th' accepted season	343
Maker of the mouth of man	37
Man, born of a woman impure	245
Man, foolish and impotent man	292
Manifested by thy light	269
Manner and time I leave to thee	375
May I not feel my comfort fled	164
May we not grant our God's request	101
May'st thou not still conceal The face	217
Me an hoary, captive king	199
Me, his own, so dearly bought	363
Me, if purposed to destroy	138
Me if thou in the desert hide	177
Me if to myself thou leave	361
Me, me who still in darkness sit	416
Meanest of Jacob's race	117
Meanest of that happy band	176
Meekest of all the sons of men	69
Men in vain with fiends combine	38
Merciful God, long-suffering, kind	56
Merciful God, thyself proclaim	54
Mercy hath a sure nail bestowed	221
Mere withering leaves is all beside	255
Messias, Prince of Peace	373
Millions more their Lord shall know	430
Mindful of my rescues passed	160
Misers, hear, by God abhorred	275
More than the consolation	307
Moses fasted forty days	56
Moses might lead to Jordan's tide	119
Moses, the minister of God	71
Moses, when dead, himself survives	119
Most destitute, most helpless I	152
Most gracious God, reveal	67
Most righteous God, my doom I bear	9
Most tenderly affected	342
Much more than our sin	324
Murmuring that God should hide his face	264
Music, as first by heaven designed	160
Must we not walk before we run	409

My days are all vanished away	253
My days are extinguished and gone	253
My evil inclination	336
My favour and good-will to gain	371
My feeble ineffectual cry	238
My God, forsake me not at last	337
My God, from whom the precept came	105
My God, I wake to call thee mine	303
My God if in Jesus thou art	308
My God, my God, on thee I call	141
My heart is clean, and free	339
My heart to every ill inclined	336
My hope of creature-good I see	254
My hope of spotless righteousness	247
My house I may in order set	198
My inbred hell was stirred	355
My joy and my song	285
My latter end is come	98
My longing heart's desire	307
My loving God, the hindrance show	236
My lust of life is gone; yet here	291
My merciful God Hath chastened His Son	326
My merit, Lord, and righteousness	99
My most long-suffering Saviour	338
My mournful face is foul with tears	252
My name be on the children? no	31
My nature, Lord, is foul as hell	247
My own inventions past	318
My people saved, my chosen seed	432
My Potter from above	461
My Saviour, my God	26
My Saviour thee, not yet revealed	420
My Shepherd found his wandering sheep	281
My sin and wretchedness	282
My sin will find me out, unless	86
My sinful wretched heart set free	328
My sins as mountains rise	460
My sordid array	288
My sorrowful night	288
My soul, a dry and barren place	400
My soul, thou know'st, is faint	463
My soul through my Redeemers care	325
My soul, till God his Spirit pours	339
My time is in thy hand, O Lord	289
My treacherous heart will turn again	280
My trouble returned	286
My utmost strength when I exert	357

Volume X

Made willing by thy powerful call	158
Make our earthly souls a field	55
Man, fallen man conceals within	290
Man may swell with towering hope	10
Man mocks a Saviour, and High-priest	429
Man, sinful man, with blind desire	268
Many a paralytic soul	457
Many eat, but are not filled	500
Many they are and dry	59
Master, can thy follower be	479
Master, for thine we cannot own	230
Master, I want thy tenderness	312
Master, I with shame confess	390
Master, I would no longer be	238
Master, (in faith I call thee so)	205
Master of his own gifts, he takes	304
Master, thou didst the same by me	319
May I, observant of the least	362
May we not to Jesus go	279
Me, and every precious grain	147
Me, the true Barabbas, me	423
Me when an enemy to God	318
Me with that restless thirst inspire	163
Meanest vessel of thy grace	127
Meeken my soul, thou heavenly Lamb	162
Men who never care for God	397
Men would charm it or remove	427
Merciful God, what crowds receive	331
Mercy as with my latest breath	17
Mercy I ask in Jesu's name	40
Mercy who show shall mercy find	163
Mercy's outward works who show	393
Messiah, full of grace	61
Midst furious winds and raging seas	283
Might he now exalted be	65

Might we now with pure desire	32	Man made of earth by earth he heals	440
Millions go smoothly on	377	Man magnifies the deeds of men	161
Mine eyes have seen his orient star	142	Man will speak accused by man	84
Mine utter helplessness I feel	253	Marching through the vale below	93
Modest, not singular in dress	358	Martha's chosen work is good[457]	198
More desperately diseased than those	293	Martha's faith in active life[458]	196
More[456] labourers in their manly age	330	Master, (as such thyself I own)[459]	328
More servants to declare his word	346	Master, if thee I rightly hear	153
More than all the prophets old	247	Master, instruct us thus to know	340
More than for ease in mortal pain	81	Master, Lord, on me confer	214
Moses and the prophets speak	305	Master of my heart and will	330
Most gracious, most tremendous Lord	396	Master, the grace vouchsafe to me	66
Must we not then with patience wait	203	Master thee we call, and Lord	504
Must you wander far and near	373	Master, what a school is thine	394
My bosom sin I would not hide	193	Masters of our every passion	278
My faithfulness I cannot see	388	May this alone my thoughts employ	183
My Father knows the things I need	190	Me by the hand thy grace hath took	16
My Friend, my bosom Friend	422	Me! did Jesus come for me?	148
My God will add the rest	190	Me, I know thine eye beheld	331
My heart doth oft to idols cleave	76	Me into thy kingdom take	259
My heart was hardened from thy fear	7	Me, me command to sin no more	419
My memory, Lord, cannot retain	413	Me, the vile deserter me	92
My mortal foe, whom for thy sake	172	Meekness and love compose his train	486
My painful sin and misery	209	Meet and right it is that thou[460]	278
My Saviour if indeed thou art	284	Men with one consent excuse	228
My Saviour lost if I have found	439	Mercy constrains me to relieve	196
My sins I may with horror own	416	Mercy doth every soul embrace	111
My soul is among lions still	71	Mere man of earthly origin	349
My soul redeemed from Satan's toils	469	Might I but do for thee	70
My spirit's whole capacity	262	Millions of sheep so dearly bought	460
My strength when thou, O Jesus, art	104	Millions the Christian name	231
Myself I cannot heal	207	Mine eyes are holden too	307
Myself I cannot humble make	360	Mine universal sin	144
		Ministers and people too	18
		Ministers of Jesus' word	104

Volume XI

		Money with God of no esteem	484
Made capable through Jesus' word	9	More odious than the birds and beasts	337
Made willing by thy gracious call	35	More than a prophet sent by God	324
Made willing in the strength of grace	471	Moses could not give the Bread	382
Make thy heavenly wisdom mine	176		
Man in ministering relief	475		
Man is cruel to his friends	204		

456. Osborn changed "More" to "men."

457. *UP* 2:126.
458. *UP* 2:123.
459. *UP* 2:216.
460. *UP* 2:189.

Most lovely night with blessings crowned	510	Me, me, thou justly may'st upbraid	8
Most sensibly, O Lord, I know	438	Me thou know'st; let that	126
Mother of Purity Divine	332	Me thou know'st, my gracious God	125
Much of myself I dare not say	75	Meek, patient Lamb, for us he gives	99
Much she loved her loving God	167	Men from her infancy have rose	295
Multitudes of souls distressed	229	Men in every age are seen	174
Murdered on earth by Jews he was	51	Men of philosophic pride	337
My business, Lord, my only care	147	Men should patiently endure	187
My darkness by thy light I see	24	Men the Divine attraction feel	382
My evil will be all cast out	48	Mercy from savages we find	446
My Father's mind I then perceive	55	Mercy has ways to find them out	245
My God, my God, was ever love	500	Messengers of Christ the Lord	274
My God, to which shall I belong	246	Mighty miracles of love	144
My heart anoint and purify	17	Mine earnest expectation	300
My heart, my life henceforth is thine	159	Mine eyes are ever unto thee[462]	235
My heart, thy meanest house, I keep	66	Miracles he multiplies!	119
My heavenly Lord, I would from thee	161	Modern Athenians, hear	338
My hunted life belongs to thee	222	More of this madness, more	430
My life is not my own	349	More precious than the gold and gems	80
My most indulgent Saviour	507	More than outward wonders show	289
My simple childlike heart inspire	402	Moses the meek man of God	165
Myself as in a glass	298	Moses truly ministered	166
Myself from sin I cannot save	35	Moses when Abraham's God is near	165
		Moses with the church abode	212
		Most are ignorant that God	356
		Moved by every wind the sea	331
		Must I not do all I can	321

Volume XII

		My faith with joy and wonder sees	93
Made by persecution strong	288	My gracious Lord I know, thou art	104
Made out of weakness strong	195	My heart is set on things above	299
Man from adoring man	291	My hope by purity I show	411
Man, guilty man, by God abhorred	98	My hope is fixed on things above	412
Man without grace may courage show	69	My latest hope alas is o'er	438
Marriage was by God designed	183	My Lord by all deserted	45
Master, I bow to thy decree	40	My mind is hatred against God	32
Master, if me thou canst employ	237	My partners in the ship	119
Master of his own word and grace	313	My sins fell off, my will was free	267
Master, they are not ours but thine	119	My sins have done the deed	90
Master, thy pitying eye	159		
May I not, Lord, of thee inquire	136		
May not a creating God	424	## Volume XIII	
May we not trust our flock to him[461]	294		
Me by thy Father's love bestowed	68	Made by the Father's gift and grace	23

461. *UP* 3:364.

462. *UP* 2:325.

Man of the world, O God, am I?	103	Nations remote and realms unknown[464]	121
Master, at thy feet I wait	222	Nations, whom once thou didst not own	207
May I throughout this day of thine	221		
May we not 'scape the killing pain	88	Nature had lost its genial power	213
Me, Lord, if thou one moment leave	254	Nay, but I yield, I yield!	268
Memory severe, and secret shame	146	Near us, assisting Jesu, stand	346
Merciful God, vouchsafe to me	223	Never let them cease to flow	289
Mercy from God and heavenly grace	173	Never shall my wandering mind[465]	18
Mightier joys ordained to know	233	Never will he thence depart	188
More and more like Jesus grow	153	Nigh with my lips to thee I draw	132
Most feeble of the feeble throng	54	No common Vision this I see[466]	118
Most gracious Lord	81	No condemnation now I dread	106
Most wretched comforters are they	124	No: for us you ever wait	365
Most wretched of all the lost race	7	No—I never will resign	325
Most wretched of the fallen race	206	No! in the death of him that dies	312
Must I be tried and tortured still?	56	No longer then my heart shall mourn	329
My calling now I clearly see	84	No longer, then, my Lord, defer	244
My days shall then be all employed	255	No more, I cried, shall grief be mine[467]	38
My double privilege I take	78	No more to lift my eyes I dare	84
My friend no more on earth appears	79	No! my best actions cannot save	226
My God, most high, most holy	74	No profit canst thou gain[468]	126
My grain of faith, my buried grain	38	No! thou blind leader of the blind	24
My hands, and lips, and heart impure	100	No! though it rouse thy utmost rage	24
My heart is hardened from thy fear	180	No, though men and fiends exclaim	286
My last decisive hour	258	No—though the ancient dragon rage	92
My ransomed spirit I	258	Nor can we thus thy wrath appease	368
My soul, escaped the fowler's net	256	Nor heaven nor earth do I desire[469]	111
My want of thankfulness, and love	78	Nor yet the earthly Adam dies	132
My works the sure credentials are	169	Not but his gracious Master here[470]	58
Myself begotten from above	180	Not even a word or look[471]	70
Myself I fain would humble, Lord	187	Not long—for he, gone up on high[472]	165
Myself to Tophet I condemn	187	Not one will call upon thy name	368
Myself how shall I ready make	238		
Mysterious gifts unseen	72		
Mystery of amazing grace!	49		

464. Henry Pitt.
465. From the French, Antoinette Bourignon.
466. Altered from John Norris.
467. George Herbert.
468. From the German of Paul Gerhardt translated by John Wesley.
469. From the French, Antoinette Bourignon.
470. George Herbert.
471. George Herbert.
472. Henry More.

Volume I

Naked from Satan did I flee[463]	348
Naked or in rough goatskins clad	220
Nations all, far off and near	185

463. From the German of Nikolaus von Zinzendorf, translated by John Wesley.

INDEX OF FIRST LINES OF POETRY BY JOHN AND CHARLES WESLEY

First Line	Page
Not so, my heart!—for fruit there is[473]	39
Nothing I am, and nothing have	253
Nothing ye in exchange shall give	205
Now arm me now for the threatening fight	179
Now Christ in us doth live, and we[474]	339
Now descend and share the earth	189
Now display thy saving power	184
Now hast thou given us, through thy Son[475]	339
Now I have found the ground wherein[476]	279
Now incline me to repent	273
Now let our darkness comprehend	237
Now let the heathens fear thy name	366
Now let their opposition cease	296
Now let them feel the tidings true	240
Now let thy face be seen	338
Now, Lord, for thee our all we leave	215
Now, Lord, to whom for help I call	263
Now the gracious Father smiles	94
Now then, my God, thou hast my soul[477]	100
Now to thyself the victim take	216
Now varied deaths their terrors spread	14

Volume II

First Line	Page
Naked of thine image, Lord	93
Nature is subject to thy word	142
Nature, perverse and rough, shall yield	50
Neither life nor death shall sever	97
Never again disclose thy face	65
Never let me go, till I	126
Never let me leave thy breast	126
Never shall I want it less	208
Nigh with my lips I drew	115

473. George Herbert.
474. From the German of Ludwig Andreas Gotter, translated by John Wesley.
475. From the German of Ludwig Andreas Gotter, translated by John Wesley.
476. From the German of Johann Andreas Rothe, translated by John Wesley.
477. From the German of Joachim Lange, translated by John Wesley.

First Line	Page
No choice, endeavour, or desire	110
No desire or will have I	76
No good work, or word, or thought	201
No, Jesus, no! thou Holy One	162
No longer am I now afraid	243
No, Lord, thy truth and grace I clear	101
No more in me thy being last	308
No, no, the witness cries!	329
No way to escape, I see	266
No work of mine, or word, or thought	149
None is there like Jeshurun's God	305
Nor can he thus their hate assuage	70
Nor did he let his censure wildly fall	122
Nor did his zeal for her his love restrain	123
Nor even in death could he forget His own	125
Nor less th' exemplary father shone	118
Nor does the tender wandering lambs	18
Nor doth his love eclipse	52
Not because I willing am	76
Not by human might or power	291
Not by my own righteousness	260
Nothing, alas! have I to plead	122
Nothing am I in thy sight	152
Nothing but drought and thorn and brake	42
Nothing have I, Lord, to pay	200
Nothing in me thy grace can move	84
Nothing the creature adds to him	53
Now I seem to taste thy love	124
Now, if thou canst, withhold the grace	288
Now in thy strength I strive with thee	295
Now, Jesu, let thy powerful death	270
Now let me gain perfection's height	323
Now let the ponderous ruin fall	108
Now, Lord, thy death, thy life bring in	122
Now, O my Joshua, bring me in	303
Now the old Adam is, I know	247
Now, this instant now, if sin	124
Now to their idol's temple brought	107

Volume III

Nay, but his bowels yearned to see	22
Nay, but this is his will	282
Never let me lose my peace	250
Never love nor sorrow was	230
Never will we hence depart	229
Nigh to thy wounds whoever draw	153
No answer yet? What, no reply?	76
No cloak for mine offence have I	42
No common fight, though fierce, and loud	138
No decree of his consigned	15
No dire decree obtained thy seal	33
No dire decree of thine is here	19
No local Deity	262
No more let Satan's offspring rise	149
No more may they offend	329
No other right have I	57
No ray of light, no gleam of hope	26
No: to be saved he made them not	67
Nor did he let his censure wildly fall	122
Nor did his zeal for her his love restrain	123
Nor even in death could he forget his own	125
Nor less th' exemplary father shone	118
Not a spirit above	372
Not all his threatened woes	54
Not all the days before or since	322
Not as uncertainty the race he ran	115
Not by the hearing of the ear	142
Not long for all her heaven she stayed	176
Not one of all that fell	90
Not then above their Master wise	339
Nothing else but love I know[478]	167
Nothing for me remains	56
Nothing have I to plead	56
Nourish us to that awful day	247
Now, even now, we all plunge in	235
Now, even now we may	HGEL 1741, 31
Now I am fall'n away	57
Now in the means the grace impart	272
Now inflict the mortal pain	333
Now let the spouse, reclined on thee	341
Now, Lord, into our souls bring in	30
Now, Lord, on us thy flesh bestow	238
Now mine eyes are opened wide	258
Now, O God, thine own I am	334
Now, on the sacred table laid	263
Now, Saviour, now thyself reveal	237
Now to thy glorious kingdom come	290

Volume IV

Naked and destitute and blind	186
Neither passion nor pride	365
Neither wars nor plagues they fear	16
Never let the world break in	229
Never, never can it be	318
News they bring us of salvation	207
No foot of land do I possess	279
No gift or comfort we	168
No help can I from these receive	452
No horrid alarum of war	126
No, I will not cease from crying	389
No, in thy strength we say	45
No longer visible	177
No longer we join While sinners invite	241
No man can truly say	196
No more shall sin its sway maintain	480
No more shall strange desires consume[479]	314
No, never will we part	45
No opening door, no way to shun	269
No possibility of hope	269
No power to stand against my sin	392
No smallest motion can I make	332
No spark of sin is left alive	290
Nor angel tongues can e'er express	161
Nor can my desperate heart conceive	269
Nor won, nor lost, subsists the fight	355
Not all their treasures shall redeem	61
Not but thou read'st our thankful heart	102
Not by a mighty host	82

---

478. Free paraphrase of the German of Wolfgang Christoph Dessler by Charles Wesley.

479. *UP* 2:453.

First Line	Page
Not by an arm of flesh, but	54
Not by many or by few	64
Not on an arm of flesh, but thine	301
Not one attempts with pious care	305
Not our providence or sword	58
Not to a single age confined	166
Not to those earliest days	178
Not without blood—thou pray'st above	158
Nothing against their might shall stand	72
Nothing is there in me	412
Nothing now can relieve	410
Nothing on earth I call my own	279
Now I languish in vain	412
Now I sin without remorse	386
Now, Jesu, now the veil remove	137
Now, Jesus, now the Father's love	324
Now let thy best endeavours plead	345
Now, Lord, if thou art power, descend	247
Now, Lord, relieve my misery	326
Now, now let me die	413
Now, now let me know	366
Now, Saviour, now the fever chide	376
Now sinner, now what is thy hope?	344
Now the benefit impart	180
Now the gracious work begin	417
Now then acknowledge us for thine	6
Now then of his receive	192
Now wilt thou mock the sons of God	346
Numbered with the transgressors thou	461

Volume V

First Line	Page
Naked, and without disguise	195
Nature would cry, my son, my son!	81
Nay, and when we remove	31
Nay, but in thy strength we rise	277
Nay, nay, but I feel	29
Near the Most High, on either hand	287
Nearer and nearer still	386
Never once wast thou betrayed	359
Never shipwrecked mariner wanted	212
Never sure was heart like mine	443
Never will I cease to mourn	133
Never will thy patience fail	184
Nigh me I find my threefold foe	6
No answer yet? no late reply	147
No curse to annoy	201
No, dear companion, no!	215
No faithless friend shall there be found	199
No grievous alloy	401
No heart-distracting passion	208
No longer now constrained	220
No longing we find	387
No matter how dull The scholar whom he	390
No more in our imperfect state	319
No more may I provoke	418
No more may we to sin submit	166
No more o'erwhelmed with terrors	217
No more; till that thrice welcome day	432
No mournful complaints	201
No; my God, if from the way	13
No, my Lamb, my Saviour, no	14
No, no, never fear	320
No other end of life I know	77
No pity or humane regard	152
No promise can their wisdom find	327
No, thou gracious God and true	160
No uneasy alloy	223
None of all thy gifts below	204
None of the sacred order I	103
Nor death, nor life can now disjoin	74
Nor pleasure soft can soothe	84
Nor slightest touch of pain	461
Nor would I him o'ertake	357
Not a doubt can arise	25
Not all the powers of hell can fright	17
Not all thy passion's bleeding power	98
Not for your needless aid	221
Not in the name of pride	468
Not one of all the rich, or great	257
Not unto me, O Lord	127
Not unto me, O Lord, the praise	8
Not without thee, my Lord, I am	110
Nothing do I seek below	161
Nothing else can I require	22
Nothing else will we know	31

Nothing less will I require	306	Not all the things we read or hear	382
Nought have I whereof to boast	196	Not even in death his friendship dies	226
Now into his dungeon shine	256	Not for our nation's righteousness	166
Now let us by thy word be tried	315	Not in a confident conceit	102
Now, Lord, appear	61	Not in my helpless self I trust	274
Now, now let me feel	305	Not of the world, while here he lived	345
Now; or whene'er thy will	431	Not one, but all our days below	431
Now pronounce the welcome word	206	Not one good word or thought	2
Now, Saviour, now (if after God	415	Not one, till Israel is passed o'er	180
Now, Saviour, now their fears remove	254	"Not so," replied the Father's love[481]	302
Now therefore a spirit receive	340	Not without hope henceforth I mourn	348
Now thy love-infusing Spirit	54	Nothing hath the just to lose	94
Now thy mercy's wings expand	134	Nothing is worth a thought beneath	433
Now to thy yoke their spirits bow	125	"Nothing," she cries, "can shake my peace	274
Now wilt thou make an end	471	Now destroy the man of sin	48
		Now, Father, send him down	393
		Now let the generous patriots rise	128

Volume VI

		Now let us give our fightings o'er	50
Never can thy word be broken	45	Now, Lord, in answer to our prayer	132
Never will we hence depart	377	Now, Lord, in their defence arise	50
No delight thy goodness hath	40	Now, Lord, into thy hands receive	341
No earthly wish detains thee here	229	Now, Lord, the gracious work begin	413
No human heart can e'er conceive	257	Now, Lord, to shake our guilty land	25
No matter which my thoughts employ	432	Now, O Christ, thy right assert	174
No more my eyes with tears o'erflow	258	*Now, only now against that hour*	27
No need of the sun in that day	198	Now reveal thy full salvation	142
No, never shall their rage prevail	106	Now, Saviour, clothe them with	
No new-made Deity	230	thy power	108
No noisy self-deceiver she	249	Now to thy drooping church return	82
No pangs of loss or care	238		
No riches had they But riches of grace	440		
No room for mirth or trifling here	432	## Volume VII	
No sudden fits of transient love	319		
Nor can it seem to souls already freed	60	Nature with little is content	420
Nor did he perish immature	234	Need we then prescribe to thee	122
Nor did I linger at my friend's desire	69	Neither greater nor less	321
Nor less the Christian husband shone	310	No distinction we find	302
Nor would I e'er disgrace the		No inferior God we praise	220
church's cause	58	No longer I endeavour	112
Nor yet the Lord his light imparts	312	No matter where or how	136
Nor yet the peaceful answer came[480]	302	*No more amused by earthly things*	106
Not all the archangels can tell	196	No: rather let my actions tell	172

480. *UP* 3:334.

481. *UP* 3:335.

No: thy passion answers no	353	Never more will I commit	442
No vain distinction we confess	219	Never shall I love my God	373
No: we have our suit made known	123	Never shall I more remove	59
None applied in vain to thee	97	No: by redeeming love the snare is broke	443
None but th' almighty Spirit can	246	No creature-good dost thou desire	117
None of a different nature can	254	No fellowship have they with thee	180
Nor can my utmost griefs or pains	100	No mercies can their rage disarm	129
Nor did their fierce abhorrence always last	437	No portion and no place have they	4
		No shadowy form dost thou require	91
Nor let the scrupulous sons of Levi fear	428	No thief he saith shall enter in	347
Nor poverty nor riches give	419	Not by the basest tools of war	286
Not from our creeds alone	305	Not for a single crime we die	349
Not harsh, imperious, or austere	159	Not for crimes which I have done	130
Not his own will, as man, to do	227	Not for himself but others made	290
Not in the tombs we pine to dwell	43	Not for his death, but life we pray	415
Not my own faithfulness	361	Not one of Adam's race	326
Not on vain imaginations	333	Nothing his rapid course can stay	304
Not that the sufferings I endure	100	Nothing more can I desire	365
Not three eternals we adore	287	Now, accepting my distress	410
Not without thy direction	91	Now admit my bold appeal	443
Not yet by the commandment slain	133	Now baptize my soul with fire	369
Nothing here can relieve	322	Now[482] cut short thy work in mine	412
Now apply the blood that cleanses	384	Now in thy own appointed hour	441
Now as yesterday the same	61	Now let him kindly condescend	351
Now by thy dying love constrain	25	Now let his guilty doom proceed	94
Now explain thy whole design	56	Now, Lord, a gracious token show	293
Now her spotless soul remove	82	Now, Lord, a gracious token give	411
Now I have thine aid bespoken	59	Now, Lord, in our behalf arise	20
Now Jesus, now, thy love impart	43	Now, Lord, the grace almighty show	153
Now let me know The grace below	190	Now, O thou love essential come	375
Now let thy dying love constrain	406	Now, Saviour, now accept my prayer	170
Now, Lord, I have to thee made known	51	Now the precious grace impart	383
Now the veil of sin withdraw	196	Now to my helpless soul draw nigh	156
Now their foundation false o'erturn	329		
Now then exert thy gracious art	187		

Volume IX

Naked into the world I came	230
Nay, but he casts the righteous down	239

Volume VIII

Nations that walked in gospel light	419	Nay, but I surely will	465
Near to relieve them at their need	72	"Nay, we have thousands got:"	438
Neither man, nor God they spare	302	No: every fallen child of man	208
Neither sin, nor earth, nor hell	235	No; for I am not yet in hell	321
Never can we know thy way	334		

482. Osborn changed "Now" to "O."

No: for the Lord is not in them 193
No good thing belongs to me 297
No goodness have ye, No goodness ye need 445
No; I would not always live 235
No longer, dearest Lord, defer 348
No longer rash to act, or speak 393
No longer then to evil prone 337
No, Lord; it cannot shortened be 69
No more can I require 310
No more shalt thou upbraided be 441
No, not if all the saints could join 237
No, thou malicious fiend! 230
No wily fiend, by magic spell 162
No wrinkle of the Adam old 107
Noah, descended from the skies 15
Nor swiftness can secure the race 357
Not all the miracles of love 49
Not all the powers of earth and hell 152
Not as a formal task to thee 302
Not every day, but oft, he falls 352
Not for a favourite form, or name 333
Not from his head was woman took 4
Not in contemplating, or prayer 185
Not in my watchfulness or care 331
Not in the strong impetuous wind 180
Not like the mothers in our day 149
Not like the warring sons of men 381
Not on the whirlwind's wings he flies 6
Not one of all mankind 248
Not one of all our fallen race 246
Not one of all our sinful race 246
Not one of all the sons of men 250
Not one of our polluted race 247
Not so the true immortal Bread 48
Not the alms, or works of man 62
Not with a loud uplifted voice 414
Nothing but sin can sinners slay 75
Nothing great may I admire 376
Nothing more can we require 429
Nothing too hard can be 18
Now for thy promise sake 383
Now I find the good of man 356
Now in the state of devils 3
Now let our monarch see 320
Now let thy chosen ones appear 85
Now let thy look inspire 463
Now, Lord, I arrested attend 269
Now, Lord, with simple faith divine 113
Now our universe create 461
Now out of our sins we go 428
Now, Saviour, now appear, appear 276
Now she without spot appears 367
Now through faith divinely strong 284
Now with enlightened eyes we see 222

Volume X

Nature cries, Deliver now! 501
Nature would fain evade, or flee 336
Nay; but his seed he often sows 389
Need I then, my God, despair 124
Never more will I transgress 5
New as the word of truth and grace 450
No evil, Lord, can I eschew 328
No evil thought shall there remain 13
No I cannot doubt thy love 453
No, I find he never will 260
No: I would not hitherto 23
No longer weep and mourn 438
No more feet from wrath to flee 352
No mortal eye the manner sees 476
No partial, outward righteousness 167
No pause or intermission 181
No peace is for the wicked found 14
No powers extraordinary I claim 154
No preachers of thy gospel they 443
No respite or repose we know 332
No shy reserve, or close disguise 238
No; the rich in faith who most 384
No, there can be no reprieve *SH* 1762, 2:194
No, they cry, it cannot be! 42
No, thou wilt not make an end 35
No turns of eloquence he 477
No, ye blind scribes of learning proud 220
None is originally good 324
Nor yet his servant he permits 494

Not all the mortal sons of grace	26	Nature impatient of delay	462
Not all those other husbandmen	345	Nature's strife will never last	79
Not brawling, popular, and loud	260	Need the true believer dread	176
Not by our best endeavours vain	114	Needy saints your privilege know	59
Not for my fault, or folly's sake	164	Never may I take the praise	178
Not for ourselves the light of grace	165	New Pharisees in every place	30
Not for the wretched sons of men	395	Nine months for a mistrustful word	104
Not from a stock of ours but thine	280	No angel from his throne	345
Not from the greatest to the least	42	No dazzling gifts or talents	193
Not honours, power, or pleasures vain	300	No greater joy the servant knows	348
Not in a king's, but servant's form	336	No help or hope I have	187
Not know the Man (that God below)	414	No hope shall the tormented know	246
Not on a frail sinful creature	301	No longer visible	70
Not on our own laborious pain	333	No matter how vile The sinner has been	359
Not one of all the rich or great	232	No proofs will for the men suffice	12
Not one of our rebellious race	149	No thanks to me my Master owes	251
Not through an all-suspecting fear	237	No; the letter profits nought[483]	504
Not to indulge our sloth and ease	240	No; the Spirit's dispensation	408
Not to surprise our Lord intends	307	No unexamined thought or word	67
Not to the just, but sinners sent	457	No: with God they greatly live	434
Not without grief an eye is lost	315	No: without thy farther light	504
Nothing can thy will withstand	227	None dares in their behalf to speak	400
Nothing can withstand thy will	480	None that is not taught by thee	313
Nothing I ask but in his name	149	Not a new-made dependent God	436
Nothing impossible shall be	311	Not a single soul excused	182
Nothing of softness or excess	247	Not all who saving faith profess	503
Now, even now, I yield, I yield	24	Not by a blind capricious will	194
Now, even now thy saints attend	374	Not by the Christian name alone	428
Now for my double sin I grieve	3	Not differing from a servant now	321
Now for thy mercy's sake	59	Not employing for his use	240
Now in the sense of cancelled sin	85	Not for the legal feast	283
Now inclined by thee, I pray	82	Not half so wise the sons of light[484]	241
Now let thy word take place	122	Not he who barely knows	57
Now, Lord, at thy command I go	485	Not like a sudden transient flood	356
Now on the verge of life I cry	195	Not one among them all, not one	418
Now the holy violence give	250	Not one upbraiding word	237
Now then put forth thy hand of grace	209	Not such the riches of his grace	209
Numbered with the transgressors, thee	428	Not the desires of men to please	336
		Not through a sad desponding fear	471
		Not to a single age or place	140

Volume XI

Naked is my heart to thee	327
Nature attempts and hopes in vain	308

483. *UP* 2:257.
484. *UP* 2:156.

Not to improve them, is to lose[485]	266
Not with these eyes of flesh and blood	321
Nothing I in secret do	207
Now, Father, now our sins forgive	201
Now he is sent down from heaven	409
Now I seek to touch my Lord	151
Now, in the end of time, revealed	335
Now, in thy Spirit of burning come	310
Now, just now, is nature's word	398
Now that the world our God arraign	493
Now thy miracles of grace	384
Numbers frequent thy house of prayer	252

Volume XII

Nature innocently may	127
Nearer the destined time and place	384
Needful thee alone we know	355
Neglecting such a time as this	414
Never unfruitful or alone	370
Never weary of well doing	326
No colour for their sin they have	31
No conqueror or hero can	362
No, I never will believe	109
No longer held by servile fear	27
No more presumptuous to foretell	137
No; my sin and shame I own	123
No neuters in the Christian war	289
No ornaments in its defence	410
No other arms but prayer she knows	264
No outward miracles we claim	155
No smooth-tongued orator is he	413
No, there is no other name	172
No; thy guilty heart must own	225
No time the prisoner needs	421
No universal head	386
No vision of my God	427
None affects dominion there	306
Nor earth nor hell its power withstands	320
Not all the hands of all mankind	377
Not by a legal righteousness	303
Not by force of arms upheld	75

Not by the crafty wizard swayed[486]	274
Not careful to foreknow	374
Not for the sake of health alone	241
Not for the vinegar they gave[487]	94
Not for the world of sinners dead	51
Not hasty, not precipitate	413
Not in a lower sphere	456
Not like an hireling vain	387
Not many rich and great	334
Not peace but a divisive sword	289
Not rigid wrath extreme	184
Not speak at all in Jesus' name	176
Not the advice of flesh and blood	240
Not through vile hypocrisy	352
Not with a cold or double heart	77
Not with angry passion fired	275
Not with worldly pomp and power	76
Nothing can escape thine eye	305
Nothing have we asked of thee	41
Nothing they could by tumult gain	404
Nothing unclean can come from heaven	246
Now behold their threatenings, Lord	179
Now in the way we go	7
Now, now he ready is	233
Now then the ceaseless shower	260
Numbered with sinners thee	84
Numbered with the transgressors see	318
Numbered with the transgressors here	434

Volume XIII

Nailed to the cross where Jesus bled	7
Nature doth to thy gracious power	14
Nature would the crown receive	133
Nature's highmindedness	16
No dread have they, lest men should prize	54
No end of this intestine war	281
No enemies to Sion's peace	282
No follower after thee I am	181
No longer I	81

485. *UP* 2:176.
486. *UP* 2:351.
487. *UP* 2:276.

INDEX OF FIRST LINES OF POETRY BY JOHN AND CHARLES WESLEY

No lot or part with us have they	213	O, do not, do not thus withdraw[491]	46
No; not after twenty years	80	O, draw me, Saviour, after thee[492]	140
No room for glorying in their grace	95	O Father, sanctify this pain[493]	130
No sooner was I called a son	127	O Filial Deity,	
No: the follower of that Lamb	59	/ Accept my new-born cry![494]	97
Not all that hear the word	4	O Filial Deity,	
Not by the blood of bullocks	138	/ Accept my new-born cry!	99
Not for our works or righteousness	114	O for a faith like his, that we	215
Not John himself presumes to trace	199	O for a thousand tongues to sing	300
Not many rich there are	167	O, give me now to speak thy word	239
Not one of all thy saints but needs	17	O, give me, Saviour, give me more!	75
Not out of nature's reach, fight on	87	O God, my God, my all thou art[495]	174
Nothing have I of my own	51	O God of God, in whom combine[496]	162
Nothing have I to offer thee	231	O God, of good th' unfathomed Sea[497]	141
Nothing of desert I claim	102	O God, of good th' unfathomed Sea[498]	143
Now in the wilderness	185	O God, thou bottomless abyss[499]	143
Now is salvation's day	202	O, guide me, lead me in thy ways[500]	130
Now is the saints' salvation come	234	O, grant that nothing in my soul[501]	138
Now Lord, as love thyself reveal	51	O, hide this self from me, that I[502]	72
Now, Lord, reveal	162	O, holy, holy, holy Lord!	245
Now, Saviour, bring the joyful hour	191	O, how diversified the scene	180
Now, Saviour, now the work begin	69		
Now, Saviour, now thy servant bless	123		
Now the gospel-grace impart	271		
Now the old dragon is o'erthrown	234		
Now the season is of love	50		
Now to every saint, and me	20		

Volume I

O, break my bonds, let sin enthrall[488]	61
O, brook not this; let not thy foes[489]	38
O, call to mind thy earnest prayers	274
O, come; for thou dost know the way![490]	40
O, could I lose myself in thee!	327
O Death, where is thy sting? where now	128
O, disclose thy lovely face	254

488. George Herbert.
489. George Herbert.
490. George Herbert.
491. George Herbert.
492. From the German of Paul Gerhardt, translated by John Wesley.
493. From the German of Nikolaus von Zinzendorf, translated by John Wesley.
494. The six-line stanzas on pages 97 and 99 beginning with the line. "O filial Deity" are identical.
495. From the Spanish of David Israel Lopez Laguna.
496. From the German of Nikolaus von Zinzendorf, translated by John Wesley.
497. The six-line stanzas on pages 141 and 143 beginning with this line are identical.
498. From the German of Johann Angelus Scheffler, translated by John Wesley.
499. From the German of Ernst Lange, translated by John Wesley.
500. From the German of Nikolaus von Zinzendorf, translated by John Wesley.
501. From the German of Paul Gerhardt, translated by John Wesley.
502. From the German of Gerhard Tersteegen, translated by John Wesley.

O, how shall I the goodness tell	91	O Love, our stubborn wills subdue[518]	163
O, how unbounded is thy love[503]	125	O Love, thou bottomless abyss[519]	280
O! if thy Spirit send forth me	314	O Love! thy sovereign aid impart / To save[520]	72
O Jesu, full of grace! the sighs[504]	90	O Love! thy sovereign aid impart / And	132
O Jesu, source of calm repose[505]	161	O, may I of thy grace obtain	24
O, kill in me this rebel Sin[506]	109	O, may one beam of thy blest light[521]	12
O King of glory, King of peace[507]	102	O, may our souls for ever pine	32
O King of Glory, thy rich grace[508]	174	O, mete not arms with man, nor stretch[522]	48
O King of Grief! (how strange and true[509]	27	O my offended Lord	267
O, leave not, cast me not away[510]	130	O, never in these veils of shame[523]	160
O, let the dead now hear thy voice[511]	350	O powerful Love, to thee we bow[524]	163
O, let thine anger rage no more	369	O sovereign Love, to thee I cry	88
O, let thine indignation burn	366	O that I as a little child[525]	140
O, let thy love our hearts constrain	298	O that I never, never more	305
O, let thy sacred presence fill[512]	110	O that I now the rest might know	371
O, let thy wondrous mercy's praise[513]	114	O that in me the sacred fire	329
O, let us find the ancient way	299	O that it now from heaven might fall	329
O, let your prayers the Saviour move	246	O that my heart, which open stands[526]	139
O, loose this frame, life's knot untie[514]	65	O that my latest change were o'er![527]	45
O Lord, how gladly would my rhymes[515]	47	O that our life might be	338
O Lord, O God of Love[516]	158	O that the bitterness were past	245
O Love, how cheering is thy ray![517]	139	O that the Comforter would come	308
		O that the mild and peaceful dove	250
		O that thou wouldst the heavens rend	366

503. George Herbert.
504. From the German of Wolfgang Dessler, translated by John Wesley.
505. From the German of Johann A. Freylinghausen, translated by John Wesley.
506. From the German of Nikolaus von Zinzendorf, translated by John Wesley.
507. George Herbert.
508. From the German of Nikolaus von Zinzendorf, translated by John Wesley.
509. George Herbert.
510. From the German of Nikolaus von Zinzendorf. translated by John Wesley.
511. From the German of Nikolaus von Zinzendorf. translated by John Wesley.
512. From the French, Antoinette Bourignon.
513. George Herbert.
514. George Herbert.
515. George Herbert.
516. From the German of Johann Angelus Scheffler, translated by John Wesley.
517. From the German of Paul Gerhardt, translated by John Wesley.
518. From the German of Nikolaus von Zinzendorf, translated by John Wesley.
519. From the German of Johann Andreas Rothe, translated by John Wesley.
520. From the German of Gerhard Tersteegen, translated by John Wesley.
521. From the German of Sigmund Gmelin, translated by John Wesley.
522. George Herbert.
523. From the German of Joachim Lange, translated by John Wesley.
524. From the German of Nikolaus von Zinzendorf, translated by John Wesley.
525. From the German of Paul Gerhardt, translated by John Wesley.
526. From the German of Paul Gerhardt, translated by John Wesley.
527. George Herbert.

IDEX OF FIRST LINES OF POETRY BY JOHN AND CHARLES WESLEY

O that thou wouldst the heavens rent	269
O the intolerable load	261
O, then, let wrath remove[528]	70
O thou that in thy chosen liv'st[529]	344
O thou, to whose all-searching sight[530]	137
O thou, who all things canst control[531]	12
O thou, who, when I did complain[532]	123
O thou, whom sinners love, whose care[533]	169
O, throw away thy rod / O, throw away[534]	69
O, throw away thy rod / What though[535]	70
O were I innocent, that I[536]	28
O, what a damp and deadly shade[537]	46
O, what a thing is man! from rest[538]	18
O, what is life without my God	251
O, what were man, if his attire[539]	19
O, when shall I my Canaan gain	303
O, when shall I no longer call	242
O, when wilt thou, my Life, appear	172
O, who shall save the man of sin?	252
O, why did I my Saviour leave	327
O ye, who joy to feed his sheep[540]	349
Obedient to his God's command	212
Of all thou hast in earth below	225
Of all thou the beginning art[541]	104
Of hope I felt no joyful ground	73
Of life the Fountain thou	98
Of life thou art the tree	98
Of whom the world unworthy was	220
Oft did I with th' assembly join	233
Oft from the margin of the grave	323
Oft hath the sea confessed thy power	323
Oft have we seen thy mighty power[542]	174
Oft when beneath the work of sin[543]	51
Oft with thy saints my voice I raise	131
On all the earth thy Spirit shower[544]	167
On God supreme our hope depends[545]	121
On right and wrong thy thoughts no more[546]	39
On thee my helpless soul is cast	322
On thee, my Priest, I call	99
On thee we fix our eyes	337
On this glad day the glorious Sun	299
One only care my soul shall know[547]	86
One with God, the Source of bliss	357
Only a sweet and virtuous mind[548]	10
Only preserve my soul from sin	237
Only thou to me be given	223
Open the hearts of all that hear	239
Open the intercourse between	225
Open the Scriptures now; reveal	238
Or, firm through him and undismayed	26
Or, if the sovereign wise decree	182
Or, if thy wiser will ordain	135
Or stoned, they glorified their Lord	220
Ordained I am, and sent by thee	239
Other ground can no man lay	358
Other refuge have I none	259
Others, as in a furnace tried	220
Our claim admit, and from above[549]	166
Our eyes on earth survey	147

528. George Herbert.
529. Altered from George Sandys.
530. From the German of Nikolaus von Zinzendorf. translated by John Wesley.
531. From the German of Sigmund Gmelin, translated by John Wesley.
532. Samuel Wesley, Sr.
533. From the German of Nikolaus von Zinzendorf. translated by John Wesley.
534. George Herbert.
535. George Herbert.
536. George Herbert.
537. George Herbert.
538. George Herbert.
539. George Herbert.
540. From the German of Nikolaus von Zinzendorf, translated by John Wesley.
541. From the German of Johann A. Freylinghausen, translated by John Wesley.
542. From the German of Nikolaus von Zinzendorf, translated by John Wesley.
543. John Gambold?
544. Henry More.
545. Henry Pitt.
546. George Herbert.
547. From the German of Christian Friedrich Richter, translated by John Wesley.
548. George Herbert.
549. Henry More.

Our life is hid with Christ in God	370	O, look not, Lord, on my desert	41
Our messias is come down	297	O let it now make haste to die	271
Our spirit is right, our heart is clean	370	O let them spread thy name	343
Out of the deep on Christ I call	273	O let thy gracious Spirit guide	255
Out of the depths of self-despair	255	O, let thy orient beams	27
Outcasts of men, to you I call	92	O let us all join hand in hand	333
		O let us by thy cross abide	332
		O let us conquer all our foes	352

Volume II

		O let us ever walk in him	222
O Almighty God of Love	104	O let us faithfully obey	137
O, begin; the way prepare	80	O let us not presume to take	331
O! but must I, Lord, return	103	O let us of thy strength take hold	350
O, cast not out my dying prayer	108	O let us on thy fulness feed	362
O compassionate High-Priest	134	O let us our own works forsake	360
O could I but escape away	160	O let us take a softer mould	334
O could we call to mind the grace	346	O Lord, if I at last discern	129
O cut short the work, and make	297	*O Lord, my God, with shame I own*	252
O for an heart to praise my God	77	*O Love Divine, what hast thou done!*	74
O give me faith and faith's increase	255	*O Love, I languish at thy stay*	73
O glorious hope of perfect love!	302	O may I hear his warning voice	254
O God, behold my troubled breast	160	O, may no gloomy crime	27
O God! (but shall I dare to pray?	91	O may we all triumphant rise!	194
O God my salvation, hear	231	O, might I have my one request	83
O God of our life, We hallow thy name	177	O might I this moment cease	297
O God, regard my bitter cry	160	O, might my heart at least relent	69
O God, thou art my home, my rest	121	O might we see in this our day	360
O God, thy record I receive	310	O might we through thy grace attain	360
O great mountain, who art thou / Immense	290	O, multiply thy sower's seed!⁵⁵¹	64
O great mountain, who art thou / That	292	O my abominable heart!	83
O heavenly King, Look down from above	177	*O my false, deceitful heart*	86
O help thy little church below	355	*O my Father and my God*	210
O holy Lord! O mighty God!	29	*O my heart, what must I do*	78
O how shall I the anguish bear	159	O my Lord, what must I do?	88
O how wavering is my mind	276	O omnipotent Redeemer	31
O Jesu, could I this believe	13	O put thy fear within my heart	130
O Jesu, full of truth and grace	295	*O respite me from self and pride*	140
O Jesu, grant this my request!⁵⁵⁰	15	O Root Divine, in this our earth	249
O Jesu, still, still shall I groan	126	*O Son of God, whose flaming eyes*	350
O joyful sound of gospel grace!	364	*O Sun of Righteousness, arise*	12
		O, supply my every want	97
		O take this heart of stone away	320

550. From the German of Johann Angelus Scheffler, translated by John Wesley.

551. From the German of August Gottlieb Spangenberg, translated by John Wesley.

O that I could all invite	316	O wretched man, from guilt to dream	304
O that I could truly wait	113	O wretched man, what must I do?	159
O that I had a cottage there	83	O wretched man, who dares divide	304
O that I had the silver wings	80	O ye of fearful hearts, be strong!	289
O that I might at once go up	303	Obedient faith, that waits on thee	312
O that I now, from sin released	321	O'er the vast howling wilderness	312
O that I now with all could part	94	Of righteousness Divine possest	255
O that I once again	118	*Oft have I cursed my natal day*	180
O that I thus resigned	85	*Oft have we passed the guilty night*	193
O that I was as heretofore	120	Oft I in my heart have said / Who shall	240
O that my load of sin were gone!	144	*Oft I in my heart have said/ Who to the*	240
O that my tender soul might fly	273	Oft thou visitest my breast	261
O that the grace were now applied	249	*Omnipotent Lord, my Saviour and King*	197
O that the life-infusing grace	338	*Omniscient God, whose eyelids try*	82
O that to thee my constant mind	273	*Omniscient, Omnipresent King*	163
O that to thee our deeds were known	347	On all mankind forgiven	343
O that we better could improve	25	On every dwelling-place of thine	250
O that we might through thee repent	346	On Jesus, my power, Till then I rely	198
O that we now might turn again	354	On me for good this token show	103
O the cruel power of sin	296	On thee we humbly wait	342
O the curse, the plague I feel	211	*On this auspicious happy day*	24
O, the dire effects of sin!	113	On us no other burden lay	352
O the grace unsearchable!	252	One deep unto another cries	145
O the length and breadth of love	212	One only refuge there remains	102
O, the load my spirit bears	113	Only love can end the strife	98
O the strength of inbred sin!	79	Only the lowly and the meek	25
O, thou dear suffering Son of God	71	Open a door to preach thy word	355
O thou Good Samaritan	157	Open a window in our breast	137
O thou meek and gentle Lamb	265	Open, Lord, my inward ear	263
O thou that dost the churches bear	345	Open my faith's interior eye	322
O thou that hast the two-edged sword	348	Open their mouth, and utterance give	344
O thou, who know'st what is in man	68	Or if I ask I know not what	130
O thou whom all thy saints adore	226	Or if in my forlorn estate	204
O thou whom fain my soul would love	166	Or if my endless groans and sighs	206
O thou whose eyes run to and fro	353	Or, if pride hath this destroyed	67
O thou whose wisdom, power, and love	20	Or let me (if I more would have	141
O! 'tis all I want below	210	Or let my Lord still hold his peace	82
O what a loathsome hypocrite	131	Or rather, if it be thy will	91
O what shall I do, my Saviour to praise	176	Other knowledge I disdain	315
O when shall all thy members rise	195	Our common foes, who thee defied	143
O when shall my tongue Be filled with thy praise	178	Our dying parents us forsake	16
O who can explain This struggle for life	198	Our Father and Lord, Almighty art thou	177
O, who shall bid this self depart	81	Our fig-leaves all be cast aside	137

Our friend in sure and certain hope	191
Our hearts are to ourselves unknown	137
Our Jesus is gone up on high	227
Our joy would soon o'erflow the banks	21
Our knees confirm, our hands lift up	352
Our Lord, and our Redeemer now	60
Our names among the living write	249
Our sister's flesh shall turn to dust	185
Our soul is changed, our heart is clean	325
Our watchful guardians, robed in light	22
Our wine with water mixt, our gold	346
Our works of faith thou once didst know	345
Out of our inmost souls expel	249
Outward comforts have I none	318
Overturn it, overturn it	32

Volume III

O all-atoning Lamb	78
O all-redeeming Lord / thy kindness I record	30
O all-redeeming Lord / Our common Friend	83
O all that pass by, To Jesus draw near!	6
O all ye ends of earth, behold	4
O arm me with the mind	78
O bid me live in thee and die	157
O bowels of love! O infinite grace!	8
O, could I always pray	61
O could I gain the mountain's height	220
O death, my hope is full of thee	163
O death, this is thy sting! O grave	26
O death, thou art on every side	158
O do not let me trust	79
O Father of all	359
O Fountain of love, O God of all grace	97
O for a trumpet voice	73
O glorious instrument Divine	300
O glorious victory of grace divine	127
O God of all grace, / thy bounty we praise	365
O God of all grace, All truth, and all power	73
O God of our forefathers, hear	309

O God, if thou art love indeed	19
O God of truth and love	252
O God of love, lay to thine hand	71
O God that hear'st the prayer	222
O God, thy word we claim	262
O God! 'tis finished now	219
O gracious, loving Lord	35
O happy soul, thy work is done	156
O hasten the hour, Send down from above	7
O hear, and show thou hear'st my call	77
O Horrible Decree	34
O how happy am I here[552]	167
O how wonderful thy ways![553]	168
O Jesu, full of grace	45
O Lamb, for sinners slain	98
O let me commend my Saviour to you!	6
O let me kiss thy bleeding feet	23
O let thy love my heart constrain	23
O let thy Spirit sanctify	330
O let us of the gift partake	358
O let us still the earnest feel	285
O Lord, thou art my Lord, my God	152
O Lucifer, bright morning star	147
O may I love like thee	79
O may we still abide	297
O might I feel the utmost power	166
O might the sacred word	252
O, my God, he dies for me	231
O my offended God	55
O our agonizing Saviour	270
O, plant in me thy mind!	93
O rock of our salvation, see	238
O Saviour of all In Adam that fell	7
O Saviour of all, Who didst not pass by	74
O Son of his love, Who deignedst to die	347
O Spirit of love, Of health, and of power	347
O Spirit of love, Whom all men may feel	98

552. Free paraphrase of the German of Wolfgang Christoph Dessler by Charles Wesley.

553. Free paraphrase of the German of Wolfgang Christoph Dessler by Charles Wesley.

O Spirit of might	353	On thee we depend	359
O take me at my word	38	On us, whom Jesus hath called forth	96
O take away the stone	46	Once thou didst my doom revoke	13
O that all men would haste	282	One angel to another cried	133
O that every thought and word	321	One with the living Bread Divine	338
O that I might yield at last	10	Only sin we call our own	319
O that our faith may never move	220	Or rather now, while lingering justice stays	127
O that the world might prove	366	Our cup of blessing from above	289
O that the world might taste, and see	166	Our fainting souls sustain	252
O that we now thy flesh may eat	298	Our faith is not vain; But death Thou didst taste	8
O the depth of love Divine	255	Our food we now with fear receive	358
O the grace on man bestowed!	262	Our hearts we open wide	273
O the infinite height	372	Our helpless unbelief remove	269
O the length, and breadth, and height	291	Our life of grace we here shall feel	243
O thou eternal Victim, slain	219	Our Lord, for whom we long did wait	155
O thou holy Lamb Divine	319	Our mean imperfect sacrifice	328
O thou Paschal Lamb of God	241	Our meanest deeds exalt, improve	358
O thou who, hanging on the cross	252	Our needy souls sustain	244
O thou who hast our sorrows took	316	*Our Passover for us is slain*	247
O thou who this mysterious bread	237	Our persons and our deeds aspire	320
O thou, whose bowels yearned to see	360	Our sins are on thine altar laid	318
O thou whose offering on the tree	307	Our sins as dunghill straw shall be	156
O 'tis a bitter thing	44	Our souls and bodies we resign	335
O 'tis enough, my God, my God!	18	Our souls eternally to save	248
O unexampled Love	73	Our spirits drink a fresh supply	236
O what a change was there! The man of birth	114	Our state if parted spirits know	157
O vindicate thy grace	37	Our wandering brethren's hearts to gain	280
O what a change will soon ensue	143	Out of great distress they came	294
O what a flame of sacred love	340		
O what a killing thought is this	316		
O what a miracle of love	300		

Volume IV

O what a soul-transporting feast	285	*O alarm the sleeping crowd*	9
O what a taste is this	336	*O all-loving Lamb*	273
O what a time for offering up	322	O Almighty God of love	64
O when shall I be taken home!	157	O Almighty Lord, we own	58
O, wouldst thou to thy church return	341	O answer the prayer Of prevalent faith	53
O wretched man of sin	62	*O astonishing grace*	119
Obedient to thy gracious word	237	O believe the record true	212
Of thee we commune still, and mourn	237	O bid it all depart	242
Offer up one sacrifice	319	O bid me look on thee, and mourn	393
Oh, how can a criminal feast	363	O bid the angry waves subside	11
On all who at his word draw near	267		
On him, who all our burdens bears	320		

O blessed word of gospel grace	260	O Jesus, our King	142
O bring him out of all	82	O Jesus, the rest	364
O Christ, my Hope, make known in me	121	O Jesus, thou know'st my sorrowful load	257
O come to a mourner in pain	478		
O confirm the gracious word	444	O King of saints, with pitying eye	40
O conquer this rebellious will	335	O Lamb of God, to thee	241
O cut short the work in me	251	O let him look to thee alone	351
O depth of sad distress	327	O let him thankfully submit	98
O earth, earth, earth attend!	395	O let it not my Lord displease	362
O Father, glorify thy Son	260	O let me have thy presence still	232
O Father of all	362	O let thy Spirit shed abroad	340
O Father of mercies restore	425	O let us pray, and never cease	22
O for thy glorious name	427	O let us thus go on	272
O for thy Jesus' sake	77	O Lord, according to thy love	6
O God of Love, to whom I pray	472	O Lord, attend; O Lord forgive	7
O God, mine inmost soul convert	316	O Lord, our God, (when all renewed	289
O God, the great the fearful God	3	O Lord, our strength and righteousness	350
O God, thy faithfulness I plead	469	O Love Divine, how sweet thou art!	341
O God, thy righteousness we own, / Laid by	62	O lover of sinners, extend	478
		O may he in thy gracious might	24
O God, thy righteousness we own, / Judgment	422	O may I cast my rags aside	236
		O may we in thy footsteps go	28
O God, to whom in flesh revealed	372	O mercy Divine, / How couldst Thou incline	122
O God who hear'st the prayer	77		
O happy, happy day	272	O mercy Divine! / When shall it be mine!	414
O happy state of grace	178		
O hell of sin! thy fiery rage	397	O might I as the harlot lie	441
O Holy Child, still let thy birth	120	O might I die that awe to prove	245
O horrid, horrid state!	398	O might I feel thy blood applied	258
O how shall a sinner perform	477	O might I hear the Turtle's voice	248
O how shall I move	412	O might I with thy saints aspire	244
O! how shall I the rebels shun	385	O might they all receive / The new-born	115
O how sore a thing and grievous	382	O might they all receive / The bleeding	144
O how sweet it is to languish	208	O might they at last With sorrow return	241
O Israel, hear, thy God hath said	298	O might we all to thee submit	104
O Jesu, full of pardoning grace	442	O might we each receive the grace	189
O Jesu, let me kiss thy name!	340	O might we mercy seek and find	103
O Jesus, if now Too many we are	90	O might we with our closing eyes	461
O Jesus, full of truth and grace	430	O my Advocate above	443
O Jesus, in pity draw near	419	*O my God, my God forgive*	420
O Jesus, my hope, / When wilt Thou lift up	411	O my God, no longer mine!	404
		O my much offended Saviour	440
O Jesus, my hope, / For me offered up	365	O my old, my bosom foe	450
O Jesus, of thee I inquire	418	O my threefold enemy	451

O never suffer me to rest	264	O thou gracious Son of God	421
O pity, and spare, And save them from death	53	*O thou hidden God unknown*	331
O praise him, and rejoice for me	246	*O thou of whom I oft have heard*	332
O save me, save me from this hour	467	*O thou that dost in secret see*	355
O Saviour, cast a pitying eye	338	*O thou that hangedst on the tree*	460
O Saviour, loose me from my pain	355	*O thou who by thy blood*	183
O Saviour of all Who trust in thy love	90	*O thou, who hast redeemed of old*	342
O send me from thy holy place	468	*O thou who seest and know'st my grief*	324
O Son of God, to thee	178	*O thou, whom once they flocked*	376
O Son of man, thy power make known	380	*O thou, whose Spirit hath made known*	263
O take away thy rod	397	O unexhausted grace	448
O that all our friends might feel	17	O were thy sufferings on the tree	471
O that all the art might know	216	O what a glorious life shall be	44
O that at last by love compelled	31	O what a length of wretched years	323
O that I always may	15	*O what an evil heart have I*	445
O that I at once had gone	387	O when shall I see An end of my pain	257
O that I could but surely know	356	O who shall help afford	394
O that I could for ever sit	342	*O why should he take thy purchase away*	53
O that I could my soul resign	396	*O wondrous power of faithful prayer*	260
O that I could repent, / With all my idols part	426	O wouldst thou again be made known	125
O that I could repent, / O that I could believe	434	O wouldst thou bring the final scene	190
O that I could revere	431	O wouldst thou cast a pitying look	29
O that I could with favoured John	342	O wouldst thou now descend	21
O that I in Mary's place	358	O wouldst thou undertake for me	375
O that I now could find	402	*O wretched man of hopeless grief*	413
O that my load were gone	401	O'er earth a banished man I rove	323
O that the cleansing tide	243	*Object of all our knowledge here*	134
O that the love of God	426	O'erwhelm him with th' amazing grace	47
O that the world might know	197	O'erwhelmed again with guilty shame	369
O that this might swallow up	420	O'erwhelmed with horrible affright	396
O that thou wouldst root out the thorn	476	Of all her sons whom she brought forth	305
O that thou wouldst stretch out Thine hand	476	Of judgment now the world convince	189
		Oft have I asked for help, afraid	445
		Oft, when he would not let me yield	445
		Oft when the pleasing ill drew nigh	445
O that we all may seek and find	98	Oh would'st thou now in all reveal	186
O that we all might see the Hand	94	*Omnipotent King, Who reignest on high*	52
O that we might to God rejoice	94	*Omnipotent Lord, Whom armies obey*	89
O that with humbled Peter I	342	Omnipotent Redeemer	237
O the rapturous height	409	On all th' affliction we look down	43
O the soul-transporting pleasure	209	On earth they lived my witnesses	33
O then impute, impart	208	On every soul that thirsts for grace	295
O this inexplicable doubt!	401	On Jesus's face	122
		On me, on all some gift bestow	271

On the margin of the grave	359
On the wings of his love	409
On thee I ever call	249
On these the Lord his wrath shall show	61
Once I could lament my state	386
Once I knew thee reconciled	458
Once thy blissful love we tasted	182
One drop of thy blood	364
One only good I here would have	385
One only way the erring mind	470
Only because thou diedst for me	472
Only pride could destroy	410
Open the gates, and open wide	286
Open their eyes and ears, to see	29
Or (for I know not what is best)	355
Or if, before the scourge return	94
Or if I did begin to taste	264
Or if the wicked will not hear	62
Or if the wicked will not mourn	81
Or, if thou wilt, keep back	435
Or if thy hand be lifted up	261
Or if yet I must not hope	357
Or if yet they will not turn	59
Or stablished and confirmed by him	160
Ought not our Lord the death to die	136
Ought not the members all to pass	136
Our Advocate there	203
Our anchor sure and fast	161
Our back we to the smiters give	37
Our Captain and King With shouts we proclaim	146
Our Conquering Lord	210
Our God, ever blest	122
Our heart is above	156
Our heathenish land	212
Our heavenly Guide	204
Our heavenly wealth shall never fail	38
Our holy heavenly Father thou	170
Our Immanuel came	120
Our Jesus is near, Whenever we sing	53
Our life is secure, And hidden above	89
Our Master's burden we sustain	39
Our mouth as in the dust we lay	422
Our newly born King By faith we have seen	113
Our old usurping sins are dead	290
Our ruined souls repair	168
Our Spirit is flown	156
Our toil and strife availed us not	291
Out of myself for help I go	343
Out of the deep I cry	249
Out of the deep I cry, and mourn	423
Out of the iron furnace, Lord	325
Outcast of God and man no more	313
Outcasts of men, to thee we fly	460
Overwhelmed with pardoning grace	444

Volume V

O all-loving Lamb	435
O bitter, bitter loss! my bosom friend is gone	188
O blessed hope of lasting peace	210
O could I break this fleshly fence	200
O do not quit thy gracious hold	241
O do not suffer him to part	34
O! do thou always warn	263
O entreat me not to leave	132
O Father receive Our heartiest praise	464
O Father, who hearest the prayer	255
O find them out some calm recess	482
O! for the honour of thy name	248
O for thy great and glorious name	166
O for thy Jesus' merit	203
O for thy only Jesu's sake	103
O for thy truth and mercy sake	229
O God, I can hold out no more	3
O God, my hope, my heavenly rest	92
O God of all grace	30
O God, thy truth, and power declare	76
O God, was ever heart like mine!	310
O happy, happy hope	214
O happy, happy place	462
O hasten the day! / he will not delay	32
O hasten the day: / thou hear'st what we say	58

O heaven! what a triumph is there	358	O my only Ease in pain	161
O! how constant is my Lord	180	O my tender-hearted Lord	343
O how gracious is thy love	188	O never suffer me to sleep	49
O how wonderful thy love	180	O put it in our inward parts	95
O Jesu, at thy feet we wait	330	O put me in the cleft, empower	92
O Jesus, appear, No longer delay	427	O! satisfy their soul in drought	232
O Jesus, appear	266	O save the father in the son	80
O Jesus, full of truth, and grace	307	O Saviour of sinners distressed	254
O Jesus, my Rest	24	O Saviour from sin	289
O Jesus, ride on Till all are subdued	116	O Saviour whose blood	29
O Jesus, the Rest	265	O sorrowful soul	200
O let it sink into our soul	312	O that all men would prove	57
O let our heart and mind	462	O that all men would raise	379
O! let the prisoners' mournful cries	231	O that all with us might prove	453
O let them all thy mind express	482	O that both might soon arise	438
O let us ever dwell	463	O that ev'n I might share	117
O let us stir each other up	478	O that every knee	57
O Love, by thee constrained at last	3	O that every soul might be	134
O Love unknown!	58	O that I at last may stand	294
O make me all like thee	23	*O that I could*	59
O make them of one soul and heart	483	*O that I could but pray*	170
O matchless grace!	59	O that I might his burden bear	434
O may I in thy strength fulfil	345	O that I might like him withstand	143
O may I never, never seek	415	O that I might so believe	293
O may the least omission pain	374	*O that I was as heretofore*	105
O may thy bowels yearn in me	96	O that my Jesu's heavenly charms	112
O! may we thus be found	261	O that my mind	59
O might I every mourner cheer	126	O that my prayers might now to thee	8
O might I, from this dungeon freed	210	O that now my spirit might fail	183
O might I now thy goodness taste	191	O that the hour were come	118
O might I now thy love retrieve	148	O that the veil might now be rent!	327
O might I soon attain	16	O that the world might taste, and see	112
O might it deeper sink, (but give	151	O that thy foes were all subdued	311
O might it now my heart constrain	148	O that to thee the world might bow	21
O might my lot be cast with these	483	O that to these poor Gentiles now	121
O might the gracious Hand	213	O that we all might now begin	124
O might thy Spirit seal	423	O the insufferable loss!	159
O might we now behold thee	455	*O this agony of grief*	160
O most compassionate High-Priest	230	O thou Father of compassions	174
O my best, my only Friend	182	O thou gentle Lamb of God	291
O my condescending Lord	185	O thou great almighty Lord	99
O my dear Master, and my Lord	156	O thou jealous God, come down	9
O my Galilean King	195	O thou our Husband, Brother, Friend	229
O my God, how long shall I	173	*O thou that on all*	436

O thou who at thy creature's bar	134	Omnipresent God, whose aid	8
O thou who hast in mercy sought	129	On both thy natures we rely	323
O thou, who plead'st the widow's	336	On earth th' usurpers reign	272
O thou whose gracious word	104	On God They cast their every care	480
O thou whose special grace	417	On me and my friend	439
O thrice-blessed hope! Even now it lifts up	201	On the Son of peace descending	53
O 'tis enough! my God, my God	191	On thee for help I call	117
O what a piteous sight is there!	147	On thee I fix my single eye	392
O what a soul-transporting sight	224	On thee, my God, on thee	418
O what an age of golden days!	480	Once again revive the dead	173
O what an evil, faithless heart	2	Only have faith in God	272
O what cordial consolation	447	Only tell me I am thine	9
O what shall we do Our Saviour to love	469	Only this do I desire	206
O what shall we do to retrieve	265	Only thou canst never be	184
O when shall I	60	Only thou God of power	203
O while thou giv'st their bodies ease	393	Open then, in great compassion	211
O wouldst thou appear	430	Or, (for it is not ours to know	471
O wouldst thou break the fatal snare	244	Or if, my faith to prove	446
O wouldst thou end the storm	235	Or if pity inclined	31
O wouldst thou, Lord, appear	189	Or if thou my soul require	10
O wouldst thou, Lord, thy servant guard	49	Or if thy great will ordain	183
Obedient faith in Jesu's blood	90	Or if, to serve thy church and thee	106
Obedient to the voice of God	71	Or let us here on Tabor stop	155
Obedient to thy will alone	65	Or, rather, if any are nigh	264
Of heavenly birth	387	Our bosom-Friend, and Brother too	478
Of his earthly all bereft	188	Our brethren, and companions dear	165
Of my earthly all bereaved	343	Our brethren we see	266
Of pain I now advantage make	209	Our Brother, Saviour, head	387
Of pardon possessed	28	Our Captain leads us on	273
Of thee alone possessed	356	Our concert of praise	284
Of this assured I rest	446	Our confident trust in him we declare	465
Oh! may I every moment see	394	Our desperate state through sin declare	124
Oh! might I rise by love restored	421	Our faith is not vain	320
Oh! that all the pain were past	445	Our foreheads proclaim	458
Oh! that the flaming chariot	454	Our friend is at rest	222
Oh! that the perfect gift were given	331	Our friend is gone before	215
Oh! that the souls baptized herein	389	Our friendship sanctify, and guide	409
Oh! the fathomless love	402	Our God would not have One reprobate die	391
Oh! the goodness of God	402	Our high, and holy calling's prize	313
Oh! the infinite cares	401	Our Husband, Brother, Friend	429
Oh! what a mighty change	460	Our Jesus appear	437
Oh! wouldst thou now receive us	455	Our Jesus is gone up on high	318
Omnipotent, omniscient Lord	513	Our Jesus surround	224

Our Jesus thee, entire, and whole	325
Our Jesus thou from future woe	324
Our loss we solemnly deplore	219
Our own desire, though weak, sincere	376
Our Safeguard thou art	27
Our Saviour we own	224
Our sinful state we partly see	131
Our sins though great and numberless	131
Our souls like God raised up	39
Our sufferings shall advance thy cause	251
Our works, and gifts, and graces past	316
Out of the deep regard their cries	231
Out of the dust of death I rise	74

Volume VI

O all-creating God!	372
O blessed estate of the dead	188
O come! thy Spirit cries	202
O could I attain to the grace	333
O could I now the faith obtain	374
O could I now to God return	374
O enlarge my scanty thought	445
O Father, I am but a child	462
O Father of all, / The great and the small	431
O Father of mercies attend	458
O for a thankful heart	420
O for the saving fear	51
O God, thou hast deceived our hope	85
O God, who dost the victory give	362
O happy, happy soul	206
O Happy state of infancy!	446
O how fickle is our mind!	404
O how much happier we than they!	417
O how shall I praise thy wonderful love?	452
O how shall I presume	1
O Israel, hear the warning word	83
O Jesus, if this be thy will	191
O Jesus, in pity appear	333
O Jesus, lead on thy militant care	195
O Jesus, on us The blessing bestow	440
O let me on the image dwell	242
O let us as from serpents, fly	426
O let us not ourselves forget	426
O let us not, when old, depart	417
O let us put on thee	208
O Light of Life, thy Spirit shed	105
O Lord, our strength and righteousness	99
O may I never, never tell	425
O may I to my ways take heed	425
O may they never seek their own	117
O might his grace victorious prove	403
O might I in my youthful days	456
O might I of thy follower learn	276
O might I, with calmest zeal	291
O might the blood of sprinkling cry	137
O might the universal Friend	112
O might thy love our loss repair	256
O might we all, like him, believe	281
O might we all our sins forsake	76
O might we by their downfall rise	76
O might we from our hearts repent	37
O might we quickly find	44
O my everlasting Lover	380
O never may the fiend steal in	99
O, Saviour, descend; No longer delay	308
O Saviour, her spirit receive	193
O Saviour of all	405
O Saviour, to thee Our souls we commend	288
O Sion, wash thy heart from sin	86
O sister in Jesus, arise	192
O take us up into thine arms	448
O that a portion of his grace	313
O that at last even I	206
O that each in the day	14
O that I, like Timothy	398
O that I may never know	442
O that my mournful days were past	247
O that our residue of days	357
O that the child of heavenly light	265
O that the friends he leaves beneath	352
O that the promised time were come	247
O that we all may thus break through	200
O that we all were landed there!	298
O that we might our faith sincere	314
O that we then, like him	245

O thou, who hast in special grace	120	Oppression laid her iron yoke	310
O thou who seest what is in man	4	Or I shall gall the mitred race	102
O thou who wouldst not have	427	Or if I needed still	2
O thou whom none hath seen or known	382	Or if the danger they confess	170
O thou, whose providential grace	412	Or if thine awful will	151
O were it, Lord, on us bestowed	266	Or shameless advocates for hell	100
O were they all on me bestowed	331	Or should they stir the people up	106
O what a blessed hope is ours!	218	Or water swelling for a vent	24
O what a heaven of heavens is this	220	Our bodies are thine	406
O what a mighty change was wrought[554]	308	Our brethren; though they still disclaim	105
O what a scene attracts our eyes!	104	Our brother the haven hath gained	189
O what a soul o'erpowering thought	200	Our country saved from sword and fire	184
O what are all my sufferings here	220	*Our earth we now lament to see*	372
O what hath Jesus bought for me!	219	Our friend is restored	210
O when shall we supremely blest	140	Our hearts and our hands	435
O when shall we sweetly remove	196	Our hearts with hopes and fears	224
O when will the Saviour extend	188	Our life is a dream	14
O where are the men with virtue endowed	440	Our lives are in our Maker's hand	166
		Our Lord appears again	47
O where shall we his equal find[555]	301	Our loving confidence is sure	167
O would he more of heaven bestow	218	Our minds to unbend	434
Of thy great unbounded power	460	Our moments below Shall pleasantly glide	441
Of whom should children sing	463		
Omnipotent to save	224	Our mourning is all at an end	198
On earth he drank the deepest cup	354	Our number and our bliss complete	247
On hell's apparent brink	36	Our old companions in distress	216
On him she fixed her single eye	319	Our own, our nation's sins confess	75
On me he rests his dying head	226	Our partner below	210
On thee our dying souls we cast	39	Our prayers to his unite	390
On thy thigh and vesture written	161	Our residue of days or hours	16
On us the grace be shown	339	Our sad devoted land go through	80
One family we dwell in him	215	Our safety on him Alone doth depend	184
One of those distinguished few	334	Our sin-avenging Lord	51
One of those happy children, me	452	Our sons henceforth be wholly thine	408
One only labour yet remains	250	Our souls to God devoted are	438
One only Place remains	36	Our souls, (we above all desire,)	388
One only task is yet behind	305	Our spirits too shall quickly join	216
One thou hast so dearly bought	352	Out of our mouth and life, O Lord	419
One with the little flock I rest	72	Out of our slumber woke	155
Open mine eyes, the veil withdraw	392	Out of themselves apostles raise	132
Open now mine eyes of faith	399	Outcasts from thee, and scattered wide	136
		Outstretching his hand O'er mountains and seas	91

554. *UP* 3:336.
555. *UP* 3:333.

Volume VII

First line	Page
O by thy bloody offering	188
O could I emulate the zeal	161
O could I first perform my Master's will	441
O could I then behold my God	360
O Father of all	8
O Father of mercies, attend	317
O Father, on me	322
O Father, Son, and Holy Ghost	295
O for love and pity sake	56
O for thy truth and mercy sake	398
O God, in Christ the Saviour	31
O God in Christ, thine embassy	217
O God of love, Come from above	190
O how shall a sinner like me	365
O immaculate Lamb!	372
O let me still the promise plead	358
O let my mournful cry	388
O let our faith and love abound	43
O let thy grief dry up her tears	66
O might each obtain a share	197
O might he live before thee	131
O might I after God wake up	372
O might I now with Jesus find	371
O might I thus through life remain	192
O might I with thy people blessed	195
O might that revealing Spirit	112
O might the love of Jesus	185
O might thy love on me bestowed	355
O might we always know	22
O might we now relenting	35
O might we one become in thee	152
O never let my children live	174
O re-assure my sprinkled heart	405
O Saviour, appear, To finish our sin	27
O Saviour, cast a gracious smile	44
O Saviour of all	9
O Son of man, assuage my woes	50
O teach me my first lesson now	163
O that all our blind gainsayers	334
O that I always may	167
O that I could my Lord receive	192
O that I first of love possessed	135
O that I might Receive my sight	187
O that I on the wings of love	386
O that it might this moment be	373
O that my son might live	78
O that our light may shine	306
O that the blood which cleanses	356
O that the joyful day were come	36
O that thou wouldst thy power exert	125
O that we all might thus believe	314
O that we now in love renewed	311
O that we now the power might feel	45
O thou that hast our sorrows borne	24
O thou who didst in our degenerate state	425
O thou, whose kind compassion	103
O thou, whose wise paternal love	98
O thou, with whom unfelt, unseen	183
O were that point secured	110
O what a God is ours! So true and just	440
O what shall we do To praise thee aright?	319
O what shall I do	79
O when shall I With rapture cry	190
O would he appear	37
O would he now himself impart	180
O would my God the veil withdraw	206
O wouldst thou inspire Our hearts with thy love	29
O wouldst thou, Lord, discover	185
O wouldst thou stamp it now on mine	327
Obedient saints, and they alone	368
Object of thy dearest love	129
O'ercome, o'erwhelmed with Mercy's power	49
O'erwhelmed at times with chilling fears	142
Of a dejected spirit	105
Of angry man th' impatience proud	163
Of Christ the Son of Man	224
Of creature bliss my nature is	187
Of Jesus our Friend We talk by the way	27
Of love, of God in Christ possessed	372
Oft as from thee I roved	392
Oft have I for thy Spirit prayed	397
Oft I have implored thy aid	357
Omnipotent God, Eternal I am	317

On Jehovah in all	321	Out of the fire of chastening love	183
On Sion's walls the watchman place	130		
On the margin of the grave	403		
On thee my health in sickness	59	## Volume VIII	
On them, on me the prayer be sealed	405	O all ye saints of his	65
On this triumphant day	13	*O all ye lands, rejoice in God*	144
On thy bleeding passion stayed	353	O could I once behold thee	359
On us the precious faith bestow	23	O do not at a distance stand!	43
One God Jehovah is the Son	212	O earth, conceal not thou their blood	285
One God to us, there is but One	229	*O for a spark of heavenly fire*	354
One inexplicably three	308	O England's desolate Church! if thee	253
One Lord in Jesus we admire	229	O enter then his courts with praise	185
One person of the Sire we praise	340	O for the weeping prophet's strains	254
One revealing Deity	294	O for thy love, thy Jesu's sake	248
One thing I now desire	102	O God, in whom I trust, appear!	259
Only thee I gasp to know	391	O God of love, thy sway we own	104
Only while she hence departs	82	*O God, thou art in Jesus mine*	138
Only while we offer up	88	O God, we of thy fame have heard	99
Open my mouth, almighty Love	399	*O how overjoyed was I*	236
Open my mouth to speak thy praise	405	O Israel, on th' Almighty Lord	247
Or come in perfect light and love	185	*O Jesus, prove thy name on me*	382
Or if thou grant a longer date	73	*O let the prisoners' mournful sighs*	342
Or in the morning of his day	53	O let thy jealously awake	301
Or let me live, of love possessed	99	O let thy love to me o'erflow	114
Or let the sleeping babe remain	52	*O Lord, in pitying love give ear!*	258
Ordained the Godhead cannot be	224	O Lord, incline thy gracious ear	9
Order if some invert, confound	161	O Lord of Hosts, O God of grace[556]	162
Others, a half-discerning few	74	O Lord of Hosts, to whom are known	321
Our church a thousand-fold increase	420	O Lord, my God, my holy one	318
Our common head in Christ we see	230	O love, essentially divine	381
Our faith, imagination	344	O love, O God, thyself reveal	374
Our faith is but a shadow vain	331	*O Love, thou sovereign good unknown*	374
Our fellowship, who Christ profess	292	O may they still approve	301
Our God, whom one in Three we praise	274	*O might I weep, and love thee now*	117
Our hearts are then convinced indeed	248	O might they, Lord, this moment rise	327
Our heavenly Father is but One	230	O peace, thou art banished and fled	335
Our heavenly Master is but One	231	O reverse their sorest doom	374
Our Isaac on the altar laid	123	O sin, my cruel bosom-foe	205
Our Lord the Father is, the Son	271	O Sun of Righteousness, appear	321
Our little one, believing	91	O that all might seek and find	247
Our naked hearts to thee we raise	45	O that at last the faithful seed	298
Our only help in danger's hour	77	O that he in the gap may stand	287
Our souls the Father keeps	270		
Our wages are sure	159	556. UP 2:246.	

O that his saints, with one accord	197
O that I could but pray!	361
O that our lives may tell	271
O that the faithful seed	418
O that the joyful hour was come	432
O that the world might feel	325
O the lingering misery	368
O thou temple of my God	238
O thou that on thine heavenly throne	238
O thou whose pitying love relieves	407
O were it poured into my heart	379
O were the work begun	314
O what a cruel war ensued	391
O what a night was that! The crowd	460
O what manna in thy word!	224
O when shall I thy spotless mind	382
O who can abide Unquenchable fire!	350
O who, when God doth this, shall live?	487
O wouldst thou in this gracious hour	408
O ye that know the pardoning Lord	194
Obedience is his pure delight	3
Obedient to his sovereign will	197
Obedient to the word Divine	411
Obedient to thy parents be	347
Observe the saint of God	85
Ocean, roar, with all thy waves	184
O'erreached, impelled by a sly Gnostic's art	443
Of gospel-peace possessed	9
Of gracious riches full, and happy days	434
Of neither evidence nor warrant	453
Of sense thou dost bereave	314
Offer your prayer and praise	8
Oft hath thine arm, in ancient days	288
Oft I to the Lord have said	256
Omniscient God, to whom alone	269
On all his chosen ones	251
On himself he takes their care	111
On the Lord my soul is stayed	21
On thee I muse with vast delight	139
On thee, O God of purity	10
On us the outcasts of mankind	342
One glorious enterprise remains	456
One is as a thousand days	412
One of Jesu's kings I reign	135
One soul into us all inspire	405
Once I could in God rejoice	96
Only spare my feeble soul	90
Only thee I serve below	227
Open my faith's enlightened eyes	24
Open now the gospel door	430
Open the gates of righteousness	206
Open their eyes, almighty grace	293
Or if still they will not yield	132
Or if the beast will but be civil	473
Or if they need a nobler trophy raise	443
Order and government they scorn	481
Our age is threescore years and ten	173
Our arm of flesh entirely fails	268
Our cities in a blaze	271
Our fathers trusted in thy aid	42
Our God alone hath power to save	152
Our God the hostile powers destroyed	274
Our harps, no longer vocal now	253
Our inmost souls thy Spirit knows	404
Our Lord is risen from the dead	48
Our nation's good, and not his own	287
Our patriot chiefs betrayed their trust	285
Our punishment accepting here	346
Our sole desire and aim	389
Our soul is to the dust bowed down	102
Our souls the book of nature draws	35
Out of the deep thy call we wait	323
Out of the deeps to thee, O Lord	246

Volume IX

O almighty Lord, rebuke	46
O could I more than feebly hope	245
O could I thus sink down	111
O Father of mercies, on me	234
O for that gracious power	232
O for that tenderness of heart	199
O for thy own compassion's sake	322
O God, at thy command we rise	225
O God in Christ, accept our prayer	309
O God, take all my sins away!	176

O God, thou art in Jesus mine	303	O thou afflicted church, forlorn	442
O how shall I praise		O thou slaughtered Lamb of God	11
The goodness Divine	320	O thou that hid'st thy face	378
O how shall we thy grace record	226	O thou, to whom I would aspire	328
O Jesus, appear	287	O thou who camest from above	58
O Jesus, full of richest grace	147	O thou who into me art come	350
O let the Dove	301	O thou, whose eyes run to and fro	213
O Lord from heaven, on earth bestowed	311	O thou whose pitying eye	266
O Lord our God, we bless thee now	205	O 'tis enough! I ask no more	206
O may I never look behind	20	O vain, vain, vain all else beside	328
O may I never, never seek	204	O were the faith on me bestowed	328
O may I still from sin depart	260	O what a change shall then ensue!	457
O may I thus confirm my friend	162	O what shall I do to retrieve	364
O may I thus resigned	232	O what shall I say?	325
O might I in the Spirit of grace	273	O where shall I wander to find	257
O might it now from thee proceed	415	O wouldst thou touch my lips	
O might the gracious words Divine	95	once more	377
O might the hidden God unknown	181	Obedience is our pure delight	92
O might we, Lord, the grace improve	268	Object of the world's desire	32
O my all-sufficient God	309	Object of thy guardian care	274
O my most condescending Lord	101	O'er[557] the highway of holiness	115
O Saviour attend	287	O'erwhelmed alas, with deep distress	92
O Saviour of sinners, from whom	320	Of all thou hast in earth below	291
O shut not up my soul within	282	Of beauty vain, of wisdom void	348
O take this plague away!	148	Of blessings infinite I read	329
O tell it not in Gath, nor spread	168	Of my boasted wisdom spoiled	392
O that all the mournful nation	275	Of my extreme distresses	154
O that all who would rely on	275	Of sad tormenting fear	355
O that I could, in every place	276	Of the true manna from above	48
O that I every moment might	379	Of thee, O Lord, I oft have heard	271
O that I knew the way to find	259	Of woman born, of flesh alone	252
O that I, Lord, in thee alone	291	Oft as I lay me down to rest	95
O that I might walk with God	13	Oft as our hearts to sin turned back	75
O that I thus on Christ reclined	393	Oft by thy judgments shook	378
O that I were as in the days	260	Oft hast thou, Lord, in tender love	462
O that my faltering heart may smite	171	Often faint, yet still pursuing	136
O that now with pardon blessed	386	Omnipotent to save	249
O that the chosen band	469	Omniscient God, to me impart	213
O that the fire from heaven might fall	179	On every side surrounded	295
O that the work were done	124	On me thy constant helper trust	411
O that thou wouldst thy servant bless	200	On the first early dawn of grace	176
O that we now could cast aside	398	On thee, O God, my soul is stayed	105
O that we now might feel	427		
O the resistless power of grace	81	557. Osborn changed "O'er" to "In."	

On those who dare his word gainsay	349	O Jesus, let thy dying cry	430
On us, Almighty Lord, bestow	77	O let thy death's mysterious power	431
On us thy Father's love	28	O Love Divine, how can it be	355
One of the stubborn, hardened race	105	O Love Divine, of thee possessed	356
Only from sin my soul restrain	380	O may I call my ways to mind	109
Opened are their eyes to see	5	O may I cry for help to thee	285
Our brethren false, with furious zeal	464	O may I ever more advert	375
Our brethren, of their foes afraid	88	O may I hear and taste the word	272
Our City of defence, to thee	87	O may I never dare despise	457
Our dead in sin and buried race	148	O may I never dare receive	359
Our God almighty to redeem	198	O may I never, never be	246
Our hearts o'erflow with praise and prayer	29	O may I never sadly prove	321
		O may I strive and not in vain	194
Our High-priest the breast-plate wears	59	O may I tempt my God no more	154
Our hymns shall record Immanuel's name	341	O may thy sweet implanted love	52
		O may we never more expose	194
Our mighty sins they need not still	74	O may we tremble at their doom	342
Our prayer, presented through thy Son	208	O might I daily in thy cause	242
Our Prince and Friend enthroned above	160	O might thy powerful word	249
Our Prophet, Priest, and King, to thee	113	O might thy word take place	209
Our sins are o'erthrown, Which rose against thee	46	O might we put thine image on	5
		O might we see our Saviour shine	303
Our surety shall the breach repair	399	O that all mankind might hear him	305
Ourselves how can we purify?	372	O that all were taught of God	140
Out of an humble heart and meek	267	O that his wrath were turned aside	85
Out of the iron furnace brought	44	O that I could like thee forget	318
		O that I could the desert find	19
		O that I none beside might see	306
Volume X		O that my life might be	378
		O that the character were mine	248
O bid my dead, dead soul arise	490	O that the Spirit of our Lord	369
O could I now in garments white	13	O that they now restored	62
O could I so perfidious be	242	O that this earth might quake	436
O could I thus my wants declare	406	O that thy heavenly fire within	93
O could I view them with those eyes	171	O that we all his words might hear	95
O could we with his calmness meet	397	O that with all thy people I	442
O for that single eye	187	O that ye might like them repent	344
O for the faith in Jesu's name	67	O the vile ungrateful race	349
O God most merciful and true	52	O thou faithful God of love	45
O God of all-redeeming grace	106	O were the happy evening come	332
O how gracious is my Lord[558]	211	O what a speaking look was there!	327
O how unlike the kingdoms here	338	O where is our Friend in distress?	478
O Jesus awake and be near	479	O wouldst thou, Lord, reveal their sins	16
		O wouldst thou now thy presence show	83

558. *UP* 2:21.

Object of our joy and hope	347
O'erwhelmed with blessings from above	282
Of him they casually inquire	339
Of my transgressions numberless	90
Of others with design he speaks	459
Of small imperfect things the day	115
Of those who learned and austere	298
Oft have I offered up the blind	127
Oft have I prayed thee to remove	194
Oft have I unconcerned passed by	48
Omnipotence alone	436
Omniscient God, to man declare	27
On all who dare confess his sway	340
On earth I ask no more	80
On every child of Adam's race	386
On me, even me, confer	122
On me that wrestling power bestow	79
On me the wisdom pure bestow	70
On me, thou bleeding Lamb, on me	423
On simple souls sincere	361
On thee, great God, we still attend	105
On thee I faithfully depend	369
On them we day and night attend	467
On thy word my soul is stayed	35
On us bestow the pardon	182
Once he in the Baptist came	135
One, by his hellish father taught	153
One moment, Lord, if thou depart	402
One only gift can justify	20
One only proof doth yet remain	396
One that overwhelmed with fear	409
Only good proceeds from God	273
Only regard my dying cries	19
Only unbelief withstands	278
Open their graves, and bring	61
Open thy mouth, celestial Lord	162
Or if thou hast a few restored	18
Or if thy people to revive	24
Ordered by thee, O Lord, I go[559]	210
Our alms and works of righteousness	257
Our base ingratitude forgive	340
Our first and last desire	179
Our ignorance 'tis thine to show	473
Our joy in a created good	95
Our life, and grace, and ministry	233
Our Lord from the skies Again shall come down	339
Our Lord's humility we praise	312
Our Master doth with sinners eat	223
Our meek, pacific Prince adore	424
Our mighty Intercessor there	441
Our Model, the meek Son of Man	323
Our Pattern if we rightly know	321
Our quick-resenting pride	413
Our scanty stock as soon as known	281
Our sovereign Priest above	466
Our strength shall with our trials last	372
Our trespasses forgive	178
Our weakness in this emblem we	462
Our zealous great High-Priest	364
Out of himself the God of love	329
Out of the deep of poverty	106
Out of the pit of sin I cry	119

Volume XI

O blessed, blessed hope!	72
O come, thou stronger than the fiend	205
O could I gain my calling's height	188
O could I now behold my Lord	312
O could I thee my pattern make	155
O end the dark hour	139
O for that cheering light	419
O glorious inability	369
O how gentle is my Lord	166
O Jesus, after thee I feel	16
O Jesus, I see	364
O may I always bear in mind	118
O may I in his love delight	118
O may I, Lord, with jealous care	395
O may we shun that subtler snare	280
O may we to ourselves take heed	279
O might I in thy likeness wake	69
O might my course like Jesu's end	304
O my God, how can it be!	197

559. UP 2:221.

O put it in our inward parts	511	Old age we second childhood name	31
O Saviour let thy pitying love	8	Omniscient God of love, impart	74
O Saviour, make thy wisdom mine	SH 1762, 2:218	On Christ while humbly they rely	470
O Saviour of all, thy word we believe	408	On his Redeemer's breast reclined	506
O Saviour, repeat	138	On the thoughtless multitude	305
O Saviour touch mine eyes again	17	On thee we in thy temple wait	317
O that I could with all my heart	25	On whom doth Jesus' censure fall?	14
O that I might humbly sit[560]	197	One God the children all confess	460
O that I my God might find	255	One, I and my Father are!	465
O that I now my heart could raise[561]	219	One of the formal worldly throng	158
O that I through faith might sit	SH 1762, 2:219	One only thing we ask to know	164
O that I thus with upright aim	403	One possessed of Jesus' mind	6
O that it now might breathe its last	90	One question puts them all to flight	413
O that like his disciples, I	509	Only on our Father's love	212
O that the joy which then o'erflowed	434	Open mine eyes of faith to see	312
O that we might begin below	55	Open, O Lord, their blinded eyes	457
O that with the faithful I	322	Open then our minds and hearts	313
O the riches of thy grace!	329	Our Advocate for ever lives	256
O the vanity of man!	426	Our Captain and triumphant head	317
O thou who hadst the world forsook	190	Our fervent zeal for God to show	337
O thou whom God vouchsafes t' inspire	131	Our God is love supreme	57
		Our goodness is not ours but thine	9
O what a life is mine!	217	Our holy God the smallest fault	104
O what cause of humble fear!	63	Our incense of prayer thou offer'st alone	102
O what multitudes at last	230	Our life on needful things depends[562]	209
O what wondrous grace that I	126	Our loving Lord the outcasts seeks	451
Obedient to his Father's will	426	Our Maker and redeeming Lord	343
Objects of his constant care	499	Our real want of needful food	334
Objects which fleshly minds amuse	275	Our Saviour and God	145
Obsequious to thy dear commands	464	Our Saviour and Lord	138
O'erwhelmed beneath the load	144	Our sins against the Saviour cry	90
Of Abraham's line The Blessing I own	265	Our souls are born again	346
Of every promised good our Lord	20	Our souls raised up to die no more	473
Of grace I never will	144	Our tears for thee will nought avail	300
Of their ignorance they show	453	Our toiling strength exhausted is	171
Offspring of God and man	130	Our whole apostate kind	265
Oft a seasonable word	106	Our zeal in men's esteem	69
Oft a soul that late begins	221	Out of an evil world of woe	456
Oft thou dost cut short their days	62	Out of the crowd he first must take	16

560. *UP* 2:124.
561. *UP* 2:144.

562. *UP* 2:137, reads: "Your life on needful things depends."

Volume XII

O could I first repent and prove	128
O could I mourn for God	192
O could I to the Lord appeal	125
O for an end like his, whose sin	128
O help my unbelieving heart	322
O how infinite the price is	219
O how kind and condescending	110
O how restless is the foe	334
O Jesus, we adore thee!	43
O joyful sound of pardoning grace	96
O let thy love constrain	192
O may I ever gaze	90
O may we constantly abide	153
O may we still the truth declare[563]	293
O might I at the goal arrive	102
O might I, like Jesus, be[564]	71
O might I none but Jesus know	388
O might I thus my warfare end	99
O might thy hallowing Spirit	300
O that all mankind were filled	230
O that all the lost kind	285
O that from instant now I might	370
O that I could but act on thee	322
O that I like him could stoop	352
O that I now my wish might have	93
O that in every house there were	324
O that, like Saul I might	395
O that like the Bridegroom's friend	281
O that now the church were blessed	240
O that such might now appear	440
O that the world with us would taste	367
O that they both in me might meet	118
O that thy Spirit of love	186
O that we could to God present	163
O that we might the Spirit find	16
O that with John's affection	129
O the depths of mercy shown	278
O thou just and holy One	396
O thou,[565] whose manifested love	426
O were we in thy Spirit joined	28
O what shall we do Who Jesus have slain	151
O who can of thy grace despair	97
O would my gracious God confer	301
O wouldst thou now thy Spirit breathe	8
O wouldst thou to my heart explain	75
Obedience to our Lord must prove	25
Obedient to our Lord's command	28
Obedient to the heavenly call	429
Occasion from my slowness take	110
Occasion of great joy and praise	296
O'erjoyed his faithfulness to'approve	385
O'erwhelmed with grief and shame I see	72
Of bliss essentially possessed	216
Of evangelic pains afraid	277
Of sinners he foretells	163
Of spices all his garments smell	92
Of whom should his apostles speak	195
Offering up his soul in prayer	218
Oft an evangelic guide	295
Oft in deaths before he dies	292
Oft thy weak disciple, I	130
Oh that the happiness were mine!	297
Omnipotent Redeemer	387
On all the house of Jacob's race	153
On the common good intent	306
On the great auspicious day	144
On this accepted day	376
On this only ground relies	451
On thyself I depend	129
On us the Christian feast bestow	153
Once embarked in wickedness	263
One door is shut, when God permits	359
One good man endued with power	440
One only Shrine he had	340
One only way doth still remain	276
One only work on earth I have	24
One single minister renewed	199
One the body mystical	216
One, though not the same, with thee	58
Only love thy heart inclined	207

---

563. UP 2:364.
564. UP 2:268.
565. Osborn changed "O thou" to "Saviour."

Only thus by stooping low	102	O might I, to sinners sent	178
Only thy expiring pain	124	O might it now my heart o'erflow	209
Open now my spirit's eyes	38	O might the blood	161
Open their hearts, almighty Lord	152	O might our every work and word	164
Opposed by earth and hell	35	O might we thus our head obey	131
Opposers of the Spirit's course	145	O Son of God, in vain	201
Oppressed we in his Spirit groan	234	O that I could	161
Or if I have turned back in heart	277	O that I could in him believe	146
Ordained, prepared, disposed	285	O that I could look to thee	152
Others he finds our faith to tell	240	O that I the souls could win	178
Ought not the rulers to suppress	350	O that the angelic choir	97
Our broken hearts prepare	285	O that the power were mine	177
Our crucified head	122	O that the promised time were come	190
Our danger is the same	443	O that the pure engrafted word	89
Our Father doth forgive	256	O that to me were given	74
Our foes may in the temple seize	188	O thou redeeming God	8
Our foes, the superstitious crowd	410	O thou who didst our frailties bear	53
Our heart hath lost by sin	6	O thou who hast the victory	232
Our implacable foe	47	O thou, whose soul-transforming grace	262
Our omnipotent Lord	445	O were the fiend expelled indeed	29
Our persecuting foes to shun	335	O would my Lord to me impart	160
Our relatives who know not God	247	Obedience is th' effect of love	209
Our Saviour and head	150	Obedience to our Lord's commands	209
Our Saviour mindful of his word	357	Object of their adoration	118
Our sins have nailed him to the wood	95	Obliged to impart	240
Our souls with faith supply	456	O'er sin and death victorious	47
Our true and faithful Lord	256	On creatures I no more rely	37
Our whole delightful task below	347	On[566] him we have nailed to the tree	260
Out of the dungeon brought	270	On this my patient soul I stay	228
		Once thou didst on earth appear	200
		One only means I see	33
Volume XIII		One with our Saviour, we defy	284
		Or if so my Lord ordain	269
O blessed hope of life to come	38	Or let me in sorrow remain	106
O could I faithfully embrace	255	Our Father, moved by Jesu's prayer	114
O for that just humility	38	Our long-expected Jesus	106
O for thy mercy sake	205	Our Lord is for us: Sin, devils, and men	14
O God in Christ, a soul behold	10	Our sins thy body bore	141
O God of peace, and pardoning love	164	Our sorrows, pure from sin, he bore	127
O King of saints come down	112	Our sufferings cannot grace procure	189
O let me then thy warnings heed	122	Our tutelary Rock, extend	268
O might I, as my Lord, survey	252	Out of the deep of late despair	252
O might I faithfully improve	74		
O might I now thy pity find	92		

566. Osborn changed "On" to "To."

Out of thy sins awake	73

Volume I

Pain, and sin, and sorrow cease	189
Painfully it now aspires	223
Pale Death with all his ghastly train[567]	123
Parent of Good, thy bounteous hand[568]	146
Parent of good, whose plenteous grace	189
Partners of a glorious hope	353
Partners of all my griefs and joys	246
Peace, doubting heart—my God's I am	135
Peace, fluttering soul! the storm is o'er	73
Perfect at first, and blest his state[569]	61
Perpetual knockings at thy door[570]	41
Pilgrims they here themselves confessed	214
Pity and heal my sin-sick soul	83
Pity from thine eye let fall	273
Plead we thus for faith alone	352
Pledge of thy promise given	101
Plenteous grace with thee is found	260
Plucked from the roaring lion's teeth	323
Plunged in th' abyss of deep distress[571]	121
Pour but thy blood upon the flame	261
Power is all to Jesus given	296
Powerful Advocate with God	115
Praise God, from whom all blessings flow	288
Praises here to thee we give	286
Prepare, and then possess my heart	76
Present to end the doubtful strife	25
Prevent thy foes, nor wait their charge	229
Primeval Beauty! in thy sight[572]	142
Prince of the hosts of God	153
Prisoner of hope, to thee I turn	237

567. Samuel Wesley, Sr.
568. From the German of Ernst Lange, translated by John Wesley.
569. George Herbert.
570. George Herbert.
571. Henry Pitt.
572. From the German of Johann Angelus Scheffler, translated by John Wesley.

Pronounce our happy doom	319
Prophet, on earth bestowed	315
Prophet, to me reveal	98
Publish the joyful year	317

Volume II

Pain and sickness, at thy word	155
Partakers of the life Divine	354
Partakers of the Saviour's grace	222
Partners of this heavenly hope	225
Passion, and appetite, and pride	313
Passion and appetite destroy	270
Past is thine oppressive hour	33
Patiently I then shall wait	68
Peace be on this house bestowed	219
Perfect then the work begun	158
Perfect then thy mighty power	298
Perform the work thou hast begun	320
Persons thou dost not respect	154
Pierce, fill me with an humble fear	272
Pity to my dying cries	158
Plant, and root, and fix in me	277
Planted awhile, or sown below	55
Pleased in borrowed plumes to shine	79
Plenteous he is in truth and grace	301
Poison now o'erflows my cup	106
Poor, alas! thou know'st I am	93
Poor, guilty, abject worms, to thee	345
Power I want, a constant power	135
Power over hell, and earth, and sin	352
Power over sins, to hew, and slay	352
Power to maintain his victory	353
Power to o'erturn, subdue, control	352
Praise by all to Christ be given	32
Present to all believing souls	340
Preserved through faith by power Divine	181
Princes, and kings, that dare withstand	55
Prisoner of hope, I wait the hour	140
Prisoners of hope, be strong, be bold	289
Prisoners of hope, lift up your heads	288
Prophet, sent from God above	261
Punished thou art, for he hath died	49

Pure as he did at first create	235
Purge me from every sinful blot	320
Put me not to eternal shame	41

Volume III

Pardon and grace impart	268
Pardon and peace in him I find	32
Pardon, and power, and peace	244
Part of his church below	225
Partner of the sinful nature	101
Paternal Deity	102
Paternal Source of Deity	350
Patient as my great High-Priest	327
Pay we equal adoration	346
Perishing for hunger, I	362
Pity their simpleness	83
Place us near th' accursed wood	232
Plant us into his death	329
Pleasure will I never taste	363
Poor heathens from far To Jesus we came	320
Poor penitents, we	324
Power to walk in all well-pleasing	271
Praise be to the Father given!	346
Praise God from whom pure blessings flow	100
Praise him who by his word	366
Prepare, the slaughtering sword prepare	149
Prince of Life, for sinners slain	232
Proceeds from thee the double grace	242
Publish we our Father's praise	103
Purge we all our sin away	275

Volume IV

Partakers of the life Divine	293
Partners of thy death and passion	148
Past human help I long have been	377
Patience its perfect work shall have	310
Patient th' appointed race to run	262
Peace, doubting heart, hath God begun	334
Peace, troubled soul, thou need'st not fear	378
People and priest are doubly dead	185
Perfect love! we long t' attain it	148

Perfect what thou hast begun	459
Perfect when we walk before thee	167
Perishing as the garb they wear	302
Plague and curse I now inherit	383
Plucked as a brand out of the fire	100
Plucked out of the flame, Thy soldiers we stand	90
Poor, pensive sojourners	230
Poor vassal! to rebel afraid	306
Poor, wretched heart, by sin oppressed	395
Praise everlasting as his love	457
Praise the Lord, ye blessed ones	253
Prepare the soul thou first shalt call	47
Preserve a life so dear	23
Prevalent now with God and man	296
Princes by thy appointment reign	24
Prisoners of hope, we meekly stand	256
Prolong his glorious race	78
Prophet, and priest, and king of peace	307
Prophets to thee thy Lord hath raised[573]	313
Punished after my demerit	383

Volume V

Pain, my old companion pain	67
Paleness his dying face o'erspreads	20
Pardon, and grace, and heaven to buy	149
Part by their own inventions led	247
Partake on earth the heavenly bliss	336
Partner of thy perfect nature	297
Pass a few fleeting days, or years	82
Pass away the empty shade	183
Peace be to this habitation!	53
Peace to the troubled heart	342
Perfect at once, and pure, and clean	249
Perfect in love, that casts out fear	299
Perfect let us walk before thee	456
Perfect when I walk before thee	297
Persist to save my soul	23
Physician, Friend of human kind	391
Pity my grief	59
Pity the day of feeble things	232

573. *UP* 2:452.

Place no longer let us give	178	Preserved so oft, we cannot doubt	160
Pleasure, and wealth, and praise no more	158	Press on to perfect holiness	318
Plunge me in the purple tide	205	Pride, only pride, can cause divorce	100
Poor abject slaves of sin	475	Principled with faith unfeigned[574]	336
Poor, abject souls! they tell thee	326	*Promised Prince of Peace, appear*	173
Poor is the man by slaves adored	405	Prostrate before the idol's shrine	437
Poor outcasts of men Whose souls were despised	390	Pursuing her, as she her Lord	357
Poor sinners below	223	Put thy hands upon my head	442

Volume VII

Poor tempted souls, with tempests tossed	231		
Pour out the promised gift on all	228		
Pour out your souls to God	43	Pain before thy presence flies	369
Praise him ye first-born sons of light	35	Pains and griefs—we soon shall lose 'em	41
Pray we, in the realms of light	179	Pardon he on our conscience seals	327
Pray we on, when all renewed	179	Pardon then to us impart	38
Pray, without ceasing pray	43	Partaker of thy purity	401
Present in spirit, howe'er disjoined	412	Parties and sects I now forego	180
Present we know thou art	468	Passed on all the sinful kind	363
Present with me in temptation	212	Passing through the dreary vale	403
Preserve me from my calling's snare	51	Peace be to our habitation	33
Prince of peace, if thou art	54	*Peace, my heart, be calm, be still*	92
Prisoners of hope, arise	329	Peace, panting soul, the storm is o'er	93
Proceeds from thee the wish to pray	175	Peace, righteousness, and joy Divine	355
Pronounce the glad word, And bid us be free	469	Persecution for thy sake	153
Propriety was there unknown	480	Plucked from the jaws of death	145
Pure into the hands of God	360	Poor and blind, condemned and lost	323
		Poor, unnoticed, and unknown	418
		Power Divine hath made us willing	40
		Praise to the blessed Spirit above	198

Volume VI

		Praise to the glorious Cause of all	309
Partakers of thy nature made	314	*Praise to the glorious Three in One*	310
Partner of my reproach, who justly claim	62	Present in thy balmy power	122
Plague, famine, and war But quicken our hope	47	Prevent, restrain, attend him	131
Plant in us thy constant mind	404	Preventing the first dawn of day	176
Plant the heavenly kingdom here	48	*Prince of everlasting peace*	38
Poor and vile in my own eyes	391	Prisoner of hope I still attend	108
Poor, meek, and patient to the end	313	Prostrate before thy mercy-seat	118
Possessed of that for which alone	277		

Volume VIII

Praise the Father for his love	464		
Prepossess my tender mind	444	Pain, and anguish, and affright	229
Presaging that her time is come	180	Pale death, with all his ghastly train	201
Present alike in every place	371		

574. *UP* 3:339.

Partaker of my flesh, impart	355	Peace at the last! eternal peace	292
Pass a few days or years	82	Peace within all her walls be found	332
Past feeling through habitual sin	348	Perfect if I were indeed	238
Patient I waited for the Lord	91	Perfect in love which casts out fear	421
Patient till death I feel my pain	425	Perhaps she thought, religion's law	166
Peace to them and power he brings	111	Physician of the sin-sick soul	47
Pierced my bones as with a sword	97	Pierced with the true religious fear	157
Planted by thine almighty hand[575]	163	Plenty is from, and with, the Lord	143
Pluck us as brands out of the flame	342	Poor abject souls that disbelieve	74
Poor, and mean, whom all reject	306	Poor needy souls athirst and faint	412
Poor, credulous slaves if he allure	483	Poor, tempted soul, what canst thou do?	437
Poor desolate souls he makes his	149	Poor vagabonds here Who shadows pursue	444
Poor desperate souls! they will not	26	Power and might are in thy hand	214
Poor guilty worms, what can we plead	344	Pride, and nature's various lusts	125
Possessed of lawless power	333	Prince of universal peace	385
Power is all to Jesus given	111	Principled with godly fear	12
Praise him, the faithful Lord and good!	185	Proud learning boasts its skill in vain	395
Praise, O God, attends on thee	141	Provoked, thou didst not quite depart	97
Praise the Lord, my thankful soul	190	Pure from the blood of Saul in vain	170
Praise the Lord, who reigns above	262	Purge me then from every sin	407
Praise the Lord, ye ransomed nations	203	Pursue the mystery!	28
Pray, my friends, and never cease	237		
Preserve my waiting soul in peace	51		
Preserved by my redeeming Lord	384	**Volume X**	
Prince of Peace, and Israel's King	334		
Princes have, with cruel rage	232	Pardoned through Jesu's grace alone	115
Prone to ill, averse from good	385	Pardoned without condition	182
Prophet of ills why should I live	416	Partakers of his nature pure	442
Protected by thy guardian grace	11	Partakers of his triumph	75
Proud, profligate, to evil sold	481	Passing through life in every stage	323
Publish, spread to all around	262	Pastors can we them confess	499
Purest love, and joy, and peace	365	Pastors corrupt their flocks induce	420
		Patient the rough repulse he bears	291
Volume IX		Peace from above revealed	101
		Peace of the tempestuous soul	479
Pardon admits of no degrees	48	Peace to the house I enter now	235
Pardon through thy wounds I have	439	Perfection is my calling's prize	173
Pardoned, still for sin I grieve	235	Physician of the fallen race	28
Partaker of my flesh below	147	Physician of the sin-sick race	43
Pass a few swiftly-fleeting years	130	Physicians of no price are they	14
Pass but another moment, Lord	314	Pity in my last distress	33
Patiently received from thee	231	Planted in the land of rest	65
		Pleading in prayer the faithful word	200

575. *UP* 2:447.

Pleading now thy faithful word	38	Praise him extolled above all height	117
Poor helpless souls whom Satan keeps!	228	Preach forgiveness to the poor	135
Poor, ignorant, illiterate men	356	Preach repentance in his name	314
Poorest of men, with comfort see	215	Preach the acceptable year	135
Power doth unto God belong	409	Preachers should with all maintain	125
Praise he bestows on faith alone	298	Prepare to meet thy hellish foe	131
Prayer is the language of the heart	177	Present before thy pitying eyes	224
Preach the heavenly kingdom near	232	Preserver of mankind	182
Preachers of righteousness arise	344	Presuming on his strength of grace	74
Preachers of the gospel word	247	Presumption, confidence, and pride	258
Prepared by sacred poverty	246	Presumptuous men through malice blind	476
Present in our assemblies we	132	Pride is the armour of our foe	205
Preserve my conscience pure	378	Prince and Saviour of mankind	356
Pretenders to the Spirit rise	368	Principled with humble grace	259
Preventing the first dawn of day	451	Professors still his name abuse[576]	221
Previous to the dreadful day	135	Prophet of Christ the Lord Most-High	114
Priests and infidels may join	357	Prophet, Priest, and King, on me	135
Profit every way we find	236	Prophets, kings far off beheld thee	196
Pure baptismal Fire Divine	146	Prostrate now the shrine before	338
Put forth the virtue of thy love	306	Prostrate, with eyes of faith I see	87
		Purchased by thy own merit	199

Volume XI

Parted from God the soul is dead	471
Parted in the act of blessing	316
Passion's turbulent excess	475
Pastors and priests to avarice sold	506
Pastors the sheep should feed	180
Pasture I find in every place	458
Peace to this house! the greatest good	191
Peace with the world and peace with God	216
Penitents the Saviour cheers	92
Period of my griefs and woes	470
Perishing for want of food	203
Peter self-confident, sincere	288
Pharisees inquire in vain	443
Pitying he hears the widow's prayers	163
Pomp and magnificence he leaves	486
Poor fainting souls our Lord relieves	378
Poor for our sake, the Lord most high	169
Possessed by sin the world and hell	23
Practice is the truth of grace	159

Volume XII

Partakers of thy ministry	54
Partially by nature taught	447
Partly false and partly true	316
Partner of the heavenly hope	432
Passion brands religion pure	348
Pastors thus the flock should leave	368
Pastors, who live at ease	356
Paul exorcised the maid possessed	317
Paul for his companions pays	448
Paul in its strongest fortress here	339
Peace the Saviour speaks again	107
Persecution's progress see!	144
Peter between the soldiers bound	272
Peter had by experience found	123
Peter musing on the vision	246
Piety respect inspires	185
Pity, Lord, thy creature's pain	21

576. *UP* 2:147.

IDEX OF FIRST LINES OF POETRY BY JOHN AND CHARLES WESLEY

Poor Agrippa! but almost	432
Poor, and ignorant, and blind	236
Poor trembling sinners we incline	428
Power to every messenger	180
Power to pray and never cease	41
Power, wisdom, learning all combine	170
Praise is the proof, the touchstone praise	290
Prayers and alms to heaven ascend[577]	244
Praying on for faith's increase	23
Preachers are called, above the rest	191
Preachers of Christ, his death we prove[578]	327
Preachers of Christ, in faith go on	359
Preferred to those that seemed the best	331
Prepared to make their Saviour known	353
Present we know thou always art	106
Present with thy people still	36
Prince of life, for sinners slain	148
Prisoner of Christ, to death pursued[579]	418
Prisoner of death, and silent here	93
Proud sinners who in learning trust[580]	344
Providence extends its care	117
Pure apostolic zeal	336
Pure from the blood of all	376
Purged from the stains of sin	294

Volume XIII

Pardon itself avails me not	193
Pardoned, if ye the grace retain	187
Part of thy Church o'er earth dispread	284
Partakers of his bitterest cup	157
Partners now in tribulation	47
Pass a few fleeting moments more	91
Pass we thus our days of mourning	18
Patient to all that I may be	92
Pent in an house of clay	47
Perfect in love which casts out fear	171
Perfection is the good	215
Place me in that happiest station	272

577. *UP* 2:335.
578. *UP* 2:378.
579. *UP* 2:422.
580. *UP* 2:330.

Power executive is thine	232
Power is all to Jesus given	218
Power o'er the world, the fiend, and sin	104
Praying faith on us bestow	267
Press to the mark, (the Spirit cries	60
Proclaiming my own holiness	78
Put him to death, the Adam old	87

Volume II

Quickly we shall all appear	224

Volume III

Quicken our dead souls again	241

Volume IV

Quench this cruel hell of doubt	421
Quicken by thy parting breath	360
Quite from the manger to the cross	344

Volume V

Quickened at once they soon shall rise	86
Quickened by power Divine	39

Volume X

Quick as the darted lightning flies	374

Volume XII

Questioned if thee indeed I love	125

Volume XIII

Quickened with our immortal head	104

Volume I

Rack me not to such vast extent[581]	48
Rage, while our faith the Saviour tries	231
Rahab by faith deliverance found	219
Raised t' inherit glorious joys	354
Rather than let it burn	269
Rebuke the seas, the tempest chide	298
Redeemed from sin, its guilt, and power	285
Redeemed, we walk on holy ground	371
Refining fire, go through my heart	329
Refulgent from afar	147
Regardless now of things below[582]	222
Regardless of the things behind	214
Reign in me, Lord, thy foes control	284
Rejected and despised of men	79
Remove this hardness from my heart	371
Renew thy image, Lord, in me[583]	162
Rescued from the fowler's snare	93
Resistless then it wins its way	14
Restore my sight! let thy free grace[584]	89
Rise I to heaven, or sink to dust[585]	48
Rise, my soul, with ardour rise	192
Risen with him, we upward move	186
Roar on, ye waves! Our souls defy	231
Roaring lion, own his power	296

Volume II

Rather let all the creatures take	258
Rather than suffer me to sin	127
Rebellious worms, they would not take	339
Regard thine own eternal prayer	334
Regardless now of flesh and blood	311
Rejoice, rejoice, ye fallen race	227
Rejoicing in hope, And patient in grief	197
Rejoicing now in earnest hope	302
Remember me, O Lord, my God	107
Remove the sins which we declare	137
Repent thee of thy peevish haste	56
Rescued from want, and vice, and shame	24
Rest for my soul I long to find	144
Rich, and increased with goods, I was	90
Rise, ye men of Israel, rise	239
Rock of my salvation, haste	104

Volume III

Raise, and enable me to stand	249
Receive my soul, which gasps for death	161
Receive us then, thou pardoning God	222
Receiving the bread	282
Rejoice, rejoice, ye fallen race	145
Repeat the Saviour's dying cry	221
Reserved, in dark, substantial chains	147
Resolved each precious moment to redeem	114
Rest to my soul I now have found	33
Restored to thine unsinning state	145
Return, and with thy servants sit	341
Returning to his Father's throne	292
Returning to his throne above	289
Reveal in every soul thy Son	278
Right precious in his sight the death	174
Righteous in all thy ways thou art	41
Rivers of salvation still	235
Rock of Israel, cleft for me	235
Root out the seeds of pride and lust	318
Ruin in him complete we have	240

Volume IV

Raised by the breath of Love Divine	263
Raised from the dead we are	144
Ready, through grace, I am	15
Ready to pierce thy trembling heart	348
Receive my gasping spirit home	386
Redeemed from all iniquity	289
Refresh us with a ceaseless shower	271

---

581. George Herbert.
582. From the German of Maria Böhmer.
583. From the German of Johann A. Freylinghausen, translated by John Wesley.
584. From the German of Wolfgang Dessler, translated by John Wesley.
585. George Herbert.

Regard me with a gracious eye	324	Rejoice in glorious hope	285
Regard the number of our foes	31	Rejoice, my friends, I go before	226
Regard, thou righteous God and true	81	*Rejoice, ye happy saints*	258
Rejoice evermore With angels above	241	Rejoicing in hope We humbly go on	427
Rejoice, the Lord is King	140	Released from all your wants and cares	361
Rejoice with us, ye angel host	457	Relieve the souls whose cross we bear	232
Rejoice in glorious hope	141	Remove the stumbling block within	415
Rejoicing now in glorious hope	226	Removed from the sure gospel hope	246
Remembering my distress	431	Resolved, her house should serve the Lord	89
Repent before the dire decree	62	*Rest, my troubled spirit, rest*	351
Resolved our Lord t' obey	46	Restrained from my own wickedness	8
Rest, till the storm is all o'erpast	292	Return from above	305
Restless grief, and pain unceasing	439	Rise, in the Spirit's rapture, rise	286
Restorer of the sin-sick mind	202	*Rise, my soul, the dawn appears*	349
Riches unsearchable	231	Rivals of the heavenly choir	274
Righteous in all thy ways	433	*Rock of everlasting love*	163
Righteous, sin-avenging God	57		
Righteousness, Lord, belongs to thee	4		
Rise all who seek the Crucified	145		
Rivers of real tears I shed	368		
Root up every bitter root	194		

Volume VI

Raised up through thee the righteous man	122
Ravished hence by sovereign love	365
Ready for her celestial home	361

Volume V

Raised to-day above my sorrow	451	Ready to fly this moment home	297
Rather I would in darkness mourn	372	Receive the answer of thy prayer	402
Rather let me snatch th' occasion	451	Recreation of mind	434
Rather let my soul depart	444	Redeemed by righteousness Divine	280
Rather my spirit take	104	Redeemed by thine almighty grace	71
Ready for you the angels wait	63	Redeemed from all iniquity	375
Ready the Father is to own	63	Redeemed from earth and pain	316
Ready the Spirit of his love	63	Redeemed from earth, the tuneful soul	247
Ready thou art the blood t' apply	122	Redemption is come, Jehovah descends	91
Reason, blind leader of the blind	158	Refreshing, soft as vernal showers	283
Rebuke the fever in this hour	79	*Rejoice for a brother deceased*	189
Redeemed from all his woes	365	*Rejoice in the Lord, Rejoice evermore!*	397
Redemption through thy blood we have	33	*Rejoice, ye sons of light*	202
Refrain my soul, and keep it low	415	*Relieve whoe'er thy succour need*	134
Regard our prayers for Sion's peace	229	Religion undefiled and true	346
Regard thy faithful ones	237	Remember, Lord, the righteous man	34
Regard thy own	60	Remember us then, And answer our call	288
Regardless of their smile, and frown	88	Repent before my vengeful ire	83
Rejoice, and sing	62	Repentance to our thanks we join	166

Repentance upon both bestow	186	Reach me out thy helping hand	234
Reposed in those Elysian seats	227	Rebellions, massacres, and blood	304
Rest, happy saint, with God secure	235	Redeem my life from Satan's power	44
Resting in this glorious hope	94	Redeemer of the sinful kind	379
Rests secure the righteous man	94	*Refuge supreme of sad despair*	352
Righteous God, whose vengeful vials	92	Regard my cruel, countless foes	51
Righteous Lord, thy people spare	39	*Remember, Lord, the ancient days*	167
Righteous, O Lord, are all thy ways	40	Remember, Lord, the cruel pride	254
Ripe for the glorious harvest made	199	*Remember, Lord, the pious zeal*	248
Rise every soul in Jesus' name	42	Rescue me, O my God, from those	159
Rise, ye dearly purchased sinners	142	Reserved by the love	421
Rising in thy dreadful might	20	Resolved at last, "To God," I cried	66
Rome with a new armada vowed	181	Restore me to my first estate	382
Root up the tares by Satan sown	115	*Returned into thy kingdom, Lord*	343
Rugged howe'er his manners seemed	350	Returned to heaven, again he lives	348
		Revive, O God of power, revive[586]	165
		Righteous I am in him, and strong	205
		Righteous in himself, the Lord	22
		Righteous Lord, attend my cry	28

Volume VII

Rapturous anticipation	336	*Righteous, O Lord, thy judgments are! / Yet*	322
Rather I would with warmer zeal	173	*Righteous, O Lord, thy judgments are! / We*	283
Rather in tender grace	79	*Righteous souls, rejoice in God*	68
Rather permit them to expire	174	Rise, the Lord of armies, rise	332
Rather resume the blessings lent	52	*Rise, ye ransomed sinners, rise*	400
Read all and understand	275	Running at his kind command	237
Ready made for my translation	367		
Reason can no farther go	311		
Redeemed from passion and from pride	410		
Reject me not, because I fear	411		
Remember thy Creators, God	272		
Remembering then thy mortal pain	412		
Reserved for this alone	145		

Volume IX

Rest of every weary spirit	32	Raised from the people's lowest lees	79
Restorer of the sin-sick race	154	Rapt to Pisgah's top, I stand	118
Restrained by heavenly grace	392	Rather thy loving Spirit Divine	414
Right notions have their slender use	324	Ready for my earthen bed	253
Righteous, O God, are all thy ways!	115	Redeemed from the foe	324
Righteous, O Lord, thy judgments are	49	Redeemer of mankind	28
Rise the woman's conquering Seed	69	Redundant as a swelling tide	440
Rock of offence at first he was	206	Reflecting on this gospel-day	83
		Refusing with our sin to part	132
		Regardless of a private wrong	189
		Rejoice in Jesu's birth!	381
		Religion pure rejects the dress	146

Volume VIII

Raised up by thee he seemed to stand	408

---

586. *UP* 2:449.

Reserves of unexhausted grace	56	Rejoice, ye rich, with humble fear	34
Resolved, O God, with all to part	24	Rejoicing in iniquity	414
Respecting Jesus in our prayer	208	Religion is their care	482
Righteous Judge, who read'st the heart	384	Religion true to visit earth	350
Rise, the woman's conquering Seed	8	Rent is the sacred flesh of him	91
Rising to sing my Saviour's praise	95	Repentance doth with fear begin[587]	251
Rivers of pure delight shall rise	412	Repentance must prepare the way	124
Rock of eternity	218	Reproved she answers not a word	334
Root them out of Adam's race	8	Resolved, I follow thee	419
		Resolved on man his grace to prove	40
		Rest, thou favoured spirit, rest[588]	198
		Retreat the mourner seeks	82

Volume X

Raised to thine everlasting throne	264	Returning from the dead	94
Rather a thousand-fold increase	15	Reverencing thy name and word	99
Reader of the trembling heart	436	Rich in faith and poverty	275
Ready is it to take place	233	Riches to love and clothing gay	242
Reason's glimmering light is vain	472	Righteous Lord thy judgments are!	453
Redeemed from passion's tyranny	256	Ritual services are passed	357
Remember, Lord, my sins no more	53	Rivals of saints supremely blessed	73
Rent by thy expiring groan	432	Room in thy capacious breast	229
Repentance permanent and deep	195	Root out the wrath thou dost restrain	156
Repentance should be preached to all	494		
Rest of my weary mind	255		
Rest succeeding work is sweet	498		

Volume XII

Retired into his secret place	76	Reason and probity forbid	364
Returns the age of golden days	131	Reason and sense would fain forget	30
Riches with unsuspected art	273	Reason he did not cast aside[589]	327
Righteous in our own esteem	458	Recorded in th' authentic book	112
Rising out of thy holy place	113	Redeemed by thine electing love	62
Rising saints forsake the tomb	433	Redeemed from all his sufferings here	204
Rising with thy faithful race	274	Redeemed through faith by blood Divine	295
		Reeds may still, if thou ordain	173
		Reflecting on thy wondrous ways	268
		Rejecting thy distress	45

Volume XI

Ranging in vice without control	234	Religion undefiled and true	452
Ready to conclude thy race	479	Reluctantly they let them go	195
Reason and faith together strive	478	Remember Lord our griefs and fears	378
Re-begotten from above	466	Remember me, O Lord my God	97
Receive him in Jehovah's name	485	Repent and believe	168
Redemption's wondrous work is wrought	510	Repent, and cast aside	224
Regardless of the things unseen	280		
Regardless of the tyrant's frown	19		
Rejoice, ye followers of your Lord	297		

587. *UP* 2:162.
588. *UP* 2:126.
589. *UP* 2:378.

Repent in heart, and word, and deed	373	*Saviour, who ready art to hear*	304
Repent, ye self-destroying race	343	Savor of life, O, let it prove	240
Respect external but unfeigned	401	Say, is thy heart resolved as ours?	341
Rest after toil is doubly sweet!	281	'Scaped from the world, redeemed from sin	340
Return, most gracious Lord, return	40	Scarce I begin my sad complaint	77
Rival meek of Jesu's passion	218	Scarce on earth a thought bestow	186
Rulers in church and state give ear	171	Scatter the last remains of sin	284

Volume XIII

Rather let my bowels move	68	Scorn to contend with flesh and blood	227
Rejoice evermore	93	Search and try out my panting heart	262
Rejoicing in hope We humbly go on	18	Secure a better life to find	220
Remembrance shakes her whip severe	144	Secure beneath its shade I sat	24
Renewed I in thy image rise	190	Secure from danger and from dread	294
Repent of thy religion vain	166	See all your sins on Jesus laid	301
Rest to my soul I gasp to find	125	See from the Rock a fountain rise!	205
Returning from his sacrifice	170	See! he lifts his hands above!	187
Righteous as my God am I?	204	See my sad inconstant state	254
Righteous God, whose awful frown	266	*See the Day-spring from afar*	158
Rock of eternity, he stood	26	See the Desire of Nations comes	78
		See then thy ransomed servant, see	96
		See, then, we take thee at thy word	302

Volume I

		See these barren souls of ours	290
Sad soothing thought! to lose my cares	244	See thy poor dust, in pity see[594]	66
Safe in the way of life, above	371	See where before the throne he stands	278
Salvation in that Name is found	270	See, ye sinners, see, the flame[595]	281
Satan, thy due reward survey[590]	347	Seek ye the Lord with timely care	207
Save me from pride, the plague expel	261	Selfish pursuits, and nature's maze	249
Saviour, if thy precious love[591]	107	Send down thy likeness from above[596]	160
Saviour, look down with pitying eyes	299	Sent by Almighty Pity down	26
Saviour of men, how long shall I	95	Servant of all, to toil for man	172
Saviour of men, my sad complaint	274	Servant of God, confess	319
Saviour of men! thy searching eye[592]	178	*Servant of God, the summons hear*	228
Saviour, the world's and mine	149	Servants of God, both yours and mine	303
Saviour, where'er thy steps I see[593]	138	Set to thy seal that I am his	25
		Set up thy kingdom in my heart[597]	49
		Shall I, for fear of feeble man[598]	177

590. From the German of Nikolaus von Zinzendorf, translated by John Wesley.
591. George Herbert.
592. From the German of Johann Joseph Winckler, translated by John Wesley.
593. From the German of Nikolaus von Zinzendorf, translated by John Wesley.
594. George Herbert.
595. From the German of Anna Dober, translated by John Wesley.
596. From the German of Joachim Lange, translated by John Wesley.
597. George Herbert.
598. From the German of Johann Joseph Winckler, translated by John Wesley.

IDEX OF FIRST LINES OF POETRY BY JOHN AND CHARLES WESLEY

Shall I my darling Isaac give	276	So many human souls divine[607]	8
Shall I, to soothe th' unholy throng[599]	178	So many tender joys and woes[608]	8
Shepherd, securely keep	319	So many wondrous gleams of light[609]	9
Shine in their hearts, Father of Light	315	*So many years I've seen the sun*[610]	8
Shine on thy work, disperse the gloom	258	So shall my every power to thee[611]	104
Show us thy Sire; for known to thee	238	So shall the word my lips have spoke	208
Sick of desire, for thee I cry	250	So when before th' angelic host	26
Silent, (alas! thou know'st how long	263	So when on Sion thou shalt stand[612]	129
Silent have we been too long	287	Soar we now, where Christ has led?	186
Sin felt of old thy power	154	Softened and vanquished by my tears[613]	102
Sin is still spreading o'er my heart[600]	40	*Solitude! where shall I find*[614]	6
Sin shall tyrannise no more	170	Son of my love, behold, to thee	206
Since by thy light myself I see	76	*Son of the Carpenter, receive*	172
Since the Son hath bought my peace	193	Sons of Belial, hear the cry	286
Since the Son hath made me free	193	*Sons of God, exulting rise*	93
Since then I many a bitter storm[601]	103	*Sons of God, triumphant rise*	170
Since thou a pitying ear didst give[602]	123	*Sons of men, behold from far*	184
Since thou hast bid me come to thee	136	Soon as his love has raised me up[615]	114
Since thou wast precious in his sight	181	Soon as I taste the heavenly bread[616]	113
Sing we now in duty bound	286	Soon as the trying hour returned	333
Sing we then in Jesu's name	350	Sorrow and sighs are fled away	120
Sing we then with one accord	289	Sorrow and self shall then expire	329
Sing, ye heavens; and, earth, rejoice	93	Sorrow and sin, and loss and pain[617]	65
Sing, ye morning stars, again!	185	Sovereign Father, heavenly King!	115
Single of heart, O! may I be[603]	13	Speak, and the deaf shall hear thy voice	271
Sinking underneath my load	256	Speak, gracious Lord, my sickness cure	83
Sinners, your Saviour see!	336	Speak to my warring passions, "Peace;"	128
Small is it in this humble sort[604]	102	Spirit they are, and life	318
Snatch me from ill to come	269	Spotless and just in thee I am	283
So even in storms my zeal shall grow[605]	86	Stamped with an infinite desert	173
So frail, impure, and weak, could I	335	Steadfast let us cleave to thee	359
So many airy draughts and lines[606]	8		

599. From the German of Johann Joseph Winckler, translated by John Wesley.
600. George Herbert.
601. George Herbert.
602. Samuel Wesley, Sr.
603. From the German of Sigmund Gmelin, translated by John Wesley.
604. George Herbert.
605. From the German of Christian Friedrich Richter, translated by John Wesley.
606. John Gambold.
607. John Gambold.
608. John Gambold.
609. John Gambold.
610. John Gambold.
611. From the German of Johann A. Freylinghausen, translated by John Wesley.
612. From the German of Christian Friedrich Richter, translated by John Wesley.
613. George Herbert.
614. From the Latin.
615. George Herbert.
616. George Herbert.
617. George Herbert.

Steadfast we then shall stand, and sure	345	Still with thy grace anoint my eyes	282
Steel me to shame, reproach, disgrace	179	Stir up thy strength, and help us, Lord	314
Still by his faith he speaks, though dead	211	Stoop from thy eternal throne	194
Still for thy lovingkindness, Lord	235	Stop this full current of thy tears	244
Still for us his death he pleads	187	Stranger on earth, I sojourn here	262
Still heavy is thy heart?[618]	127	Strive in joy, with angels strive	93
Still hide me in thy secret place	305	Strive we, in affection strive	350
Still I ask, nor yet receive	257	Strong in Christ, we thee defy	297
Still if I wail not, (still to wail[619]	43	Strong in the Lord, divinely strong	345
Still let me run, or end my race	307	Strong in the Lord's almighty power	228
Still let thy love point out my way[620]	141	Struggling in the fowler's snare	257
Still let thy tears, thy groans, thy sighs[621]	233	Subdue in us the carnal mind	298
Still let thy wisdom be my guide[622]	90	Sudden expired the legal strife	299
Still, Lord, from thy exhaustless store[623]	130	Suffer me no more to grieve	193
Still may his love thy fortress be	181	Suffered awhile to want my God	95
Still may we continue thus	358	Suffice for me, that thou, my Lord	234
Still nigh me, O my Saviour, stand	136	Suffice it, Lord, I now believe	336
Still, O Lord, (for thine we are,)	361	Suffice that for the season past	288
Still, O Lord, our faith increase	353	*Summoned my labour to renew*	172
Still, O my soul, prolong	151	Superior far to mortal things	14
Still shall I urge, with endless toil[624]	39	Surely against thy holy Son	295
Still the small inward voice I hear	106	Surely for us he humbled was	79
Still then may prayer with me remain[625]	125	Surely our God will bid him live	207
Still vexed and troubled is my heart?	244	Surely thou wilt. thou canst not send	293
Still we gasp thy grace to know	291	Surrounded by his power I stand	326
Still, while our mouths are filled with good	190	*Sweet Day, so cool, so calm, so bright*[628]	10
Still will I hope for voice and strength[626]	52	*Sweet Rose, so fragrant and so brave*[629]	10
Still will I watch, and labour still[627]	89	*Sweet Spring, so beauteous and so gay*[630]	10
		Sweeten at length this bitter bowl	62
		Sweetly now we all agree	362
		Sworn to destroy, let earth assail	270

618. From the German of Paul Gerhardt, translated by John Wesley.
619. George Herbert.
620. From the German of Paul Gerhardt, translated by John Wesley.
621. From the German of Paul Gerhardt, translated by John Wesley.
622. From the German of Wolfgang Dessler. translated by John Wesley.
623. From the German of Nikolaus von Zinzendorf, translated by John Wesley.
624. George Herbert.
625. George Herbert.
626. John Gambold?
627. From the German of Christian Friedrich Richter, translated by John Wesley.

Volume II

Satan, hear the name of Jesus	31
Satan, wilt thou now defy us?	33
Satan, with all his arts, no more	296
Save me for thine own great name	266
Save me, Lord, from sin and fear	97
Saviour, for this I thank thee now	232

628. George Herbert.
629. George Herbert.
630. George Herbert.

Saviour from sin, I wait to prove	132	Shall Satan into prison cast	348
Saviour, from thy wounded side	201	Shall still the proud Philistine's noise	335
Saviour, I thank thee for the grace	149	She died in sure and steadfast hope	184
Saviour of all, to thee we bow	361	She now the fight of faith hath fought	184
Saviour of my soul, draw nigh	157	Shepherd of Souls, his tender care	51
Saviour, purify my soul	106	Shortened is thy hand, O Saviour?	31
Say, then, ye abject worms, to whom	55	Should I say, that aught in me	76
Say, then, ye worms of earth, to whom	53	Should we be wanting to rejoice	19
Say, which of you would see the Lord	340	Shout in the midst of us, O King	194
'Scaped from the world of pride and lust	249	Show me, as my soul can bear	263
Secure beneath thy shadow sit	250	Show me how foul my heart hath been	322
See, gracious Lord, with pitying eyes	216	Sick of anger, pride, and lust	153
See how his back the scourges tear	70	Sin hath poisoned all my soul	66
See, I give up all at last	112	Sin hath tyrannized too long	239
See me lying at the pool	153	Sin in me, the inbred foe	268
See me, O Lord, athirst and faint	73	Sin is now my sore disease	154
See me the reverse of thee	97	Sin, my strongest sin, is dead	239
See my utter helplessness	124	Sin only let me not commit	129
See the lawful captive taken	32	Sin, only sin, in me I find	148
See the porches open wide!	153	Sin shall not always live	329
See the promise-word takes place	238	Sin shall not have dominion now[632]	247
See the vast tribes that crowd the face	53	Sin shall not have dominion now[633]	254
See then the sinner stript of all	110	Sin shall not in our flesh remain	249
See there! his temples crowned with thorns	71	*Sinners, your hearts lift up*	229
See thy poor afflicted child	213	Sin's deceitfulness hath spread	119
See where enthroned in Christ we sit	195	Since first I felt by grace removed	181
See where the servants of their God[631]	62	Since 'tis thy sentence I should part[634]	11
Seek, O seek me, Lord, again	277	Single, a thousand foes I chase	314
Send, O send me now away	151	Sion, ascend the mountain-top	51
Senseless alike of sin and thee	69	Sion, shout thy Lord and King	252
Sensible delights on me	213	Slay me, and I in thee shall trust	271
Sent of God, we thee receive	218	Slay me, and I shall live indeed	122
Serpent, see in us thy Bruiser	33	Smell the sweet odour of our prayers	362
Servant of sin too long I was	248	Smooth as the generous-nurtured beast	59
Set upon thyself my feet	105	Snatched from the death of sin, my soul	254
Shake off the bands of sad despair	168	So I may thy Spirit know	215
Shake off the dust that blinds thy sight	168	So shall I bless thy pleasing sway	143
Shall he still the souls enthral	257	So shall I do thy will below	143
Shall magnify the sovereign grace	335	So shall our lives thy power proclaim[635]	64
Shall now, in Jesus taught to trust	173		

631. From the German of August Gottlieb Spangenberg, translated by John Wesley.
632. Line 2: "Or in my body reign."
633. Line 2: "Or in my mortal body reign."
634. Altered from John Norris.
635. From the German of August Gottlieb

So shall the world believe and know	334	Stripped of every boasted grace	283
So shall thy grace our souls preserve	356	Stript of my boasted gifts, I fall	90
So shalt thou grant to all that fight	363	Strong I am, for he is strong	251
So teach us, Lord, to number out	29	Stronger than the strong man, thou	256
So when his eyes behold thee near	216	Stubborn heart, ungrateful, hard	88
Sober, and just, and godly here	325	Such faith in God through thee I have	308
Son of God, arise, arise	293	Suffer him no more to harm her	30
Son of God, if thy free grace	125	Suffer not an Egyptian night	41
Son of thy Sire's eternal love	336	Suffering, sin-atoning God	179
Soon as I find myself forsook	202	Summoned to answer at thy bar	109
Soon as Satan gives the word	284	Surely, he said, Mine own they are	57
Spare me till I my strength of soul	281	Surely he will lift me up	318
Speak; and an holy thing and clean	132	Surely he will not delay	221
Speak but the reconciling word	333	Surely I shall, the sinner I	287
Speak the word, and we shall be	256	*Surely in the Lord we have*	110
Spirit of faith, within us live	228	Surely in us the hope	245
Spirit of grace, and health, and power	336	Surely now the bitterness	158
Spirits like him he made us be	235	Surely now the charm is broken	33
Sprinkle it, Jesu, on my heart!	321	Surely they all shall know my name	169
Standing now as newly slain	200	Surely thou canst, I do not doubt	282
Steadfast our anchor is and sure	331	Surely thou canst not let me die!	14
Still do I live, not Christ, but I	95	Surely we did thy faith receive	354
Still (for I put my trust in thee)	77	Sweetly he strove their hearts to gain	58
Still hold my soul in second life	254		
Still hold the stars in thy right hand	341		
Still I cannot part with thee	151	**Volume III**	
Still I see his unfelt grace	318	Sad mutual causes of decay	340
Still let him with my weakness stay	272	Saint of the Lord, my soul is sin	264
Still let it on th' assembly stay	226	Saints begin the endless song	293
Still let me live thy blood to show	281	Saith he what he never meant	87
Still let my bleeding heart be torn	164	Salvation to God, / Who carried	334
Still let thy gracious Spirit strive	347	Satan his kingdom's fall shall see	149
Still let us own our common Lord	139	Satan shall be at last brought low	153
Still, O my God, thy power display	254	Satan stirs a tempest up[636]	167
Still thou answerest not a word	150	Save me now, and still deliver	278
Still thou journey'st where I am	157	*Saviour, and can it be*	246
Still to thee, my God, I come	151	*Saviour, and Friend of sinners, see*	27
Still we listen to our foe	283	*Saviour of all, by God designed*	32
Stir ourselves up, renounce our ease	354	*Saviour of all, our thanks receive!*	177
Stony heart, which nought can move!	87	*Saviour of my soul from sin*	249
Straitened I am till this be done	196		
Strengthened by thy great example	31		

636. Free paraphrase of the German of Wolfgang Christoph Dessler by Charles Wesley.

Spangenberg, translated by John Wesley.

INDEX OF FIRST LINES OF POETRY BY JOHN AND CHARLES WESLEY

Saviour, Prince, enthroned above	296	Sinners, turn while God is near	88
Saviour, thou didst not come from heaven	242	Sinners, turn; why will ye die / God, the Spirit	85
Saviour, thou didst the mystery give	253	*Sinners, turn; why will ye die? / God your Maker*	84
Savour of life, and joy, and bliss	255		
Say, are his consolations small?	175	Sinners, turn; why will ye die? / God your Saviour	85
Searcher of hearts, in ours appear	268		
Secure of the celestial prize	157	Six thousand years are now past by	239
See from his wounded side	267	Six wings each heavenly herald wore	133
See him dragged out to open light	67	So dear the tie where souls agree	339
See me looking for my doom	13	So when the first degenerated man	111
See, sinners, in the gospel glass	20	So when the woman did of Jesus tell	113
See the slaughtered Sacrifice	228	Some men of simple heart	83
See then, I all at last resign	158	*Son of God, thy blessing grant*	250
See there the quickening Cause of all	299	Soon as I found my heart set free	135
See where our great High-Priest	313	Soon as I taste the liquid life[638]	169
See where the God incarnate stands	20	Soon as the morn of opening life begun	109
See where the lame, the halt, the blind	21	*Soothing, soul-composing thought*	162
Seized by the rage of sinful man	217	Spare, my friends, your vain expense	362
Send me, my answering spirit cried	135	Spectators of the pangs Divine	220
Shall make him apt to teach and reign	142	Spirit of faith, come down	268
Shall we let him die in vain	233	Spirit of power, and health, and love	101
Shall we let our God groan	323	Sprinkled with the blood we lie	315
Shouldst thou o'er the desert lead[637]	167	*Stay, thou eternal spirit, stay*	176
Shout to the great Jehovah's praise	353	Still all-involved in God we are	318
Sin shall no more in thee have place	141	Still, gracious Lord, on us bestow	370
Sin shall no more in them have place	144	Still in his instituted ways	259
Since first with Adam's sons he strove	44	Still, Lord, with joy we bless thee	371
Since God might justly let all die	67	Still my cruel sins oppress me	278
Sinful, and blind, and poor	265	Still my imprisoned spirit waits	158
Sing we to our God above	345	Still, O Lord, our strength repair	241
Sinner, with awe draw near	243	Still shall the hellish doctrine stand	5
Sinners, abhor the fiend	35	Still the wounds are open wide	307
Sinners, believe the gospel word	21	Strangers shall then to thee be joined	145
Sinners, for full redemption hope	141	Strengthened by this immortal food	299
Sinners, hear my dying call	16	Stricken by thine anger's rod	326
Sinners, how oft would he HGEL 1741, 31		Strong in the strength herewith received	340
Sinners on every side step in	257	Strongly upheld by thy right hand	95
Sinners, regard your friend who speaks though dead	118	Stung by the scorpion sin	72
Sinners, see, he dies for all	315	Such was the man by men and fiends abhorred	119

637. Free paraphrase of the German of Wolfgang Christoph Dessler by Charles Wesley.

638. Free paraphrase of the German of Christian Friedrich Richter by Charles Wesley.

Suffer sin no more t' oppress us	270
Sure and real is the grace	256
Sure instrument of present grace	285
Sure pledge of ecstasies unknown	290
Sure pledges of his dying love	266
Surely I once believed	46
Surely if thou the symbols bless	257
Surely now the prayer he hears	232
Surely the gospel day shall come	145
Surely the grace doth once appear	65
Surely the righteous man	49
Surely thy dying prayer is heard	69
Swift as air my moments fly	162
Swift as the panting hart I fly[639]	169
Swift, as their rising Lord to find	254

Volume IV

Safe as devoted Peter	238
Safe in the fiery furnace	86
Safe in the lions' den I lie	468
Salvation to God, / Will I publish abroad	274
Salvation to God Who sits on the throne!	52
Salvation to our souls brought in	285
Satan, cease thine empty boast	450
Satan, the world, and sin too long[640]	314
Satan's strongholds o'erthrown shall be	287
Save, Jesu, save the sinking ship	11
Save me! I ask not how	399
Save me, through faith in Jesu's blood	228
Save us by grace through faith alone	460
Save us in thy great compassion	117
Saved beyond the dread of falling	148
Saved from the Romish fowler's snare	100
Saviour and Prince of Peace, / The double	434
Saviour and Prince of Peace, / thy saying	177
Saviour, cast a pitying eye	389
Saviour, dost thou bid me rise	443
Saviour, Lord, who at thy death	180

639. Free paraphrase of the German of Christian Friedrich Richter by Charles Wesley.
640. *UP* 2:453.

Saviour, Prince, enthroned above	405
Saviour, Prince, enthroned on high	388
Saviour, Prince of Israel's race	357
Saviour, see my troubled breast	359
Say, if prepared for death thou art	345
Scandal of the Christian name	8
Screen my faint devoted head	360
Seated at God's right hand again	226
Secure from danger, as from dread	285
Secure on earth who dwell	20
Secure on liquid waves I tread	456
Secure us of his royal race	26
See him between the dying thieves	347
See him set forth before your eyes	277
See how his meteors glare!	12
See how they fly to set us free	97
See in that Infant's face	110
See, Lord, the purchase of thy death	31
See me in my last distress	462
See me, Saviour, from above	406
See th' eternal Son of God	109
See the poor patient at thy feet	376
See then I at thy feet once more	424
See then, with eyes of mercy see	381
See there! The new-born Saviour see	124
See thy creature most distressed	421
See where o'er desert wastes they err	251
Send the Comforter to raise us	167
Send us the Spirit of thy Son	166
Sent by my Lord, on you I call	275
Sent down to make us meet	169
Sent in his name thou art	192
Shake my inmost soul with fear	357
Shall glory in my saving name	309
Shall I believe, Who made the eye	392
Shall I then the strife give o'er	428
Shall learning show the Sinner's Friend	124
Shall soon his fallen Sion raise	300
Shall we of earthly kings inquire	124
Shame on my soul! The dire disgrace	337
She mocks my unavailing cry	424
She seizes, holds, and weighs me down	423
Shed on the altar of thy cross	157
Shepherd of souls, thy sheep behold	43

Shepherd of souls, with pitying eye	251	Son of Man, will he despise	118
Short of thy love I would not stop	236	Soon as thou hast our place prepared	159
Shorten the days of inbred sin	356	Soon as thy hand the balm applies	376
Show him thyself at God's right hand	48	Soon as thy slighted grace	447
Show me the naked sword	432	Sorrow, and loss, and shame	437
Show them they never yet received	185	Sorrow and sins increase	266
Shut up in unbelief I groan	325	Sovereign Arbiter, arise	64
Simple shepherds us he raises	108	*Sovereign of all, whose will ordains*	21
Sin only hath your ruin been	54	Speak, Lord, and let him find thee near	350
Sing to the church in that glad day	293	Speak then once more, and tell my soul	454
Sing we with the host of heaven	108	Spirit immense, eternal Mind	199
Sing, ye ransomed nations, sing	117	*Spirit of Faith, come down*	196
Sinking on him for help I call	456	Spirit of Faith, on thee we call	188
Sinners, believe he died	147	*Spirit of Grace, we bless thy name*	199
Sinners, dismiss your fear	131	*Spirit of holiness, and Root*	201
Sinners, I rose again to show	134	Spirit of Holiness	255
Sinners, lift up your hearts	168	Spirit of meek and godly fear	201
Sinners my gracious Lord receives	276	*Spirit of Power 'tis thine alone*	200
Sinners, obey the gracious call	54	Spirit of pure and holy love	201
Sinners, obey the heavenly call	307	*Spirit of sanctifying grace*	190
Sinners of old thou didst receive	374	*Spirit of Truth descend*	191
Sinners, rejoice; your peace is made	159	Spirit of Truth, in all begin	185
Sinners shall hear thy threatening rod	288	Spoiler, take all! We will not grieve	38
Sinners, the call obey	12	Sprinkle thy blood upon my heart	349
Sion, for thee thy God shall care[641]	313	Stand by us in this evil hour	30
Sion I will no more expose	75	Stand forth the self-instructed seers	296
Sion, thy suffering God behold[642]	315	*Stay, thou insulted Spirit stay*	370
Slaughter and cruel threats they breathe	30	Still art thou silent at my tears?	362
So apt his mercy to forget	445	Still do I languish for thy grace	288
So be it, Lord, for whom we stay	67	Still do I urge my sole request	401
So be it then, I sink into	370	Still every means in vain I try	323
So fallen from grace	414	Still hide from me thy face	403
So heavenly mild	122	Still let the publicans draw near	252
So shall I charm the listening throng	244	*Still let us in our rising song*	97
So shall we pray, and never cease	166	Still let us, Lord, with love be blest	226
So soon I abuse	415	*Still, Lord, I languish for thy grace*	335
So will we render thee the praise	54	Still may he by thy special grace	24
So will we trust in man no more	54	Still my carnal mind withstands	417
So wretched and obscure	230	*Still, O Lamb, to thee I pray*	417
Some put their trust in chariots	88	*Still, O Lord, for thee I tarry*	352
Son of God, for thee we languish	182	*Still out of the deepest abyss*	270
		Still the long hour of darkness lasts	354
641. UP 2:452.		Still they provoke thy glorious eyes	63
642. UP 2:453.		Still we wait for thy appearing	116

Stir up thy strength, appear, appear	21	Salvation in his name there is	302
Straight as the rule, the written word	382	*Salvation is in Jesu's name / For all who*	335
Strangers and pilgrims here below	262	*Salvation is in Jesu's name, / The Lord of*	298
Strangers shall serve at your command	308	Salvation to God, / Who bought us with blood	57
Strength in the Lord my righteousness	326	Sanctify our mutual care	425
Strict and general temperance	195	Satan his thousand arts essays	233
Stript of all my boasted power	331	Satan shall be repelled	37
Stronger his love than death or hell	341	Satan's slaves against me rose	384
Struggles my soul, and gasps for ease	396	Save me now from all my fears	206
Subsists as in us all one soul	280	Saved by a miracle of grace	108
Sufferers like them beneath	42	Saved from the guilt and power of sin	335
Suffering here, we threaten not	35	Saved is the life for Jesus lost	150
Suffice for this the season past	244	Saviour, bring near the joyful hour	73
Sufficient is his grace for thee	348	*Saviour, Friend of lost mankind*	385
Sufficient is the season past	330	Saviour from sin we thee receive[644]	331
Sufficient to restrain from sin	468	Saviour from sin we thee receive[645]	334
Sure as I now his cross sustain	469	Saviour, I with guilty shame	13
Surely his healing power is nigh	453	*Saviour of all, what hast thou done*	148
Surely I shall as gold come forth	468	*Saviour of sinful men*	458
Surely I will my people save	56	*Saviour, to thee we humbly cry*	244
Surely in me (your God replies	55	Saw ye not the cloud arise	121
Surely now in part we feel	69	Scattered o'er all the earth they lie	481
Surely the faithful seed at last[643]	314	*See, dearest Lord, thy servant see*	421
Surely the hindrance lies	432	*See how great a flame aspires*	120
Surely th' incorruptible seed	312	*See, Jesu, see that much loved soul*	415
Surely thou hast called me now	133	*See, Jesus, thy disciples see*	469
Surely thou wilt, we dare believe	170	*See, Lord, our wavering brethren see*	241
Surely we are possessed	49	*See, Lord, the object of thy love*	237
Surely we do in God believe	40	*See, Lord, with pity see*	236
Surely we now believe and feel	40	*See, Lord, with tenderest pity see*	239
Swallowed up in sad despair	389	See my burdened, sin-sick soul	306
Swallowed up in sin and sadness	167	See on the mountain's top	271
Swelled to an host, the daring few	96	See, sinners, see	58
Swift to the slaughter and the spoil	72	See that happy soul in me	352
		See the celestial bodies roll	382
		See the soul whose fall we weep	240
		See the souls that hang on thee	476

Volume V

Sacred, salutary ill	68
Safe in thine all-victorious love	5
Safe on the happy shore	208
Saints without holiness are they	327
Salvation from our foes within	299

643. *UP* 2:452.

644. Lines 2–4 read: "From all indwelling sin, / thy word, we steadfastly believe, / Shall make us thoroughly clean."

645. Lines 2–4 read: "From all indwelling sin, / thy blood, we steadfastly believe, / Shall make us pure within."

See then at last I all resign	195	Sinners, behold the Lamb of God	112
See there, ye misbelieving race	225	*Sinners look up, by grace forgiven*	286
See us now, as side by side	438	*Sinners, obey the gospel word*	63
See, where the Lamb in glory stands	168	Sinning on so oft, so long	184
Seldom alas! thy silken cord	404	Slain for a sinful world, and me	135
Send forth the everlasting word	125	Slaves to our lusts we all have been	130
Send forth thy pure, unerring light	315	Smitten, we turn the other cheek	252
Send our long desired messias	174	Snatched from ten thousand snares	
Send the Witness from above	439	I prove	413
Sent forth I am to reap the field	114	Snatched from the rage of cruel men	108
Set for this if, Lord, I am	281	So be it then, if thou ordain	71
Set my face, and fix my heart	383	So early to remove	83
Shall I back to Egypt go	12	So ignorant of God	367
Shall I force thee still to take	444	So shall the world believe	236
Shall I go to courts and kings?	12	So weak, so impotent, so blind	310
Shall I my old toil renew	12	*Soldier of Christ, adieu!*	219
Shall I resent my slighted love	192	*Soldiers of Christ, arise*	40
Shall I the haughty wish instil	395	Son of my womb, my joy, my hope	81
Shall I then my state bemoan	343	Son of my womb, to evil sold	396
Shall make us free indeed	475	Sons of God, your Saviour praise	121
Shall my most suspected love	444	Soon as in hymns the mystic four	288
Shall soon behold our God	464	Soon, or later then remove	303
Shall taste the manna of his grace	317	Sorrow and fear are gone	342
Shall we there in plaintive passion	448	Sorrow is solid joy, and pain	150
Shepherd, appear, the Great, the Good	97	Spangled with eyes before, behind	288
Shepherd Divine, at whose command	245	Speak, and by thy word detain	14
Shepherd Divine, our want relieve	176	Speak but the word of grace and power	127
Shepherd of Israel, hear	234	Spirit of grace, inspire	56
Shepherd of souls, if thou indeed	96	Spite of myself resolved t' obey	431
Shepherd of souls, lay to thine hand	248	Spread throughout the earth thine own	282
Shine on the work thyself hast wrought	314	Stand by them in the fiery hour	232
Shivering beneath those rags he stands	19	Stand then against your foes	40
Show them the blood that bought		Stand then in his great might	40
their peace	231	Still at Jerusalem abide	471
Sick, and in prison will I find	20	Still at thy feet I lie	117
Silent for them, for them he pleads	147	Still, gracious Lord, delight to shed	75
Sin, only sin could close	128	Still in thy mercy's arms embrace	130
Sin, only sin we deprecate	167	Still in weariness, and pain	187
Sin shall not have dominion now	33	Still let me preach thy word	118
Since first she felt the sprinkled blood	87	*Still let me on my Pattern gaze*	147
Since first the maze of life I trod	193	Still let your feet be shod	41
Since first we heavenward turned our face	152	Still let thy Spirit, Lord	23
Since thou wouldst have us free from sin	331	Still let us, gracious Lord	429
Sinners, and saints at once they are	327	Still let us on our guard be found	399

Still, Lord, we ask, and urge thee still	167	*Saviour of life, and Prince of peace*	49
Still may I walk as in thy sight	373	Saviour of men, through whom we live	186
Still may they on the world look down	254	Saviour, regard my vehement prayer	276
Still the old Dragon bites his chain	251	*Saviour, thou hast bestowed on me*	451
Still we continue in thy word	331	Saviour, thy mercy's praise	400
Still will I strive, and labour still	18	Saviour, thy unexhausted love	159
Still would I pour my mournful tears	337	*Say, ye companions of her youth*	359
Stir up, O Lord, thine utmost power	239	'Scaped from a life of pain	223
Strangers to truth, how can it be	405	Searched the Scriptures day and night	377
Strength and righteousness	25	*See from the world's politest school*	437
Strengthened by the cordial blessing	456	*See, Lord, a nation at thy feet*	176
Stripped of her choicest blessing here	218	See the stars from heaven falling	145
Struggle through thy latest passion	216	See us, when from the Papal fire we came	59
Stumbling on shame's offensive rock	248	Seeing the great Invisible	340
Such honour all thy saints possess	197	Sent in Jesu's mighty name	376
Such power belongeth unto thee	313	Sent of the Lord his bolts to deal	183
Such thy fair example was	360	Servant of God, my yoke fellow and friend	60
Sufferer for sin my Master was	156	*Servant of God, well done!*	316
Suffice that for the season past	162	Shall I,—amidst a ghastly band	428
Superior to ourselves we rise	219	Shall I, his creature, I	396
Superior to their smile, or frown	136	She at the welcome word	202
Surely I have pardon found	306	She cast the tempting fiend behind	321
Surely I now my Saviour see	20	She flew preventing their request	360
Surely I now rely on thee	346	*She flies! the soul as lightening flies!*	277
Surely if thou pronounce the word	79	She knew not, till the God unknown	358
Surely thou didst unite	423	She lived a burning shining light	274
Surely we now your souls embrace	479	She lived to serve the God unknown	240
Surely you have kindly dealt	132	She loved, but leaned no more on man	273
Surrounded by an host of foes	301	She loved even that most straitened sect	321
Swearers, and whoremongers and thieves	122	She loved them both in word and deed	241
Swept from the earth away	460	She more than shared his woe and weal	296
Swift to my rescue come	52	She never left her former love	272
		She sinks beneath her ambient flood	27
		She spake, and by her looks expressed	297

Volume VI

		She speaks, and bows her willing head	274
Sad, disconsolate, alone	291	*She thus, adorning every state*	361
Save them from pride, and worldly love	118	She took your guardian angel's part	242
Saved by the merit of his Lord	279	She was (let all her worth confess	264
Saved from all evil words, he speaks	375	She was (what words can never paint	264
Saved from the love of all below	375	*Shepherd of souls, the great, the good*	107
Saviour and Lord of all	11	Should the earth this moment cleave	24
Saviour, Desire of all mankind	177	Should those who sit in Moses' seat	106
Saviour from sin, from death, and hell	374		

Shout all the first-born church above	285	Stand, the omnipotent decree	94
Shout all the people of the sky	141	Stay, thou departing Spirit, stay	82
Shout, ye heirs of sure salvation	278	*Stay thou triumphant spirit, stay*	239
Show them, their strength and safety lies	118	*Steady, faithful soul, adieu*	290
Silent follower of the Lamb	334	Still, as we grow in years, in grace	449
Simple, ignorant of ill	443	Still in fearful expectation	169
Sin, only sin, his soul abhorred	351	*Still in the arms of faith and prayer*	123
Sing to the great Jehovah's praise	16	Still in the doubtful balance weighed	10
Sing to the Lord! the Lord alone	181	*Still let us keep the end in mind*	421
Sing to the Lord by whom we live	167	*Still let us on her virtue gaze*	294
Sing to the Lord, for he alone	177	Still let us steadily pursue our end	63
Sinner's Advocate, appear	221	*Still, Lord, the little ones receive*	134
Sion, my first, my latest care	108	Still may I in the truth delight	425
Sloth is the accursed root	423	*Still may the righteous ten prevail*	130
Small learning they had, And wanted no more	440	Still the drowsy nations shake	174
Smiling on his mourner there	337	Still to us they speak, though dead	377
So be it! let this system end	28	Still we bear about thy dying	209
So be it, Lord! if thou ordain	101	Stir up the praying seed to stand	175
So be it, Lord, our labours speed	412	Stir up the souls by them begot	117
So modest, diffident, and meek	345	Strange fire will in this bosom burn	102
So shall I see thy face with joy	425	Stranger to guilty fears	204
So shall we every moment feel	386	Strengthen them in the gap to stand	126
So wholly formed for social love	299	Strong and fervent for an hour	404
Sole self-existing God most high	139	Strong let us in thy grace abide	449
Son of God, come down, come down	223	Strong towers, and massy walls	35
Soon as from earth I go	427	Struck from above with sacred fear	179
Soon as our broken hearts repent	374	Such happiness, O Lord, have we	95
Soon as th' appointed sickness came	329	Such is the nation, Lord	90
Soon as the heavenly Guest arrives	226	Summoned before the throne t' appear	242
Soon as the warning angel came, / thy convoy	229	Sun and moon are both confounded	144
Soon as the warning angel came, / That called	249	*Sun of Righteousness, appear*	352
Soon as their guides are taken home	107	*Sun of unclouded Righteousness*	137
Soon as thy heart did feel	205	Superior to the storms below	42
Soon our best desires decay	404	*Supinely negligent and proud*	157
Sorely tempted and distressed	252	Surely he will not long delay	219
Sorrow, and sin, and death are dead	298	Surely the time is come, for God to rise	61
Sovereign Majesty of heaven	77	*Surely ye judged her faithful then*	271
Spare the death-devoted city	169	Surrounded by a flaming host	448
Spring of all good, thy will I own	385	Surrounded by his power I stand	329
Spirit of heavenly counsel, come	127		
Stabilised in truth and righteousness	83		

Volume VII

Save her by thy righteous merit	63

Save her, thyself of woman born	64	Sing to the Prince of life and peace	94
Save, Jesus, save! my hour is near	51	Single his eye, transparently sincere	438
Save us for thy own nature's sake	254	*Sleep that soothingly restores*	128
Saved by the Son, the Lord our God	210	Slighting nature's every feeling	333
Saved from ten thousand deaths and snares	377	So be it, O my God, my Lord	184
		So foolish, ignorant, and blind	146
Saviour, all my wretchedness	357	*So near the haven brought*	391
Saviour and Prince of life and peace	387	So shall the ransomed sinner give	65
Saviour, his slumbering spirit call	152	So the first missioners in Jesu's name	433
Saviour, I would not take	138	So when thou dost with clouds appear	234
Saviour, inspire him with thy grace	124	Soften, sanctify the anguish	63
Saviour, lavish of thy blood	352	*Son of God, to thee I pray*	407
Saviour, let thy will be done	153	Son of the living God, appear	332
Saviour of men, incline	6	Son of the Most High, appear	366
Saviour, on thy faithful love	416	Soon as he thus lifts up his trumpet voice	434
Saviour, speak the blessing ours	15	Soon as in Christ we truly are	218
Saviour, thou hast deliverance sent	129	Soon as in thee we gain a part	45
Saviour, till thou declare thy will	119	Soon as of thee possessed I am	385
Saviour, to me thy Spirit give	150	Soon as our pardoned hearts believe	310
Saviour, we at thy hands receive	88	Soon as reason's glimmering ray	68
Scarcely I presume to pray	415	Soon as the antepast I feel	406
Searcher of hearts, to thee I fly	151	Soon as the mighty change I know	410
See, where he flies! As if by heaven designed	431	Soon as thou dost in me proclaim	378
		Soon as thy passion tells me	113
Seize, O seize his tender heart	68	Soon as thy Spirit shows	213
Senders and Sent we praise	275	Soon may the all-inspiring Dove	133
Sent thy Father to proclaim	16	Sorrow and sin are chased away	178
Servant of Christ, on him I call	170	Sound an alarm, the gospel-trumpet blow	429
Set our hearts at liberty	11		
Shall I not then engage	5	Speak with that voice which wakes the dead	30
Shall I through indolence supine	162		
Shall tell the drooping sons of men	399	Speechless am I, Till thy kind sigh	187
Shall we then with sin comply	284	Spirit of consolation	335
Shall yet again thy tokens see	183	Spirit of faith, discover	35
Sharer of thy dereliction	341	Spirit of faith, my soul convince	332
She lives to extol thy wonderful name	143	Spirit of faith, reveal in me	247
Shepherd of Souls, the great, the good	420	Spirit of God, Jehovah come	264
Shout to the great Jehovah's praise	310	Spirit of life, and love, and power	69
Show me what I wanted then	56	*Spirit of love, return*	21
Show thyself the Lord of glory	383	*Spirit of supplication*	34
Sick, and in pain, why should I grieve?	103	Spirit of truth, essential God	249
Simple folk and undiscerning	149	Spirit of uncreated Light	289
Sing all on earth like those on high	200	Spiritual life t' impart	291
Sing to the Lord of the earth and sky	197	Spotless, sincere, without offence	243

Stand omnipotently near	403	Say, ye assembled sons of men	128
Stay with us, Lord, our Guide unseen	295	Scattered o'er the earth they lie	306
Still let me in thy Spirit pray	375	Searcher of hearts, thine eye hath seen	76
Still let us to each other cleave	18	*See and save me in distress*	231
Still may we to our Centre tend	44	*See, gracious Lord, with pitying eyes*	403
Still, O thou patient God of love	358	See, in yon glorious azure height	35
Still on thee I cast my care	58	See, Lord, a dying sinner see!	259
Still mine eyes for him o'erflow	153	See my soul, in pity see	95
Still we believe, almighty Lord	249	*See, O Lord, my foes increase*	6
Stir up thy saving power	345	See the gospel-church secure	113
Stop the hurrying spirit's haste	196	See the Lord thy Keeper stand	236
Strangers or foes to God	165	*See the true ancient Church appears*	424
Stretch out thine arm, almighty King	347	See, where th' impetuous waster comes	267
Stripped of all, we trust in thee	96	See where the Protestant crusade	451
Submissive to thy just decree	412	Send me succour from above	29
Such for a length of year his glorious race	435	Set forth a spectacle to all	346
Such our whole employment be	47	Shall I my innocence declare	347
Such power belongs to thee alone	407	*Shall see thy footsteps in th' abyss*	305
Suffering for another's sin	89	Shall truly by thy Spirit know	371
Suffering in the sinner's place	127	Sharp are the arrows of thy love	103
Suffice that more than threescore years	375	*Shepherd of souls, the great, the good / Who*[646]	161
Summoned to thy judgment-seat	153		
Supply what every member wants	44	*Shepherd of souls, the great, the good / thy*	397
Supreme in majesty and power	289		
Sure evidence of things unseen	314	Shocked at the hypocrites profane	424
Surely thou wilt provide	138	Shorn of all my strength, I languish	13
		Shortened our days by wrath Divine	173
		Should bloody arms entrusted be	468
Volume VIII		Shout the God enthroned above	110
		Show me thy salvation, Lord	214
Saints shall possess the land	84	Show thyself now, arise, O Lord	178
Satan, thy reigning hour is past	18	Shrivelled and dried up am I	221
Satan vexes them no longer	78	Sick of sin, to thee I cried	59
Save me from the wicked, Lord	30	Simple, teachable, and mild	247
Save me, Lord, by thy great name	120	Sin, the world, and hell oppose	231
Save me, Lord, from all my foes	256	Sing the new, the gospel song	68
Save me, O God! my griefs abound	154	Sing to the Lord, ye people sing	145
Saved from the burning pit	272	Sing unto God, his praise proclaim	149
Saved, they rest from their distresses	78	*Sing we to our conquering Lord*	183
Saviour and Friend of all mankind	341	Sing, ye saints, unto the Lord	59
Saviour, I thankfully adore	120	Sinners have beset my way	222
Saviour, thou dost their threatenings	267	Sinners have drawn the sword	82
Saviour, thy promised aid I claim	402		
Saviour, whom our hearts adore	299		

646. UP 2:446.

Sinners have thy law broke through	221	Spoiled and hated for thy sake	217
Sinners, hence! be far away	225	Springs the watered wilderness	144
Sion again shall lift her head	245	Sprinkling us with thy own blood	335
Sion hath heard his word	182	States and empires rise, or fall	306
Sion's God is all our own	114	Stay, then, with those that know Thy peace	80
Slay them not, O God of grace	131	Still at his feet I humbly own	394
Small I am in mine own eyes	229	Still beset with various evils	278
Snatched from the flames by grace Divine	326	Still do I for the kingdom pant	405
So, as the sons of Epicurus	467	Still I owned thee for my Lord	212
So, if almighty wisdom will	469	Still if my iniquity	369
So sailors when the storm is o'er	470	Still if unbelief withstands	369
So shall I, Lord, to all proclaim	379	Still in grateful songs of praise	132
So shall I magnify thy name	157	Still in his hallowed courts to dwell	54
So shall I render thee thine own	432	Still let the word of truth prevail	103
So shall I sing the Saviour's name	117	Still let thine eye his steps pursue	423
So shall our happy monarch see	291	Still let thy praying seed prevail	292
So shall the saints surround thy throne	14	Still my foes with rage and scorn	186
So shall thy people sing	333	Still support me in thy ways	29
So when ferocious Omar comes	459	Still the battle is the Lord's	331
So will I magnify thy grace	76	Still when to thee for help I cry	54
So will we not from thee go back[647]	165	Still thou art Israel's sure defence	150
So will we sing and praise thy name	275	Still thou hear'st the mourner's sighing	292
Solemn, memorable day	409	Still to bolder mischiefs rise	140
Some in chariots put their trust	40	Still to search the sacred word	215
Some pledge of good bestow on me	171	Still will I invocate his name	30
Son of the living God most high	355	Still with lowly thanks declare	141
Sons of earth, the triumph join	110	Still would I keep the Lamb in view[649]	427
Sons of God, triumphant rise	113	Stop the rage of persecution	78
Sons of men, be still, and know	109	Stop their lying mouths, and turn	131
Soon as I have learned thy ways	209	Stranger in the vale of woe	90
Soon as my power of acting came	390	Stranger to repose and peace	89
Soon as the breath of man expires	261	*Stranger to sin, and guilty fears*	437
Soon as thou hear'st their contrite moan	340	Strangers alas! to thee and peace	398
Source of happiness thou art	210	Strangers to my God have rose	120
Sovereign, everlasting Lord[648]	15	Strangers to thy saving grace	231
Sovereign, everlasting Lord	17	Strengthen the powers thou didst ordain	270
Sovereign, everlasting, Lord, / thou art	228	Strengthen their hands, almighty Lord, / Their	279
"Spare me, O my God!" I said	188	Strengthen their hands, Almighty Lord, / Incline	327
Spent with my own complaints and cries	154	Stricken so oft, we mourn	313
Spirit of revelation	372		

647. *UP* 2:449.
648. The eight-line stanzas on pages 15 and 17 beginning with this line are identical. Line 2 reads: "How excellent thy name!"

649. *UP* 1:315.

Stricken with the stroke of death	411	Save me, gracious Lord, for why?	275
Stripped[650] in that dark, satanic hour	407	Saved at my latest hour receive	82
Succour and strength in God I have	15	Saved to the utmost here	117
Such as brought Immanuel down	369	Saviour, from thine open side	49
Such as thou didst first ordain	222	Saviour, I long to testify	321
Such faithful leaders we allow	483	Saviour, I now with shame confess	448
Such generals never can aspire	483	Saviour, my latter end is come	98
Such their country's cause to fight	329	Saviour, my nature's pride t' abase	97
Suffered by thee, their swift allies	317	Saviour of the world, come down	450
Suffering for ills which we have done	342	Saviour, thus o'errule thy foes	82
Support him with thy guardian hand[651]	165	Saviour, to me in pity give	199
Supreme by his eternal birth	45	Saviour to thee	300
Supreme, immortal Potentate	300	Saviour, we wait the day	67
Sure I am, divinely sure	257	Scarce have we put the harness on	182
Sure I am, it is thy will	442	Secure in Christ I dwell	114
Sure I am, thou able art	442	See here the miracle renewed	34
Sure of thy dying love to me	381	See the great Antitype arise	139
"Surely now," the Lord hath said	23	See the power of God displayed	192
Surely, O Lord, we once were thine	163	See the standard lifted up	387
Surely, our God his arm shall show	134	See the true Elijah flies	187
Surely our God shall vengeance take	254	See, through him, the heavenly King	175
Surely thou wilt full vengeance take	294	Self thy word would fain diminish	91
Surely thou wilt thy grace impart	115	Selfish, and proud, in mind and will	370
Surround him with thy guardian power	424	Send forth a ray of faith Divine	317
Surrounded with temptations	359	Send forth one ray of heavenly light	420
Sustained by thine almighty hand	34	Send then thy servants forth	470
Swallowed up with fervent zeal	229	Sent, through Jesus, from the skies	61
Sweet is the odour of thy name	104	Seraphs the fiery horses were	186
Sworn on me to wreak their hate	130	Servant of God, and Son of Man	413
		Shall foolish, weak, short-sighted man	242
		Shall I in thy care confide	346

Volume IX

		Shall man direct the sovereign God	239
Safely we may our Isaacs give	24	Shall our corruptions stand	121
Saints anticipate the day	462	Shall teeming earth at once	465
Salvation from the Lord	263	Shall the mighty lose his prey	434
Salvation gladly I embrace	322	Shall we mistake the morning-ray	345
Salvation I desire	323	Shall we the Spirit's course restrain	71
Samson the strong, the weak, we blame	139	She could not live, she could not rest	29
Samson the theatre o'erthrew	142	She saw; she took; she ate	4
Satan himself fulfils thy word	8	Shout to the Lord, who stands between	45
Satan, with all his worldly powers	314	Shrinking from the cold hand of death	33
		Shut up in unbelief I groan	243

650. Osborn changed "Stripped" to "Robbed."
651. *UP* 2:449.

Silence when the Almighty broke	241
Silence, ye unbelieving fears	73

Sin is the desperate wound	298	Spirit of faith, the cross lift up	449
Sin, only sin, can there appear	401	Spoiled of the bliss to Adam given	11
Since first we did from Egypt fly	77	Steadfast in faith, I rest resigned	170
Since what I lend or give to thee	149	Steady in continued prayer	51
Sing we merrily to God	312	Still I for thy coming stay	284
Sing ye heavens, and earth rejoice	430	Still—I in thy presence am	299
Sinner, alarmed by judgment near	159	Still I enquire and weep, and pray	244
Sinners, behold the sacred flame	155	Still may the holy seed	378
Sinners my witnesses shall see	413	Still, O my gracious God, and just	424
Sinners our immortal King	429	Still on a precipice I stand	22
Sinners, the vain delusion see	353	Still the great God resides below	175
Sion, look round with joyful eyes	452	Still the old serpent doth deceive	4
Sion, look round with strange delight	431	Still to make our numbers less	33
Slack not thine hand, but hasten down	124	Still, whene'er in love renewed	238
Slow of speech, and slower still	36	Still will my Redeemer tarry	297
Sluggard, out of thy sleep arise	346	Still wilt thou put a worm to grief	245
Smite down the strength of Moab's pride	84	Stirred up once more—what can I do	259
Smitten by thee my heart is sore	234	"Stone the blasphemers vile," they cry	76
So be it Lord; my foes bring down	96	Straitened in God we cannot be	190
So by the Spirit of holiness	138	Strangely at his table fed	52
So dear it cost for sin t' atone	265	Strangers, and foreigners we were	148
So dearly-bought I must be thine	366	Strengthened by thy command	104
So oft preserved in perils passed	162	Stupendous grace of the Most High!	19
So powerful both by sea and land	214	Subscribing to Jehovah's word	130
So sacred if the symbol be	165	Such as we are, without disguise	222
So strongly to all sin inclined	297	Such comfort I find	285
So, when the Saviour shows his face	39	Such honour all thy saints receive	134
Sole Governor of earth and skies	128	Such is my soul, confused and void	1
Sole self-existent God supreme	422	Such is the heart of man to God	184
Sole, self-existing God and Lord	150	Such is the life my servants live	444
Some angel tell me where to find	258	Such is the stubbornness of man!	40
Son of God's eternal love	168	Such may our young Josiah prove	433
Son of Man, we long to see	374	Suitable grace to him is showed	186
Sons of God by faith we came	462	Summoned to my heavenly home	251
Soon as in earnest we begin	37	Sure the word which God doth say	389
Soon as Shiloh came, the Jews	31	Sure token of redemption near	37
Soon as with conscious grief I said	316	Surely, before my Lord withdrew	217
Sore assailed, o'erpowered, oppressed	200	Surely for Christ the isles shall wait	454
Souls from the death of sin to raise	191	Surely in Christ by faith revealed	423
Spare me a little longer	294	Surely now thy pitying eye	388
Speak again the world from nought	462	Surely the promise is for me	405
Speak, Lord, that I my work may know	181	Surprising turn of heavenly grace	418
Speak, thou true Interpreter	103	Surrounded, sunk in deepest night	270
Spirit of faith, come down	138	Sweet is the odour of thy grace	360

Swift as an eagle soaring	409

Volume X

Salvation from our sins we found	140
Salvation is the work of God	94
Satan himself will push them on	460
Satan the instrument defies	310
Save, for myself I cannot save	30
Save, Lord, because unsaved by thee	216
Saved from the guilt and power of sin	92
Saviour,[652] apply the powerful word	240
Saviour, at thy command I speak	411
Saviour at thy feet I fall	470
Saviour, cleanse us from all sin	63
Saviour hear a sinner's prayer	210
Saviour I in thee confide	474
Saviour I still to thee apply	269
Saviour, inspire with unknown awe	166
Saviour, instruct us to declare	477
Saviour, let thy dying love	432
Saviour, my double want I feel	236
Saviour now to thee I cry	393
Saviour, remove the vanity	175
Saviour, speak into my heart	239
Saviour,[653] the fond delusion stop	476
Saviour, the human house is thine	262
Saviour, thou canst with equal ease	454
Saviour, thou didst the glory bear	117
Saviour, thou hast bid me come	285
Saviour, thou know'st us all	217
Saviour, thou seest the fear	400
Saviour, thy balmy grace impart	29
Saviour, thy sacred day	257
Saviour, thy Spirit's power exert	454
Saviour, thy weak disciple hear	371
Saviour, till thy face I see	501
Saviour to us through faith impart	322
Saviour, when the storm is high	286

652. Osborn changed "Saviour" to "Now, Lord."
653. Osborn changed "Saviour" to "Thou then".

Saviour, while after thee we mourn	99
Saviour, who dost with anger see	340
Saviour-God, thine Israel here	47
Scourged by wicked, cruel men	424
Scourged for my sin, the frown of God	99
See the hypocrite profane	497
See the murderer's rage and power	308
See the patience of our God	465
See, the sad fruit of sin appears	415
See the soul redeemed indeed	484
See the true evangelic child	314
See the wretchedness of sin	218
See with what vehement eagerness	293
Seeking in Christ thy face	90
Self-destroyed for help I pray	80
Self-diffidence may souls abase	488
Selfish and vain desires in me	12
Self-loathing at thy feet I lie	208
Send forth the Spirit of thy Son	171
Send the multitude away?	500
Sent forth by Christ indeed	466
Sequestered from the noisy crowd	283
Servant of Christ, thy talent see	457
Servants of souls, they take the pay	341
Set my soul upon the tower	404
Shall a saved sinner then receive	324
Shall I be of that wretched crowd	205
Shall I my righteous zeal suppress	192
Shall I stand idle still	SH 1762, 2:178
Shall I suffer them to live	423
Shall I through prudent fear forbear	484
Shall man to God a method show	96
Shall we by resistance vain	465
Shepherds, and chosen labourers raise	230
Should we not the dread retain	481
Show my faith thy hands and feet	254
Show thy converting grace on me	39
Shut up within himself he dwells	481
Sight incomprehensible	425
Sin cannot duty supersede	193
Sin entered by the eye, and made	155
Sin that we may serve no more	34
Sing to the God of faithful love!	73
Sing with joyful acclamation	112

Sing, ye happy souls, that press	37	Still the faithless world deride	490
Sinner secure, the writing see!	70	Still the prophetic curse takes place	91
Sinners, by Jesus bought, obey	250	Still the two clashing sects appear	299
Sinners formed out of the ground	295	Still thou go'st about to teach	160
Sinners if thou cam'st to call	459	Still thy genuine gospel, Lord	233
Sinners, in that grovelling herd	218	Still to the pinnacle he brings	152
Sinners, in this great verity	252	Still we see our Lord below	426
Sinners our Master doth receive	SH 1762, 2:154	Stopped by my persevering prayer	337
		Strangers to every priestly vice	493
Sinners should lament and wail	312	Strengthened by thee to persevere	200
Sinners, that doubt his healing love	309	Strengthened by thy Spirit's word	250
Sinners the Lord our God receives	319	Stricken for mine iniquity	89
Sinners the most abandoned now	347	Struggling for mastery within	79
Sinners who bewail your dead	489	Stupendous love of God Most High!	253
Sinners, with joy look up!	100	Such is the heart of those that hear	267
Sinners with true repentance turn	448	Such may all my anger be	463
Sion shall then in safety dwell	89	Such, miser, is thy end, or worse	417
Slight who ever bid you quit	373	Such power belongs to thee alone	231
Slowly doth thine anger rise	51	Such was our ignorant desire	335
Smitten the Shepherd was	124	Suffice, O Lord, the season passed	186
So dear thy sinful pleasures cost	381	Suffice that known to God they are	144
So gentle toward my basest foe	407	Sun of Righteousness, arise	134
So high, so holy, and so great	458	Superfluous luxury they hate	234
So late enlightened from above	302	Supreme, incarnate Deity	146
So shall their pure oblations please	131	Sure earnest of the joys above	444
Some desperate souls the God of grace	310	Surely then if sick and poor	465
Son of God 'tis thine alone	382		
Sons of the church, yourselves who deem	145		
Soon as I know my guilt removed	454		

Volume XI

Salvation is in Jesus' name	351
Salvation is of faith alone	385
Satan once the body tore	137
Satan tempts our faith t' o'erthrow	376
Saved by faith from sin and fear	168
Saved by that blood from death and hell	288
Saving faith is not alone	168
Saviour, am not I thine own?	499
Saviour, and Prince, appear	217
Saviour extend thy hand of grace	26
Saviour for this alone I live	146
Saviour, for thy own promise sake	384
Saviour, I listen for thy voice	194
Saviour, I want that ardent zeal	338

Soon as one fight is done	447
Soon as that efficacious blood	23
Soon as we truly willing are	426
Sovereign, universal King	140
Speechless the Saviour stood	419
Stand by me in this evil day	401
Stand we in the good old way	15
Stands the promise of our Lord	376
Stationed by my Redeemer's grave	435
Still I long for his returning	49
Still in every trial new[654]	285
Still let the world with haughty pride	424
Still may the preachers of thy word	164

654. UP 2:29.

IDEX OF FIRST LINES OF POETRY BY JOHN AND CHARLES WESLEY

First line	Page	First line	Page
Saviour in death, the grace by one	303	Shall man exalt himself, or boast	226
Saviour of men, to thee we cry[655]	252	Shall men, the great, the learned and wise	362
Saviour, on me the faith bestow	463	Shall those who evil act or speak	157
Saviour shut up my feeble heart	282	Shall we discourage or repel	339
Saviour, thy flesh is meat indeed!	390	She had no friend or patron kind	256
Saviour, thy witnesses	70	She had no promise to succeed	255
Saviour to thee in sufferings joined	296	Shedding at length a martyr's blood	128
Saviour, to thee my soul looks up	45	Shod with the gospel-peace	238
Saviour, we nothing have to fear	193	Silent before the king he stood	300
Saviour, we on the word rely	100	Silent long the Prisoner stood	81
Saviour, who ask to reign with thee	36	Simple men who nothing know	164
Saviour who by thy balmy blood	367	Sing, all in heaven at Jesu's birth	117
Saviour, with kind compassion see	467	Sing, every soul of Adam's line	117
Scripture, a second servant, came	50	Sing, rejoice, and leap for joy	152
Sealed his lips with wisdom's seal	84	Sinner, come down at Jesus' call	263
Sealed with the baptismal seal	120	Sinner in love with guilty joys	28
Searching Lord, if thou art he	466	Sinner the painful truth admit	429
Secretly allured by grace	165	Sinner who dost not bear[659]	126
See a soul with pardon blessed[656]	359	Sinners, a pardon I proclaim	315
See and believe! it cannot be	88	Sinners, approach, the Lamb is slain	90
See the fruit of faithful prayer	186	Sinners by gentleness he wins	487
See the heavenly Man of God	406	Sinners redeemed, yet still inclined	506
See the salutary stream[657]	292	Sinners, your bosom sins let go	217
See the source of human care	208	Sins he bears, but not his own	83
See then ye haughty worms of earth	500	Sin's immeasurable distance	10
See ye blushing sons of pride	115	Slaves we all by nature are	427
Seeming contrarieties[658]	494	So slow and backward to believe	96
Self-love which strikes us blind	154	So the lying prophets lived	153
Self-righteous Pharisees	481	Sole independent God most-high	446
Selling all our happiness	212	Sole Object of thy Father's love	370
Senseless no more in sin I dwell	480	Sole self-existing God, I own	320
Sent down from above Who governs the skies	408	Some token, gracious Lord, impart	488
		Sometimes the faith, at once bestowed	313
Sent from Jehovah in the skies	496	Son of Man, the hour is come	489
Set on slippery ground is he	221	Soon as thy yearning bowels move	365
Severely tried by inward want	131	Soon out of the house of God	427
Shall I be left in sin to die	254	Sore amazed is God's own Son	77
Shall I my Lord and God adore	287	Souls are by temptation shown	393
Shall I the Lord of hosts defy	232	Souls from Jesus separated	177
		Souls to win is Jesu's meat	360
		Source of my holiness	174

655. UP 2:162.
656. UP 2:229.
657. UP 2:296.
658. UP 2:255.

659. UP 2:86.

Sovereign Lord for this we wait[660]	278
Sovereign Lord of life and death	479
Speak, Divine Interpreter	135
Spirit of Jesus, tell	120
Spirit of unity, come down	216
Spotless, meek and holy Lamb	326
Sprinkled with th' atoning blood	357
Stands the world in being still	62
Still by faith we see him wait	58
Still by the holy matrons led	91
Still every faithful minister	269
Still he doth to sinners turn	166
Still I knock, and ask, and seek[661]	203
Still in spite of earth and hell	467
Still let them in thy footsteps tread	31
Still let thy grace abound	266
Still may we tremble and take heed	65
Still, O my dear redeeming Lord	46
Still on the soul of fallen man	319
Still our adversary's nigh[662]	287
Still the streams of pity run	268
Still with bowels of compassion	10
Stop him by prayer alone	261
Stopped by a sinner's prayer	37
Strange malignity of men!	444
Strangers both to themselves and thee	456
Strangers to his converting grace	448
Strangers to Jesu's blood	482
Strangers to Jesus and his grace	3
Strangers to nature's mystery	342
Strangers to your redeeming Lord	430
Stripped of his Maker's character	172
Stupendous height of heavenly love	114
Stupendous miracle of love!	390
Subject to thy parents thee	123
Submissive to thy Father's will	461
Such is the desperate wickedness	366
Such the Father seeks and owns	358
Such thy unchangeable decree	483
Suffering death without the gate	86
Suffering in the sinner's place	327
Suffering saints with comfort mourn	406
Supernally strengthened to bear	491
Super-substantial[663] bread	72
Surely if we ought, we may	254
Surrounded by thy power and love	15
Surrounded with the golden blaze	22
Swollen with concupiscence and pride	224

Volume XII

Safety and strength in thee we have	68
Salvation's of the Jews	392
Satan his zealous servants hath	328
Satan in his allies withstands	275
Satan must tremble and give place	223
Saul, the furious Saul, confesses	219
Save me that I may proclaim	173
Saved by thy blood applied	157
Saved from the legal curse I am[664]	100
Saved from the present guilt they feel	321
Saviour and Friend of men	285
Saviour and Prince enthroned on high	48
Saviour and Prince, I lift	258
Saviour, by thy permissive will	311
Saviour, in thy church appear	154
Saviour of all, lay to thine hand	252
Saviour of men, and Prince	192
Saviour, reverse my righteous doom	22
Saviour, take my sins away	17
Saviour the time is come	34
Saviour, thou dost my soul restore	268
Saviour, thou know'st the things of earth	204
Saviour, thou need'st not say	42
Saviour, thy preaching servants bless[665]	293
Saviour, we know, thou art	157
Saviour, whose manifested love	426
Scourged by the world's opprobrious tongue	146

---

660. *UP* 2:189.
661. *UP* 2:127.
662. *UP* 2:194.
663. Osborn changed "Super-substantial" to "Jesus, substantial."
664. *UP* 2:278.
665. *UP* 2:363.

Searcher[666] of hearts, 'tis thine alone	140	Sinner behold what thou hast done!	79
Secret things belong to God	130	Sinners, believe, and now be free	172
See a rough draught of human life!	115	Sinners drawn forth out of the deep	120
See from a single chamber spread	138	Sinners' hearts are in thy hand	148
See here an apostolic priest[667]	181	Sinners, if Christ ye truly seek	362
See in the strong impetuous sign	142	Sinners, to God your Maker turn	372
See the fierce beast, whose rage umtamed	221	Sinners to seek and save he came	66
See the first expiring witness	219	Sinners what have ye done	162
See the first fatal step to part[668]	196	Sinners, ye all remain	226
See the last brutish refuge, see	286	Skin for your skin, and all ye have	437
See the whole church retired in prayer	139	Slow of heart, thou know'st I am	109
See ye misbelieving race	200	Slower of heart than Thomas I	110
Send forth a kind convincing ray	426	So a superior order wills	418
Sent to the great, and rich, and wise	191	So lately to each other known	382
Servants and lord, when God they fear	245	So let my light to others shine	24
Servants of Christ, the same expect	193	So Lord, let it be	128
Servants of God, by Jesus' love	371	So many influenced by one	444
Servants of God, your treatment see	350	So worship I my fathers' God	410
Servants of the Lord Most-High	316	Sole Deliverer of thine own	173
Severed from Christ the root SH 1762, 2:260		Some put their trust in chariots	405
Shackled, death-devoted Peter	265	Soon as his death confers the grace	91
Shall a poor worm of grace be proud	248	Soon as in you our word takes place	330
Shall I in desperate straits despair	206	Soon as Moses prophesied	165
Shall men of name and dignity	286	Soon as the Saviour's messenger	223
Shall not we as zealous prove	335	Soon as thy cross appears	259
Shall we in time of need	399	Soon as thy wounds I see	427
Shall we on tradition vain	131	Sorrow may enter and remain	37
Shall women too the fight maintain	286	Sound in the faith, though weak and slow	111
Sharpness exercised on one	276	Spirit of true holiness	39
Shepherd of souls, the lambs and sheep	68	Spirit of truth, from Jesus come	38
Should we not on our labour live	119	Spirit of truth, the Comforter	32
Signs alas! cannot suffice	200	Stand we for a season still	247
Silence! Tertullus speaks!	409	Statesmen, here your pattern see	227
Silenced, but not convinced, the foes[669]	199	Still at a loss, ye know not how[670]	175
Silent we turn the other cheek	72	Still at the stated hours we pray	158
Silver and gold he none possessed	415	Still busy, still for Christ employed	351
Sin and doubt to chase away	109	Still in the gall of bitterness	224
Sin, unempowered by grace	20	Still let the world their charge repeat	71
		Still let us earthly matters leave	197
		Still the Holy Ghost descends	358
		Still the promise is fulfilled[671]	360

666. Osborn changed "Searcher" to "Teacher."
667. UP 2:298.
668. UP 2:305.
669. UP 2:309.
670. UP 2:294.
671. UP 2:392.

Still thou dost thine arm reveal	10	Servants of Christ, your rule is plain	30
Stoics with the sons of ease	336	Shall we glory in our grace	23
Stranger far the miracle	161	Shall we live on like thoughtless	182
Stranger to pride and stateliness	371	Shorten the great extreme distress	241
Strangers he secretly inclines	416	Sick of every disease that a spirit	245
Strangers to faith we cannot trust	444	Sin could not (we then shall show)	247
Strangers to thy love are they	11	Sing we to our God above	246
Strength for us his sufferings buy	84	Sing with glad anticipation	238
Stripped of his rags, with double power	424	Sing ye inhabitants of heaven	235
Stupendous mystery	21	Sinner, in thine own esteem	223
Such a witness for my Lord	372	Sinner, that know'st not God	73
Such honour all the people gain	391	Sinner, thy lost condition see	162
Such ministers, O Christ ordain	199	Sinner, who dost thyself deceive	108
Sufficient is that sight alone	8	Sinners, attend the dreadful word	216
Superior grace he cannot boast	398	Sinking at last in just despair	192
Superior happiness we prove	112	Slandered in the cause of Jesus	183
Superior joys above	243	So when thou shalt on earth appear	225
Surely he asked his Lord to spare	444	Soldier of Christ, in his great might	103
Surely if thou direct my heart	137	Sole basis of our faith and hope	26
Surely thou dost even now partake	250	Son of God, thine anger show	204
Swept from the face of earth	228	Soon as I render up the ghost	39
Swift are the steps of angry zeal	408	Soon as I win the vast reward	227
Swiftly it runs from east to west	139	Soon as the blood has touched my heart	190
Swiftly the man whom Jesus loves	101	Soon as thou hast the pardon given	100
		Soon as thou wilt the world forsake	108
		Soon as we every moment feel	196

Volume XIII

		Soon, if I cease to watch and pray	121
Save, till all these tempests end	264	Sore buffeted, I ask again	56
Saved by faith we once have been	13	Space to repent without the power	225
Saviour, his heart is in thy hands	98	Spirit of grace, spring up in me	255
Saviour, I know thy gracious will	231	Spirit of interceding grace	13
Saviour, on me the grace bestow	228	Sprinkle, and make my conscience pure	147
Saviour, the fond delusion chide	32	Sprinkled on me	161
Saviour, to thee for help I sue	55	Stay then, my aid in time of need	254
Saviour, with thankful awe I see	116	Stay, thou too happy sinner, stay	101
'Scaped from a world of anxious grief	268	Still in mine agony I pray	56
See the fruit of worldly cares	103	Still with and in thy people dwell	242
See the power of God to save	179	Stranger to holy joy and peace	191
See, thou wretched slave accurst	30	Strengthened by Christ alone	111
See, ye heirs of sure salvation	218	Strengthened by thy Spirit's might	41
Send forth the Spirit of thy Son	12	Stupendous mystery of grace!	231
Senseless now of all its heat	247	Stupendous word of power Divine!	39
Separate now from sinful men	137	Such, Lord, did thine apostle know	99
		Such may I delight to be	59

INDEX OF FIRST LINES OF POETRY BY JOHN AND CHARLES WESLEY

Such the credulous dotard's dream	80	The day, the signal day is come[679]	119
Such the man whom God forgives	59	The deadly Slumber soon I feel[680]	12
Suffice for this the season past	251	The deadly writing now I see[681]	347
Superior to all fear and shame	3	The dew unsought each morning falls[682]	40
Sure, when I my soul resign	154	The dictates of thy sovereign will[683]	173
Sustained by the pity Divine	100	The earth, in token of his grace	209
		Th' Egyptians, daring to pursue	218
		Th' elixir this, the stone[684]	31

Volume I

		The Ethiop then shall change his skin	271
Take my poor heart, and let it be[672]	265	The father curbed his swelling grief	215
Take this poor wandering, worthless heart	134	The fever turned its backward course	75
		The fleet Astronomer travels o'er[685]	16
Talk with me, Lord: thyself reveal	304	*The flower now blooms, now hangs its head*[686]	30
Teach me at last thy love to know[673]	29	The folly thrived, and came in sight[687]	52
Teach me, my God and King[674]	30	The Gentiles too may see	317
Teacher Divine, we ask thy grace	238	The greater world knows no decay[688]	48
Tear the bright idol from his shrine	228	The happy band whom Christ redeems	171
Tell me again, my peace is made	326	The heavens thy glorious power proclaim	210
Thankful I take the cup from thee	128	The helmet of salvation take	229
That energy, which quells the strong	15	The holy, the unspotted Lamb[689]	347
That path with humble speed I'll seek[675]	110	The lesser stars that shone	316
Th' atonement of thy blood apply	283	The love of Christ does me constrain[690]	178
The battles of the Lord they fought	219	The mansion for thyself prepare	84
The best of men to evil yield[676]	59	The meek, the still, the lowly mind[691]	233
The blessing of thy love bestow	76	The men of worldly wealth possessed	171
The bliss thou hast for me prepared	372		
The bondage of corruption break!	33		
The burden, for me to sustain[677]	232		
The church through all her bounds[678]	157		
The daily death I prove	267		
The day of small and feeble things	276		
The day, the dreadful day's at hand!	179		

672. From the German of Nikolaus von Zinzendorf, translated by John Wesley.
673. George Herbert.
674. George Herbert.
675. From the French, Antoinette Bourignon.
676. George Herbert.
677. From the German of Paul Gerhardt, translated by John Wesley.
678. From the German of Johann Angelus Scheffler, translated by John Wesley.
679. Altered from John Norris.
680. From the German of Sigmund Gmelin, translated by John Wesley.
681. From the German of Nikolaus von Zinzendorf, translated by John Wesley.
682. George Herbert.
683. From the German of Nikolaus von Zinzendorf, translated by John Wesley.
684. George Herbert.
685. George Herbert.
686. George Herbert.
687. John Gambold?
688. George Herbert.
689. From the German of Nikolaus von Zinzendorf, translated by John Wesley.
690. From the German of Johann Joseph Winckler, translated by John Wesley.
691. From the German of Paul Gerhardt, translated by John Wesley.

The mighty, from their native sky	120	Thee I can love, and thee alone[702]	111
The nimble Diver with his side[692]	16	Thee I exult to feel	100
The pain of absence still I prove	255	Thee let us feel benignly near	299
The people that in darkness lay	287	Thee let us taste; nor toil below	190
The poor thou liftest from the dust[693]	122	Thee my restless soul requires	223
The Potter thou, and we the clay	369	*Thee, O my God and King*	96
The prelude of contempt they found	220	*Thee, O my great Deliverer, thee*	285
The promised Comforter impart	96	Thee seven whole days, not one in seven[703]	102
The recent horrors still appear	74	Thee shall my music find: each string[704]	28
The rich have pined amidst their store	120	Thee then, my God and King	97
The sacred means thyself ordained	369	Thee through thyself we understand	210
The scanty verse himself supplies[694]	47	Thee to laud in songs Divine	114
The secret voice invites me still[695]	71	Thee to perfection who can tell?	230
The sinner, when he comes to thee	302	Thee we address with humble fear	32
The Spirit breathe of inward life[696]	166	Thee when the dragon's pride	154
The Spirit of convincing speech[697]	166	Thee when with awful pomp arrayed	25
The Spirit of faith, in this thy day[698]	166	Thee will I love, my joy, my crown[705]	177
The Spirit of refining fire	166	*Thee will I love, my strength, my tower*[706]	176
The subtle Chemist can divest[699]	16	Their faith the gracious Father sees	214
The things unknown to feeble sense	210	Them, only them his will decreed	312
The trees of God shall deck the soil	209	Them shall he claim his just desert	81
The trees shall clap their hands and sing	208	Them, the elect, consenting few	312
The various tribes of earth obey[700]	122	Then bend once more thy knees and pray[707]	42
The weapons of thy warfare take	227		
The wonders thou for them hast wrought	367	Then let me vie with thee in love[708]	27
The word pronounced, the Gospel-word	171	Then let us join our God to bless	303
The world, sin, death oppose in vain[701]	161	Then mirth be ever banished hence[709]	43
The worthies these ancient days	214	Then, O my soul, be never more[710]	123
Thee all the seers of old	316	Then, only then our eyes shall see	315
Thee every tongue shall then confess	315	Then shall heaven's hosts with loud acclaim[711]	349
Thee he loved e'er time begun	360		

692. George Herbert.
693. Samuel Wesley, Sr.
694. George Herbert.
695. From the German of Gerhard Tersteegen, translated by John Wesley.
696. Henry More.
697. Henry More.
698. Henry More.
699. George Herbert.
700. Samuel Wesley, Sr.
701. From the German of Johann A. Freylinghausen, translated by John Wesley.
702. From the French, Antoinette Bourignon.
703. George Herbert.
704. George Herbert.
705. From the German of Johann Angelus Scheffler, translated by John Wesley.
706. From the German of Johann Angelus Scheffler, translated by John Wesley.
707. George Herbert.
708. George Herbert.
709. George Herbert.
710. Samuel Wesley, Sr.
711. From the German of Nikolaus von

IDEX OF FIRST LINES OF POETRY BY JOHN AND CHARLES WESLEY

First line	Page
Then shall I bear thy utmost will	294
Then weep, my eyes, for God doth grieve[712]	43
Then with my heart I first believed	300
Thence she never shall remove	94
There behold the Day-Spring rise	185
There for me the Saviour stands	272
There he helps our feeble moans	189
There its peculiar influence known	13
There lay thy Son; but left his rest[713]	64
There let him ever, ever dwell	96
There let me rest, and sin no more	243
There the pompous triumph waits	187
There the simple cannot stray	291
There, there before the throne thou art[714]	223
There we shall in glory shine	355
There we shall with thee remain	188
These are thy wonders, Lord of power[715]	45
These are thy wonders, Lord of love[716]	46
These by th' apostles' counsels led	171
They stopped the lions' mouths, the rage	219
Thine be the choicest store	318
Thine eye observed from far	97
Thine eye surveyed the fallen race	311
Thine eye surveyed my pain	149
Thine is the work, and thine alone	234
Thine is whate'er we are: thy grace[717]	340
Thine, Lord, is wisdom, thine alone[718]	145
Thine, wholly thine, we pant to be	34
This I would—that humbly still[719]	108
This life belongs to things of sense[720]	57
This spotless robe the same appears[721]	348
This through ages all along	93
This we now rejoice to know	355
Thither he willed his bones to go	217
Thou art my daily bread	98
Thou art my inward Guide	101
Thou art our food: we taste thee now	192
Thou art th' Eternal Light[722]	156
Thou art the truth: I now receive	282
Thou art the Truth, the Way	318
Thou art thyself the seal	101
Thou bidd'st; and wouldst thou bid us choose	313
Thou bidd'st me search the Sacred Leaves	234
Thou callest me to seek thy face	304
Thou canst not mock the sons of men	313
Thou canst o'ercome this heart of mine	271
Thou, even thou art he	320
Thou everywhere hast way[723]	126
Thou for our pain didst mourn	156
Thou God of power, thou God of love[724]	349
Thou God, that answerest by fire	341
Thou hast my flesh; thy hallowed shrine[725]	160
Thou hast o'erthrown the foe[726]	156
Thou hast pronounced the mourner blest	258
Thou hidden love of God, whose height[727]	71
Thou, Jesu, art our King[728]	155
Thou, Jesu, on th' accursed tree[729]	66

Zinzendorf, translated by John Wesley.
712. George Herbert.
713. George Herbert.
714. From the German of Maria Böhmer.
715. George Herbert.
716. George Herbert.
717. From the German of Ludwig Andreas Gotter, translated by John Wesley.
718. From the German of Ernst Lange, translated by John Wesley.
719. George Herbert.
720. George Herbert.

721. From the German of Nikolaus von Zinzendorf, translated by John Wesley.
722. From the German of Johann Angelus Scheffler, translated by John Wesley.
723. From the German of Paul Gerhardt, translated by John Wesley.
724. From the German of Nikolaus von Zinzendorf, translated by John Wesley.
725. From the German of Joachim Lange, translated by John Wesley.
726. From the German of Johann Angelus Scheffler, translated by John Wesley.
727. From the German of Paul Gerhardt translated by John Wesley.
728. From the German of Johann Angelus Scheffler, translated by John Wesley.
729. George Herbert.

Thou know'st the baseness of my mind	77	Thou tarriest, while I sink, I die[741]	67
Thou Lamb of God, thou Prince of peace[730]	129	Thou the Father seest alone	360
Thou leav'st thy Father's blissful face[731]	125	Thou the good Shepherd art	98
Thou, Lord, and only thou canst tell[732]	46	Thou, true and only God, lead'st forth[742]	145
Thou, Lord, art good, and thou alone[733]	104	Thou who all my ways hast seen	321
Thou, Lord, art light; thy native ray[734]	104	*Thou, who hast given so much to me*[743]	41
Thou, Lord, art love; from thee pure love[735]	104	Thou wilt not break a bruised reed	275
Thou, Lord, hast blest my going out	305	Though earth her ancient seat forsake[744]	121
Thou, Lord, my power and wisdom art	63	Though heaven be moved, may I remain[745]	49
Thou, Lord, my spirit oft hast stayed	322	Though hills be in the ocean lost[746]	121
Thou, Lord, the dreadful fight hast won[736]	129	Though I groan beneath thy frown	325
Thou meetest him that dares rejoice	367	Though in affliction's furnace tried	137
Thou my impetuous spirit guide	269	Though late, I all forsake	268
Thou, O Christ, art all I want	260	Though, signed and written with My blood[747]	347
Thou, O my God, thou only art	225	Though the floods lift up their voice	296
Thou on my neck didst fall	97	Though the sons of night blaspheme	297
Thou on the Lord rely[737]	126	Though there were forty heavens or more[748]	48
Thou only, Lord, the work hast done	287	Though thou bruise in us his heel	296
Thou seest me deaf to thy commands	263	Though waves and storms go o'er My head[749]	280
Thou seest, my heart's desire[738]	69	Thousands of notions swift did run[750]	107
Thou seest my tortured breast	267	Through earth diffused, the active flame	14
Thou seest our weakness, Lord[739]	127	Through faith we know the worlds were made	210
Thou shin'st with everlasting rays[740]	142	Through racks and fires pursue thy way	229
Thou Son of God, thou Son of man	252	Through thee he treads the shining way	25
		Through thy rich grace, in Jesu's blood[751]	339

730. From the German of Christian Friedrich Richter, translated by John Wesley.
731. George Herbert.
732. George Herbert.
733. From the German of Johann A. Freylinghausen, translated by John Wesley.
734. From the German of Johann A. Freylinghausen, translated by John Wesley.
735. From the German of Johann A. Freylinghausen, translated by John Wesley.
736. From the German of Christian Friedrich Richter, translated by John Wesley.
737. From the German of Paul Gerhardt, translated by John Wesley.
738. George Herbert.
739. From the German of Paul Gerhardt, translated by John Wesley.
740. From the German of Johann Angelus Scheffler, translated by John Wesley.
741. George Herbert.
742. From the German of Ernst Lange, translated by John Wesley.
743. George Herbert.
744. Henry Pitt.
745. George Herbert.
746. Henry Pitt.
747. From the German of Nikolaus von Zinzendorf, translated by John Wesley.
748. George Herbert.
749. From the German of Johann Andreas Rothe, translated by John Wesley.
750. George Herbert.
751. From the German of Ludwig Andreas

Through waves and clouds and storms[752]	127	Thy power I pant to prove	150
Throughout the deep thy footsteps shine	230	Thy power was to our fathers known	367
Thus Abraham, the friend of God[753]	348	Thy powerful Spirit shall subdue	271
Thus in the presence of their God	171	Thy prayer is heard, thy will is done	275
Thus may he comfort thee below	182	Thy secret voice invites me still	71
Thy breastplate be his righteousness	229	Thy single arm, Almighty Lord	287
Thy bright example I pursue	172	Thy Spirit, breathing in the word	282
Thy cheering beams we bless	316	Thy will so vast a distance is[763]	69
Thy condescending grace	268	Thy wisdom here we learn t' adore	230
Thy conquering arm with terror crowned	120	Thy witness with my spirit bear	241
Thy darling attribute I praise	310	Till then, to sorrow born, I sigh	50
Thy dew came down—my heart was thine[754]	51	'Tis burden all, and pain, and strife	255
		'Tis done! my God hath died	150
Thy everlasting truth[755]	126	'Tis done! my justice asks no more	81
Thy fallen tabernacle raise	370	'Tis done! the precious ransom's paid[764]	117
Thy gifts, blest Paraclete	100	'Tis hence my ravished friends I mourn	247
Thy gifts, if called for, I resign[756]	111	'Tis here thy unknown paths we trace	230
Thy glories, Lord, in all things shine[757]	63	'Tis in that peace we see and act[765]	35
Thy Godhead we revere	317	'Tis mercy all, that thou has brought[766]	71
Thy life on earth was grief: to this Thou still[758]	44	'Tis mystery all! th' Immortal dies!	105
		'Tis not the outward food we eat	191
Thy love I will turn back on thee[759]	28	'Tis not the pain I seek to shun	243
Thy love provides the sober feast	190	'Tis now by faith's enlightened eye	282
Thy mercy pleads, thy truth requires	236	'Tis now the meaner creatures join	190
Thy mind now multitude of thoughts[760]	35	'Tis thine a heart of flesh to give	82
Thy name, O Lord, upon my bed[761]	175	'Tis thine a help! Forget me not![767]	67
Thy Name to me, thy Nature grant	372	'Tis Zeal must end this inward strife	13
Thy parent hand, thy forming skill[762]	144	To clothe the sun, no dress too fine[768]	107
		To do thy will, while here I make	303
		To God, through all creation's bounds[769]	60
		To him my eye of faith I turn	136
		To him that in thy name believes	210
		To him through earth-born cares ye pass	246
		To him who reigns enthroned on high[770]	124

Gotter, translated by John Wesley.
752. From the German of Paul Gerhardt, translated by John Wesley.
753. From the German of Nikolaus von Zinzendorf, translated by John Wesley.
754. John Gambold?
755. From the German of Paul Gerhardt, translated by John Wesley.
756. From the French, Antoinette Bourignon.
757. George Herbert.
758. George Herbert.
759. George Herbert.
760. John Gambold?
761. From the Spanish of David Israel Lopez Laguna.
762. From the German of Ernst Lange,

translated by John Wesley.
763. George Herbert.
764. Samuel Wesley, Sr.
765. John Gambold?
766. From the German of Gerhard Tersteegen, translated by John Wesley.
767. George Herbert.
768. George Herbert.
769. George Herbert.
770. Samuel Wesley, Sr.

To Jesu's name if all things now	264
To leave my Captain I disdain	294
To love is all my wish	150
To please thee thus (at last I see)	233
To rescue me from woe	268
To scorn the senses' sway[771]	31
To serve his God is man's estate[772]	29
To speak for God, to sound Religion's praise[773]	52
To thee, benign and saving Power	75
To thee for refuge may I run	305
To thee my earnest soul aspires[774]	111
To thee my longing soul aspires[775]	342
To thee, O Lord, my tender years[776]	51
To thee, O Lord of Life, I prayed[777]	123
To thee our humble hearts aspire	209
To thee, the only wise and true	237
To thee, then, O vouchsafe me power	226
Too much to thee I cannot give[778]	233
Torture and sin prepared his way	74
Touch me, and make the leper clean	326
Trembles the King of Fears	154
Trembling in dread suspense I stand	250
Trembling, we taste: for ah! no more	32
Triumph and reign in me	155
Truly our fellowship below	341
Turn again to God thy Rest	330
Turn, O turn us, Lord, again	159
Turn the full stream of nature's tide	33
'Twas not the searching pain within	73
'Twas then my soul beheld from far	334
'Twixt God and them he still shall stand	81

771. George Herbert.
772. George Herbert.
773. John Gambold.
774. From the French, Antoinette Bourignon.
775. Altered from John Norris.
776. John Gambold?
777. Samuel Wesley, Sr.
778. From the German of Paul Gerhardt, translated by John Wesley.

Volume II

Take all, Great God, I will not grieve[779]	11
Take away my darling sin	89
Take me into thy people's rest	301
Take my broken reeds away	80
Take my nature's strength away	214
Take us into thy people's rest	332
Tallest of the earth-born race	237
Tell me, Jesus died for me	67
Tell me no more it cannot be	287
Tell me no more, ye carnal saints	162
Tell me, O Lord, if thine I am	300
Tell us, "I am the First and Last	341
Ten thousand times ten thousand, sing	236
Thanks to thy grace, if I begin	90
That blood which he for all did shed	325
That crown the conqueror *here* receives	357
That dreadful thought comes thundering back	162
That I thy mercy may proclaim	319
That law, by our kind patron's care	23
That power which stopped the mid-day sun	330
That says to Israel's mournful race	170
The abjects spit upon that face	70
The acceptable year	329
Th' Almighty be their strong defence	21
The blessing of another day	140
The blest, eternal Trinity	22
The bliss of those that fully dwell	244
The blood-sweat trickling from thy face[780]	15
The boundless love that found out me	232
The breath from heaven we did receive	24
The captive exile is released	184
The captive exile makes his moan	161
The children to the birth are come	100
The choicest of thy blessings shower	19
The day of thy great power I feel	143
The devilish and the brutal lust	138
The devil's factors still we hear	349

779. Altered from John Norris.
780. From the German of Johann Angelus Scheffler, translated by John Wesley.

IDEX OF FIRST LINES OF POETRY BY JOHN AND CHARLES WESLEY

The dreadful, dire, oppressive hour	242	The painful thirst, the fond desire	322
The earth could to her centre quake	71	The patient, meek, and lowly mind	347
The enemy his tares hath sown	335	The poor and needy from the dust	19
The Father hears him pray	324	The power of godliness we show	325
The foul reproach I groan to bear	83	The power of hell, the strength of sin	242
The fulness of eternal bliss	362	The power we daringly deny	359
The Gentiles shall hear the life-giving call	171	The promise stands for ever sure	290
The glorious crown of righteousness	365	The promised land from Pisgah's top	365
The glorious presence of my God	253	The prophets of smooth things we hear	351
The glorious prize I now pursue	326	The rich, the poor, the mean, the great	20
The glory of the Lord displayed	50	The rocks could feel thy powerful death	72
The glory of thy truth and grace	286	The secret of the Lord thou art	74
The God of truth himself hath sworn	365	The service which our fathers paid	351
The grace I surely shall receive	72	The sin-atoning blood	330
The graces of my second birth	288	The souls peculiarly his own	338
The gracious fruits of righteousness	322	The spirit of an healthful mind	281
The guilt and power, with all thy art	304	The string of death, our sin, is gone	186
The hatred of my carnal mind	320	The suffering, sin-atoning God	172
The heavenly manna faith imparts	362	The Sun of Righteousness on me	175
The heavens his glorious power proclaim	54	The terrible, all-conquering king	186
The hireling longeth for his hire— / But only	145	The thing for which thou bidd'st me pray	287
		The thing surpasses all my thought	311
The hireling longeth for his hire, / The watcher	163	The thing thou dost I know not now	164
		The tree of immortality	346
The Holy Ghost, if I depart	227	The true and faithful Witness he	338
The Holy One shall live	330	The tyranny of sin is past	181
Th' inhabitants of earth from thence	54	The unbelieving world shall wail	339
The judging, burning Spirit inspire	249	The vile idolater belies	54
The land we fondly deemed our own	61	The water issuing from thy side[781]	15
The living, he shall praise thy love	217	The Well of life to us thou art	225
The Lord hath saved my soul from death	218	The word is now gone forth from thee	310
The Lord is king, and earth submits	334	The word of God is sure	246
The Lord of Hosts in all appeared	59	*The world he made he still sustains*	56
The Lord our Righteousness	245	The world of liars and their god	287
The Lord shall clear his way through all	50	The world on him they doomed to die	172
The Lord shall in your front appear	171	The worst of sinners would rejoice	14
The Lord unto my Lord hath said	142	The worthy successors of those	342
The Lord your God shall quickly come	50	Thee, all-lovely as thou art	75
The meanest worm that creeps on earth	20	Thee, at thy word, we come to meet	137
The mourners go about the streets	29	Thee I serve, my Lord, my God	266
The name and city of thy God	357	Thee I shall serve without constraint	287
The nations shall receive his word	172		
The nations with their God compare	53		
Th' oppressors with insulting boast	169		

781. From the German of Johann Angelus Scheffler, translated by John Wesley.

Thee I shall then for ever praise	132	They hear; and each his will performs	55
Thee, Jesu, thee, the sinner's Friend	299	They held it fast in evil days	349
Thee, King of nations, we proclaim	226	They here shall be redeemed from sin	355
Thee, only thee, I fain would find	258	They speak; and we to ill inclined	349
Thee, Sovereign Lord, let all confess	336	They teach them things unclean to eat	351
Thee the great Jehovah deigns	305	They vexed; and forced his wrath to rise	58
Their alms in blessings on their head	17	Thine outstretched arm was bared for me	312
Their daily delight Shall be in thy name	176	Thine own peculiar servant claim	133
Their hearts from things of earth remove	342	Things most impossible shall be	309
Their names thou wilt vouchsafe to own	355	Things that are not, as though they were	310
Their radiant hosts he marshals right	55	This corruptible body soon	186
Their willing souls, from sin set free	57	This delight I fain would prove	99
Them by the hand of Moses led	59	This heart shall be his constant home	365
Them wilt thou lead, them wilt Thou keep	18	This is our glorious calling's prize	357
Then all the advocates for sin	356	This is the bond of perfectness	139
Then help me to receive thy word	102	This is the dear, peculiar race	326
Then let me every good resign	109	This is the dear redeeming grace	305
Then let or earth or hell oppose	138	This is the fellowship of saints	326
Then let us gladly bring	246	This is the rest, the life, the peace	364
Then let us in his footsteps tread	18	This is the way to find my Lord	122
Then let us in his service spend	16	This moment would I take it up	145
Then let us patiently attend	166	This, only this, is all my hope	146
Then let us sit beneath his cross	75	This record do I leave behind	101
Then let us wait to see the day	191	This still shall be our grateful theme	21
Then only can we fall no more	250	This unbelief, these cruel fears	65
Then only, when by grace renewed	149	Thither may we be safe conveyed	25
Then pour thy vengeance on my head	66	Those other lords no more are mine	253
Then shall we to thine only name	138	Thou a spark of hallowed fire	260
Then thaw this ice, and make my frost retreat	10	Thou art both Judge and Saviour, Lord	41
		Thou art darkness in my mind	291
Then th' accursed lust of praise	278	Thou art not slack touching thy word	103
Then, when the mighty work is wrought	136	Thou art the anchor of my hope	295
Then would I swiftly fly away	81	Thou callest all men to repent	361
There let me ever, ever dwell	321	Thou canst cut short the work, and heal	128
There let me lay my burden down	95	Thou chiefly dost thy boundless power	21
There let us all with Jesus stand	226	Thou hast a great deliverance wrought	312
Therefore shall ye draw with joy	251	Thou hast bought, and thou wilt have us	33
Therefore unto my gift I stand[782]	13	Thou hast obtained for us a power	361
These clouds of pride and sin dispel	12	Thou hast shown thyself the stronger	32
They, by thy mercy reconciled	354	Thou hast the spirits, seven and one	353
They groaned beneath the tyrant's chain	169	Thou hast undertook for me	263
		Thou holdest my soul In spiritual life	178
		Thou know'st for my offence he died	309
782. Altered from George Herbert.		Thou know'st we take in vain thy name	353

PART 1: *THE POETICAL WORKS OF JOHN AND CHARLES WESLEY*

Thou know'st what keeps me out of thee	95	Thy cleansing blood, by faith applied	356
Thou, Lord, for me a sinner made	295	Thy controversy, Lord	328
Thou, Lord, hast saved both man and beast	77	Thy dear preserving grace	269
Thou, Lord, wilt give him a white stone	350	Thy enemies destroy in mine	143
Thou mak'st the world obey thy will	23	Thy enemies ursurped the place	252
Thou my life, my treasure be	276	Thy faithful mercies let me find	322
Thou no longer shalt oppress us	33	Thy Father *here* thou didst reveal	357
Thou only canst our wills control	333	Thy fatherly chastisements own	361
Thou only know'st, who did obtain	244	Thy gifts, alas! cannot suffice	150
Thou, only thou, the kind and good	343	Thy heart, I know, thy tender heart	300
Thou rather wouldst that we were cold	359	Thy judgments all our thoughts transcend	195
Thou seest, alas! I am not dead	95	Thy love, by which redeemed I am	253
Thou seest me lost in shame	118	Thy love hath cast out servile fear	254
Thou shalt make me white as snow	148	Thy love I soon expect to find	244
Thou shalt on me thy Spirit pour	285	Thy love the conquest more than gains	144
Thou the Potter, I the clay	147	Thy med'cine puts me to great smart[783]	11
Thou thine hand on me hast laid	260	Thy mercies found out me	269
Thou wilt, I know thou wilt, appear	271	Thy nature, dearest Lord, impart	78
Thou wilt, I steadfastly believe	141	Thy only glory let them seek	344
Though all the advocates for sin	296	Thy only will be done, not mine	142
Though earth and hell at once engage	348	Thy[784] outstretched arm was bared for me	312
Though earth and hell thy rule oppose	332	Thy people are all sanctified	364
Though he now triumphant reigns	134	Thy perfect comeliness	117
Though heaven and earth away shall pass	309	Thy pity, and paternal care	60
Though in my flesh I feel the thorn	103	Thy poor unworthy servant view[785]	9
Though men blaspheme the liberty	285	Thy presence, Lord, the place shall fill	141
Though my sins as mountains rise	119	Thy sacred Spirit on Jordan's stream	23
Though nature fail, and flesh and blood	285	Thy salvation to obtain	76
Though nature gives my God the lie	296	Thy sanctifying Spirit pour	320
Though now to every sin inclined	141	Thy Son thou hast on all bestowed	311
Though once ye intermeddled not	185	Thy Spirit lifts the standard up	313
Though Satan all thy truths deny	285	Thy strength and thy power I now can proclaim	178
Though thy wrath against me burned	251	Thy tender heart is still the same	78
Though we our hands do not lift up	331	Thy truth and faithfulness I own	308
Through the long night of doubts and fears	250	Thy truth, and power, and love I plead	311
Through the wide world of sin and woe	121	Thy watchman shall the voice lift up	170
Through unbelief I stagger not	286	*Thy will be done, thy name be blest*	253
Throughout his soul thy glories shine	364		
Thus didst thou guide thy chosen race	59		
Thus let us all for ever lie	236		
Thus may we all our parting breath	184		
Thy angels shall around their beds	28		

783. Altered from John Norris.
784. Osborn changed "Thy" to "Thine."
785. David Lewis.

Thy will by me on earth be done	286	*To thee, O Lord, our God and King*	26
Thyself, through sufferings perfect made	216	To thee shall earth and hell submit	144
Till thou anew my soul create	273	To thee the glory of thy power	311
Till thou from all our sins shalt cleanse	250	To those calm happy seats may he	20
'Tis all in vain to hold thy tongue	174	To thy cross, thine altar, bind	123
'Tis done; my prayer hath pierced the skies	289	To us our own Barabbas give	70
		Touched by an unction from above	360
'Tis he who stretched them out, 'tis he	54	Touched by the loadstone of thy love	139
'Tis Love! 'tis Love! thou diedst for me	175	Transform my nature into thine	196
'Tis not a bare release from sin	133	Tremble our hearts to find thee nigh	226
'Tis not the desert, or the cell	81	Trembling I expect my fate	147
'Tis not the punishment I dread	127	*Triumphal notes, and hymns of joy*	23
'Tis of thy mercies, Lord	269	Triumphantly she laid it down	185
'Tis vain, I find, from self to flee	84	True and faithful Witness thou	229
To all, through faith which is in thee	137	Truly thou art a secret God	194
To all who his appearing love	191	*Try us, O God, and search the ground*	136
To all whom thou hast given an ear	357	Turn aside, a sight t' admire	213
To destroy his work of sin	256	Turn back our nature's rapid tide	225
To dig the ground, they all bestow[786]	63	Turning to my rest again	315
To every one whom God shall call	227	'Twas love Divine, 'twas sovereign grace	23
To every soul it comes unsought	324		
To Father, Son, and Holy Ghost, / Glory	236		
To God the Father, and the Son	25	## Volume III	
To God the Father, God the Son	21		
To God the Father, Son	27	*Take, and eat, the Saviour saith*	291
To him my body I present	248	Take, eat, this is my body, given	215
To him that conquers in thy might	350	Take my soul and body's powers	333
To him that overcomes at last	347	Take our happy seats above	288
To him ye Hallelujah cry	239	Take the ransomed captive home	173
To my soul in sore temptation	96	Take when thou wilt into thy hands	326
To praise my God I only live	217	Tasteless all the world to me	362
To psalms and hymns we may aspire	24	Tears, and eyes, and heart shall fail	161
To testify the grace of God	228	Ten thousand thousand times restored	41
To the blest co-eternal Three	20	Tenant of my troubled breast	161
To the haven of thy breast	206	Tenderest branch, alas! am I	250
To the never-ceasing cries	257	*Terrible God, severely just*	41
To the sheep of Israel's fold	151	*Thankful for our every blessing*	367
To the Source of all our good	223	*Thanks be to God, whose truth we prove*	370
To thee, for all men lifted up	344	That all may turn and live	91
To thee inseparably joined	139	That arm that smote the parting sea	247
To thee, O Father of mankind	19	That blessed Spirit praise	351
		The covering o'er the people cast	154
		That heavenly life in Christ concealed	290
		That living death, that sin which parts	154

786. From the German of August Gottlieb Spangenberg, translated by John Wesley.

That Man of Sin is now cast down	146	The Lamb of God, who takes	103
That vast unfathomable sea	144	The Lamb that with his Father reigns	180
That Wicked One he shall reprove	142	The light of life eternal darts	290
The anger shall not always last	141	The light of thy redeeming love[787]	170
Th' atonement thou for all hast made	271	The lion like the ox shall graze	143
The badge and token this	224	The lion with the calf shall dwell	143
The blackest crime upon record	60	The living Bread sent down from heaven	238
The blood removed our guilt in vain	242	The Lord hath founded on a rock	151
The bread dried up and burnt with fire	216	The Lord he sought allowed his creature's claim	112
The church triumphant in thy love	286		
The city of confusion now	152	The Lord his glory shall display	154
The constant miracle we own	95	The Lord of Hosts hath so decreed	150
The cross on Calvary he bore	306	The Lord of Hosts his rod shall raise	141
The cup of blessing, blest by thee	238	The Lord of Hosts, the mighty Lord	149
The dear remains of sin are gone	151	The Lord shall in this mountain spread	153
The death sustained for all mankind	222	The lords to whom thou bowedst thy neck	145
The dire occasion of my fall	24	The mediator stands between	68
The double stream in pardons rolls	239	The men of narrow hearts, who dare restrain	123
The dreadful sin-consuming fire	25		
The earth is of his glory full	134	The mercy I feel To others I show	6
Th' effects of his atoning blood	267	The motions of our head	313
The Father of men	352	(The mournful cause let Jesus tell	21
The feet which did to evil run	318	The nails that fixed thee to the tree	272
The fixed, unchangeable decree	150	Th' oblation sends as sweet a smell	218
The fruit of the vine (The Joy it implies	286	Th' oppressive foe that dwells within	140
The God of love passed by	36	*The people that in nature's night*	137
The God of truth commands	81	The Philistines at last have found	24
The God that answereth by fire	77	The poor shall on his promise feed	151
The gospel mystery	366	The power unseen which bade his wandering cease	111
The gospel ordinances here	261		
The grace which I to all bequeath	216	The prayer, the fast, the word conveys	254
The grace which sure salvation brings	238	The righteous God consigned	35
The gracious word of his command	145	The sacred signs thou didst ordain	340
The great, supreme, almighty God	139	The sacred, true, effectual sign	236
The heavenly host it passes far	261	The saved and Saviour now agree	317
The heavenly ordinances shine	260	The Saviour hath died For me and for you	337
The holy to the holiest leads	287	The Saviour shall spread forth his hands	156
The horrid crew, that dare their Lord deny	123	The Saviour's hand is stretched out still	151
		The seraphim, a glittering train	133
Th' inbred sin in that great day	141	The sheaf and harvest is but one	317
The instruments that bruised him so	217	The sheaf was waved before the Lord	317
The Lamb as crucified afresh	310		
The Lamb for sinners slain	336	787. Free paraphrase of the German of Christian Friedrich Richter by Charles Wesley.	
The Lamb his Father now surveys	310		

The simple and weak Pluck out of his net	74	The worth domestic let his consort tell	118
The sin-atoning blood apply	238	The zeal of our Almighty Lord	139
The sin mine anger shall destroy	141	Thee every soul may find	30
The sin of all the world he bears	77	Thee, Father, Son, and Spirit we	368
The sin on him which was not laid	17	Thee, Holy Ghost, we praise, / Giver of	98
The smoke of thy atonement here	301	Thee, Holy Ghost, we praise, / thy sweet	103
The Son shall make them free indeed	155	Thee in thy glorious realm they praise	286
The soul of man shall be my shrine	148	Thee, Jesus the Son	352
The Spirit adore	348	Thee, King of saints, we praise	287
The Spirit of burning Love shall come	138	Thee, Redeemer of mankind	223
The Spirit of faith, Of faith in thy blood	7	Thee, Saviour of mankind, we bless	100
The Spirit of godly, filial fear	142	Thee, Saviour, to know	365
The spirit of their father speaks	71	Thee, Spirit of Love, we gladly praise	97
The Spirit of thy love	31	Thee the purchase of my blood	172
The Spirit of wisdom from above	142	Their Lord, unto his own he came	4
The stoical fiend Root out of our heart	74	Their sins he shall to death condemn	142
The stream that from thy wounded side	242	Their souls from chains of flesh released	340
The strong shall therefore fear thy name	152	Then let our faith adore the Lamb	218
The sucking child shall safely then	143	*Then let us go, and take, and eat*	217
The Sun of Righteousness shall rise[788]	171	Then let us still in hope rejoice	284
The sure, irrevocable word	69	Then let us still profess	224
The temple's veil is rent in twain	234	Then let us submit his grace to receive	6
The tempter now withdrew	52	Then save me for thy mercy's sake	44
The tender life of God	361	Then shall the Lord his power display	144
The Three that are One	354	Then shall thy saints rejoice	84
The tokens of thy dying love	238	Then, then let us see	283
The trees of righteousness rejoice	147	Then we walk in means no more	224
The upper and the lower choir	349	Then, when the Lord hath given thee rest	146
The vilest need not doubt	91	*There I shall my lot receive*[790]	168
The walls of sin shall be laid low	156	There let the untamed bullock lay	76
The water cannot cleanse	267	There, there we shall see	353
The whole benefit of thy passion	270	These thoughtless souls his happy change deplored	116
The wine which doth his passion show	284	They all shall speak and think the same	143
The Wonderful his name shall be	139	They each, in different glory bright	261
The world can no refreshment give[789]	169	They joy in their Redeemer's sight	138
The world shall all his call obey	154	They may, but will not all believe	135
The world's Desire and Hope	31	They me, I did not them, pass by	135
The world's fierce ruler, and their god	146	They shall not vex it so	51
		They steer the pilgrim's course aright	261
		They think thee not sincere	34

788. Free paraphrase of the German of Christian Friedrich Richter by Charles Wesley.

789. Free paraphrase of the German of Christian Friedrich Richter by Charles Wesley.

790. Free paraphrase of the German of Wolfgang Christoph Dessler by Charles Wesley.

IDEX OF FIRST LINES OF POETRY BY JOHN AND CHARLES WESLEY

They think with shrieks and cries	36	Thou, Lord, hast made thy Mercies known	138
They would not the pure truth receive	70	Thou meetest them that joy	223
Thine holy ordinance contemned	341	Thou, my faithful Friend and true[792]	167
Thirsty so long, and weak, and faint[791]	169	Thou oft hast called in vain	90
This duteous son his piety knew to bear	122	Thou our faithful hearts prepare	240
This earth, I know, is not my place	164	Thou our sacrifice receive	321
This eucharistic feast	218	Thou said'st, "Where'er I am	314
This for thy dear sake we do	223	Thou seest me lying at the pool	257
This is my blood which seals the new	216	Thou standest at the door	90
This is our God, (they then shall say	155	Thou standest in the holiest place	301
This is that Horrible Decree!	67	Thou, the poor slave of Satan, thou	146
This is the ground of all our hope	94	*Thou very Paschal Lamb*	251
This is the purpose of my grace	150	Thou wouldst not let me go away	272
This is the richest legacy	245	Though twice four hundred prophets swear	75
This is the state which all may know	151	Though you continue not	48
This last, and every sin of mine	17	Three in person, One in power	346
This, this is he that came	267	Thrice happy soul, thy Lord appears	175
This token of thy love	298	Thrice happy soul, whom Jesus gave to know	113
This vale of tears and misery	160	Through faith in Jesu's name	56
Thither the Gentile world shall flow	144	Through grace, we hearken to thy voice	66
Those feeble types and shadows old	308	Through vain pretence of clearer sight	280
Thou all the debt hast paid	103	Throughout his life the new creation shines	115
Thou art earlier restored	172	Throughout the desert way	251
Thou art willing to forgive	14	Throughout their spotless lives was seen	339
Thou art with all thy members here	323	Thus let me thy free mercy prove	29
Thou, as in Midian's dreadful day	138	Thus may me still in thee be blest	246
Thou bidd'st us call thy death to mind	234	*Thus saith the Lord, th' Almighty Lord*	140
Thou canst not now thy grace deny	32	Thy blessing feeds us in the food	369
Thou dost not mock me, Lord	62	Thy blood was shed upon the cross	263
Thou dost not mock our race	31	Thy creature, in thy hands I am	325
Thou dost not stand in need	79	Thy death exalts thy ransomed ones	302
Thou drawest all men unto thee	94	Thy death hath brought the power	58
Thou God of boundless power and grace	259	Thy deserts to us make over	270
Thou God of sanctifying love	239	Thy faithfulness, Lord, Each moment we find	6
Thou hast all in Christ elected	101	Thy flesh for our support is given	247
Thou hast compelled the lost to die	5	Thy goodness I accused	91
Thou hast for all a ransom paid	68		
Thou hast made manifest thy power	152		
Thou hast obtained the grace	57		
Thou hear'st the pleading Spirit's groan	341		
Thou Lamb that sufferedst on the tree	302		

791. Free paraphrase of the German of Christian Friedrich Richter by Charles Wesley.

792. Free paraphrase of the German of Wolfgang Christoph Dessler by Charles Wesley.

Thy grace, when conscience cries aloud	153	To save what was lost, From heaven He came	6
Thy gracious readiness	92	To serve thy blessed will	73
Thy long-suffering is salvation	102	To the blood that speaks above	304
Thy mercy then takes place	92	*To the meek and gentle Lamb*	9
Thy mighty ecstasies I feel	175	To thee his passion we present	310
Thy offering doth to ours impart	328	To thee I make my bold appeal	77
Thy offering still continues new	219	To thy foul and helpless creature	278
Thy presence shall the cloud dispart	243	"To thy pardoning grace receive them"	225
Thy promised grace vouchsafe to give	268	*Tremendous love to lost mankind*	247
Thy sacrifice with heavenly powers	328	*Triumphant soul, the hour is come*	173
Thy sacrifice without the gate	298	Tophet is for the king prepared, / But I must	25
Thy sun no more goes down by night	156	Tophet is for the king prepared, / The sorest	147
Thy undistinguishing regard	3	True followers of our bleeding Lamb	323
Thy wounds have wounded me	329	True Light of mankind	283
Thyself our utmost price hast paid	312	True piety impartial to commend	124
Till all who truly join in this	289	True principles of life Divine	300
Till first we partake	324	Truth is the girdle of his reins	143
'Tis done! th' atoning work is done	234	*Truth of the paschal sacrifice*	245
'Tis done; The Lord sets to his seal	279	Turn from me thy glorious eyes	304
'Tis done: your hearts with sin o'erflow	76	Turn, he cries, ye sinners, turn	88
'Tis finished! thou hast bought our peace	68	'Twas grace from hell that brought us up	95
'Tis God we believe	282	'Twas grace, when we in sin were dead	94
'Tis here he meets the faithful line	249	'Twas not a useless rib he lost	300
'Tis here he nourishes his own	259	'Twas thus my wretched heart	54
'Tis not a dead external sign	254	'Twas thus the royal saint, by God approved	120
'Tis not by works that we have done	93	*'Twas thus the subtle foe*	52
'Tis not for us to set our God	259		
'Tis thus, thou loving Lamb	82		
'Tis we, the wretched abjects we	5		
Title to eternal bliss	292		
To all flesh thy grace is given	102		
To all men impart	283		
To damn the world, and not to save	66		

Volume IV

To Father, Son, and Holy Ghost, / *Who*	100
To Father, Son, and Holy Ghost, / *One God*	349
To Father, Son, and Spirit	349
To God, who reigns enthroned on high	346
To heaven the mystic banquet leads	289
To limit thee they dare	35
To make our right and title sure	243
To me this token give	63
To most, as devils teach	80

Take all, take all our sins away	54
Take the dear purchase of thy blood	340
Take this heart of stone away	417
Taking up our daily cross	34
Taught obedience to my God	479
Tell them, their sins are all forgiven	277
Terrible God! and true	13
Terror their heart assails	18
Thankful we now the earnest take	158
Thanks be all ascribed to thee	221

Thanks be to God, the God of power[793]	95	The depth of all-redeeming love	446
Thanks be to God, the God of power	96	*The dreadful day is come*	14
Thanks to the atoning Lamb	16	The earth shall at his word her blood	65
That all-informing breath thou art	198	The earth shall then cast out its dead	292
That arm which is not shortened now	303	Th' eternal God from heaven came down	120
That blood we felt through faith applied	32	The everlasting God comes down	119
That blood, which speaking once for me	392	The faith they persecute, embrace	31
That comfort was mine	408	The Father of my dying Lord	429
That covenant-blood	367	The Father shall thy Spirit send	174
That fulness of thy pitying love	429	The fire of persecution	86
That glorious wreath which now I see	67	The gift I embrace	214
That haughty Babylon within	287	The gift unspeakable impart	227
That heavenly Teacher of mankind	179	The gift which he on one bestows	253
That hope is in my end declare	356	The God who doth from sin restrain	469
That peace of God, that peace of thine	179	The grace, but not the Spirit of grace	175
That plague of your own heart	217	The grace I have abused, alone	393
That promise made to Adam's race	179	The grace shall on thy sons descend	295
That rob me of my utmost power	310	The grave of hell stands open wide	467
That sudden flash of heavenly light	385	The heavenly treasure now we have	281
That token of thine utmost good	375	The heaviness of soul	437
That we may thyself inherit	183	The Holy Ghost, whom we partake	175
That we the promise might receive	157	The holy mountain of our God	6
The Alien's sons your vine shall dress	309	The holy seed shall soon spring up	295
The anchor of my steadfast hope	472	The hour shall come, the gospel hour	292
The Ancient of Days	114	Th' intolerable load sustain	269
The angels she knew	122	Th' irreparable loss repair	269
Th' apostates toil with fruitless pain	174	The joy that swells a bridegroom's breast[795]	313
The barren souls shall be restored	300	The Judge of quick and dead	192
The blessing is free	214	The kingdom take, for all prepared	33
The blood of goats and bullocks slain	157	The Lamb that was slain	274
The Body breathes, and lifts his head[794]	130	The least shall say, the Lord's I am	296
The burning pit she open throws	424	The length and breadth of love repeal	179
The captive exile pines for ease	304	The life of our indwelling God	175
The cause is all in thee alone	333	The Lord by his right hand hath sworn[796]	314
The cleansing blood t' apply	169	The Lord hath glorified his grace[797]	315
The Comforter shall surely come	174	The Lord hath sent his only Son	307
The Counsels vain of earthly kings	78	The Lord himself thy husband is[798]	313
The Creator of all	119	*The Lord is King, ye saints rejoice*	78
The day, the dreadful day draws nigh	60		
The day, the gospel day draws near	285		

793. The six-line stanzas beginning with this line on pages 95 and 96 are identical.
794. UP 3:112.

795. UP 2:452.
796. UP 2:453.
797. UP 2:454.
798. UP 2:452.

The Lord is risen indeed[799]	144	The Sabbath of my soul I see	382
The Lord of Hosts is he	154	The Saviour God of love I clear	337
The Lord of Hosts, th' Almighty Lord	293	The sea is calmed, the troubled soul	293
The Lord of life is risen indeed	130	The sea shall then its dead restore	292
The Lord our God shall give th' increase	312	The servant of thy church below	376
The Lord shall bring a sudden snare	61	The shepherds behold	123
The Lord shall to his people say	75	The sin avenging God	398
The love of God-man	274	The sinners we see, Who Satan obey	53
The loving powerful Spirit shed	271	The soul that will not taste my love	294
The man who sits on the red horse	103	"The Spirit himself thou wilt not give"	175
The man whose heart approves	178	The spirit of an healthful mind	453
The mariners are struck with fear	10	*The Spirit of the Lord my God*	307
The means his wisdom chose	99	The Spirit of their God	171
The meed of all thy labours this	34	The Spirit of thy grace	82
The men whose hearts deny his love	60	The Spirit that raised him from the dead	291
The morning of my life is past	322	The stone cries out, I do not love	265
The Morning Star, that glittering bright	234	The stone to flesh again convert	442
The name inscribed in the white stone	233	The storm of sin can never cease	393
The nations are distressed	17	The sun no more shall rule the day	72
Th' opposers admire	211	The sun shall black as sackcloth turn	76
Th' oppressor's rage thou every day	304	The sword which first bereaved abroad	81
The pain of life shall there be o'er	303	The things eternal I pursue	278
The pit its mouth hath opened wide	252	The third auspicious morn is come[800]	130
The plenitude of God	193	The thorn which in my flesh I feel	467
The power of his rise We know and declare	146	The treasure in the gospel-field	233
The powers of heaven he shakes	17	The tree of life, that blooms and grows	233
The prayer is sealed, the soul fled	246	The trees of righteousness shall rise	295
The Presence Divine	204	The waster of Rome Is now on his way	89
The Prince of life and peace	146	The waves lift up their voice	267
The Prince of Peace on earth is found	124	The waves of the sea Have lift up their voice	51
The Promise of our God and Lord	174	The widowed church shall married be[801]	313
The purchased Comforter is given	165	The wise men adore	123
The pure in heart thy face shall see	233	The wonderful messias	111
The reprobates dare Their Master proclaim	52	The wondrous works in Jewry wrought	375
The rich and poor, the high and low	4	The word hath passed thy gracious lips	266
The righteous God and true	436	The word of reconciling grace	430
The righteousness of Christ our Lord	188	The world admire my mystic grief	339
The righteousness of saints I wear	311	The world and Satan's malice	239
The Rise and End, the First and Last	296	The world and their infernal god	30
The rivers of delight	50		
The royal edict to proclaim	307		

799. *UP* 3:112.

800. *UP* 2:112.

801. *UP* 2:452.

The world did not before us fall	291	There is my house and portion fair	279
The world obedient to their god	455	There we shall meet again	272
The world she sets in fierce array, The murderers	423	There, where thou art gone before us	149
		There with you we trust to lie	254
The world, to prove thy saying true	27	Therefore the Lord, the jealous God	5
The worst unto my supper press	276	These cruel buffetings of sin	467
The wounded dragon raged in vain	303	These eyes shall see them fall	272
The wrath is come, the curse takes place	293	These, (if our hearts may now conceive	33
Thee all the choir of angels sings	224	These threatening clouds look through	18
Thee for my Lord, and God I own	347	They all shall sit beneath the vine[802]	314
Thee have I shadowed with my hand	305	They all shall spread the gospel hope	308
Thee in dreadful indignation	101	They cry, and never hold their peace[803]	313
Thee let the witnesses confess	41	They from the death of sin shall rise	292
Thee let us still obey	20	They its threatening point defy	16
Thee, Lord, before thy foes we dare	32	They now of double grace possest	309
Thee more peculiarly I give	305	They now the holy people named[804]	315
Thee, Sion, thee: so long compelled	306	They only can our bodies kill	43
Thee, the great Prophet sent from God	135	They sowed the ground, and did not reap[805]	314
Thee we revere, the faithful Lord	3		
Thee with my spirit have I desired	288	They that be whole, thyself hast said	377
Thee without faith I cannot please	227	They who the will Divine have done	286
Their boughs with fruit ambrosial crowned	56	Thine arm hath safely brought us	238
		Thine arm is still unshortened	84
Their even course let nothing stop	315	Thine, Jesus, thine alone I am	382
Their feeble hearts confirm, unite	40	Thine own musician, Lord, inspire	244
Their glory shall their shame exceed	309	This base unworthy breast	426
Their newly born King	122	This day the Scripture is fulfilled	145
Their seed by characters Divine	311	This God hath bid us do	46
Their souls are impassive above	240	This is my only hope, (might I	393
Then all that on the Lord rely	76	This is my shame, my curse, my hell	265
Then every saint of his	50	This is my sin and misery	339
Then let us adore, And give him his right	52	This is my utmost hope	399
Then let us all our burden bear	40	This is the faith we humbly seek	461
Then let us behold messias the Lord	113	This is the saving power of God	232
Then let us believe	114	This is the time, no more delay	277
Then let us lawfully contend	282	This is the triumph of the just	287
Then let us rejoice	204	This is thy will, I know	435
Then let us turn no more aside	124	This Jesus is restored	147
Then let us wait the sound	273	This only labour shall employ	441
Then remember me for good	358		
Then, Saviour, then my soul receive	317	802. *UP* 2:453.	
Then the whole earth again shall rest	190	803. *UP* 2:452.	
Then, then, the gospel day shall rise	75	804. *UP* 2:454.	
Then shall the Lord his truth display	76	805. *UP* 2:453.	

This, only this do I require	264	Thou know'st my sad case	411
This only woe I deprecate	370	Thou know'st on works, and means, and men	471
This the universal bliss	213	Thou know'st the undissembled pain	475
This, this is all my plea	242	Thou know'st the way to bring me back	442
Thither in all our thoughts we tend	262	Thou Lord, alone, hast laid them low	94
Those longings were they not sincere	369	Thou, Lord, our relief In trouble hast been	241
Those strong convulsive throes	217	Thou, Lord, shalt take thy people's part	79
Thou all their memory hast erased	290	Thou, Lord, who hast the keys of death	385
Thou art into thy kingdom come	461	Thou lovedst before the world began	266
Thou art our flesh and bone	162	*Thou lovely Lamb, who on the tree*	336
Thou art the end of doubtful care	201	Thou, O Lord, in tender love	215
Thou art the sinner's Friend	15	Thou, O Lord, my portion art	215
Thou art the Universal soul	198	(thou only didst the blessing give	22
Thou art to thy Father gone	193	Thou only dost the Godhead know	264
Thou awful God, whose righteous ire	69	Thou only know'st the fallen man	185
Thou bidd'st us knock, and enter in	325	*Thou, only thou my servant art*	297
Thou didst th' outrageous dragon wound	222	Thou pleadest in the living stones	202
Thou didst thy fallen creature see	199	Thou saidst, I will the Father pray	173
Thou didst thy mighty wings outspread	198	Thou Saviour of all	211
Thou dost by thine almighty grace	200	Thou seest me wretched, and distressed	373
Thou dost conduct thy people	80	Thou that hast drunk the deadly wine	305
Thou dost create the earth anew	198	Thou that revealing Spirit art	200
Thou dost the first good thought inspire	199	Thou then, O God, thine hand lay to	339
Thou dost the living power exert	202	Thou thy messengers hast sent	59
Thou dost the vital seed infuse	200	Thou wilt not leave me in the snare	469
Thou gavest me to speak thy word	232	Thou wilt not let me hence depart	472
Thou God of glorious majesty	316	Though I have most unfaithful been	370
Thou God of harmony and love	243	Though I have steeled my stubborn heart	370
Thou great God of war, thine Israel bless	89	Though seventeen hundred years are past	374
Thou great mysterious God unknown	235	Though the world will not believe it	209
Thou great, tremendous God	432	Though they call our hope delusion	209
Thou hast conquered beneath	143	Though thou seem to cast me out	459
Thou hast in unbelief shut up	247	Though thy judgments are abroad	9
Thou hast long withdrawn thy grace	391	Though twice ten thousand souls are fled	63
Thou hast not dropped thy quarrel, Lord	103	Though war's devouring surges rise	78
Thou hast oft my refuge been	464	Thousands of ours are vile to his	24
Thou hast the prophecy fulfilled	165	Thousands to their account are fled	103
Thou hast thy praying remnant heard	100	Through persecution bold	41
Thou hidden God, for whom I groan	246	Through selfish desire	415
Thou in danger's darkest hour	57	Through thee the flesh we mortify	202
Thou in thy saints art glorified	290	Through thee thy goodness we proclaim	289
Thou know'st (but must I tell thee so?)	265	Through thee we now together came	280
Thou know'st for thy dear sake alone	32	Through thee we render God his due	202

Through thee, who all our sins hast borne	263	Thy righteousness the world shall see[808]	312
Throughout my fallen soul I feel / thy only	360	Thy servant, Lord, in torment is	379
		Thy sins, which like a wide-spread cloud	297
Throughout the world its breadth is known	446	Thy sovereign grace to all extends	446
		Thy Spirit revives	211
Thus saith the Lord of earth and heaven	296	Thy tenfold vengeance knew to quell	302
Thus will I make the covenant sure	310	Thy wisdom from below	46
Thy awful judgments first awoke	288	Thy work we now acknowledge	238
Thy awful righteousness	438	Till added to that heavenly choir	166
Thy blood and righteousness	208	Till all the earth renewed	155
Thy blood shall quench this fire of hell	472	Till God appear the faithful God[809]	314
Thy blood to all our souls apply	461	Till that welcome day I see	429
Thy blood, which alone	365	Till then I forego	363
Thy call if I ever have known	195	Till then, thou holy Jesus	112
Thy duteous sons to thee shall cleave[806]	313	Till then with us vouchsafe to stay	226
Thy faithful, wise, and mighty love	470	Till thou the mountain load remove	338
Thy few returning sheep behold	31	'Tis all our soul's desire to know	288
Thy garment, O thou pardoning God	377	'Tis all thy loving heart's desire	336
Thy glorious grace what tongue can tell?[807]	312	'Tis done: my all-redeeming Lord	276
		'Tis God who bids contentions cease	78
Thy goodness I praise	274	'Tis here, in hope my God to find	453
Thy grace I languish to receive	259	'Tis I who bought you with my blood	455
Thy hardy soldier, Lord, inure	47	'Tis mine the drooping soul to raise	308
Thy judgments we revere	20	To all our souls apply	191
Thy love is all my plea	259	T' avenge them of their tyrant foe	308
Thy love that o'ercame	143	To chastise me for my pride	459
Thy marks we in our body bear	36	To-day, while it is called today	393
Thy mercy is my prop	242	To death delivered in our stead	145
Thy minister for good	77	To fill my soul it emptied thee	344
Thy nature and name my portion shall be	257	To gain that heavenly prize	36
Thy nature I long to put on	270	To help their grovelling unbelief	308
Thy only blood can be my balm	355	To him let us restore	100
Thy only dying love I plead	333	To hoary hairs be thou his God	25
Thy only love do I require	342	To make an end of sin	169
Thy only name can be my balm	268	To make them trees of righteousness	308
Thy own joy to us impart	194	To purest joys she all invites	235
Thy people, Lord, are sold for nought	252	To purge thy guilty stain	131
Thy power, and truth, and love Divine	377	To shipwreck our weak faith and hope	455
Thy power be in his weakness seen	66	To sinners bruised, and meek, and poor	307
Thy prodigal in Christ receive	430	To suffer now is sweet	42
		To take a poor fugitive in	270

806. *UP* 2:452.
807. *UP* 2:451.
808. *UP* 2:450.
809. *UP* 2:453.

To the desert, or the cell	215
To the Fountain I go	412
To the inn they repair	123
To thee and to each other draw / While midst	41
To thee I lift my mournful eye	335
To thee let him in faith look up	47
To thee we in our trouble turned	290
To thee with our heart And spirit we cleave	90
To this heavenly prize	120
To those who thee in him obey	22
To thy little flock of sheep	68
To whom but thee, thou bleeding Lamb	471
To you is born on this glad day	106
To you the Gentile world shall flow	309
Token of thy richest grace	332
Tongue cannot declare	411
Touched by thine all-restoring hands	377
Touched from above with fear Divine	70
Triumph in our Saviour's love	118
Trouble the souls who know not God	186
True Witness of our sonship thee	203
Trust in the Lord, ye sons of men	286
Turn, almighty as thou art	35
Turn, and your sins of deepest dye	29
Turn then to God, ye sinners, turn	62
Turn, thou Friend of sinners, turn	471
'Twas an heaven below	408
'Twas not a feeble arm of ours	93
'Twas not the number of our hosts	98
'Twas thus the saints of God	42

Volume V

Take all my heart, my thanks, my love	378
Take the dear purchase of thy blood	230
Take the guilt and power of sin	291
Take the purchase of thy blood	134
Take these broken reeds away!	179
Taught of God, like him we love	406
Teach me, O my Guide, my Friend	341
Teach me the happy art	23

Teach me to cast my net aright	126
Teachers he gives our souls to feed	318
Tell me, or thou shalt never go	484
Tempted, detained in sore distress	362
Ten thousand blessings on his head!	434
Ten thousand snares my path beset	17
Thankful from thy blessed hands I take	422
Thanks be to God alone	348
That blessed sense of guilt impart	124
That blood which cleanses from all sin	230
That bloody banner see	36
That God who saved the faithful three	109
That great mysterious Deity	169
That happy man whom Jesus loves	405
That heavenly bliss, when language	227
That highest point of love Divine	318
That hurrying strife far off remove	400
That I never shall sin	304
That moment be now	266
That moment is past!	223
That taste of thy grace	437
The babes in Christ should nothing know	335
The beast, and devil I deny	158
The best I shall prove	28
The blessed messenger is sent	226
The blessing we want	437
The blessings all on you be shed	479
The blind are restored Through Jesus's name	116
The blood of the Lamb Shall wash our hearts clean	334
The body with the head is nigh	472
The captive exiles make their moans	231
The chaff of sin, th' accursed thing	315
The civiller crowd	283
The counsel of thy love fulfil	331
The covenant of forgiveness seal	95
The covenant of redemption he	299
The day of God shall then be ours	278
The deaf hear his voice, And comforting word	116
The Delilah within	262
The dreaming, visionary fiend	233

The drunkards, and thieves. And harlots return	115	The heavenly prize Is ever in view	427
The drunkards proclaim	283	The holy ark they bear	45
The earnest I prove	304	The human beast and fiend	48
The earnest in my heart I feel	79	The infinite store	29
The earth and all the works therein	82	The joy, and desire of our eyes	265
The earth is the Lord's, And all it contains	384	The joyful day we soon shall see	278
The everlasting doors	285	The King of the place	201
The fatal blow I feel	446	The Lamb on the throne	458
The Father hath his word fulfilled	298	The lepers are made clean	129
The Father of our Lord	474	The lepers from all Their spots are made clean	116
The Father shining on his throne	169	The life, which in my spirit dwells	225
The Father, Son, and Holy Ghost	64	The lion bold their heart displays	288
The Father then revealed his Son	86	The lion roaring for his prey, / Ah! do not	165
The few that truly call thee Lord	482		
The fiercer the blast	388	The lion roaring for his prey, / With ravening	233
The fiery sun's directest ray	190		
The flesh, alas! thou know'st is weak	155	*The Lord of earth and sky*	55
The flesh is weak, and will prevail	326	The Lord, the Lord, and God of love	93
The floods with horrid discord raged	109	The loss I by the first sustain	310
The friend, whom once I wanted	203	The love which brought thee from the skies	97
The friendly properties that flow	392		
The fulness of my great reward	94	The Lover of your souls is near	112
The fulness of thy grace receive	482	The Man of Sin, the mystery	310
The gasping patient lies	365	The man that will thy follower be	154
The gate shall soon unfold to you	90	The Man who hung upon the tree	477
The gates of hell cannot prevail	481	The meek and lowly heart	364
The glorious ministry Divine	318	The men of careless lives, who deem	244
The God of love hath touched his breast	412	The modest and meek This earth shall possess	385
The God of love, to earth he came	123		
The God who kills, and makes alive	105	The more my sufferings here increase	70
The godly grief, the pleasing smart	64	The more the outward man decays	71
The grace which kept us to this hour	466	The most impossible of all	300
The great archangel's trump shall sound	381	The new-born babe desired the word	88
The great I AM	62	The oath he hath to Abraham sworn	299
The great salvation thou hast wrought	326	Th' o'erwheming power of saving grace	64
The greedy sea shall yield her dead	382	The outcasts of men Their Saviour pursue	115
The grief beyond expressing	202	The peace and joy of faith	387
The guiltless shame, the sweet distress	64	The pledge of future bliss	363
The guilty I will never clear	93	The poor, and the blind, The halt, and the lame	115
The hallowed delight, With thanks I receive	419		
		The power of our Lord Doth all things subdue	333
The hallowing Spirit's prayer	83		
The heavenly choir	31	The praying spirit breathe	52

The promise apply	437	The things that were not his mercy bids live	391
The promise is sure, / It shall always endure	26	The touchstone, and the proof of grace	150
The promise is sure / To the helpless and poor	30	The truth that makes us free indeed	331
The prophets of the Lord	460	Th' unchangeable decree is past	301
The publicans all	115	The vale I took through	201
The random blows of chance	449	The Victim slain Arose again	62
The ransomed sons of God	386	The walls are compassed round	47
The reaper too receives his hire	113	The wary world, as Julian wise	250
The reconciling word	330	The waves and storms of passion	217
The ripest fruit he gathers there	113	The wayfaring men, though fools	390
The rougher our way	388	The winter's night, and summer's day	279
The saints of ancient days	459	The word, the awful word is true	156
The same in your esteem	367	The word thy blessed lips hath past	307
The sayings of our Lord	369	The word, which struck them to the ground	142
The Scriptures they in vain deny	152	The world and its god	28
The seal is secure	304	The world are always nigh	261
The secret pride, the subtle sin	399	The world cannot withstand	37
The servant of thy servants bless	346	The world cast out your name like ours	361
The Shepherd who died his sheep to redeem	115	The world that mocked, and slandered thee	97
The sight display	61	The world, who take thy name in vain	259
The sin-subduing power Divine	6	Thee, high enthroned above all height	135
The slaves of excess	283	*Thee, Jesus, full of truth and grace*	164
The slumber from my soul I shake	49	Thee I awfully adore	187
The solemn day draws nigh	46	Thee I shall constantly proclaim	111
The Son of God	62	Thee, Jesus, thee	60
The sorest plague thou hast to send	2	Thee let us praise our common Lord	400
The soul hath o'ertaken her mate	357	Thee let us praise with one accord	471
The soul superior soars	85	Thee, Lord, I receive	26
The soul transforming word	236	Thee, Lord, let every tongue confess	229
The soul whom more than life I loved	337	Thee, Lord, we adore, And dwell on thy praise	465
The speaking saint, though dead, I hear	87	Thee may I set at my right hand	51
The Spirit of his power	38	Thee, Saviour, thee	61
The Spirit of interceding grace	177	Thee, Son of Man, by faith we see	164
The Spirit of my God	367	Thee the first-born sons of light	279
The Spirit of power, and health, and love	329	Thee, thine ally, the heaven-born muse	403
The Spirit's living law it writes	312	Thee to procure how fond their boast!	404
The stony from their hearts remove	122	Thee we expect, our faithful Lord	470
The strength of sin is lost	47	Then dig about our root	55
The stress of our salvation, we	376	Then help us meekly to sustain	253
The task thy wisdom hath assigned	51	Then let me on the mountain top	177
The things he hath prepared	475		

INDEX OF FIRST LINES OF POETRY BY JOHN AND CHARLES WESLEY

Then let me with meekness attend	182	Thine arm did o'erthrow	28
Then let us agree Our Jesus to praise	35	Thine earthly course is ended	218
Then let us all at once aspire	472	Thine image is love	27
Then let us all proceed	39	This be here our whole employment	275
Then let us all thy fulness know	316	This is his acceptable will	319
Then let us attend	424	This is the straight, and royal way	149
Then let us ever bear	423	This languishing desire	461
Then let us follow on, to prove	336	This mountain load of care	213
Then let us go on, Till Jesus appear	321	This only thing do I require	483
Then let us in his praises join	398	This sovereign antidote expels	312
Then let us love our Lord alone	478	This still is the cry	57
Then let us make our boast	467	This, this is our high calling's prize	95
Then let us not stop	321	This, this is the prize	28
Then let us still proceed	462	Thither collect thy little flock	482
Then[810] let us stir each other up	478	Thither he still points out my way	413
Then let us wait to hear	286	Thither our faithful souls he leads	281
Then, Lord, when pure in heart	119	Thither we all repair	215
Then, Saviour, for my spirit call	66	Thou again shalt appear	26
Then shall I be clean	305	Thou all our works in us hast wrought	375
Then shall I labour to approve	99	Thou art greater than my heart	303
Then shall my tongue delight to own	98	Thou art just to thy word	30
Then the blissful sight be given	298	Thou art Mary's good part	25
Then, when our sufferings all are past	233	Thou art my own, I know thou art	74
Then, when the perfect life of love	230	Thou canst from every sin secure	4
Then, when the work is done	17	Thou canst not there bemoan	220
There all our griefs are spent	461	Thou canst, thou wilt for one short day	5
There all the tempestuous blast	182	Thou didst at first the grace impart	414
There all thy sufferings cease	220	Thou didst the meek example leave	149
There is the place beside thy throne	92	Thou every simple heart	234
There let them lie secure, and take	234	Thou feelest all the woes we feel	75
There my flesh shall rest in hope	339	*Thou God of love, and truth, and power*	166
There, only there, we shall	423	*Thou God of truth and love*	422
There we fix our place of meeting	452	*Thou God, that hear'st the prayer*	441
There we shall with transport meet	349	*Thou God, that hear'st the whispered prayer*	395
There will I my burial have	133	Thou hast healed me in part	30
These are they that owned my name	354	Thou hast laid the sure foundation	297
They bring his golden lyre	85	Thou hast not to my soul declared	91
They load us with reproach, and shame	259	Thou hast the hungry filled	116
They seek him, and find, They ask, and receive	115	*Thou heavenly Love, from whom*	429
They, under him, his church shall build	318	*Thou hidden Source of calm repose*	50
They will, thyself hast said, they will	144	Thou in Jesu's words and ways	360
		Thou in thy youthful prime	215
		Thou, Jesu, thou my breast inspire	137

810. Osborn changed "Then" to "O."

Thou, Jesus, thou my mouth hast been	110
Thou Judge of quick and dead	260
Thou keepest us in perfect peace	33
Thou know'st his distress	435
Thou know'st my heart's desire	203
Thou know'st the black desponding fear	102
Thou know'st the tenfold rage	104
Thou, Lord, art rich in grace to all	7
Thou, Lord, beyond their reach didst bear	109
Thou, Lord, by him, and thou alone	433
Thou, Lord, the fatal ill prevent	395
Thou, Lord, thy promise hast fulfilled	78
Thou, Lord, who hast ravished away	339
Thou Man of Griefs, I fain would be	196
Thou, my great redeeming God	384
Thou my one thing needful be	21
Thou never didst the wicked join	404
Thou never wilt relinquish	442
Thou, O Love, my portion art	22
Thou only canst relieve	356
Thou only didst our spirits join	411
Thou only didst reveal	323
Thou only didst the gift bestow	411
Thou only didst the souls incline	78
Thou only dost the power transfer	414
Thou only know'st the load I bear	245
Thou out of great distress	221
Thou seest him sore tormented	442
Thou seest my feebleness	263
Thou seest my heart's desire	15
Thou seest the dire malicious fiend	102
Thou seest the threatening of our foes	101
Thou seest their wants thou know'st their names	233
Thou seest this feeble heart	104
Thou slaughtered Lamb	59
Thou Son of God, whose flaming eyes	431
Thou Son of Man, with equal ease	238
Thou very present Aid	341
Thou who at thy creature's bar	383
Thou willest, and it must be done	313
Thou wilt cut short thy work of grace	72
Thou wilt not leave thy work undone	72
Thou wilt not shut thy bowels up	253
Thou wilt not slight the feeblest grace	3
Thou wilt to us make known	468
Thou wilt to us thy name impart	324
Thou wilt, we steadfastly believe	257
Thou wouldst not have thy children stray	314
Thou wouldst not let thy captive go	194
Thou wouldst that I from man should cease	338
Thou wretched man of sorrow	206
Though earth and hell the word gainsay	300
Though my flesh and spirit languish	344
Three innocents lie buried here	85
Thrice-blessed bliss-inspiring hope!	169
Thrice happy employ! We there shall enjoy	31
Thrice-happy remove To a country above	222
Thrice happy soul! by special grace	227
Thrice, three thousand, times have I	160
Through calumny, and pain	459
Through faith in our dear Lord	39
Through grace we take the purchased grace	335
Through him thou hast restored my hope	434
Through Jesus alone	379
Through much distress and pain	37
Through pride and desire Unhurt we have gone	469
Through thee, my God, through thee alone	8
Through thee we can in faith abide	33
Thrown, as an useless vessel, by	377
Thus I from my birth have been	443
Thus let me pass my days	270
Thus let us still maintain	221
Thus may he still his faith approve	416
Thus, thus let us lie	224
Thus, thus let us stay	321
Thus, thus we bestow	284
Thus while we bestow	424
Thy blessing of grace	267
Thy blood did all my sorrows calm	66
Thy blood from all iniquity	312
Thy blood makes us clean	28
Thy blood shall wash me white as snow	67

Thy body torn	61	Thy side an open fountain is	122
Thy days of pain and mourning	217	Thy soul for sin an offering made	148
Thy dying love hath sealed my peace	73	Thy Spirit breathe into my breast	146
Thy every faithful promise, Lord	307	Thy Spirit gave me utterance now	110
Thy every perfect servant, Lord	149	Thy Spirit in their hearts did cry	78
Thy favour alone can supply	340	Thy Spirit let us now receive	131
Thy favour to know	440	Thy Spirit of grace we daily grieved	130
Thy feet were nailed to yonder tree	122	Thy Spirit send me from above	96
Thy former gift is vain	16	Thy Spirit witnesses to mine	143
Thy gifts I clamour for no more	163	Thy thoughts and ways are not as ours	314
Thy gifts that are past	304	Thy victory we share	221
Thy goodness gave success	117	Thy visage marred with tears and blood	20
Thy goodness I taste, thy goodness proclaim	420	Thy weakest confessors defend	253
		Thy will be done, whate'er it be	432
Thy goodness, O all-gracious Lord	313	Thy will I cheerfully obey	338
Thy goodness, obstinate to save	194	Thy wonders of grace	31
Thy grace for all divinely free	311	Till farther still by faith we go	318
Thy help we every moment feel	33	Till God the full delight reveals	113
Thy holy will be done, not mine	150	Till he our life reveal	364
Thy holy will be ever mine	65	Till I from all my sins am freed	73
Thy Jesus alone	401	Till that welcome hour I see	181
Thy kingdom restore	436	Till then in fixed despair	207
Thy kingly power in us exert	324	Till then in thy blest hands I am	393
Thy love, that found the wandering sheep	242	Till then we hold your memory dear	361
Thy mercy in the stroke I see	338	Till thou the perfect love impart	177
Thy messenger of peace	127	Till we like you behold his face	473
Thy mighty name salvation is	50	'Tis done! he hears his Spirit's cry	168
Thy miracles of grace	129	'Tis done: through faith our hands we join	472
Thy mouth, O Lord, hath spoke, hath sworn	301		
		'Tis he! the Prince of Peace!	464
Thy name is release From sorrow, and sin	465	'Tis not of him that wills or runs	377
		'Tis there I shall meet him again	182
Thy name the fainting soul restores	65	'Tis thus the righteous Lord	273
Thy nature impart	304	'Tis thus ye learn to be	258
Thy panting heart for sinners bleeds	231	To baffle the wise, And noble, and strong	391
Thy poor, oppressed disciples, Lord	249	To buy, and make me free indeed	67
Thy power and saving grace to show	136	To damp our earthly joys	261
Thy power into my heart inspeak	145	*To do, or not to do; to have*	162
Thy powerful blood can clothe again	67	To God again I turn	449
Thy powerful hand in all I see	111	To God your spirits dart	43
Thy precious blood hath washed away	323	To heaven I lift my mournful eyes	199
Thy righteousness to cloak their sin	246	To help our soul's infirmity	176
Thy sanctifying word is sure	312	To him let every member cleave	477
Thy servant in the gospel, I	101	To him our request	385

To Jesu's name give thanks and sing	478	Turn me, Lord, and turn me now	303
To Jesus they performed their vows	480	*Two are better far than one*	452
To keep your armour bright	42	'Twas I that caused thy mortal pain	98
To know my final state	451	'Twas Jesus checked his straitened chain	381
To languish for his native air	199	'Twas Jesus raised our bodies up	381
To magnify thy awful name	399	'Twas on these terms alone	446
To me thy powerful presence show	126	'Twas there our peace he bought	38
To men of simple heart	267		
To pain and grief inured	207		
To pray, and wait the hour	260	## Volume VI	
To Satan's malice left	189		
To seal the universal doom	281	Take me young into thy school	450
To suffer all things for thy sake	156	Take to thee thy royal power	48
To suffer as my Lord I come	142	Taught by the Spirit of thy grace	403
To the fountain of thy blood	204	Taught of God himself to please[811]	335
To thee alone	61	Teach me, as I older grow	464
To thee, and thy great name	417	Teach me then betimes t' obey	401
To thee let all the nations flow	228	*Teacher Divine, with melting eye*	131
To thee, O Christ, the praise we give	323	*Teacher, Guide of young beginners*	380
To thee, great God of love, I bow	94	*Teacher of babes, to thee*	392
To thee, the true eternal Light	277	Ten thousand to their endless home	215
To thee, when sin draws nigh	22	*Terrible thought! shall I alone*	428
To those dear wounds we calmly fly	33	*Thanks be to God alone*	204
To those who would their Lord embrace	107	*Thanks be to God in Christ, who gives*	317
To us, and to them, Is published the word	116	Thanks be to God, the God of love	306
Together let us sweetly live	34	Thanks be to God, through Christ alone	199
Tongue cannot explain	30	Thanks be to God, through Christ, His Son!	351
Too long alas, we lived in sin	130	Thanks be to God who gave	286
Too long this corruptible clay	209	*Thanks be to God, whose faithful love*	199
Tormented, destitute, distressed	175	*Thanks be to God, whose truth and power*	306
Torn from thy friends below	220	That all might Jesu's witness hear	304
Torn with an endless war within	231	That latest labour o'er	231
Torn with the whips, and nails, and spear	21	That mercy I languish to feel	463
Touching this thing we all agree	314	That Spirit of faith and power divine	177
Tremble; yet O! with love draw near	286	That Spirit of love to each impart	99
Tried to the uttermost	46	That tender sense of infant grace	236
Trouble, and loss, and grief, and pain	193	That vision of the One in Three	323
True, and faithful is my Lord	353	*Th' Almighty will be done*	229
True daughter of affliction she	86	Th' angelic army sings	205
True pleasures abound	24	The blessed spirit enthroned above	299
True to thy great Master thou	359	The blood by faith applied	3
True Witness of the Father's love	125	The brethren—false, by stealth crept in	115
Turn again, my children turn	132		
Turn as he will, the eyes Divine	286		

811. *UP* 2:338.

The buffeting fiend Who pushed him so sore	287
The car that carried up our friend	293
The cause of all, our nation's sin	32
The champion of religion pure	121
The child, of whom we seem bereaved	259
The children in their earliest days	452
The Christians of old, United in one	439
The cities shall be all forsook	88
The crowd alarmed with short surprise	31
The crowd, the poor unthinking crowd	22
The dear tokens of his passion	143
The earth he hath long since forsook	81
The earthquake turned its fatal course	76
Th' eternal mind at last is known	345
The Father above	465
The friend by grace and nature dear	295
The God whom here his faith beheld	306
The golden rule she still pursued	268
The good and faithful servant, blessed	317
The gospel-trumpet hear	13
The grace which saved our happy friend	363
The guardians of religion true	126
The hairs of our head Are registered all	47
The happiest hour is come at last	242
The harmless youth who freely loved	359
The heart whose charity o'erflows	6
The hope of a sudden release	332
The hour of their temptation's come	49
Th' incarnate God his sight restored	282
Th' invader comes with furious haste	84
The inward change, that second birth	414
The Judge of all shall soon come	459
The labour of my aching breast	255
The Lamb hath brought us through the fire	227
The lamb-like innocence	204
The Lamb of God alone	244
The languishing head is at rest	194
The last vindictive times	51
The leopard fierce, who watches o'er	176
The lids he so seldom could close	194
The lion from his brake is come	84
The Lord allowed his bold request	284
The Lord, he is a man of war	178
The Lord, he knows the thoughts of men	403
The Lord himself our portion is	439
The Lord our favoured child hath blessed	261
The Lord, the true and faithful Lord	425
The meadow and field	435
The meek Lamb of God From heaven came down	405
The men of Nineveh shall rise	79
The men, who daily sigh and grieve	80
The men who dare disown	231
The mighty shock seems now begun	26
The mortal hour is past	204
The mourner there rejoices	343
The nation suddenly o'erthrown	88
The nations to rebuke	35
The object of his kindest love	311
The one thing needful we pursue	438
The pain, whose lingering strife	224
The pardon on my conscience seal	375
The pillars of the earth are thine	25
The plague, and dearth, and din of war	95
The pleasure and gain Of them that believe	397
The poison spreads throughout our veins	436
The[812] prayer is heard, and, saved at last	355
The prisoners, as confined with them	134
The purchase of thy death I am	305
The race we all are running now	217
The rich to thy dread courts repair	165
The ripe shock of corn Corruption defies	307
The sacrilegious hope is vain	275
The saints in his presence receive	198
The Saviour of all	211
The Saviour saw our strife with pitying eye	67
The Searcher of my heart can tell	254
The servants most unlike their Lord	4
The servile progeny of Ham	138
The sight her ravished spirit fires	243
The sign which men and demons flee	80
The simple men of hearts sincere	49

812. Osborn changed "The" to "his."

The sinners how blest, Who pardon receive	47	Their foulest sin my own I made	5
The slaves of pride, ambition, lust	104	Their lands alas! and they	43
The smoke of the infernal cave	137	Their Master she revered in them	273
The soul is now at rest	245	Their teachers edge their thirst of fame	411
The souls whom most he prized below	355	Then at thy reconciling word	131
The spirit of my foes I caught	4	Then let me suddenly remove	218
The spirit that in Moses prayed	176	Then let the thundering trumpet sound	27
The spirits of the just	203	Then let the zealous orthodox appear	56
The spoiler as a cloud shall rise	85	Then let us begin	399
The standard Sion-ward set up	84	Then let us bless his name	464
The star (in thy right hand no more	139	Then let us cheerfully pursue	353
The sword, which he reluctant drew	124	Then let us cordially again embrace	68
"The temple of the Lord are we!"	5	Then let us in his name sing on	430
The tempter all his wiles essayed	311	*Then let us look with comfort up*	297
The tempter asked and urged in vain	305	Then let us record The conquering Name	195
The things impossible to man	409	Then let us render him his own	430
The thousands whom our hands have slain	185	Then let us steadily pursue	318
		Then let us thank him for his grace	447
The tokens of thy presence show	82	Then let us to our Saviour turn	20
The travail of my soul is past	255	Then let us with thy gifts receive	388
The tyrannizing power	224	Then, Lord, by thine almighty power	384
The tyrant was not worth a thought	362	Then, when thy work is wrought	339
The universal King	433	Then, when we served our God through fear alone	69
The vile abusers of thy grace	115		
The wandering sheep of England's fold	100	Then wilt thou in the saints reside	180
The weightier matters of the law	268	Thenceforth an Israelite indeed	269
The widows desolate, distressed	135	Thenceforth, entirely ruled by grace	294
The wisdom that departs from sin	28	There all the ship's company meet	190
The witness of his hallowing grace	264	There let us ever, ever sleep	448
The witness which through life she bore	330	There their tortured bodies lie	378
The women sad, whose hour is come	133	There, there the ecstasy is full	300
The world's and sin's, and Satan's prey	410	There they lie, alas, how long!	378
The wrath Divine doth fiercely burn	85	*There with the virgin-choir she sits*	275
The year of release Even now is begun	13	Therefore is the plague begun	39
Thee, Conqueror of our foes, we greet	167	Therefore the earth beneath us reels	25
Thee, Jesus, the Son	453	These are the bulwark of our land	129
Thee let all mankind admire	161	They drink the deifying stream	220
Thee let thy prosperous servant own	122	They now are our guard	406
Thee, Lord, in all events we praise!	349	They soon shall convey	211
Thee, Lord, we hope t' adore	400	They tell me thou art good indeed	452
Thee, Maker of the world, we praise	394	Thine, O Lord, I surely am	415
Thee may I for my portion choose	452	Thine the kingdom, power, and glory	160
Thee with sacred envy moved	290	Thine was the power, the wisdom thine	182
Their first concern, their foremost aim	128	This dying life shall soon be past	277

This earth is affected no more	194	Thou neither canst be felt, or seen	371
This fatal vanity of mind	436	Thou never canst thy foes consume	34
This is our confidence of hope	159	*Thou, O God, art good alone*	383
This is the day the Lord hath made	429	Thou, O God, art wise alone	460
This is the day which God hath blessed	430	Thou seest my heart's desire	393
This, Lord, is our sincere desire	414	Thou the first happy pair	372
This token for Good We thankfully take	184	*Thou the great, eternal Lord*	460
Thither her Godlike spirit soared	320	Thou the holy God and pure	461
Thither on that 'pointed morn	233	Thou to the cry of thine elect	185
Thorns and briers our spirits wound	364	Thou who hast our place prepared	48
Those amaranthine bowers	44	*Thou, whom angel-choirs proclaim*	455
Those heavenly smiles distinctly tell	250	Thou, whom angels serve and fear	401
Those waving hands no more shall move	253	Thou wilt not hide the thing decreed	158
Thou art gone to thy reward	232	Thou wilt cut short my years	207
Thou art in every age the same	40	*Though envy foul its poison shed*	271
Thou art merciful to all	382	Though famine, plague, and sword	126
Thou art our only God and King	179	Though men despise our infancy	448
Thou art thyself the Way	428	Though men our simpleness despise	453
Thou awful Judge of quick and dead	402	Threatening I did and slaughter breathe	4
Thou by the Christian hero stand	124	Through all her words the soul within	269
Thou call'st us here to seek thy face	419	Through him let us to God look up	422
Thou canst not trust us with success	129	Through him to Britain's realms restore	121
Thou canst the meditated blow	159	Through him who called her up to reign	293
Thou couldst not rest among the dead	228	Through his own Spirit's power	230
Thou didst his heaven-born spirit draw	236	Through Jesus' name	210
Thou didst live to God alone	443	Through Jesus' name, and strength, and word	280
Thou everlasting Strength Divine	116		
Thou, for our sake, a man wast made	374	Through life inviolably just	354
Thou hast, from earth conveyed	238	Through the last dreadful conflict brought	279
Thou hast lifted up thy hand	174		
Thou hast to us thy secret shown	158	Through whom in paradise we meet	227
Thou justly hast chastised thy foes	166	*Throughout Jerusalem declare*	84
Thou know'st, and canst to us make known	172	Throughout this day thy mercy show	450
		Thus explain the mystery	457
Thou know'st in the spirit of prayer / I groan	191	Thus may we all our warfare end	199
		Thus the saints of ancient days	376
Thou know'st in the spirit of prayer / We groan	196	Thus the whole assembly joined	376
		Thy beauty cannot take their eyes	89
Thou know'st, th' usurping Man of sin	113	Thy brow a radiant circle wears	344
Thou, Lord, against our foes	90	Thy cheerful soul obeyed	205
Thou, Lord, who art the Truth, the Way	425	Thy doings have procured the woe	86
Thou lov'st whate'er thy hands have made	372	Thy favour we find	431
Thou my better portion art	444	Thy generous, good, and upright heart	344
Thou, my God, art good and wise	390	Thy God forbade the son to bear	235

Thy gracious eye which never sleeps	451	To thee, by whom we live	11
Thy humility impart	401	To thee, O Christ, to thee	338
Thy lifted hand, restrained by prayer	78	To thee our steadfast hearts shall cleave	418
Thy love hath our protection been	176	To those thou shalt with us entrust	411
Thy meat was to fulfil	230	To thy wise and gracious will	212
Thy mercies all our thoughts transcend	172	To us thy love show	405
Thy mercy and truth In the days of our youth	431	To us who in thy blood believe	307
		To waft from the valley of tears	192
Thy mercy hath brought	432	To whom her plighted faith she gave	361
Thy more enduring treasure	343	Token of our own translation	278
Thy name we adore, thine attributes praise	184	Too long, alas! We gave to Satan place	67
		Touching the legal righteousness	324
Thy providence hath cared	420	Train up thy hardy soldiers, Lord	409
Thy single arm the victories gave	163	Trained up in the true way	416
Thy Spirit in our councils sat	182	Transparent as the crystal stream	319
Thy tokens we with joy confess	95	Tremble, ye Christless crowd	34
Thy voice ever-sounding I hear	333	Trembling for religion's cause	77
Thy words behind their back they cast	31	*Tremendous God of Israel, hear*	80
Thyself the men refrain	125	Tremendous God, to whom alone	157
Till then, disdaining all relief	293	*Tremendous Lord of earth, and skies*	21
Till then preserve the faithful seed	114	Tried to the last, but not forsook	285
'Tis done, the soul is entered there	235	Triumphant while his soul ascends	355
'Tis done, the soul is fled	237	True prophets once they surely bred	131
'Tis done! the sovereign will's obeyed!	246	Turn from him, turn, officious thought!	253
'Tis finished! All his course of pain	259	'Twas aimed at him, the deadly dart	296
'Tis finished! 'tis done! The spirit is fled	195	'Twas love ordained so short a date	259
'Tis finished! 'tis past, his conflict below	287	'Twas thus the dying Christian spoke	304
To ask his death shall I presume?	356	Twice a week they fasted then	377

Volume VII

To-day, while it is called to-day	303		
To die, her only business then	274	Taught by our Father in the skies	231
To falsehood an eternal foe	269	*Teacher, Friend of foolish sinners*	148
To God the Comforter	286	*Tell me, affrighted reason, tell*	386
To God the Creator of all	457	Ten thousand talents, Lord, remit	408
To him we will our trophies raise	177	*Thankful the Father's grace we own*	200
To him will we give Our earliest days	405	Thanks be to God enthroned above	177
To his meritorious passion	142	Thanks to our heavenly Adam give	198
To keep her here in vain we strove	356	That everlasting joy of his	198
To little ones, and not to men	453	That from his kind Creator	131
To make my sinful nature pure	456	That God-revealing Spirit of grace	184
To me thy compassion extend	462	That heavenly kingdom, Lord, within	367
To mourn, and to suffer, is mine	195	That rest from oppression bestow	365
To mourn for thy coming is sweet	197		
To propagate the truth I fought	5		
To that Jerusalem above	217		

That saving power extend to me	399	The Father, Son, and Spirit of love	340
That Spirit purchased by thy death	398	The Father, Son, and Spirit praise	339
That virtue doth from Christ proceed	324	The Father we proclaim	296
That wandering star who blazed and fell	347	The Father's grace allures me	338
Th' affectionate sensation	189	*The Finger of our God most high*	257
Th' almighty Lord of earth and heaven	207	The God of grace, who all invites	18
The attributes Divine	216	The gospel-pearl, the truth Divine	171
The awful doubt is solved at last	93	The grace affectionate infuse	367
The blessing we claim Now, Father impart	79	*The grace of Jesus Christ our Lord*	278
The blessings of grace If others conceal	28	The grace thou didst for me procure	361
The[813] blood, which did my pardon buy	411	*The great God ever-blessed*	320
The breathless body of our Lord	294	The heavenly principle of faith within	436
The broken, contrite spirit give	141	*The heavenly three their record bear*	279
The cause express Of my distress	190	*The Holy Ghost in part we know*	248
The cause in its effect I find	115	The house is built; and shall God provide	432
The cause of my salvation	188		
The confidence Divine impart	94	Th' indubitable Witness	253
The cry of our heart thou waitest to hear	38	The keys of death and hell are held	52
The dark apostasy shall end	183	The King of saints, the Lord of Hosts	207
The day of Christ, the day of God	243	*The kingdom he, as Man, receives*	223
The death thou didst for me sustain, / Shall	387	*The kingdom is not thine to give*	228
		The Lamb from the throne	81
The death thou didst for me sustain, / O let	396	The law-fulfilling power of love	368
		The leprosy That cleaves to me	186
The Deity Trine One Being we name	318	*The living, they thy love shall praise*	125
The doting excess Of nature remove	79	*The Lord, and the eternal Word*	281
The end of sin and death is near	222	*The Lord is risen indeed*	13
The everlasting Father bless	287	*The Lord of Hosts himself alone*	205
Th' experience of salvation	359	The Lord of Hosts, the Lord most high	337
The Father alone	302	*The Lord our God is only One*	282
The Father is both God and Lord	340	*The Lord who did by David speak*	259
The Father made of none	299	The love which brought him from the skies	100
The Father multiplies my peace	304		
The Father owns him from the skies	279	The man of God, whom God delights t' approve	432
The Father sits and judges right	270		
The Father and Son And Spirit we praise	297	The meaning of thy Spirit's prayer	402
The Father and the Son	296	The meetness for that rapturous sight	368
The Father freely justifies	325	The merciful God, The hallowing three	297
The Father, full of love unknown	225	*The mighty deeds in Jesus' name*	227
The Father greater than the Son	232	The misery of my fall I feel	50
The Father, Son, and Spirit agree	279	The most Holy and High	321
The Father, Son, and Spirit dwell	293	*The name peculiarly Divine*	282
		The nature, both of God and Man	240
		The nature which its power receives	223

813. Osborn changed "The" to "thy."

The night of death will quickly come	401	The things and purposes of man	254
The one, true, only God most high	215	The things invisible / Of that new	415
The only wise almighty God	236	The things invisible, Divine	254
The opposite extremes I see	162	*The Trinity in Unity*	283
The orthodox renowned in fight	325	The Trinity we Alone can attest	336
The pains which soul and body part	376	The Triune God is found below	339
The pardon grant for which I pray	408	The Triune God we cannot know	314
The Partner of our flesh and blood	232	The truth I seemingly possess	315
The peace which man can ne'er conceive	108	The truth that makes us free indeed	325
The persons unconfused abide	211	The unbelieving veil remove	25
The philosopher vain	320	The undivided Godhead	316
The poison boiled in every vein	95	The unspeakable grace	175
The Portion of the poor thou art	158	The unsuspicious stranger	131
The power to bless my house	5	The virtue to his servants given	227
The praise of our Lord Impatient	28	*The voice of God the Father sounds*	210
The precious promises in him	238	*The way of all the earth I go*	366
The promise stands for ever sure	169	*The will of God is Jesus' will*	285
The prophet of the Lord most high	209	*The will of my Creator*	359
The realizing power	185	*The wisdom owned by all thy sons*	272
The sacred three conspire	338	The witnesses in heaven adored	313
The salvation is sure	373	*The wonders of grace Redeemed we proclaim*	26
The same Divine perfection	316		
The Saviour by men, And angels confessed	213	*The Word was independent God*	219
The self-same act of grace Divine	245	The world of misbelievers	344
The servant faithful and discreet	161	Thee a heritage from God	69
The sharers of my victory	229	*Thee faithful and true, O Jesus, we praise*	143
The sin which long beset my soul	354	*Thee, Father, Son, and Holy Ghost*	339
The sinners suddenly convince	19	*Thee, great tremendous Deity*	314
The Son his cleansing blood applies	304	Thee, holy Father, we confess	280
The Son of God revealed in me	371	Thee let thy bleeding love compel	383
The Son of man supplies	136	*Thee our strength and righteousness*	144
The Source and End of all I am	221	*Thee, Saviour, I confess*	364
The sovereign Lord of Hosts is One	207	Thee that I may my Father know	332
The Spirit his love imparts	296	Thee the bright harmonious choir	300
The Spirit is Life, we know and feel	290	Thee we sing, almighty Lord	269
The Spirit of a healthful mind	262	Their eyes against the light they close	262
The Spirit of Jehovah came	264	Their omnipotent Lord	301
The spirit of man is man indeed	263	Their shadowy faith embracing	344
The Spirit purchased with his blood	327	Their souls and bodies I commend	419
The Spirit quickening him, again	295	Themselves they call the church of God	328
The Spirit testifies of him	279	Then am I ready for my Lord	410
The Spirit's residue is thine	421	Then, because thou first hast loved	342
The sun at last shall lose his way	194	Then cut short our days of mourning	343
The testifying Spirit	330	Then in the last extreme of hopeless grief	427

Then let his wakened soul arise	170	Thou art the co-eternal Son	219
Then let me tenderly entreat	160	Thou co-essential Spirit, shine	254
Then let this body drop	388	Thou couldst not, Lord, thy help deny	120
Then let us glory in his grace	198	Thou didst in tender mercy look	124
Then let us see that day supreme	243	Thou didst not blame the father's prayer	120
Then lowly I enter the rest	365	Thou didst the lost sinners receive	27
Then my ready soul receive	358	Thou dost, in answer to our prayer	123
Then, O my God and Father, then	409	Thou dost not yet relief afford	121
Then, partaker of thy nature	367	*Thou, even thou alone*	237
Then shall I never more offend	374	Thou gav'st on this condition	117
Then the earnest I inherit	384	Thou giv'st us now our want to feel	24
Then, then acknowledge, and set free	19	Thou God of unexhausted grace	126
Then, then I feel redemption nigh	368	Thou God unknown, For whom I groan	190
Then, then, mature for my reward	385	*Thou God who hear'st the prayer*	116
Then, then my wandering toil is o'er	136	Thou God who sin forgivest	344
Then, then where'er thy will below	136	Thou hast been the sinner's Friend	408
Then, when all her work is done	98	Thou hast bought us with thy blood	11
Then would I joyfully proclaim	206	Thou hast his house prepared	415
There—but we know not what to say	119	Thou hast in patient love	380
There by wrestling faith obtain	47	Thou hast in the weak and feeble	149
There inscribe thy favourite name	357	Thou hast in triumph led	240
There is a God we truly call	270	Thou hast, O God, in special grace	417
There is none good but God alone	222	Thou hast pacified God	372
There let our mingled ashes lie	119	Thou hast redeemed in troubles past	141
There the bitter root we find	90	*Thou hast restrained my soul from sin*	373
There, there at his seat	199	Thou hear'st the unspeakable groan	318
They tempt the Lord most high	284	Thou his feebleness sustain	122
Thine acceptable will	166	Thou in mortal flesh revealed	323
Thine it is to bless and heal	90	Thou its infinite desert	241
This blessing is ours	36	Thou know'st I wait for this alone	409
This earth, I know, is not my home	386	Thou know'st if not a foe professed	152
This glorious Trinity	300	Thou know'st the trials yet behind	359
This I ask with strong desire	128	Thou know'st their unrelenting hate	171
This instant now I cease from sin	110	Thou know'st thy pleading Spirit's will	130
This keenest sense of deep distress	64	Thou Lamb of God, who bear'st away	332
This moment come, and touch his hand	148	Thou must admit the sinner's plea	147
This only blessing I implore	106	Thou never wilt thine own forsake	393
This, only this, I stay to know	371	Thou only canst my soul prepare	410
This single good I humbly crave	99	Thou, only thou canst soothe my grief	178
This sorrowful petition	117	Thou seest I cannot journey on	180
This, this is all my heart's desire	394	*Thou shalt not tempt the Lord thy God*	255
This, this is the true God supreme	217	Thou shedd'st thy blood that I might find	407
This unbelieving sin	393	Thou sittest on the throne	320
Thou alone didst inspire	322	*Thou Son of God, whose flaming eyes*	30

PART 1: *THE POETICAL WORKS OF JOHN AND CHARLES WESLEY*

Thou to thine apostate creature	337
Thou Triune God of pardoning love	326
Thou unsearchable Three	321
Thou, we know, hast died to save us	149
Thou wilt, I humbly trust, impart	55
Thou with equal ease and skill	98
Though age benumbs my active	402
Though late, I yield me to thy will	257
Though long by following multitudes admired	437
Though my sins reach up to heaven	341
Though of dying afraid	372
Though the worms this flesh devour	366
Three persons equally Divine	280
Three persons there are	302
Thrice happy estate of the dead	364
Thrice Holy and High, thy goodness and power	319
Thrice holy God, admit	312
Thrice holy God, in whom	306
Thrones I appoint to you my friends	228
Through his abundant toils, with fixed amaze	436
Through the perfect righteousness	213
Through the purple fountain brought	92
Through thee approaching now the gracious throne	442
Through thy death and righteous merit	381
Throughout my veins A fever reigns	186
Thrust out from them I served so long	181
Thus her parents' grief she cheers	83
Thus, only thus I surely know	305
Thus prepared for my dismission	390
Thus will I, Lord, my seal set to	400
Thy absence from my heart	388
Thy all-restoring love impart	24
Thy arm omnipotent to save	94
Thy bleeding love declare	362
Thy blessing, grace, and peace we claim	277
Thy boundless charity Divine	155
Thy bowels melt at his distress	147
Thy call to lay this body down	397
Thy confessor I stand alone	171
Thy Divinity's adorer	341
Thy faithful word and oath we plead	12
Thy favour and thine image, Lord	409
Thy favour how shall I obtain	411
Thy gifts are bestowed On all the lost kind	319
Thy Godhead whole was in thy Son	215
Thy goodness formed, and turned his mind	152
Thy goodness wills the kind delay	417
Thy hands must the foundation lay	20
Thy healing work begun	145
Thy heartfelt love alone can save	351
Thy hoary, helpless servant hear	399
Thy living law of love reveal	256
Thy love so strong and fervent	189
Thy love which did their souls redeem	420
Thy manifested favour	111
Thy mercy evermore the same	120
Thy mild humanity Divine	121
Thy nature's purity reveal	374
Thy own kind purpose to fulfil	407
Thy pity heard our softest tears	123
Thy servants prepare With wisdom for this	79
Thy Spirit hath the difference made	19
Thy Spirit now if thou infuse	109
Thy Spirit's attestation	110
Thy wisdom and thy power shall join	181
Till entering thy celestial joy	400
Till he awakes I cannot rest	152
Till thou direction send	137
Till thou thy secret will declare	183
Till thy love's design we see	98
Time to repent thou dost bestow	396
'Tis all my soul's desire	356
'Tis finished he cries	370
'Tis finished, 'tis done! By messias alone	372
'Tis fit we should to dust return	412
'Tis life, eternal life to know	273
'Tis mercy alone	80
To all he rendered what to all he owed	438
To destroy idolatry	220
To enlighten and cheer	322
To execute thy kind intent	327
To Father, Son, and Holy Ghost / We	232

To Father, Son, and Holy Ghost / Be	274
To Father, Son, and Holy Ghost / Our	346
To find the heart by Jesus bought	367
To God the great Jehovah	316
To my latest moment crying	389
To my primeval state restored	383
To persons thou hast no respect	159
To sanctify those By mercy foreknown	297
To the hope displayed before us	32
To thee devoted from the womb	413
To thee, great God, in Jesus' name	53
To thee in Christ my Peace	101
To thee on the throne We lift up our voice	317
To thy blessed will resigned	62
To what am I reserved! Great God	180
To whom should I for succour fly	54
To whom should I in grief complain	126
Tortured in his tender frame	89
Touched by the healing hand Divine	67
Touched thyself with human pain	128
Touching this we both agree	122
Trampled as dirt beneath his feet	168
Transgressors of his righteous law	256
Trembling, lest without thy power	58
Tremendous God, with humble fear	412
Tried above what I can bear	58
Triumph, happy soul, to whom	307
Triumphant host! they never cease	313
Triumphant I am	370
Triune God of pardoning love	345
Triune God, the New-Creator	342
True, absolute Divinity	218
True believers have seen	175
True Witness of thy swift return	244
Truth himself the word hath spoken	6
'Twas prayer alone that turned the scale	93
'Twas there he dared his father's God pursue	426
Twixt God and his own Spirit we	255

Volume VIII

Take all the power of sin away	114
Take, O take thy plague away	90
Take to thee thy power, O Jesus, and reign	41
Teach me, Lord, the perfect way	213
Teach me, O Lord, thy perfect way	170
Teach me thy commands to do	212
Tears have been my daily bread	96
Ten thousand now unite their cries	320
Terrible things thine own right hand	103
That fire for devils was prepared	341
That good and full conclusions came	462
That grace unspeakable	363
That I in thee appeased may know	355
That I th' habitual pure delight	378
That poison of the Romish sect	424
(That purchase of thy dying groan	371
Th' abominable thing by thee	356
Th' apostles false far off remove	404
The blessed day of my release	425
The blessed, tempted man, who always feared	433
The boar out of the German wood[814]	164
The book of covenanted grace	36
The bottomless pit Expects us we know	350
The chapels were a good beginning	457
The children of thy faith and prayer	245
The church is built in troublous times	304
The co-eternal Son of God	344
The comfort of thy help restore	116
The countless storms of life brought through	384
The Crescent to the Cross shall yield	487
The Earnest and the Witness	372
The earth, with all her fulness owns	47
The factious enemies to peace	327
The father of his people bless	267
The fear of God restrains from sin	37
The fervent prayer thou oft hast heard	413
The First and Second George were wise	447

---

814. UP 2:448.

The floods, O Lord, lift up their voice	265	The Lord I will for ever bless	27
The floods, with angry noise	177	The Lord most high is our defence	272
The fool hath in his heart denied	25	"The Lord," my faithful heart replies	175
The foe comes on insulting loud	121	*The Lord my great salvation is*	53
The gates of hell can ne'er o'erthrow	418	The Lord out of his holy place	127
The generous mob, too brave to martyr	453	The Lord protects and cheers his own	166
The glorious gospel-truth receive	133	The Lord regards with watchful eyes	73
The God of all-redeeming grace	203	The Lord shall make good his kindness to me	256
The good word of truth from me	215	The Lord shall pluck thy soul away	119
The goodness of the Lord remains	118	The Lord shall suddenly reveal	129
The great salvation thou hast wrought	92	*The Lord, th' almighty Lord of hosts*	283
The great shall to his sway submit	45	The Lord that calmly sits above	4
The great vindictive day's begun	319	*The Lord, the all-redeeming Lord*	150
The hearts of kings are in thy hand	351	The Lord th' amazing work hath wrought	207
The heathen, too, could see	242	The Lord, the righteous Lord and true	245
The heavens in his descent he bowed	31	The Lord thy God, O Sion, reigns	261
The hills were covered with her shade[815]	163	*The Lord unrivalled reigns*	181
The hills were melted down	181	*The Lord who saved me by his grace*	200
The humble prayers which pierce the skies	485	*The Lord whose saving love I feel*	71
The humble shall behold his grace	157	The Lord will save his people here	18
Th' idolatrous priest	395	The Lord's command is plain, and free	37
The ignorant who miss their way	266	The Lord's right hand hath wonders wrought	206
The ill we cannot fear	325	The loyal if he first invite	482
The infinite I AM	364	The man of sin who reigns at Rome	419
The judgments of the Lord are true	38	The man who o'er Britannia reigns	279
The keepers warned, in time prepare	454	The man who truly fears his God	402
The kings of the earth thee, Jesus, shall praise	255	The man whose hands and heart are clean	48
The knowledge of thy love	379	The man with heavenly courage bold	290
The life thy tender love bestowed	159	The many-headed beast	63
The light of grace is sown	182	The meek he will in mercy guide	50
The lion, ready to devour	14	The men that humbly fear their Lord	71
The little of the just	82	The men who dared their king revere	284
The Lord again shall take our part	180	The mercy asked in Jesu's name	351
The Lord for me doth ever live	34	The mercy which he sought from man	352
The Lord from heaven in thunder spoke	32	The nations thou hast made shall all	170
The Lord hath heard my groans and tears	12	The offering of a broken heart	343
The Lord hath made my goings strong	91	The one unpardonable sin	353
The Lord hath oft declared	137	The parting sea at his command	145
The Lord hath sorely chastened me	206	The people of thy wrath abase	277
The Lord himself my portion is	27	The people still to evil sold	276
The Lord, I now can say, is mine	204	The pit of bottomless despair	312
		The ploughers ploughed upon my back	245

815. *UP* 2:447.

The power must then from thee proceed	376	The voice of joy, and love, and praise	206
The prayer is sealed: we now foresee	80	The voice of my complaint attend	56
The prayer of faith hath raised the dead	399	The watery stores discovered were	32
The pure desire unquenchable	354	The wicked are thy sword and rod	283
The reconciling word apply	169	The wicked borrower owes	83
The remnant that prayed thou couldst not disown	280	The wicked eyes the good	84
		The wicked plots the death	82
The rich shall lay their riches down	105	The world through him	366
The riches of his grace	252	The world with fruitless pain	8
The righteous Lord is kind and good	49	The wretches, Lord, who thee blaspheme	301
The righteous man on every side	73	Thee all the earth shall soon adore	144
The righteous shall his ruin see	119	Thee, before the dawn of day	230
The righteous shall observe and praise	199	Thee, by the highest heavens adored	154
The ruin of thy church they seek	178	*Thee, Father, I praise*	420
The savage tribes, an injured race	487	Thee how often doth he save	190
The sea beheld his power, and fled	200	Thee I have remembered, Lord	216
The secret of the Lord is known	50	Thee in evil's scorching day	236
The silent laws have lost their force	317	Thee, Jesus, King of kings, and Lord	106
The sin-consuming power	181	Thee let me still my refuge know	356
The Son of Abraham, and thine	320	Thee, Lord, I humbly claim	61
The sons of violence surround	403	Thee, Lord, I with my heart believed	202
The soul shall be glad, In Jesus restored	40	Thee, Lord, my latest breath shall bless	138
The soul that sins, if God is true	343	Thee, Lord, with joyful lips we praise	207
The Spirit pleading in the bride	420	Thee no alarms of war can fright	175
The Spirit which raised thee from the dead	413	Thee, O Lord, I still obey	215
		Thee, O Lord, the good, the just	216
The spotless church on earth shall rise	46	Thee, only thee, have I defied	115
The statutes of the Lord are right	37	Thee, Saviour, let thy church adore	152
The sure-succeeding night and day	36	Thee, Saviour of mankind, I bless	161
The testimony of the Lord	37	Thee the Christian-infidels	328
The things which we desire we have	400	Thee the dead cannot declare	60
The threatened jails, an hour before	455	Thee, thee my restless heart requires	138
The tokens of thy favour show	168	*Thee will I love, O Lord, my power!*	30
The truth of thy salvation show	156	Thee will I praise among thine own	128
The tumult so loud No farther proceeds	280	*Thee will I praise with all my heart*	17
The vengeance decreed Yet farther shall go	41	Thee without love I cannot know	378
		Their brethren turned by grace Divine	25
The vineyard which thine own right hand[816]	164	Their cruel guile, and cursed art	123
		Their faithful seed shall still increase	157
The virtues of thy balmy name[817]	421	Their fury cannot move	177
		Their God let Israel glorify	44
		Their heart, O Lord, thou know'st	333
816. *UP* 2:448.		Their hell without a covering lies	269
817. *UP* 3:286. This line reads "The virtue of thy saving name" in AM 8(1785):64.		Their joints and soul dissolved they feel	197

Their mouth is full of bitterest lies	26	Therefore will I love thee more	227
Their oaths have caused the land to mourn	312	These poor for whom we wrestle still	399
		They all have left the heavenly way	25
Their rage defeat, their malice blind	74	They caught me in my evil day	33
Their souls shall drink the crystal stream	80	They daily wrest the words I speak	125
Their violence I have felt and seen	122	They dare the anger of the skies	235
Their ways to swift destruction tend	26	They kept me in on every side	205
Them, as much as lies in me	402	They that in thy law delight	232
Them his love delights to spare	188	They the innocent beset	140
Them in thy secret place	64	Thine everlasting righteousness	92
Them thou dost as dross at last	226	Thine eye beneath the fig-tree saw	391
Then, according to thy word	300	Thine eye observes, thy Spirit knows	484
Then all religious Babels cease	487	Thine it is, O Lord, to save	7
Then, and not before, shall I	209	Thine own, thine own, for respite cries	297
Then as the rivers of the sea	270	Thine undissembling lips refrain	72
Then he shall regard the cries	187	This alas, I always feel	385
Then hear the contrite sinner's prayer	118	This is the chosen royal race	48
Then in his soul the secret tell	425	This strong propensity to sin	382
Then let thy people's suit succeed	298	This the Lord himself hath done	330
Then my soul shall bow before thee	78	This, this is all my hope	362
Then, O my soul, be never more	201	This, this is his boast And triumph, that God	41
Then reveal thy perfect love	428		
Then shall he in his wrath address	5	Thither he bids the poor repair	198
Then shall I teach the world thy ways	117	Those blindfold leaders of the blind	398
Then shall thy whole design be seen	308	Those that have my soul surrounded	158
Then shall we all go forth in peace	321	Those that have thy precepts known	220
Then shall we Hallelujah sing	308	Those whose earnest expectation	158
Then shall we, Lord, surround thy throne	287	Thou always hear'st thy favourite Son	320
Then the Gentile world shall praise	187	Thou art my God, and thee I praise	208
Then, then I see	367	Thou art my hiding-place: in thee	66
Then to perfect holiness	148	Thou art not slack to keep thy word	360
Then when the work is done	334	*Thou awful God of righteousness*	315
Then, without a wish, I wait	383	Thou canst with equal ease make whole[818]	422
Then would their vain concern	325	Thou didst my drooping spirit cheer	180
There are Aaron's mitred sons	237	Thou didst, O God, thy blessing pour	150
There his triumphal chariot waits	48	Thou didst the heathen stock expel[819]	163
There shall the horn of David bud	249	Thou dost the malice know	273
There the chosen tribes go up	237	Thou from all my sins redeem	89
There thou diedst for me to buy	369	Thou givest us plenteous draughts of tears[820]	162
There thy last expiring groan	369		
Therefore a sad reverse we find	315		
Therefore he hath his Spirit shed	104		
Therefore the dire decree takes place	284		
Therefore the sword abroad bereaves	316		

818. *UP* 3:286.
819. *UP* 2:447.
820. *UP* 2:447.

Thou God of grace	366	Thou Man of griefs, thou Man of love	380
Thou God that answerest by fire	416	*Thou most compassionate High-priest*	266
Thou God unknown	366	Thou my only God and Saviour	98
Thou God who hear'st the faithful prayer	420	*Thou my portion art, O Lord!*	217
Thou God who hear'st the prayer	272	Thou, O God, my vows hast heard	134
Thou great Unsearchable, Unknown	371	*Thou, O Lord, my Maker art*	219
Thou hast abhorred thine heritage	100	Thou, O Lord, shalt all fulfil	23
Thou hast an evil spirit sent	316	Thou reignest supreme in goodness and power	41
Thou hast charged us, Lord, t' obey	209	Thou shalt, for thy own glory's sake	153
Thou hast chastised thine own, O God	132	Thou shalt judge the nations right	147
Thou hast girded me with joy	60	Thou shalt not spend thy strength in vain	244
Thou hast numbered out my days	89	Thou shalt not take my name in vain	347
Thou hast, O God, thy servants tried	145	Thou shalt, to thy promise just	187
Thou hast, O God, thy work begun	270	*Thou Sovereign Good, for whom I groan*	365
Thou hast oft my shelter been	134	Thou still art ready to forgive	169
Thou hast on me bestowed	9	*Thou still shalt save the poor oppressed*	33
Thou hast ordained the powers that be[821]	164	Thou Strength of thine anointed ones!	57
Thou hast our guilty nation shook	133	Thou sufferest now the evil done	295
Thou hast received the promised grace	152	Thou, the God of power and grace	15
Thou hast saved me heretofore	7	Thou the needy dost deliver	78
Thou hast thy people's doom repealed	167	Thou the true wrestling Jacob art	48
Thou hatest all that evil do	10	Thou, the unbeginning Word	189
Thou in the Lord be still	81	Thou, therefore, O Lord, Shalt put them to flight	41
Thou in the Saviour hope	85	*Thou who giv'st the wish to pray*	367
Thou in thy turn shalt be brought low	254	Thou wilt, I steadfastly believe	385
Thou in truth and righteousness	142	Thou wilt the mournful spirit cheer	116
Thou, Jesus, art gone up on high	151	Thou wilt the path of life display	28
Thou keepest me from hour to hour	95	Thou wilt! thou wilt! my hope returns	24
Thou know'st for more than seventy	377	Thou, with all that keep thy word	189
Thou know'st for this alone I live	381	Thou wouldst not restrain The wicked from sin	280
Thou know'st the depth of their design	275	Thou wouldst not suffer me to rest	390
Thou know'st thine own appointed time	294	Though ye among the pots have been	150
Thou, Lord, a God of mercy art	171	Thousands who unconsumed remain	483
Thou, Lord, hast girded me with might	34	Thrice happy all who trust in him	6
Thou, Lord, hast heard the prayer	21	Through avarice and ambition, blind	482
Thou, Lord of lords, and King of kings	278	Through every rank and order spread	311
Thou, Lord, our dwelling-place	171	Through him the just shall enter in	207
Thou, Lord, shalt drive them from thy face	11	Through mercy set free, The grace we receive	280
Thou lovest ill, and hatest good	119	Through thee I will thy word proclaim	125
Thou mak'st us a reproach and scorn	100	Through thee resolved I am	53
Thou man of double tongue and heart!	234		

---

821. *UP* 2:449.

Throughout my life of death afraid	384	Thy speaking rod they will not hear	414
Thus shall the man be blessed who owns	244	Thy statutes, Lord, are sure	178
Thy angels plant around her bed	403	Thy strong antipathy to sin	356
Thy blessing with the remnant stays	419	*Thy unworthy servant, Lord*	211
Thy captive, Lord, myself I yield	429	Thy ways to me, O Jesus, show	49
Thy children, faithful in the fire	415	Thy weighty right hand Shall find out thy foes	41
Thy dying love in me reveal	376	Thy welcome will concerning me	92
Thy faith in him shall not be vain	175	Thy wife shall as the fruitful vine	244
Thy favour will I seek again	55	Thy will, O God, I fain would do	50
Thy glory, Lord, I will display	45	Thy wonderful power Of saving exert	350
Thy hatred of the hellish seed	356	Thy word dispenses life and death	172
Thy heavenly charms the virgins move	104	Thy words are my delight and guide	38
Thy heavenly kingdom then restore	270	Thy wrath doth on my soul abide	43
Thy help to the distressed afford	266	Thy wrath on these shall soon be showed	275
Thy lawful servant, Lord, I owe	202	Thyself the Finisher reveal	356
Thy love did once my heart inspire	155	Till that welcome hour I see	47
Thy love doth all delights exceed!	138	Till then, from wilful sin restrain	38
Thy love her soul and body heal	404	Till then I to the Lord will pray	123
Thy love I ever shall proclaim	25	Till then, thou bidd'st thy servants	286
Thy love must send whate'er is best	411	Till with thy mind and Spirit blessed	380
Thy love sustains the world it made	79	Time may gently bring relief	410
Thy love which did my soul redeem	386	'Tis God instructs my hands to war	34
Thy love which passeth thought	388	'Tis God who vindicates my right	35
Thy loving son	367	'Tis *here* I look up, And grasp at thy mind	441
Thy mercy, and love, And truth I proclaim	255	'Tis Jesus commands, Come all to his house	252
Thy mercy bade my strugglings cease	391	'Tis now cut down, and burned with fire[822]	164
Thy mercy placed my parents good	392	*'Tis of thy mercy, Lord*	271
Thy mercy still will I proclaim	120	"To a fond father's arms return"	433
Thy messengers run to and fro	322	To buy for me th' uniting grace	378
Thy mighty right hand Their fury shall tame	256	To George in majesty supreme	279
Thy mind we surely know	389	*To God in trouble I applied*	234
Thy ministers to us for good	279	To God, my God, with plaintive cry	31
Thy name I therefore will reveal	44	To God they in their trouble cried	194
Thy nature pure partaking	370	To God they then in trouble cried[823]	195
Thy power was on our side	271		
Thy presence, and thy help afford	431		
Thy promise with the church t' abide	418		
Thy providence reversed our doom	288		
Thy purer eyes abhor to see	318		
Thy righteousness is far above	161		
Thy sacred hairs are numbered all	176		
Thy searching eye beholds him now	287		

822. *UP* 2:448.

823. The first three lines of the stanzas on pages 195 and 196 beginning with this line are identical. The last three lines on page 195 read: "he brought them from the depth again, / Pardoned their sin,

To God they then in trouble cried	196	Truth shall spring up, the truth of grace	168
To God will I in trouble cry	127	Turn away my dire disgrace	214
To him I cried, mighty to save	146	Turn away my roving eyes	214
To Jesus, mighty to redeem	71	Turn thee again, O Lord our God![825]	164
To labour in my Master's cause	404	Turn then, my Lord, my God unknown	348
To swallow up my soul they came	53	Turn then to me, thy mercy show	171
To the dust my spirit cleaves	212	Turn to me, Lord, in mercy turn!	51
To the hills I lift mine eyes	235	Turn us again, O God! and show[826]	162, 165
To the Lord I cried; the cry	6	Turn us again, O Lord	242
To thee, and to each other draw / thy mercy	420	*Turn us again, our Saviour God*	297
To thee, by day and night, I cry	42		
To thee let all my foes submit	128		

Volume IX

To thee, my Lord, my Rock, I cry	56	Take me from the evil, Lord	446
To thee, O Lord, my soul I raise	49	Take not the sacred signs away	44
To thee, the sinner's Friend, I prayed	201	Taste him in Christ, and see	290
To thee with boldness we look up	400	Taught as by thorns and briars, we know	145
To thy only will resigned	385	Taught by long experience, Lord!	356
To us our gracious God	242	Teach me, O God, thy will to do	102
To us our nursing-fathers raise[824]	164	Teach me what I never can	268
To us thou grievous things hast shown	133	Tell him—you feel your pardon sealed	395
Touch my lips with hallowing fire	430	Thanks to my redeeming Lord!	161
Travailed thy soul to ransom mine	355	Thanksgiving and praise To Jesus belongs	416
Trembled the earth before thy frown	149	That blood Divine, so freely spilt	247
Trembling at thine altar stand	442	That careless fool am I	349
Tremendous God unknown	379	That chariot, in my life's short day	186
Tremendous God, thy work we see	413	That envious sect and most confined	335
Troubled and distressed I am	224	That hand hath opened wide mine eyes	70
True and faithful is the Lord	23	That Hiding-place I long to find	400
True is the oracle Divine	294	That I heavenward may move	362
True is the patriotic word	482	That place where once I walked below	456
True to his everlasting word	261	That secret place afford	116
Trust in the Lord alone	137	That solemn mystery Divine	371
Trust in the Lord, and still	81	That thy stock may never cease	177
Trust in the Lord, ye saints of his!	260	That true remorse, that grief Divine	449
Truth and grace unsearchable	219	That voice which speaks Jehovah near	180
		That wisdom, Lord, on us bestow	224
		Th' Almighty God is he	382
		The angels are at home in heaven	205

---

and burst their chain, / And loosed, and bade them go in peace." The last three lines of the stanza beginning with this line on page 196 read: "he sent his all-reviving word, / Their body to full health restored, / Their soul to perfect holiness."

824. *UP* 2:449.

825. *UP* 2:448.

826. The four-line stanza beginning with this line appears twice on page 162 and once on page 165 and in all three instances is identical. *UP* 2:447, 449.

The angels gazed to see their God	438	The literal, outward house we love	227
The author dire of sin and death	142	The Lord a cheerful giver loves	203
The beast that meets him shall be slain	137	The Lord allows of sin in none	168
The blessings God on man bestows	57	The Lord doth in his Son delight	75
The bliss of those above I knew	109	The Lord hath to his servants shown	47
The brightness of thy glories leaves	242	The Lord himself is on our side	76
The cedars shall obey my nod	455	The Lord is King	317
The child whom struggling into light	138	The Lord is king till that great day	47
The church shall then appear	466	The Lord is my might: Redeemed by His grace	46
The cities that for ages past	440	The Lord resolved in death to save	141
The crafty manages the fool	243	The Lord that I sincerely love	317
The creature fails, if thou art near	233	The malice of thy church's foes	133
The cruel taskmasters oppress	35	The man whom God so freely loved	83
The difference now I know and feel	210	The meanest then may mercy claim	341
The eagle fond her charge awakes	108	The men to sin and Satan sold	347
The eagles' wings	301	The men whom God pronounces just	264
The ear of your heart, Whoever incline	445	The middle wall is broken down	441
The enemy within	116	The nation that thy laws disdains	455
Th' expected good, the bliss unknown	394	The object of his kindest care	108
Th' external house of the Most High	220	The parent indolently mild	172
The faithful soul doth not make haste	394	The people of God	324
The Father in his saints delights	343	The people out of Egypt brought	112
The flesh against the Spirit lusts	302	The people that in darkness lay	380
The fool in his own judgment wise	349	The pleasant land displayed before	88
The foulest heart that ever beat	246	The powers that did from Chittim come	85
The fruit of your indulgence see	153	The presence of my Saviour	310
The Gentiles shall my church adorn	431	The promise to myself I take	120
The ghastly wastes which sin hath made	428	The quiet solitary place	305
The God of faithful mercies	295	The redeemed of the Lamb	288
The good in man is not his own	157	The rest be mine	301
The great redeeming Angel, thee	31	The saving promise is for all	79
The guardian of an heart sincere	263	The scattered clouds are fled	364
The heavenly comforts share	466	The secret curse, the bosom sin	122
The highest seats no longer take	353	The seed which I resolve to bless	459
The hills and mountains may depart	442	The sins which men at thy command	87
The hope of Christ how good!	329	The solemn day draws nigh, when all	398
The host is now gone forth: to fly	104	The souls that Israel leave	143
Th' incurable disease	213	The spark which from thy Spirit came	361
The inextinguishable fire	306	The Spirit of redeeming grace	109
The joy and desire of mine eyes	365	The Spirit of revelation	256
The just man falls to rise again	352	The stream of swelling words subsides	394
The Kingdom, Lord, is thine alone	204	The sure foundation laid	218
The land of uprightness	120	The table of my heart prepare	94
The land where Jesus should be known	401		

The test of truth and righteousness	380	Then infuse the teaching grace	392
The thoughtless brute his master knows	369	Then let me die to see my Lord!	11
The thunders of thy law	354	Then let the patient, perfect man	239
The time I to thy wisdom leave	397	Then let the worms demand their prey	255
The top our faith adores	27	Then let us abide Through Jesus's name	400
The true Cyrus I see!	419	Then let us urge our way	121
The Truth determined to obey	351	Then mankind shall magnify	450
The violence of self-will is passed	394	Then shall I answer thy design	236
The voice of my Beloved sounds	363	Then shall I see the bliss prepared	322
The weapons men or devils frame	443	Then shall my soul recover	257
The weary steps that still remain	345	Then shall the Lord our Righteousness	399
The wicked in that net is snared	230	Then shall thy church superior rise	398
The word of God continues sure	331	Then shall we exercise	374
The word thy sacred lips has passed	423	Then shalt thou fear thy foes no more	443
The work of righteousness is peace	277	Then shalt thou say with glad surprise	432
The world and its prince No longer are found	46	Then, Sion, thou shalt fully know	434
		Then the last judgment-day shall come	254
The world and their infernal god	34	Then the world shall surely know	435
The world may boast their knowledge vain	264	Then, then our barren souls shall bloom	401
		Then, then we shall obtain	122
The world, O Lord, will not receive	195	Then, when thou dost possess me whole	248
The world on every side entice	344	There in the smiling wilderness	413
The world shall impotently rage	443	There in the temple of thy Son	175
Thee I adore, my sovereign Lord	345	There needed, Lord, no act of thine	40
Thee I confess, my God, my Guide	344	There the soft dew distils	117
Thee in the watches of the night	303	They are, as withered grass they are	334
Thee Jesus, I praise, Who kindly hast spread	304	They must be as the troubled sea	449
		Thick swarming from the dark abyss	194
Thee, Lord, alone do I require	348	Thine image if thou stamp on me	57
Thee, Saviour, at my greatest need	147	Thine own in Samson's state behold	140
Thee, Saviour, I my refuge make	129	Think not the law through faith made void	119
Thee, Saviour-Prince, our souls adore	129		
Thee that I may no more forsake	110	Think, thou busy, prosperous man	99
Thee that my sacrifice may please	58	This Altar ever lives	406
Thee the angelic armies praise	226	This Altar is the Lord	406
Thee the paternal Grace Divine	416	This anguish of a wounded soul	235
Thee thy first disciples saw	185	This be ever on my mind	104
Thee will I wield by grace renewed	411	This earth without regret I leave	207
Their first concern alas, is mine	6	This evil above all	306
Their sinful spot the heathen have	107	This filthiness of pride	249
Their wealth the children of the East	453	This happiness be mine	354
Them snatched out of the flame	469	This is the joy my soul desires	225
Then every countenance shall shine	350	This is that holiness	249
Then, Father, and never till then	234	This moment I thy truth confess	392

Thither with our heavenly Guide	429	Thou wast my Guide in infancy	299
Thou art the man—in David's case	169	Thou who all our works hast wrought	374
Thou art the man—that lives secure	169	Thou who dost my soul require	251
Thou art the thing, th' eternal Word	309	Thou who from infancy to age	308
Thou bidd'st me ask whate'er I will	173	Thou who hast brought my body down	321
Thou call'st my former sins to mind	245	Thou who hast suffered me so long	294
Thou canst a clean and holy thing	250	Thou who so long hast saved me here	308
Thou canst destroy our pardoned sin	436	Thou wilt be merciful, thou wilt	419
Thou canst not, Lord, a beggar spurn	143	Thou wilt in death my weakness bear	424
Thou dost indeed conceal thy face	379	Thou wilt not crush the poor and weak	414
Thou dost with sweet complacence see	208	Though all the precious promises	238
Thou, even thou, art God alone	225	Though every sinful act increase	12
Thou Giver of songs in the night	269	Though I am condemned to die	228
Thou God, that answerest by fire	179	Though kings may not so far presume	216
Thou God unsearchable, unknown	420	Three kings expecting at his gate	189
Thou hast enlarged thy church's bound	16	Thrice happy all who wait for thee	397
Thou hast in part forsook	326	Thrice happy, might I urge my flight	301
Thou hast into the furnace cast	425	Thrice welcome word to those who live	112
Thou hast my kind Preserver been	423	Through Christ our living way	28
Thou hast on us the grace bestowed	204	Through fear of feeble man	63
Thou hast our bonds in sunder broke	381	Through hope of perfect love delayed	348
Thou hast saved me from sin	286	Through labour exhausted, and pain	308
Thou hast undertook my cause	407	Through many a night of distress	390
Thou heavenly Solomon Divine	359	Through the dark distressing hour	403
Thou hidden God, unsearchable	258	Through unbelief I stagger not	248
Thou in the time appointed	283	Throughout my fallen soul I own	247
Thou, Jesus, of the chosen seed	421	Throughout my fallen soul I feel	
Thou, Jesus, thou, my Maker know'st	321	/ The want	278
Thou, Jesus, thou that Umpire art	240	Thus, almighty Lord, may I	272
Thou know'st, I know not what to do	214	Thus do I my bed prepare	254
Thou know'st what thou to me hast done	182	Thus may I humbly hide my face	34
Thou lately, Lord, in special grace	221	Thus, out of its state forlorn	368
Thou Man of affliction and love	261	Thus, thus may I happily grieve	234
Thou must for thy own sake forgive	418	Thus to meet my Lord I go	446
Thou need'st the kind command repeat	100	Thus will I, Lord, thy grace employ	196
Thou, O Christ, our altar art	172	Thy call, O God, to man conveys	156
Thou, on whom thy church depend	435	Thy causeless unexhausted love	55
Thou seek'st thine own who thee reject	435	Thy children, all inspired by me	443
Thou seest my feebleness of heart	162	Thy covenant this, that I shall know	325
"thou shalt not suffer her to live:"	52	Thy dying love my heart constrains	182
Thou Shepherd of Israel, and mine	362	Thy faithful God, shall I	465
Thou that by a touch Divine	219	Thy favour and love I prefer	303
Thou to me, O God, hast sent	355	Thy furious foes implacable	410
Thou waitest still, when thee I know	396	Thy God and thee who never knew	454

Thy goodness and thy truth to me	55	To make thy truth and goodness known	425
Thy grace, and loving-kindness	342	To me, by thy own presence	257
Thy hand we still unshortened see	436	To mine inmost soul restore	218
Thy happiest state is come at last	458	To my own net I dare	22
Thy killing and thy quickening power	110	To save from sin, convinced I own	278
Thy kingdom, Lord, we long to see	85	To save my helpless soul from sin	313
Thy land, which long lay waste and void	431	To sin, the world, and Satan sold	438
Thy mercy, Lord, is better	323	To teach the wretched man	232
Thy messenger we hear	88	To the chastening God I pray	265
Thy mighty arm, in Israel's sight	125	To the temple of the Lord	52
Thy nature doth itself impart	335	To this my heart applying	315
Thy people by the world abhorred	144	To this stronghold whoever turn	351
Thy people in the wilderness	226	To traverse hills and dales is vain	188
Thy people, Lord, if thou command	40	To whom with my complaints should I	191
Thy people saved are virgins wise	361	To work for God is good	67
Thy presence is the secret place	289	Too strong I was to conquer sin	135
Thy presence, Lord, the fountain brings	132	Too well that Amalek I know	85
Thy promise I confide in	336	Tophet its mouth hath opened wide	306
Thy providential care	66	Touched from above with sacred woe	155
Thy sceptre of redeeming love	229	Transient our life, and dark, and vain	205
Thy servant if I am indeed	280	Treaty of peace 'twixt God and man	428
Thy servant, Lord, inspire	315	Tremendous oracle Divine!	23
Thy sons they in their arms shall bear	433	Triumphant o'er his baffled foes	139
Thy sway among men to maintain	261	Triumphing we go	324
Thy visage marred to me reveal	252	Troops of violent sins and lusts	33
Thy wisdom all my folly sees	305	Trouble and sin are hard at hand	280
Thy word, O God, as right and just	86	Troubled by th' Almighty I	259
Till by thy mighty signs compelled	39	Troubles and sins, a countless crowd	296
Till then, on him thy spirit stay	437	True and faithful Witness, thou	385
Till Tophet takes me in	41	Trusting in the strength Divine	131
Times without number have I prayed	41	Truth of the legal sacrament	47
'Tis not a sudden stroke of grace	96	Try me then, and try me still	259
'Tis not in pain to move	217	Turning then from earth away	356
'Tis not so much the bulk of grace	48	'Twas thus in nature's sleep I lay	108
'Tis there with the lambs of thy flock	362	Two shadows of one substance see	50
'Tis thus the Lord his judgment shows	20	Type of Christ, the servant gains	191
'Tis thus the Lord my God descends	178		
To all believers visible	44		
To bring my former sins to mind	178		
To build this house, O Lord, display	333		
To cure the spirit's leprosy	193		
To guard our guilty trembling race	334		
To him we fly, at thy command	272		
To keep me from presumptuous sin	278		

Volume X

Take this stumbling-block away	56
Taught by thee, in doing well	228
Teach me, O Lord, to fight like thee	151

Teach me the Prophets smooth to shun	202	The condescending grace Divine	313
Teachers and priests perversely blind	341	The conscience of chief-priests admire	417
Tell me "'Tis I—that died for thee"	285	The covenant we this moment make	46
Temple of the Deity	410	The crowd in every age and place	340
Tempted, and persecuted here	69	The cure we have found Through faith in his name	287
That blessed law of thine	41	The daughter gay both hates and fears	241
That blood the mighty deed can do	23	The death of sin is but a sleep	225
That covenant of eternal grace	43	The dire occasion of my fall	415
That ground of fellowship with God	89	The double source of error see	353
That health of soul I gasp to know	29	The earnest of that joy supreme	389
That heavenly principle within	275	The elder serves the younger now	92
That just and holy One	421	The evangelic blessing give	110
That kingdom of the Lord most high	72	Th' example which to man we owe	185
That kingdom of the saints below	71	The faith opposed by all mankind	373
That Man, the surety of our peace	486	The father hates his gracious child	241
That mighty faith on me bestow	293	The felon comes our souls to steal	378
That Satan never more may find	265	The first and great command, we own	353
That silence of th' eternal Word	411	The first effects of dying love	433
That soap from inward sin	130	The first faint spark of good desire	116
That Spirit Divine, that Water clean	446	The first of saints, the Bridegroom's friend	498
That thou may'st kindly smile on me	149	The first will prove the last	328
That universal love sincere	368	The floods of ungodliness swell	478
The adversary's seed	289	The force of unity Divine	493
Th' ambassador of Jesus see	234	The forwardness of listening Jews	453
Th' appointed teachers now	358	The friendship of my heavenly Friend	434
The ball, the feast, the flowing bowl	279	The fulness of thy graces	180
The balm for every soul-disease	172	The gift unspeakable confer	84
The Baptist and his heavenly Lord	494	The God of love, he oft delays	227
The bare external word	473	The God of love our nature bore	159
The blessings which through faith I claim	209	The God of truth, and power, and love	250
The blood of Abel cries	364	The good which Pharisees gainsay	463
The blood of innocents I bear	6	The gospel by our Saviour blessed	282
The book (let all bow down and read)	138	The grace if actions cannot prove	263
The bowels of that Shepherd good	291	The grace if men refuse t' improve	367
The cause of my misgiving fear	189	The great command which here we know	355
The cause of this perpetual pain	82	The great King of earth and sky	350
The causeless curse is lost on me	172	The guilt and power of sin remove	83
The character a servant bears	235	The harmless inoffensive man[827]	390
The children with their sires compare	417	The[828] harshness in his words appears	309
The Christian apostolic man	266		
The Christian who to Christ affords	342		
The Church his Spirit's kingdom stands	329		
The comfort lost, and soon restored	143		

827. *UP* 2:45.
828. Osborn changed "The" to "Though."

The harvest of my joys is past	17	The pains I have so long endured	4
The heart of man, the ground accursed	267	The partner of our flesh and blood	324
The heart unoccupied by God	267	The past no longer in my power	191
The heavenly Householder at last	345	The pastor good with pious care	404
The hope of thy redeeming love	475	The patient, meek, and heavenly mind	84
The Householder in Canaan's land	345	The patriarchs and prophets viewed	270
The Householder in this our day	346	The Pharisees rage At Jesus's power	229
The humble man of heart	408	The plague which all my soul o'erspreads	487
The image of a sinner see	291	The plan and finished discipline	69
Th' insidious foes of truth become	463	The poor supply thy place[831]	398
The interests of his Master dear	244	The portion this, the lot appears	307
The[829] judgment is revealed	377	The power is on the Man bestowed	440
The kingdom of grace Shall soon be restored	93	The power of vital piety	288
		The preachers ye defame	361
The law which Jesus gives	303	The precious promise made to all	105
The least apostle of the Lamb	249	The principle of grace Divine	274
The life by miracle restored	491	The promise of my chastening God	76
The light in us must shine	166	The promise we for Israel plead	8
The lion roars, before he tears	89	The prophets old, and rough, and true	164
The loaves by distribution grow	282	The proud mistake a dream for grace	284
The Lord is King, let earth be glad!	117	The publicans may still draw near	222
The Lord to save his chosen care	371	The rest we in the desert seek	280
The Lord unto my Lord hath said	118	The rich and great in every age	301
The love of God is found again	356	The root of every ill	399
The lusting flesh, the carnal mind	83	The sacrilegious three	497
The magistrate is oft inclined	420	The saints alone can understand	355
The man of God, like Christ, gives place	259	The saving work thou hast begun	369
The Man of sorrow now[830]	403	The Saviour oft his help denies	308
The Master comes and speaks again	330	The schools of scribes, and courts of kings	157
The men in tents who meanly live	121	The scorching fever of desire	213
The men of a place Where Jesus hath been	286	The secrets of the Lord are known	478
The men of human learning proud	220	The self-confiding man	407
The men who slight thy faithful word	16	The servant by his Master led	279
The mind of earthly savour	183	The servant faithful once and wise	379
The mingled tribes where'er they lie	9	The servant of unbridled lust	495
The more a preacher toils to save	494	The sheep their faithful Shepherd leave	402
The mountain dark that stands between	199	The sheep thou hast redeemed of old	230
The Name be known from east to west	128	The simple despicable poor	338
The Name we still acknowledge	75	The sinner big with creature love	370
The number of the called is great	335	The smallest things, the weakest means	225
The only God supreme thou art	128	The Son obeys the will Divine	144

829. Osborn changed "The" to "Thy."
830. UP 2:47.
831. UP 2:46, where the first line in a different meter reads: "Yes; the poor supply thy place."

PART 1: *THE POETICAL WORKS OF JOHN AND CHARLES WESLEY*

The soul is unto Tophet thrust	391	Thee I seek, my pardoning Lord	49
The soul o'ercome by vile desires	482	Thee in our creeds we still confess	25
The soul of man is Jesus' due	329	Thee, Jesus, Lord of lords we know	126
The souls committed to his trust	244	Thee, Jesus, our true Jonas, thee	264
The Spirit that our deliverance wrought	109	Thee, Jesus, thee our hearts adore!	416
The spirit unclean will still remain	311	Thee Jesus, thee thy foes confess	428
The spring of sin is proud self-love	487	Thee, Lord, I joyfully confess	334
The strong man armed this moment bind	469	Thee, Lord, I just and faithful own	334
The summer of my youth is passed	17	Thee Prince and Saviour we adore	118
The sun shall set in endless night	87	Thee to seek by thee inclined	437
The temple of the Lord—they pull	16	Thee we cannot trust in vain	437
The thing my God doth hate	44	Their gross unfeeling heart oppose	269
The time of death and pain	399	Their reward they have, not thine	176
The trodden worm will turn again	170	Their sacred charge who undertakes	159
The true heavenly David give	54	Them thy wrath, most righteous Lord	376
The truth a Pharisee offends	288	Themselves instructed from above	443
The truth of each prophetic word	214	Then every murmuring thought and vain	53
The two commands are one	356	Then every soul his Lord shall know	105
Th' ungrateful unbelieving crowd	492	Then Jesus, then, the good bestow	84
The various shapes of worldly woe	272	Then, Jesus, then, when seven times tried	131
The vigilance our Lord demands	378	Then let th' unrighteous mammon go	188
The virtue of thy Spirit	180	Then only, when by sore distress	94
The watery flood destroyed	377	Then our ready souls remove	147
The way I through thy grace have found	202	Then shall I my Physician praise	30
The wicked and the just	392	Then the slaves of Satan know	308
The wicked may, through pride affect	495	Then, then th' intestine war is o'er	106
The wicked one is slain	101	Then, then the true repose I find	256
The wide, original domain	97	Then thou art come for me	224
The wise applaud; but all beside	251	Then thou wilt pardon me	46
The witnesses ye praise	363	Then to perfect peace restored	480
The word in every one	473	Then when I feel thy Spirit mine	172
The word is unaccomplished still	86	Then wilt thou on thy throne appear	66
The word of all-preventing grace	142	There is a time for souls to toil	159
The word of Christ alone	258	These are the works thou dost require	304
The world against their Maker cry	169	They always, Lord, who money love	439
The world is at his coming moved	339	They bear the spurious character	372
The world is one great wilderness	295	They called the miracles he wrought	367
The world unknowingly fulfil	269	They might perceive that Christ is he	269
The world with courtesy like his	407	They shall be numbered with the sheep	392
The world with feeble saints agree	29	Thine anger at what I have done	103
The world with spurious wisdom blind	492	This dawn of grace, this glimmering ray	116
The world would by my words ensnare	353	This day with this day's bread	178
Thee, almighty God, we praise	456	This dire concupiscence within	413
Thee, Father, Son, and Holy Ghost	46	This inbred enemy to rest	20

This is that sin of sins	263	Thou wonderest at our unbelief	492
This is the soul divinely great	314	Thou would'st that I should holy be	209
This is the word in every age	443	Though now out of thy presence driven	94
This strong propensity to ill	217	Through earth the blessing spread	139
This till Christ pronounce me blessed	394	Through faith our friends we bring to thee	310
Thither the saints shall soon repair	374	Through false pretence of honouring thee	174
Those who seem at first rejected	232	Through life your change of mind express	448
Thou art the Door: I knock at thee	200	Through our fiery trial, Lord	125
Thou art the thing my soul requires	84	Through zeal for piety sincere	243
Thou bidd'st me ask, and while thy word	195	Throughout my fallen soul I feel / Repentance	39
Thou bidd'st me seek, and thy command	199	Throughout my fallen soul I feel / The strength	69
Thou by thy energy of grace	441	Throughout my sinful soul I know	216
Thou call'st us at our latest hour	331	Thus in temptation I	408
Thou canst not want the power	207	Thus, Lord, throughout my life would I	71
Thou dost in all thy people dwell	143	Thus may I the kingdom seize	249
Thou dost not say, The seed springs up	476	Thus may I with alternate care	405
Thou feeble soul unsaved from pride	460	Thus, O Lord, the world convince	65
Thou goest about in every age	229	Thus, thus may I the prize pursue	174
Thou great Incomprehensible	199	Thus would I watch till life is o'er	375
Thou hast, O God, the work begun	113	Thy blood can save from inbred sin	13
Thou hast, O Lord, thine Israel blessed	8	Thy church, O God, shall find fulfilled	116
Thou hast to me my case made known	456	Thy confessor in deed and word	239
Thou Holy One and Just	364	Thy death supports the dying saint	431
Thou in thy humanity	453	Thy debtor at thy feet I fall	319
Thou Jesus alone	221	Thy Deity to prove	62
Thou kindly camest to stand between[832]	240	Thy faithful promise I receive	243
Thou know'st, and thou, O God, hast shown	10	Thy glorious power, O Christ, employ	120
Thou, Lord, its Finisher shalt be	115	Thy good and holy will	178
Thou lovely, meek, and gentle Lamb	260	Thy grace invisible	207
Thou my little faith increase	481	Thy gracious Lord shall soon for thee	108
Thou offerest, Lord, to all thy love	268	Thy hand, O Lord, o'er us extend	464
Thou only canst confer	260	Thy handmaid in the softer kind	241
Thou only dost the Father know	252	Thy hands shall never more hang down	107
Thou, the great Power of God in man	217	Thy kingdom of internal peace	119
Thou universal Saviour, come	97	Thy kingdom's fruits mature	181
Thou who didst for all atone	139	Thy kingdom's restoration	180
Thou who hast purchased them of old	91	Thy love the day designed	258
Thou will'st thy followers to request	196	Thy nature be my law	41
Thou wilt; but why not now?	208	Thy own word I bring to thee	472
Thou wilt what thou hast spoken, do	58		
Thou with thy own perfections blest	401		

832. UP 2:26.

Thy presence doth my bliss ensure	44	To sense and pride by nature prone	22
Thy right acquired by mortal pain	428	To suffer, and abstain	303
Thy sanctifying word is sure	28	To the broad frequented ways	350
Thy Spirit, Lord, can sin subdue	84	To thee my heart I open wide	143
Thy Spirit of inspiration	180	To those that believe Salvation is sure	287
Thy Spirit's energy exert	83	*To those who on thy truth rely*	SH 1762, 2:174
Thy virtue, Lord, if thou exert	224	To us he doth his love reveal	270
Thy virtue, O almighty Lord	231	To whom should thy disciples go[833]	223
Thy will, O Lord, whate'er I do	205	To work at his command we go	331
Thy word of evangelic grace	456	Too strong for this weak soul of mine	37
Thy wrath shall not for ever last	7	Transporting word for all that hear	388
Till Jesus come to seek and send	331	Tremble, ye families profane	21
Till Jesus' hand the sinner take	226	Tremble, ye fond of human praise	360
Till the grain becomes a tree	275	Tremendous Lord, thy voice we hear	105
Tired with the greatness of my way	253	Tremendous words! they all contain	400
'Tis always nature's cautious care	317	Tried is every faithful man	124
'Tis not enough, at thy command	315	Triumph ye ransomed worms of earth	444
'Tis not for sin which thou hast done	430	Troops of priests and doctors proud	499
'Tis there we soon shall find	439	True and faithful as thou art	32
'Tis thus he blasts the pride of Rome	232	True followers of their Lord	399
'Tis thus our heavenly Master slights	232	True ministers of gospel grace	493
'Tis thus the world in every age	409	Trusting in thy word alone	45
T' abase the loftiness of man	467	Truth never shuns the light	475
To all that life of righteousness	246	Truth of the Paschal sacrifice	397
To all the souls he owns for his	305	Truth will not be suppressed	475
To all who watch his sepulchre	435	Turn again, ye faithless race	10
To ask a second grace we join	316	Turn, into flesh the stony turn	162
To bless me, Lord, this day begin	110	Turn then, thou good Physician turn	225
To carry thy disciples word	438	Turned by thy Son's victorious blood	40
To Christ the tempted I	448		
To Christ who would not gladly give	395		
To damn us by our own desires	155	## Volume XI	
To each thy hallowing spirit give	322		
To earthly things they cleave	377	Taught by their incredulity	248
T' elude the force of truth severe	492	Taught of himself my God to fear	386
To him in all our steps we tend	325	Teach me, Jesus, how to pray	200
To Jesus's name Hosanna we sing	342	Teach me, Saviour, by thy grace	352
To Jews the gospel-faith impart	8	Tell me again that thou hast healed	368
To judge the wretch in sin secure	380	Tell me, O my Life, my Hope	189
To meet my God	90	That all might savingly believe	51
To men of their own knowledge proud	477	That apostolic ship[834]	141
To Salem, as their central place	9		
To save the lost he came	316	833. *UP* 2:22.	
To seal the universal doom	392	834. *UP* 2:91.	

That blood Divine had brought the grace	91	The Father's delight Shall surely be ours	129
That every soul may make thee room	125	The Father's Fellow, and his Son	489
That hand beneficent, Divine	218	The father's fondness for his son	362
That heavenly Light appeared below	437	The feast of tabernacles	396
That holy Child bestowed	107	The feeble first desire	199
That my fears may all be over	311	The fellowship below	283
That plainly in the gospel-glass	489	The fiery law by Moses given	322
That strange excess of love unknown	511	The first effect of faith is praise	119
That the doubly dead might live	458	The first great work of God	381
That we may in patient hope	277	The first of duties is the last	124
Th' Almighty can employ his power	77	The foes of our Lord, Who multitudes see	219
The angels fell through pride o'erthrown	112	The Fountain of my life, and head	389
The arm of the Almighty	495	The Fruit of Mary's womb	107
The Author of our joy we bless	486	The fulness of the Deity	184
The awful day and hour unknown	67	The furious world rejecting those	451
The Babe unseen his power displays	107	The gift which our own flesh we owe	5
The birth of thy Son	106	The gifts thou didst thyself bestow	35
The body and the head are one	505	The God of love himself imparts	31
The carnal Jews misunderstood	54	The good he doth through grace regain	226
The cause of human ruin see!	234	The good we eagerly require	473
The change of my heart my life shall express	264	The gospel of grace	145
The change we all may feel and show	343	The gospel stands in Moses' place	417
The children of that wicked one	429	The grace of our head his Members receive	129
The Christ, by raptured seers foretold	117	The great Angel of the Lord	102
The Christ foretold by ancient seers	400	The great ones of the earth delight	297
The Christian law alone	154	The great, th' ambitious, and the proud	132
The church they call their proper care[835]	274	The heart corrupt with all his care	158
The church's Principle and Seed	490	The heart that believes Is Jesus's home	265
The cock had crowed in vain	82	The heart to creature-love inclined	325
The creature in those realms of bliss	54	The heavenly Man The God we adore	128
The deaf, we to his voice attend	9	The heavenly principle within	343
The devils that reign	138	The holy God himself they blame	165
The dogs some small relief afford	243	The house which seems so clean	206
The earliest fruits of bleeding love	305	The image of the earthy now	21
The earnest of his glorious hire	361	The infidel his doom shall bear	98
The everlasting God is he	350	The Jews beheld the Lord most-high[836]	220
The faith thou dost even now bestow	464	The judgment blind of erring man	373
The faith thou dost on us bestow	473	The judgment of the world how blind	400
The faith which in my heart I feel	363	The justice of God	306
The faithful acceptable word	100	The lasting peace of mind	492
The faithful in their Saviour's sight	469		

---

835. UP 2:186.

836. UP 2:147.

The law points out the Victim slain[837]	328
The law thy servant Moses gave	403
The least of thy disciples I	490
The Light for a few moments shines	438
The Light into the world is come	497
The Lion might have torn his foes	293
The little child, the twice-born man	188
The Lord of hosts, the God most-high	117
The Lord unto my Lord hath said	272
The Lord, whose mercies never end	50
The love impartial and sincere	511
The lower at his feet we stoop	253
The man that to himself adheres	122
The Man, the God, they Jesus call	442
The man who Christ hath truly known	161
The man who hath his Saviour found	329
The man whom covetous desire[838]	459
The man whom God to this hath wrought	452
The Man whose word is life and power	367
The manger mean, and bleeding cross	121
The mark on every face impress	512
The marks of wicked pastors see!	450
The meek humility Divine	111
The men who seek their portion here[839]	240
The mercy to our fathers showed	113
The messengers rejected	495
The miser doth his riches store	211
The modern Jews who bear his name	54
The modest man, the meek in heart	507
The more my Lord prolongs his stay	68
The more our Lord exalts, the more	110
The most apostate spirit below	269
The mystery of Jehovah's birth	111
The mystery of thy grace	108
The one great God supreme	71
The one religion see	56
Th' original disease	173
Th' original of evil see	431
The people can a prophet know	269
The people still go forth to meet	485
The perishable things below	210
The persecutor's rage refrain	191
The Pharisees see And murmur in vain	264
The pile magnificent may please	275
The place of John I covet	507
The poor rejoice to hear	116
The poor, the death-devoted crowd	412
The poor wayfaring man	448
The poor, we joyfully confess	412
The power is not revoked or lost	193
The power which thy command conveys	477
The prayer which God delights to hear	467
The preacher doth not all condemn	127
The preacher vehemently requires	27
The pride of haughtiest kings is seen	285
The promise made but not fulfilled	409
The promise made our fallen race	493
The prophets spake of Jesu's grace[840]	361
The proud he doth far off behold	257
The reaper of thy fields receives	360
The righteous real Abel cries	304
The righteousness that never ends	200
The ring, the Spirit's seal	238
The saint indeed, the humble man	323
The saint who of his grace presumes	81
The saints shall at thy table sit	287
The same in every age thou art	26
The Saviour-God so long foretold	474
The Saviour, Priest, and Sacrifice	85
The Saviour sad replies no more	75
The Saviour still delights to find	367
The Saviour then his promise seals	61
The scorn of men, the worldling's fool	401
The Scriptures all with Christ are filled	308
The Scriptures never can be known	55
The secret of the Lord is known	507
The secret whisper of thy love	461
The seed infused, the good desire	341
The Sender (for it cannot be)	425
The serpent speaks in guileful men	415
The servant of the Lord	280

837. *UP* 2:216.
838. *UP* 2:244.
839. *UP* 2:156.
840. *UP* 2:231.

The sheep with meek docility	463	Th' unfathomable mystery!	389
The sheep with true simplicity	463	The universal Light thou art	319
The Shepherd good indeed thou art[841]	459	The veil removed we then perceive	487
The Shepherd good, thou dost approve	459	The virtue of thy perfect love	337
The signs of our Redeemer nigh	279	The ways of God are dark to man	342
The sin that cleaves to Adam's race	325	The weakest instrument Divine	440
The sinful father of mankind	341	The wicked, Lord, and they alone	272
The single miracle	292	The widow's and the orphan's Friend	255
The sinner blind is always poor	441	The will of man must bow before	40
The sinner poor thy word believes	248	The wisdom and the power of God	456
The sinner saved is Jesu's guest	484	The wisdom of our God made man	462
The slave of fashionable sin	478	The woman testifies	95
The slave of hell and sin	293	The wonders wrought in this our day	447
The slave to nature's filthy sin	172	The word fulfilled in this our day	268
The slave to vile affections sold	172	The word his sacred lips hath passed!	28
The slothful worldly throng[842]	270	The word, the seed of righteousness[844]	170
The Son of Man, the Man of woe	37	The Word, the uncreated Son	318
The sons of God with faith sincere	432	The words thou dost from God declare[845]	351
The soul in which his work is done	342	The words we speak, we speak them not	61
The soul that would on thee rely	384	The works of thy grace Exulting we sing	219
The Sovereign God affects	57	The world an outward temple praise	60
The Spirit of our head	181	The world, and all we valued here	184
The sport of his own creatures made	293	The world his abject poverty	136
The stubborn and rebellious	58	The world in darkness lies	89
The sudden faith thou hast bestowed	452	The world offended at our Lord	410
The tempted church for help relies	288	The world rebuke in vain	37
The things we most affect and prize[843]	484	The world their hands can never lay	410
The things which I desire in prayer	48	The world who only seek their own	484
The things which we th' occasion make	192	The world will always love their own	398
The tongues, the hands, the hearts of men	405	The world with persecuting spite	398
The trees their swelling buds disclose	279	The world with useless care	380
The truth, and blessedness, and need	340	The worldly man of wealth possessed	33
The truth his confessors defend	410	The world's bright Day did then appear	439
The truth I now declare	174	Thee I behold with steadfast eye	326
The Truth, the Deity	72	Thee, if they finally deny	320
The Truth thou say'st, the Truth thou art	432	Thee, Jesus, full of truth and grace	320
The truth thy witnesses have known	344	Thee, Jesus, God supreme, the Son	371
The truth who with our hearts believe	170	Thee Jesus, thee I fall before	457
The truths he speaks are not his own	402	Thee, Jesus, thee th' eternal Lord	423
The ulcers which I hide from man	365	Thee, Jesus, thee we glorify	147
		Thee, King of kings, I faint to see	488

841. *UP* 2:244.
842. *UP* 2:182.
843. *UP* 2:252.
844. *UP* 2:104.
845. *UP* 2:225.

Thee let me drink, and thirst no more	355	They did not keep thy charge enjoined	9
Thee let our actions glorify	119	They drag her out to public view	415
Thee let thy own love constrain	309	They, only they, the Lord invite	333
Thee Lord our law and rule we see	186	They promise all, seduced by one	76
Thee, Lord, that I may serve aright	4	They prove thine acceptable will	464
Thee, Lord, thy church confess	51	They see their meek expiring Lord	299
Thee, Lord, thy love constrains	216	They still a God unknown adore	55
Thee, Lord, we our Example see	222	They who never knew the Son	421
Thee, Lord, who on the tree	346	Thine Advocate in Jesus see!	418
Thee, Redeemer of mankind	427	Thine anger casts the sinner down	121
Thee, Son of the Most-High	323	Thine hand beneficent extend	30
Thee that I at last may please	207	Third of the glorious One-in-Three	129
Thee the Principle and Food	383	This demonstration of thy grace	336
Thee, the thrice holy God, I want	48	This figurative custom	84
Their debts to God who paid alone	227	This filth we first should purge away	4
Their deep calamity he sees	300	This happiness is mine	62
Their horror of assured disgrace	496	This happiness, O Lord, is mine	349
Their indolence would shun	220	"This night thou shalt deny me thrice"	75
Their Shepherd rising from the dead	95	This unbelief of heart	261
Their sin extorts th' indignant groan	476	Those hands on which my hopes depend	316
Their successors in vain	142	Those who will not seek him now	407
Then I may happy be	SH 1762, 2:253	Those who will not while they may	406
Then jarring sentiments shall cease	461	Thou art that Bread of life	381
Then let me patiently attend	250	Thou art the basis laid	52
Then let us hear the trumpet sound	201	Thou art the Christ of God	181
Then let us patiently attend	103	Thou bidd'st us take away the stone	477
Then let us urge our meek request	334	Thou by thy example guide	353
Then my dust his voice shall hear	470	Thou by thy foes confined	79
Then, my God, and not till then	428	Thou camest from above	215
Then our spotless spirits hide	257	Thou cam'st from God, we know	420
Then shall the lamp diffuse its blaze	207	Thou canst not Lord subsist alone	420
Then the prophets false we hear	276	Thou canst not speak distinct from him	402
Then, then his full ire On sinners is come	128	Thou canst not to our keeping trust	339
Then, then ye shall with anguish own	192	Thou city of the living God	20
Then we eat before thy throne	178	Thou didst foretell the fearful doom	422
There I shall transported see	63	Thou didst forsake thy throne above	310
These are the souls he sends	94	Thou didst once for sin atone	328
These lords thy subject have oppressed[846]	267	Thou didst thy Son bestow[847]	346
These the greater things which I	332	Thou dost for thy disciples care	289
They bid the Lord's disciples too	333	Thou dost from thy disciples part	317
They brand him whom they will not know	432	Thou dost in closest bonds unite	335
		Thou dost my helpless case behold	365

---

846. *UP* 2:178

847. *UP* 2:222.

Thou dost my pardon seal	262
Thou dost not Lord the rich condemn	274
Thou dost on whom thou wilt bestow	370
Thou dost out of the temple go	436
Thou dost the Spirit confer	323
Thou dost thy Godhead testify	436
Thou dost thy suppliant hear	261
Thou dost to every longing heart	483
Thou epicure not yet in hell	244
Thou hast a lovely one indeed	SH 1762, 2:256
Thou hast brought forth for me	238
Thou hast in me displayed	492
Thou hast o'ercome the world and sin	273
Thou hast took us by the hand	176
Thou hear'st me for salvation pray	44
Thou in the Gospel hast made known	499
Thou know'st what I would say	237
Thou long sought God of grace	43
Thou, my God, and thou alone	213
Thou need'st not feel th' infernal woe	245
Thou, O God, a Spirit art	358
Thou only by thy prayer and blood	183
Thou promisest thyself t' impart	356
Thou Saviour dost the wish impart	262
Thou say'st, the law is good and just	415
Thou tell'st me, "I thy King will be	109
Thou tell'st me, O most gracious Lord	109
Thou who art both God and man	199
Thou who forward art to hear	160
Thou who know'st a father's heart[848]	204
Thou wilt this secret bar remove	25
Thou workest all the works Divine	351
Though God in Christ reveal	170
Though long he seemed as distant far	49
Though men thy yoke disdain	296
Though now the good and evil meet	246
Thoughtless of what the world intends	405
Thrice solemn, thrice repeated word	29
Through sufferings our exalted head	308
Through thee and thine atoning blood	458
Through vanity I will not tell	442
Thus may I with faith sincere	165
Thus might I from man retreat	76
Thus throughout our course below	249
Thus, to save us it became	314
Thy church is here with saints supplied	31
Thy counsel is, to save me now	46
Thy day is come but never passed	435
Thy Father gave thee all mankind	384
Thy great commission to fulfil	498
Thy hand medicinal extend	224
Thy hand upon thy creature lay	16
Thy hands upon our children lay	32
Thy kingdom come, with power and grace	200
Thy kingdom, Lord, I fain would see	183
Thy law is in their inward parts	401
Thy love constrains thee to proclaim	140
Thy mercy grants the sinner's prayer	471
Thy murderers, now we learn of thee	425
Thy mystic body we	181
Thy peace into my troubled soul	141
Thy[849] people can a prophet know	269
Thy pound hath gained the pounds, not I	266
Thy precious sacrifice	216
Thy presence bids our troubles cease	471
Thy previous grace, which now I feel	16
Thy providence preserves, maintains	369
Thy saints in holiness complete	336
Thy Spirit, Lord, the water pure	503
Thy Spirit's hand apply	145
Thy touch medicinal we prove	440
Thy voice outspeaks, and strikes us dumb	417
Thy word enables me to rise	366
Thy word in the bare literal sense	392
Thy work, O God, they will not see	217
Thyself thou dost from them conceal	400
Thyself thou wouldst to sinners give	320
Till Jesus casts the veil aside	288
Till thou return to fetch thy bride	317
'Tis all foretold, th' impostor's art	64
'Tis all my longing soul's desire	488
'Tis all our blessed business here	65
'Tis not enough for me to know	363

---

848. *UP* 2:128.

849. Osborn changed "Thy" to "The."

'Tis not enough to speak for God	329	Troubled at heart and grieved within	506
'Tis not, O Lord, th' eternal part	404	Trouble's flood assaults in vain	160
'Tis now the woman's heavenly Seed	130	True Light of the whole world, appear	319
'Tis there the law is void at last	23	Tumults and wars serene he sees	61
'Tis thine, O God of grace	52	'Twas there I washed my sins away	441
'Tis thus a follower of the Lamb	421	Two and two, not one and one[852]	190
'Tis thus he for his followers cares	95		
'Tis thus he teaches them t' aspire	93		

Volume XII

'Tis thus the world thy love repays	369	Taught by our Lord we will not pray	64
To all our guilty brethren	330	Taught to teach thy people here	309
To all the twelve thou wouldst not show	23	Teacher of hearts, 'tis thine alone	140
To an unrighteous judge she came	255	Tears of saints! how can it be	380
To change the soul's ignoble taste	336	Temple, or house, or barn, or school	359
To Christ ascribing my success	192	Ten thousand thousand in our isle	348
To David's Son and sovereign Lord	298	Terrible thy judgments are	140
To each seducer they give ear	60	That all may think and speak the same	29
T' escape thy persecuting foes	395	That change entire of life and heart	257
To him the Doorkeeper above	455	That day by earliest saints confessed	366
To me that Spirit of wisdom give	309	That Fire enflames the heart	143
To rectify my crooked will[850]	125	That gladness of heart	156
To simple souls alone	116	That happiest day I long to see	14
To tend the great Jehovah's heirs	227	That irresistible I AM	66
To that sacramental feast	399	That kingdom of his Which Jesus imparts	454
To the hedges and highways	230	That Man among the sons of men	112
To thee I now draw near	173	That none of thine elect may boast	53
To thee our lawful Sovereign	88	That Spirit pure of truth and love	55
To this, O God, thou hast us wrought	386	That thou art God Most-High	9
To thy holy saving name	119	That warmth without excess	383
To thy poor unfaithful creature	310	Th' accursed love of money leads	317
To us a Child of royal birth	117	The actions of the sent	134
To us at thy feet The Comforter give	408	The affections of grace	156
To whom but Jesus shall we run	171	The angel from Jehovah sent	244
Tormented I confess	187	The angel might have preached his Lord	244
Touched by thine efficacious grace	163	The angels too, th' accusing fiends	417
Transformed by the ecstatic sight	322	Th' apostle gloried in distress	371
Traveller, see thy gracious day	494	Th' apostles fly the faithless race	287
Tremble thou careless minister[851]	266	Th' ascending Son of God	138
Tremble who slight the word ye hear	192	The authors of their flock's distress	305
Tremble whoe'er thou art	154	The awful prophecy	282
Tremble ye that preach the word	134	The battered ship, by tempest tossed[853]	444
Triumph we the sons of grace	116		

---

850. UP 2:86.
851. UP 2:175.
852. UP 2:116.
853. UP 2:431.

The bleeding Lamb before our eyes	177	The Gift unspeakable thou art	41
The blessing I implore	159	The glare of royal pageantry	420
The body he did once assume	164	The glory of God's only Son	58
The body pure of flesh and blood	164	The God made man	378
The Breath of Christ, that Spirit is	107	The God of all grace	167
The captain doth the priests defeat	406	The gospel some with scorn refuse	345
The cause is in yourselves unknown	453	The gospel then ye hear in vain	454
The chief of saints may well express	384	The grain of wheat, the quickened grain	204
The church engrosses all their care	310	The great are compassed round by those	275
The church his house and kingdom	204	The great Invisible, unknown	7
The church in ancient days	157	The greatest miracles of grace	175
The church's servant should be wise[854]	255	The hatred of our ancient foe	29
The city they with uproar fill	329	The heart which in thy Son confides	301
The Comforter bestowed	370	The heathen dreads his righteous doom	414
The company of faithful men	355	The heathens still thy creatures are	305
The confessor of Jesus	405	The heavenly light to all appeared	395
The consolation from above	441	The hoary saint for heaven mature	127
The counsel learned in the laws	408	The Holy Ghost, th' eternal Lord	453
The counsel of the Lord	376	The holy Jesus rests in hope[857]	99
The coward Peter had denied	87	The holy unconcern	375
The creature of my God	439	The human beasts they rouse	390
The creature was created good	246	Th' imperial dignity alone	416
The cruel murderers of our God[855]	78	Th' infernal jailer stood before	266
The desperate crowd	186	The innocent atoning Lamb	132
The dire effects of envious pride	175	The instruments to save their souls	444
The door which Christ displays	455	The judge corrupt and most unjust	408
The dust shook off, shall rise	286	The judge his innocence confessed	422
The emblem had in trembling haste	64	The kinsmen of the Lord	139
The everlasting gospel hear	249	The Lamb, they say, disturbs the stream	330
The evils which the church befall	178	The law and prophets all foretold	430
The faith of Paul they see	443	The law our irksome duty shows	302
The Father of our Lord	193	The life of a true pastor	134
The fault, if fault indeed there was	310	The long-predicted things	35
The fierceness of men Who threaten so loud	365	The Lord hath spoke, the faithful Lord	441
		The Lord Most-High on earth was seen	146
The firmness of one, Who follows his call	386	The Lord of all, he knows	422
The fishers of men In love should agree	114	The Lord our persecutors knows	325
The flight of those by Jesus sent[856]	290	The Lord to every soul is good	249
The foes of truth, by malice joined	402	The Lord who sends by whom he will	353
The full meridian blaze	394	The Lord whoever truly hears	315
		The love of Jesu's cross how rare!	37

854. *UP* 2:343.
855. *UP* 2:270.
856. *UP* 2:360.
857. *UP* 2:204.

The love which worldly men pretend[858]	362	The prisoner of the Lord	449
The Man of griefs by all despised[859]	79	The progress of thy word	134
The man that hath, that still remains	354	The promised Spirit of holiness	151
The man who praise from man receives	272	The prophecies foreshowed	281
The Man who suffered in our stead	344	The prudence which thy love bestows	366
The martyrs thus their strength received	88	The publicans hear his peace-giving word	455
The meanest saint who Jesus knows	354	The pure baptismal Fire	256
The means of life to gain	436	The reconciling word	19
The members here and head above	234	The reign of sin and death is o'er[861]	100
The members one with Christ their head	417	The rich and great of Festus learn	420
The men who human praise desire	77	The rich they set below the poor	330
The men who public peace maintain	409	The Rock is smote by Moses' rod	89
The men whom thou hast inly moved	141	The sacred book on man bestowed	308
The messengers they cannot miss	287	The sacrilegious power bestowed	232
The modern infidels are bold	145	The saint whom those outrageous Jews	416
The modern Sadducees	402	The Saviour doth in various ways	113
The moment we direction need	227	The Saviour never supersedes	442
The more like thee we live	26	The Saviour we love	122
The mournful church, of James bereft	264	The seers and holy men of old	167
The mystical sign	135	The Shepherd good rejoiced to keep	52
Th' omniscient Lord	44	The sight without the touch compelled	111
The only sinless Man and just	92	The sinful will of man	163
The outcasts of men, The reprobate race	454	The sinners unclean Are washed in his blood	251
The pagan deities of old	364	The sinners who his counsel slight	438
The pastor called a soul to aid	101	The solemn interdict of blood	307
The pastor when his flock he leaves	311	The Son of God himself he made	80
The paths of life to thee he showed	150	The sons of violence misuse	329
The people praise a pardoning God	178	The sons of wickedness	284
The people saved below	157	The sovereign Cause and End of all	249
The persecuted man	400	The sovereign everlasting Lord	230
The persecuted pair	346	The Spirit had to them foreshown	381
The person sanctifies the place	318	The Spirit of that heavenly Man	146
The Pharisee was proud and blind	235	The stubborn fiend will not give place	361
The Pharisees maintain	402	The stupendous things of God	338
The place apostates know	65	The sufferers who his name confess	321
The poor afflicted saints[860]	242	The tempest may roar	440
The poor and blind receive their sight	452	The tools of bad revengeful men	317
The poor might well embrace	242	The truly Christian man alone	262
The power of efficacious love	303	The type in Moses we confess	206
The prayer of those that Jesus love	269	The types and figures are fulfilled[862]	100

858. *UP* 2:395.
859. *UP* 2:271.
860. See *UP* 2:333.
861. *UP* 2:278.
862. *UP* 2:278.

IDEX OF FIRST LINES OF POETRY BY JOHN AND CHARLES WESLEY

The unbelieving heart's unclean	299	Thee, the truth we testify[865]	76
The universal fault[863]	364	Thee we never could have chose[866]	27
Th' unrighteous world with malice blind	417	Thee we preach to sinful men	229
The unspeakable Grace	284	Their advocate with others I	412
The veil is rent in Christ alone[864]	100	Their dazzling state let faith compare	421
The view of heavenly things	137	Their hate they can no further show	177
The vision doth a church present	245	Their ignorance, we find	35
The vision of those glorious scars	106	Their impotent foes	156
The war against thy people dear	233	Their narrowness of heart they show	253
The wary magistrate we praise	349	Their prayer calls down th' eternal King	319
The waves of the sea When highest they rise	365	Their successors we find	114
The way to God thou art	5	Their unsuspected guilt reveal	426
The wisdom of our God adore	232	Their wonder plainly showed	269
The witness of the Lord is sure	298	Themselves the false conclusion draw	389
The witnesses appear	162	Then behold the heavenly Lamb	226
The witnesses by Jesus sent	425	Then I shall to thee reply	124
The witnesses who cried so loud	412	Then let us all beware	282
The word conditional he knew	441	Then let us each to other give	96
The word is crowned with more success	170	Then Lord—but trembling I forbear	128
The word of pardoning grace	18	Then, Lord, thy fallen murderers raise	426
The world did thus thy saints entreat	318	Then shall my actions show	10
The world exult to see pursued	70	Then, then to their immortal state	379
The world fulfil their Saviour's word	144	Then we testify his grace	266
The world in every age the same	326	These, these are Israel's horsemen	405
The world may thus our words deny	32	They creep on earth who gold adore	255
The world our unrelenting foe	30	They felt the sharp two-edged sword	193
The world sometimes their rage suppress	189	They had nothing to plead	304
The world which lies in wickedness	330	They heard the strange unwonted sound	319
The world, who know not God	34	They heard the voice so rarely heard	319
The worldling shrinks at famine near	262	They promised him again to hear	345
The wretch so impious and profane	390	They spake more boldly than before	288
The written word, entire and pure	411	They vow he shall no longer live	390
Thee Jesus, and thy church below	304	They will not enemies withstand	189
Thee Jesus, I adore	25	They would not obstinate appear	326
Thee, Jesus, I believe the Son	230	Things which from without befal[l] us	246
Thee Jesus we confess	6	This comfort is for you	117
Thee, Lord, and thee alone	20	This earth on which awhile we stay	201
Thee may I ever keep in view	81	This fervency of good desire	283
Thee the theme of all their praises	105	This is our consolation, Lord	29

---

863. UP 2:397.
864. UP 2:278: "The veil is rent, the Way is shewn."
865. Osborn switches the first and third lines of this poem and makes line three the first: God descended from the sky.
866. UP 2:264.

This is the consecrated way[867]	293	Through faith we then are saved by grace	303
This the doctrine new receive	338	Through fear of the self-righteous Jews	91
This the work of thy right hand	146	Through him empowered I am	42
Those callous hands extended see	379	Through humility and patience	83
Those many things at first unknown	39	Through the ministry of man	161
Those sacred hands on sinners laid	379	Through the name and sprinkled blood	179
Those steps I never should have took	268	Through the pure evangelic word	64
Those voluntary bonds of thine	73	Thus from error's endless maze	313
Those who quaked and could not bear	165	Thus my few remaining days	258
Thou didst by thy garment's hem	10	Thus the truth of God we witness	127
Thou didst inspire his mortal frame	108	Thus thy Father's kind intent	59
Thou didst rejoice t' obey	25	Thus thy testimony give	289
Thou dost his name to men declare	48	Thy days of flesh are ended	43
Thou hast employed thy servants	387	Thy Father's mind through thee we know	8
Thou hast enrolled our names above	4	Thy friends instructed are by thee	27
Thou his name unspeakable	61	Thy gospel-minister	375
Thou know'st my mediator's mind	41	Thy grace our souls revives	21
Thou know'st, that now I love thee not	124	Thy least disciple, I	119
Thou laid'st on earth the steadfast base	49	Thy love's an emanation	24
Thou, Lord, and thou alone	279	Thy members must their trial take	54
Thou, Lord, art greatly to be feared	184	Thy members with thyself are one	14
Thou Saviour by thy sacred bands	72	Thy painful days of flesh are o'er	63
Thou seest my helplessness	159	Thy peace to rule my heart and mind	136
Thou the Saviour of mankind	229	Thy poor external worshipper	339
Thou them in their distress	233	Thy power doth now their rage confine	81
Thou who freely didst resign	124	Thy prayer I daily feel	42
Thou who hast cast me down	427	Thy prayer the world sustains	42
Thou who hast undertook our cause	4	Thy presence makes the hallowed place	302
Thou who once didst shake the place	180	Thy promised grace I dare not say	137
Thou wilt set thyself before us	217	Thy prophetic word we find	178
Thou wouldst not from the people take	79	Thy providence explains thy will	232
Thou wouldst on every soul bestow	48	Thy servant here I still remain	429
Though a few might suffice	250	Thy servants, Lord, in every age	318
Though our vessel be broke	445	Thy servants, Lord, they must dismiss	68
Three days he bears th' Egyptian load	235	Thy Spirit helps them to believe	428
Three days he groans deprived of sight	235	Thy Spirit of faith from above	211
Thrice happy prisoner of the Lord	384	Thy voice that dying sinner cheers	96
Thrice he promised to confess	73	Thy weak disciple I	33
Through faith in the God-Man	343	Thy wonders wrought already	388
Through faith their pardoned sin they know	428	Thy word of grace sufficient is	379
		Thy zeal to save my ransomed soul	124
		Thyself lay hold on me	160
		Till the Crucified appears	124

867. UP 2:364.

Till then I would my hands employ	241
'Tis all our joy, while here below	383
'Tis finished! all the debt is paid[868]	100
'Tis finished! the messias dies[869]	99
'Tis here my nature's state I see!	266
'Tis not a slight offence to start	310
'Tis not for sin which thou hast done[870]	98
'Tis not the name, but thing	334
'Tis thus our baffled foes	401
'Tis thus our fierce unrighteous foes	74
'Tis thus the legalists mistake	389
'Tis thus with faithful Paul	443
To be thy ministers above	27
To beasts we aptly may compare	255
To each he severally applies[871]	353
To each sinful inclination	212
T' elude his wonders and suppress	175
To envy's general calumny	417
To God each other they commend	311
To groundless lies and slanders bold	406
To Jews and Gentiles sent we feel	428
To magistrates of God ordained	423
To me, almighty Saviour, give	315
To opposite extremes so prone	447
To save an infidel from sin	396
To succour man whate'er is done	378
To the multitude enraged	363
To the saints of thine election	135
To the temple of God	156
To the world and Satan sold	225
To us the new command he gives	96
Tongues are multiplied again	143
Tongues at first were multiplied	143
Touched by the blood your souls are clean	152
Transported by prophetic zeal[872]	401
Tremble thou hypocrite profane	182
Tremendous change! the reverend guide	139
Triumphant through thy mortal pain	106
True Light of mankind	284
True love will readily give place	335
True Paschal Lamb, to thee I look	90
Truth, not ourselves, to justify	431
Turn, sinners, turn from such away	333
Turning with contrite hearts to God	151
'Twas not the way of Pagan Rome	419
'Twas then the heavenly messenger	266
Twelve at first must testify	140
Two are better far than one	351
Two or three in Jesus' name, / According	382
Two or three in Jesus' name / met	434
Tyrants of the sea and land	436

Volume XIII

Taught by the oracles of God	27
Tell me my faith hath made me whole	191
Tempted by their besetting sin	53
Tempted like us our Saviour was	127
Tempted souls, your Lord descry	246
Thanks upon thanks to God we owe	77
That childish ignorance of ill	36
That finished holiness alone	160
That finished holiness / my calling's prize	159
That liberty from sin	64
That patience of unwearied hope	90
That sea of love in me be found	98
That steadfast faith Divine	112
That work of faith the novice blind	89
That wretched man accursed am I	43
Th' abominable thing unclean	52
The babes are weak, the youths are strong	198
The blood of goats and bullocks slain	139
The blood which made our conscience pure	13
The body and the deathless soul	187
The brightness of his face	74
The cause of separation	46
The caution is not vain	215
The children every one partake	156
The children's mark I surely bear	155

---

868. UP 2:277.
869. UP 2:277.
870. Osborn changed to: 'Twas not for sin which thou hadst done.
871. UP 2:387.
872. UP 2:412.

The Christian rule to few is known	69	The mystery so long unknown	84
The church in her militant state	239	The name, the cross we love	112
The city drunk with martyrs' blood	252	The news of his coming I hear	239
The Comforter assures our hearts[873]	25	Th' occasion of my every fall	196
The crooked things shall at thy word	256	The old congenial man of sin	6
The desert to the garden brought	127	The peace and the power, Ye sinners embrace	248
Th' effect must from the cause proceed	208		
The elder serves the younger now	14	The peace thy people know	5
The faith distinct from works is dead	168	The power and excellence Divine	46
The faithful saying of my Lord	99	The power of faith his works begot	170
The Father from his bosom gave	50	The preacher of the Gospel word	281
The father of the faithful seed	169	The process of that dreadful day[875]	27
The flesh and Spirit's strife	185	The promise here of perfect love	147
The foolishness of preaching hear	22	The promise is free	240
The form of godliness remains	107	The promise sure to Abraham made	63
The gift, the blessing, and the grace	63	The rich in every place and age	168
The gift unspeakable procured	63	The riches of thy pardoning grace	4
The gift unspeakable	72	The righteousness thy law requires	10
The good, which we could never find	158	The saints who die of Christ possest	236
The gospel-husbandman, like him	175	The same I yesterday did prove	162
The gospel mystery	85	The secret lessons of thy grace	110
The grace and peace of God	115	The self-existing God supreme	211
The grace I every moment want	129	The sentence passed on Adam's race	140
The grace of a pacified God	7	The sinner's Sacrifice	257
The grace of God in thee	9	The smoke alas, must still ascend	236
The grace with Christ bestowed	217	The solemn hour is come	257
The heaven above our head	265	The solemn thoughtfulness impart	262
The heavenly way to find	184	The Son, at God's right hand he sits	142
The holiest, who their watch remit	89	The souls whom separated for his	143
The honours worldly men admire	211	The state of fathers, who shall tell	198
The kingdom of his grace alone	174	The steadfast word of God and sure	156
The law of glorious liberty	138	The sufferings which the body bears	83
The legal priests as servants stood	142	The things thy free unbounded love[876]	25
The living power, which saves from sin	107	The thirsty are called to their Lord	239
The living principle of grace	212	The treasure of celestial grace	45
The Lord to us who now believe[874]	25	The trials still behind	33
The man by faith who truly lives	216	The true and faithful Witness, we	210
The men that know not God	83	The true believer's challenge hear	169
The merit of Jehovah's Son	60	The truth of our God We boldly assert	248
The mirth of fools, the jest unfit	263	The unbelief that holds me still	281
The moment we begin our race	151	The word doth Christ, the Word, declare	259

873. *UP* 2:460.
874. *UP* 2:461.
875. *UP* 2:462.
876. *UP* 2:461.

INDEX OF FIRST LINES OF POETRY BY JOHN AND CHARLES WESLEY

The word if thou vouchsafe to give	109	This blessed word be mine	111
The word of God by all confessed	258	This dire propensity to ill	11
The word which we declare and feel	263	This flesh at the last gasp restores	39
The work of faith with heaven begun	89	This hope of holiness	82
The world, and its god	235	This instant now I may receive	140
The world he must not seek to please	282	This is the time: I surely may	51
The wrath of frantic man[877]	166	This moment, Lord, thou ready art	51
Thee may we every moment see	268	This my sole employment be	153
Their counsels aggravate my grief	124	This pain, this consecrated pain	158
Their earthly task who fail to do	17	This solemn exhibition	260
Their instrumental aid unknown	119	This stubborn bent to evil	197
Them, Lord, we in thy strength pursue	283	This the fruit of Jesus' passion	91
Then am I bound (if charity	76	Thou art gone up on high	72
"Then know thy place," (a novice cries	79	Thou bidd'st me put my sins away	194
Then let me calmly flee[878]	166	Thou by that immortal hope	154
Then let me meet my three-fold foe	232	Thou canst thy weakest servant keep	254
Then let me see my Saviour's face	160	Thou didst not work, that I secure	181
Then let me thee my Pattern trace	181	Thou God of my salvation	197
Then let thy peace	81	Thou great, mysterious Three in One	238
Then let us still his cross sustain	158	Thou hast by thy hallowing blood	233
Then my soul with strange delight	101	Thou know'st the treachery of my heart	254
Then, only then my God I know	204	Thou, Lord, on whom I still depend	223
Then shall the word on me take place	227	Thou, Lord, who didst our faith bestow	225
Then should I with my Saviour sup	231	Thou Man of affliction and woe	105
Then, then my soul with rapid speed	125	Thou man of an unbridled tongue	166
Then, then our full Redemption be	23	Thou Man of griefs, remember me	129
Then we whose flesh is troubled here	96	Thou seest I know not what to do	256
Then would I cheerfully resign	215	Thou send'st his Spirit into my heart[879]	25
Then would your guides their charge attend	29	Thou waitest now to show thy grace	51
		Thou, who didst so greatly stoop	101
There, at thy throne of grace we meet	128	Thou who gav'st the word to all	40
There he ever lives to plead	126	Thou who my utmost Saviour art	200
There is no fear in love	208	Thou wilt in me thy arm reveal	254
There is one God, thou dost believe	169	Thou universal Lover	44
There we see our great High-Priest	143	Though our mighty sins demand	266
There your exalted Saviour see	86	Though slow of heart, we comprehend	157
These are the followers of their Lord	96	Thrice acceptable word	49
These evil thoughts, these foul desires	252	Through him the Crucified I know	259
They on the hidden Manna feed	224	Through him who did for sinners die	136
Thine image of true holiness	195	Through Jesus our Divine High-Priest	128
This be the genuine proof of mine	213	Through life's short waking dream	92

877. UP 2:470.
878. UP 2:471.
879. UP 2:461.

Throughout my fallen soul I feel / Salvation	160	T' exalt myself I would not speak	261
Throughout my fallen soul I find	281	To him our willing hearts we give	86
Thus may I give, when man I praise	95	To his royal proclamation	218
Thus may I show thy Spirit within	167	To none of the believing race	157
Thus only may I trust in man	97	To save my soul from endless woe	68
Thy blood was shed for me in vain	146	To the Father of mercies we show	260
Thy blood which pleaded on the cross	252	To the glory of the Lord	34
Thy call I exult to obey	239	To thee my last distress I bring	130
Thy covenant of redeeming grace	138	To this poor heart of mine	85
Thy cross on soul and body lay	165	To whom should I fly for relief	188
Thy God's mysterious grace	186	To Zion's sacred top	217
Thy hand, thy gracious Spirit exert	252	Tossed too long by every wind	41
Thy hasty servant, Lord, restrain	207	Triumphant with the saints above	248
Thy kingdom come in power	197	True and faithful Witness, thee	219
Thy love must be the seal	258	Trusting in his faithful word	148
Thy mind throughout my life be shown	167	Trusting in our Lord alone	126
Thy passion, Lord, and not our own	120	'Twas thus, not yet awakened, dead	229
Thy patience forces me to hope	188		
Thy servant, Lord, prepare	177		

Volume I

Thy Spirit doth the power infuse	259	*Unchangeable, Almighty Lord, / The true*	236
Thy Spirit doth the truth reveal	259	Unwearied may I this pursue[881]	139
Thy Spirit in my heart explains[880]	26	Upborne on this, I mount, I fly[882]	114
Thy Spirit in our inward parts	11	Uphold me in the doubtful race[883]	177
Thy Spirit which wholly sanctifies	115	Upward on wings of love I fly	304
Thy trials yet behind	186	Us into closest union draw	298
Thy vengeful wrath's resistless power	187		
Thy wounded side, to which alone	268		

Volume II

Thyself Jehovah's Son	250	*Unchangeable Almighty Lord, / Our souls*	333
Till he knows it is best	163	Under the law no more enslaved	247
Till thou the answer give	265	Unto righteousness I still	241
Till thy welcome will is done	270	Unto salvation kept I am	243
Tired with the follies of mankind	251	Unto thee, my help, my hope	268
'Tis here I seek and hope to find	259	Unto this thrice happy state	297
'Tis then my faith attains its end	58	Up into thee, our living head	136
'Tis this essentially divides	207	Uphold me, Saviour, or I fall	272
'Tis this must banish my complaints	113	Upon me lay thy mighty hand	140
'Tis thus we in our manner say	236		
To all, who hallowing grace obtain	77		
To Christ a wretched stranger	44		
To-day, while it is called to-day	122		
To every ransomed creature	198		

880. *UP* 2:462.

881. From the German of Paul Gerhardt, translated by John Wesley.

882. George Herbert.

883. From the German of Johann Angelus Scheffler, translated by John Wesley.

Upon my head his candle shone	120	Unutterable things I see!	340
Upon thy gracious promise, Lord[884]	9	Unwarned of her release so near	362
		Unworthy of her longer stay	263
		Unworthy of the blessing lent	292
		Upheld by thine almighty hand	163

Volume III

Unless to all thy bowels move	65
Unseal the volume of thy grace	237
Unsustained by thee I fall	250
Until their cities are destroyed	137
Upon my mouth he gently laid	134

Upright she walked in open day 328
Urged to the last extremity 157
Us, for the sake of Christ, he loves 447
Us, whoe'er the gift receive 376

Volume VII

Unconscious of the yawning deep	409
Under the galling iron yoke	168
United with thy sacrifice	406
Unless restrained by grace we are	76
Unless thou wash my life from sin	368
Unnumbered deaths and snares	392
Us by thy peace assure	13

Volume IV

Unhurt I bear the fiery test	468
Unsearchable the love	110
Unto thy heavenly kingdom keep	67
Unworthy to be called thy son	429
Us by thy Spirit certify	158
Us, who before the sons of men	32

Volume V

Unchangeable, almighty Lord, / The promise	126
Unfold the hidden mystery	336
United in the closest bands	477
Unknown to men, and meanly born	197
Urge on your rapid course	36
Us, and our brethren in distress	243
Us into thy protection take	34
Us, who join on earth t' adore thee	456

Volume VIII

Unappalled by guilty fear	47
Unhappy Charles, mistaken and misled	445
Unhappy Langdale! Who could see	460
Unhurt thou shalt on adders tread	176
Unite my heart to all that bear	405
Universal Saviour, thou	299
Unless the king his troops withdraw	472
Unless the stony thou remove	371
Unless, while at the point to die	381
Unsearchable thy judgments are	79
Unto God, my Rock, I say	97
Upborne aloft on venturous wing	191
Upon thy servant make	63

Volume VI

Unassisted by thy grace	383
Unconscious of the grace received	249
Unconscious of the love bestowed	295
Unite the pair so long disjoined	408
Unless the Most High For Israel had stood	183
Unless the power of heavenly grace	410
Unspotted from the world, and pure	408

Volume IX

Unauthorised by right Divine	165
Uncertain what my end shall be	250
Under the yoke, O God, to thee	146
Unholy, of an holy God	62
Unlike my God I cannot rest	277

884. David Lewis.

Unsavoury all our offerings are	58
Unstable, Lord, by nature I	31
Unveil the beauties of thy face	360
Unwearied let us still request	20
Up to my Saviour given	284
Upright both in heart and will	357
Urged by the world and Satan I	231
Us that his righteous Spirit grieved	272

Volume X

Unadorned and unarrayed	351
Unbaptized, in sin I live	446
Unclean, of life and heart unclean	224
United in a common cause	299
United to our head	316
Unprofitable all and vain	189
Unworthy to live, Our Saviour we own	48
Us in their hands the angels bear	153
Us who climb thy holy hill	55
Usurpers of the Christian name	313

Volume XI

Under thy shade, O Christ, we sing	335
Unless a constant watch I keep	78
Unless thy warnings we despise	64
Us through rebellion lost	265
Us, when our Lord the victory gives	133
Useless disputes, reflections vain	409

Volume XII

Unawed by man's authority	176
Under the conduct of thy grace	268
Ungrateful as I am	45
United in heart Together we go	114
Unless we faith receive	19
Unmoved by human hope or fear	277
Unmoved the pillars stand	220
Unspeakably blessed	448
Unworthy of the ministry	307
Up from the sleep of nature stirred	333
Upon thy faithful mercies stayed	12
Urged by his old infernal lord	320
Us each to other he commends	96

Volume XIII

Unless thy Spirit the truth reveal[885]	36
Unmixed with faith, the Scripture gives	124
Upright now my heart and true	144
Urged, surrounded with temptations	147
Us, who would do the Saviour's will	147

Volume I

Vain man has measured land and sea[886]	27
Vain the stone, the watch, the seal	185
Vain thy entertaining sights[887]	17
Veiled in flesh, the Godhead see	183
Visit, then, this soul of mine	225

Volume II

Vain, delusive world, adieu	315
Vain man, of mortal parents born	28
Vanishing out of my sight	277
Vanity, the serpent-seed	79
Vengeance Divine is always near	121
Vessels of mercy, sons of grace	171
Vilest of all the sons of men / him in his	172
Vilest of all the sons of men, / When I	232
Vouchsafe to keep my soul from sin	140

Volume III

Vain in themselves their duties were	307

885. *UP* 2:464: "Unless thy Spirit the truth reveal."
886. George Herbert.
887. From the French, Antoinette Bourignon.

INDEX OF FIRST LINES OF POETRY BY JOHN AND CHARLES WESLEY

Victim Divine, thy grace we claim	301
Vilest of the fallen race	333

Volume IV

Vain are thy tears and late remorse	348
Vanishes hence whate'er is seen	301
Viler still, if that can be	58
Vilest of all th' apostate race / I have	392

Volume V

Vilest of all th' apostate race, / Who dare	123
Virtue Divine, balsamic Word	64
Visit, Lord, with thy salvation	54
Vouchsafe to keep me, Lord, this day / Without	4
Vouchsafe to keep me, Lord, this day, / And	5
Vying with that happy choir	280

Volume VI

Vanish then the world of shadows	93
Vapours and damps confessed their God	32
Vengeance on thy foes to take	23

Volume VII

Very man, and very God	241
Vessels, instruments of grace	47
Victorious, with thy cross in view	66
Vouchsafe us eyes of faith to see	24

Volume VIII

Vain help, alas, which never came	461
Vainly in our protection join	396
Vapours, fire, and hail, and snow	330
Virtuous, wise, without pretence	302
Visit me in tender love	220
Vouchsafe me then the wish sincere	355

Volume IX

Vessels of thy free election	390
Viler than Manasses I	218
Vilest of the sinful race	157
Visit us, bright Morning-Star	388
Vouchsafe the grace for which I pray	169

Volume X

Vainest man affects applause	489
Vanity, concupiscence	81
Vanquished by the word Divine	222

Volume XI

Vanish then this old creation	66
Vengeance doth to God belong	189
Very God I thee confess	294
Very man of very man	338
Vile and wretched as the worst	6
Voice of all the prophets old	466
Vouchsafe us, Lord, that humble fear	134

Volume XII

Virtue by few embraced	85
Virtue still proceeds from thee	173

Volume XIII

Vain man, who dost dispute the need	156
Vain of your gifts and boasted grace	186
Vain, wretched man, whose fond desire	236
Vanquished by injurious ill	19

Volume I

Waft me to that happy shore	257
Wait, ye righteous spirits, wait	366
Was there a man thou doom'st to die	309
Was there a single soul decreed	309

Wash me, and make me thus thine own	283	What in thy love possess I not?[896]	140
Wash out its stains, refine its dross[888]	137	What is a worthless worm to thee?[897]	222
Wayward they haste, while Nature leads[889]	59	What lingering anguish must corrode[898]	35
We are now in Jesus found	289	*What morn on thee with sweeter ray*	180
We behold (the abjects we)	290	What mortal formed of fading clay[899]	122
We boast of our recovered powers	231	What pleasures could I want who served[900]	36
We deem the saints from mortal flesh[890]	15	What shall I say thy grace to move?	84
We feelingly believe thou art	211	What strange pollutions does he wed[901]	59
We now our elder brethren meet	221	What streams of sweetness from the bowl[902]	113
We now the writing see	337	What then is he whose scorn I dread[903]	178
We, O Christ, have thee received	359	What though I cannot break my chain	270
We our elder brethren meet	363	What though my sins against me cried[904]	102
We the evil angels doom	298	What though once we perished all	186
We too by faith the world condemn	212	What though the floods lift up their voice	231
We wait; for since the world began	367	What though the throne I then should fill[905]	30
We, we would die for Jesus too!	346	What though thou rulest not?[906]	127
We with them to God are come	363	What though we all as wandering sheep	79
Wealth, honour, pleasure, or what else[891]	111	Whate'er I fondly counted mine	132
Weary of struggling with my pain	82	Whate'er our ardent souls require[907]	125
Welcome, Contempt! Stern, faithful guide	25	Whate'er the Father views as thine	173
Welcome, delicious sacred cheer[892]	113	*When all the secrets of my heart*[908]	61
Welcome from earth!—Lo! the right hand	341	*When Christ had left his flock below*[909]	165
Well have I weighed it, Lord, and find[893]	28	When darkness intercepts the skies	136
Well thou know'st I cannot rest	254		
What are our works but sin and death[894]	266		
What has not man sought out and found[895]	17		
What have I felt, while torn within	335		
What have I known since thee I knew!	335		
What have I then wherein to trust?	277		
What if here awhile thou grieve	330		

888. From the German of Nikolaus von Zinzendorf, translated by John Wesley.
889. George Herbert.
890. Monsigneur De Renty.
891. From the French, Antoinette Bourignon.
892. George Herbert.
893. George Herbert.
894. From the German of Nikolaus von Zinzendorf, translated by John Wesley.
895. George Herbert.
896. From the German of Paul Gerhardt, translated by John Wesley.
897. From the German of Maria Böhmer.
898. John Gambold?
899. Samuel Wesley, Sr.
900. George Herbert.
901. George Herbert.
902. George Herbert.
903. From the German of Johann Joseph Winckler, translated by John Wesley.
904. George Herbert.
905. George Herbert.
906. From the German of Paul Gerhardt, translated by John Wesley.
907. George Herbert.
908. George Herbert.
909. Henry More.

IDEX OF FIRST LINES OF POETRY BY JOHN AND CHARLES WESLEY

First line	Page
When first my feeble verse essayed[910]	107
When first thou didst entice my heart[911]	36
When first thy gracious eye's survey[912]	103
When from the dust of death I rise[913]	348
When fully he my faith hath tried	326
When God invites, shall man repel?	313
When, gracious Lord, ah, tell me when	250
When I thy promised Christ have seen	74
When I was a little child	320
When man was lost, Love looked about[914]	64
When my warmed thoughts I fix on thee[915]	86
When, O my God, shall I	150
When, O, when wilt thou appear?	224
When on the margin of the grave	73
When pain o'er my weak flesh prevails[916]	129
When passing through the watery deep	136
When rising floods my head o'erflow[917]	137
When shall concupiscence and pride	83
When shall I hear the inward voice	307
When shall I see the welcome hour	328
When shall my eye affect my heart	134
When shall our souls regain the skies	191
When shall thy love constrain	267
When thou arisest, Lord[918]	126
When thou for sin rebukest man	62
When thou, my Lord, my God art nigh[919]	69
When thou shalt call in that great day[920]	348
When thou shalt look us out of pain[921]	103
When to him I would not look	321
When will the dear deliverance come?	245
When wilt thou my whole heart subdue?	241
When wilt thou sin and grief destroy	62
Whence to me this waste of love	272
Where am I now, or what my hope?	234
Where earth and hell no more molest	345
Where has my slumbering spirit been	23
Where have they hid the world so long	23
Where humbly low our fathers bowed	369
Where is my God? What secret place[922]	68
Where is the blessedness bestowed	258
Where, my soul, is now thy boast?	324
Where none but the all-seeing eye	250
Where shall I lay my weary head	261
Where shall my wondering soul begin	91
Where shall we find its high abode?	13
Where the ancient dragon lay	291
Where thy Indubitable Seal	308
Where thorns deformed the barren ground	209
Where thou, and only thou art loved	243
Where Zeal holds on its even course	14
Wherefore I cry, and cry again[923]	41
Wherefore in confidence I close	307
Wherefore with all my strength and art[924]	102
Wherewith, O God, shall I draw near	276
Which shall I leave, and which pursue?	24
While all, in sweet devotion joined[925]	165
While dead in trespasses I lie	264
While, full of anguish and disease	264
While groaning at thy feet I fall	85
While in these regions here below[926]	110
While in thy word we search for thee	237
While midnight shades the earth o'erspread	49

910. George Herbert.
911. George Herbert.
912. George Herbert.
913. From the German of Nikolaus von Zinzendorf, translated by John Wesley.
914. George Herbert.
915. From the German of Christian Friedrich Richter, translated by John Wesley.
916. From the German of Christian Friedrich Richter, translated by John Wesley.
917. From the German of Nikolaus von Zinzendorf, translated by John Wesley.
918. From the German of Paul Gerhardt, translated by John Wesley.
919. George Herbert.
920. From the German of Nikolaus von Zinzendorf, translated by John Wesley.
921. George Herbert.
922. George Herbert.
923. George Herbert.
924. George Herbert.
925. Henry More.
926. From the French, Antoinette Bourignon.

While sad my heart, and blasted mourns[927]	44	Why do the deeds of happier men[937]	51
While sickness shakes the house of clay	242	Why do these cares my soul divide	131
While thou art intimately nigh	306	Why hopes for help my drooping heart	274
While through the sea by faith they past	218	Why seek ye that which is not bread	206
While torn by hellish pride, I cry	264	Why sleeps my principle divine	94
While we walk with God in light	353	Why then in this unequal strife	274
While Zeal its heavenly influence sheds	15	Why then with unavailing rage	295
Whither, O whither art thou fled[928]	68	Why should a sinful man complain	247
Whither, O, whither should I fly	323	Why should I longer stay and groan?[938]	65
Whither should my glad soul aspire	242	Why should this weary world delight[939]	64
Who can escape his bow?[929]	70	Why wear'st thou then this crimson dye[940]	118
Who could his heavenly birth declare	80	Wide earth's remotest bound[941]	157
Who hath believed the tidings? Who?	78	Wildly shall I from thine turn back	234
Who in heart on thee believes[930]	281	Will gifts delight the Lord Most High?	276
Who points the clouds their course[931]	126	Wilt thou not regard my call?	259
Who, who, my Saviour, this hath done?[932]	232	Wisdom is due to thee	153
Who, who shall in thy presence stand	270	Wisely he chose the better part	217
Who would have thought my withered heart[933]	44	With all the servants of his Lord	218
Who would know Sin, let him repair[934]	27	With bended knees, and aching eyes[942]	66
Who would not now pursue the way	299	With faith I plunge me in this sea[943]	280
Whoe'er admits; my soul disowns	309	With fraudless, even, humble mind[944]	129
Whoe'er enslaved to grief and pain[935]	39	With him we are gone up on high	230
Whoe'er to God for pardon fly	312	With his blood he us hath bought	289
Whoe'er to thee themselves approve	277	With labour faint thou wilt not fail	275
Whom his eternal mind foreknew	311	With me is plenteous mercy found	208
Who's this, who like the morning shows[936]	343	With me, O, continue, Lord	254
Whose firm foundations never move	213	With me still let thy Spirit strive	251
Why didst thou bid my terrors chase	96	With me, your chief, you then shall know	301
Why didst thou the first gift impart	95	With other eyes I now could see	334
		With outstretched hands, and streaming eyes[945]	12

927. George Herbert.
928. George Herbert.
929. George Herbert.
930. From the German of Anna Dober, translated by John Wesley.
931. From the German of Paul Gerhardt, translated by John Wesley.
932. From the German of Paul Gerhardt, translated by John Wesley.
933. George Herbert.
934. George Herbert.
935. George Herbert.
936. Altered from George Sandys.
937. John Gambold?
938. George Herbert.
939. George Herbert.
940. Altered from John Norris.
941. From the German of Johann Angelus Scheffler, translated by John Wesley.
942. George Herbert.
943. From the German of Johann Andreas Rothe, translated by John Wesley.
944. From the German of Christian Friedrich Richter, translated by John Wesley.
945. From the German of Sigmund Gmelin,

First Line	Page
With outstretched wings my temples shade	303
With simple faith, to thee I call	83
With studied words each rising thought[946]	107
With thee conversing, I forget	304
With thee gone up on high	149
With thee heaven's favourite Son, when made	26
Withered my heart, like barren ground[947]	66
Within no narrow bounds confined	309
Within that Eden we retire	371
Without this best, divinest grace	76
Witness Divine he thus obtained	211
Witness, within us place	319
Witnesses that Christ hath died	351
Women their quickened dead received	219
Wondering I ask, Is this the breast	74
World, adieu, thou real cheat![948]	17
Worthies, who all recorded stand	219
Worthy, O Lord, art thou	153
Would aught with thee my wishes share	132
Wouldst thou know Love? behold the God[949]	27
Wrathful, impure, and proud I am	260

Volume II

First Line	Page
Wait we all in patient hope	192
Wash out my old original stain	321
Wavering, frail, inconstant heart	87
We all are one who him receive	222
We all shall find, (whom in his word	288
We all shall think and speak the same	333
We believe that Christ our head	186
We call thee Lord, thy faith profess	358
We can, dear Jesu, for thy sake	193
We cannot see without thy light	331
We come, great God, to seek thy face	226
We dare not give our God the lie	356
We dwell where Satan keeps his seat	349
We have now begun to cry	256
We know in whom we have believed	185
We know thou wilt not long delay	357
We lift our hearts to thee	26
We live in pleasures, and are dead	358
We look for that thrice blessed hope	325
We magnify the gift of God	324
We say that we with goods abound	359
We see him on his dazzling throne	235
We soon shall reach the boundless sea	226
We suffer them for sin to plead	349
We surely shall obtain	329
We talk of harvests; no	42
We then the power of faith shall prove	348
We tried him by the written word	345
We, we are called by thy great name	61
We will not close our wakeful eyes	193
We with our Lord shall always live	339
Weaken, bring me down to nought	215
Wean my soul, and keep it low	212
Weary and sick of sin I am	128
Weary of life through inbred sin	181
Welcome as the water-spring	207
Welcome friend, in that great name	218
Were it not better to bestow[950]	13
What a mystery am I	282
What, alas! I once have been	111
What avails the creature's strife	262
What can we offer our good Lord[951]	64
What did thy only Son endure	13
What have I then wherein to trust	149
What have I thy grace to move	147
What is our calling's glorious hope	304
What is redemption in his blood	304
What is this world, this meat	42
What means this struggling in my breast	129
What shall I do, or whither turn	100

---

    translated by John Wesley.
946. George Herbert.
947. George Herbert.
948. From the French, Antoinette Bourignon.
949. George Herbert.
950. Altered from George Herbert.
951. From the German of August Gottlieb Spangenberg, translated by John Wesley.

What shall I do, my God, my God?	148	Where'er the faithful workers turn[952]	63
What shall I do my God to love	72	Wherefore of him I make my boast	289
What shall I do? 'Tis worse than death	122	Wherefore of thy love We sing and rejoice	178
What shall I do to 'scape the hell	101		
What thou hast lent we all may use	361	Wherefore should I doubt the grace	294
What though all I am is sin?	316	Wherefore should I longer doubt?	241
What though earth and hell engage	316	Wherefore through thee to sin I say	308
What though my shrinking flesh complain	174	Wherefore to thee all honour, praise	339
		Wherefore to thee my soul I raise	314
Whate'er I ask I shall receive	308	Whether or no my heart of stone	101
Whate'er I ask in faith I have	309	While thus we walk with Christ in light	222
Whate'er I have, or can, or am	270	Whither, ah whither shall I go?	159
Whate'er in me seems wise, or good	203	Who blasphemously call thee Lord	303
Whate'er is human ebbs and flows	26	Who bore thy cross shall wear Thy crown	363
When all, into subjection brought	50		
When, dearest Lord, when shall it be	258	Who can before my Captain stand?	313
When from the arm of flesh set free	259	Who can now lament the lot	190
When God is mine, and I am his	244	Who can tell the happiness	187
When he vouchsafes our hands to use	17	Who falsely call themselves thine own	356
When I feel it fixed within	278	Who hath slighted or contemned	292
When I had forfeited my peace	232	Who held my fleeting soul in life	204
When it doth in me appear	277	*Who is this gigantic foe*	237
When Jesus makes my soul his home	305	Who Jesu's sufferings share	246
When, longing oft to be restored	122	Who madly plead for sin's remains	304
When man forsakes thou wilt not leave	259	Who my misery can relate	92
When, my Saviour, shall I be	214	Who now our scanty offerings bring	196
When others fell we faithful proved	235	Who pierced him by their sins beneath	339
When shall mine eyes behold the Lamb	44	Who placed a shepherd o'er the rest	59
When the boasted grace is gone	79	Who publishes the joyful sound	170
When this unspotted robe we wear	360	Who sow in tears in joy shall reap	166
When thou dost in my heart appear	244	Who, who can all thy counsel see	195
When thou the work of faith hast wrought	287	Who with the great Omniscient God	52
		Who would not do what God ordains	17
When thy love is my defence	98	Whoe'er thy Being dare dispute	21
When 'tis deeply rooted here	278	Whom thou dost guard, O King of kings	28
When to the left or right I stray	272	Why did I this forget	117
When to the right or left we stray	136	Why didst thou my ransom pay	275
When to the temple we repair	19	Why hast thou hid thy lovely face	60
When twice ten thousand times I fell	204	Why hast thou on me bestowed	275
Where am I now? From what a height	121	Why, then, O Lord, if ours thou art	60
Where is he now—their God, their Guide!	59	Why then, O my Saviour, why	111
Where is my strength, my faith, my God	107		
Where is the King of Glory now!	71		
Where is thy strength to conquer sin?	60		

952. From the German of August Gottlieb Spangenberg, translated by John Wesley.

First line	Page
Willing now to be made free	238
Wilt give him the bright Morning-Star	353
Wilt thou cast a sinner out	99
Wilt thou not once thy face display	65
Wilt thou not yet to me reveal	174
Wilt thou, O Lord, regard my tears[953]	9
Wilt thou suffer me to go	274
Wisdom, and power, and strength, and might	314
Wisdom and strength to thee belongs	228
With confidence I now look up	242
With eagle's wings their souls shall rise	57
With ease our souls through death shall glide	139
With guilty self-condemning fear	358
With holy indignation filled	314
With holy souls we here may meet	24
With me he dwells, and bids thee come	197
With me I know, I feel, thou art	366
With me, I know, thy Spirit dwells	243
With my sling and stone I go	238
With sin I joyfully complied	253
With sin I strove, alas! too long	202
With tears of joy our eyes o'erflow	185
With thee my virtue is but vice	149
With thee the potsherds strive	328
With what resembling care and love	22
Wither my strength, destroy my will	94
Withering as grass is humankind	50
Withhold whate'er my flesh requires	270
Within its mouth I was	269
Within me thy good Spirit place	320
Without money, without price	201
Witness Divine, the Just and True	330
Woe is me! that wretched man	105
Woe is me! what tongue can tell	156
Wondrous things the Lord hath done	252
World, and sin, and Satan, go	284
Worldly good I do not want	99
Worms of the earth, to you, we own	235
Worthy, we walk with him in white	325
Wretched heart, with woes opprest!	87
Wretched, helpless, and distrest	92
Wretched, naked, poor, and blind	274

Volume III

First line	Page
Waiting for the Comforter	361
Wakeful eyes, for your repose	161
Was it to save, or to condemn	28
Watchful the heavenly wisdom to instill	119
We bless the saving name	104
We cast our sins into that fire	323
We eat the offering of our peace	263
We glorify the Dove, / Who peaceful	103
We glorify the Dove, / Who strives	105
We have in the desert tarried	274
We here shall gain our calling's prize	243
We his image shall regain	291
We in thy birth are born	314
We join with all our friends above	96
We look on thee our dying Lamb	316
We magnify the grace	105
We nail th' old Adam to the tree	317
We need no reprobates to prove	96
We need not now go up to heaven	302
We now forgiveness have	297
We now their faithful saying feel	151
We on thee alone depend	319
We see the blood that seals our peace	236
We stake our interest in thy blood	64
We that on thy goodness feast	367
We wait t' obtain them now	223
We with our friends above	351
We yield thee thine own	334
Weary of life, in pain I breathe	159
Weep o'er your Desire and hope	231
Welcome, weariness and pain	161
Welcome whate'er my God ordain!	325
Well I know the promise sure	362
Well may heaven be clothed with black	231
What are these arrayed in white	294
What could my Redeemer move	11
What could your Redeemer do	87
What good can we need	372

---

953. David Lewis.

PART 1: *THE POETICAL WORKS OF JOHN AND CHARLES WESLEY*

What he did for our use ordain	262
What if I foully fell	53
What if I sinned sometimes	53
What is it keeps me back	89
What naughty men be they	51
What shall I say to move	45
What soul those drawings never knew?	4
Whate'er we cast on him alone	319
When all the rays of vengeance beat	152
When Nature felt the deadly blow	322
When on thy love we turned our back	94
When Satan drove the furious blast	153
When shall we see the day	370
When thou hast spoke my nature clean	159
When twice ten thousand times we fell	95
Where is Elijah's jealous God	74
Where is the answer to your prayer?	75
Where is the pure primeval flame	340
Where shall this memorial end?	287
Wherefore are thy garments red	227
Wherefore, my God hath tasted death	28
Whether I shall ever yield	15
While faith th' atoning blood applies	312
While now for us the Saviour prays	322
While the bitter herbs I eat	326
While to thy upper courts	297
Whither should our full souls aspire	289
Who can the will Divine withstand?	150
Who eats unworthily this bread	255
Who hath done the direful deed	11
Who here commemorate his death	279
Who is as the Christian blest?	164
Who is as the Christian wise?	164
Who is as the Christian great?	164
Who is this that comes from far	227
Who loved in death's sad shade to dwell	137
Who made the world a wilderness	149
Who seek redemption through his love	259
Who shall gain that heavenly height	165
Who that beholds thy lovely face	33
Who thee remember in thy ways	279
Who then the gracious wonder shall explain	110
Who thus our faith employ	219
Who thy mysterious supper share	338
Who under foot their Saviour trod	4
Whoe'er receive his power t' obey	139
Whoever receives The life-giving word	7
Wholly devoted now to God alone	114
Whom I reject, do you receive	27
Why did my dying Lord ordain	253
Why hast thou, Lord, forsook thine own?	216
Why is the faithful seed decreased	340
Why then, thou universal Love	5
Will you die because his grace	87
Wilt thou not bid me rise?	45
Wisdom and strength to thee belong	61
With all that loved the bleeding Lamb	179
With awful thanks we now receive	369
With bread from above	282
With him, the Corner-stone	313
With Jesu's constant presence blest	339
With joy we feel its sacred power	261
With mystical wine he comforts us here	286
With pity, Lord, a sinner see	272
With pure celestial bliss	273
With reverential faith we claim	234
With solemn faith we offer up	309
With us together sing	105
Withhold my foot from every snare	61
Worship, and praise, and power	351
Worship, honour, thanks, and blessing	346
Worthy, O Lamb, art thou	105
Worthy the Lamb of endless praise	243
Would Jesus have the sinner die?	22
Would the Saviour of mankind	314
Wretch that I am, while unrenewed	159

Volume IV

Warned by thy Spirit's gracious call	63
We all partake the joy of one	253
We are his ransomed people	88
We drink the consecrated cup	39
We for thy fleshly presence here	174
We have no 'biding city here	262

We have no outward righteousness	460	What shall I do? by guilt oppressed	392
We have not hearkened to the word	4	*What shall I do my God to love?*	
We have not, Lord, thy gifts improved	422	*/ my God*	265
We have seen the King of Glory	108	What shall I do my God to love?	
We in thy strength can all things do	37	/ my loving	446
We in thy word believe	13	What shall I do my suit to gain?	340
We know that his word And promise are past	89	What shall I do to keep	448
		What shall I say to move	249
We know that our head	143	What then wilt thou, canst thou do	318
We lift our joyful eyes	161	*What tongue alas! can tell*	328
We now divinely bold	161	*What would I have on earth beneath?*	216
We own our punishment is just	460	Whate'er a Christless soul can wound	423
We search the outward church in vain	124	Whate'er in me obstructs the way	430
We seek, thou know'st, we seek thy face	170	Whate'er obstructs thy pardoning love	237
We shall soon enjoy the favour	208	Whate'er the ancient prophets spoke	137
We sing of his love While sojourning here	146	Whate'er thou hear'st above	191
		Whate'er thy heart can wish, is poor	235
We the sons of men rejoice	109	Whatever thy will And wisdom ordain	90
We who have counted loss	44	When after each foul sinful fall	445
Weary of this war within	220	When every human friend is fled	66
Weary of my sad complaining	389	When his judgments are abroad	16
Weary of wandering from my God	442	When humbly on thee Alone we depend	90
Weary souls, who wander wide	212	When I had forfeited my peace	474
Weary world, when will it end	250	When my relief shall most display	330
Weary, weary, and oppressed	418	When ready to be offered up	67
Weeping to thee I lift mine eyes	356	When shall the fiery trial end?	356
Welcome tidings! to retrieve us	107	When shall this shadowy sabbath end	248
Well may our nature fear	14	When thou hadst rendered up thy breath	225
Well-pleased in him thyself declare	271	When thou in our flesh didst appear	125
Were this thy will concerning me	473	When will the affliction be o'er	240
What a wonder of grace	122	Whene'er my feeble hands hang down	477
What can our destruction stop	58	Where is now my strife and care	404
What ecstasy of bliss is there	244	Where is the helpless sinner's Friend?	414
What hast thou done for me?	250	*Where is the holy heaven-born Child*	123
What have fiends to do with thee?	443	Where is the promise then	49
What hope or help remains for thee?	348	Where is the way? Ah! show me where?	470
What is it, Lord, that keeps me back?	336	Where is the wise, foreknowing man	296
What is it makes my Saviour stay	29	Where pure essential joy is found	303
What moved the Most High so greatly to stoop	113	Where two or three thy presence claim	380
		Where wilt thou ease or comfort take?	345
What must a poor prodigal do	425	Where'er they turn, the people fail	72
What recompence, or meet reward	100	*Wherefore he now in mercy cries*	73
What shall a sinner say	328	Wherefore in never-ceasing prayer	480
What shall an helpless sinner do	422	*Wherefore the utmost sufferings here*	43

Wherefore to him our souls we raise	79	Whoe'er behold their heavenly grace	311
Wherefore to thee our souls we trust	37	Whoe'er beneath his shadow dwell	55
Wherefore to thee the Lord hath said	306	Whoe'er to this high prize aspire	56
Wherefore we now for mercy pray	226	Whoever then thine aid implored	374
While in affliction's furnace	79	Whom all the angels worship	111
While in our Shepherd's breast	46	Whose mercies exceed	416
While still to thee for help I call	480	Why am I then, ah! show me why	431
While thus ye love your souls t' employ[954]	129	Why did I not resign my breath	400
While void of care, the cheerful crowd	102	Why did thy love submit to die	333
While we walk with him in light	16	Why did thy providential power	473
Whither, ah! whither must thou go?	345	Why didst thou gently draw me on	473
Whither, ah! whither should I go?	335	Why didst thou in my youthful age	473
Who against me would madly dare	294	Why didst thou in this vale of tears	343
Who, ah, who deserves to feel	317	Why didst thou leave thy throne above	341
Who believes the tidings? who	317	Why didst thou, Lord, my load remove	473
Who basely all forsook their Lord	134	Why hast thou to thy people joined	474
Who can now presume to fear?	133	*Why, (in the dust I ask,) O why*	400
Who can that awful day declare?	61	Why should a man complain	403
Who ever asked for help in vain	334	Why should I longer live	328
Who galls the nations with his yoke	189	Why should not the dreadful sentence	7
Who hold the truth in righteousness	286	Why should the foe thy purchase seize?	252
Who is the trembling sinner, who	378	Why should the heathen aliens say	74
Who kick against the pricks in vain	31	*Why should the Lord a worm pursue*	440
Who knows but he may now return	73	Why should they still be stricken, Lord	63
Who now their hellish malice show	289	Why then art thou cast down	131
Who now would be great	123	Why then do thy fears return	318
Who patiently endure	218	Why then heave again thy sighs	320
Who pine for heavenly food	217	Why, then, if thou for me hast died	135
Who see their Lord at parting	149	Why then should I complain	436
Who slight my miracles of love	76	Wild as the untamed Arab's race	28
Who stumble at the cross	218	Wild as the untaught Indian's brood	252
Who that hath ever known	402	Will his majesty disdain	118
Who thee beneath their feet have trod	29	Will the fight be never over?	352
Who thee remembers in thy ways	286	*Will the pardoning God despise*	359
Who thy lovely pattern knows	34	Willing to save, I know, thou art	430
Who to my righteousness submit	297	Wilt thou bid a sinner seek	463
Who trust to be redeemed from sin	286	Wilt thou not the promise seal	176
Who was it then dispersed the snare	96	Wisdom and strength belongs	99
Who would not cheerfully sustain	44	Wisdom Divine! who tells the price	234
Who would not fear the Lord	12	With a diamond's point it stands	404
Who would not then, for such an hope	44	With all my soul I seek thy face	257
		With angels and archangels	258
954. *UP* 3:112: "While thus ye long your souls t' employ."		With consolations from above	39
		With faith, and every grace beside	311

With favour look upon his face	21	Walking in thy pleasant ways	386
With guilty, unbelieving dread	10	Wash out the deep, original stain	230
With gushing eyes their deeds I see	28	Water of life Divine	369
With him I reside	123	We all shall commend	32
With him we walk in white	231	We all shall gain what we pursue	319
With Jesus Christ together we	281	We all shall see the golden blaze	278
With joy I embrace	273	We all the truth shall know	474
With lowly reverential fear	454	We are now his lawful right	332
With me if of old thou hast strove	195	We beckoned to our friends for aid	249
With me is full redemption found	309	We by his Spirit prove	364
With me the ghastly spectre walks	423	We cannot rest in sin subdued	334
With patience then I yield	403	We cannot speak one useful word	375
With penitent sighs	364	We cannot think a gracious thought	175
With pity, O thou gracious Lord	74	We come at thy call	437
With publicans and harlots I	373	We dare avow the gospel hope	334
With tears of desire, I humbly require	368	We dare not believe	320
With trembling awe we humbly pray	10	We do not shamefully desert	466
With Tubal's wretched sons no more	243	We feared to wait thy leisure, Lord	243
With zeal, and heavenly wisdom filled	308	We feel it, and pray	57
Withering as grass he fades, and dies	304	We have not an high-priest in thee	242
Without a gracious thought	436	We have not believed in vain	332
Witnesses of th' atoning blood	32	We his life on earth shall live	332
Woe to the souls at ease	19	We know thou wilt not long delay	76
Workers with God, they now shall rear	308	We laugh to scorn his cruel power	34
Worldly grief be far away	420	We like all thy host adore thee	275
Worms of earth, on gods we call	254	We march hand in hand	388
Worship, and thanks, and blessing	237	We mourn, till thou appear	459
Worst of all th' apostate race	8	We now affix our seal	371
Worthy esteemed through grace	20	We now shall more than win	38
Worthy in her great Saviour's worth[955]	312	We now thy promised presence claim	388
Would I not in thy name believe?	430	We rest in his protection here	381
Would to God, that I had died	404	We rest on his word	320
Wouldst thou have stirred them up to pray	474	We shall attain what we pursue	336
Wouldst thou not rather have me fly	401	We shall be wholly sanctified	335
Wouldst thou the body's health restore	375	We shall gain our calling's prize	333
Wrapped in swathes th' immortal Stranger	107	We shall our time beneath	463
Wretch that I am, what help, or hope	391	We shall the end of faith attain	317
Written for me the gospel page	379	We steadfastly believe	235
		We that are Christ's have crucified	32
		We the paths of death pursued	385
		We tremble in our evil day	102
		We wait till thou the gift impart	471
		We, while the stars from heaven shall fall	382
		We who in Christ believe	363

Volume V

Wake in him the strong desire	438

955. *UP* 2:451.

We would not, Lord, ourselves conceal	316	Whate'er thou dost on one bestow	409
We would not of ourselves conceive	315	Whate'er ye ask, whate'er ye want	225
We would not our own souls deceive	314	Whatever we need his bounty shall give	385
We wrestle not with flesh and blood	32	When called to testify thy grace	197
We yield to be redeemed from sin	322	When he first the work begun	120
Weak, and coward as I am	205	When inbred sin is all destroyed	416
Weak, and wayward as I am	184	When justice bared the sword	55
Weary, burdened, and oppressed	100	When nature sunk beneath her load	142
Weary of my friends below	183	When our lovely Lord appears	447
Weary world of sin, and anguish	212	*When shall I lay down my head*	205
Weep, ye common mourners, weep	340	When shall I my haven find	205
Welcome alike the crown or cross	163	When stronger souls their faith forsook	465
Well maintain the post assigned	281	When thou the work of faith hast wrought	301
Were I from all my pain	189		
What a mercy is this	402	When time is no more	32
What a mighty blessing this!	181	When we would have spurned his Mercy and grace	469
What a rapturous song	458		
What am I, O thou glorious God!	1	When weary oft I faint, and droop	412
What are the sorest plagues I bear	192	When with joy we remove	321
What are thy gifts, compared to thee!	415	Where are in Christ the creatures new	328
What can I desire beside?	185	Where are Jesu's witnesses	353
What did my Lord from sinners bear?	141	Where are the spirits to Jesus joined	328
What doth this low earth afford	444	*Where is my God, my joy, my hope*	6
What hath their malice done	220	Where is the glorious church below	328
What is the reason of my hope	308	*Where is the gourd, that sudden rose*	190
What joy shall abound	222	Where is the king of terrors? where	225
What mighty troubles hast thou shown	465	*Where is the passionate regret*	81
What shall I do my God to love	420	*Where shall I rest my weary head*	355
What shall I say	61	Where shall I wander now to find	480
What thou dost I know not now	162	Where thou goest, I still will go	133
What thou dost on one confer	433	Wherefore from us depart	368
What though a thousand hosts engage	302	Wherefore on you we ever call	35
What though my every lucid hour	414	Wherefore should I complain	445
What though my soul with shame is filled	192	*Wherefore should I make my moan*	80
What tongue cannot tell	304	Wherefore then, thou gracious God	162
What troubles have we seen	466	Wherefore to thee I all resign	159
Whate'er I ask in faith, I have	4	*While angel choirs their harps employ*	218
Whate'er I ask, the Truth hath said	4	While I thus my soul recline	185
Whate'er I speak, or do	56	While in the heavenly work we join	399
Whate'er my heavenly Father wills	67	*While pride and wrath remain within*	296
Whate'er my sinful flesh requires	158	While with a single eye	128
Whate'er offends thy glorious eyes	316	While with just peculiar kindness	425
Whate'er our pardoning Lord	364	Who are these but sinners poor	119
Whate'er the rage of fiends, and men	143	*Who are these that come from far*	119

Who can tell the solid bliss	351	With all my soul, O Lord, I give	81
Who dares approach those towers?	44	With all who chant thy name on high	279
Who first the precious blessing lent	338	With calmly reverential joy	400
Who, for his sake, count all things lost	478	With grace abundantly endued	480
Who for thy coming wait	475	With humble thankfulness I own	8
Who hath a right like us to sing	398	With joy we approve	30
Who, I ask, in amaze	402	With joy we shall behold	463
Who in Jesus confide	457	With loving surprise	222
Who in the Spirit walk, and live	296	With me he doth even now reside	78
Who is this, that now comes up	352	With patience persevere	46
Who kept his garments white	84	With pure celestial day	267
Who left the sky	63	With shame the fatal cause I own	5
Who now to every ill submit	153	With solemn dread my life, my fame	191
Who of the great, or wise	368	With speeches fair, and glozing lies	319
Who of twain hath made us one	453	With steadfast faith for this I wait	144
Who on earth can conceive	457	With thanks I rejoice	401
Who on the part of God will rise	397	With the High and Lofty One	350
Who only seek in thee our rest	151	With thee, O Christ, on earth I reign	70
Who suffer for our Master here	169	With these, and every sin-sick soul	393
Who suffer in Jesus's shame	181	With those that went before thee	217
Who that trusted in the Lord	383	With us no melancholy void	279
Who the good fight of faith have fought	416	With us thou art assembled here	470
Who will not be by love constrained	247	With us through life abide	227
Who would go from health to pain	13	Without a groan the Christian dies	227
Who would the life of God regain	151	Without a murmuring wish I give	82
Who wrought the work shall have the praise	114	Without blemish, or blot	26
Whoever seek to know	368	Witness my undissembled tears	227
Whom but thee have we in heaven	309	Witnesses of th' all-cleansing blood	410
Whom have I on earth below?	21	Woe to him, whose spirits droop	453
Whom next to God I love	349	Woman, and man, and beast	48
Whom now we seek, O may we meet!	470	Wondering the calm despisers stand	250
Whom thou hast bound, O Lord expel	232	Work a sudden work of grace	206
Whom thy dying love o'erpowers	274	*Worn out with long fatigue, and pain*	209
Whom thy grace to me hath lent	432	Would he I should closer cleave	341
Why hast thou cast our lot	422	Wounded in the tenderest part	188
Why should a child of thine give place	241	Wretched, and void of God, and blind	431
Why should a living child of man	192		
Why then was I cast down	450		
Why wilt thou not for all my life	5		
Willing he is, that all should live	5		
Wilt thou lop the boughs of sin	291		
Wisely let me mourn my dead	340		
With all her heart she clave to God	88		

Volume VI

Walking in her house with God	335
Warned of her dissolution near	321
Wars, and plagues, and great distresses	45
We after our translated friend	277

We, alas, remain below	364	We want the spirit of humble fear	314
We all his kind protection share	446	We weep with those that weep below	111
We all shall see our life appear	200	We will not let our sorrow go	263
We by idleness expose	423	We with our ears have heard	149
We came into the world to do	385	We wrestle for the ruined race	111
We come, depending on thy name	101	*Weary of all this wordy strife*	71
We dare the evil day to come	156	Weary to death, she spreads her hands	89
We do not dream the danger past!	165	What a bold and foolish lie	423
We do with joy look up	47	What a glorious title this	444
We do with thanks receive it now	418	What a gracious God is ours!	233
We, even we, the scourge demand	185	What ails thee, O thou sea	52
We fear, the saved unthankful throng	171	What but th' essential Truth Divine	140
We for no worldly pleasures plead	439	What but thy love's almighty power	116
We in his favour shall retrieve	422	What can'st thou more for sinners do?	79
We know, by faith we know	207	What fulness of rapture is there	190
We know in whom we trust	287	What hath thy death for sinners gained?	374
We know not, Lord, thy dread decree	81	What have I else whereof to boast?	315
We know thou wilt not long delay	298	What I into thy hands commend	384
We lack the wisdom from on high	388	What is redemption unpossessed?	303
We lift our thankful hearts to thee	413	What is there here to court my stay	217
We mourn, but as men Rejoicing in hope	307	*What matters it to pray*	389
We mourn the slaughtered sons of Gaul	185	*What shall we say? It is the Lord*	248
We must have died that second death	394	What then can their protection be?	107
We need not come there	406	What then have thine elect to dread	173
We never will the grace forget	32	What then remains for us on earth to do	63
We now, by his good Spirit led	394	What then shall of our souls become	385
We offer up our weak desires	167	What though she in the desert pined	249
We only fear to lose our loss	293	What though the earth remove	36
We ourselves, not him, deplore	364	What tongue her hidden worth can tell	241
We own thy mercy in the stroke	32	Whate'er these threatening wars portend	167
We praise him with a stammering tongue	446	Whate'er thou wilt, in earth below	372
We praise thee for our hope to know	422	Whatever ill the world befall	96
We praise thee for our master's care	422	When called the mystery to explain	360
We praise thy constancy of love	307	*When, dear Lord, ah! tell us when*	403
We pray, but with our lips alone	389	When, dearest soul, shall we	239
We pray that these dry bones may live	104	When first sent forth to minister the word	63
We rashly for our offspring claim	261	When God, to prove her love sincere	361
We render thanks with one accord	140	When I, from all my burdens freed	108
We, Saviour, at thy footstool lie	306	*When Jesus darts his glorious light*	455
We shall with many stripes be beat	418	When language failed, her silence spoke	322
We speak, because they hold their peace	103	*When late translated to the skies*	120
We still the bloody harness wear	186	When men and fiends against her rose	268
We thy judgments have abhorred	39	When most displeased thou shakest the rod	78
We to the Lamb's atoning blood	417		

IDEX OF FIRST LINES OF POETRY BY JOHN AND CHARLES WESLEY

When reason fled the rack of pain	234	Who can sound the depths unknown	461
When they once are entered there	379	Who can tell if late repentance	168
When thou didst our Isaac give	251	Who could forbid the outward sign	228
Whene'er we think on God Most High	456	Who did for her the kingdom buy	363
Where have I been so long	1	Who earth and heaven commands	463
Where is the fair Elysian flower	234	Who fancy righteousness in man	426
Where knowledge vain, unsanctified	131	Who filled me with those jealous fears	259
Where now are all thy fears	342	Who for so poor a creature care	329
Where now is the invader's boast	181	Who good pursue, and evil fly	392
Where now thy lamentations	343	*Who hunt our souls with cruel scorn*	135
Where Satan keeps his gaudy throne	267	*Who languish on a bed of pain*	133
Where shall this dreadful havoc end?	175	Who live her life her death shall die	244
Where shall true believers go	378	Who may abide his frown	52
Wherefore again we say, Rejoice	396	Who most withstand the gospel-word	115
Wherefore did he stoop so low?	457	Who now against each other rise	112
Wherefore I safely lay me down	451	Who now with humble zeal go on	318
Wherefore, let every creature give	372	Who rest beneath th' Almighty's wings	168
Wherefore our lives shall show His praise	43	Who shall arise in their defence	411
		Who shall join the acclamation	459
Wherefore to thee we cry	390	Who shall now the orphans feed	291
Wherefore to thine almighty hand	100	Who share it above, They never can lose	397
Wherefore when we met below	366	Who soon their innocency lose	417
Whether he eats, in faith, or drinks	376	Who then upon earth can conceive	196
Which of the saints by Rome adored	179	Who weeping build our infant's tomb	257
While all my old companions dear	428	Whoe'er beheld, pronounced her blessed	294
While Britain's sons their trophies raise	184	Whom I into thy hands commend	108
While Christ with all his heart he sought	283	Whom the heavens cannot contain	457
While distant climes resound his name	123	Whom then, when every vain pretenders cast	57
While inflamed with vengeful ire	168		
While more obdurate still, thy word	75	Whom thou by us hast gathered in	107
While nature's will remained alive	294	Whom thou dost for thy glory choose	123
While others spent their strength for nought	272	*Why should my tears for ever flow*	225
		Why should our hearts for ever bleed	256
While they enjoy his heavenly love	429	*Why should our parents call us good*	425
While thus he toiled, a sudden cry	282	Wide as our conquering arms extend	164
While thus we confide In Jesus's blood	47	Will not the righteous Judge bestow	200
While to the work their lives they give	117	Will they believe the spoiler nigh	170
While weeping there the sinner lay	302	Willing thou that all should know	382
While yet we call, the prayer is sealed	122	Wilt thou, Lord, be yet entreated	168
While, zealous for thy righteous law	324	Winged with infinite desire	366
Who all the bright train Angelical made	451	*Wisdom ascribe, and might and praise*	9
Who always liberal things devised	354	With all that angel-host, with all	140
Who can escape the wreck	35	With all the Spirit's powers she prayed	340
Who can resolve the doubt	427	With angels and archangels join	306

With ease her quick discerning eyes	272	Walk with me through the dreadful shade	375
With foul and riotous excess	104	*Warned from the body to depart*	404
With furious error blind	90	Warned of the sure-approaching day	409
With glory decked, and clothed with power	261	*Warned of my dissolution / Unfit to die*	356
With her to range th' eternal plains	299	*Warned of my dissolution near*	374
With joy she flew her all to sell	267	We by faith behold him too	209
With joyfulest news Your prisons resound	14	We censure them, ourselves untried	77
With kind distinguishing regard	33	We found the presence of our God	23
With lowly reverential joy	167	We give glory to God	321
With lust of fame and pleasure fired	437	*We God the Father praise*	338
With mixed concern her flight we view	243	We grow in grace, abound in hope	346
With pure superior wisdom fraught	261	We have laid up our love	198
With reverential joy	97	We, if so thy will require	87
With saints enthroned on high	316	*We lift our hearts to thee*	299
With sober joy, and conscious fear	166	We live, but not by bread alone	157
With songs of pure thanksgiving	342	We live to praise and magnify	346
With steadfast faith and hope	203	We live to testify the grace	23
With thine army of cross-bearers	142	We on thy only word depend	158
With those redeemed of old	349	We remember the word	176
With timely sorrow we confess	81	We rise with the sun, To commune of him	26
With what different exclamation	145	We see our kind Supporter's hand	46
With what submissive lowliness	381	We soon shall wake, with you to sing	36
With wholesome discipline severe	5	We teach the mystery	296
Witness, her companions here	337	We that amidst a people dwell	262
Witness his old companions there[956]	309	*We the Father's law receive*	284
Witness his one extreme desire	234	We through sin no longer drooping	7
Witness, ye children of her prayers	241	We tremble at the danger near	72
Witness, ye once to evil sold!	326	*We wait for the returning*	214
Witness ye servants of her Lord	271	We wait the glad hour	9
Witness, ye souls to her allied	326	We want our wishes to suspend	119
Woe! to the men on earth who dwell	25	We who have in Christ found favour	7
Worship and power to God belongs!	164	We would in every step look up	70
Worthless are our best offerings	447	We would our earthly bliss resign	118
Worthy is God, and God alone	396	Weary of all below	387
Wrapped up in their Lord, his service and love	440	Weary of contention here	414
Wretched souls, who live in sin	377	*Weary of my own complaints*	390
		Weary of this daily dying	111
		Weary, why should I farther go	134
		Weeping where'er mine eye I turn	134
Volume VII		*Welcome incurable disease*	99
		Well the Holy Ghost, the Lord	260
Walk with me through the lion's den	359	Well thou know'st the fear and sorrow	58
		Well thou know'st we cannot rest	15
956. UP 3:336.		What after God he asks can God deny	440

What but my faithful thinking	105
What but thy manifested grace	135
What by the Lord of Hosts was said	262
What day I shall from earth remove	400
What follies abound	80
What is that preparation	114
What mighty works the prayer of faith can do	432
What multitudes repent, and then believe	435
What Jesus' blood for me did buy	107
What matters it to me	138
What must a dying sinner do	355
What nation is so high	269
What profit is there in my death	399
What recompense for all his endless toil	432
What shall I do to love thee	188
What shall I say thy love to gain?	351
What then is change of place to me?	134
What though the sinners' chief I am	333
Whate'er for man I do	167
Whate'er I have of evil done	395
When all have heavenward set their face	418
When all his friends are saved at last	222
When borne aloft on angels' wings	158
When crowds for counsel or relief applied	438
When I feel his blood applied	403
When I from all my labours rest	130
When nature's strength and sense were gone	67
When nature's strength, and spirits fail	376
When near the slippery paths of vice	133
When Satan strove the brethren to divide	439
When sick of sin I languish	105
When stripped of all but sin they grieve	329
When the creature-streams are dry	96
When the Spirit thou bestow'st	251
When thou didst converse below	97
Whence the earnest expectation	381
Whene'er our day of Pentecost	248
Whene'er thou dost thy love reveal	49
Where first I preached the word of grace	182
Wherefore did she visit earth	83
Wherefore in me reveal the grace	226
Wherefore thy righteousness I own	116
Wherefore with joyful lips and heart	67
Wherefore with meekest awe to thee	184
Wherewithal shall I appear	127
Whether thy will ordain my stay	184
While all that breathe acknowledge	132
While, hanging on thy faithful word	359
While here our Samuel we present	89
While struggling in the toils of death	360
While the army above	301
While thou didst on earth appear	47
While thou dost her soul renew	144
While we in thy name assemble	306
While we labour for him	158
While we yet invoke thy name	122
While yet I am calling, appear	318
Whisper to my parting soul	407
Whither shall a creature run?	260
Who but the souls that savingly believe	427
Who can forgive but God alone	226
Who gave all things to be	81
Who giv'st me yet a longer space	405
Who God in Christ discover	343
Who have with faith Divine believed	264
Who intimate communion feel	292
Who into temptation led	252
Who is so great a God as ours	123
Who Jehovah's mind hath known?	268
Who know the thing by God designed	285
Who on thine only truth depend	181
Who seek redemption in thy blood	30
Who sent the Son is true	287
Who shall the rapturous sight explain	385
Who shall the will and work divine oppose	429
Who so near the birth hast brought	60
Who strive resisting unto blood	228
Who tempted Christ, the faithless race	211
Who the Holy Ghost receive	251
Who the Saviour and Son	81
Who to the Holy Spirit lied	250
Whom but now thy mercy gave	82
Whom have I in heaven but thee?	408
Whom the Paternal Grace bestowed	225

Whom thyself hast died to save	369
Whom thyself hast planted there	96
Whose spirits bow to Jesus' name	232
Why in the neighbourhood of hell	169
Why is he called, that Man adored	261
Why should my faltering tongue disown	126
Why then am I cast down	392
Why wast thou there of God forsook	352
Why would my prayer detain him here	129
Will he forsake his throne above	194
Will it not all thy children shame	399
Wilt thou not, Lord, my offer take?	182
Wilt thou not our guilt remove	21
Wise to foresee my latter end	409
Wisdom, and praise, and glory be	337
With a believing master blessed	172
With all my heart I then shall love	398
With all-sufficient grace supply	164
With cries and tears unceasing	356
With earnest desire	176
With glorious clouds encompassed round	194
With glorious pomp descending	214
With God the Son and Saviour	253
With heart enlarged, with confidence increased	433
With humble faith his death I plead	395
With humble fear I now draw near	186
With lust of pleasure, wealth, and fame	74
With notions fraught, the Stoics sour	74
With our weakness and temptation	58
With pity then the anguish see	65
With ready minds th' Americans receive	431
With resigned simplicity	34
With sin and grief beginning	112
With singing we praise	199
With thankful heart I ask for more	129
With thankfulness and fear	362
With thanks we approve	199
With the children of men	81
With us residing here	21
Without that sense of pardoning grace	411
Witness and messenger of peace	183
Witness, seal of sin forgiven	367
World of vanity, farewell!	366
Worship, and power, and thanks, and love	88
Worship and praise belong	305
Worthy the Lamb extolled to live	177
Wrestling on in mighty prayer	48
Wretched, and miserable	188

Volume VIII

Warning, ye sons of rapine, take	346
We grant it, the associate host	477
We have the wages of our sin	349
We long entangled in their net	145
We now with thy protection blessed	265
We the works of ancient days	112
We too the joyful sound have heard	248
We trace thy footsteps in the deep	295
We will glory in thy name	39
Weary alas! of living	358
Weary, faint, through long delay	220
Weary of my unanswered groans	12
What ailed thee, O thou trembling sea	200
What angel in that darkest hour	469
What but a miracle of grace	393
What but thy hallowing blood could cleanse	381
What can th' Omnipotent withstand	359
What can their purpose fell defeat	463
What doth then my hopes prevent?	442
What hinders now the fell banditti	459
What hope of safety for our realm	480
What is a modern man of fashion?	479
What is man, that thou, O Lord	16
What is that mysterious Name	371
What man is he that fears the Lord?	50
What means this melancholy ditty	470
What need of government assistance	471
What shall I do my doom to shun	347
What shall I do to love thee	358
What shall I render to my God	202
What shall I say my suit to gain?	377
What streams of blood already shed	465
Whate'er the plagues that intervene	296

IDEX OF FIRST LINES OF POETRY BY JOHN AND CHARLES WESLEY

When all are sweetly joined	250	Who consciously doom Ourselves to the flame	350
When burdened I cried For pardon to thee	255	Who deal in lies and perjury	139
When destruction was nigh	420	Who for thy coming wait	242
When devils and men Against us arose	280	*Who in the Lord confide*	240
When God did on my part appear	31	"Who is this King of glory, who?"[957]	48
When God made bare his arm in fight	151	"Who is this King of glory, who?"[958]	49
When Israel out of Egypt came	199	Who lead their followers down the way	398
When left by all, and void of hope	55	Who may the trial, Lord, abide	246
When my heart is circumcised	364	Who my nature didst partake	372
When nothing can their force resist	454	*Who on the Lord Most High*	325
When, O my Saviour, shall I find	380	Who, passing through the mournful vale	166
When once reconciled to our God	336	Who planted the attentive ear	179
When our redeeming Lord	241	Who plough with ships the watery road	197
When plagues the land o'erflow	323	Who seed immortal bears	242
When shall my grief and pain	363	Who shall with my Lord compare?	78
When sick and languishing he lies	93	Who the convict liars see	141
When the number is fulfilled	306	Who their own countrymen destroyed	481
When thou hast sealed thy peoples' peace	118	Who then for filthy gain betrayed his trust	443
When thou hast wrought a will in me	355	Who to their sins draw back	241
When thou, O Lord, didst greatly lead	149	Who vainly trust in lies	62
When thy foes are swept away	299	Who would not here from slanders cease	119
When thy judgments are abroad	306	Whoe'er beholds th' event shall say	130
When young, and full of sanguine hope	428	Whoe'er like horse and mule withstand	67
Whenever on the Lord I cry	126	Whoe'er withstand a pardoning God	5
Where they all thy laws have spurned	299	Wholly at thy dispose I am	429
Where unity is found	250	Whom hostile multitudes surround	288
Where unity takes place	250	Whom man accounts not fit to live	352
Where'er we turn our blasted eyes	460	Whom thy viceregent we confess	351
Wherefore beneath thy hand we bow	305	Whom to me thy goodness lends	402
Wherefore I soon my wish shall see	204	Whose refuge is the Lord most high	176
Wherefore I will exalt thy name	35	Why art thou, my soul, oppressed?[959]	96
Wherefore I will thy goodness sing	161	Why art thou, my soul, oppressed?	97
Wherefore, I will with joy obey	133	*Why do the christened heathens rage*	484
Wherefore my heart doth now rejoice	28	*Why do the Jews and Gentiles join*	4
Wherefore of him his people boasts	397	*Why do the zealots of Geneva rage*	446
Wherefore should we be stricken more	277	Why dost thou to thy servants show	317
Wherefore then, my restless spirit	98		
Wherefore, to all I cry, "Believe!	55		
Wherefore to him, ye kings, submit	5		
Wherefore with lowly thanks I will	146		
Wherefore with soft and silent pace	425		
While my foes are in my sight	88		
Who can against the ruffians stand	462		

957. Page 48, line 2: "The Lord that all his foes o'ercame."
958. Page 49, line 2: "The Lord of glorious power possessed."
959. The four-line stanzas beginning with this line on pages 96 and 97 are identical.

Why, O thou man of lawless might	118	Wonderful in saving power	111
Why send us troops who cannot need'em	471	*Wonderful thy statutes are*	227
Why should I live another day	359	Worn away with endless pain	186
Why should I longer, Lord, contend	416	Worship the co-eternal Son	6
Why should the specious fiend deceive	293	Would have me love my God	380
Why standest thou, O Lord	20	Wouldst thou for fifty righteous men	320
Why then, great God, should we despair[960]	289	Wrestling with Abraham's faithful seed	289
Why then hast thou abhorred thine own	163	*Wretched soul, the strife forbear*	373
Why would ye then, ah, tell us why	477	Wretches!—'tis all their joy	136
Why, ye ambitious mountains, why	151		
Wicked men who thee oppose	140		
Wild, independent anarchy	316		

Volume IX

Will they not charge my fall on thee?	24	Wake my soul to sleep no more	216
Willing, and strong to save thou art	341	Walking in the church below	64
Wilt thou thine own for ever chide	167	Warmed by fond nature's wild desire	62
Wise to believe in time of need	179	Warned of my dissolution near	315
With angels above	395	Was ever grief like thine	438
With deepest sympathy	324	Was it a sin in Nebat's son	177
With every sufferer	324	Was not our Father Abraham tried	25
With fasting and prayer my Saviour I seek	440	Watched by the world's malignant eye	224
With favour look on	406	We are the men, mankind must own	243
With giant-strength he comes from far	36	We blame the fiend, ourselves to clear	7
With grateful joy we comprehend	305	We claim the promise, Lord, for ours!	439
With love beyond expression	372	We gather up with pious care	187
With pity, Lord, thine outcasts see	134	We have nothing to pay	420
With pity mark her silent tears	410	We in our Lord's command	90
With poverty of spirit blessed	438	We know, it must be done	470
With severest anguish torn	340	We lift our hearts to God in thee	333
With sin and wickedness	357	We seek the New Jerusalem	427
With Sinai's thunderings, Lord, begin	340	We think on her desolate stones	320
With sinners sweep me not away	56	We wait in patient pain	121
With tender affection inspired	335	We wrestle not with flesh and blood	127
With terror arm, and virtuous zeal	279	Weakened by my bosom-sin	140
With the blessing Divine	406	Weakest, when I strongest seem	215
With the flagitious multitude	320	Well doth a summer leaf explain	460
With thy kind protection blessed	409	What advantage to God	287
With thy shield my weakness cover	78	What angel can explain	95
With zeal for God, with love of souls inspired	434	What but thy strength-inspiring eye	219
Without the law I lived awhile	391	What can I say, what can I do	237
		What can we ask or covet more	17
		What cannot the Almighty do?	336
		What could have been done less, to save	377
		What do these solemn words portend?	163

[960]. UP 2:448.

IDEX OF FIRST LINES OF POETRY BY JOHN AND CHARLES WESLEY

What doth the ladder mean	27	Wherefore thy gates shall open stand	455
What doth the Lord require of man?	100	While banished from thy blissful sight	267
What evil thing is this ye do	227	While nations unenlightened lie	452
What have his servants then to fear	244	While Satan fills th' unerring chair	86
What is in man for God t' approve?	202	While the world is wrapped in night	42
What lost the king his regal power?	158	While those who persecute and hate	434
What man or angel can explore	150	While thus I went on	286
What now is my object and aim?	293	While yet the ground I cumber	315
What pity 'tis, to cross his will	173	While yet they hear the rebels' cries	80
What power against a worm can stand	135	While wandering in the wilderness	179
What profit hath th' ambitious man	229	Who but th' Almighty can	249
What profit your religious shows	370	Who can a wounded spirit sustain	352
What profits prayer itself, unless	122	Who can soothe the soul's distresses	291
What saith a younger prophet's zeal	193	Who can the benefits explain	256
What say the false faint-hearted spies	72	Who can thy strict tribunal face	155
What thou hast spoke I have not done	53	Who comes unto thee	444
What wisdom from thy lips distils	210	Who dares blame thy justice, Lord	90
Whate'er I ask, I surely know	149	Who first inspired the breath of lives	151
Whate'er my God ordain	68	Who for their unborn children care	137
Whate'er th' Almighty wills is done	365	Who for us went up, we know	59
When by the harp's harmonious aid	190	Who forge the instruments of death	443
When first he freely justified	109	Who in the painting art excel	196
When first we of thy promise heard	18	Who in thy word confide	66
When God, discovered from above	273	Who is the weak believer, who	436
When God in man his Son reveals	350	Who is this we see ascend	368
When God receives his servants up	184	Who loves me so well, my helper has been	304
When he frees our souls from prison	276		
When mortal man resigns his breath	151	Who madest thus the earth and skies	3
When once the devils are entered in	79	Who make to heaven your bold appeal	241
When quiet in my house I sit	94	Who murmur in the wilderness	81
When saints forsake our mean abode	188	Who musters the celestial host	133
When shall I walk before thee	319	Who of the rich hath ears to hear	302
When the just God, the Lord most high	375	Who our trust in princes place	341
When the loving King of kings	201	Who seek to be blessed, But labour in vain	444
When wilt thou come unto me	319		
Whene'er my Father in the skies	171	Who shall live to see that day	367
Where angels in his presence stand	405	Who that promised Seed receive	25
Where are thine old intestine foes?	410	Who the strength of God distrust	79
Where but on yonder tree?	257	Who to thy wounds for refuge flee	129
Where have they been in secret bred?	432	Who truly trust, O Lord, in thee	394
Where is the hebrews' God	66	Who, what are these, that as a cloud	454
Where is the just, unblemished man	270	Who wills us, if his soul we love	347
Whereas thou hast forsaken been	456	Who would not quit his sins for thee	372
Where'er I am, whate'er I do	18	Whoe'er for sensual pleasures burn	69

Whoe'er the King of kings adore	206	Without a voice he cried	44
Whom God declares a perfect man	256	Without that sin-consuming fire	178
Whom Jesu's blood doth sanctify	112	Witness of my extreme distress	38
Whom once they hated and despised	456	Woe to them who will not own	103
Whom we everywhere may find	52	Woman, thy faith is great	192
Whom we here by faith behold	389	Workmen, and soldiers of the Lord	224
Why am I, Lord, at life's sad close	241	Worldly wretch, let go thy hold	345
Why do I not the call obey	236	Worthy of death, afraid to die	183
Why dost thou, Lord, conceal thy face	244	Would God himself his people lead	49
Why dost thou this affliction send	240	Would God, his greatness to display	51
Why not now, my God, my God	318	Would the great God his rebels spare	77
Why should a living man complain	62	Would we after Christ fulfil	78
Why should a mortal man complain	10	Wouldst thou for fifty righteous men	19
Why should believing Israel fear	45	Wouldst thou insult the fallen man	106
Why should I doubt his love at last	235	Wretched as sin can make	282
Why should I of his grace despair	223		
Why should I seek what cannot save	233		
Why shouldst thou fear, when I am thine	410		

Volume X

Why this profusion of thy grace	462	Waking at our plaintive cry	480
Will a meek, modest man of God	57	Walking in this heavenly path	15
Will they not now your words receive?	267	War with the fiend they wage	466
Will ye plead for sinning on	135	Warned of that vindictive day	104
Will ye the hateful relics spare	87	Was ever charity like thine!	214
Willing made my God t' obey	131	While with my lips I call thee Lord	12
Wilt thou from me withdraw thy grace	300	We cannot know th' eternal Son	300
Wilt thou not a difference make	42	We cannot rest, who Jesus know[961]	502
Wisdom, because we ask, he gives	207	We fear lest when thy grace o'erpowers	323
Wisdom Divine I long to know	207	We gain, in solitude and prayer	159
Wisdom is the hoary hair	351	We in his ministers and word	159
With all my heart, O Lord, I pray	332	We must in our requests succeed	177
With all the new-born babes I fed	109	We now who Jesus' Spirit breathe	301
With all who for redemption groan	208	We preach in Jesus' name in vain	205
With confidence lift up thy face	440	We run in distress To Jesus our tower	100
With darkness palpable oppressed	270	We see the unbelieving crowd	463
With deepest shame, with humblest fear	359	We should have been doomed With devils to dwell	48
With faith's most fixed attention	408		
With forward zeal well meant	165	We sing as in those earliest days	74
With gospel-songs triumphant tell	426	We two, O Lord, on earth agree	316
With graces from above	467	We wish our children rich and great	321
With him I on Sion shall stand	405	Weary of earth, my soul receive	157
With Jesus to reign Whoever aspire	400	Weary of passions unsubued	253
With longing eyes and restless heart	329	Weighed in the scale, thou wanting art	70
With restless expectation	408		
With thy benefits surrounded	391		

961. *UP* 2:57.

Welcome my Saviour's word to me	237	When Jesus hath a sinner healed	488
Welcome the bright millennial day	88	When maliciously they seek	418
What are these wounds, so deep, so wide	123	When once we let the tempter in	399
What avails th' external sign	445	When our neighbour's wants declare	461
What but Omnipotence can raise	491	When raised out of the dust I stand	111
What can feeble nature do?	409	When rash into the snare we run	414
What can I do but lay me down	77	When Satan fails the souls to shake	152
What canst thou do to me, whose good	77	When shall I share, O Lord, with thee	157
What Christian crowds the kingdom lose	212	When shall th' imperial standard spread	375
What crowds in every age receive	271	When shall thy Spirit reign	178
What crowds, O Lord, thy name profess	487	When the house of Jacob's sons	64
What end of man's apostasy	414	When the King of Israel came	351
What fatal madness to delay	370	When the trying hour is passed	481
What harm to raise a fortune fair	272	When thee in part I truly know	111
What hath this wretched world to give	70	When thou didst to life return	410
What have devils to do with thee?	218	When thou the bond of sin hast broke	255
What hypocrite so base as he	380	When thy Spirit we receive	376
What if we pine for want of bread	257	When undistinguishing I prayed	201
What is an heart with envy fraught	464	Whene'er[962] the pure baptismal rite	446
What is the chaff, the word of man	31	Whene'er thou dost thy grace bestow	210
What kind of man is this	217	Whene'er thou leav'st me in distress	408
What multitudes the curse shall feel	SH 1762, 2:187	Where are the learned and rich and great?	338
		Where but at his Saviour's feet	452
What numbers call the Saviour Lord	290	Where is my power to watch and pray	77
What posture should I use, who see	403	Where social virtue never comes	482
What though a Sadducee maintain	495	Where'er thou dost thy grace bestow	248
What, to man my follies own!	444	Wherefore in confidence of grace	485
What tongue the greatness can explain	239	Which of the old prophets dared	167
What violence and convulsive throes	449	While faults in others I reprove	192
What wisdom can in sinners dwell	16	While God his judgments sure defers	370
What words of horror can explain	258	While in the flesh we tarry	181
What would dying sinners give	384	While Jacob for a wife doth wait	80
Whate'er is not of God	288	While Jesus receives The grace He imparts	342
Whate'er to magistrates belong	170		
Whate'er we can of Jesus know	301	While thou dost our souls restore	63
Whatever knowledge from his Lord	281	While thus I testify of thee	485
When all my unbelief is gone	20	While we in his sight review	499
When Antichrist erects his throne	371	While with my lips I call thee Lord	205
When faith, almighty faith, is mine	227	Who a bare profession make	382
When from thee we cannot turn	37	Who armed with Christ's commission goes	236
When he did our flesh assume	41		
When he hath begun our cure	458		
When I use the proffered power	23	962. Osborn changed "Whene'er" to "Where'er."	
When in thine image I awake	40		

Who avarice with religion veil	340	Who simple innocence approves	322
Who bids the careless lilies grow	189	Who slights the warning word	367
Who boast their forms, without the power	358	Who soften and corrupt the word	450
Who camest self-emptied from the sky	245	Who teach that the most righteus man	203
Who can reconcile and make	62	Who teach their children to admire	156
Who comprehends the reason why	430	Who the first elements would know	477
Who dares religion's power deny	289	Who the high office can display	248
Who do the will Divine	470	Who their own good declare	289
Who dost that awful day forget	381	Who to his people came unsought	73
Who ever of a mountain heard	342	Who to his Saviour's messengers	243
Who feign a zeal for God	361	Who to the poor and needy gives	386
Who fiercely with each other fight	297	Who truly know his name	44
Who first their hands imbrued	122	Who trust in a supposed decree	403
Who follow Christ in good delight	464	Who untried himself can know?	474
Who hath engaged my heart t' address	35	Who waits for the applause of man	283
Who hear, and cast the word behind	271	Who walking like their Saviour here	387
Who hears the word and disbelieves	348	Who weakly once to sin gives place	414
Who herod did of old inspire	144	Who will reject thy richest grace	251
Who in his nature's weakness lies	221	Who with the smallest act begin	498
Who in his Spirit walk and live	149	Who would not dread the frown of him	239
Who in the faith of Abraham tread	212	Who would not start from avarice	398
Who is that servant good and wise	386	Whoe'er by thy command impart	491
Who is the idol Shepherd? who	120	Whoe'er for happiness relies	272
Who Jesus for their Lord receive	204	Whoe'er for sin and Satan plead	203
Who knowingly the truth oppose	433	Whoe'er rejects thy sacrifice	470
Who labours in the church of God	234	Whoe'er submits to sin's commands	261
Who like the thoughtless many live	202	Whoe'er th' authority impeach	167
Who may his day abide	130	Whoe'er the cross of Christ oppose	302
Who now lament and grieve	438	Whoe'er their indolent delight	265
Who now thy living church admire	491	Whoe'er to thee, O Christ, belong	237
Who, of authority possessed	462	Whole nights we to ambition give	406
Who of other help despair	160	Whom Christ his brethren owns	439
Who of the rich or great appear?	467	Whom God pronounced his favourite Son	151
Who of the rich will e'er believe	326	Whom I to thy grace commend	45
Who on Jesus' love rely	206	Whom Jacob once in Bethel found	80
Who on Providence depend	296	Whom nature joins he often parts	159
Who preach the genuine word of God	454	Whom the Lord vouchsafes to feed	296
Who publish his authentic word	471	Whom the only fear of men	279
Who sail with our Lord in the ship	478	Whom wilt thou thy people call	125
Who see, must surely feel	122	Why am I stripped of all my power?	390
Who seek the Crucified	437	Why do I not receive it now?	198
Who sends his servants forth by pairs	493	Why hath God concealed the day	376
Who shall explain the mystery?	9	Why is my heart so dark and void	268

Why should a sinful man complain	51	Warm, vehement, positive, and loud	75
Why should I ask the future load	191	Warned of God to watch and pray	290
Why was he doomed to endless pain?	391	Wast thou not sent, my Lord, for me	385
Why, what evil hath he done	422	We ask a soul no longer blind	442
Will man be diligent to serve	188	We bless thee Saviour for the grace	485
Will th' Almighty God of grace	211	We bow submissive to the will	97
Willing to be rescued now	308	We by thy bloody conquest	88
Wilt thou as such the cowards own	439	We cannot wish our neighbour more	191
Wilt thou not, Lord, the word repeat	220	We every earthly love forsake	149
Wisdom himself surprised would be	487	We have no benefit from thee	502
With anger, pride, and worldly love	273	*We have them too; and Christ beside*[963]	247
With Christ what shall I do? / What use	421	We hear, but cannot think with them	446
With Christ what shall I do? / The Prince	422	We here the sinner's history read	162
With envious, fierce, vindictive pride	418	We in our celestial Friend	202
With full indignation fired	422	We kindly share a mourner's woe	472
With humble joy the word who hear	474	We long to worldly pleasures cleave	149
With humble prayers and contrite sighs	106	We now the great salvation claim	113
With Magdalene and me	437	We of every good below	40
With man this is impossible	26	We ought not to his word alone	372
With me, Lord, I know, thou art	35	We ought to wash before we eat	4
With mine enemies surrounded	185	We see not why the Man Divine	7
With rigorous abstinence austere	251	We shall behold our Saviour shine	65
With shame and sorrow I confess	210	We shall stand before his face	240
With signs their high commission seal	442	We soon shall meet him in the sky	486
With sin we must entirely break	483	We still among the poor may find	446
With specious shows, and state, and ease	299	We still the old objection hear	411
With these may I my lot receive	107	We travel through this desert	396
With unrelenting heart they see	344	We trust thy providential power	289
Without reluctance or delay	448	We will not chide thy followers, Lord	188
Witness to the truth he bears	418	We worship our exalted Lord	316
Woe to the man, eternal woe	315	Weakened when our faith we find	306
Wonders and signs by Satan's aid	372	Weaker for each he lies	187
Worldlings in vain the truth approve	272	Weakest of thy disciples, young	80
Worldly consolations see!	427	Weary of publishing thy grace	448
Would the wise malicious fiend	469	Weary on the well reclined	353
Wouldst thou be truly mortified?	185	Weary, weary, and oppressed	470
Wouldst thou require what cannot be?	173	Weary, with thirst and hunger faint	250
Wretched in myself, I would	254	Weeps the Saviour o'er his foe	268
		Welcome to the souls of men	41
		Welcome, weariness and pain	354
		Well-pleasing to our God above	87
		What angel can the grace explain	321

Volume XI

Waiting at his Saviour's feet	27
Wandering souls, lift up your eyes	353

[963]. *UP* 2:160.

What avails it, Lord, to know[964]	505	When our God the gospel gives	410
What but mercy could impose	314	When our incarnate God[967]	141
What but the love of truth and thee	19	When people and priest, United in prayer	102
What can I do but offer	439	When shall the happy moment come	184
What cannot Christ in sinners do	35	When shall we hear his trumpet sound[968]	201
What cannot the Almighty do	105	When six great days of God are passed	20
What comfortable words are thine	452	When th' almighty Jesus cries	479
What could the curious passion do	179	When the captious Pharisee	13
What crowds acknowledge thee	158	When the evangelic sound	108
What endless scenes of wonder rise	22	When the sacramental cup	284
What I cannot hide from thee	357	When the time was now fulfilled[969]	227
What is everything beside[965]	198	When thou appear'st below	143
What is it then, thy flesh to eat	389	When thy wise permissive will	405
What is the fruit which Christ requires	42	When time and all its works are passed	275
What is the proof of perfect love	156	When to his sober mind restored[970]	235
What meekness, grace, and love Divine	225	When to the house of prayer we go	257
What multitudes to God draw near	4	When virtue's advocate replies	404
What multitudes who never know	425	When wine they want th' almighty Lord	334
What my gracious Saviour spoke	123	When with eyes of faith we see	476
What profits it alas, to hear	497	Whence is it that my Lord	107
What profits it the great and wise	179	Whene'er thou dost a sinner heal	366
What then is all beside	SH 1762, 2:219	Where are the men that called so loud	418
What we love for its own sake	213	Where are the nine? alas, my God	253
What will it profit me to know	215	Wherefore should I doubt his power	175
What wisdom in our heavenly Lord	416	Wherefore should we droop or fear	189
When Abraham was not born, I AM	435	Wherefore we thankfully believe	430
When captious Pharisees are near	53	Wherewith shall I be seasoned now?	29
When Christ and purity is near	172	Whether they praise us, or condemn	54
When Christ doth to the soul appear	21	Whether thy little flock we feed	250
When given up to brutish lust	173	Which wilt thou serve? The world or God?	242
When God resigns his parting breath	90	While all his holy angels	330
When in his arms he held[966]	120	While at the bar he stands	83
When in Jesus' name we pray	12	While feebly gasping at thy feet	392
When Jesus at his feet he saw	501	While for us he undertakes	84
When Jesus bade me first believe	440	While he sits at meat, reclined	165
When Jesus first pronounced the word	371	While in faithful hearts we bear	98
When Jesus for his murderers prays	302	While in their hands the angels bear	133
When Jesus in the clouds ye see	391		
When Jesus we presume to praise	411		
When mercy's day is o'er	301		

964. *UP* 2:258.
965. *UP* 2:126.
966. *UP* 2:82.
967. *UP* 2:91.
968. Osborn changed to: "Then let us hear the trumpet sound."
969. *UP* 2:150.
970. *UP* 2:155.

IDEX OF FIRST LINES OF POETRY BY JOHN AND CHARLES WESLEY

While in this wilderness we stray	310	Who in the Saviour sent confides	373
While in this wilderness we dwell	388	Who in the steps of Jesus	463
While myself I faint to bear	148	Who in the worldly spirit	398
While nature yielding to despair	102	Who in thy faithful word	74
While our grief for sin we show	167	Who is this condescending	32
While the world and sin oppress us	277	*Who is this tender-hearted friend*	
While we of his mysteries	312		SH 1762, 2:207
While with tears of true contrition	311	Who is this that sin forgives	168
Whither shall we go from thee	394	Who Jesus' spirit knows	292
Who all our infirmities knows	491	Who knows the evils that	284
Who all thy springs of action knows	132	Who lies in unbelief confined	477
Who at his cross had stood	93	Who love the praise of men	397
Who blush their Lord to own	182	Who marvel at his power admire	188
Who came to make his Father known[971]	129	Who miracles demand in vain	89
Who can resist th' almighty will	385	Who Moses and the prophets hear	21
Who changes water into wine	337	Who now his flesh and blood partake	390
Who dar'st oppose the popular cry	413	Who on thy mystic body fall	271
Who did his servant's fall foretell	289	Who shall accuse th' elect of God	418
Who did the rebel angels quell	111	Who suffer for thy sake	52
Who didst from him thy mission know	500	Who suffer in their Saviour's cause	412
Who[972] dost all worldly state decline	379	Who tastes the truth, and Jesus sees[975]	184
Who doth through Jesu's grace repent	303	Who the host celestial made	291
Who earth and heaven and Hell commands	63	Who the true disciples are	282
		Who the work of God oppose	445
Who every thought and motion knows	74	Who their authority maintain	285
Who first by reason's scanty line	343	Who their own desires pursue	397
Who first conversed with Christ	412	Who thy Deity confess	123
Who follows Christ with heart sincere	230	Who to the world restorest thy heart	190
Who from the world retreat	92	Who trusts his own intrepid heart	73
Who gladly to his home invites	226	Who will not now the word believe[976]	344
Who God devoutly dreads	120	Who works the works of God	396
Who God in truth adore	450	Who worldly good pursue	69
Who happy without God would be[973]	234	Who would not descend his Saviour	264
Who hears his warnings with disdain[974]	509	Who would not eagerly desire	27
Who himself to babes reveals	494	Who would not serve a Lord	35
Who his mind on God hath stayed	422	Whoe'er his Master's money wastes	241
Who his wisdom can surprise	208	Whoe'er the gospel hate	62
Who in his mean condition here	270	Wholly sacrificed to God	286
Who in the faith of Abraham tread	429	Whom the Lord of life denies	209
		Why hast thou, Saviour, by thy grace	366
		Why have I, Lord, so often been	225

971. *UP* 2:88.
972. Osborn changed "Who" to "Thou."
973. *UP* 2:155.
974. *UP* 2:260.
975. *UP* 2:111.
976. *UP* 2:221.

Why is he doomed to endless pain	245			
Why should I smaller gifts request	47			

Volume XII

Why is he doomed to endless pain	245	Waits my heart insensible	258
Why should I smaller gifts request	47	Warned by the Comforter	374
Why should that a hindrance prove	229	Warned of thy approach I wait	236
Why? thou thyself hast told us why	403	Was ever grief like his	84
Will carnal thoughts of carnal men	54	Was it his nature's stubbornness	385
Will my Lord be so unkind	309	Was it not thy kind design	208
Will the foes of Jesus own	464	Watchman of Israel I	375
Will they not? alas for them	374	We all are sprung from Adam's line	341
Wisdom and power to God belong	483	We all obedient to our head	366
Wisdom we gain, O Lord, from thee	23	We, and the men whose wrath we feel	325
Wisdom with all its fulness dwells	124	We are from all our sins released	95
With all my small remains of grace	46	We cannot be withheld	195
With envious impotent desire	235	We do not, Lord, in thee confide	366
With eyes of faith we see	323	We grossly misconceive	5
With faith thy saying we receive	473	We have surely found him here	60
With his our office is the same	114	We hear the word which faith conveys	205
With infinite desire	283	We know he is the Lord	121
With lowly fear and shame	174	We lift our hearts (for God is here)	248
With meekness and majestic grace	433	We live, and move, and are	342
With mercy's quickest eyes	236	We live to make the Saviour known[977]	197
With that acclaiming choir above	317	We look for our returning Lord	304
With thee substantially the same	425	We may in all the creatures find	342
With truth we benefactors call	285	We must speak on, forbid by all	190
Within the promise now, I sing	109	We never can recriminate	451
Witness of thy death am I	315	We nothing catch with all our care	120
Witness of truth, and Channel too	387	We out of thee, the Way	6
Witnesses of Jesu's death	315	We speak because we have believed	177
Witnesses of th' atoning blood	413	We still may his epistles read	367
Woe to the men whom Jesus leaves	422	We the linen garments need	103
Woe to you, eternal woe	153	We think by truth Divine impressed	397
Woe to you who always full	152	We too of Jesus sing	255
Woe to you who laugh and play	152	We triumph in the word's success	257
Woe to you who riches prize	152	We wish his longer stay	253
Woe to you whom all commend	152	We witness for our Prince	192
Wonders we daily see	382	We yet shall to the people speak	188
Worldlings ye may, but will not see	14	Weakness still with ignorance	174
Worldly men whom interest parts	298	Well the bodily possession	222
Worn out with grief, and want, and pain	244	Were his alms and ceaseless prayers[978]	243
Would God decree his creature's pain	223	What a beautiful sight	155
Would you own with humble grief	454		
Wrestling on in ceaseless prayer	256		

977. *UP* 2:307.
978. *UP* 2:335.

What but the power which wakes the dead	320
What but the Spirit of faith Divine	301
What but thy grace that went before	268
What can persecution do	259
What could earth and hell do more	265
What heart can e'er conceive	242
What honour for the follower poor	384
What I publicly proclaim	372
What is all the world to me	131
What is that unity?	56
What Jesus for his soul hath done	394
What must I do? who hears my heart	323
What numbers like th' Athenians, mean	345
What shall I answer thee?	23
What shall I ask but thee	23
What shall the Spirit's will defeat	264
What the prediction meant	256
What then are they that dare forbid	333
What to thee thy Father gave	58
What tongue can express	212
When Christians lukewarm grown, and cold	343
When full four thousand years are passed	47
When God hath touched our souls, and brought	118
When he could himself defend[979]	81
When I have run my earthly race	241
When I my Saviour love	375
When Jesus gives the word	117
When Jesus imparts The truth to our hearts	44
When Jesus' meanest messenger	251
When man cast off his Maker's yoke	343
When man presumes a law t' enjoin	190
When ministers make known	294
When on that celestial land	120
When our benign almighty Lord	188
When passion in the judge prevails	82
When reason can no further go	141
When Satan rules and urges on	66
When superior pastors show	198
When the church of thine election	154
When the gospel of grace	186
When the great God his Spirit pours[980]	147
When the Spirit was come	156
When the stumbling-block is gone[981]	198
When[982] the word his blood applying	222
When the work and cause of God	292
When thou hast disposed a heart	229
When thy mercy appears	284
When to the counsel of our Lord	386
When vanquishing our sloth and ease	101
When we must our raiment shake	347
Whene'er thou dost our crimes efface	164
Whene'er we preach our pardoning Lord	452
Whene'er we preach the dying God	155
Where are humility and peace?[983]	196
Where are the venerable men[984]	346
Where can we now a city see	335
Where first by us it came, we there	240
Where is now the feeble reed	173
Where is the boastful tyrant's power	270
Where the true Joseph is not seen	204
Where the word his blood applying	222
Where were the venerable men	451
Where'er our Lord is pleased to send	427
Wherefore on thee we fix our eyes	82
While a weak worm passed by	186
While at my mouth the outcasts hear	298
While Canaan he to Israel gives	278
While feebly in thy paths we tread	12
While God their baffled rage averts	452
While hanging on the shameful cross	95
While his watchful friends are weeping	205
While Jesus doth to heaven ascend	51
While obstinate I disbelieved	395
While on thy blood relying	300
While severed from the Root	20
While sinners in thy name they call	261

979. *UP* 2:273.
980. *UP* 2:288.
981. *UP* 2:308.
982. Osborn changed "When" to "Where."
983. *UP* 2:305.
984. *UP* 2:382.

While standing at the bar	422	Who Jesu's word esteem	201
While th' afflicted people weep	380	Who Jesus our Example know	158
While the glad tidings we proclaim	152	Who Jesus revere	303
While the Holy Spirit reigning	135	Who Jesus to the world confess[988]	239
While the power of faith I prove	22	Who Jesus' work resolves to do	199
While the succession true	356	Who John's sincere disciples are	357
While their host with loving zeal	324	Who laid the ground alone	215
While thine earthly course was ending	105	Who lately shed the martyrs' blood	239
While thy religious actions show	250	Who live O God in thee	342
While with a fleshly arm	403	Who long the nations dark beguiled[989]	316
While yet thou livedst a Man of woe	53	Who love to reign installed on high	187
Who act the persecutor's part[985]	216	Who now dispense the pardoning word	288
Who after Paul and Jesus tread	410	Who now his work revives	283
Who after the first Christians tread	368	Who now the water can deny	251
Who all our sin and weakness knows	91	Who only seeks his Lord to raise	261
Who always took his people's part	332	Who our conduct scrutinize	170
Who bare the title then	334	Who our mortality put on	91
Who believes the prophets true	431	Who our weaknesses have known	160
Who boast their form of godliness	446	Who preach the truth, the gospel-word	169
Who but th' apostles of the Lamb	296	Who put their guides to flight	287
Who but the Holy Ghost can make	377	Who seeks the souls of men	312
Who can compass or contain	215	Who sees the miracle believes	276
Who can count his worshippers	228	Who shall make the Father known	9
Who can, O God, thy counsels tell![986]	196	Who shall presume t' explore	220
Who can resist the Saviour's word	138	Who that moment's price can tell	433
Who can tell the consolation	449	Who then shall needless things impose	307
Who can the grace explain?	26	Who to some brutish lust submit	213
Who can the sudden turns explain	291	Who to those gracious words of thine	32
Who can the yoke of Moses bear?	302	Who trust in his protecting grace	332
Who dares the gospel truth blaspheme[987]	347	Who want the form of godliness	254
Who doth indeed believe	44	Who wilfully refuse	7
Who faith's sincere obedience showed	205	Who would not his advice pursue[990]	442
Who first received th' engrafted word	53	Who would not look on thee	80
Who furious for the truth contend	69	Who yield their hearts the sordid Throne	83
Who heard him speaking from the skies	97	Whoe'er in thy hand The instrument be	365
Who heard the heaven-instructed man	367	Whoe'er, like Lucifer, aspire	272
Who his Lord and pattern knows	292	Whom first to thee thy Father gave	50
Who in Jesus believe	250	Whome'er he doth for servants take	244
Who in thine oracles delight	379		
Who is so great a God as ours!	205		

985. UP 2:313.
986. UP 2:305
987. UP 2:383.
988. UP 2:329.
989. Osborn changed to: The nations dark who long beguiled.
990. UP 2:430.

INDEX OF FIRST LINES OF POETRY BY JOHN AND CHARLES WESLEY

Whose words they can no more withstand[991]	200
Why should believers droop?	148
Why should I longer stay	397
Why were they left to disagree?	310
Willing that all his death should know[992]	94
Wilt thou in that bloody place	417
Wilt thou not soon display thy heart	340
Wisely ye may consult, contrive	194
With Divine instructions fraught	314
With hasty grief and fear	103
With joy we now approve	294
With me, I find, thou still dost dwell	8
With me thy Spirit shall abide	68
With milk thou dost the infants feed	39
With patience I attend	203
With sorrow Lord and fear	65
With the goods and ills below	36
With the humble filial fear	241
With the Omniscient Spirit filled	275
With thee we put it on	279
With them we lift our voice	295
With thy commission Lord, we go	428
With thy pure Spirit filled	181
With trembling crowds surrounded	439
With true humility inspired	248
With us we know he dwells	13
With vain magnificent excess	420
With what indifferent carelessness	419
Women, excused from public care	314
Women in days of old	334
Women we own the foremost still	315
Worldlings, anticipate the day	437
Would we attend the voice Divine	210
Wounded and bruised and drenched in blood	392
Written with an iron pen	86

Volume XIII

Walking in thee, I go in peace	190
Was it a fruitless fond desire	59
We are safe in his hands	163
We find the better hope brought in	135
We first beheld the promise made	150
We have not an High-priest above	126
We, Jesus, will on thee attend	88
We know, by faith we surely know	210
We know, the solemn day draws nigh	176
We look for mercy still	217
We, only we believe indeed	213
We preach a rest from sin and fear	123
We still experience them the same	168
We that are Christ's, have crucified	66
We that the Lord have known	199
We the one sure foundation lay	6
We trust in our Lord, Our Saviour and King	246
We who in thy death confide	233
We wish your full perfection here	28
We work, till thou pronounce, "Well done!"	90
Weary life of sin and grief	52
Weary of life, with guilt opprest	125
Were all the race already run	152
What are those marks th' apostle bears?	69
What but thy right hand of power	222
What depths of wisdom and of grace	116
What doth my gracious Saviour say?	132
What doth that silence mean?	234
What doth thy Gnostic faith avail	168
What good remains in me?	226
What have I else whereof to boast?[993]	256
What heart can e'er conceive	85
What is that gospel-hope?	82
What is that meetness for the skies?	82
What is the pleasure of my Lord?	97
What may I not expect from him	63
What must I do, shut up alone	8
What, never, never more to sin!	203

---

991. *UP* 2:309.
992. *UP* 2:276: "Willing that all his truth should know."
993. Osborn notes that this is a poem of J. Leifchild.

PART 1: THE POETICAL WORKS OF JOHN AND CHARLES WESLEY

What, never speak one evil word	173	Who can a pastor's heart express	115
What saith the word infallible	15	Who can tell the worth of Jesus?	179
What say the happy dead?	149	Who can worthily commend	220
What then are they, who dare deride	216	Who daily bleed and die with thee	120
What thou gav'st me once to know	153	Who every hasty growth reject	175
What though ten thousand witnesses	206	Who gently leadest those with young	210
What though the faithless world gainsay	206	Who in our father's footsteps tread	134
What victims doth our God demand?	16	Who in their own perfection boast	196
Whate'er the hypocrites pretend	5	Who laboured by the law to live	135
Whate'er the members must endure	84	Who never hast affliction known	156
When all thy waves and storms are passed	183	Who on thy word relying	106
When death thy soul and body part	102	Who pardon preach through faith alone	6
When his coming from above	269	Who see the light of Jesu's face	133
When I am weak, then I am strong	58	Who shall my soul deliver? Who	9
When I see my brother's fault	67	Who the calm can understand	264
When Satan hath in me no part	190	Who then art thou that darest reject	32
When shall I be crucified?	62	Who truly thinks, and surely knows	33
When shall the Judge descend	111	Who trust in our Redeemer's blood	143
When that philanthropy Divine	114	Who walk enlightened by thy light	226
When the old Adam was	184	Who would not be partaker	260
When thou hadst all thy foes o'ercome	229	Whoe'er by thy good Spirit are led	12
When thou hadst found the grace	184	Whoe'er the joyful news believes	3
When we all things do in love	42	Whoe'er the patient word retain	227
Whene'er in error's paths we rove	110	Whoe'er their heavenly Father fear	156
Where is that faith, whose fervent prayer	176	Whoe'er their own perfection boast[994]	196
Where is thy promise? where	32	Whoe'er through ignorance, or pride	6
Where then shall I appear	183	Why hast thou apprehended me	79
Wherefore let every soul beware	17	Why have not I my pardon sealed?	174
Wherefore thy goodness we implore	195	Why should I till to-morrow stay	51
Wherefore, ye saints, with resolute zeal	87	Why should they be stricken more?	270
Wherever our Lord his Spirit imparts	30	Will the chief of saints declare	24
Whether by slow or swift degrees	7	Winds and storms their charge fulfil	266
Whether the word be preached or read	123	Witchcraft! enchantment! Sorcery	66
Which of the old apostles taught	132	With countless burdens pressed	48
Which of the petty kings of earth	118	With Elijah's faith endowed	267
While after Jesus we proceed	151	With love we receive The power to obey	30
While, as thy oracles enjoin	94	With me how canst thou longer bear	188
While I sensibly decline	269	With me, most gracious Lord	113
While I thus my Pattern view	153	With pride that I may never swell	261
While in the flesh I languish	46	With simple faith like his	150
While now thine oracles we read	110	With the first spark of good desire	15
While thus the life of faith she showed	172		
While tossed about with every wind	53	994. Osborn changed to: "Who in their own perfection boast."	
Whilst preaching gospel to the poor	261		

315

With thee in full paternal might	226
With them we march securely on	118
With true celestial wisdom filled	173
Witness thou righteous man	184
Wood, stubble, hay,—of creeds untrue	27
Wood, stubble, hay,—of lifeless forms	27
Worldlings in the shadow rest	182
Worthy the Lamb for sinners slain	233
Worthy the Lamb that died for man	248
Would my Saviour have me do	132
Wrestling on for faith's increase	191
Write upon me the Name Divine	228

Volume I

Ye earthly loves, be far away![995]	109
Ye faithful souls, confide in God	256
Ye nations, who the globe divide[996]	124
Ye of fearful hearts, be strong	291
Ye priests of God, whose happy days[997]	122
Ye sons of men, here nought avails[998]	86
Ye that round our altars throng	170
Ye that tremble at his frown	290
Yea, Father, ours through him thou art[999]	340
Yea, let man rage! since thou wilt spread[1000]	178
Yea, let thy Spirit in every place[1001]	167
Yea, thou true Witness, spotless Lamb[1002]	109
Yes, Lord; we hearken to thy call	213
Yes; since with thee my lot is cast	26
Yes; the divorce at last is made	248
Yes; the future work is done	297
Yet am I lost, (shouldst thou depart,)	293
Yet ask not in mere ease and pomp[1003]	36
Yet can I mark that herbs below[1004]	68
Yet darkly safe with God thy soul[1005]	35
Yet even the sharpest, heaviest grief[1006]	58
Yet higher still our farthest aim	191
Yet him th' Almighty Father's will	80
Yet I partake thy grace	100
Yet if one haply longing stands	25
Yet in thy Son, Divinely great	230
Yet must I, though oppressed, submit[1007]	37
Yet nought whereof to boast I have[1008]	348
Yet, O, I cannot burst my chain	253
Yet, O! ten thousand lusts remain	134
Yet sin is dead; and yet abide[1009]	67
Yet take thy way: thy way is best[1010]	48
Yet thy unwearied love went on[1011]	41
Yet vain the fierce Enthusiast's aim	14
Yet while, at length, who scorned thy might[1012]	146
Yet will I share the conquest too[1013]	29
You can brave th' eternal laws	286
You for my own I then shall take	206
Your willing ear and heart incline	206

Volume II

Ye all may freely take	229
Ye angels that in strength excel	236

---

995. From the German of Nikolaus von Zinzendorf, translated by John Wesley.
996. Samuel Wesley, Sr.
997. Samuel Wesley, Sr.
998. From the German of Christian Friedrich Richter, translated by John Wesley.
999. From the German of Ludwig Andreas Gotter, translated by John Wesley.
1000. From the German of Johann Joseph Winckler, translated by John Wesley.
1001. Henry More.
1002. From the German of Nikolaus von Zinzendorf, translated by John Wesley.
1003. John Gambold?
1004. George Herbert.
1005. John Gambold?
1006. George Herbert.
1007. George Herbert.
1008. From the German of Nikolaus von Zinzendorf, translated by John Wesley.
1009. George Herbert.
1010. George Herbert.
1011. George Herbert.
1012. From the German of Ernst Lange, translated by John Wesley.
1013. George Herbert.

Ye cast your crowns before his throne	236	Yes, our sins have done the deed	232
Ye happy sinners, hear	245	Yes, thy sacrament extends	263
Ye that pass by, behold the Man!	70	Yet all the faithful shall not fail	137
Ye who faint beneath the load	192	Yet come, thou heavenly Guest	246
Ye whose loins are girt, stand forth!	192	Yet for thy commandment sake	362
Ye worms of earth, our God admire	234	Yet I may be saved I know	14
Yes; for the broken contrite heart[1014]	9	Yet in this ordinance Divine	323
Yes, Lord, I put my trust in thee	243	Yet may we celebrate below	309
Yes, Lord, I shall see The bliss of thine own	177	Yet not from these the power proceeds	260
		Yet, O Lord, I still believe	14
Yes, Lord, we must believe thee kind	289	Yet O! my God (I said) how long	136
Yes, the Christian's course is run	189	Yet shalt thou be brought down to hell	148
Yes: with my shield of faith I part	109	Yet still, alas! there are	80
Yet God is above men, devils, and sin	198	Yet still an higher seat	287
Yet hast thou in the Gospel glass	195	Yet still I cannot ask	62
Yet if thou stay'st, why must I stay?	42	Yet these, even these his pity knew to bear	124
Yet, Lord, for thee again we mourn	61		
Yet now I choose to breathe my last	127	Yet thy wrath I cannot fear	11
Yet now, thou know'st, I fear	115	Yet will he plead the sinner's cause	142
Yet O! how quickly, Lord, hast thou	345	Yet will I all my word fulfil	140
Yet soon my wretched heart	117	You, his own peculiar race	87
Yet still the servants of their Lord[1015]	62	You must for ever live	48
Yet still we glory in thy name	359	You never can forget	47
Yet we are thine, though dispossest	61	You never can receive	47
Yet when the fullest joy is given	140	You, on whom he favours showers	86
Yield to me now; for I am weak	175	You, who own his record true	86
		You, whom he ordained to be	86
		Your meat and your drink offerings throw	319

Volume III

Ye are, and I was once, forgiven	27
Ye faithful souls, who thus record	279
Ye fear to use the grace ye have	136
Ye fools that throng the smooth infernal road	127
Ye hear, and will not understand	136
Ye men that live in riotous excess	117
Ye royal priests of Jesus, rise	319
Ye will not, what ye see, perceive	136
Yes, Lord, we are thine	334

1014. David Lewis.
1015. From the German of August Gottlieb Spangenberg, translated by John Wesley.

Volume IV

Ye all my glory shall declare	309
Ye are my witnesses, to you	297
Ye heavenly choir, Assist me to sing	107
Ye heavens rejoice In Jesus his grace	298
Ye men of Israel, hear	146
Ye mountains, and vales, In praises abound	298
Ye now afflicted are	218
Ye saw him in the courts above	160
Ye servants of God, Your Master proclaim	51

IDEX OF FIRST LINES OF POETRY BY JOHN AND CHARLES WESLEY

Ye simple men of heart sincere	106
Ye simple souls, that stray	230
Ye souls of the righteous, appear	240
Ye tempted souls, that feel	217
Ye vagrant souls, on you I call	277
Ye who believe his record true	277
Ye who now enjoy his favour	383
Yes, Lord, thy word for ever stands	286
Yes, Lord, we adore, though all Men deny	52
Yes, our exalted Jesus	150
Yes, thou art surely gone before	159
Yes, thou shalt soon pronounce His doom	190
Yes, to her the Master came	132
Yes, without thy help I must	462
Yet, alas, we cannot rest	176
Yet do not drive us from thy face	422
Yet for the faithful remnant's sake	81
Yet for the honour of thy love	63
Yet for the righteous remnant's sake	70
Yet for thy own mercy sake	417
Yet hast thou left thyself a seed	70
Yet here alas! in pain I live	28
Yet let me urge my one request	351
Yet long I withstood	273
Yet must I, Lord, to thee complain	275
Yet must we, Lord, with shame confess	275
Yet now, O Lord our God, at last	5
Yet now, my chosen servant, hear	295
Yet O! I doubt thy gracious will	361
Yet O! my enemy hath found	400
Yet, O my God, at last	439
Yet O! the chief of sinners spare	370
Yet O thou wilt not quit	447
Yet O! we look for more	49
Yet still we all share his happiness	156
Yet there when I am	274
Yet thou hast the cause unfolded	182
Yet what is all I bear	438
Your grounds forsake, your oxen quit	275
Your hearts, and not your garments rent	73
Your sons and daughters at that day	75

Volume V

Ye advocates for sin, and hell	4
Ye different sects, who all declare	480
Ye felt the cruel torturing fear	362
Ye followers of the bleeding Lamb	472
Ye followers of the Lamb	473
Ye happy souls, no longer tossed	361
Ye liars, and blasphemers too	123
Ye monsters of unnatural vice	123
Ye neighbours, and friends Of Jesus, draw near	115
Ye now have took the field	272
Ye people all pass on	45
Ye servants of God, Who trust in his Son	322
Ye sons of grace	62
Ye souls that own the common Lord	477
Ye that have here received	285
Ye that in strength Divine excel	473
Ye virgin souls arise	284
Ye watchmen of Israel, declare	265
Ye who his call obey	271
Ye wise and pious few	258
Yes, Lord, I drink thy bitter cup	157
Yes, Lord, I now perceive	366
Yes, Lord, thy promise-word is true	251
Yes, Lord, with deepest shame we own	243
Yes, Lord, with joy, and grief, and love	20
Yes, the lion is once more	380
Yes, thou dear lamb-like Son of God	146
Yes, with a solemn oath the Lord	299
Yet can I not rest	304
Yet do I this resign	118
Yet (for he bids us keep in view	361
Yet for thy desolate Sion sake	75
Yet I can thy mercy praise	188
Yet hear me, for thy people hear	95
Yet hear, ye souls that cleave	370
Yet, Lord, if it be	439
Yet not many wise his summons obey	391
Yet now in life detain	236
Yet of these if God's decree	406
Yet onward I haste	24
Yet since thy will ordains it so	77

Yet will I offer in thy might	159	Yet on thy virgin-bier	238
You on our minds we ever bear	479	Yet, ready to depart in peace	304
You, though in body distant far	477	Yet should we on her memory dwell	319
You, whom I have brought to God	13	Yet still the Lord, the Saviour reigns	28
Your claim, alas! ye cannot prove	481	Yet still thy lingering pity spares	130
Your Rock can never shake	42	Yet still to us she speaks, though dead	244
		Yet thou know'st what pangs of love	252
		Yet, though her choice was still to sit	359

Volume VI

		Yet vainly of our ancestors we boast	59
Ye rob Britannia of her shield	165	Yet we know our mediator	161
Ye servants of God, Acknowledge		Yet when she heard the gospel sound	240
Him near	91	Yet while I warmly, for her faith contend	57
Ye servants of the Lord	46	*Young men and maidens, raise*	433
Ye slaves of sin and hell	13	Your sins for vengeance call	35
Ye spirits enslaved Your liberty claim	13		
Ye who have sold for nought	13		

Volume VII

Ye worms of earth, arise	10		
Yea, Amen! let all adore thee	133	Ye seraphs nearest to the throne	313
Yes, every secret of my heart	402	Yes, O thou all-redeeming Lamb	100
Yes, happy soul, so closely pressed	275	Yet ah! my troubled spirit knows	108
Yes, the prize shall now be given	145	Yet as thy own command requires	130
Yes, thou hast found an home	238	Yet here my soul detain	387
Yes; though now his spirit reigns	363	Yet I in my lost condition	390
Yet first the stricken earth shall mourn	88	Yet lo! The Lord our God for ever lives	441
Yet for myself, not him, I grieve	347	Yet now permit the sad request	118
Yet forty days thy justice cries	78	Yet shall we, Lord, our hearts disguise	119
Yet hath thy kind compassion spared	75	Yet spare him—for his only sake	116
Yet hear us, for the labourers hear	117	Yet spare us, O thou God supreme	256
Yet if our sin demands	125	Yet, spite of our resolves, we fear	77
Yet if so thy will ordain	212	Yet teach me still by special grace	400
Yet if thou hast not fixed our doom	175	Yet though I am sometimes afraid	54
Yet if thou must thy foes chastise	130	Yet we still indulge our tears	242
Yet in no narrow bounds confined[1016]	301	Yet we, with Peter, own	233
Yet lo! I now the blessing find	239	*Young and old, and men and maidens*	6
Yet may thy last expiring prayer	236		

Volume VIII

Yet, mindful of her friends below	362		
Yet neither earth nor hell could move	272		
Yet not forsook, but sorely tried[1017]	309	*Ye citizens of London, why*	468
Yet nought have we whereof to boast	417	Ye gentle citizens, attend	474
Yet now before thy gracious throne	166	Ye faithful souls, rejoice in him	67
Yet, O most patient God, forbear	165	Ye humble followers of my Lord	71
		Ye kingdoms of the earth, arise!	153
		Ye Londoners, with smiles regard	475

1016. UP 3:333.
1017. UP 3:336.

Ye men of childlike hearts draw near	72	Ye upstart priests, your sentence know	216
Ye powerful to oppress	137	Ye watchmen of Israel, declare	364
Ye servants of God, Whose diligent care	252	Yes; for we are not yet in hell	222
Ye sinners, stand in awe	8	Yes, I thee my helper know	297
Ye sons of men, lift up your voice	185	Yes; if the Lord his mind reveal	156
Ye worms, that wear an earthly crown	57	Yes, the Lord my God hath blessed	89
Year after year, thy patient grace	315	Yes; though thou fill my flesh with pain	241
Yes: the justified shall give	257	Yet come, thou radiant morning Star	84
Yet again, O God, my God	96	Yet conscious of my guilt I dare	237
Yet again to thee, O Lord	60	Yet dost thou, Lord, thy wrath forbear	424
Yet hast thou, Lord, a remnant still	316	Yet for a time he strives with all	14
Yet hath thy tender mercy spread	133	Yet for thy promise sake	266
Yet having your dear country freed	476	Yet if I do at last relent	210
Yet if our brethren's doom be sealed	285	Yet in the bottom of my heart	327
Yet if they have not sinned the sin	294	Yet, Lord, I ask a further grace	115
Yet if thou hast not fixed our doom	284	Yet Sion stands secure	464
Yet instruments of thy design	307	Yet still I humbly sue for more	132
Yet not for all this blasphemy	101	Yet still we wait the end	468
Yet not in this I trust	52	Yet till thy time is fully come	396
Yet O! we would, we would believe	344	Yet wilt thou not the guilty clear	56
Yet oh! thou gracious God and true	414	Your means (of sin, instead) of grace	371
Yet on the point of being sacked	456	Your sin-detesting virtue show	267
Yet Satan hath too oft prevailed	419	Your tempers with judicious love	395
Yet since he from my heart is torn	422	Your works of faith, let them commend	353
Yet still my Lord possessing	370		
Yet still, unconscious of its wound	407		
Yet th' infatuated crowd	329	## Volume X	
Yet though for all we feel	324	Ye angels, put the sickle in	87
Yet when beneath his wrath they stoop	199	Ye bold t' explain, describe, define	476
Yet, when I survey the skies	16	Ye envious Scribes who tread	363
"Yet will I bring," the Lord hath said	152	Ye gods of earth, expect to dwell	251
Yet will I in thy strength go forth	160	Ye high in gifts, who lift your head	146
Yet without thee	366	Ye must, ye must be born again	313
You ask the cause of all this pother	446	Ye partisans of every sect	193
Your heart shall find a heaven below	45	Ye pitiless, hard-hearted men	320
		Ye rich in works of righteousness	344
		Ye rich who bear the Christian name	215
## Volume IX		Ye saints, the most advanced in grace	348
Ye daughters of Sion, declare	365	Ye Scribes and Pharisees	361
Ye deserts so wild, Your offerings bring	416	"Ye shall be perfect" here below	174
Ye hate my truths and witnesses	372	Ye that do your Master's will	104
Ye seafaring men his footsteps adore	416	Ye that of power and riches proud	251
Ye that in royal mansions live	228	Yes; for thou wilt thy Son reveal	9

PART 1: *THE POETICAL WORKS OF JOHN AND CHARLES WESLEY*

Yes, from this instant now I will	6	Ye will not bear it in your mind	14
Yes, I steadfastly believe	211	Yes, by faith's enlightened eye	5
Yes, my Lord may justly leave me	265	Yes; for thou hast received[1019]	232
Yes, the law is like its Giver	167	Yes: he hath the Gentiles sought	407
Yes, the purest saint below	148	Yes, Lord: I steadfastly believe	474
Yes; their slanderous lies I hear	419	Yes, my gracious God and Lord	331
Yes, there is, there is, my God	18	Yes, O my suffering God	39
Yes, thou didst my soul release	4	Yes, unless thou hold me fast	393
Yes, thou hast told thy church before	372	Yet ah! how few his kingdom own	133
Yes we joyfully confess	275	Yet bold his neighbour to explore	226
Yes; we know, our Lord will come	135	Yet[1020] do not rest secure	205
Yet every one that seeks, shall find	201	Yet every tongue at last shall own	122
Yet guarded by thy word alone	298	Yet for my sinless Saviour's sake	238
Yet I cannot proudly scorn	473	Yet I seldom blush or groan	207
Yet in the midst of us thou art	24	Yet if I truly trust in thee	76
Yet not in outward veils of grace	225	Yet millions still uncalled remain	460
Yet, O most patient Lord	54	Yet more and more abandoned still	235
Yet still the sin to which he cleaves	483	Yet must we not presume to know	334
Yet still the worldly fool desires	273	Yet none of all our fallen race	344
Yet still we look for happier days	8	Yet O, a time I dare not set	250
Yet surely, Lord, I may expect	27	Yet the incorruptible seed[1021]	170
Yet the curious pride of man	376	Yet thou my Saviour art	143
Yet thousands, Lord, the honour claim	SH 1762, 2:155	Yet well he knows himself the same	441
		Yet will we not their sentence fear	451
Yet, when in faith the storm we bear	283	Yet will we still the truth maintain	447
Yet will I in my God confide	225	You who revel every day	182
Your house, no longer mine	365	Your pride and want of faith lament	376

Volume XI

Ye aged saints whose one concern	122
Ye envied rich, who nothing fear	SH 1762, 2:215
Ye know not, for ye will not know	448
Ye patient of applause and fame	375
Ye rich who live yourselves to please	243
Ye rich, your poverty confess	241
Ye scribes with learning fraught	450
Ye shepherds of the Romish fold	5
Ye thirsty for God To Jesus give ear	407
Ye venerable men	481
Ye who curiously desire[1018]	485

1018. *UP* 2:252.

Volume XII

Ye adders deaf, who stop your ears	166
Ye apostolic men	197
Ye dare not turn to God and live	453
Ye elders of the first degree	370
Ye Jews of our days Who heathens reject	251
Ye men who Christ profess to know	166
Ye murmur and accuse in vain	254
Ye now are joined in love[1022]	218
Ye now into our deeds inquire	171

1019. *UP* 2:153.
1020. Osborn changed "Yet" to "Then."
1021. *UP* 2:104.
1022. Osborn changed to "Now are ye."

Ye of the Christian sect	33	Ye just, the faithful God and true	217
Ye sacrilegious race	224	Ye see, who willing are to see	171
Ye sages of the world, be wise	194	Ye sordid slaves of avarice	73
Ye scorn the tyrants' frown	34	Ye talkers of your perfect love	28
Ye see the wonders of his hand	172	Ye that uncalled the power assume	129
Ye sprinkled heathen hear	340	Ye will, unless ye watch and pray	133
Ye that in rich attire delight	421	Year after year for this I live	194
Ye that now the news proclaim	398	Yes; but with the fleshly lust	65
Yes; another King we own	331	Yet children now here partake the prize	199
Yes; I own the crime abhorred	213	Yet now I feel a gleam of hope	128
Yes, the promised tribulation[1023]	46	Yet still the chief of saints below	196
Yes, thou hast my manners borne	278	Yet when the work is done	221
Yes; ye all may comprehend	337	Young men the victory have won	198
Yet, by the prince of darkness bound	430	Your humble confidence hold fast, / For	133
Yet conscious of his Lord's design	239	Your humble confidence hold fast / Till	199
Yet curious man whose reasoning eye	350		
Yet drawn by thine alluring grace	340		
Yet heathens still by Satan taught	368	## Volume II	
Yet here your curious pride	339	Zealous of all good works they live	326
Yet him we trust who went before	115		
Yet if in me thy Spirit dwell	302		
Yet in that Man deformed for thee	80	## Volume IX	
Yet Jesus regards Their services passed	114	Zealous I for my Lord have been	181
Yet lo, the Holy Ghost commands	273		
Yet must I more desire	9		
Yet something still thou know'st will be	300	## Volume X	
Yet till thy sovereign grace permit	429		
Yet while thou dost restrain	34	Zion, be glad, rejoice, and sing	107
Yet will we not the world upbraid	31		
Yet with the mind of Jesus steeled	385	## Volume XII	
Your call is to dispense	197		
Your ears ye stop, afraid to hear	453	Zeal to prefer our Maker's will	191
Your eyes through obstinate despite	453	Zeal will nothing leave undone	389
Your learned rulers too	162	Zealots though unregenerate men	403
Yourselves must judge it meet and right	176	Zeno and his followers still	336

Volume XIII

		First Lines not included in *PW* and *UP*	
Ye children of God, Your Father adore	245		
Ye faithful, patient souls, attend	176	### *Arminian Magazine*	
Ye faithful souls, who Jesus know	86		
Ye full, of confidence unsound	28	A scripture text to tell, and try *AM* 4 (1781)	456

1023. *UP* 2:264.

Fisher of men, ordained by Christ alone	
AM 4 (1781)	344
Here's an end of the story, and end of the dance	
AM 5 (1782)	167
Nor labour such for souls in vain	
AM 4 (1781)	456
Supported by the power of grace	
AM 7 (1784)	59–60
When zeal impetuous urged her vot'ries on	
AM 2 (1779)	47
Where are Geneva's doughty champions fled	
AM 2 (1779)	47
Why are they changed to George the third	
AM 4 (1781)	340

Hymn for Mary Langson (1770)[1024]

Hymn I

For the joy he sets before thee	11
Waiting to receive thy Spirit	11

Hymn II

Now I see with joy and wonder	12
O thou God of my salvation	12
This has set me all on fire	12
Tho' unseen, I love the Saviour	12
While the angel choirs are crying	12

I. Hymn [for the King][1025]

A king whose heart thy laws approves	5
But ought we, unconcerned, to see	5
Jesus, who bow to thy command	5
Outraged by the audacious croud	5

1024. Hymns published in [Thomas Olivers.] *A Short Account of the Death of Mary Langson, of Taxall, who died January 29th, 1769*, 12. [np] 1770.

1025. For this and the remaining hymns see the website of the Center for Studies in the Wesleyan Tradition and the section "Charles Wesley Manuscript Verse." The page numbers refer to those of the above entries on the website.

Thy power omnipotent exert	6
With pity, Lord, the rebels view	5

II. Hymn for the Queen[1026]

Born to insure her Consort's peace	7
Ev'n now the gracious token give	8
Long may our gracious Princess reign	7
No sex or rank the ruffians spare	6
On our inhospitable shore	6
The Earnest of their heaven bestow	7
Their blooming progeny increase	7
Thou Friend to Virtue in distress	6

On the Rev'd John Wesley[1027]

Born in the Churches Pale, and bred	1

[III.] Hymns for King George, 1769.[1028]

A thorny crown on earth he wears	1
Cloth all his enemies with shame	3
Fierce as the beast with iron teeth	2
Keep as the apple of thine eye	3
O God, the help of righteous kings	1
The Great—in wickedness and vice	1
Thine Image let the people see	3
Tired of a mild pacific Prince	2
See when the Beast of many heads	2
With fair pretence of public weal	1
Yet, O thou God of patient grace	2

[Untitled]

Would Peter's zeal have sold[1029]	41

1026. Ibid., MS Hymn for King and Queen 1780.

1027. Ibid., MS Tribute to John Wesley 1787.

1028. Ibid., MS Hymn for King George 1769.

1029. See "Assorted Looseleaf Manuscript Verse" on the website cited in fn. 1025.

PART 2

Alphabetical Index of First Lines of All Stanzas of Poems in *The Unpublished Poetry of Charles Wesley*, Volumes 1–3

First line, Volume of *UP*, and Page

A bird escaped the fowler's snare	3:170	A little more delicious sleep	3:314
A bishop primitively good	2:108	A look like that what heart can bear!	2:198
A blessing to the church below	3:331	A minister of grace	2:323
"A Child of 8 years old" I grant	1:282	A minister of Jesus	2:400
A Child of sorrow from the womb	1:314	A mission to the ministry	2:326
A Chosen, Saved, Peculiar Race[1]	2:455	A moment here I still remain	3:320
A Christian should with Christ remain	2:64	A moment more had Lot delayed	2:166
A conscious unbeliever, I	2:408	A moment more I would not stop	3:355
A conscious unbeliever see	2:325	A peace which never could have been	1:99
A difference in their favor make	3:56	A peace, whose evils know no bounds	1:99
A doer of the word he heard[2]	3:336	A penitent indeed	2:169
A faithful brother now	2:327	A persecutor I	2:329
A faithful minister	2:337	A pilgrim whilst on earth I rove	2:442
A faithful Seed there yet remains	1:81	A plain indisputable case[3]	2:319
A faithful soul that ceaseless prays	2:111	A preacher should himself conceal	2:78
A false pretended zeal	2:96	A preacher should with freedom use[4]	2:117
A flood of general wickedness broke in	3:394	A present help in deep distress	3:125
A fancied strength presumption gives	2:262	A prince who bears the Christian name	2:348
A Friend to us, but not our sins	2:101	A prisoner for the gospel-hope	2:414
A glorious Prize is still behind	3:158	A ready way repentance makes	2:85
A gospel-minister disdains	2:300	A Remedy, that never fails	1:239
A language unknown	2:341	A righteous judge can never boast	2:274
A life of poverty and toil	3:49	A righteous man who fears	2:81

1. The stanza beginning with this line appears in *PW* 4:316.
2. The stanza beginning with this line appears in *PW* 6:309–10.
3. The stanza beginning with this line appears in *PW* 12:222.
4. The stanza beginning with this line appears in *PW* 11:191.

A Scripture test—to tell, and try	3:391	Accursed by all, his memory shall rot	1:102
A servant in his earliest years[5]	3:355	Adieu! dear Linnell! from the shades of night	3:325
A servant of the Lord	2:421		
A servant of th'incarnate God	2:407	Adverse to Brothers, when we seemed to stray	3:436
A share did I say	1:285		
A sinner blind, to sight restored	2:58	Advocates (?) with flesh and blood	3:419
A sinner tottering o'er the grave	3:269	Affection unfeigned	2:290
A sinner's blindfold will	2:197	After my L[or]d resolved to go	3:351
A smile it will from Sister gain	1:281	After our ministerial toil	2:108
A soul detached from all below	3:342	Again I ask, this torturing ill	2:468
A soul that hath the truth received	2:58	Again I come my friends to meet	3:108
A State for judgment ripe as this	1:83	Again, my Howel, lend a patient ear	1:190
A stranger to that faith divine	1:305	Again, my soul, to Jesus turn	1:306
A Strife we are to all around[6]	2:447	Again they practised all their wiles	1:129
A stupid nation doomed	3:212	Against our Church, the gates of hell	1:78
A thousand different causes joined	1:113	Against the good & just	2:421
A thousand different paths I view	3:205	Against the instrument of ill[8]	1:315
A thousand ways thou canst prevent	3:425	Against the truth they stop their ears	2:316
A thousand ways to man unknown	3:140	Agreed, and meeting in thy Name	3:288
A troop of Jeroboam's priests appears	3:92	Ah, do not, Lord, the tempted leave	3:236
A widow on the poor bestowed	2:332	Ah, give them, Lord, the rod to bear	1:122
A worthy labourer of the Lord	2:373	Ah! leave me not to dream	2:460
A wretched, weak, intangled thing	3:356	Ah! leave them not in error's maze	3:310
Abandoned to the will of man	2:201	Ah! look not at what I have done	3:312
Able thou art the proud t'abase	3:40	Ah! Lord, depart not far from me	1:223
Above every name adored	2:393	Ah! Lord, I do, I do repent	3:154
Above our civil forms & ways	2:386	Ah! Lord, I know not what to say	1:222
Above the world (that gulph profound	1:245	Ah! lovely Pair, which shall we most admire	1:207
Above what I can ask or think	1:260		
Absent from the sepulcher	2:206	Ah, send me not up hence	3:138
Absent from those whom most he loves	2:279	Ah! what avails it, that our friendly Care	1:174
Abundant grace indeed	2:297	Ah! what have I to do with Peace	3:145
Accept from me the cordial praise	3:345	Ah! what shall I say	1:284
Accepted in the well-beloved[7]	2:278	Ah! where are all his Promises and Vows	3:87
Accomplishing his gracious word	2:78		
Accomplishing his kind intent	2:292	Ah! wherefore is thy former Zeal decayed?	1:191
According to thy will	3:272		
		Ah! whither, or to whom	3:362
		Ah! why should I longer remain	3:353
		Ah! woe is me, a man of woe	1:320
		Ah! woe is me, a Wretched Man	3:126

5. The stanza beginning with this line appears in *PW* 6:308.

6. The stanza beginning with this line appears in *PW* 8:447.

7. The stanza beginning with this line appears in *PW* 12:99–100.

8. See *PW* 8:427.

Ah! woe is me, my Friend is gone	3:357	All ye that seek the Lord who died[12]	3:111
Ah, woe is me, whom thrones surround	3:435	Allows my Howel's heart ye Saviour's Claim?	1:189
Ah, wretched souls, who, lifted up	2:89	Allured, and bought with Gallic gold	1:98
Alack & alack	1:283	Almighty God, be thou their Shield	1:290
Alas for us, who need beware[9]	2:186	Alms cannot alone, we know	2:87
Alas! I dare no longer hope	3:151	Already ye the men behold	2:402
Alas! I know not what to say—	3:358	Ambition in our bosom strives	3:45
All are not prophets of the Lord	2:26	Ambitious, covetous, and vain	2:183
All glory to thee	2:30	Among the most corrupt of men	2:303
All-good, All-gracious to redeem	3:159	An angel of the church below	2:401
All good, all wise, almighty Lord	1:217	An Apelles alone, as the Learned relate	1:153
All hail, ye venerable Band	1:161	An apostolic minister[13]	2:387
All her delight and joy below	3:330	An earthquake hath the Cavern shook[14]	3:112
All her happiness below	3:364	An emblem of the Gentiles see	2:336
All in their wretched selves alone[10]	2:223	An endless War, yet free from Rage	3:161
All its passionate excess	3:274	An happy change for him, I see	1:162
All merciful, almighty Lord	3:367	An hellish sorcerer may seize	2:319
All my comfort in distress	3:274	An hypocrite will oft appear	2:321
All my Happiness is fled	3:150	An impotent desire I feel	2:234
All other gain I count but loss	3:347	An Outcast for my Master's sake	3:129
All parties furiously contend	2:164	And am I in the body still	3:346
All Power and Majesty are his	3:189	And can I doubt thy gracious will	2:375
All power, authority, and grace	2:119	And can we now deserted be	1:90
All power in heaven & Earth is thine	1:230	And canst thou look us in the Face, & say	1:211
All Thanks and Praise to God belong	3:189	*And first thy Person (with thyself) we own*	1:204
All that go by pluck off her Grapes[11]	2:448	And first, while pleased thy Principles to beg	1:207
All th' angelic powers adoring	3:436	And first your sacred hands are laid	3:97
All the foul secrets of my heart	3:320	And if the Patriots still prevail	1:129
All the Virtue of thy Passion	3:110	And if we lawfully pursue	3:425
All the world's disputers vain	2:241	And is it come to this? and has the Man	3:87
All things to thy command submit	2:98	And is it come to this at last	3:251
All thy benefits restore	3:265		
All we, like sheep, have gone astray	3:295		
All who use, in means confide	3:410		
All-wise, almighty Lord	3:141		
All wise, omniscient as thou art	3:65		

9. The first six lines of the twelve-line stanza beginning with this line appear in *PW* 11:273 as a six-line stanza.
10. The stanza beginning with this line appears in *PW* 11:347.
11. The stanza beginning with this line appears in *PW* 8:163.
12. The stanza beginning with this line appears in *PW* 4:129.
13. The stanza beginning with this line appears in *PW* 12:353.
14. The stanza beginning with this line appears in *PW* 4:129.

And is it come to this? Poor ruined Friend	1:180	Armed with thy mind and doubly blest	2:364
And is our final doom decreed?	1:136	Arrested, seized by mercy's power	3:285
And is the Dream of Friendship past	1:266	As a lion once he walked	3:409
And is the happy moment come	3:331	As all the high-born slaves of vice	1:87
And is there Hope for me	1:231	As banished long from human thought	2:254
And let the world for Jesus' sake	2:407	As beasts that on each other prey	3:285
And must I give him up, and never more	1:175	As born their appetites to please	2:166
And must I still in groans complain	3:162	As Cromwell with his desperate crew	1:72
And must they not at last prevail	1:77	As eagles hastning to the pray	1:66
And O! if I might be so greatly blest	1:199	As gold from the refining flame	1:78
And O their faithful hearts inflame	3:39	As long forgot and out of mind	2:206
And shall I not with thanks receive	3:239	As now abandoned to our fate	1:118
And shall I now of wrong complain	1:299	As One whom heaven delights to bless	3:237
And shall I then lament & droop	1:240	As pestilent, seditious men	2:417
And shall not we the same require[15]	2:277	As sheep appointed to be slain	1:116
And shall the ransomed sons of men	2:80	As Snow behold his Garment white[16]	3:112
And shall we scorn to fear	2:459	As strong, & glorying in my might	2:281
And shall we think it strange, or new	2:235	As the caught adulteress	3:256
And tho' our Bodies part	3:209	As well may lambs with tigers dwell	1:118
And what are we, who still withstand	2:344	Ashamed of having hoped for Rest	3:145
And wilt thou leave us in Distress	1:231	Ask Will, why he refused to join	1:103
And ye, my Brethren, whom I leave behind	1:186	Asking for thy righteousness	2:128
Angels the virgin-mother bless	2:131	Assume thy power, and reign below	3:217
Angry at th'ungrateful Jews	2:272	Assure my trembling Soul	1:232
Answer, O thou mighty One	3:182	Assured thou wilt direct our ways	3:70
Answering to thy Spirit's groan	3:280	At every Shew of Creature Good	1:261
Anxious thought to avarice tends	2:138	At the Marriage-Feast above	1:262
Appear, and chase these endless sigh	3:356	Attached to earth he sees me lie	2:122
Appear, the true eternal light	3:288	Athens indolent and vain	2:381
Arise, O God, arise, / thy people	1:119	Attend to my earnest Request	3:352
Arise, O God, arise, / thy righteous	3:135	Attentive to his people's needs	2:394
Arise, thou jealous God, arise	3:235	Athirst for Jesus and the word	3:253
Arm of the Lord, awake, awake, / Nor utterly	1:107	Author of everlasting Bliss	3:180
Arm of the Lord, awake, awake, / Such power	1:122	Author of everlasting peace	3:216
		Author of faith, the grace bestow	3:177
		Author of penitential woe	3:318
		Author, Prince of lasting Peace	3:281
Armed with thy mind / I come resigned	2:280	Averse from us, our King who loved	1:125
		Averse from us who take their part	1:127

---

15. The stanza beginning with this line appears in *PW* 12:94.

16. The stanza beginning with this line appears in *PW* 4:130.

Avert it, Lord, the Woe avert	1:269	Believers of old who Jesus confessed[18]	2:290
Avert the vain relenting thought	1:260	Beneath that Load I now stand up	1:260
Awake, Old Soldier, to ye fight half won	1:188	Beneath the hidings of thy face	3:232
		Beneath the honours of thy Name	3:51
Away, ye dreams of vain relief	3:261	Beneath thy kind protection keep	3:313
Away, ye wrathful Passions! hence	1:268	Besieging still thy gracious throne	3:245
		Beyond his persecutors' sight[19]	2:398
		Beyond the Grave my Views extend	1:244
Back to the world shall I return	3:260	Bid him now himself mistrust	1:297
Baffled by his inferior foes	1:97	Bind up my wounds by opening thine	2:122
Balm of the wounded Spirit	3:128	Bishop of souls, where shall we see	2:103
Baptized into the name of God	2:389	Bishops by superstition steeled	2:426
Be it known to all our race	2:286	Bleeding Tenderness, farewell	3:343
Be it thro' life my sole delight	3:348	Blessing, and thanks, and power, and praise[20]	3:335
Be it to Adam's offspring known	2:356		
Be not into bondage brought	3:411	Blessings thou dost to sinners give[21]	2:22
Be satisfied, We long for thee[17]	2:277	Blest be his Name, for ever blest!	3:220
Be this our only crime, To trust	2:425	Blest be the Hand, forever blest	1:259
Be this their single aim	3:58	*Blest Redeemer, bow thine ear*	3:442
Be thou his sure resource	1:144	Blest the house, and doubly blest	2:124
Be thou omnipotently near	3:130	Blest with perfect Resignation	1:241
Be with him in the lion's den	1:306	Blest with thy Abiding Spirit	1:249
Bear my afflictions all above	3:420	Blind in our natural estate	2:426
Because his self-deceit I show	2:468	Bliss or Mis'ry never ending	1:240
Because I did receive the Seed	3:157	Blooming, heart-bewitching Maid	3:380
Because the prophets hold their peace	3:37	Bold the attested truth to tell	2:343
Before he purge my sin away	2:472	Born and bred up within the Pale	3:60
Before he sinks among the dead	3:250	Born to trouble, grief and care	3:404
Before it sees this outward light	3:274	Bought by thee, shall Satan have me	3:124
Before Jehovah's awful throne	1:113	Bound by the prophetic word	2:416
Before the Comforter's descent	2:211	Bowels of pitying Love divine	3:230
Before the inbred poison spread	3:188	Break my heart in kind Compassion	1:252
Before they taste the mortal tree	1:288	Brethren, the gospel hear	2:354
Begin, ye worms, yourselves to know	2:113	Bring all the Proofs into my Mind	3:358
Beguiled like poor, unwary Eve	3:245	Britain shall her foes devour	1:63
Behold me on the brink of fate	1:245	Bright kindred saints around his bed	3:341
Behold me with thy Flaming Eyes	1:243		
Being of Beings, Lord of all	1:273		
Believing against hope	3:271		
Believing in thy name	2:410		

17. The stanza beginning with this line appears in *PW* 12:94.

18. The stanza beginning with this line appears in *PW* 12:155.

19. The stanza beginning with this line appears in *PW* 12:365.

20. The stanza beginning with this line appears in *PW* 6:308.

21. The first two lines of the stanza beginning with this line appear in *PW* 10:224.

Bring the sweet Spices of your Sighs[22]	3:111	But grant the Bishops *shoued* bow down	3:100
Britons their bleeding Brethren see	1:133	But grievous ills you apprehend	3:100
Brought by a way they never knew	1:98	But *has Almighty Love* vouchsafed to hear	1:196
Bruise, in me, thy hateful foe	2:439		
Burst, strugling Soul, the Bands of sin	3:156	But hast thou, Lord, thy church forsook	3:68
Burst the barriers of the tomb	2:252	But he that reads, thy Spirit perceives	3:71
Burthens which ourselves did bear	2:366	But hear (for O, thou know'st I fear)	1:245
But ah! not one was found to stay	1:80	But hear my agonizing prayer	1:305
But all your policy is blind	2:295	But heathens will their prisoners hear	2:408
But are outward wonders ceased	2:72	But here thou mayst awake, and call	3:314
But arm us with wisdom, Lord	2:182	But here thy Modesty insists again	1:212
But art thou not a Saviour still	3:221	But hide him, Lord, beneath thy wings	1:79
But blackened, and refused our due	3:136	But how have I, alas, repaid	3:437
But bless us, Lord, and prosper still	3:66	But how is loyalty regarded	1:97
But by a providential stroke	3:285	But I now my want bemoan	3:277
But can we ask (when thou art Ours,)	1:234	But if, before the fixt decree	3:349
But can you hope by means like these	1:152	But if his stubborn pride disdain[23]	2:161
But canst not thou a difference make	1:66	But if I aim at aught beside	2:132
But canst thou impart	3:266	But if I always humbly fear	3:48
But careless of the Public Good	1:133	But if I love thee not	2:263
But cast in this your gracious day	2:413	But if Justice hath decreed	1:76
But chiefly for his Own he cares	1:111	But if on Christ ye dare rely	2:357
But chiefly he, whose single aim	2:428	But if our faith to try	3:136
But chiefly those in Moses' seat	3:61	But if the aids of life we need	1:140
But chiefly *we* the Scourge require	3:306	But if the clam'rous tribe	2:422
But chiefly when their Lord's intent	2:350	But if the fire thy work consume[24]	2:463
But did he not at last awake	1:128	But if they triumph in my Fall	3:121
But did he spare a rival Chief	1:125	But if thou didst on me bestow	1:300
But do ye thus your Gratitude approve	1:183	But if thou favour our design	3:424
But Faction's Sons, from Gaul set free	1:124	But if thou here his Saviour art	1:311
But few th'incarnate Word receive	2:221	But if thou the Father show[25]	2:230
But first by heaven's permissive will	1:72	But if thou wil'st the load t'abide	2:64
But first, thou all-refining Fire	3:67	But if thy sovereign will, severe yet just	3:403
But for thou know'st my feeble heart	1:243	But if what I think Best	1:229
But from his old oppressors freed	1:161	But is it possible to find	2:473
But give I God a sacrifice	1:304	But kindly first he bids you all beware	1:213
But God his messengers hath sent	2:380	But let me first the Justice clear	3:156
But God, the jealous God of love	3:283	But let me first with tears lament	3:347
But God was pleased to raise	2:352		
But God who o'er the heathen reigns	1:95		
But grant him his superior Parts	1:141		

23. The stanza beginning with this line appears in *PW* 11:248.

24. The stanza beginning with this line appears in *PW* 13:28.

25. The stanza beginning with this line appears in *PW* 11:360.

22. The stanza beginning with this line appears in *PW* 4:129.

But let my prayers at last take place	1:299	But O, what endless woes	2:42
But let not those in darkness dwell	2:456	But Oh, could longing paint the deep distress	3:398
But let the holy Child Divine	2:31	But Oh how short my interval of woe	3:398
But let the season past suffice[26]	2:270	But one for Jesus gained we see	2:381
But let the witnesses stand forth	2:424	But piety cannot suffice	2:306
But let them have their judgment here	1:80	But raised out of the people's lees	3:84
But Life I see in death appear	2:122	But raised to rule us for an hour	1:163
But lo! I from this moment turn	3:347	But shall a sinful man complain	1:321
But lo! in faith on thee we call	1:108	But shall it fall? my Soul your Hope defies	1:186
But lo, the men who most decried	1:164	But shall they, Lord, succeed	1:82
But lo, the sentence to prevent[27]	2:177	But shall we rest in Pardning Grace	3:157
But lo, the tooth of calumny	2:431	But shall we their disciples be	2:164
But lo! thro' a fond Father's Aid	3:82	But shining in the faithless heart	2:215
But, Lord, I must confess	3:166	But she soon unfaithful proved	3:364
But may we not expect to see	2:305	But should not the First Minister	1:101
But men are blind, presumptuous men	2:371	But small at first thy kingdom, Lord	2:145
But more amazed I prove	2:92	But soon a countless race	2:178
But more than all thy Greatness I admire	1:210	But soon from earth removed	2:51
But most disturbed the wicked are	2:348	But soon or late we moan	2:52
But my GOD, thou wilt not leave	1:250	But sufferers in a righteous cause	3:133
But now enervated by age	2:282	But taught, O Lord, of thee	2:459
But now (if we believe the fiend)	2:350	But the effects I cannot hide	3:46
But now the glorious Gospel-Sound	1:266	But the Lord once more hath shook me	3:147
But now the love of earthly things	3:44	But the Punster's vain boast	3:390
But now the mist is cleared away	1:163	But thee thy saints revere	2:271
But now, we fear, we would much rather	3:438	But those that labour in the word	3:62
But not to conquer or suppress	1:124	But those who most the caution need	2:132
But O, how desperate he & blind	2:261	But thou by a Look Their Race canst restrain	3:138
But O, how suddenly cast down	1:73	But thou canst redeem her here	3:241
But O, if hope doth still remain	3:368	But thou canst turn aside the ill	3:424
But O, it cannot, cannot be	2:111	But thou, expiring on the tree[28]	2:465
But O my God, shall all be lost	3:56	But thou shalt take our part	2:135
But O! my tortured Conscience cries	3:151	But thro' the world's insidious arts	3:74
But O thou faithful God and just	1:60	But to clear up the doubt	1:283
But O thou God of boundless power	1:138	But trouble will not always last	1:314
But O thou Shepherd great & good	3:39	But true Englishmen hope, that the Nation	1:147
But O, to every messenger	3:36		
But O, what answer at the throne	2:175		
But O, whate'er obstructs thy will	2:376		

26. The stanza beginning with this line appears in *PW* 12:78.
27. The stanza beginning with this line appears in *PW* 11:267.
28. The stanza beginning with this line appears in *PW* 13:36.

But warned out of the flames he fled	2:166	By faith we possess	2:318
But was it all a Dream	3:349	By Foes opprest, by Friends betrayed	1:136
But we bewail their wretched state	3:101	By God's right hand exalted	2:312
But well thou knowst thy Grandeur to maintain	1:205	By feeble flesh opprest	3:281
		By grief and sin's enormous load	2:64
But what my Lord is pleased t'impart	3:268	By him ye all are justified	2:357
But what thou art, *thou thinkest,* cannot be guest	1:213	By hunger in this desert tried	2:18
		By Jesus' Cross sustained	3:184
But when him thou dost remove	3:302	By Love Divine bestowed	2:338
But when I ceased from Man in calm despair	1:201	By many, or by few	3:218
		By pangs extreme	2:280
But when on earth I cease to live	2:156	By Patriots who their Country sold	1:124
But when she wakes in dread surprize	3:240	By Pilate urged in vain to speak	2:274
But while he yields his parting breath	3:251	By pomp ye charm the people's sight	2:413
But while I to my doom submit	3:126	By rebels armed with cruel power	1:121
But while it doth in me remain	2:450	By rising from the dead	2:356
But while thy way is in the deep	1:312	By Satan into prison cast	3:311
But who can paint the Conjugal Intrigues	1:193	By silent, slow, unnoticed means	2:145
		By smooth Seducer's skill	3:243
But who sufficient is to *shew*	1:256	By tasting him we know	2:217
But who th' Ambassadors despise	2:119	By ten thous[an]d Snares beset	3:182
But who the End can see	1:70	By that unspoken word of thine[30]	2:232
But who thy warning voice attend	3:284	By the ordinance divine	2:250
But who with open arms receives	1:139	By the paternal love decreed	3:73
But who the fugitives received	1:128	By the Spirit of thy Grace	3:182
But why should my degrading Fancy dare	1:213	By the Spirit's instinct led	2:369
		By the Spirit's power convince	3:242
But will not God the just arise	1:135	By the toils of hell o'ertaken	1:63
But wilt thou, O my Trust, my Fear	1:224	By thee if rightful Monarchs reign	1:62
But worse than all the factious throng	1:62	By thee renewed	2:280
But ye his offers have withstood	2:315	By their Saviour's Spirit led	2:396
But you, who modern Rome foreswear	2:423	By thine from Earthly Love set free	1:264
		By th'indwelling God restored	3:164
By a show of good misled	3:93	By this the followers of our Lord	3:196
By all their power unterrified	2:384	By this we know our Passage here	3:196
By ceaseless toils of humble love	3:38	By thy heaviest wrath opprest	2:445
By civil and religious ties	3:60	By thy passion's exhibition	2:302
By day and night my Keeper be	3:127	But I have lost my bower again	3:262
By Death prevent the Evil Day	1:220	But you who censure his ductility	3:92
By faith I know thee near	1:290	By reiterated Crimes	3:152
By Faith we ascend	3:119		
By faith we now the cloud look thro'[29]	1:74		

29. The stanza beginning with this line appears in *PW* 8:486.

30. The stanza beginning with this line appears in *PW* 11:362.

By violence from the body driven	3:320	Cause of our calamities	1:75
By water he came, and by blood	2:474	Cautious their sayings he received	3:337
By whom thou wilt the rescue send	3:214	Charged with crimes we never knew	2:273
By whom thou wilt thy pleasure show	2:409	Cherished beneath our Country's wings	1:123
By wild impetuous passion led[31]	2:270	Children ye must be All again	3:190
		Choose for Us our whole Condition	3:211
Call on him Now, ye Watchmen, call[32]	2:453	Christ from his power diverts our mind	2:113
Called by the gospel messenger[33]	2:232	Christ hath paid the mighty price	3:168
Called forth to earn my daily bread	3:224	Christ himself, unless he wrought	2:246
Called from above, I rise[34]	2:410	Christ is the head, the corner stone	2:293
Called my Master to confess	2:64	Christ, my Life, my Only Treasure	1:248
Called to give up my Isaac here	1:267	Christ our merciful High-priest	3:93
Calm and quiet is the zeal	2:125	Christ the Lord, the woman's Seed	3:245
Calm from such she turned away	3:338	Christ the Truth, the Life, the Way	3:177
Calm with meek submission mourn	3:300	Christian the World of Drunkards is	3:198
Calmest Peace & meekest Patience	1:241	Christians, who know the price of grace	2:370
Can I be near the mingled pool	2:323	Claim as thy lawful Right	3:178
Can I enough the outstretched Arm admire	1:201	Cleave to ye Souls, who as thy own sincere	1:199
Can I the perfect beauties trace	3:260	Clodius, inspired with fierce inveterate hate	1:108
Can kings be cruel and unjust	1:91	Clothed with humility and grace[36]	3:286
Can sufferings without grace avail	2:203	Close beneath the cursed Wood	3:183
Can they forget our loyal zeal	1:90	Close not thy wounds against my soul	2:211
Can they succeed, unblest by thee	1:130	Closely urged on every Side	3:182
Can we in Satan's mind	2:459	Closer, and closer yet embrace	1:287
Can we, Lord, the path decline	2:256	C[oke] in his spritely youth for Honor tried	3:86
Can we with unconcern behold	1:134	Come, and bring her pardon back	3:301
Canst thou in such a Cause *begin* to fear	1:202	Come and take intire possession	3:125
Canst thou suffer me to stray	1:251	Come, and thy precious Self reveal	2:473
Captain of my Salvation hear	3:160	Come away to the Chase! —The Republican Pack	1:146
Cast the mighty from their thrones	1:68	Come divine Interpreter	3:177
Casting a dying look[35]	2:69	Come, Father, Son, and Holy Ghost, / Who thyself	3:189
		Come, Finisher of sin and woe	1:314
		Come, Holy Ghost, whose breath inspires	1:309

---

31. The stanza beginning with this line appears in *PW* 12:78.
32. The stanza beginning with this line appears in *PW* 4:314.
33. The stanza beginning with this line appears in *PW* 11:362.
34. The stanza beginning with this line appears in *PW* 12:397.
35. The stanza beginning with this line appears in *PW* 11:90.
36. The stanza beginning with this line appears in *PW* 8:422.

Come in thy gracious kingdom[37]	2:180	Comfort hence, ye saints, receive	2:202
Come, Jesus, & show thyself on the Wave	3:138	Commemorating our dying Lord	2:193
Come, Jesus, our peace	3:186	Commemorating the Death	3:185
Come, lead me forth to pastures green	2:442	Conceived, and wholly born in sin	1:287
Come, let us anew / Our Saviour pursue	2:239	Concluding worse than he began	1:125
Come let us away, / And his summons obey	3:289	Confirm in me the Pure Desire	1:243
		Confirm the gracious Wish I feel	3:361
Come let us away, To Jesus, his Throne	1:274	Conform my heart to thine	2:47
Come, let us join the wrestling race	3:246	Conformed to an expiring God	2:83
Come, my beloved Saviour, come	3:341	Confounded and condemned I am	2:375
Come, O thou mighty Lord	3:178	Congress repeats its furious boasts	1:72
Come, prick up your ears	3:389	Conquerors of sin, the world, and hell	1:292
Come, Saviour Friend of human kind	1:323	Conscience, & fear, & shame are o'er	2:260
Come then at his call Our Jesus to meet	2:253	Conscience seared by Sin's hot Iron	3:147
Come then, dear Lord, for sinners slain	1:323	Conscience, the Worm that never dies	3:156
Come then, dear Lord, the love declare	3:290	Conscious of my Condemnation	3:147
Come then, my heavenly Bridegroom, come	1:244	Conscious of our lost condition	1:63
		Conscious the laws are on our side	2:398
Come then, my loving heart's desire	1:316	Constrained at last, thou dost Thyself display	1:203
Come then, my Only Hope	3:363	Constrained with men to deal	3:142
Come then, my soul, thou restless exile, come	3:395	Conversion is by just degrees	2:324
		Converting into flesh the stone	1:299
Come then, O my heart's desire	3:164	Convert our nature into grace	2:219
Come then, old Comrade, to my Arms again	1:196	Convinced his foot hath slipt, uphold	3:309
		Convinced that thy great will is done	3:296
Come then, thou great messiah, come	3:275	Convinced to thee, O Lord, we come	2:231
Come then, ye threatening Sons of Rome	3:129	Corrupt, and daringly prophane	1:65
		Could friendship self so deep concern express	3:401
Come, thine exiles to remove[38]	2:189	Could God's peculiar people fight	2:399
Come, thou, dear pardoner (?) of my soul	3:420	Could I ask the promised Grace	3:132
		Could I in such Distress my G[ambold] leave?	1:182
Come thou, our living head	2:53	
Come, thou Prophet of the Lord	2:229	Could neither Seal nor Stone secure[39]	3:112
Come thyself, her soul to raise	3:301	Counseled by a friendly Child	3:380
Come up hither, it cried	3:119	Covered with honorable shame[40]	3:333
		Crawl on the earth, nor ever more	2:89
		Crown my Infinite Desire	1:252

37. The first five lines of the ten-line poem beginning with this first line appear in *PW* 11:267 and are combined with the last five lines of the poem beginning with the line, "Descending from the mountain."

38. The stanza beginning with this line appears in *PW* 11:278.

39. The stanza beginning with this line appears in *PW* 4:130.

40. The stanza beginning with this line appears in *PW* 6:302.

Cruelly mocked, and sourged, and bound	1:114	Destroyers of the public peace	2:396
		Detached from every earthly good	2:118
Crushed with heavy Grief & Fear	1:240	Detained in a long vale of tears	3:329
Cut off from all dependance / Of human help	3:131	Detained in the Refiner's fire	3:279
		Determined here I still abide	3:72
Cut off from all dependance vain	1:138	Devils my parting soul surround	3:317
Cut off from all retreat	3:270	Did he not love the Poor & Good	3:358
Cut off from every hope	1:86	Did not each soul throughout the isle	2:433
		Did not our feeble ministers	1:112
		Did not they trust the Cause to Those	1:112
Daily he doth his people teach	2:181	Didst thou not give the seed	2:349
Daily sent in Jesus' name	2:150	Didst thou the Gift of Faith from Man receive	1:194
Daily we ourselves deny	2:109	Discoursing from the written word[43]	2:378
Dare we hope her safe above	3:343	Dismayed I should not be	2:84
Dare ye reject my Love? reject, but know	1:185	Dissolve the charm which long hath held	3:245
Daring as Charles's spurious brood	1:156	Dissolve their compact dire	3:218
Dark alas! and doubly blind	1:253	Dispersing the infernal gloom[44]	1:74
Dark as I am, bereaved of sight	2:456	Distant at first my danger I survey	3:398
Dark, I mourn, till thou appear	3:276	Do it thyself in me[45]	2:119
Darkness and light as well agree	1:95	Do thou, my best of friends, the word receive	1:187
Daughter of Abraham, and thine	3:287		
Day & night they chant above	3:168	Do thou restrain the baffled Foe	3:240
Dead, dead in sins and trespasses	2:99	Does he assume the name in vain	1:109
Dead, dead to GOD, but still alive	3:154	Doomed to late but vain Repentance	3:146
Dead he now in pleasure lives	1:294	Dost thou with-hold thy pardning love	2:374
Deaf to his expiring prayers	3:243		
Deaf to our cries and dying groans	1:116	Double honour they claim	2:433
Death, hell, & Sin are now subdued[41]	2:279	Down to the dust, but not to hell	3:77
Deceived by each appearance fair	3:73	Draw we then with Boldness near	3:193
Deeds and words a bishop praise	2:209	Drawn by the Spirit of grace	2:81
Deeply the sore affront ye feel	1:95	Dreadful, sin-chastising God	3:150
Deists and Sectaries agree	2:448	Drive the Old *Fatal*ist to hell	3:162
Deny yourselves, the cross embrace	2:469	Driven by stronger grace[46]	2:130
Deprived of every gracious gift	2:177		
Descending from the mountain[42]	2:179		
Destitute of holiness	3:367		

41. The stanza beginning with this line appears in *PW* 12:99–100.
42. The first five lines of the ten-line stanza beginning with this line appear in *PW* 11:267 and are combined with the last five lines of the stanza beginning with the line "Sent from thy Father's bosom."
43. The stanza beginning with this line appears in *PW* 12:327.
44. The stanza beginning with this line appears in *PW* 8:486.
45. The first four lines of the eight-line poem beginning with this line appear in *PW* 11:196.
46. The stanza beginning with this line appears in *PW* 11:205.

Duty and inclination, Lord	3:245	Ever in thy Spirit near us	3:110
Dying, while in pain she lives	3:279	Ever nigh to those who call	2:444
		Every one that asks shall have	2:128
		Every ordinance of man	2:78
Each presents the officers	2:308	Every real worshipper	2:242
Eager that all should upward press	2:23	Every throne, & every mansion	3:436
Earth to earth, & dust to dust	3:369	Every word and act shall show	3:282
Eager to repair the wrong[47]	2:328	Every word of God is sure	2:191
Earth's conquerors seek with fire and sword	2:118	Evil & few my Days have been	3:354
		Evil before his Presence flies	3:117
Easy to be intreated, mild	2:377	Evil by thy presence chase	1:76
Eat, drink, and play, and take thine ease	1:87	Ev'n now his fierce assaults begin	1:246
		Ev'n now, in deep prophetic woe	2:402
E'er my soul and body part	3:370	Ev'n now their powerful prayer I feel	3:264
Elected by thy Father's grace	2:33	Ev'n now th'omniscient God perceives	2:303
Elders & scribes be sure are there	2:309	Ev'n now thy searching eye perceives	3:234
Empty the word cannot return	3:179	Ev'n then, while in my sins and blood	3:252
Encompasst by the Dogs of hell	2:465	Except the Lord conduct the plan	3:425
End these dire Effects of Sin	3:150	Excused, our privilege we own	3:213
Enough for him who only means[48]	2:194	Excusing their contempt, they say	1:281
Enough, the pattern mild to show	2:195	Expecting then before thy throne	3:140
Enter then thy mean abode	3:219	Explain, great God, the mystery	2:473
Entered into their labours we	2:231	Expiring in the Sinners' stead[50]	2:276
Entring into the ministry	2:97		
Entring on Life's meridian Stage	2:259		
Envious of the peasant's lot	3:406	Fain I would retrieve his Fav[ou]r	3:147
Episcopalians, now no more	3:89	Fain we would distinctly see	1:235
Equal to the great God supreme	2:243	Fain would I weep my life away	3:298
Erase the deep, original stain	3:127	Faintly hoping against hope	3:259
Error, ye Pharisees sincere[49]	2:427	Fairer than all the sons of men	3:420
Essence of Holiness Divine	2:356	Faith comes by hearing of thy word	3:71
Eternal Son of God most high, / Whose glory	2:472	Faith & the Holy Ghost bestowed	2:346
		Faith I surely have in thee	3:149
Eternal Son of God most high, / Whose only	3:227	Faith to be healed I surely have	3:222
		Faithful to death he owned his Lord	3:341
Eternal Sun of righteousness	3:228	Faithless & ungrateful men	2:238
Eternal GOD, be Present now	1:264	Far better 'tis that righteous men[51]	2:422
Even love cannot repress	2:405	Far, in body far removed	3:194
		Far from my Native Land removed	3:128
		Far from Passion, and from Pride	1:250

47. The stanza beginning with this line appears in *PW* 12:238.
48. The stanza beginning with this line appears in *PW* 11:290.
49. The stanza beginning with this line appears in *PW* 12:425.
50. The stanza beginning with this line appears in *PW* 12:94.
51. The stanza beginning with this line appears in *PW* 12:418.

Far from the cheerful Ways of men	1:221	Father, thy speaking rod I hear	3:263
Far from the new Jerusalem	2:120	Father, thy whole design to know	1:111
Farewell, my all of earthly hope	1:304	Father, to thee our joint request	3:349
Farewell! thou Man of complicated strife	3:326	Father, to thy just Decree	3:148
Father yet farther from eternal truth	3:396	Father, we praise thy guardian Care	3:237
Fast let me hold the good I find	3:207	Father, we thro' thy favourite Son	3:432
Father, accept my fervent prayer	3:297	Father, who dost in secret see	1:289
Father, accept our praise	3:169	Father, whose goodness knows no bound	3:248
Father & Friend, & Lord of all	1:244	Father, whose mercies never end	1:115
Father & Friend of all mankind	3:70	Fatigued with his victorious toil	1:46
Father and friend of the Opprest	1:137	Favour & Peace on Earth & Praise in heaven	3:106
Father, behold with pitying Grace	1:261	Fear, & Grief, & sore Temptation	3:146
Father, beneath whose Hand I groan	3:351	Feeble, & self-betrayed, the Prophet hears	3:91
Father by all confest	1:84	Few of the wealthy fear	2:172
Father, for his sake convert	1:75	Fill then your measure up	2:41
Father, Friend of Human Race	3:182	Fill up, and change his faith to sight	3:233
Father, hear the Faithful Prayer	1:255	Filled may I be	2:280
Father, how great thy love to man	2:269	Filled with the Spirit of faith and love	2:465
Father, in Jesus' powerful Name	1:288	Finished the First Transgression is	2:278
Father, in the prevailing name	3:246	Fired with the thought, ev'n now I see	1:152
Father, into thy hands receive	3:233	Firm as a rock that cannot move	2:97
Father, let thy will be done	3:293	First for themselves the Patriots care	1:156
Father, my wretched heart I find	2:450	Fixt in solemn Expectation	1:240
Father of all, the prayer attend	3:188	Five hundred witnesses arose	3:337
Father of compassions, hear	1:235	Flows a Fountain from thy Side	3:149
Father of everlasting grace, / Of infinite	1:60	Follower of Christ, thy calling see	2:96
Father of everlasting grace, / thy awful	3:311	Foolish and blindfold guides	2:39
Father of Jesus Christ, and mine	1:246	"Foolish child," he suavely cried	3:409
Father of Jesus Christ my Lord	2:204	Fools with repetition vain	2:44
Father of kind compassions thou	1:298	Forever be thy grace adored	2:193
Father of light, & God of grace	3:295	For farther light I then shall sue	2:408
Father of our glorious Lord	2:356	For God originally made	2:180
Father, regard the cry	2:68	For half a mournful century	2:234
Father, regard the sprinkled blood	3:248	For him they first a table spread	2:376
Father, regard the faithful fervent Prayer	1:187	For him thou didst the Spirit impart	3:359
Father, since thou permittest	2:82	For Jesus' sake forgiven	3:111
Father, Son and Holy Ghost / In thine	3:191	For Jesus' sake release me	3:155
Father, Son, and Spirit, come, / Manifest ...	3:219	For King, (at last you let us know)	3:95
Father, that I thy child may be	3:206	For liberty why should we strive	1:166
Father, thou know'st I need	3:72	For mercy's sake suspend	1:82
Father, thou know'st whate'er we need	3:423	For now the Prize is gained	3:340
Father, thy awful righteousness	1:299		

For other Sects' & Churches' sake	3:66	Friend to his flesh alone	2:110
For our abuse of sight t'atone	2:198	Friends, and men, and Sins oppress us	2:441
For Sion's sake I will not cease[52]	2:451	From all Earthly Expectation	1:248
For the blind multitude distrest	1:60	From all iniquity avert	3:127
For the Object of my care	1:295	From all Remains of self & Pride	3:201
For the sick of sin we plead[53]	2:71	From dire Rebellion's rage we fled	1:139
For this alone on Earth I wait	1:221	From drunken, riotous excess	1:305
For this continually I wait	3:223	From earth & sin set free	2:368
For this do we earnestly groan	3:360	From every secret bias free	2:423
For this I unto Being came	1:242	From every Touch of Evil guard	1:260
For this in quiet Hope	1:226	From heaven he shall once more	2:288
For this the kind angelic bands	3:264	From her eyes the Scales remove	3:244
For this the meekest Awe we wait	1:231	From, or *in* the evils here	1:293
For this thou didst my soul allure	3:170	From presumptuous sins defend me	3:125
For this, thou faithful Lord, I come	1:325	From sloth, and pride, and passion free	3:174
For this thou hast hedged up my ways	1:321	From the Dead, if such thy Pleas[ur]e	3:212
For this we first together came	3:379	From the gulph of desperation	1:63
For this we met, with lowly Fear	3:379	From the lust of lawless power	1:67
For this with childlike Awe I wait	1:242	From the old deceiver's snare	2:62
For thy Determining Command	1:218	From the poets we learn, that an Artist of Greece	3:388
For thy own compassion's sake	3:274	From the poor they turn away	3:417
For thy truth & mercy sake	2:409	From thee his fav'rite, why	2:68
For us, for all he died and rose	2:379	From thee this good desire proceeds	3:206
For when I fall into the grave	3:172	From these the Tempter laboured to remove	1:172
Forbid it, gracious Lord, forbid	3:298	From thee his fav'rite, why	2:68
Forgive me, O thou injured GOD	1:263	Full many a war has been for woman waged	3:303
Forth in thy Name I go	1:227	Full of impurity	2:112
Forty long & mournful years	3:149	Full of Satan's subtlety	2:351
Foul lepers, by ourselves abhorred[54]	2:162	Full oft have I besought thee, Lord	2:467
Founder of thy Church, and Lord	3:305	Fulness of the Deity	2:226
Fountain of life and happiness	3:273		
F[ox] in his hole may safely lie	1:93		
Free from the partial, blind respect	1:311	Gainers ye by others' loss	3:414
Freely, where'er I would, I went	2:281	'Gainst the truth he stops his ears	3:94
Fresh fatigue for Jesus' sake[55]	2:401	Gallop on my grey Nag	1:283
Fresh matter of joy	2:366	Gather the Outcasts in	3:178
		Genevensis a Friend's inconsistency blames	3:375
		Genteelity we now affect	3:44
		Gentiles and Jews, by malice joined	2:360

52. The stanza beginning with this line appears in *PW* 4:312.
53. The stanza beginning with this line appears in *PW* 11:99.
54. The stanza beginning with this line appears in *PW* 11:251.
55. The stanza beginning with this line appears in *PW* 12:369.

Gentle Inglisina, say	3:380	Go thro' the Gates ('tis GOD commands[60]	2:454
Gently into the valley lead	3:236	God almighty to deliver	1:64
Gently she their will inclined[56]	3:339	God at last in anger said	2:143
G[iardini], B[oyce] and all	3:383	God bestows on everyone	2:128
Give him, Saviour, above all	3:265	God by the ministry of man	2:322
Give me an inlightened mind	3:277	God did indeed come down	2:362
Give me but this, I ask no more	3:123	God employs whome'er he will	2:345
Give me Faith to hold me up[57]	3:203	God has, you say, a two-fold Will	3:391
Give me love, or else I die	3:366	God hath chose the simple poor	2:240
Give me thy only will to seek	3:143	God hath on us his Spirit bestowed[61]	2:460
Give me thy saying to receive	3:419	God hearkens, and hears	2:333
Give them on thee to call	2:327	God his grace on them bestows	2:37
Give them with other eyes to see	1:62	God his mighty power displays	2:187
Give us, of thee reborn, to shine	1:309	God in thee, O Christ, is Love	3:366
Give us that power of godliness	1:308	God in whom I move, and live	3:195
Give us the Double Blessing, Lord	1:236	God is the judge and sets up one	1:111
Give us this day our daily bread	1:315	God knows his own, wheree'er they are	2:334
Giver of nature's every gift	1:287	God laughs at the designs of men	2:300
Giver of penitence, begin	2:85	God let his vineyard out to man[62]	2:62
Giver of power to them that faint	3:255	God never can his own reprove	2:47
Giver of repentance, thee	2:301	God of all grace and patience, hear	3:306
Giver of the humbling grace	1:297	God of All-inviting Grace	1:249
Gladly I now to Love submit	3:203	God of all-sufficient grace	1:293
Glide into the Pleasing Snare	1:250	God of all-sufficient love	3:281
Glory, and power, and thanks and praise	3:197	God of grace & patience, hear	1:60
Glory doth to thee belong	2:203	God of eternal power & grace	1:271
Glory, honour, thanks and praise	3:415	God of infinite compassion	1:63
Glory to God above	3:339	God of love, incline thine ear	3:274
Glory to the Redeemer give[58]	3:332	God of love, who hearst the prayer	3:264
Glory to thee, almighty God	1:319	GOD of my Life & Refuge, hear	3:361
Go bid the shipwracked Man forbear	3:353	God of my life, to thy decree	3:362
Go, happy saint, by Jesus blessed	3:331	God of my life, I seek thy Face	1:219
Go not after empty schemes	3:410	God of redeeming love	1:69
Go tell the Followers of your Lord[59]	3:113	God of resistless power and love	3:247
		God of the Patriarchal Race	1:266
		God of unbounded Grace	1:232

56. The stanza beginning with this line appears in *PW* 6:335.
57. The stanza beginning with this line appears in *PW* 4:450.
58. The stanza beginning with this line appears in *PW* 6:300.
59. The stanza beginning with this line appears in *PW* 4:130.
60. The stanza beginning with this line appears in *PW* 4:315.
61. The stanza beginning with this line appears in *PW* 13:24–5.
62. The stanza beginning with this line appears in *PW* 11:49.

God of unbounded patience, hear	3:52	Hail, happy Prince, in whom combined we see	3:108
God of unbounded power and grace	3:85	Hail, happy Soul! no more a Prisoner here	1:199
God of uncreated love	3:163		
God of unfathomable grace	1:313		
God omnipotent in grace	3:216	Hail, happy Souls, by mercy snatched away	1:184
God omniscient as thou art	2:101		
God over all, deliverance send	1:110	Hail, successful levellers	3:418
God over all in power supream	2:245	Hail the bright auspicious Day	3:381
God resists the proud and vain	2:170	Hail the bright Auspicious Morn	1:254
GOD, the GOD that heareth Prayer	1:253	Hail the sad, memorable day	3:330
God the world in mercy spares	2:43	Hail, ye nursing fathers' god[66]	3:418
God through the world extends His Sway	2:450	Hands on himself he laid, and *took*	3:89
		Happy America, whose ruinous wars	3:89
God to Apostolic men[63]	2:369	Happy, forever happy, I / Suffered to	3:129
God to chastise our sin	3:212	Happy, forever happy, I / Indulged at	3:144
God when we desire to please	2:206	Happy he, whose wickedness	2:149
God who bad the grave restore	2:355	Happy, if for our Doom prepared	1:137
God, who only canst abase	1:296	Happy in each other then	3:282
God who out of Christ adore	2:228	Happy in thee alone	3:272
God who sends by whom he will	3:412	Happy in thy love revealed	3:372
God, whom all are bound to fear	3:294	Happy might we at last obtain	3:293
Godly in Christ resolved to live	3:59	Happy our highly favoured Race	3:221
Grace, if thou forbear to give	3:194	Happy place that could afford	2:250
Great Author of the mystick Grace	3:379	Happy the age and place	2:42
Great God of all-victorious Love	3:248	Happy the child of misery	2:159
Great GOD of Truth & Love	1:237	Happy the days in which we see	1:158
Great God, who never dost pass by	3:43	Happy the days when Charles and John	3:82
Great God, with humble awe we own	1:91	Happy the Man by Jesus' grace subdued	3:107
Great howe'er their guilt hath been	1:61	Happy the man divinely led	2:343
Great Judge of all opprest with wrong	1:120	Happy the man who ever bears	2:113
Great Peacemaker 'twixt God and man	1:71	Happy the multitude[67]	2:295
Great the nuptial mystery	2:34	Happy the saints that followed thee	2:69
Great things ordained for thee to do[64]	2:326	Happy the soul, whom death shall find	2:332
Greater miracles than these[65]	2:391	Happy the souls who feel and know	3:200
Grieved for having lost our Lord	2:208	Happy they whoe'er obtain	3:257
Guide of my early thoughtless Days	1:223	Happy whome'er the God of grace	2:217
Guiltless the saint by all declared	2:429	Happy ye Souls that can in Christ confide	1:202
		Hardened in his impenitence[68]	2:161

63. The stanza beginning with this line appears in *PW* 12:309.
64. The stanza beginning with this line appears in *PW* 12:238.
65. The stanza beginning with this line appears in *PW* 12:360.
66. Shorthand uncertain, perhaps "good."
67. The stanza beginning with this line appears in *PW* 12:180.
68. The stanza beginning with this line appears in *PW* 11:248.

Hard-labouring for the body here	2:168	He fills from first he hath prepared[73]	2:454
Hark, how the rabble roar	2:406	He first receives him here	2:81
Hark, how they groan beneath ye yoke	1:137	He folds his arms to rest again	3:314
Harrietta is She	1:284	He hath his consolation here	2:160
Harshly thou dost thy mother treat	2:218	He hath his promises fulfiled	2:77
Has he a British heart, who sees	1:164	He hears their insolent demands	1:105
Has Satan the advantage got?	3:309	He is, he is at last possest	3:331
Hast thou not known them such, my rescued Friend	1:202	He holds her, still in life detained	3:328
		He is indeed ascended	2:288
Haste then, ye Souls who first believe[69]	3:113	He keeps my Sinfull Soul from Sin	3:201
Haste to our help, thou GOD of love[70]	2:446	He keeps us above	3:120
Haste, ye advocates for sin	3:414	He lets the pastor fall, t'explain	2:197
Hasty in spirit, I	3:141	He lifts me now to Pisgah's Top	3:201
Haters of all righteousness	2:352	He lives to God, he greatly lives	3:341
Hath not the heavenly Potter power	3:238	He made, he keeps us one in heart	3:197
Have any separated, and sped	3:55	He may enter into life	3:417
Have I not heard, & known	1:272	He may his bosom-lust confess	2:321
Have they not for a length of years	1:159	He now beholds us strugling with our Fate	1:181
Have they not took the Sufferers' side	1:159		
Have you so suddenly forgot	1:162	He practices his subtlest wiles	3:50
He at the helm appears	2:91	He sees, and if he pities too	3:317
He cannot now his Pattern trace	2:262	He shall in me himself reveal	3:201
He clave the sea by his command	2:88	He soon his prodigies will show	2:288
He bids me cast my care on him	1:307	He spake, and Jesus' word alone[74]	2:233
He breaks to all the mystic bread	2:109	He speaks: when lo! the man app[ea]rs unsou[gh]t	3:90
He calls us to the skies	3:185		
He comes his people to redeem	2:34	He that in the temple prays	2:410
He comes, the conquering hero comes	1:152	He testified to all around	3:332
He comes to raise the dead again	2:99	He thirsted for this soul of mine[75]	2:276
He comes triumphant from above[71]	2:463	He thirsted, to redeem his foe	2:277
He dares not arrogate or share	2:224	He urges me (so rich in grace	3:51
He did not proclaim To all that passed by	2:29	He uses men to serve his will	1:111
		He waits; to manifest his grace[76]	2:247
He dies—a death of pain and shame[72]	2:202	He who formed our curious frame	2:139
He falls; but not alone; the Ruin spreads	1:173	He will not speak a greater word	2:469
		He's come!—to set the prisoner free	3:327

69. The stanza beginning with this line appears in *PW* 4:130.
70. The stanza beginning with this line appears in *PW* 8:446.
71. The stanza beginning with this line appears in *PW* 13:28.
72. The stanza beginning with this line appears in *PW* 11:301–2.
73. The stanza beginning with this line appears in *PW* 4:315.
74. The stanza beginning with this line appears in *PW* 11:362.
75. The stanza beginning with this line appears in *PW* 12:94.
76. The stanza beginning with this line appears in *PW* 11:468–69.

Head of thy church, attend our cry	3:62	Her danger *past* O may she see	3:240
Head of thy church, our prayers attend	3:54	Her hunted life in mercy spare	3:273
Healer of my languid soul	3:144	Her in affliction's furnace chuse	3:278
Hear, Britons, hear, and tremble at the Rod	1:109	Her in the arms of faith I bring	1:271
Hear this, who now abuse your power	2:412	Her sins of ignorance forgive	3:245
Hear this, ye Jewish elders, hear	2:423	Her smiling Lord appoints his bride	3:434
Hear thy afflicted People's Prayer[77]	2:446	Here all the mystic Powers of sound	3:382
Hear us for a chosen child	3:246	Here first I learnt to catch an empty name	3:396
Hearing the Bridegroom's voice	2:52	Here for our Country's sake undone	1:128
Heathen scoff the Saviour's name	3:418	Here from the Cross, on which I bleed	1:268
Heathens baptized, who never knew	2:363	Here, if thou darest, suffer *r m m* tell[81]	3:402
Heaven is for all alike prepared[78]	2:32	Here in truth and righteousness	2:34
Heaven is now with Jesus given	1:249	Here let me pause, my former Friend survey	1:174
Heavenly Counsellor Divine	1:218	Here lies, who late a living emblem lay	3:326
Heav'nward when we turn our face	2:114	Here may I covet no reward	3:49
Hedge up his way with legal thorns	1:292	Here my spirit took the alarm	3:411
Heir of that everlasting curse	3:249	Here then a sinner at thy feet	2:458
Heirs of the prophecies are we	2:292	Here then I all my hopes forego	3:261
Hell from beneath is moved to meet	1:88	Here then I at his footstool lie	3:318
Help him in his greatest need	3:264	Here then I rest my fainting Soul	1:261
Help, Jesus, help in time of need	1:245	Here then, O Lord, we rest	1:238
Help, Lord, the weakest Instrument	3:48	Here then we humbly, Lord, confess	2:372
Help me, Lord, thy works to praise	3:408	Here then while sojourning below	3:65
Help me, Saviour, from this day	2:412	Here we would thro' life remain	2:126
Help me then to search the word	3:295	Herod and his men of war	2:199
Help, O my gracious Saviour	3:128	Hide him from the things designed	3:93
Help of them that succour need	3:144	Hide me in the peaceful shade	1:322
Help us for them in faith to pray	3:57	Hide thou her pretious Life above	1:260
Help us, Lord, shew forth thy Power	2:441	High is the Church, whoe'er oppose	2:397
Help us to make the poor our friends[79]	2:157	Highminded they refuse to hear	3:54
Helper of the poor opprest	1:68	Him as on the Altar laid	3:183
Her as the Apple of an Eye	1:260	Him by wicked arts beguiled	1:295
Her Boughs she stretched from Sea to Sea[80]	2:447	Him if the tempter shake	2:112
		Him in his life and death we trace[82]	2:70

---

77. The stanza beginning with this line appears in *PW* 8:446.
78. The stanza beginning with this line appears in *PW* 10:332.
79. The stanza beginning with this line appears in *PW* 11:241. *SH* 1762, 2:226, line begins "help me."
80. The stanza beginning with this line appears in *PW* 8:447.
81. This line is part of a poem from MS Shorthand. The letters *r m m* have not been deciphered.
82. The first four lines of the stanza of eight lines beginning with this line are combined with the first four lines of the stanza of eight beginning "Still by the

Him the self-existent God	3:177	His Rights they challenge for their own	1:165
Him who for his servant cares	3:428	His sacred flesh the scourges tear	2:271
Himself must first at Pilate's bar	2:59	His secret ones to God are known	2:205
Himself prepares his People's hearts[83]	2:454	His shining Steps I followed from afar	1:175
Himself the standard bears	2:416	His sickness to heal	3:267
His blood the cement was[84]	2:295	His sight he first receives[86]	2:327
His Charge, departing to the Wolf he leaves	3:88	His slumbers loth to discompose	3:314
His church will approve	2:365	His Son, of little interest	1:140
His Counsel we see	1:275	His soul, attuned to heavenly Praise	3:330
His dangers in this beaten road	1:295	His spiritual want	3:266
His dangers in this rugged road	1:302	His Spirit in these mysterious leaves	3:173
His dear Redeeming Grace I prove	3:203	His Spirit into my soul inspire[87]	1:315
His death could not revoke	1:301	His Talents take into thy hand	3:237
His death the prophecies fulfilled[85]	2:378	His troubled breast, and tearful eyes	3:342
His face unless he hide	2:52	His wary, quick, judicious eye	3:337
His firmest friends, unbought, unknown	1:80	His wrath he with his love reveals[88]	2:288
His foes by lawful means he tries	2:413	His written will to all displays	3:392
His forfeited peace	3:266	Holy, & just are all thy ways	3:154
His friends from principle increase	1:80	Holy Ghost, I trust in thee	2:136
His friends the happy prisoner see	2:419	Holy Ghost, my heart inspire	2:366
His grief be lost in joy's excess	3:342	Hope in my end, my latest hour	2:456
His heart, constrained by love divine	3:317	Hope of the sinsick, dying soul	3:167
His hour of suffering is not yet	2:406	Hoping against hope, I wait	3:370
His innocence to all appears	2:424	Horribly the waves and wind	2:239
His life to save with vain desire	2:200	Horror of Offending thee	1:254
His love was once my daily bread	3:261	Hosanna to God	3:187
His Love the pardoned sinner shows	2:251	How are the mighty from their height	1:132
His meek humility	2:405	How are you least in your own eyes	2:113
His members, one in heart and mind	2:293	How blind, & slow my heart to see	1:321
His mighty Chiefs have cast us in	3:130	How blind the heart of man	2:171
His Ordinance Divine	3:184	How blind the judgment of the croud	2:200
His precious soul in life detain	3:344	How can I hate what nature loves	3:220
His Providential Will	1:238	How can I then mistrust	1:272
His resurrection's power	2:418	How can our wretched nation see	1:76
		How can we 'scape the curse extreme	3:307
		How chearful among the gay mead	3:431
		How could the Leader of so wise a Sect	1:194
		How desperate is the state of man	2:120

holy matrons led" to form a stanza of eight lines.

83. The stanza beginning with this line appears in *PW* 4:315.
84. The stanza beginning with this line appears in *PW* 12:180.
85. The stanza beginning with this line appears in *PW* 12:328.
86. The stanza beginning with this line appears in *PW* 12:238.
87. See *PW* 8:427.
88. The stanza beginning with this line appears in *PW* 12:147.

IDEX OF FIRST LINES OF POETRY BY JOHN AND CHARLES WESLEY

How did I ev'n contend to lay	3:438	How wretched is the man possest	2:160
How dreadful is the Place	3:184	H[owe] might have giv'n another reason	1:96
How few by his example led	2:238		
How for Grace in vain we languish	3:146	How'e'er our hasty nature fret[91]	2:104
How furiously now do the Patriots strive	1:145	How'e'er the laboured Babels rise	2:462
		Howl the defrauded Fiends beneath	3:117
How gladly then should I resign	2:110	Humble, dispassionate, and meek	3; 62
How great thy love, to stop and turn	2:99	Humble, penitential zeal	3:432
How happy the men[89]	2:289	Humbly I lift my streaming Eye	3:204
How hast thou my soul secured	3:404	Hurrying on with eagerness	2:125
How have I pined to see this joyful Day	1:200	Husband of thy church below	2:35
		Huzza for liberty and laws	1:150
How have they persevered in good	1:160	Huzza for Wilkes and liberty	1:149
How hopeless is a sinner's case[90]	2:260		
How is it possible to hide	3:98		
How is the Mighty fallen from His height	3:88	I am never at one Stay[92]	3:202
		I am not now condemned within	1:270
How like those Worthies, in ye Lists of Fame	1:213	I ask thee not to take them hence	3:310
		I both see thee & hear	2:414
How long, how often shall I pray	2:457	I can believe thy faithful Word	1:244
How long shall I complain	3:165	I can thro' thee the World resign	1:220
How long shall Patriots prophane	1:122	I cannot doubt the power Divine[93]	2:237
How many rich in pleasures live	2:138	I cannot live, or die in peace	3:269
How needless then our anxious Fear	1:273	I count not fit to be compared	1:307
How oft to save thy Modesty the Pain	1:208	I dare not ask thy pain	2:115
How powerful our Redeemer's cries	2:69	I fasted, read, and wept, and cried	3:252
How rapid the course	1:283	I fear this Evil heart	1:273
How safe & happy we	1:238	I fell, but not by his Decree	3:157
How shall his zeal in judgment rise	2:383	I have not yet received	3:350
How shall I 'scape, so close beset	1:246	I heard the voice among the trees	3:262
How shall I thank thy love	2:93	I hid me in the secret shade	3:251
How shall I walk as in thy sight	3:224	I in Jesus' Name have sworn	3:182
How shall I wash my heart	2:455	I in thy strength proceed	3:139
How shrill the Gospel-Trumpet sounds	1:324	I know, if thou thy hand withdraw	2:260
		I know not what to do, / But lift	1:301
How strange a sight at court appears	1:105	I know not what to do, / But till	3:138
How then can I conceive	1:231	I know not what to do—but wait	3:139
How then, O my simple heart	3:412	I long with thee to bow my head	2:204
How thick this Outward Darkness lies	2:466		
How vainly do the heathen strive	3:198		

89. The stanza beginning with this line appears in *PW* 12:155.
90. The stanza beginning with this line appears in *PW* 11:508.
91. The stanza beginning with this line appears in *PW* 11:170.
92. The stanza beginning with this line appears in *PW* 4:449.
93. The stanza beginning with this line appears in *PW* 11:372.

I meet the Providential blow	3:238	If by thy Spirit moved I am	3:348
I mix with theirs my feeble cry	3:35	If Christ the word bestow	2:434
I must my salvation doubt	3:126	If cleansed by thee ev'n now I am	2:20
I now as from the grave restored	3:170	If envy and self-interest rule	2:399
I now discern thy gracious aim	3:263	If fiercely some the truth deny	3:62
I pray thee let me pass the Flood	3:355	If first thy Wisdom prove	1:227
I publish abroad	2:56	If God upon the action shine	3:426
I reason, and resolve in vain	3:269	If gratified in his request	2:106
I see the gospel-summer past	3:163	If he for a time withdraws	2:207
I see the Opening Door of Hope!	3:359	If his soul is on the wing	3:302
I see their cruel Waste with streaming eyes	1:179	If hitherto, intirely thine	3:344
		If Jesus bless, and break the bread	2:209
I shall, if thou bestow the power	2:18	If Jesus, the Immortal Tree	2:201
I sing Grimalkin brave & bold	1:280	If justice should abridge my days	3:263
I sing thy Grace Divinely free	3:159	If now I had forgot to grieve	3:145
I the barren figtree am	2:143	If now in Lamenting for GOD	1:258
I trust thy mercy to restrain	3:206	If now, O GOD, thou hast begun	1:233
I wait the powerful look	2:301	If now thy time be fully come	3:288
I want a permanent release	3:190	If still, his faith to try	1:144
I want the gospel-purity	2:342	If still my faith to prove	1:226
I wanted still I knew not what	3:252	If such the counsel of thy will	3:134
I was (himself can tell) sincere	3:251	If swelled with self-important pride	3:48
I will give you drink, and feed[94]	2:150	If taught by thy Intending Grace	1:243
I will not harbour in my Mind	1:269	If the ancient faith thou give	2:72
I who long have called him Lord	2:389	If the just God himself consent	2:272
I woud be governed by thy will	3:256	If the strength and joy of grace	3:257
I would not a Parent see	3:299	If thou art H[arri]s still, awake, arise	1:189
I would not use the proffered Power	3:154	If thou avert thine angry eyes	1:245
I would not vex thy glorious eyes	3:268	If thou canst pardon me once more	3:438
I would not live to cross thy Will	1:220	If thou forgive my debt immense	1:315
I would not, Lord, the Doom decline	2:121	If thou hast called her by her name	3:278
I would not my own Soul deceive	1:218	[If] thou, indeed, desir'st this heart	2:443
I would not to thy Creature cleave	1:243	If thou mayst intreated be	3:302
Idle I in the vineyard stood	3:347	If thou my loving labour speed	3:299
Idle, mercenary, proud	2:183	If thou my unbelief remove	3:222
If anger once begin to rise	3:143	If thou pronounce the word	1:85
If banished from the human race	1:91	If thou the fishers guide	2:92
If blest with faith that works by love[95]	2:235	If thou the power of faith bestow	3:163
		If thou the word bestow	2:349
		If thou the word of truth revoke	3:40
		If thou their ministry ordain	2:325
		If thou thwart my best design	2:372
		If thy Decree, which rules our Mind	1:222
		If thy Justice, Lord, demands	3:148

94. The stanza beginning with this line appears in *PW* 11:227–8.
95. The stanza beginning with this line appears in *PW* 11:371 with a variant first line: "Blessed with the faith that works by love."

If to me in Drawing Love	3:132	In outward things alone[96]	2:95
If virtue, Lord, from thee proceed	3:167	In part, before he reached the sky	3:334
If want or pestilence be near	2:245	In perfect power divine	1:145
If while this principle for thee remains	3:403	In Peter's threefold fall we see	2:197
		In pity for our helpless race	2:216
If with us thou art	3:186	In search of the Religion true	3:174
If worship were, to bow the knee	2:66	In simple innocency drest	1:320
If yesterday thou canst recall	3:151	In sin we rush impetuous on	2:324
If yet thou mayst intreated be	1:84	In Sins we were dead	3:119
Ignorant of what is best	1:250	In *Solemn League* with death and hell	1:64
Impatient to be disbelieved	2:464	In sweet convincing Love come down	1:242
Impeled by active love, I come	2:71	In swift preventing Love appear	1:244
Impious priests in every age	2:252	In that land of endless rest	3:370
Impossible commands	2:455	In that oblivious Land of Rest	1:224
In a Good Land of Corn and Wine	3:201	In that suffering Son of man	2:109
In absolute, extreme despair	3:140	In the slippery paths of youth	3:195
In an angelical disguise	3:351	In this Accepted Hour	3:178
In answer to my labouring heart	3:188	In this howling Wilderness	1:219
In answer to our prayer	3:59	In this precarious situation	1:132
In Body removed from a Friend	1:256	In the Beloved accepted	2:471
In British realms you wa[i]ve your Right	3:96	In the city or place	2:318
		In the Spirit of holiness	2:328
In calm despair I bow my head	1:320	In the Spirit of inspiration	3:125
In ceremonies nice	1:40	In the toils of death I lay	3:407
In chains of conscious fear	3:271	In these thy Spirit's days as near	3:222
In faith against their sin we pray	1:79	In trouble and distress	1:69
In fixt attention wait	2:139	In vain against the stream you strive	1:148
In haste their measure to fulfil	3:306	In vain alas! I strive to check	3:353
In him, as in a faithful glass	1:300	In vain his thousand wiles ye Tyrant tried	1:197
In Immanuel we	3:120		
In infancy their hopes and fears	3:83	In vain the Partisans of Rome	3:71
In jealous self-mistrusting Fear	1:222	In vain their malice hoped to see	3:197
In Jehovah's incarnation	2:76	In vain our treacherous brethren tried	1:136
In Jesus Christ we see	2:185	In vain to pride and pleasure prone	1:246
In Jesus found, for him we cry	3:248	In vain we Causes false assign	1:83
In Jesus his name	2:388	In vain would Christ's insidious foes	2:241
In judgment then, great God arise	3:134	In view of such transcendent bliss	1:307
In life's extremest hour	3:166	In wisest love thou dost delay	2:468
In Love to Man thou dost thy Merits shew	1:209	Indifference is a crime in all	2:130
		Infatuated by wrath divine	1:91
In my last distress relieve me	2:428	Infidels, if God compel	2:393
In myself a feeble worm	3:192		
In our unregenerate state	2:19		

96. The stanza beginning with this line appears in *PW* 11:150.

Infinite Love, & Truth, & Power	1:314	Jesu, preserve her to that Day	1:268
Injoy the evils ye have done	1:94	Jesu, Shepherd of the Sheep[98]	3:202
Injured, bereaved—what shall we say	3:283	Jesu, thro' whom again I breathe	3:431
Inkindled at the word	2:139	Jesu, thy goodness I proclaim	1:325
Innocence in youth, how rare	2:60	Jesus, a soul afflicted, see	2:21
Inspire me with the grace	2:263	Jesus a traitor chose	2:54
Inspire his soul with faith to soar	3:342	Jesus, all thy subjects here	2:43
Inspired with penitential fear	3:188	Jesus, Almighty to redeem	1:135
Instant in prayer, I cannot rest	1:298	Jesus & heaven is all my Own	3:202
Instruct me, Lord, with tenderest zeal	3:298	Jesus, arise, thy cause maintain	1:108
Instructed by his Spirit, we know	2:360	Jesus, assume thy right divine	3:214
Intangled in their calling's snares	3:292	Jesus, at thy command I come	3:348
Interest and superstition joined	2:396	Jesus, avenge us of the Foe	1:114
Into absolute Subjection	1:249	Jesus, behold the men	3:277
Into their longing hearts	3:272	Jesus, believing in thy Name	3:308
Into thy hands my soul receive	3:329	Jesus' bliss the church inspires	2:153
Inured to want, in spirit poor	3:239	Jesus, come, the Spirit cries	1:76
Invisible near	2:239	Jesus commends the good in man	2:98
Is it for thy dear sake alone	1:269	Jesus conveys himself away	2:235
Is it in all thy Depths of Love	3:151	Jesus, dear redeeming Lord	3:303
Is there a second time for them	2:310	Jesus declines the umpire's place[99]	2:136
Is there in my Distress	1:225	Jesus, dig about my root	2:144
Is there no balm in Gilead found	3:167	Jesus doth the truth declare	2:170
Is there no medicine for her wound	3:273	Jesus, end the bloody Fray	1:68
Is there some cursed thing unknown	2:374	Jesus, evermore the same	2:411
Is this, O Lord, the sign	2:79	Jesus expiring on the tree	2:342
Israel's God & strength, arise	3:241	Jesus' feet her refuge are	2:247
It is the Lord, whose sovereign will	3:282	Jesus, fix it in my heart	2:187
It matters not how small	2:173	Jesus, friend of the distrest	3:280
It matters not, if Both are One	3:89	Jesus *from*, not *in*, our sins	2:17
It seems impossible that Grace	3:151	Jesus from them we learn t' obey	2:350
It speaks a weak ignoble Soul	1:270	Jesus, from thy Servants taken	3:109
It would not be by Wrath compelled	3:203	Jesus, full of balmy grace	3:164
Jacob of old to gain a Wife	3:159	Jesus, God of love, appear!	3:279
Jealous, close, reserved, afraid	1:297	Jesus, hear, my God, my All	1:252
Jealous for thy People be	3:132	Jesus, help as weak a soul	3:258
Jehovah sends by whom he will	2:291	Jesus, help the Woman's Seed	3:300
Jehovah to Jehovah	2:289		
Jehovah's praise declare	3:168		
Jesu, I believe thee Now[97]	3:202		

[97]. The stanza beginning with this line appears in *PW* 4:449, but the first line has different wording: "Jesus, I behold thee now."

[98]. The stanza beginning with this line appears in *PW* 4:449.

[99]. The first four lines of a six-line stanza beginning with this line are combined with the last two lines of the next stanza of the same poem to form one poem in *PW* 11:209.

IDEX OF FIRST LINES OF POETRY BY JOHN AND CHARLES WESLEY

Jesus himself to works appeals	2:27	Jesus replete with truth and grace	2:93
Jesus *his* times and moments knows	2:56	Jesus risen from the dead	2:355
Jesus, if by thy light I see	3:291	Jesus sent a messenger	3:364
Jesus, if such thy love's design	2:247	Jesus, sheltered in thy name	3:428
Jesus, if thou thy Spirit give[100]	2:148	Jesus, spoil him of his prey	3:244
Jesus, in every time and place	3:127	Jesus spoke the powerful word	3:407
Jesus in the spirit groans	2:247	Jesus still with favour see	2:345
Jesus in wisdom and in love	2:326	Jesus, supreme, almighty Lord	3:179
Jesus is glorified	2:287	Jesus takes the sinner's part	2:102
Jesus is of his church possest	2:225	Jesus tastes the bitter cup	2:66
Jesus is within the vail	2:439	Jesus, that precious grace of thine	2:369
Jesus, Jehovah, God supreme	3:321	Jesus the child by growing shews	2:83
Jesus justifies expence	2:46	Jesus, the Crucified for all	3:319
Jesus' love I cannot feel[101]	2:328	Jesus, th' essential Power divine	3:231
Jesus, manifest thy grace	3:372	Jesus, the everlasting Son	2:257
Jesus, mighty Intercessor	2:302	Jesus, the God of love	2:42
Jesus, my hope, my life, my Lord	3:50	Jesus, the matter take	3:135
Jesus, my long sequestered God[102]	2:88	Jesus, the only God and true	2:236
Jesus, my Residue of years	1:259	Jesus the Lord by man forsook	2:65
Jesus now gone up on high[103]	2:153	Jesus, the Man Divine thou art!	2:242
Jesus, now his heart inspire	3:265	Jesus, the power impart[104]	2:140
Jesus of Nazareth / thou hearst	2:339	Jesus, The promise made by thee[105]	3:286
Jesus of Nazareth, appear	3:232	Jesus, the world was made by thee	2:215
Jesus, on thy saving Name	3:144	Jesus, th'incarnate God, we praise	2:99
Jesus, our absent Brethren bless	3:230	Jesus thine heir Anointed	2:83
Jesus, our merciful High-priest	1:305	Jesus, this feeble heart of mine	2:331
Jesus, our true and faithful Lord	3:65	Jesus, tho' late I now submit	3:159
Jesus persisting to deny	2:383	Jesus, thou hast spoke the word	2:101
Jesus present to the heart	2:57	Jesus, thou hast with pity seen	2:163
Jesus, preserve thy grace in me	2:175	Jesus, thou our Rabbi art	2:217
Jesus, Prince of pastors, fill	2:146	Jesus, thou Son of David, hear	3:275
Jesus, pronounce my spirit loosed	3:191	Jesus, thou tak'st thy servant's part[106]	2:384
Jesus, purge our foul transgression	2:471	Jesus, thro' every age the same	3:345
Jesus, quickning Spirit, come	2:249	Jesus, thro' thine o'erpowering Grace	1:218
Jesus, refused by sinners	2:312	Jesus, thro' thy death alone	2:200
		Jesus, thy all-atoning blood	1:308

100. The stanza beginning with this line appears in *PW* 11:222.
101. The stanza beginning with this line appears in *PW* 12:239: "Jesu's love I cannot feel."
102. The stanza beginning with this line appears in *PW* 11:130.
103. The first four lines of the eight-line stanza beginning with this line appear in *PW* 11:233.
104. The stanza beginning with this line appears in *PW* 11:213.
105. The stanza beginning with this line appears in *PW* 8:421.
106. The first six lines of the eight-line stanza beginning with this line appear in *PW* 12:348.

Jesus, thy church inspire[107]	2:298	Jesus, with pity see	3:271
Jesus, thy faithful love I praise	3:239	Jesus, with thy disciples stay	3:232
Jesus, thy hated Servant own	3:304	Jesus would be declared to none	2:59
Jesus, thy kind command	2:361	Jesus' zeal can never bear	2:181
Jesus, thy only grace can heal	3:163	Join all the Friends of Jesus	3:110
Jesus, thy vengeful power exert	3:229	Joined to a sinful multitude	2:304
Jesus, thy witnesses increase	3:69	Joy of our eyes, our heart's desire	1:79
Jesus to heaven is gone[108]	2:182	Joyful tidings of their Lord	2:207
Jesus, to her help descend	3:246	Joys all earthly joys transcending	3:371
Jesus, to thee I fly	1:272	Judas did first himself betray	2:257
Jesus, to thee in faith we cry	3:318	Judgment is at thy house begun	3:75
Jesus, to thee my child I bring	1:291	Judicious Barrington, whose searching eye	3:384
Jesus, to thee our wants we tell	2:218	Justice hath given the Rebels up	1:133
Jesus, to thee thy Church looks up	3:133	Justly is his case deplored	2:37
Jesus to those he most approves	2:46		
Jesus, to us apostles raise[109]	2:299		
Jesus, today appear	2:327		
Jesus, vanished from my sight	2:262	Keep (for I nothing else desire)	1:304
Jesus vouchsafes his own to praise	2:193	Keep from me thy loveliest Creature	1:249
Jesus, we come to do thy Will	3:196	Keep me, Lord, by day & night	3:370
Jesus, we hear thine actions speak	2:100	Keep not silence at my Tears	1:251
Jesus, we now with pure delight[110]	2:230	Keep up the intercourse between	1:271
Jesus, we thy promise claim	3:243	Keep us, O thou lowly Lamb	3:36
Jesus weeps for sinners blind[111]	2:248	Kelway's Sonatas who can bear	3:382
Jesus, what shall I do	2:143	Kept by the virtue of thy name	1:319
Jesus who assumes our nature	2:76	Kindly minding my request	3:281
Jesus, who now thy cause maintain	2:330	King of heaven's exalted powers	3:168
Jesus, who omnipresent art	1:302	King of saints, he meekly bears	2:275
Jesus, who sent them out	3:84	Kings of earth, to Christ bow down	2:65
Jesus whom once I knew	2:84	Know, ye zealots proud and blind	2:102
Jesus whom the world forsake	2:53		
Jesus, whom thy grace constrains	2:205		
Jesus with his undaunted zeal	2:390	Labours his struggling soul	2:170
Jesus, with human eyes	1:290	Labourers dreadful to the fiend	2:399
		Lamb of God, I would like thee	2:323
		Lame preface, lame transition too	2:416
		Late let him find his destined place	1:131
		Lay thy mighty Cross on me[112]	3:202
		Lay your zealous scruples by	3:411
		Learning and authority	2:199

107. The stanza beginning with this line appears in *PW* 12:181.
108. The stanza beginning with this line appears in *PW* 11:270.
109. The stanza beginning with this line appears in *PW* 12:181.
110. The stanza beginning with this line appears in *PW* 11:360.
111. The stanza beginning with this line appears in *PW* 11:475–6 as the second stanza of a two-stanza hymn.
112. The stanza beginning with this line appears in *PW* 4:449.

IDEX OF FIRST LINES OF POETRY BY JOHN AND CHARLES WESLEY

Least[113] the enemy prevail	3:132	Let thy well-known sign appear	2:189
Least this my dreadful end should be	2:260	Let us in Continual Prayer	1:241
Least we miss the dubious Way	1:235	Let us on his Faithful Love	3:193
Left by thee in danger's day	2:194	Let us rejoice, give thanks, and sing	3:219
Left to his will how could we be?	1:100	Let us the shining path pursue[117]	3:333
Left to itself, the soul of man	2:210	Let us thy great glory seek	3:37
Less than the least in my own sight	3:35	Let us with our Lord retreat	2:195
Less than the least who Jesus know	2:149	Life of the world, I worship thee	2:203
Let all mankind abase	2:76	Lift the dejected sinner up	3:228
Let all mankind give ear	2:355	Lift up for All Mankind to see[118]	2:454
Let all th'Incarnate God adore	2:77	Light lie the earth on our Forefathers dead	1:143
Let all who know the Sinner's Friend	3:157	Light of dreary Souls appear	1:251
Let earth be glad, the Lord is King	1:95	Lightened by a ray of grace	2:228
Let every tongue my Saviour Praise	3:169	Like Others of thy Rank (like kings that go	1:204
Let fools and infidels revere	3:171	Like them I long on thee to gaze	3:160
Let God arise & let his foes	3:312	Like those of old, a stiffnecked race	1:59
Let heathens murmur, or resent	1:269	Lion of Judah's tribe, arise	3:229
Let her, as thy laws require	3:242	Listening I wait to hear	2:361
Let him blaspheme thy Grace no more	3:162	List'ning to my feeble cry	3:144
Let infidels and heathen mourn[114]	3:332	Live to employ thy gifts aright	3:314
Let Jews and Greeks as folly deem	2:80	Loath, I seem to take the field	1:253
Let me cry for help to thee[115]	2:30	Lo, again the silent fiend	3:416
Let me from men forever cease	3:420	Lo, at thy feet we bow	1:87
Let me not from thee e'er swerve	2:445	Lo, I in thy house attend	2:411
Let me only live to see	1:75	Lo, in the arms of faith and prayer	2:93
Let me wander not unseen	1:284	Lo! the Beastly Mark is seen	3:149
Let Midas judge, and what will follow	3:383	Lo, the ruthless felon comes	2:243
Let mine injurious brother own[116]	2:161	Lo! they expose to view the naked Plan	1:193
Let my disciples go	2:265	Long as he did reside	2:51
Let not the pit infernal close	1:135	Long as in me thy Breath remains	3:161
Let not their counsel stand	1:85	Long have I forfeited my Peace	1:263
Let saints rejoice with fear	2:130	Long have I wept, & prayed	1:225
Let Satan still their tongues employ	2:432	Long he on Tabor's top abode[119]	3:336
Let Scribes & Pharisees blaspheme	2:94	Long in affliction's furnace tried	3:331
Let the sprinkled blood that cleanses	3:125	Long in the conflict, long	3:339
"Let there be light" if thou command	1:288		

113. Least = Lest.
114. The stanza beginning with this line appears in *PW* 6:301.
115. The stanza beginning with this line appears in *SH* 1762, 2:169 but in a different meter.
116. The stanza beginning with this line appears in *PW* 11:248.
117. The stanza beginning with this line appears in *PW* 6:301.
118. The stanza beginning with this line appears in *PW* 4:315.
119. The stanza beginning with this line appears in *PW* 6:309.

Long in the heart of man concealed	2:145
Long in the toils of death she lay	3:328
LONG MAY HE LIVE, for England's Good	3:304
LONG MAY HE LIVE, to serve Thy cause	3:304
Long on man their hopes were stayed	1:68
Long on Tabor's top abode	3:336
Long the triumphant Villains cried	1:73
Long, undesired, with foes he stayed[120]	2:386
Long undisturbed the tempter keeps[121]	2:129
Longsuffering, pitiful, and kind	3143
Look me then into thy Peace	1:250
Look on my honest, open face	1:154
Look on them with thy flaming Eyes[122]	2:448
Look to thy Cause, I ask no more	3:122
Loosed by the power of grace	2:170
Loosed from the ties of flesh and blood	2:218
Lord, from sinful worshippers	2:313
Lord, I dare not ask a sign	2:22
Lord, I will not let thee rest	3:258
Lord, if my sin-sick soul[123]	2:107
Lord, if thou call me by my name	2:326
Lord, if thou didst the wish inspire	3:420
Lord, if thou hast my blindness healed	2:59
Lord, if thou know'st it good for me	1:221
Lord, if thy love doth still abound	3:255
Lord, in my contrite heart reveal	2:46
Lord, in whom I fain would trust	3:299
Lord, into thy harvest send	2:371
Lord, mine eyes are holden too[124]	2:208
Lord of life, thy people hear	3:302
Lord of the gospel-harvest, hear	3:35
Lord of the harvest, hear	3:58
Lord, on thee I cast my care	1:294
Lord over all, thy people hear	3:37
Lord, that I to friend & foe[125]	2:268
Lord, the love of truth impart	2:357
Lord, the virtue of thy love	2:161
Lord, thou dost for ever live	3:431
Lord, thou see'st my heart's desire	2:337
Lord, we believe against his foes	3:311
Lord, we for thine absence mourn	2:106
Lord, we long to know thy Pleasure	1:240
Lord, we will not let thee go	3:242
Lord, we with joy confess	2:185
Lord, when thy love begins to reign	2:56
Lost, distracted I inquire	1:253
Lost in an endless maze	1:86
Lost to all sense of shame or fear	1:99
Louder than that his hands have shed	3:249
Love only can renew my heart	3:153
LOVE only doth the loss ordain	3:238
Love, only love, their purpose dared to oppose	3:401
Love, perfect Love, shall cast out Sin	3:201
Love, the power of humble love	2:163
Lover of every Sect, attached to none	3:327
Lover of Lazarus, and Friend	3:344
Lover of man's apostate kind	3:221
Lover of souls, on thee I call	3:420
Low at thy mercy-seat	1:301
Lowliness meets in him	2:185
Lulled in a Satanic dream	3:246
Lunardi for ever!	3:389
Made, and redeemed by Love divine	3:319
Made free, & willing to obey	2:409
Mad-men, who us for madmen take	2:426
Make her Duty her delight	3:243

120. The stanza beginning with this line appears in *PW* 12:352.
121. The stanza beginning with this line appears in *PW* 11:204.
122. The stanza beginning with this line appears in *PW* 8:164.
123. The stanza beginning with this line appears in *PW* 11:174.
124. A similar stanza beginning with the line "Mine eyes are holden too" appears in *PW* 11:307, but the remaining lines vary considerably.
125. The last four lines of the six-line stanza beginning with this line in *UP* appear in *PW* 12:71, where they are combined with four other lines to form an eight-line stanza.

Make her thy peculiar care	3:301	Meantime by our pacific measures	1:132
Make me thro' thy wondrous Name	3:195	Meek, patient, humble, wise above His years	1:176
Makers of wrecks, a desperate race	1:155	Meek, patient Lamb for us he gives	2:204
Man may soul and body part	2:135	Meer mercy doth repeat	2:142
Man & God for sinners slain	2:379	Meet and right it is that thou[130]	2:189
Man, sinful man, to labour born	3:426	Members of his Church we know	2:67
Man would all the reasons know	2:106	Men the choicest gift abuse	2:151
Manner and time to thee we leave	3:288	*Mene tekel!* here the days	3:412
Man's soul, the vineyard of the Lord	2:62	Merciful God, the grace impart	1:117
Many a bold, presumptuous guest	2:37	Merciful God, what shall I do?	1:220
Mark every thought that rises there	3:420	Merciful God, with pitying Eye	1:263
Martha renews her pious care	2:251	Merciful, just, almighty Lord	1:121
Martha's chosen work is good[126]	2:126	Mercy thou dost for thousands keep	3:367
Martha's faith in active life[127]	2:123	Might I live to see him freed	1:296
Martin would have plucked out, we own	3:438	Might I now to heaven repair	3:258
Martyr of fidelity	3:343	Mild my Advocate replied	2:143
Mary could not envy feel	2:124	Millions of fellow-subjects lost	1:135
Mary, devoted Mary, lies	2:251	Millions of mournful souls have seen	2:209
Master, (as such thyself I own)[128]	2:216	Mine eyes are ever unto thee[131]	2:325
Master of the gospel-feast	3:36	Mine inmost Soul to thee is known	1:223
Master, thy Greatness needs not me	3:47	Miracles of uncommon grace	2:75
Matthew, and Mark, and Luke, and John	2:375	Misers, the name belongs to you	2:137
May we not now look up	2:189	Mistaken comforter! Could tears remove	3:400
May we not trust our flock to him[129]	2:364	Mob undiscerning took their word	1:160
Me, and my works canst thou approve	3:433	Mocked with her comrades in distress	3:434
Me, & my happy Partner seize	1:244	Modern, as ancient priests, presume	2:420
Me, Father, to myself make known	3:284	Money! the direful love of thee	2:257
Me he hath not quite rejected	3:147	Monsters of iniquity	1:61
Me how often didst thou save	3:405	Monsters unnatural, who dare	1:76
Me if thou never more incline	3:155	More courageous than the men	2:207
Me if thou vouchsafe to give	3:294	More odious than the birds and beasts	2:219
Me let thy dying love constrain	3:177	More inclined to ill than good	3:294
Me, me, thy meanest messenger	3:304	Moses may frown, if Jesus smiles	2:242
Me thou hast sent, a thing of nought	3:47	Most gracious God, our hearts incline	1:77
		Mould me to thy will resigned	3:195
		Mourn, all who love the all-redeeming Lamb	1:178
		Mourners for ourselves alone	3:372

126. The stanza beginning with this line appears in *PW* 11:198.
127. The stanza beginning with this line appears in *PW* 11:196.
128. The stanza beginning with this line appears in *PW* 11:328.
129. The stanza beginning with this line appears in *PW* 12:294.
130. The stanza beginning with this line appears in *PW* 11:278.
131. The stanza beginning with this line appears in *PW* 12:235.

Moved by our united prayer	3:94	My one, momentous business here	3:291
Much goods for many years laid up	2:138	My other Self, but more beloved	1:320
Multitudes cannot distress	2:385	My other Self, to Eden borne	3:357
Musing on the ancient days[132]	2:446	My Passover, O Christ, thou art	2:192
Must not he sing in the abyss	1:158	My Ransomer he died	3:350
Must with the Man of Sorrows grieve	2:111	My Saviour to the utmost here	2:473
My affections fix above	2:439	My Saviour's friends by men despised	3:253
My bitter persecuting Foes	3:434	My sins have raised the stormy sea	1:84
My Brother comes with Armed Bands	3:121	My Son committed to his hands	1:307
My days are as a shadow fled	3:356	My spirit doth in God rejoice	2:225
My double want supply	3:72	My spirit magnifies the Lord	3:170
My Duty, Wisdom, Gain	1:229	My thoughts, O God, are not as thine	2:463
My eager thirst of creature-bliss	2:227	My trust is in thy blood alone	3:321
My Earthly Father's Shade	1:225	My wealth, my friends, my plans I leave	3:285
My evil things content I am	1:265	My will I would to his resign	3:299
My faith is to the utmost tried	3:50	My worthless life, O Lord, receive	3:123
My faith thou dost bestow	2:460	Myriads hosanna cry	2:179
My fallen soul create anew	3:191		
My Father's Hope, my Father's Fear	1:220		
My Friend (alas no longer mine)	1:268		
My Friend and mediator	3:165	Naked of Christ ye now are found	2:392
My Friend, himself devoid of selfish Art	1:174	Nations who did in Treaties trust	1:98
		Nature, by the cross kept down	3:404
My God alone I fain would love	1:314	Nature cannot comprehend	2:174
My God, be thou my Guide	3:141	Nature in vain would hide its fears	3:297
My God expiring on a cross	2:67	Nature thy gifts requires	2:240
My God, for help I cry to thee	3:127	Nature would shine above the rest	2:149
My God, my God, I hear thy call	3:153	Nature's impotent condition	2:318
My God omnipotently nigh	3:200	Nature's talents to improve	3:294
My goodness now I cannot boast	2:45	Needful for the good of man	2:125
My hastiness is stayed	2:398	Needy, impotent to good	2:152
My heart (how contrary to thee!)	3:153	Neglected lay the unkindled spark within	3:396
My heart which cannot cease from sin	3:163	Neither asks, nor looks for healing	3:147
My heart's supreme desire	2:146	New terms of fellowship we frame	2:344
My impotence to him is known	2:71	No abstinence severe	2:52
My Leader, my Lord	3:265	No! be the veil forever cast aside	3:399
My more than Friend, accept the Warning Lay	1:171	No: but thou calldst them forth to be	3:41
My more than life to thee I give	1:271	No cause of death, no slightest blame	2:354
My nature's haste restrain	3:142	No faintest Ray of distant Hope	1:265
My nature's weakness I confess	1:316	No fanciful Enthusiasts we	3:199
My new & strange Distress	1:232	No farther let their Rage proceed	3:313
		No good in man can be	2:107

132. The stanza is incomplete.

IDEX OF FIRST LINES OF POETRY BY JOHN AND CHARLES WESLEY

No helps medicinal have I	3:167
No longer now my drooping hands I rear	3:402
No longer now their watch the Watchmen keep	1:172
No, Lord, thy Bowels answer No!	1:231
No marvel he should soon mislead His Guide	3:91
No matter what—if God be here	2:312
No more I rashly turn aside	2:17
No more shall strange Desires consume[133]	2:453
No, my most gracious God	1:226
No overplus, or need	2:296
No Power a Band of Soldiers have	3:112
No red-hot Zealot thou, whose furious Mind	1:201
No relief on earth is found	2:445
No right the house of God to cleanse	2:220
No, Saviour, no: it cannot be	3:261
No secret practices that shun	2:428
No succour in myself I have	3:126
No; the letter profits nought[134]	2:257
No; the servants of the Lord	2:417
No true humility and love	2:472
None can tell but those that bear it	3:146
None for our lives or safety cares	1:127
None hath a right to throw	2:91
None on earth can conceive	3:289
Nor art thou less benevolent than great	1:205
Nor generous hope, nor servile fear	3:269
Nor slightest Touch of blame	3:209
Nor time nor means my Lord can need[135]	2:144
Nor works, nor sufferings, can atone	1:308
Nor yet from my dim Eyes thy form retires	3:381
Nor yet retired the principle divine	3:397
Nor yet the peaceful answer came[136]	3:334
Nor yet would treacherous reason's timely care	3:398
Not all the first-born Sons of Light	3:159
Not all thou canst in Life bestow	1:224
Not artificial wants to feed	3:293
Not as distinguished from the rest	3:59
Not as his inclination leads	2:25
Not biassed by a party zeal	3:334
Not by Angelic ministry	2:315
Not by the crafty wizard swayed[137]	2:351
Not by the door ye enter in	2:243
Not by their own resistless powers	1:72
Not by voice Angelic taught	2:322
Not content with Christ to live	2:68
Not for his death, but life, we pray	3:304
Not for sin or splendid vice	2:60
Not for some condemning all	2:385
Not for the vinegar they gave[138]	2:276
Not governed by his word	2:196
Not half so wise the sons of light[139]	2:156
Not in temples made with hands	3:219
Not like the simple croud misled	1:311
Not long enjoyed my soul the pure relief	3:400
Not meerly human policy	2:413
Not of a blemished character	1:306
Not one particular alone	3:173
Not out of earth the trouble springs	3:283
"Not so," replied the Father's love[140]	3:335
Not that I dare my God blaspheme	3:419

133. The stanza beginning with this line appears in *PW* 4:314.
134. The stanza beginning with this line appears in *PW* 11:504.
135. The last four lines of the eight-line stanza beginning with this line appear as part of a longer poem in *PW* 11:218–19.
136. The stanza beginning with this line appears in *PW* 6:302.
137. The stanza beginning with this line appears in *PW* 12:274–75.
138. The stanza beginning with this line appears in *PW* 12:94.
139. The stanza beginning with this line appears in *PW* 11:241.
140. The stanza beginning with this line appears in *PW* 6:302.

Not that my sufferings can procure	1:308	Now thy Spirit brings to mind	3:406
Not the wild Authors of a Sect	3:59	Now to your utmost height you rise	3:96
Not to improve them, is to lose[141]	2:176	Now with thorns hedge up her way	3:244
Not to indulge our sloth and ease[142]	2:26	Numberless hosts and fleets combined	1:61
Not to the vain Desires of men	3:199	Numbers have left the narrow way	3:306
Not with outward pomp and state	2:163	Numbers for custom['s] sake	2:107
Not with the doctors of the law	2:335		
Nothing beneath my heart commands	3:129		
Nothing is too hard for thee	3:281	O All-embracing Love Divine	3:162
Nothing more the wealthy need	2:151	O be not rigorously extreme	3:47
Nothing on earth but Christ we know	2:426	O beget my soul again	3:196
Nothing shall, sir, appease my Rage	1:282	O by the Comforts of thy Grace	1:233
Nothing we thought too much t'endure	1:90	O cast not out my dying prayer	3:191
Nought we love which man can give	2:135	O could I now discern thee near	3:276
Now avenge her of her Foe	3:242	O could I hear that inward Voice	1:323
Now, dearest Lord	2:281	O could I that Asylum find	1:224
Now, ev'n now, the kingdom's near	2:174	O could I to my Saviour pray	1:98
Now, Father, now thy terrors dart	3:250	O could I to the Desart fly	1:320
Now I dare my hellish foe	3:415	O could I view them with *thine* eyes	1:270
Now I live to Jesus joined	2:35	O could we with the Sign receive	3:185
Now I see with other eyes	3:413	O could we to our Smiter turn	1:117
Now, in Jesu's name I pray	2:439	O Depth of exquisite Distress!	3:357
Now is the season to repent	2:146	O dire effect of party zeal	1:135
Now, let me Now give up the Ghost	2:204	O Father, impart	3:289
Now let them feel the torturing fear	3:318	O Father of mercies, incline	3:360
Now let them to the dunghill look	3:80	O for a kind, pitying ray	3:260
Now, Lord, apply thy powerful word	2:26	O for a spark of heavenly fire	3:207
Now, Lord, (if we know	2:353	O for a steady Mind	1:228
Now, Lord, we have made known	3:278	O for a Zeal like his, who scorned to fear	3:108
Now my spirit's cure begin	3:144		
Now, now the dire contagion stop	3:78	O for an end like his	2:82
Now, O my God, the havock see	2:466	O for his only sake	1:86
Now, or whene'er it is thy will	1:298	O for his prayer and passion sake	3:249
Now our heart again is hardened	3:147	O for my dear Saviour's sake	3:297
Now, Saviour, now our hearts prepare	3:236	O for one Cordial Drop	3:363
Now, Saviour, now thy latest cries	3:314	O for the strength of fervent zeal	3:255
Now then, if now I pray	1:291	O for thy Truth & mercy sake	1:222
Now then let us turn	3:181	O gentle Shepherd, hear my cry	2:441
Now then the Spirit of holiness	1:289	O God, from whom our blessings flow	3:424
Now thy convincing work begin	3:247	O God, my Refuge in Distress	1:243
		O God of my forefathers, hear	1:292
		O God of unlimited Power	3:352
		O God, our refuge in distress	3:229

141. The stanza beginning with this line appears in *PW* 11:266.
142. See *PW* 10:240.

O God, stir up thy Jealousy	3:122	O may I ever be	2:152
O God, to whom for light I look	3:172	O may I every moment feel	3:51
O God, thy promised aid impart	2:442	O may I never seek my own	2:238
O God, what a Strength of Desire	1:257	O may I never take the praise	3:311
O God, who didst out of the dust	3:46	O may I never teach my Lord	2:29
O God, who didst the Seers inspire	3:71	O may we ever keep in view	3:380
O God, who dost for ever live	3:341	O may we still the truth declare[145]	2:364
O God, who dost the motives know	3:73	O may we watch, and pray, and strive	2:167
O God, who hast my manners borne	3:286	O merciful Creator	3:155
O God, who hear'st thy people's prayer	1:89	O might I all present to thee	3:310
O gracious Father! why to man	2:440	O might I her Portion share	1:255
O had he died before that day	3:85	O might I, like Jesus, be[146]	2:268
O had he kept the Post by Heaven assigned	1:176	O might I now lay down my head	3:124
		O might I now with calmest Haste	3:355
O had I lived, and languished then	3:221	O might I thus my Warfare end	2:204
O Happy, happy Place	3:210	O might I thus thro' life endure	2:69
O happy Life of Faith & Love	3:200	O might my heart, to ill inclined	3:127
O helper of sinners distrest	3:312	O might my useless warfare end	3:356
O how are they increased	3:137	O might our nation now repent	1:71
O how distant from my hope	3:164	O might the blood that flowed for him	3:298
O how gracious is my Lord[143]	2:21	O might the prayer of faith prevail	3:240
O how ought we to hear	2:105	O might they now receive	2:341
O how pretious is his blood	3:365	O might they now the blessing find	3:230
O how ready is the Lord	3:215	O might thy Spirit intercede	3:122
O how shall I attain	2:27	O might we each distinctly grieve	1:83
O how sore a Thing & grievous	3:146	O might we gain that heavenly Rest	3:62
O how unlike the thoughts of man	2:145	O might we seek the kingdom first	3:427
O how winning your address	3:413	O might we truly bear	2:368
O Jesus, appear	1:275	O most compassionate High Priest	3:228
O Jesus, in thee	2:414	O my Father, God and King	3:404
O Jesus our head	3:180	O my God, my God, forbear	3:152
O Jesus, thou knowst	3:266	O my God, my gracious God	3:131
O let him by thy quickning word	3:346	O my God, what hast thou done?	2:201
O let it not our Lord displease	1:233	O my unsettled Soul	1:272
O let us steadily pursue	1:271	O Saviour, sanctify this pain	3:232
O Lord of Hosts, O GOD of Grace[144]	2:446	O set not an ungodly Man	1:106
O Lord of lords, & King of kings	1:111	O Son of God, whose flaming eyes	3:51
O Lover of Sinners distrest	1:258		
O make on his soul	3:267		

143. This stanza appears in *PW* 10:211 in a six-line format, but in *UP* 2:21 it has eight lines.

144. The stanza beginning with this line appears in *PW* 8:162.

145. The stanza beginning with this line appears in *PW* 12:293.

146. The last four lines of the six-line stanza beginning with this line appear in *PW* 12:71, where they are combined with four other lines to form an eight-line stanza.

O Son of Man, O God most high	3:77	O thou who at the gospel-feast	2:149
O tear it now away	1:229	O thou, who didst an help ordain	1:255
O terrible, but just Decree	2:465	O thou, who didst my Burthen bear	3:121
O that all would apply	2:56	O thou, who dost in secret see	3:278
O that crouds in this our day	2:308	O thou who dost not put to pain	2:373
O that he *now* might tremble there	1:300	O thou who dost the proud withstand	3:77
O that his afflicted mind	3:265	O thou, who dost vouchsafe to chuse	3:47
O that his Masters never here had been	1:179	O thou who hanging on the tree	3:434
O that I could my Soul possess	3:158	O thou who hast our sorrows took	2:222
O that I might humbly sit[147]	2:124	O thou, whom winds and seas obey	3:231
O that I might never feel	3:204	O thou, whose kindly constant Care	1:241
O that I might the power receive	2:470	O thou, whose Pointing Hand	1:228
O that I now my heart could raise[148]	2:144	O thou, whose wise mysterious love	3:276
O that more might see us live	2:253	O were I like him sincere	2:217
O that our dear Redeemer's fame	2:100	O were it in my heart made known	2:110
O that our lives henceforth may raise	1:89	O were my soul shut up in thee	2:28
O that redeemed from worldly cares	3:291	O what a Conscience, what an heart is theirs	1:199
O that the God of pardning grace	1:119	O what a fall was there! The giddy youth	1:177
O that the miracle of grace	3:220	O what a Flame within thy Bosom burned	1:195
O that the tuneful Tribe like him	3:388	O what a hardned Wretch was I	3:158
O that there might at last appear	1:110	O what a Mighty Change	3:209
O that we all who now believe	2:345	O what a mighty change was wrought[149]	3:336
O that we could obtain by prayer	2:237	O what a mighty Loss is mine	1:320
O that we could the malice shun	1:119	O what a scene before us lies	1:104
O that we who have believed	2:393	O what a stubborn heart have I	3:203
O that with ancient harmony	2:306	O what an endless treasure lies	2:88
O that ye miracle of grace	1:319	O when shall we his equal find[150]	3:333
O the Blood, the pretious Blood	3:183	O where is now my hunger gone	3:294
O the Grace on Man bestowed	3:193	O who can paint the joy that blest	3:253
O the grievous agonies	3:407	O who, when God doth this, shall live?[151]	1:75
O the strength of Jesus' zeal	2:261	O would my God return at last	3:262
O the Tormenting Doubt	1:225	O wouldst thou by thy special grace	3:268
O thou meek, and injured Dove	3:121	O wouldst thou, Lord, thy blood apply	3:356
O thou that dost in darkness shine	3:278		
O thou, to whom all hearts are known, / my latest	3:365		
O thou to whom all hearts are known, / Who dost	3:66		

147. The stanza beginning with this line appears in *PW* 11:197.
148. The last four lines of the eight-line stanza beginning with this line appear as part of a longer poem in *PW* 11:218–19.
149. The stanza beginning with this line appears in *PW* 6:308–309.
150. The stanza beginning with this line appears in *PW* 6:301.
151. The stanza beginning with this line appears in *PW* 8:487.

O wouldst thou now thine arm display	3:245	On This depends our Weal or Woe	1:220
O wouldst thou try me, Lord, once more	1:264	On this mysterious Tree	3:184
		On us a sober mind bestow	2:191
O wouldst thou condescend	1:273	On us, O Christ, thy mission prove	2:100
O wouldst thou grant my Soul the Power	3:122	Once I knew the Master's mind	3:259
		Once in a new world of light	3:259
Obstinate prejudice remove	3:174	Once in Jesus' work employed	2:54
Occasions sure to meet	2:266	Once on a time, a gallant Ship	1:157
O'erwhelmed with conscious fear	2:169	One diseased, tormented soul	2:392
O'erwhelmed with gratitude & fear	3:47	One God in essence and in power	2:245
Of careless pastors ye complain	2:117	One in Jesus' work employed	2:54
Of civil priviledges here	2:411	One in will, and heart, and mind	3:282
Of heavenly origin divine	2:336	One only thing do I desire	3:369
Of his ignorance convince	3:94	One only way for both remains	2:367
Of ill-got wealth and power possesst	1:129	One only Wish detains me still	3:355
Of long-continued prayer	1:144	One thing is lacking still	2:171
Of pardon possest, my God I adore	1:29	One who hangs on yonder tree	2:67
Of these if some their charge betray	3:61	One who Mary's lot injoys	2:124
Of this we rest secure	1:237	One woman of grace	2:333
Of wars & rumoured wars we hear	3:76	One would fain his follower be	2:116
Of your redundant store	2:298	Only me in special love	1:76
Offensive to thy glorious eyes	1:64	Only one faint glimmering ray	3:370
Offered by an heart sincere	2:335	Only preserve us, Lord, from pride	3:36
Oft, alas, the penal night	2:239	Only thou the work hast done	3:216
Oft as the God of grace	2:315	Only thou thy blessing guard	3:294
Oft hast thou seen my soul aspire	3:239	Open, Lord, my willing Ear	3:132
Oft have I groaned my Lot to bear	3:354	Open my faith's interior eye	3:276
Oft have I heard, O Lord, and read	2:232	Open my mouth, and utterance give	3:179
Oft have I sunk o'erwhelmed, opprest	3:354	Open their eyes the signs to see	3:69
Oft repulsed by sinful men	2:35	Opened indeed, but what to see?	1:164
Oft the dreadful king was seen	3:365	Or by the stroke of death removed	1:322
Oft when the Cause appeared as lost	1:103	Or if my Light itself withdraw	2:18
Oh what availed it that, from sins got free	3:398	Or if, our humble faith to try	3:287
		Or if thou hast the sentence sealed	3:231
Omnipotent Lord, We sing of thy Power	3:138	Or, if thou wilt not yet reveal	2:440
		Or if thro' self-presuming pride	3:206
Omnipotently great	2:273	Or if thy soul must vengeance take	1:77
On Earth I shall not always live	1:260	Or if thy unwearied Love	3:205
On God I attend	3:266	Or if thy wise and righteous will	3:250
On him I fix my faithful eye	3:238	Or, if so my Lord ordain	3:300
On his throne of radiant azure	3:436	Or let his warlike Brother own	1:102
On me those eyes of mercy turn	2:198	Or let Monsieur sincerely say	1:103
On myself if I rely	3:192	Or let our poor degraded Brother say	1:180
On thee, Omnipotent to save	3:335	Or rather (if thy GOD allow)	3:357

Or shorten my extreme distress	3:127	Our nation's and Religion's foes	1:78
Ordained to long laborious pain	2:307	Our only care thy grace to gain	3:76
Order and government they scorn	1:156	Our only wisdom is, to trace	2:24
Order thou my whole Condition	1:248	Our Particular Church contained	3:305
Ordered by thee, O Lord, I go[152]	2:21	Our Patriots here, a restless Party	1:103
Other followers of the Lamb	3:411	Our Peacemaker, & Peace	2:322
Other wisdom I disclaim	2:188	Our prayers presenting with thine own	3:307
Our Advocate prays	3:120	Our Priest we declare	2:388
Our all-redeeming Lord	2:368	Our record is the same	2:296
Our all-sufficient Bliss thou art	1:234	Our Rulers have to Rebels sued	1:109
Our ancestors, without remorse	1:167	Our sacrilegious wickedness	2:417
Our bodies tottering o'er the grave	2:95	*Our* Scribes and Pharisees we see	2:38
Our brethren, countrymen, and friends	1:113	Our sins and woes to end	1:87
Our brethren have their flesh denied	1:115	Our sins were the Cause	3:181
Our carnal joys & pleasures here	2:270	Our souls in holiness restored	3:64
Our Champion for a length of years	3:92	Our spirits were dead And buried in sin	2:253
Our children whom we long have fed	1:70	Our soldiers abroad they forbid to oppose	1:147
Our Christian savages expect	2:431	Our souls and bodies to redeem	2:77
Our Connoisseurs their plausive voices raise	3:385	Our souls confirmed by solemn prayer	2:320
Our darkest ignorance of pride	2:28	Our sovereign Lord by right divine	1:62
Our fathers' piety	2:86	Our Spokesman with the Father	2:289
Our first Resolve we first declare	1:149	Our thirsty souls the wine require	2:219
Our freedom & rights we can never secure	1:166	Our utmost Saviour thou	2:190
Our furious foes who sought our harm	1:89	Our warmest thanks ye justly claim	1:161
Our God the true religion forms	2:313	Our way by reason's glimmering light	3:427
Our gracious & almighty Lord	3:78	Our wine with water mixt, our gold	3:307
Our gracious King and good	1:143	Our work performed, when She or I	1:274
Our gracious Lord gives back the day	2:96	Out of the deep in vain we cry	1:117
Our great Example and our head	2:178	Out of the deep of inbred woe	2:374
Our growing Happiness & Love	3:379	Outcast of God and Man no more	2:452
Our High-Priest in heaven he lives	3:193	Outcasts of men by all forsook, / For varied	1:116
Our inbred foes' unnatural rage	1:89	Outcasts of men by all forsook / To whom	1:123
Our King they threaten and revile	1:110		
Our latest Hope was fixt on him	1:136	Ourselves with Jesus' mind we arm	2:432
Our manners and our crimes so long	1:66	Outward Jews, who vainly still	2:359
Our ministry we prove	2:321		
Our Monarch fill with inward peace	3:215		
		Pains which might a father aid	3:243

152. See *PW* 10:219 but with variant readings.

Pardon for my offences past	3:365	Pomp & equipage & state	2:401
Pardon itself would profit nought	3:191	Poor guilty worm, or'ewhelmed with fear	3:249
Pardon less than power I want	3:257	Poor heathens confess	2:365
Partisans of a narrow sect	2:60	Poor men, acknowledge your Offence	3:190
Partner of all my Cares, on thee I call	1:171	Poor, piteous youth, while innocent of thought	1:177
Partner of thy nature then	3:368	Poor sinful souls, diseased, and blind	2:223
Passions, though nicely varnished o're	2:397	Possessors of the Saviour's mind	2:114
Patience in doing good we need	2:104	Possest of him I doubt no more	3:174
Patience we need the word to keep	2:104	Possest of their ambitious hope	1:73
Patient of Life, for thy dear sake	1:261	Pour on Both the Pleading Spirit	1:241
Patient till death I feel my pain	1:312	Poured out from above, thy Spirit in him	2:241
Peace be within her walls, and grace	3:66	Power supreme to thee is given	2:441
Peace, lasting Peace, inhabits there	1:224	Power to ask, in Jesus' Name	1:235
Peace, joy, & righteousness brought in	2:293	Praise and majesty and power	3:406
Peace must be by Entreaty gained	1:131	Praise be to the Father given	3:436
Peace, sorrowful heart, or apply	1:258	Praise to the Wonder-working God	3:117
Peace surpassing all expression	2:264	Prayers & alms to heaven ascend[154]	2:335
Peace thro' Britain's happy Isle	3:216	Preachers of Christ, his death we prove[155]	2:378
Peace to ask we now designed	3:215	Prepared by the refining flame	1:107
Peace, troubled heart, be calm, be still	1:258	Present if really thou art	3:185
Peace which the world can never give	1:79	Preserve, and still detain him here	1:130
Peace with the world, how short its stay	2:394	Preserve, that he may never know	1:310
Perfection if I boldly claim	2:472	Preserve them from th'infectious race	1:292
Perform the task thy laws ordain	3:224	Preserved in perfect peace	1:82
Permit him not to start aside	3:308	Prest, or'ewhelmed with sore temptation	3:124
Perplexed, ye know not what to do	2:294	Prevent the proud Philistine's Boast	3:152
Perverters of the sacred word	2:402	Prevented by thy love	2:227
Peter with himself compare	2:293	Pride in the church! (how can it be?)	2:31
Philip the Lord our Righteousness	2:317	Principled with faith unfeigned[156]	3:339
Physician, Friend of sinsick man	3:236	Priest, Prophet, and King	2:389
Pierced our hearts with pungent sorrow	1:63	Priests of the Lord, we stand between	2:307
Pierced with his want of purity	1:311	Prisoner at large, by Jesus' will	2:419
Pierced with the Sense of mercies past	1:223		
Pitch could I touch, and yet be clean	3:285		
Pity my Grief, and Fear, and Shame	3:123		
Pity to the Tempted show	3:241		
Planted by thine Almighty Hand[153]	2:447		
Pleased he is, who cannot need	2:116		
Pleased with importunity	2:127		
Point out the means if means there be	3:287		
Point out the works for him prepared	3:345		

153. The stanza beginning with this line appears in *PW* 8:447.

154. The stanza beginning with this line appears in *PW* 12:244.

155. The stanza beginning with this line appears in *PW* 12:327–8.

156. The stanza beginning with this line appears in *PW* 6:336.

Prisoner of Christ, to death pursued[157]	2:422	Raised from the people's lowest lees	3:307
Professors good in their own eyes	2:168	Raised up by an Almighty Hand	2:303
Professors still his name abuse[158]	2:147	Rankin replies, "If none is slain	1:96
Prone to ill, averse from good	3:194	Rankin withdraws—not unpursued	1:96
Prophet Divine, who knowst alone	3:433	Rather, O God, than I	2:460
Prophets to thee thy Lord hath raised[159]	2:452	Rather with humble fear	1:69
		Readers, accept at this thrice solemn Time	3:105
Prosper, for our Redeemer's sake	3:425	Ready for their full reward	2:44
Prosperous in ill, at nothing stop	1:88	Ready that I may be	2:140
Prostrate in the dust, and crying	2:428	Ready to render up the breath	3:369
Protection if allegiance draws	1:134	Reason, and truth, and justice fail	2:201
Proud of our numbers, and success	3:44	Reason he did not cast aside[161]	2:378
Proud profligate, to evil sold	1:156	Rebels, whose Independent Rise	1:100
Proud sinners, who in learning trust[160]	2:380	Rebels, your iron-sinewed neck	2:314
Publish it not in Askelon, to make	3:88	Rebuke their proud tyrannic boast	3:312
Punished for their Leaders' sin	1:67	Rebuking the malicious fiend	2:467
Pure in heart, in word, and deed	2:135	Recall not, Lord, our sins to mind	1:64
Pure, independent life divine	2:237	Receive me! and accept my pain	1:304
Pure, inward, genuin piety	2:294	Receive our every good from him	3:220
Pure the soul at first was made	2:154	Receive whom we commend	1:120
Purged from all Self-esteem, & Self-regard	1:189	Redeem them in their last distress	1:138
		Redeemed from earth, renewed in love	1:313
Put him in fear; this moment, Lord	3:247	Regard, regard my vehement cry	3:124
		Refrain our Souls, & keep them low	3:223
Quench not the last spark of hope	3:244	Rejoice, who bow to Jesus' Name	3:340
Quenched by ingratitude, the Heavenly fire	1:178	Rejoice, ye happy spirits above	3:329
		Rejoice, ye proud Philistines	3:130
Questioning a clam'rous crowd	2:407	Relieve whoe'er thy succour need	3:313
		Religion pure is chased away	1:65
		Repent, ye impious tribe, repent	2:320
		Repentance alone	2:353
		Repentance doth with fear begin[162]	2:162
		Repentance is a grace	2:86
		Repentance preached we never hear	2:85
		Repentance sincere	2:353
		Repentance true on each bestow	3:41
		Rescued by thy powerful prayer	2:144
		Rescued by thy Spirit's groans	3:94
		Resolved now a nobler Prize to gain	3:86

157. The stanza beginning with this line appears in *PW* 12:418.
158. The first four lines of the eight-line stanza beginning with this line are combined with the first four lines of the stanza beginning "Who would not for their Master own" in *PW* 11:220–1.
159. The stanza beginning with this line appears in *PW* 4:452.
160. The first four lines of the eight-line stanza beginning with this line appear in *PW* 12:344. They are combined with the last four lines of the eight-line stanza beginning "They mock his resurrection's power."
161. The stanza beginning with this line appears in *PW* 12:327.
162. The stanza beginning with this line appears in *PW* 11:251.

Resolved our nation to chastise	1:112	Saved from sin and condemnation	2:441
Resolved their calling to pursue	3:57	Saved from sin thro' faith we found	2:17
Rest is in labourers a crime	2:176	Saved from the death of sin & hell	2:222
Rest, thou favoured spirit, rest[163]	2:126	Saved from the Legal Curse I am[166]	2:278
Rest to my weary mind	2:27	Saviour and Friend, my soul prepare	3:291
Restless, malicious hate	2:419	Saviour and Prince, enthroned on high	3:307
Revive, O GOD of Power, revive[164]	2:449	Saviour & Prince, I lift	2:300
Riches, as fast as they increase	2:251	Saviour, at thy benign command	3:69
Riches by fraudful crimes acquired	2:158	Saviour, by the world unknown	2:54
Righteous Judge, thou wilt, we know	3:301	Saviour, Friend of sinful Man	3:133
Righteous, O God, thy judgments are, / Which lay	1:133	Saviour, from these defend thine own	2:158
		Saviour, how few there are	2:115
Righteous, O God, thy judgments are, / If now	3:136	Saviour, I in thy word confide	2:245
		Saviour, in whom by faith we live	2:345
Risen with Christ, in newness	3:111	Saviour of a rebellious Race	3:158
Rivers of Salvation flow	3:183	Saviour of All, whose Bowels move	3:159
Root out that curst self-seeking pride	3:54	Saviour of men, I ask no more	2:220
Rulers, high-priests, and scribes employ	2:181	Saviour of men, Physician good	2:202
Rulers themselves transgress the laws	2:360	Saviour of men, to thee we cry[167]	2:162
Run not after means of grace	3:409	Saviour, on me thy mind bestow	2:387
Run to and fro, whoe'er proclaim	1:80	Saviour, on the cross forsook	3:279
		Saviour, the human Fiends convince	1:157
		Saviour, the laws of selfish man	2:97
Safe in all events and blest	3:428	Saviour, thou readst what is in man	3:233
Safe in his Name's celestial Power	3:118	Saviour, thou with equal ease	2:21
Safe on that happy Shore	3:362	Saviour, thy preaching servants bless[168]	2:363
Safely then set up your rest	3:411	Saviour, till thine eye recalls	2:268
Saints in Jesus' Spirit one	2:404	Saviour, to thee our hearts we give	2:255
Saints in old Times there were (the world allow)	3:106	Saviour, we would thy counsel take	2:191
		Saviour, who liftest up my head	3:347
Salvation doth to God belong	3:200	Saviour, who omnipresent art	1:295
Salvation to God, / Who freely	3:118	Say, thou Almighty Jesus	3:165
Sam for his three first years the Secret kept	3:384	Say, ye prophets smooth and still	3:417
		'Scaped from a World of anxious Grief	1:325
Satan admits of no delay	2:261		
Satan all his arts essayed	3:408	Scarce had my soul fixed her director eye	3:397
Satan heard, and trembling fled	3:408		
Satan the title soft imparts	2:394		
Satan, the World, & Sin too long[165]	2:453		

163. The stanza beginning with this line appears in *PW* 11:198.
164. The stanza beginning with this line appears in *PW* 8:165.
165. The stanza beginning with this line appears in *PW* 4:314.
166. The stanza beginning with this line appears in *PW* 12:99–100.
167. The stanza beginning with this line appears in *PW* 11:251.
168. The stanza beginning with this line appears in *PW* 12:293.

Scarce had the morn of pining life began	3:395	Senseless of its lost Condition	3:146
Scripture doth Christ The WORD declare	3:175	Sent by our faithful Lord	2:432
		Sent down to make us meet	2:287
Searcher of hearts, the Wise, the Good	1:233	Sent forth they *were* to prophesy	3:37
		Sent from the heavenly Father down	2:225
Searcher of the deceitful heart	3:284	Sent from thy Father's bosom	2:179
Secure he now the sacred Pale o'erleaps	3:88	Sent of God to do his will	2:230
See a soul with pardon blessed[169]	2:229	Sentenced the first Adam was	2:195
See from his Throne by the Archangel driven	3:105	Servant of servants, hail! but O! ye words	1:210
See here an Apostolic priest[170]	2:298	Servants of Christ, arise	2:139
See him (and O, with biting sorrow see	1:177	Servants of Christ the witness vain	2:373
See, how the bold, rapacious Great	1:105	Servants of Sin, by Nature led	3:180
See, Lord, the Cause of our distress	3:296	Set forth before our eyes	3:186
See, Lord, thy meanest servant set	3:176	Shaking the weak house of clay	3:365
See, O thou Rock of Israel, see	3:199	Shall I resent my slighted love	3:361
See the brave men of British race	1:104	Shall man, a worm of earth, a child of dust	3:390
See the first fatal step to part[171]	2:305	Shall one in perfect love renewed	2:142
See the heavenly Shepherd's zeal	2:226	Shall the haters of the Lord	3:241
See the salutary stream[172]	2:196	Shall the war be abandoned, or still carried on?	1:146
See the strength that is in man	2:268	Shall we on such a day	1:69
See that all beneath your power	2:65	Shame on his Teachers! Wanton to subdue	1:181
See us to the Future blind	1:250	Shapen in guilt, conceived in sin	2:443
See we then the sinners poor	3:416	She dies on earth to die no more	3:433
See ye blushing sons of pride	2:79	Shed it on our hearts abroad	3:282
Seeing the great Invisible	3:328	She languishes, in life detained	3:328
Seeming contrarieties[173]	2:255	Shepherd of Souls, for whom alone	3:309
Self-love cannot conceive	2:85	Shepherd of Souls, *the Great, the Good*[174]	2:446
Self-love would imitate thy zeal	2:88	Shepherds indigent and plain	2:80
Send down thy Spirit on us to rest	3:435	Shew them his blood and righteousness	3:189
Send me not hence unless thy Love	1:242	Shining in his strength & height	2:427
Send the Angels now to chear	3:301	Shoued Fashion singling out (if that could be)	3:386
Sends his intrepid Suffragan before	3:91	Should vile, unworthy sinners dare	2:61
		Should we not hold our peace	2:347
		Should we not young beginners spare	2:368

169. The stanza beginning with this line appears in *PW* 11:359.
170. The stanza beginning with this line appears in *PW* 12:181.
171. The stanza beginning with this line appears in *PW* 12:196.
172. The stanza beginning with this line appears in *PW* 11:292.
173. The stanza beginning with this line appears in *PW* 11:494.
174. The stanza beginning with this line appears in *PW* 8:446.

Shout to the mighty Jesus' Name	3:117	Sire, With indulgent smiles receive	1:147
Show him the Enemy's Design	3:309	Small their Acquaintance with their Betters	3:82
Shut up by unbelief, within	2:223	Smile on us still from heaven	3:169
Silenced, but not convinced, the foes[175]	2:309	Smiting this polluted breast	3:164
Simple love no evil thought	3:409	Snatched so often from the grave	3:280
Simple we remained and poor	3:44	So be it, Lord! by thee decreed	1:322
Sin for vengeance cries aloud	2:273	So be it then: if God's Decree	1:139
Sin shall not in my Flesh remain	3:201	So be it then! the harmless Man of peace	1:207
Since first my earthly course begun	3:368	So easily are Bishops made	3:89
Since first we Believed	3:118	So foolish, ignorant, and blind	3:139
Since first the Master bad us quickly go	1:171	So good Doctor, if now	1:279
Since he had the Saviour known	2:412	So in a Sister-Church, that cannot err	1:192
Since thou hast left thyself a seed	3:307	So in Death's Capitol th'Athenian Sage	1:198
Sinking now into the deep	2:57	So in his Shrine the Indian Pagod sits	1:204
Sinks my weary, feeble mind	3:259	So in our days a Gang we see	1:157
Sinner, who dost not bear[176]	2:86	So may the Lord thy Usefulness restore	1:195
Sinner's Advocate, again	3:256	So mingled is her Soul with mine	1:257
Sinners by the commandment killed	2:342	So shall he magnify thy Name	3:346
Sinners, come by faith, and add	2:229	So shall I sing thy praise	1:291
Sinners, lift up your hearts	2:287	So shall our lives declare	3:219
Sinners of old, for ease, or food	2:32	So shall the Church surround Thy throne	3:134
Sinners self-condemned he chears	2:170	So shall they in thy presence live	1:288
Sinners shall be surprized again	2:166	So shall we cheerfully forego	1:234
Sinners she with pity saw	3:338	So shall we in the judgment stand	2:192
Sinners, the day is near	2:339	So shall we meet in Jesus' Name	1:234
Sinners, the Promise is for you	2:285	So shall ye Captives freed with Songs return	1:202
Sinner, the warning take	2:400	So teach us, Lord, to count our Days	1:274
Sinners, this instant day & hour	2:380	So the gay Nation whose capricious law	3:385
Sinners, to the shades may run	2:134	So the grand Monarch lays his State aside	1:205
Sinners, to you the source we show	2:137	So they promise and vow who triumphantly sing	1:146
Sinners, your idols vain forego	2:362	So will we praise and magnify	3:308
Sion, for thee thy GOD shall care[177]	2:452	So when Erostratus, with fruitless aim	3:87
Sion, kind Mother of degenerate Sons	1:186	So when *Old Noll* our Church & State o'erthrow	1:206
Sion, thy Suffering GOD behold[178]	2:453	So when thy waves and storms are all passed o'er	3:403
		So will we exalt thy praises	1:64

175. The stanza beginning with this line appears in *PW* 12:199–200.
176. The stanza beginning with this line appears in *PW* 11:126.
177. The stanza beginning with this line appears in *PW* 4:313.
178. The stanza beginning with this line appears in *PW* 4:315.

So will we not from thee go back[179]	2:449	Still deceived with eager Strife	1:250
Soft! attend that awful Sound	3:371	Still doth thy lingring Indolence require	1:188
Sole Arbiter and Judge of kings	1:106		
Something unmarked by human eye	3:426	Still farther have I roved from thee	1:263
Son of God, to thee I look	3:172	Still for my Son thou hearst me pray	1:310
Son of man, thou didst not come	2:115	Still, gracious Lord, our portion be	3:283
Son of the living God from heaven	2:30	Still he bids me look to him	3:415
Sons of God, your Father praise	3:168	Still his ready soul detain	3:302
Soon as I take my gloomy flight	3:320	Still in the flesh for this I stay	3:366
Soon as on Earth I disappear	3:152	Still I knock & ask & seek[182]	2:127
Soon as the slaughtered Lamb appears	3:290	Still in every trial new[183]	2:29
Soon as thy cross appears	2:301	Still in the sacred page they stand	1:319
Soon as thy lovely Face appears	1:234	Still let our enemies prevail	1:117
Soon as to thee for help they look	3:231	Still let the little leaven spread	3:67
Soon as we saw our native shore	1:128	Still let the little ones	3:58
Sore beset on every Side	3:131	Still let thy secret power	1:302
Sound words the world can never bear	2:331	Still let us earthly matters leave	2:307
Sovereign Lord, for this we wait[180]	2:189	Still let us labour to fulfil	3:293
Sovereign Lord of earth and heaven	3:125	Still let us taste the grace of God	3:220
Spare the poor Advocates of Sin	3:162	Still may he hold the earnest fast	3:342
Speak, and at the powerful word	3:275	Still may I in thy presence stay	1:247
Speak, Sav[iou]r, speak the welcome word	3:124	Still my soul was in thy hand	3:405
		Still our adversary's nigh[184]	2:194
Spectators of the grand Event	1:111	Still our dear redeeming Lord	2:97
Spirit and life, thy words, convey	3:72	Still the invisible	2:182
Spirit I do not want, or will	1:282	Still the promise is fulfilled[185]	2:392
Spirit of faith in Jesus' blood	2:366	Still the world misrepresent	2:379
Spirit of faith, to things divine	3:189	Still when they hear his pardoning word	2:429
Spirit of love, thyself impart	3:371		
Spirit of power and life, inspire	3:255	Still will I wrestle on with thee	3:298
Spirit of truth, thy mind he knows	3:296	Still with us of England's Pale	3:305
Spirits perturbed, ye now may rest	1:93	Still would I keep The Lamb in view[186]	1:315
Stablished in his state above	2:310	Stir up thy faithful people, Lord	3:86
Staff of his declining age	3:242	S[tonehouse], my Answered Prayer My life restored	1:200
Standing to thy wise Decision	3:211		
Still at a loss, ye know not how[181]	2:294		
Still at the stated hours of prayer	2:336		
Still by the holy matrons led	2:70		

179. The stanza beginning with this line appears in *PW* 8:165.
180. The stanza beginning with this line appears in *PW* 11:278.
181. The stanza beginning with this line appears in *PW* 12:175.
182. The stanza beginning with this line appears in *PW* 11:203.
183. The stanza beginning with this line appears in *PW* 10:285–6.
184. The stanza beginning with this line appears in *PW* 11:287.
185. The stanza beginning with this line appears in *PW* 12:360.
186. See *PW* 8:427.

Stop, foolish Tears! The God of Love	1:239	Suffers us our Sin to cover	3:146
Stop th' exterminating sentence	1:63	Suffice that at my latest Hour	1:260
Stop the innocent Thief	1:285	Suffice the Time in Pleasures past	1:266
Stop thou their mouths, confound their pride	3:234	Summoned to put off my clay	1:75
Straining the old Felon's chain	3:301	Sun of righteousness, arise	3:276
Strange indeed he is to you	2:379	Superior though he stands alone	2:304
Strange lovers of their Country these	1:122	Supported by the power of grace	3:332
Stranger now to thee, and peace	3:264	Support him with thy guardian Hand[187]	2:449
Stranger to himself and thee	1:294	Supporter of rebellion's cause	1:88
Stranger to the way of peace	3:405	Supreme, Almighty Lord	3:217
Stranger to Vice, with early grace imbued	3:325	Supremely wise, supremely kind	2:371
		Supported by the power of grace	3:332
Stranger unknown, thou art my God	2:122	Sure from his dear returning Lord	2:123
Strength alas! in me is none	3:182	Sure he went and came again	3:412
Strength from the Lord, & righteousness	3:235	Surely a meager Tongue sufficient was	1:179
		Surely at first our hearts were right	3:43
Stretch out thy mighty arm	1:84	Surely faith's minutest gain	2:162
Stretched out on the tree	3:181	Surely I would in thee believe	2:374
Strong I seemed, and rich in grace	3:259	Surely, if God permit our foes	2:317
Stronger at length the heavenly instinct grew	3:397	Surely, Lord, the fear is vain	1:219
		Surely, O Lord, we once were thine	2:447
Struck, but with no remorse within	2:106	Surely the Faithful seed at last[188]	2:452
Strugling long with wind & tide	2:430	Surely the Sons of grace	3:350
Stupendous height of love divine!	3:263	Surely the worldly god	2:346
Stupendous mystery	3:106	Surely their redeeming God	2:376
Subject to the laws of man	2:421	Surely thou hast in Babylon	1:303
Submissive to the Stroke again	3:145	Surely thou wilt from heaven descend	2:305
Such a desperate Self-deceiver	3:147		
Such is the crooked Statesman's hire	1:157	Surrounded by the conquering Foe	1:59
Such is your Church, above the rest	3:98	Surrounded with a world of ill	1:289
Such power belongs to God alone	1:110	Sustained by thy sufficient grace	3:228
Such Strength of Sanctified Desire	1:230	Swanwick the Loyalist am I	1:154
Such the Divinity, & such ye *Words*	1:191	Sweet Day, so cool, so calm, so bright	1:270
Such the Folly of Mankind	1:250	Swift on the wings of love & prayer	3:199
Such the Inducements, such the prosperous Arts	1:182	Swol'n with the insolence of power	1:114
		Sworn Enemy to All his Art	3:161
Such wisdom, watchfulness and love	2:368	Take the filth of sin away	3:369
Such ye were too long to me	3:414	Take their cause into thy hand	1:68
Sudden o'ercome and plunged in vast delight	3:397	Take this concupiscence away	2:457

187. The stanza beginning with this line appears in *PW* 8:165.

188. The stanza beginning with this line appears in *PW* 4:314.

Sudden, unexpected death 2:141
Suddenly the Light sprung up 2:19
Suffered a few more hours to live 3:317

Take us both into thy hand	3:282	The bitterness of death is past	2:122
Talkers of a grace unknown	2:90	The blackest crimes I should have done	2:193
Taught by thy example, Lord	2:311	The blessed day of my release	1:312
Taught of God himself to please[189]	3:338	The blessing more than once bestowed	1:322
Teacher, Guide of helpless Sinners	3:211	The blood of goats & bullocks slain	2:357
Teachers and priests corrupt assail	2:199	The Boar out of the *German* Wood[192]	2:448
Teaching his house to serve the Lord	2:343	The Body breath[e]s, & lifts his Head[193]	3:112
Tear from them, Lord, their figleaves tear	3:234	THE Brethren They! *the* Children & *the* Bride!	1:192
Tell it to none, is Christ's advice	2:59	The captive, Lord, myself I yeild	2:282
Tell us of Punic faith no more	1:134	The cause of kings and thine is one	1:106
T' exalt myself I would not speak	3:49	The chaff shall fly, thou sayst it shall	3:56
Thankful I accept the grace	2:195	The Chief his bold design approves	1:96
Thankful the token I receive	3:172	The *Christian* world is wiser grown	2:319
That almighty word of thine	2:249	The church they call their proper care[194]	2:186
That Altar in the skies	2:39	The church which keeps its Lord's commands	2:250
That angel kind, in time of need	1:97	The church's servant should be wise[195]	2:343
That apostolic ship[190]	2:91	The Church that did from Christ proceed	3:172
That blessing to secure	2:140	The church they labour to divide	2:403
That city of the living God	2:120	The City so famed for their exquisite Taste	1:146
That happy loss I long to know	2:167	The cleansing blood t'apply	2:287
That he never can rest	1:279	The cock had crowed and Peter hears	2:197
That lost unloving Wretch I am	2:465	The Comforter assures our hearts[196]	2:460
That tree thou never ca[n]st forget	3:319	The counsel of the Lord shall stand, / And out of evil bring	1:101
That truth I in the means may find	3:174	The counsel of the Lord shall stand, / For all bow down	3:424
That we may thy mercy feel	1:75		
That which most my Soul requires	1:249		
Th' advantages of riches see	2:61		
Th' ambassador of the Most High	2:224		
Th' Americans, we all allow	1:41		
Th' Anointed of the Lord	1:144		
The angel-quires their voices raise	2:80		
The Anointed of God	2:388		
The Antichristian power	1:120		
The Apostolic word	2:361		
The arms we lost by rebel power	1:127		
The Articles curtailed must be	3:97		
The basis of his church below	2:184		
The battered ship, by tempests tost[191]	2:431		

189. The stanza beginning with this line appears in *PW* 6:335.
190. The stanza beginning with this line appears in *PW* 11:141.
191. The stanza beginning with this line appears in *PW* 12:444.
192. The stanza beginning with this line appears in *PW* 8:164.
193. The stanza beginning with this line appears in *PW* 4:130.
194. The first six lines of the twelve-line stanza beginning with this line appear in *PW* 11:274 as a six-line stanza.
195. The stanza beginning with this line appears in *PW* 12:255.
196. The stanza beginning with this line appears in *PW* 13:25.

The covenant old in types concealed	2:309	The fisher chuses to remain	2:334
The Crescent to the Cross shall yield[197]	1:74	The first superlative reward	2:33
		The flight of those by Jesus sent[199]	2:360
The criminal prefered to thee	2:269	The flock they would in pieces tear	3:38
The croud they into madness drive	1:77	The flouds, O God, lift up their voice	3:214
The crown with holy violence seize	1:271	The foe hath thrust me at full sore	3:50
The cruel Loss, the grievous Wrong	1:259	The Foe in an unguarded hour	3:308
The cruel murderers of our God[198]	2:270	The foe is as a floud come in	3:290
The darkness doth to light succeed	2:112	The foes to us and peace	3:135
The days of abstinence were come	2:350	The fools' companion is not wise	2:267
The dead in trespasses convince	3:227	The foretast[e]s of alluring love	3:234
The dear portion of my Lord	2:188	The foulest falsehoods they invent	1:77
The dearest partners of our heart	1:90	The friends whom most we wish to save	2:372
The dearest Sharer of my heart	1:320		
The deed we commend	2:290	The Fulness of thy Blessings grant	1:260
The depths of hell they have not known	3:56	The generous men who, on our side	1:94
		The genuine Apostolic word	2:118
The dire contagion is begun	2:467	The gift thou hast on us bestowed	3:425
The doctrine is old, and obsolete too	1:165	The gift who receives, And hastens to tell	2:29
The drop thou didst to me bequeath	2:64		
The eager for esteem and gold	2:158	The Giver of my faithful guide	2:267
The Eternal God my Refuge is	3:200	The glaring Gospel I declare	3:355
Th' elect on wings of eagles borne	2:168	The glory which all thought transcends	2:111
The enemy of God and man	3:214		
The evangelic minister	2:176	The God of Abraham we adore	2:311
The evangelic Spirit give	2:103	The God of awful power displays	2:440
The Devilish, & the sensual Crowd	3:198	The God of faithfulness and love	2:77
The fact historical is plain	3:173	The God of love our souls prepares	2:338
The fasting days are these	2:23	The God of love with cordial praise	2:311
The fatal cause I see not yet	3:254	The God of nature, and her sovereign king	3:394
The Father by his clamours prest	2:154		
The Father doth intrust	2:339	The God of truth and grace	2:355
The Fever, which rebuked by thee	3:346	The God of universal grace	2:334
The fiend hath laid mine hon[ou]r low	3:123	The God unknown his Servant knew	3:334
		The godly jealousy inspire	3:43
The Fiend who counterfeits thy Seal	3:161	The good thou dost for Jesus' sake	2:20
The fiercest Cats before his power	1:280	The goodness placed by parents good	3:437
The fire shall at thy word	1:120	The gospel is his saving power	2:93
The first Apostle of the Lamb	2:215	The grace I have found, O Jesus, with thee	2:29
The first effect of grace Divine	2:233		

197. The stanza beginning with this line appears in *PW* 8:487.
198. The stanza beginning with this line appears in *PW* 12:78.
199. The stanza beginning with this line appears in *PW* 12:290.

The grace to insure, The treasure concealed	2:29	Th' Imaginary Power	1:236
The gracious power that conquered mine	1:300	Th' immediate Authors of our woes	1:83
		The inextinguishable fire	2:443
The great in power and wickedness	1:115	Th' inordinate excessive love	2:255
The great in their defence arose	1:124	The Infinite of Grace Divine	3:151
The great Restorer of Religion pure	3:88	The Jews beheld the Lord most high[203]	2:147
The great thro' all restraints have broke	1:65	The Jews we convince	2:388
		The Joy that swells a Bridegroom's Breast[204]	2:452
The greatest Blessing heaven bestows	1:262	The Joy within, the Passionate Surprize	1:196
The Grief & Fear shall hasten on	1:259	The joyful news of pardoned sin	2:390
The ground of every heart is known	2:299	The kind Release, the Fatal Blow	1:259
The happy Souls who Jesus know	3:354	The King of saints, with glory crowned	2:87
The harmless, inoffensive man[200]	2:45	The kingdom promised and foreshowed	2:159
The hateful light they shun	2:134		
The haven of the good old Cause	1:74	The kingdom rises from a grain	2:28
The hearts of All are in thy Hand, / Submissive	1:230	The kingdom took from Them, by God	3:55
		The Lamb before his Father's eyes	2:307
The hearts of all are in thy hand, / Defender	3:134	The law commands, Do this and live	2:121
The hearts of all this nation turn	1:136	The law points out the victim slain[205]	2:216
The heathen judge will not condemn	2:420	The laying on of hands implies	2:320
The hellish tyrant of mankind	2:395	The least of Jesus' little ones	2:466
The high and lofty God shall stoop	3:36	The legal way they wisely shun	2:398
The Hills were covered with her Shade[201]	2:447	The Levite stern approaches nigh	2:121
		The light reflected from his face	2:427
The hire more than the sheep he loves	2:245	The little flock of feeble sheep	3:310
		The living water of thy grace	2:226
The holy Jesus rests in Hope[202]	2:204	The Lord by his Right-hand hath sworn[206]	2:453
The Horror of Offending him	1:259		
The House of Woe I soon shall quit	1:240	The Lord hath Glorified his Grace[207]	2:454
The human herd, unbroken and untaught	3:393	The Lord himself thy Husband is[208]	2:452
		The Lord is King! ye saints be glad	3:197
The humble man by Jesus sent	2:216		
The humble Petition	1:279		
The humble prayers which pierce the skies	1:79		
The humble starts at danger near	2:76		

200. The stanza beginning with this line appears in *PW* 10:390.
201. The stanza beginning with this line appears in *PW* 8:447.
202. The stanza beginning with this line appears in *PW* 12:99.
203. The stanza beginning with this line appears in *PW* 11:220–21.
204. The stanza beginning with this line appears in *PW* 4:313.
205. The stanza beginning with this line appears in *PW* 11:328.
206. The stanza beginning with this line appears in *PW* 4:314.
207. The stanza beginning with this line appears in *PW* 4:315.
208. The stanza beginning with this line appears in *PW* 4:313.

The Lord of hosts is on our side	1:130	The men with their Commanders join	1:126
The Lord of Life is ris'n indeed[209]	3:112	The members must their head pursue	2:254
The Lord our fathers chose	2:352	The men who dared their loyal love	1:137
The Lord shall soon his angels send	2:63	The men who 'gainst their Sovereign stood	1:108
The Lord, the sovereign Lord	2:400		
The Lord, the wise, almighty Lord	3:238	The men who God profess to know	2:422
The Lord to us who now believe[210]	2:461	The men who nothing understand	1:131
The Lord, who gave, & takes away	1:267	The men who seek their portion here[216]	2:156
The Lot, the Fatal Lot	1:236	The messenger of peace	2:406
The love of ease and earthly things	3:38	The methodists must all allow	3:82
The love which worldly men pretend[211]	2:395	The modern Pharisee is bold	2:169
The major part, the stronger side[212]	1:148	The moment I to sin incline	2:451
The man by passion swayed	2:405	The more his faith by works he shows	2:177
The Man of griefs, by all despised[213]	2:271	The more his outward man decays	3:237
The Man of sorrow now[214]	2:47	The mountains at his presence flowed	1:270
The man that had no evil done	2:429	The mouth which our Almighty Lord	2:391
The man that on himself relies	2:267	The multitude of worldly cares	2:94
The man who God devoutly feared	2:337	The national calamity	1:61
The man who meek and upright seems	3:435	The Object of my tenderest Cares	1:259
The man whom covetous desire[215]	2:244	The office we from thee receive	2:148
The man whose sacrilegious pains	1:167	The ointment's on the members spilled	2:251
The marks of thy expiring love	2:211	The only work on earth I have	3:348
The martyrs' blood, the church's seed	2:359	"The *old* Apostles" (trembling I pursue	1:192
The masters of our Israel may	2:221	The old thief and murderer	2:244
The meanest gifts, my substance here	2:157	The omnipotent God	2:388
The meekness next demands th' applauding Song	1:206	The only Love sufficient is	1:221
		The only task was yet behind	1:126
The men who as Gamaliel wise	3:61	The pastor good & humbly wise	2:20
The men who did not count the cost	3:67	The Patriarchal God	2:291
The men who have their savour lost	3:39	The patriot-clans, by treason unawed	1:165
		The patriots all were long at work	1:167
		The peace mysterious he bestows	2:338
		The peace thou didst to man bequeath	2:279
		The people should look out & find	2:306
		The people swimming with the tide	1:128
		The perfect liberty	2:190
		The perilous, vindictive times	3:74
		The pious Mantel o'er his Dotage spread	3:88
		The poor, as Jesus' bosom-friends	2:404
		The poor I to the rich prefer	2:90
		The poor misguided croud	1:85

209. The stanza beginning with this line appears in *PW* 4:130.
210. The stanza beginning with this line appears in *PW* 13:25.
211. The stanza beginning with this line appears in *PW* 12:362.
212. There is a question as to whether this line begins a new poem or is a continuation of the previous lines.
213. The stanza beginning with this line appears in *PW* 12:79.
214. The stanza beginning with this line appears in *PW* 10:403.
215. The stanza beginning with this line appears in *PW* 11:459.
216. The stanza beginning with this line appears in *PW* 11:240.

The power he had from God received	2:347	The Saviour knows and eyes his own	2:167
The power of Christ is seen	2:178	The Scribes a sinner load	2:133
The power of praying faith and love	3:35	The self-exalting worms abase	3:77
The power the sinful bent controuls	1:287	The Sense of thy Smart	3:181
The praise of Christ offends the ear	2:180	The sentence past on all	2:87
The preacher of thy gospel-word	2:51	The sentiments of those that know	2:434
The preachers should forbear to speak	2:60	The sepulchre ye white	2:40
The present life our passage is	2:105	The servant of a Master poor	2:403
The principle of grace divine	2:55	The Shepherd good indeed thou art[222]	2:244
The prize for which our Fathers fought	1:135	The sinner left by Truth Divine	2:148
The process of that dreadful day[217]	2:462	The sinner sad, who void of thee	3:133
The promise of preserving grace	2:415	The sinner that hath, O Jesus, from thee	2:241
The promise to our fathers made	2:425	The sinners' Sacrifice	2:75
The prophets, saints, and patriarchs old	2:121	The slaves of lust & avarice	2:259
The prophets spake of Jesus' grace[218]	2:231	The slothful worldly throng[223]	2:182
The proselyte ye make	2:38	The smallest spart of self-respect	2:464
The proud & envious cannot bear	2:316	The Smoak that issues from the Pit	3:162
The purport of thy strange command	2:27	The soldiers struck their God unknown	2:198
The reasoning selfishness of man	2:19	The sole immortal Potentate	2:349
The Reign of Sin and Death is o'er[219]	2:278	The solemn hour is come	2:75
The reign of sin and Satan cease	2:129	The Son our mortal flesh assumes	2:77
The Rescuer of bold Burgoine	1:97	The sons of consolation these	2:299
The rest must all give place[220]	2:332	The soul exception from thy grace	3:368
The rich who delicately live	2:334	The soul possest by base desires	2:105
The righteous man awhile concealed	2:205	The sovereign God would stoop so low	2:200
The rock of error and offence	2:467	The Spark which first from Britain came	1:124
The sacred charge they undertook	2:347	The Spirit doth the power infuse	3:176
The sacrifice of Christian love	2:347	The Spirit doth the truth reveal	3:176
The same Almighty Hand	2:346	The spiritual blind Their Saviour behold	2:30
The same in every place	2:339	The Springs of Human Deeds to thee	1:241
The same necessity	2:165	The steps of man's conversion see	2:155
The savage Tribes, an unjust Race[221]	1:74	The streams of holiness	2:227
		The stumbling block of self & pride	3:310
		The subject has his Rights, we own	1:166

217. The stanza beginning with this line appears in *PW* 13:27.
218. The stanza beginning with this line appears in *PW* 11:361.
219. The stanza beginning with this line appears in *PW* 12:99–100.
220. The poem beginning with this line has sixteen lines. Lines nine through sixteen appear in *PW* 12:242, as the opening stanza of a five-stanza poem, which begins "The poor afflicted saints."
221. The stanza beginning with this line appears in *PW* 8:487.
222. The first four lines of the eight-line poem beginning with this line appear in *PW* 11:459.
223. The stanza beginning with this line appears in *PW* 11:270.

The succour we desire	3:271	The universal fault[228]	2:397
The sufferer without faith or hope	2:203	The valiant in his valour trusts	2:330
The suffering I this moment prove	2:246	The value I receive	2:184
The sun and moon eclipsed shall be	2:288	The veil is rent, the Way is shewn[229]	2:278
The Sun of Righteousness	1:226	The venerable priest may see	2:121
The sweetness of thy pardning love	3:273	The vessels of thy mercy fill	2:219
The Sword is drawn, the Breach is made!	3:55	The vilest minister	2:55
The talents to my offspring lent	3:423	The Vineyard which thine own right Hand[230]	2:448
The tanner to a merchant wise	2:336	The virtue of thy hallowing blood	3:344
The Temple of the Lord are We	3:198	The virtues of thy balmy name[231]	3:286
The temple ye despise	2:39	The visits of unusual grace	2:210
The thieves have robed, and stript, and bound	2:120	The wanderer from his Father's face	2:155
		The water & the Spirit join	2:220
The thieves have torn away my dress	2:120	The water pure must go before	2:63
The thing I ask thou wilt bestow	3:222	The weak, the simple, and the poor	3:57
The thing thou dost I know not now	1:312	The weak with prudent fear should shun	2:267
The thing whose consequence unknown	3:424	The Wesleys must be somewhat bigger	3:386
The things thy free unbounded love[224]	2:461	The wicked still our Lord oppress	2:66
The things we most affect and prize[225]	2:252	The wickedest of men prophane	1:72
The Third Auspicious Morn is come[226]	3:112	The Widowed Church shall married be[232]	2:452
The threatning will be soon fulfiled	2:166		
The thrice-repeated vision seals	2:342	The widows desolate, distrest	3:314
The times & seasons when to give	2:262	The wisdom of our Lord would chuse	2:24
The times of ignorance are still	2:380	The wise will not with rage oppose	2:303
The times of Jesus' grace	2:164	The Witness of thy truth I need	3:173
The tokens of paternal love	3:263	The wonders they claim	2:340
The triumph he himself decreed	1:125	The word, and care, and labouring zeal	2:176
The troubled sea can never rest	2:348		
The true, eternal Word	3:107	The word Divine we rightly hear	2:160
The truth let honest Oswald tell	1:101	The word in which I would believe	3:207
The truth which all his martyrs made	2:199	The word of God, by all confest	3:175
The truth who from their heart obey	2:224		
The types and figures are fulfilled[227]	2:278		
The tyrannous Winds Are subj[ec]t to thee	3:138		

224. The stanza beginning with this line appears in *PW* 13:25.
225. The first four lines appear in *PW* 11:484.
226. The stanza beginning with this line appears in *PW* 4:130.
227. The stanza beginning with this line appears in *PW* 12:99–100.
228. The stanza beginning with this line appears in *PW* 12:364.
229. The stanza beginning with this line appears in *PW* 12:99–100: "The veil is rent in Christ alone."
230. The stanza beginning with this line appears in *PW* 8:164.
231. The stanza beginning with this line appears in *PW* 8:421.
232. The stanza beginning with this line appears in *PW* 4:313.

The word of reconciling grace	2:338	Thee, Jesus, thee whoe'er confess	3:75
The word of righteousness	2:409	Thee, Lord, I would in all things see	2:132
The Word of thy Grace	3:119	Thee, Lord, in all my Ways I own	1:217
The word of truth & grace & power	2:433	Thee, Lord, my prostrate soul adores	3:143
The word proceeding from that Rock	3:207	Thee present in thy Courts we find	3:63
The word, the seed of righteousness[233]	2:104	Thee, Saviour that I may	2:227
The word they may with joy receive	2:103	Thee that we may no more deny	2:275
The word which cries to all, Repent	2:380	Thee the foe cannot surprize	3:192
The word whose energy we feel	2:370	Thee, we never could have chose[236]	2:264
The words thou dost from God declare[234]	2:225	Their Apostolic claim we own	3:61
The work, alas, too often I	3:46	Their chief and most religious joy	1:116
The work miraculous begin	1:288	Their Coat I shall preserve from harm	1:281
The work of grace is then begun	2:351	Their countrymen, and sworn allies	1:90
The work, the time, the manner show	3:426	Their doctrine sinsick spirits healed	3:38
The workman's worthy of his food	2:244	Their even Course let Nothing stop	2:454
The world he must not seek to please	2:51	Their fainting souls with hope he feeds	2:430
The world immerst in Satan lay	2:129	Their foes as countenanced by thee	1:121
The world may well complain	2:395	Their goods were free for all	2:295
The world that bear the Christian name	2:174	Their impious scheme in Britain planned	1:118
The world thine oracles despise	2:165	Their monarch to requite	1:144
The world we now, like Noah's, see	2:165	Their outward call to minister	3:68
The World's Infernal King exclaims	3:130	Their prayers for Us thou oft hast heard	3:54
The worst, the foulest slaves of sin	2:367	Their prey impatient to devour	1:118
The wrath of frantic man[235]	2:470	Their Rabbi cannot be by Us adored	1:193
The wretch profane who without dread	2:259	Their rage and malice we defied	1:90
The wretched hereticks profane	2:309	Their tame submission to prevent	1:115
Thee Almighty to deliver	2:441	Them by thy Spirit now convince	3:80
Thee descended from the sky	2:228	Them to the mercy he commends	1:100
Thee, Father, we praise	3:119	Themselves they never yet have known	2:168
Thee I cannot see and live	3:369	Then a fig for the Old Constitution and Laws	1:145
Thee I cannot seek in vain	2:372	Then a long fast we keep	2:53
Thee I remember on my bed	3:366	Then all our blisful business here	1:310
Thee if thy foes confess	2:329	Then all religious Babels cease[237]	1:74
Thee in all thy Ways confessing	1:241	Then all th'opposing mountains flow	3:426
Thee innocent in deed & thought	2:272		

233. The stanza beginning with this line appears in *PW* 11:170.
234. The stanza beginning with this line appears in *PW* 11:351.
235. The stanza beginning with this line appears in *PW* 13:166.
236. A six-line form of the eight-line stanza beginning with this line appears in *PW* 12:27–8, in which only the first four lines are identical.
237. The stanza beginning with this line appears in *PW* 8:487.

Then emerging from thy grave	2:110	Then we shall triumphant stand	3:301
Then Father, Son, & Holy Ghost	2:451	Then thou wilt thine own receive	3:281
Then from the midst of Babylon	1:306	Then thy watred church below	2:371
Then hear us, O thou suffering God	3:293	Then, to terminate my race	3:195
Then help them with their parting breath	3:320	Then, when all his heart is prayer	3:265
Then if their single eye is lost	2:132	There are, as idle gossips talk	1:280
Then let her, conscious of her fall	3:240	There are, by fond Mama supplied	1:280
Then let me calmly flee[238]	2:471	There from sin preserved by thee	3:192
Then let me drop him; & with wonder new	1:210	There is a righteous God and true	1:100
		There is a Time, when merit is allowed	1:203
Then let me while I breathe my last	2:466	There let every ransomed Nation[239]	2:303
Then let our Jesus' fame	2:348	There let me find him in that day	1:321
Then let our Saviour GOD have all ye praise	1:188	There reposed among the blest	1:76
		There the pure inraptured Spirit	3:371
Then let the gates be opened wide	3:345	There, there in patient peace	2:471
Then let the glittering world allure	1:247	There with his sweet Imperial lyre	1:128
Then let the Lord thy GOD be still thy Guide	1:195	There we shall find the friends we lost	1:119
		There we to each other known	1:262
Then let the spreading fire of love	3:57	Therefore upon our guilty head	1:59
Then let thy own compassions plead	3:269	Therefore the just, avenging Lord	1:133
Then let us lift up	1:275	These lords thy subject have oppressed[240]	2:178
Then let us still delight to wait	3:63	These sightless orbs on thee I turn	3:275
Then, Lord, in thine appointed hour	3:279	They all shall sit beneath the Vine[241]	2:453
Then may we ever keep in mind	3:293	They all shall then their Saviour see	2:310
Then my sin no more shall grieve thee	3:125	They all with one consent give heed	2:317
Then, only then, when clean in heart	3:201	They already *are* gone	3:120
Then possesst of my desire	1:75	They could have no injurious power	3:137
Then redeemed from all below	1:293	They could not offer up a prayer	1:60
Then, Saviour, then thyself descend	3:179	They count him now their lawful prize	3:93
Then shall I in the Word abide	2:242	They crown with prickly thorn	2:271
Then shall the church in thee abide	2:306	They cry, & never hold their Peace[242]	2:452
Then shall the ransomed Seed	1:120	They did not run, in sudden fright	2:316
Then shall our vain contention cease	1:310		
Then the sinner seeks thy grace	2:154		
Then, then intrusted with thy word	3:348		
Then, then their humbled souls indue	1:122		
Then, then these eyes shall view	2:190		
Then, then this quickened dust shall rise	1:313		
Then, then we joyfully confess	3:74		

238. The stanza beginning with this line appears in *PW* 13:166.

239. This is the first line of the last stanza of a four-stanza poem. Stanzas one through three consist of eight lines each. The fourth stanza, consisting of only four lines, is incomplete.

240. The stanza beginning with this line appears in *PW* 11:267.

241. The stanza beginning with this line appears in *PW* 4:314.

242. The stanza beginning with this line appears in *PW* 4:313.

They do not with the world conspire	2:205	This earnest wish if thou bestow	3:205
They force their Country to receive	1:98	This earth, I know, is not my place	3:291
They have his faithful Servants been	3:319	This heav'n-descended Man[245]	2:153
They heard, they listened to the soothing Tale	1:172	This is our only crime	2:419
		This is our rejoicing here	2:263
They live by rapine. The unwary guest	3:395	This is the Man (the Man himself avers)	1:208
They live the outcasts of mankind	2:33	This is the Bond of Perfectness	3:197
They make themselves, not God, their End	3:292	This is the consecrated way[246]	2:364
		This is the faith we humbly seek	2:232
They mock his resurrection's power	2:380	This is the miracle I need	2:233
They need not wait their Lord to know	2:456	This is the Proof, the Badge, the Seal	3:196
		This Languishing Desire	3:209
They now may savingly believe	2:457	This moment put him, Lord, in fear	3:309
They now preeminence affect	3:38	This only Happiness be mine	1:264
They Now, the Holy People named[243]	2:454	This only have we done	2:418
They saw the Ship by many a Tempest tossed	1:186	This silent grave, it doth embrace	3:325
		This soft infirmity forgive	3:297
They sowed the Ground, & did not reap[244]	2:453	This the high, the heav'nly Prize	3:203
		This, this is our Aim	3:120
They tell me, that my dying cry	3:320	This, this is the Prize	3:120
They tell me, who the Judge have known	3:320	This token, Lord, for good	3:139
		This urges you to let him see	3:99
They urged the Elder Presbyter	3:84	Tho' crouds may uncommissioned run	2:63
They vent their fiercest rage on him	1:77	Tho' foes surround before their face	2:442
They vow, the blood shall soon atone	1:117	Tho' he seems as left by thee	1:296
They *will* be rich, whate'er betide	3:292	Tho' his glorified estate	2:208
They will not see th'impending ills	3:55	Tho' in my sprinkled heart I feel	2:463
They would not take the tempter's part	3:56	Tho' nothing by myself I know	2:463
Thick planted on the adverse side	1:97	Tho' poor, and ignorant, and weak	2:25
Thine Arm thou soon shalt bare	1:237	Tho' rebel methodists excite thy Passion	1:206
Thine eternal Power and Glory	2:441		
Thine image & thy favor	2:83	Tho' she takes the Tempter's part	3:242
Thine Oracles the answer give	3:175	Tho' they bear thy name in vain	1:61
Thine Overruling Hand	1:227	Tho' 'tis beneath his State to view	2:450
Thine Unction we partake	2:339	Those hireling Priests whom we despise	3:45
Th' ineffable delight	2:304	Those objects of my former love	3:264
Th' inviting wide-exhausted field	1:126		
This, alas, I always feel	3:195		
This all thy life, this all thy death contest	3:327		

243. The stanza beginning with this line appears in *PW* 4:315.

244. The stanza beginning with this line appears in *PW* 4:314.

245. Lines five and six of the six-line stanza beginning with this line appear in *PW* 11:232 as the concluding lines of the stanza beginning with "Yes; for thou hast received."

246. The stanza beginning with this line appears in *PW* 12:293.

Those Reverend Drones who fill *our* place	3:45	Thou God of Faithful mercies, hear	3:223
Those who think he tarries long	2:141	Thou, God, to whom alone I live	3:354
Those whom most the Saviour loves	2:58	Thou GOD, in whose Love we agree	1:257
Thou a self-condemning Soul	3:148	Thou God that answerest by fire	3:304
Thou art a present Saviour	3:165	Thou God, whose Will to know	1:227
Thou art king, and reign'st alone	3:415	Thou hast broke his deadly blow	3:300
Thou art my confidence and power	1:247	Thou hast, if to thy wounds we look	2:444
Thou art my Glorious Calling's Prize	1:244	Thou hast in our degenerate years	3:63
Thou art not to one Sect confined	3:48	Thou hast made my terrors cease	3:415
Thou art with all thy fulness nigh	2:192	Thou hast ordained the Powers that be[251]	2:449
Thou awful God, by All unknown	1:265	Thou hast rescued me from death	3:408
Thou awful God, whose Judgments are	1:267	Thou hast ten thousand tokens given	3:63
Thou awful God, whose Smile or Frown	1:230	Thou heardst in me thy Spirit's Groans	3:359
Thou bidst the ministerial host	2:123	Thou helper of All in Distress	3:359
Thou bidst us patiently attend	2:285	Thou in life his soul detain	3:280
Thou canst animate the dead	3:281	Thou, Jesus, hast been	3:118
Thou canst from man his purpose hide	3:140	Thou kindly cam'st to stand between[252]	2:26
Thou canst my inbred foe expel	2:375	Thou know'st my every Hope & Fear	1:243
Thou canst perform the thing	1:85	Thou knowst my feebleness of mind	3:205
Thou canst, thou wilt abase the ground	3:48	Thou know'st my neverceasing Care	1:223
Thou canst with equal ease make whole[247]	3:286	Thou knowst, O Lord, in thy great Name	3:130
Thou David after God's own heart	2:259	Thou knowst our feeble wav'ring H[ear]t	3:180
Thou didst, ascending up on high	2:123	Thou knowst the burthen of my heart	3:297
Thou didst give me to despise	3:405	Thou knowst, the fiend hath set them up	3:235
Thou didst not send thy Son	2:222	Thou knowst the full Brethren she bears	3:359
Thou didst the heathen Stock expel[248]	2:447	Thou knowst the hellish aim	3:218
Thou didst thy Son bestow[249]	2:222	Thou knowst the ill our Foe intends	1:107
Thou didst to thine Apostles give	2:212	Thou knowst the number of our Foes	3:180
Thou dost forsake thy Son	2:68	Thou know'st the State of shortlived Man	1:273
Thou dost hedge up his way	1:302	Thou knowst what I would have Thee do	3:275
Thou dost Jehovah's children lead	1:309	Thou knowst with humble heart sincere	1:247
Thou dost not yet the plague remove	2:468		
Thou dost the forms commend	2:219		
Thou giv'st us plenteous Draughts of Tears[250]	2:447		

247. The stanza beginning with this line appears in *PW* 8:422.
248. The stanza beginning with this line appears in *PW* 8:447.
249. The stanza beginning with this line appears in *PW* 11:346.
250. The stanza beginning with this line appears in *PW* 8:162.
251. The stanza beginning with this line appears in *PW* 8:164.
252. See *PW* 10:240.

Thou, Lord, appearing on our side	1:89	Thou who know'st a father's heart[254]	2:128
Thou, Lord, direct my Ways	1:232	Thou who paidst my Price shall have me	1:248
Thou, Lord, dost still the fruit produce	2:318	Thou whom the winds and seas obey	3:217
Thou, Lord, hast bid th' Afflicted pray	3:122	Thou wilt not let us hence remove	3:425
Thou, Lord, hast suffered me to fall	3:171	Thou wilt our captive King	1:145
Thou most compassionate High-priest	3:271	Thou wouldst not have cut off in life's decay	3:437
Thou my sole Disposer be	1:250	Thou wouldst not let the Fiend prevail	3:50
Thou never couldst ye proud Oppressor brook	1:197	Though filled the fountain was[255]	2:455
Thou never-failing Friend	3:270	Though I have thy Spirit grieved	2:269
Thou never wilt forget	2:266	Thousands of secret Traitors wait	1:62
Thou never wilt our King forsake	1:79	Thousands when the wealthy give	2:187
Thou on his newborn soul impress	1:306	Three volumes of yours	1:279
Thou once a Man of woe	3:363	Thrice happy day that shall reveal	2:62
Thou only canst my loss repair	1:323	Thrice happy we, and all that live	1:160
Thou only canst great wonders do	1:288	Thro' avarice and ambition blind	1:156
Thou only canst in him and me	1:309	Thro' faith in thy blood	3:187
Thou only dost the rage restrain	3:169	Thro' grace the threefold yoke	2:352
Thou only knowst what is in man	3:176	Thro' hatred of the saintly sin	1:64
Thou Pharisee who, blind and proud	2:158	Thro' him the Crucified I know	3:176
Thou pitiest all who go astray	1:305	Thro' Jesus' Righteousness alone	3:157
Thou read'st the care that heaves my breast	1:242	Thro' life the Servant of thy will	3:308
Thou read'st th' unutterable Care	1:217	Thro' pride and malice blind	2:42
Thou righteous God, whose Plague I bear	3:145	Thro' the power of thy grace	3:187
		Thro' thee, superior to their frown	3:290
Thou seest my fears lest thee their God	3:423	Thro' thee to heaven I lift my Hand	3:160
Thou seest, Omniscient as thou art	2:384	Throughout our Lives to vindicate	1:256
Thou seest our faith, bestowed by thee	2:94	Throughout our mournful days	2:53
Thou seest the ground of every heart	2:95	Th' unworthiest of thy ministers	2:286
Thou seest their dark design	3:270	Thus if our hearts to earth adhere	2:431
Thou send'st his Spirit into my heart[253]	2:461	Thus in a gracious state	2:459
Thou sinners' Advocate with God	3:230	Thus let me All my Days, or Years	3:204
Thou suffer'st Parricides t' abase	1:107	Thus let us God withstand no more	2:344
Thou teacher blind, and proud	2:40	Thus longing for the welcome word	3:332
Thou to whom all hearts are known	3:367	Thus may I in my measure strive	2:387
Thou too to thine eternal Rest art gone	1:184	Thus may we still improve	2:346
Thou who hast endured so long	1:61	Thus my few remaining days	2:302
		Thus shall the Lord his sway maintain	1:73

253. The stanza beginning with this line appears in *PW* 13:25.

254. The stanza beginning with this line appears in *PW* 11:204.

255. The stanza beginning with this line was transcribed from shorthand but is incomplete.

Thus they fill their measure up	2:36	Thy power be in his weakness seen	1:310
Thus we reward their faithful zeal	1:138	Thy Priests be clothed with righteousness	3:68
Thus when the wonderful High-German Sage	1:209	Thy Priests commanded to revere	3:68
Thy alms and works of righteousness	2:20	Thy promise to the Church at large	3:63
Thy blessing makes our work succeed	3:70	Thy righteousness the world shall see[258]	2:450
Thy blood alone can purge his guilt	3:250	Thy servant, Lord, I fain would be	2:255
Thy captive, Lord, myself I yield	2:282	Thy servants in their youthful days	1:289
Thy choicest blessings from above	1:271	Thy sovereign word obeyed	2:169
Thy counsel, Lord, shall stand alone	1:312	Thy Spirit alone can root out sin	2:458
Thy counsel we regard	1:70	Thy Spirit in my heart explains[259]	2:462
Thy death to every heart reveal	3:229	Thy Spirit of Grace	3:119
Thy deed shall soon in judgments rise	1:88	Thy whole design we know	1:70
Thy deeds can never be forgot	1:88	Thy will can every bar remove	1:62
Thy duteous Sons to thee shall cleave[256]	2:452	Thy will is freely to forgive	1:288
Thy Ethiop-Soul, as black as night	1:88	Thy wisdom and thy light	2:134
Thy Face I shortly hope to see	3:51	Thy wise permissive will be bliss	3:311
Thy flock out of their hands redeem	3:39	Thy word thou hast to us fulfilled	3:65
Thy foes shall be thy footstool	2:289	Thy work is begun: But O, let it be	2:30
Thy garments made by hands of men	2:202	Thy wounded Side, to which alone	1:325
Thy Glorious Grace what Tongue can tell?[257]	2:451	Thy wounds thou dost to sinners show	2:211
Thy grace be in his sufferings showed	1:131	Thyself with thy great Father come	1:234
Thy great Design to know	1:238	Till GOD appear, the Faithful GOD[260]	2:453
Thy guilt and merits infinite	1:88	Till that happy day I see	2:248
Thy hand upon thy Servant lay	3:143	Till thee, the Glory of the Lord	3:39
Thy healing work in him begun	3:346	Till then I hug my load of pain	3:261
Thy heart the deep distress	1:301	Till then my punishment I bear	2:456
Thy judgments, Lord, in ages past	2:165	Till then, on you I call, ye *Sinners* poor	1:182
The judgments shall the earth devour	1:78	Till then thou dost a table spread	3:64
Thy judgments soar beyond our sight	1:313	Till then with thee concealed	3:272
Thy Love is equal to thy Power	1:230	Till thine Arm made bare before us	1:240
Thy Love th' Angelic Army sings	3:160	Till thou appear again	2:140
Thy mercies which for ever last	3:433	Till thou create me pure within	2:376
Thy merciful Word	3:119	Till thou dost his soul awake	1:294
Thy messenger, I	2:414	Till thy welcome will is done	3:300
Thy ministers of righteousness	3:133	Till washed, and thro' thy blood applied	1:311
Thy name, O Christ, I bear	2:184	Till with purest Passion panting	1:249
Thy only Peace can be the Seal	1:233		
Thy patient in thy hands I lie	2:123		

256. The stanza beginning with this line appears in *PW* 4:313.

257. The stanza beginning with this line appears in *PW* 4:312.

258. The stanza beginning with this line appears in *PW* 4:312.

259. The stanza beginning with this line appears in *PW* 13:26.

260. The stanza beginning with this line appears in *PW* 4:314.

T' insure success infallible	1:124	To cherish an unthankful race	1:71
Tired with the greatness of my Way	3:156	To crown these infinite desires	2:473
'Tis done! the deed adventurous is done!	3:91	To die in Christ is greatest Gain	1:239
'Tis finished! All my Guilt & Pain	2:278	To die is unspeakable gain	3:352
'Tis finished, all my guilt and pain	SH 1762, 2:234	To each he severally applies[264]	2:387
'Tis finished! all the Debt is paid[261]	2:277	To Father, Son, and Holy Ghost, / The God	2:450
'Tis here I seek, and hope to find	3:175	To gain the multitude	3:277
'Tis here thy mind I know	2:80	To good averse, to ill inclined	3:155
'Tis finished, he cries	3:187	To him my grateful heart I lift	1:270
'Tis finished! O Almighty Love	3:330	To him our earliest Fruits we bring	3:190
'Tis finished! the messias dies[262]	2:277	To him we innocently live	3:190
'Tis fixed: Rebellion mounts the throne	1:116	To Jesus' name if all things bow	3:248
'Tis not for us to rule the state	3:213	To make an end of sin	2:287
'Tis not th'effect of chance	3:212	To make your character compleat	1:94
'Tis not confined to time or place	2:233	To no single sect confined	2:228
'Tis not for Jesus' messengers	2:137	To opposite extreams so prone	2:432
'Tis not in foolish man	2:386	To our tremendous Lord	1:81
'Tis now cut down, and burnt with Fire[263]	2:448	To pluck the Prey out of his Teeth	3:161
'Tis slaughter in the outward sign	2:341	To rectify my crooked will[265]	2:86
'Tis there my Soul shall rest	3:362	To save his wandring soul from sin	1:303
'Tis thus, convinced in their own heart	2:424	To save the faithful race	3:218
'Tis thus, O God, they picture thee	3:392	To save the lost thing	2:173
'Tis thus the Leaders of our nation	3:382	To save the rich from hell	2:173
'Tis thus the men whose dictates we obey	3:385	To show forth all thy praise	3:58
		To silent streams his flock he leads	3:64
'Tis thus, when Satan's instrument	2:417	To suffer all thy will I come	1:300
'Tis time, O Lord, for thee	1:86	To that almighty prayer divine	3:249
'Twas here reposed for months he lay	1:53	To that sure Refuge in Distress	1:239
To a father's fond embrace	3:244	To the Lord in deep distress	2:445
To a good warfare, Lord	3:142	To the lost sheep of England's fold	3:57
To actions of the great	2:187	To the sweet City-waits altho'	1:281
To ask the Grace we humbly join	3:288	To thee for help I cry	2:164
To Battle in thy Strength I go	3:161	To thee for Light we still apply	1:233
To both at once their Lord revealed	3:83	To thee, great Friend of helpless man	3:268
To check my forward Will	1:228	To thee, great GOD of Truth & Power	3:379
		To thee my feeble heart I tell	3:121
		To these, O God, thou hast regard	1:81
		To thee espoused, & thee alone	1:264
		To thee, great Friend of helpless man	3:268

261. The stanza beginning with this line appears in *PW* 12:99–100.
262. The stanza beginning with this line appears in *PW* 12:94.
263. The stanza beginning with this line appears in *PW* 8:164.
264. The stanza beginning with this line appears in *PW* 12:353.
265. The stanza beginning with this line appears in *PW* 11:125.

To thee I do not offer up	1:267	Trembling he doth his sin confess	2:324
To thee my worthless name I give	3:160	Trembling on the Brink of Ruin	1:251
To thee the needy Patriot gives	1:100	Tremendous doom, when God the just	2:192
To These my murdered (?) son unite	1:303	Tremendous God, in mercy frown	3:250
To thine own Eternal Glory	3:109	Tremendous God, severely just	3:74
To think more highly than you ought	2:458	Tremendous God, thy hand we see	1:98
To those who guide the tottering state	3:215	Triumph we, the sons of grace	2:79
To us commissioned in thy name	3:65	Triumphant in his favour	2:471
To us impute thy own desert	2:191	Triumphed the Great in deeper guilt	1:129
To us, most wise, most gracious Lord	2:24	True faith with unremitting strife	2:70
To us our Nursing-Fathers raise[266]	2:449	True followers of the gallant H[owe']s	1:127
To whom but God shall we complain	1:78	True Israelites, we now believe	2:425
To whom for conscience sake opprest	1:115	True love holds on its even way	2:70
To whom for refuge shall we run	1:90	True to his Principle, the sinner poor	1:174
To whom for refuge should we fly	1:107	Truly baptized into the Name	2:389
To whom in peril and distress	3:76	Trusting his own weak heart	2:266
To whom should thy disciples go[267]	2:22	Truth divine must not be hid	2:131
To you, dear Doctor, I appeal	1:281	Try me, O Lord, & search my heart	1:269
Too happy in his love I was	1:320	Turn again, thou trembling Reed	3:194
Too long insensible I lay	2:121	Turn thee again, O Lord our God[270]	2:448
Tophet is now my just Reward	3:157	Turn then to him, ye heathens turn	2:363
Tophet its mouth hath opened wide	2:443	Turn us again, O GOD, and shew[271]	2:447
Tormentor of myself I rove	3:269	Turn us again, O GOD, and shew	2:449
Tortured into legal fear (?)	3:407	Turn us again, thou GOD of Might	2:446
Tost on life's tempestuous wave	3:257	Turn while grace may yet be found	2:352
Touched with exquisite Compassion	3:109	Twelve inspired Apostles new	2:390
Traitors at home with These conspired	1:133	'Twas GOD alone which joined our hands	1:271
Transplanted to a foreign land	1:123	T'ward the mark ye need not press	3:410
Transported by Prophetic zeal[268]	2:412	T'were Madness, they cry, in a Monarch to trust	1:166
Transported in Prayer	3:120	Two and two, not one and one[272]	2:116
Transported we receive	2:304		
Trav'ling thro' the vale of woe	2:127		
Tread on a worm, he'll turn again	1:282		
Tremble, thou careless minister[269]	2:175		
Tremble, thou favoured saint, on whom	2:142	Unless he at our greatest need	1:77

266. The stanza beginning with this line appears in *PW* 8:164.
267. The first four lines of the six-stanza poem beginning with this line appear in *PW* 10:223.
268. The stanza beginning with this line appears in *PW* 12:401.
269. The stanza beginning with this line appears in *PW* 11:266.
270. The stanza beginning with this line appears in *PW* 8:164.
271. The four-line stanzas beginning with this line appear in *PW* 8:162, 165. They are identical in *PW* and *UP*, where they appear on pages 447 and 449.
272. The stanza beginning with this line appears in *PW* 11:190.

Unless thou wash my heart with blood	3:191
Unless thy Spirit the truth reveal[273]	2:464
Unmoved by avarice or pride	3:73
Unnumbered miracles	2:362
Unspeakably blest	2:433
Unspotted from the World, and Sin	3:189
Unutterable things I see—	3:329
Urged by the hostile world, unless	2:267
Us in their hands ev'n now they bear	2:63
Us to thyself by love divine	1:309
Us whom thy mind & Spirit arm	3:76
Use them a while thy hopes to crown	1:87
Using the grace his Saviour gives	2:177
Vainly at first my labouring bosom strove	3:399
Vanished my last attempt to pray	3:254
Venerable gamesters play	2:67
Victim of an angry God	2:275
Victims of ambitious pride	1:67
Victorious o'er the world and hell	1:290
Vile prostitutes, who write for bread	1:77
Vilest of all the ransomed Race	3:160
Virtue and him they hate	1:82
Visible thro' faith I know	2:229
Void of Christ, the real Light	2:256
Void of offence tow[ard] God & man	3:340
Voters of Middlesex, forbear	1:151
Vouchsafe (to bring them safely thro'	1:292
Wait we now resigned and still	3:302
Waits my heart insensible	2:301
Wake him now out of his dream	1:296
Waking out of my Dream of Hope	3:145
Walking in her house with God	3:338
Wandring o'er inchanted ground	3:246
Warned by their fall, we woued be wise	3:292
Warned by their loving Pastor's care	3:55
Warned to put off this mouldring clay	3:355
Wash us from every guilty stain	1:308
We add our vehement suit to theirs	1:114
We, alas, can nothing do	3:94
We all shall be thro' Faith made whole	2:446
We allow him at present, a pitiful thing	1:166
We are the men—of Wealth & State	3:199
We ask (but not to tempt thee, Lord)	1:233
We blame the rabble who prefered	2:65
We blame the Savage King whose Cruel Word	3:107
We both shall see our Saviour's face	1:307
We cannot follow Christ in vain	2:32
We cannot from destruction fly	1:77
We cannot rest, who Jesus know[274]	2:57
We concerning this agree	3:94
We could not aid their black design	1:117
We could not all our oaths break thro'	1:118
We enter then into the cloud	2:112
We for them the promise claim	1:61
We for our dearest Country feel	3:60
We from this moment vow	3:213
We have them too; and Christ beside[275]	2:160
We hear a Romish founder say	3:93
We hear the Providential call	3:70
We hear the word divine and do	2:131
We here the dire Occasion see	1:65
We, Jesus, have heard thy wonderful fame	2:253
We know not what estate is best	3:283
We live, by miracle, we live	3:171
We live to make the Saviour known[276]	2:307
We loved to rest under his shade	1:90
We must acknowledge his address	1:140
We must believe his promise sure	1:91
We never can confide in them	1:83

273. The stanza beginning with this line appears in *PW* 13:36: Unless thy Spirit thy Truth reveal.
274. The stanza beginning with this line appears in *PW* 10:502.
275. The stanza beginning with this line appears in *PW* 11:247.
276. The stanza beginning with this line appears in *PW* 12:197.

We now have weighed you in the sacred Scale	1:185	Welcome from the Rocks and Waves	3:303
We now prescribe the peaceful law	1:149	Well thou knowst, I chiefly would	3:257
We put his tender bowels on	3:60	Well thou knowst, if now my heart	3:204
We run before the grace divine	2:23	Were his alms & ceaseless prayers[278]	2:335
We seek the Saviour of mankind	2:216	Were the last fatal mom[en]t come	3:349
We served our King with warmest zeal	1:137	Were they not heard for years to groan	1:73
We shall our Time beneath	3:210	W[esley] beset, assailed on every side	3:90
We sink as every moment down	2:105	W[esley] himself & Friends betrays	3:81
We spread the odour of his name	2:57	W[esley] permits ambitious C[oke] to rule	3:92
We taste that God is good	2:292	What are the sorest plagues I bear	3:360
We tell the proud indignant race	2:90	What are their dreams of bliss below?	3:292
We then our righteous doom shall meet	3:45	What are their sins compared to Ours	3:306
We then shall each with each agree	2:63	What avails it, Lord, to know[279]	2:258
We thirst to drink thy healing blood	2:277	What but th'omnipotence of grace	2:325
We tremble at thy rod	1:82	What can harm the friends of God?	2:135
We trust our never failing Guide	3:74	What can I do but humbly call	3:46
We thus our legacy receive	2:279	What can resist thy powerful word	2:391
We thus to meet our God prepare[277]	3:76	What can the friend of Jesus dread	2:330
We to the temptation yield	2:196	What can your hoarded life avail	2:138
We walk throughout our evil Day	3:130	What cannot Fashion do? with magic ease	3:386
We who for all a table spread	1:139	What could the Author of so foul a scheme	1:194
We who Jesus' Spirit know	2:115	What did I not, before his rage begun	1:178
We who our Saviour's word receive	2:188	What divine humility	2:84
We who would on thee rely	1:60	What do they to their Sovereign leave	1:164
We with the faithful *remnant* sue	1:134	What doth this grievous trouble mean	3:351
We would thine aged followers give	2:276	What harm, if ministers agree	1:102
We would thou knowst, *we* would be thine	3:224	What help alas, or hope	2:340
We your Majesty's dutiful subjects & Leiges	1:153	What help or Hope remains for me	3:156
Weak, unarmed, of sin afraid	3:409	What hinders then, I still inquire	2:375
Weak, wavering *Rogers* too the Work gives o'er	1:175	What hope of safety for our Realm	1:155
Weary alas! thou knowst I am	3:354	What in us is lacking still	2:61
Weary of the war within	3:406	What is everything beside[280]	2:126
Weary I come for rest to thee	3:163	What is it that in all their meetings sounds?	1:192

277. This is the first line of stanza five of a six-stanza poem, the second line of which reads: "By constant watchfulness and prayer." Charles Wesley wrote a marginal note in shorthand with an alternative to the second line: "Labouring and watching into prayer." See *UP* 3:76n and 437.

278. The stanza beginning with this line appears in *PW* 12:243.

279. Lines one, two, and four of the eight-line poem beginning with this line appear in *PW* 11:505.

280. The stanza beginning with this line appears in *PW* 11:198.

What is it then which now constrains	3:254
What is that Rock, but Christ alone	3:173
What is the grace I fain would prove	3:190
What Joy unknown, unspeakable	1:324
What multitudes have thought	2:320
What numbers now are found	2:341
What Pharisees can do	2:133
What pity that the Masters great	3:387
What shall I do? declare it, or suppress	1:194
What shall I say, Preserver, Lord	3:151
What should ye do, who see	2:249
What Statesman for a triffle strives	1:101
What then have I to fear	1:229
What tho' she daily died	2:340
What though my soul with shame is filled	3:361
What was it then that kept thee in their hands	1:198
What we think would bring us nigher	3:211
What wonder then, if the true seed	1:129
What would I give to feel and know	3:153
What wouldst thou have me do	3:141
Whate'er my Lot or State below	1:222
W[ha]te'er of weak, or human in his Plan	3:88
Whate'er the instrument or means	2:331
Whate'er the messenger he sends	2:24
Whate'er thou dost to us intrust	2:157
Whate'er we have 'twas God bestowed	2:363
When a saint is quite mature	2:55
When all the Gentiles are brought in	2:310
When Christ himself reveals	2:107
When Christ we preach the sinner's Friend	2:425
When cited at the bar t'appear	3:292
When envious indignation filled	2:358
When first I feel thy blood applied	2:367
When first thy Ministerial Course begun	1:190
When God awakes, the vengeful God	1:99
When God declares me reconciled	2:18
When God permits, revive	2:41
When God severely kind	2:171
When God vouchsafes the soul to bless	2:210
When half my course, alas, is run	3:347
When he could himself defend[281]	2:273
When he was swept to his own place	1:73
When him alone they praise	2:348
When his coming from above	3:300
When his troubled members feel	2:248
When humbly thus our sins we own	1:84
When impending storms appear	2:445
When in his arms he held[282]	2:82
When Jesus comes, in this our day	2:25
When Jesus first appears	2:52
When Jesus first pronounced the word	2:236
When Jesus hath his kingdom sown	2:55
When Jesus imparts	2:358
When Jesus' kingdom is revealed	2:159
When Jesus knows it good for me	2:330
When Jesus languished on the tree	2:83
When Jesus' prosperous messenger	2:331
When judgment has consumed thy foes	1:66
When many in the service join	2:383
When of themselves they thought	2:459
When our Incarnate God[283]	2:91
When prostrate in the dust they grieve	3:41
When reason is by wrath supprest	2:397
When sinners have the call obeyed	2:358
When states and kingdoms are o'erthrown	1:78
When the celestial light appears	2:324
When the fiend to shape of man	3:405
When the great God his Spirit pours[284]	2:288
When the great God intends	2:409
When the prey is in their net	3:417
When the Spirit and the word	2:322

281. The stanza beginning with this line appears in *PW* 12:81.
282. The stanza beginning with this line appears in *PW* 11:120.
283. The stanza beginning with this line appears in *PW* 11:141.
284. The stanza beginning with this line appears in *PW* 12:147.

When the stumbling-block is gone[285]	2:308	Where is the God of Shadrach? where	3:129
When the time was now fulfiled[286]	2:150	Where is the sect or party free	2:114
When the wicked seek to slay	2:246	Where, my best, my bosom-Friend	1:262
When their chief I put to flight	3:416	Where'er I turned my willing feet	3:262
When those on whom our hopes were stayed	1:112	Where'er thou hast thy work begun	3:227
		Wherever we go	2:359
When thou dost my soul release	1:76	Wher[e]fore, if thou the grace permit	3:72
When thou from sin hast set us free	2:163	Wherefore in self-mistrust I flee	3:206
When thro' the gloomy shade I roam	2:442	Wherefore in time, dear MUN, attend	1:167
When thus my bosom, torn by raging love	3:402	Wherefore now on thee we press	2:54
		Wherefore on thee alone	1:228
When to his sober mind restored[287]	2:155	Wherefore should I stay to shame	1:253
When want, and pain, and death besiege our gate	3:421	Wherefore to thee alone we look	3:287
		Wherefore to thee with faith I cleave	2:451
When we before our Judge appear	2:175	Wherefore was she formed to please	3:343
When we have the Master's mind	2:372	Wherefore we calmly wait the day	1:91
When we long the word to hear	2:357	Wherefore we, humbled in the dust	1:71
When will the pardning God appear	3:261	Wherefore with earnest cries	3:350
When wounded by thy Spirit's sword	3:235	Wherefore with soft and silent pace	1:313
When young & full of sanguine hope	2:281	Wherever we go	2:365
Whence come wars and deadly feuds	1:67	Whether he damns or passes by	3:161
Whene'er he thinks fit	3:390	Whether I shall e'er regain it	3:148
Whene'er the joyful sound we hear	2:118	Which of a thousand different roads	3:296
Whene'er thou dost the grace bestow[288]	2:20	Which of the Christians now	2:297
Whene'er thy Providential Voice	3:223	Which of the prophets old	2:314
Where are all Patriots, not one	1:139	While, as a Jew, thy word I read	2:354
Where are humility and peace[289]	2:305	While at the sepulchre I stay	2:71
Where are the venerable men[290]	2:382	While blackest clouds involve the skies	3:75
Where have ye the sinner laid?	2:248	While blackning clouds o'respread the sky	3:213
Where he appoints, & when	2:386		
Where is old England's glory fled	1:109	While discord's swelling tides run high	1:123
Where is that ancient power	2:296	While earning our bread	3:289
Where is the Fury of our Foe	3:117	While envious Foes against thy Fame conspire	1:203
		While from fallacious man I cease	3:71
		While full of the malicious fiend	2:192
		While gospel-husbandmen repose	2:28
		While heaven with angry frown	1:69
		While helpless at thy feet they lie	1:138
		While House to House, & Field to Field	3:199
		While hovering on the brink of fate	3:267
		While I hang upon thy passion	2:470
		While I sensibly decline	3:300

285. The stanza beginning with this line appears in *PW* 12:198.
286. The stanza beginning with this line appears in *PW* 11:227–8.
287. The stanza beginning with this line appears in *PW* 11:235.
288. See *PW* 10:219 but with variant readings.
289. The stanza beginning with this line appears in *PW* 12:196.
290. The stanza beginning with this line appears in *PW* 12:346–7.

While I sojourn in the Vale	1:251	While with us his Spirit stays	2:256
While hovering on the brink of fate	3:267	While without strength we were	2:360
While in the fiery furnace tried	1:306	While wounded by thy Spirit's sword	3:318
While in the furnace tried	1:119	While yet on ruin's verge ye stand	2:89
While in the Weeping Vale I stay	1:239	While yet we call, his spirit arrest	3:247
While Jesus lets his followers eat	2:53	Wh[itefield] begins his Course, and rises fair	1:176
While kept I every moment find	2:468	Whither, ah, whither shall I go	3:260
While labouring in the church below	2:384	Whither, when his Saviour leaves[294]	2:136
While mercy wills the kind delay	3:287	Who act the persecutor's part[295]	2:313
While on thee, my God, I wait	3:428	Who an army can withstand	2:400
While One removed by sudden death	3:171	Who bear the vessels of the Lord	3:67
While pleasure's fairest baits allure	1:291	Who beat thy confessors & wound	2:377
While plunged in wickedness and vice	3:60	Who before the Saviour lies	2:102
While preaching gospel to the poor	3:49	Who blame the sin of Jews abhored	2:270
While sheltered by my Saviour's hand	2:440	Who bow to thy supreme command	3:75
While the Bridegroom seems to stay	2:43	Who builders should by office be	2:184
While the city walls are sparkling	3:435	Who built this universal frame	2:362
While the guilt of sin remains	3:256	Who call thy death to mind	3:186
While thee remembering in thy ways	3:63	Who came to make his Father known[296]	2:88
While thee we own in all our ways	2:411	Who can against the Rebels stand	1:116
While there in fancied pomp ye reign	2:464	Who can all their virtues paint!	3:413
While they their calling here pursue	3:292	Who can defeat the Saviour's plan	2:300
While thou dost the veil remove	1:297	Who can against thy counsel stand	3:240
While thousands listened to his soft Command	1:197	Who can deliver, who	3:270
While thus I worthily adore	3:175	Who can enough admire and praise	1:159
While thus we record	3:181	Who can Jesus' mind explain	2:207
While thus they lead him in a string	1:165	Who can, O God, thy counsels tell![297]	2:305
While thus ye long your Souls t' employ[291]	3:112	Who can speak the Mutual Greeting	1:252
While to the temple we repair	2:181	Who can stay her violence? who	3:244
While tortured here with lingring pains[292]	2:234	Who can stop his flowing tears	1:67
While walking in the mortal vale	3:64	Who can the dreadful state explain	2:180
While warm with undiscerning zeal	2:23	Who can the joy express	2:321
While weeping there the sinner lay[293]	3:334		

291. The stanza beginning with this line appears in *PW* 4;129.
292. The stanza beginning with this line appears in *PW* 11:365, but with one variation: "While thus ye love your Souls t'employ."
293. The stanza beginning with this line appears in *PW* 6:302.
294. The last four lines of the eight-line poem beginning with this line appear in *PW* 11:200.
295. The stanza beginning with this line appears in *PW* 12:216.
296. The stanza beginning with this line appears in *PW* 11:129.
297. The stanza beginning with this line appears in *PW* 12:196.

Who can the odd Phenomenon explain?	3:91	Who Jesus' warning words receive	1:167
Who can the Prodigy explain	1:140	Who kindled, and kept up the fire	1:110
Who cleave to earth and sin	2:172	Who knows the joy we feel	2:304
Who coued so choice an instrument refuse	3:90	Who labours in the word from man	2:117
		Who listen to our clam'rous foes	2:424
Who dares the gospel-truth blaspheme[298]	2:383	Who lose the salt of grace	2:152
		Who love his name, and keep his word	2:183
Who did for all mankind atone	2:473	Who made my peace, 'tis he, 'tis he	2:450
Who didst deliver them	2:353	Who might not hear the word before	2:391
Who dost from man his purpose hide	3:73	Who minister the gospel-word	2:349
Who doth not in the Son believe	2:223	Who much receive should much restore	2:142
Who envy now behold	2:254	Who nobly for their Country stood	1:134
Who first the foul Apostasy began	1:173	Who now participates thy death	2:254
Who fought against their sovereign Lord	1:127	Who now themselves the church profess	2:358
Who gave his life mankind to save	2:261	Who now, when Z[inzendorf] a Fact has told	1:211
Who gave our Israel to the sword	1:59	Who of himself as something thinks	2:469
Who gavest me my work to do	3:224	Who of themselves too highly think	2:466
Who glory in your ripest grace	2:464	Who on his word rely	2:182
Who happy without God would be[299]	2:155	Who persecute the sons of light	3:313
Who has not heard of Rankin's proffer	1:96	Who refuse the truth t'obey	2:359
Who have the gospel truth believed	2:319	Who saves his own and neighbour's soul	2:44
Who hears his warnings with disdain[300]	2:260	Who shall tell me if the strife	3:431
Who held on earth the lowest place	2:32	Who still of Jesus testify	2:331
Who his coming shall abide	2:183	Who take at first the Saviour's side	2:275
Who his truth and mercy know	3:303	Who take the name of Christ in vain	2:407
Who in the steps of Abraham tread	2:292	Who tastes the truth, and Jesus sees[302]	2:111
Who is the trembling sinner, who	3:443	Who the baptismal rite receive	1:221
Who is this that comes from Edom	2:302	Who the cunning can declare	3:413
Who is this Stripling (let my Friend inquire)	1:189	Who the truth and us oppose	2:418
		Who their own countrymen destroyed	1:156
Who Jesus and his grace has lost	2:155	Who then can paint her soft confused distress	3:399
Who Jesus seek with zeal sincere	2:71	Who then shall say whence second life began	3:396
Who Jesus to the world confess[301]	2:329	Who thus to God devotes her days	2:332
		Who thy doctrine would obey	3:295
		Who to me the Blessing gave	1:254

298. The stanza beginning with this line appears in *PW* 12:347.
299. The stanza beginning with this line appears in *PW* 11:234.
300. The stanza beginning with this line appears in *PW* 11:509.
301. The stanza beginning with this line appears in *PW* 12:239.
302. The stanza beginning with this line appears in *PW* 11:184.

Who rashly ran uncalled, unsent	3:66	Whom yesterday I could forgive	1:316
Who truly in our Lord believe	2:80	Whose hope on ignorance is built	2:141
Who wait in view of gospel-peace	2:285	Whose seal so long her Hierarchy maintained	3:87
Who wealth possesses here	2:172		
Who *will* be rich, (thy word declares,)	3:284	Whose words they can no more withstand[305]	2:309
Who will not let their idols go	2:193		
Who will not now the word believe[303]	2:221	Whose works, & lives, & hearts were good	2:237
Who will not to their Saviour go	2:177	Whose wrath our evil day decreed	1:113
Who wisely for her offspring cares	2:370	Why boastest thou thy baleful power	1:87
Who with hate implacable	2:253	Why did God on earth appear?	2:152
Who with that Zeal thy fervent Spirit stirred?	1:195	Why didst thou at all depart?	1:296
		Why didst thou form him of a Mind	3:358
Who won for God the wandring Souls of men	2:87	Why didst thou in the worst of Times	3:358
Who would not for their Master own	2:147	Why do our factious Tyrants boast	1:112
Who would not his advice pursue[304]	2:430	Why do the lawless Great conspire	1:130
Who would not wish to have the skill	3:109	Why have I not my suit obtained	3:368
Whoe'er admires as Excellence	3:383	Why should a living child of man	3:360
Whoe'er have our destruction sworn	1:108	Why should he crush the *hutted* Few	1:125
Whoe'er in him believes	2:340	Why should sin cause [ ][306] pain?	3:410
Whoe'er the fiery spirit feel	3:61	Why should that a hindrance prove	2:151
Whoe'er the heavenly kingdom preach	2:108	Why should the fond admiring throng	2:290
Whoever stands or falls, the word	3:236	Why should we now renounce our ease	1:149
Wholly at thy dispose I am	2:282	Why should I hope thy Confidence to shame	1:212
Whom God exalts, he humbles too	2:89		
Whom have I but thee to plead	2:444	Why should I in unhallowed pain	1:321
Whom his own *vain thoughts* expose	1:297	Why should I live in fruitless pain	3:124
Whom in thy arms thou long didst bear	1:299	Why should the Nation's weal or woe	1:100
		Why should They be the last that bring	3:67
Whom incarnate fiends intice	1:293	Why should they lose their sufferings past	1:121
Whom I did from thee obtain	3:274		
Whom Jesus for his followers owns	2:31	Why should we now a church forsake	3:64
Whom now we to thy grace commend	2:95	Why then dost thou detain	3:137
Whom on earth but thee have I	2:444	Why then hast thou abhored thine own[307]	2:448
Whom rebels up to slaughter give	1:134		
Whom shall the many-headed Brute	1:152	Why then should the Professors aim	3:387
Whom the heavens cannot contain	2:79	Why then to heaven do I desire to bow	3:402
Whom thou didst for ages cherish	1:63	Why, 'tis enough to make one wild	1:281
Whom we cannot undeceive	3:94	Why were thy Gifts on him bestowed	3:344

303. The first four lines of the eight-line poem beginning with this line appear in *PW* 11:344.
304. The stanza beginning with this line appears in *PW* 12:442.
305. The stanza beginning with this line appears in *PW* 12:200.
306. There is a gap here in MS Shorthand.
307. The stanza beginning with this line appears in *PW* 8:163.

Why would my cruel Friends suppress	3:353	With Garlands to the Altar brought	1:261
Why would you aim at things so high	3:99	With generous industry he strove	2:382
Wild havoc of the flock they make	3:78	With grief a father must foresee	2:402
Wilful, ignorant, and blind	1:297	With grief their flinty bosoms tear	3:318
Will a good name, or fortune fair	3:260	With humble, meek, submissive fear	3:419
Will murtherers the guiltless spare?	1:118	With indiscriminating zeal	3:44
Will ye claim my friendship now	3:414	With infernal malice fraught	2:385
Willing made her God t'obey	3:242	With Jesus crucified and dead	2:206
Willing made for thee alone	3:280	With Jesus' sympathy we cry	3:214
Willing that All his Truth should know[308]	2:276	With Joy we see th' auspicious Day return	3:108
Willingly I heard them speak	3:412	With Joy we shall behold	3:210
Wilt thou, Lord, thine own forsake?	1:219	With him, of thee we make our boasts	1:89
Wilt thou thy Property forego	3:319	With Love Divine our Wishes crown	1:234
Wilt thou not bless me with the skill	2:157	*With* me let thy Spirit dwell	3:196
Wisdom and Power Divine	2:185	With me, Lord, today abide	3:192
Wisdom by all her children here	2:101	With nature for his guide	2:265
Wisdom I in thee possess	2:35	With pity, Lord, the men behold	3:234
Wise to redeem the time below	3:345	With pride that I may never swell	3:49
With all his members one	2:419	With readiness and lowly fear	3:427
With all his spoils the hero sails	1:126	With shame and sorrow I confess	2:45
With all the servants of my Lord	3:35	With Shame my Wishes I recant	1:263
With all the Spirit's powers she prayed	3:328	With sinners I cast my lot	3:285
With an hostile world surrounded[309]	2:265	With stedfast, calm, deliberate Might	3:160
With Angels above	3:119	With stedfast Faith & Love	1:232
With awe the Name tremendous I adore	1:200	With strength of guardian grace	3:277
		With stronger love for him they sigh	2:210
With Bristol-Organists not yet	1:282	With such tranquillity of mind	2:259
With childlike Awe, & humble Hope	1:243	With tears we own, They *did* run well	3:38
With diligence attending	2:401	With that celestial Prize in view	1:274
With eager joy I ran, I flew	3:252	With Those that do thy Father's will	3:54
With ease a wise, unbiassed man	2:415	With thy grace anoint my eyes	3:172
With ease the rebels he o'erthrew	1:125	With thy pure Spirit filled	2:298
With equal Modesty, & equal Grace	1:212	With thyself her life conceal	3:301
With every gospel-minister	2:329	With what glee he declares	3:389
With exquisite Pleasure & Pain	1:257	With what madness and rage do they now lay about	1:146
With Fellowship sweet	3:120	Witness his old companions there[310]	3:336
		Witness of thy saving power	1:298
		Witness the listning quire above	3:253
		Witness the venerable man	1:127

308. The stanza beginning with this line appears in *PW* 12:94, but with one variation: "Willing that all his Death should know."
309. The last four lines of the eight-line stanza beginning with this line appear in *PW* 12:46.
310. The stanza beginning with this line appears in *PW* 6:309.

Witness the victories he gained	1:125	Ye Levites hired who undertake	2:298
Witness, ye echoing hills and dales	3:262	Ye little Foxes, who our Vinyard spoil	1:185
Woe to Judas' successors	2:286	Ye Lords of earth, for your own Interest wise	1:213
Woe to the men, by whom thy wrath is stirred	1:208	Ye make the outside clean	2:40
Woe to the men that cry	2:133	Ye men of Jewish zeal	2:418
Women, & men, & children too	2:317	Ye men sent forth in Jesus' name	2:399
Wonderful oeconomy	2:66	Ye ministers of wrath divine	1:70
Wonders ye have already done	1:162	Ye must applaud our act so good	2:415
Wondring he must express	2:92	Ye nations hear! A Monarch great and good	3:388
Words cannot prove	2:280	Ye need not now despair	2:329
Work for the weak, & sick, & poor	2:403	Ye pillars in your own esteem	2:159
Worldlings the gospel hear in vain	2:103	Ye Pilots of the British state	1:94
Worldly men thro' worldly views	2:420	Ye prudently forbear	2:418
Worldly things to worldly men	2:116	Ye reverend thieves & robbers hear	2:243
Worn out with toil, defamed, opprest	3:123	Ye Saints and Servants of the Lord	2:449
Worthy in her great Saviour's Worth[311]	2:451	Ye stand with all your deeds	2:41
Worthy the pure primeval man	3:419	Ye sufferers who your Lord confess	2:429
[Worthy i]s the slaughtered Lamb	3:363	Ye that all your powers exert	2:351
Worthy of double honour they	2:382	Ye that now dispense the word	2:386
Worthy the great Apostle's zeal	2:404	Ye threaten us in vain	2:315
Would faction's sons neglect th' occasion	1:104	Ye vipers who your Parent tear	1:71
Would King's weak reasons have prevailed	3:96	Ye weak, mistaken worms, believe	3:392
		Ye who curiously desire[312]	2:252
Would men like these the presence hear	1:129	Ye who madly love your sins	2:263
Would Paul himself as quite secure	2:469	Ye who minister the word	2:258
Wouedst thou increase of faith receive	2:236	Ye, who the name of Jesus take	2:392
Would, but O! I want the Pow[e]r	3:148	Ye who your sin have spared	2:291
Wounded by the Spirit's sword	2:393	Ye worthy Ministers of Righteousness	3:105
Wretched far above the rest	2:36	Ye zealous Citizens of London	1:151
Wretched indeed thou know'st, I am	1:265	Yes, an heavier Curse besets us	3:146
Wretched Sinner that I am	3:149	Yes; for thou hast received[313]	2:153
Wretched world! the call who slight	2:36	Yes, I know, thou canst, thou wilt	3:182
		Yes, if sufficient proof he give	2:161
		Yes, Lord, I now my Calling see	1:268
Ye Aliens, shout against me	3:131	Yes, Lord; I will, I do embrace	3:239
Ye awful ministers of death	1:94	Yes; the poor supply thy place[314]	2:46
Ye brave *associated* Supporters	1:151		
Ye followers of the Lord	2:429		
Ye great and good in your own eyes	2:468		

311. The stanza beginning with this line appears in *PW* 4:312.

312. The stanza beginning with this line appears in *PW* 11:485.

313. Lines one through four of the six-line stanza beginning with this line appear in *PW* 11:232.

314. The poem beginning with this line

Yes, the promised tribulation[315]	2:264	Yet not thy hope of pardon,	
Yes, the sufferings of our head	2:109	or its crown	3:327
Yes, thou silent Man of woe	2:274	Yet, O Almighty Lord	1:237
Yes; unless thou hold me fast	2:240	Yet O my soul would fain decline	3:420
Yes, ye still Tyrants, Death shall set them free	1:184	Yet One, and only One, I thought secure	1:180
Yet better to the Law Divine submit	1:185	Yet quick perhaps as other folks	1:282
Yet careless on the brink of hell	3:317	Yet resolute these to win the prize	3:55
Yet commanded to divine	2:405	Yet shall thy jaws the Bridle feel	1:88
Yet danger national requires	3:213	Yet since he from my heart is torn	1:304
Yet do not rest secure	2:130	Yet skilful Masters of the tuneful string	3:383
Yet did he not his offspring leave	2:363	Yet spite of all the Brethren's pious Pains	1:193
Yet dost thou wipe thy Mouth & take thy Ease	1:212	Yet spite of Envy, thy bewitching Smile	1:206
Yet ev'n in these licentious days	1:81	Yet still thy saints attend	2:272
Yet ev'n where Satan keeps his seat	1:114	Yet still when Antichrist prevails	3:198
Yet for mercy sake restore	1:254	Yet the incorruptible seed[318]	2:104
Yet for thy Cause & People's sake	3:152	Yet then, O God, thy church shall see	1:99
Yet for thy Compassion sake	3:152	Yet unconcerned the Many meet	1:99
Yet for thy sovereign Will demands	1:267	Yet we at least should spare the weak	3:81
Yet God doth not his Spirit give	2:461	Yet who their Saviour truly knew	2:209
Yet hardened still ye will not yield	2:294	Yet will I feebly cry	3:166
Yet hasting riches to acquire	3:284	Yet will I touch the Apple of his eye	1:191
Yet have they mist for once their surest aim	1:198	Yet will I, urging my request	2:457
Yet hear us, O thou patient God	3:40	Yet will we speak, if haply some	1:123
Yet impeached they live, and reign	1:110	Yielding to an early call	3:364
Yet if thy gracious will consent	1:271	YOU JUDGE IT BEST	
Yet if thy wise Eternal Will	1:221	(& much you love	3:100
Yet in no narrow bounds confined[316]	3:333	You like Rome with laws dispense	3:418
Yet is thy *Converse* (if thyself we hear)	1:205	You look the nation in the face	1:162
Yet not a selfish party's cause	2:434	You say, "Th' Americans distrest	3:95
Yet not for my relief, or ease	1:298	You that on Britain built your hope	1:121
Yet not forsook, but sorely tried[317]	3:336	You that survive the wreck, attend	1:158
		Your conscious hearts the answer give	2:423
		Your country has deceived your trust	1:121
		Your courts unspiritual, unjust	2:423
		Your duty let th' Apostle show	2:403
		Your friends ye need no longer fear	1:93

---

appears in *PW* 10:398, but in a format of six lines and a different meter. It appears in MS Matthew (319) in a format of eight lines and its first line reads: "The poor supply thy place."

315. The first four lines of the eight-line stanza beginning with this line appear in *PW* 12:46.

316. The stanza beginning with this line appears in *PW* 6:301.

317. The stanza beginning with this line

appears in *PW* 6:309.

318. The stanza beginning with this line appears in *PW* 11:170.

Your horrid deeds which shun the light	1:93	Your strict and only care	2:39
Your ill shall serve th' Almighty's ends	1:95	Your superstition vain	2:38
Your labour which proceeds from love	2:404	Your unprovoked Rebellion brings	1:71
Your life on needful things depends[319]	2:137	Your zeal, as ancient Story sings	1:151
Your little Sketch, and Sage advice	3:95	Yourself or good, or perfect call	2:458
Your Liturgy so well-prepared	3:97		
Your patriotic care is o'er	1:93		
Your sires inflamed with hellish zeal	2:314	Zealots the Church of Christ oppose	2:408

---

319. The stanza beginning with this line appears in *PW* 11:209, but reads: "Our life on needful things depends."

www.ingramcontent.com/pod-product-compliance
Lightning Source LLC
Chambersburg PA
CBHW081147290426
44108CB00018B/2471